Common Culture

Reading and Writing about American Popular Culture

Fourth Edition

Edited by

Michael Petracca
Madeleine Sorapure

University of California at Santa Barbara

Upper Saddle River, New Jersey 07458

Library of Congress Cataloging-in-Publication Data

Common culture : reading and writing about American popular culture / edited by Michael Petracca, Madeleine Sorapure.
p. cm.
Includes bibliographical references and index.
ISBN 0-13-182545-3
1. Popular culture—United States. 2. United States—Social life and customs—1971- 3. United States—Civilization—1970- 4. Popular culture—Study and teaching—United States. 5. United States—Social life and customs—1971—Study and teaching. 6. United States—Civilization—1970—Study and teaching. I. Petracca, Michael, 1947- II. Sorapure, Madeleine. III. Title.
E169.04.C65 2004
306'.0973—dc21

2003008308

Editor-in-Chief: Leah Jewell
Senior Acquisition Editor: Corey Good
Assistant Editor: Karen Schultz
Executive Managing Editor: Ann Marie McCarthy
Production Liaison: Fran Russello
Project Manager: Jessica Balch, Pine Tree Composition, Inc.
Prepress and Manufacturing Buyer: Mary Ann Gloriande
Art Director: Jayne Conte
Cover Designer: Robert Farrar-Wagner
Permission Specialist: Mary Dalton-Hoffman
Director, Image Resource Center: Melinda Lee Reo
Manager, Rights & Permissions: Zina Arabia
Interior Image Specialist: Beth Boyd-Brenzel
Cover Image Specialist: Karen Sanatar
Image Permission Coordinator: Cynthia Vincenti
Photo Researcher: Sheila Norman
Marketing Manager: Brandy Dawson

Cover Art: USA team—Archambault Photography, Inc.; Simpsons™—20th Century Fox Film Corp/1993/Phtofest; Oscar—© A.M.P.A.S.®/Dorling Kindersley

This book was set in 10/12 Palatino by Pine Tree Composition, Inc., and was printed and bound by Maple Vail Book Manufacturing. The cover was printed by Coral Graphics.

Printed in the United States of America

10 9 8 7 6 5 4 3 2 1

ISBN 0-13-182545-3

Pearson Education LTD, London
Pearson Education Australia PTY, Limited, Sydney
Pearson Education Singapore, Pte. Ltd
Pearson Education North Asia Ltd, Hong Kong
Pearson Education Canada, Ltd., Toronto
Pearson Educación de Mexico, S. A. de C. V.
Pearson Education–Japan, Tokyo
Pearson Education Malaysia, Pte. Ltd
Pearson Education Upper Saddle River, New Jersey

For my sister, brave explorer of nerve pathways,
healer of wounded neckbones,
dedicated connoisseuse *of the half-hour sitcom.*
—M.P.

For my mother, whose odd tastes I inherited,
and whose grace and courage I admire.
—M.S.

Contents

Preface

When we started teaching composition courses that examined television, pop music, movies, and other media-generated artifacts, we looked for a text that would cover a full range of topics in the field of popular culture from a variety of theoretical perspectives. We discovered that no satisfactory text existed, and therefore we began putting together assignments and reading materials to meet our needs. From this compilation *Common Culture* emerged.

The more we've taught writing courses based on popular culture, the more convinced we've become that such courses are especially appealing for students and effective in improving their critical thinking, reading, and writing skills. Students come into the writing classroom already immersed in the culture of Britney, Benetton, Beastie Boys, and Barry Bonds. The advantage, then, is that we don't have to "sell" the subject matter of the course and can concentrate on the task at hand—namely, teaching students to think critically and to write clear and effective prose. Obviously, a course that panders to the lowest common denominator of students' taste would be a mindless, unproductive enterprise for all concerned. However, the underlying philosophy of a pop culture-based writing course is this: By reading, thinking, and writing about material they find inherently interesting, students develop their critical and analytical skills—skills which are, of course, crucial to their success in college.

Although students are already familiar with the many aspects of popular culture, few have directed sustained, critical thought to its influence or implications—that is, to what shopping malls might tell them about contemporary culture or to what they've actually learned from watching "The Jerry Springer Show." Because television shows, advertisements, and music videos, for example, are highly crafted artifacts, they are particularly susceptible to analysis; and because so much in contemporary culture is open to interpretation and controversy, students enjoy the opportunity to articulate and argue for their own interpretations of objects and institutions in the world around them.

Although popular culture is undeniably a sexy (or, at least, lively) subject, it has also, in the past decade, become accepted as a legitimate object of academic discourse. While some may contend that it's frivolous to write a dissertation on "Buffy the Vampire Slayer," most scholars recognize the importance of studying the artifacts and institutions of contemporary life. Popular culture is a rich field of study, drawing in researchers from a variety of disciplines. Because it is also a very inviting field of study for students, a textbook that addresses this subject in a comprehensive and challenging way will be especially appealing both to them and to their writing teachers.

Common Culture, fourth edition, contains an introductory chapter that walks students through one assignment—in this case, focusing on the Barbie doll—with step-by-step instruction in reading carefully and writing effectively. The chapters that follow open with a relevant and catchy cultural artifact (for example, a cartoon, an ad, an album cover) that leads into a reader-friendly, informative introduction; a selection of engaging essays on an issue of current interest in the field of pop culture; carefully constructed reading and discussion questions; and writing assignments after each reading and at the end of the chapter. This fourth edition also contains new sections on visual literacy and conducting research on popular culture, along with a selection of color and black & white images that students can analyze and enjoy.

Common Culture approaches the field of popular culture by dividing it into its constituent parts. The book contains chapters on advertising, television, music, cyberculture, sports, and movies. Most of the chapters are divided into two parts: the first presents essays that address the topic generally, while the second offers essays that explore a specific aspect of the topic in depth. For example, in the chapter on advertising, the essays in the first group discuss theories and strategies of advertising, while later essays explore images of women in advertising.

We've purposely chosen readings that are accessible and thought-provoking, while avoiding those that are excessively theoretical or jargon-ridden. The readings in this book have the added advantage of serving as good models for students' own writing; they demonstrate a range of rhetorical approaches, such as exposition, analysis, and argumentation, and they offer varying levels of sophistication and difficulty in terms of content and style. Similarly, the suggested discussion and writing topics move from relatively basic concerns to tasks that require a greater degree of critical skill. Because of this range, instructors using *Common Culture* can easily adapt the book to meet the specific needs of their students.

Acknowledgments

As California instructors and therefore participants in the growth-and-awareness movement, we'd like first to thank each other for never straying from the path of psychic goodwill and harmony, and then to thank the universe for raining beneficence and light upon this project. And while on the subject of beneficence and light, we'd like to thank our original editor, Nancy Perry, as well as Harriett Prentiss, who helped us with the second edition, Vivian Garcia, who patiently shepherded us through the third, and Karen Schultz, our present editor.

We also want to thank Muriel Zimmerman and Judith Kirscht, former Directors of the Writing Program at UCSB, for lending moral and intellectual support to the original project, and Susan McLeod, our current Director. Thanks also to Larry Behrens and Sheridan Blau for lending their expertise in the area of textbook publishing.

Michael Petracca
Madeleine Sorapure

1
Reading and Writing about American Popular Culture

You've Got Mail!
iPod.
The Gap.
Caesar's Palace.
Tiger Woods.
The Simpsons.
Elimidate.
Super Bowl.
Ozzfest.

If any of these names and phrases sounds familiar—and it would be a great surprise if some didn't—it's because we spend our lives immersed in popular culture. There's no escaping it. Like hydrogen atoms and common-cold viruses, pop culture is everywhere. You absorb it at home watching television, listening to the stereo, or reading a magazine or newspaper; passing billboards or listening to the radio on the street; chatting over coffee at work or having a burger with friends; going out to movies and dance clubs, health spas, fast-food restaurants, shopping malls and sports arenas; even noticing the graffiti that glares out at you on building facades and highway overpasses.

In fact, unless you're isolated in a mountaintop cave, you can hardly avoid the influence of popular culture. Television, radio, newspapers, and magazines shape your ideas and behavior; like family, friends, and school, pop culture is part of your learning environment, supplying ready-made images, ideas, and patterns of behavior that you draw from, consciously or unconsciously, as you live your daily life. Exactly how you learn and just what you learn may not be all that certain, but it is undeniable that popular culture is one of your most powerful teachers.

One reason to study popular culture is that by paying closer attention to this daily bombardment of information you can think more critically about how it affects you and others. You may start by asking relatively simple questions—"Do I really need my breath to be 'Mentos fresh and full of life'?"—and work your way to far more significant ones—"How can we keep young women from starving themselves in their desire to conform to the images they see in advertisements?" Analyzing pop culture with a critical eye allows you to begin to free yourself from the manipulation of the media; it is an important step toward living an examined life.

WHAT IS POPULAR CULTURE?

What do we mean by popular culture? The term may at first seem contradictory. *Popular,* in its broadest sense, means "of the people," while we often associate *culture* with refinement and intellectual superiority, "the best which has been thought and said," as Matthew Arnold put it. We might ask how culture, traditionally reserved for the elite, the educated, and the upper class, can simultaneously belong to the common mass of humanity.

One way to resolve this seeming dilemma is to think of culture in an anthropological sense, as the distinct practices, artifacts, institutions, customs, and values of a particular social group. This is the way, for instance, that we distinguish the culture of the United States in the early twenty-first century from the culture of our great-grandparents or from that of societies in other times and places.

We can also define popular culture by distinguishing it from its counterparts: *high culture* and *folk culture.*

High culture consists of the artifacts traditionally considered worthy of study by university academics and other educated people:

classical music by composers such as Beethoven and Brahms; "fine" art from the impressionists and expressionists; literature and philosophy written by the likes of Shakespeare and Sartre.

At the other end of the spectrum, folk culture refers to artifacts created by a specific community or ethnic group, usually a relatively isolated nontechnological society such as the pygmies of Africa's Ituri Forest or certain communities in our own Appalachian Mountains. While high culture is primarily preserved and studied in the academy, folk culture is generally transmitted through oral communication; both, however, place a high value on tradition, on artifacts produced in the past, and on the shared history of the community.

By contrast, popular culture encompasses the most immediate and contemporary elements in our lives—elements which are often subject to rapid changes in a highly technological world in which people are brought closer and closer by the ubiquitous mass media. Pop culture offers a common ground, as the most visible and pervasive level of culture in a given society. If the Metropolitan Opera House represents high culture, then Madison Square Garden represents pop. If the carefully crafted knives used in Asian cooking rely on a folk tradition, then the Veg-O-Matic is their pop counterpart.

Several other terms help us establish a working definition of popular culture. *Mass culture* refers to information we receive through print and electronic media. While mass culture is often denigrated as juvenile or "low," it has to be treated as an important component of popular culture by virtue of the immense size of its audience. The terms *subculture* and *counterculture,* on the other hand, suggest a desire to resist the pressures, implied or explicit, to conform to a common culture. Subcultures are specific segments of society outside the core of dominant culture. Minority groups in the United States might be called subcultures, just as certain groups such as artists, homosexuals, lawyers, or teenagers can be thought of as having cultural markers distinct from the broader culture. A counterculture, on the other hand, is a group or movement which defines itself specifically as opposing or subverting the dominant culture. Hippies of the 1960s and punk-rockers of the 1980s defined themselves as countercultural groups.

Although we may place ourselves in specific folk or high cultures, subcultures or countercultures, we are still aware of and immersed in the broader popular culture simply by virtue of living in society. As Edward Jay Whetmore notes,[1] "Popular culture represents a common denominator, something that cuts across most economic, social, and educational barriers." If the notion of culture reflects a

---

[1]Whetmore, Edward Jay. *Mediamerica: Form, Content, and Consequence of Mass Communication.* Belmont, CA: Wadsworth 1989.

certain degree of social stratification and differentiation, then popular culture represents the elements of everyday life, the artifacts and institutions shared by a society, and a body of common knowledge.

Another distinguishing characteristic of popular culture is its transitory nature. New images appear on our TV screens, replacing the popular images of years or seasons before; new phrases supersede former favorites in our popular lexicon; unknown entertainers become celebrities overnight, while others fade just as quickly from the spotlight. Britney takes the place of Madonna, who took the place of Gidget; "Elimidate" replaces" "Change of Heart," which replaced "Studs," which replaced "Singled Out," which took over from "The Dating Game"; the expression "Just do it!" was for the 1990s what "Ring around the collar!" was for the 1970s.

Interestingly, if an icon of popular culture survives, it can often make the leap into high culture. For example, Wilkie Collins's nineteenth-century horror stories were read as avidly as Stephen King's novels are today. His works survive among today's elite audiences but are virtually unknown to most popular audiences. We might ask then, what of contemporary popular culture might survive beyond the immediate here and now and ultimately speak to future audiences at a higher, more specialized level?

What, then, is pop culture? Although it's notoriously difficult to define, some elements of a definition emerge from this discussion: pop culture is the shared knowledge and practices of a specific group at a specific time. Because of its commonality, pop culture both reflects and influences people's way of life; because it is linked to a specific time and place, pop culture is transitory, subject to change, and often an initiator of change.

WHY STUDY POPULAR CULTURE?

Though pop culture is increasingly accepted as a legitimate object of academic inquiry, educators still debate whether it should be studied. Some critics contend that it would be more valuable to study the products of high culture—Shakespeare rather than Spielberg, Eliot rather than Elvis. Their arguments often center on the issue of *quality*, as they assert that pop culture, transitory and often trendy, lacks the lasting value and strong artistic merit of high culture. Further, they argue that, because pop appeals to a mass audience rather than an educated elite, it is necessarily of low quality, no better than average. Although few critics of pop culture deny its pervasive influence, many argue that this influence should be considered negative, and they point to the violence and sexual explicitness of song lyrics, television programs, and movies, as well as to the triviality and downright foolishness of many popular trends. Pop culture debases us, these critics contend, turning us into passive recipients of low-quality goods, distracting us from higher pursuits.

It's important to note that very few proponents of pop culture—pop cultists, as Marshall Fishwick[2] calls them—take a wholesale, uncritical approach and approve all things popular. Many, for example, accept the argument that products with mass appeal are often qualitatively inferior to those intended for an educated, elite audience. However, pop cultists remind us that the gap between the two isn't always so wide; that the same basic activities of creation, refinement, and reception are involved in both popular and high culture; and that, as we've noted, the "popular" works of one era can become the "classics" of another.

Moreover, pop cultists argue for the validity of studying MTV, *The National Enquirer,* video games, and the Miss America Pageant because such mass phenomena serve as a kind of mirror in which we can discern much about ourselves. George Lipsitz,[3] for instance, suggests that "perhaps the most important facts about people have always been encoded within the ordinary and the commonplace." And as Ray Browne,[4] a noted scholar of pop culture, puts it, "Popular culture is a very important segment of our society. The contemporary scene is holding us up to ourselves to see; it can tell us who we are, what we are, and why."

We see reflected in pop culture certain standards and commonly held beliefs about beauty, success, love, or justice. We also see reflected there important social contradictions and conflicts—the tension between races, genders, or generations, for example. To find out about ourselves, then, we can turn to our own popular products and pastimes.

Another argument for studying popular culture focuses on the important influence it exerts on us. The media and other pop culture components are part of the fund of ideas and images that inform our daily activities, sometimes exerting a more compelling influence than family or friends, school or work. When we play sports, we mimic the gestures and movements of professional athletes; we learn to dance from the videos on MTV; we even name our children after popular

---

[2]Browne, Ray B., and Marshall Fishwick. *Symbiosis: Popular Culture and Other Fields.* Bowling Green, OH: Bowling Green University Press, 1988.

[3]Lipsitz, George. *Time Passages: Collective Memory and American Popular Culture.* Minneapolis: University of Minnesota Press, 1990.

[4]Browne, Ray B., and Marshall Fishwick. *Symbiosis: Popular Culture and Other Fields.* Bowling Green, OH: Bowling Green University Press, 1988.

television characters. More importantly, we discover role models; we learn lessons about villainy and heroism, love and relationships, acceptable and unacceptable behavior; we see interactions with people from other cultures. Even if popular culture is merely low-quality amusement or a means of escaping the demands of the "real" world, it delivers important messages that we may internalize and later act on—for better or for worse. We should examine and analyze pop culture, then, in order to assess—and sometimes resist—its influences.

The readings and assignments in *Common Culture* give you the chance to explore these issues and determine for yourself the role of popular culture in shaping society and in shaping you as an individual. The book includes chapters on important components of popular culture: advertising, television, music, cyberculture, sports, and movies. You may already know quite a lot about some of these topics, and you may have relatively little interest in or exposure to others. Either way, as an engaged participant or a disinterested observer, you can bring your critical skills to bear on phenomena of the contemporary world. The readings and assignments encourage you to observe carefully, to question, and to construct and defend your own interpretations of some of the institutions and events, the beliefs and practices, the media and the messages in your everyday life.

Before beginning, we will look at methods of reading and writing that will help you participate fully and critically in reaching the goals of this book.

ACTIVE READING

We've discussed the importance of paying attention to the "common culture" that surrounds you in order to recognize its meanings and influences on your life. In this section, we present specific reading strategies that you can apply both to pop culture and to the essays in this book. Whether you're watching TV or reading an essay about TV, the habit of active, engaged interpretation will make the experience much more worthwhile. While you may have been encouraged to be an active reader of print material, the essays throughout this book also encourage you to be an active reader of the culture around you, including the images in which popular culture immerses you. We use the term "reading" here to apply to both texts and images, although in a later section we suggest specific strategies for reading and interpreting images.

There's a crucial difference between passively receiving and actively reading. Passively ingesting information requires very little effort or interest, and it gives very little in terms of reward or stimulation.

Active reading demands more of your time, effort, and thought, but it is ultimately much more useful in helping you develop a better understanding of ideas.

Although reading a text or an image is generally a solitary activity, it helps to think of active reading as a discussion or dialogue with another person. You look and listen carefully; you compare what the person tells you to what you already know; you question statements that strike you as complicated, confusing, or incorrect; you identify ideas that are particularly interesting and important to you; you respond with ideas of your own. As a result of your active participation, you come away with new insights and a clearer sense of your own position. You may even be stimulated to seek out more information from other sources in order to clarify your thoughts.

When you read actively—whether printed texts or visual products of popular culture—you use very similar strategies, questioning and responding and speculating about what you're reading. You are no longer a disinterested bystander simply "listening in"; rather you are a participant who is energetically engaged with an author's ideas.

Strategies for Actively Reading a Text

There are a number of specific stages and strategies involved in active reading. In the **preparatory** stage you develop a general sense of what the essay will be about. In the **reading** stage, you begin the actual dialogue with the author by paying close attention to what he or she has written, identifying key points, responding to certain ideas, and asking questions. Next comes the **re-reading** stage, in which you go back through the essay to get a clear and firm understanding of what you've read. Finally, in the **reviewing** stage, you take time to draw conclusions, evaluate the author's position, and develop your own responses; often you'll want to go back to the essay and read certain sections even more carefully or to turn to other sources to help you formulate your response. In the actual practice of active reading, these four stages circle back on one another as well as spiral outward, prompting you to do further reading and exploration.

As you see, actively reading a text is quite different from passively receiving or consuming information. By reading actively, you'll be able to clarify and develop your own ideas and your responses to the influences operating on you in your everyday life. You can become a more proficient and accomplished writer, increasing the range and precision of your vocabulary, using different options for constructing sentences and paragraphs, creating different stylistic effects, and, in general, improving your "feel" for written language.

An Active Reading Casebook: Three Selections about Barbie

This section includes three reading selections—a poem and two essays about the Barbie doll—that demonstrate the strategies of active reading and suggest the kind of reading you'll be doing in later chapters. In the color insert at the center of the book, you will find two images of Barbie (p. CI-1) that you can interpret using strategies discussed in the "Reading Images" section.

We've chosen to begin with a look at Barbie because of her longevity, popularity, and cultural significance. Since her "birth" in 1959, Barbie has achieved celebrity status in United States culture and, indeed, worldwide. More than 775 million Barbies have been sold in the last thirty-five years, and Barbie products continue to bring in hundreds of millions of dollars every year for Mattel, Inc., her owner and America's biggest toy company. In 1994, Mattel estimated that 95 percent of girls aged three to eleven own at least one Barbie, while the average is seven. Barbie lives in nearly every United States and Canadian household that includes children and in more than sixty other countries as well. In addition to her extensive accessories and her many friends (among them, her boyfriend, Ken, and her African American pal, Shani), Barbie has her own magazine and fan club and her own corps of press agents, advertising executives, and "personal secretaries" to answer her fan mail. Yves St. Laurent and Bill Blass have designed clothes especially for her; Tiffany created a sterling silver version of Barbie; and New York City's Fifth Avenue became "Barbie Boulevard" to mark her twenty-fifth birthday.

For three decades, girls (and boys, too) have been playing with and learning from Barbie, and thus she serves as an important force in conveying cultural values and attitudes. Barbie's influence is undeniable, but opinions vary as to the quality of that influence on the children who play with her and on the adults they become. Barbie's critics argue that her influence has been largely detrimental, that her improbable measurements (36-18-33), her even more improbable hair, and her inexhaustible supply of clothes and accessories help perpetuate an inappropriate model of women's interests and lives. However, defenders argue that her influence has been positive, at least in part. They point out that Barbie has recently had careers such as corporate executive, airline pilot, medical doctor, animal rights activist, and even presidential candidate, offering girls a chance to envision themselves being successful in the working world. Although Barbie's wedding dress is one of her most popular outfits, she's never officially married Ken (or G.I. Joe), and she remains a single, independent career woman, providing, some observers say, an alternative to the view that women's primary roles are as wives and mothers.

You can see that Barbie has served as a symbolic reference point for broader debates about femininity and masculinity, about beauty and success, about consumerism and lifestyle in our culture. Barbie is a good example of the way elements of popular culture can be interpreted in order to reveal some fundamental aspects of our society.

While reading this background information on Barbie, you may be thinking of your own experience as a child playing with Barbie or with other dolls and toys, and speculating about their formative influence on you. If so, you've begun to prepare for reading, by orienting yourself to the topic, by exploring your own ideas and experiences, and by thinking about the issues at hand.

Preparing to Read Let's turn now to our first selection, a poem about Barbie written by Hilary Tham. All the readings in this book are accompanied by headnotes, which briefly explain what the reading is about and give some background information on the author. In this sense, headnotes are like the front and back covers of many books, providing an overview of what will follow and serving as the place to begin thinking about the topic. Here is the headnote for the poem "Barbie's Shoes":

> Our first selection is a poem by Hilary Tham. Tham was born in Kelang, Malaysia, and currently lives in Virginia with her husband and three daughters. She teaches creative writing in high schools and has published several books of poetry, including *No Gods Today, Paper Boats, Bad Names for Women,* and *Tigerbone Wine.*

You can get an idea of what to expect from the poem both by reading the headnote and by recalling what you know about poetry in general. The headnote tells you that Hilary Tham is originally from Malaysia and now lives in the United States. You might conclude from this information that Tham brings a dual perspective to the Barbie doll and other features of United States pop culture. The headnote also points out that Tham has three daughters and teaches high school students. Before you read the poem, then, you might speculate on how being a mother and a teacher would influence Tham's thoughts about the Barbie doll.

Reading and Annotating In the reading stage, one of the most useful strategies you can use is *annotating* the text. When you annotate you use a pencil or pen to mark key words and phrases in the text and to write questions and responses in the margins. You underline words that you need to look up in a dictionary and phrases that you find particularly interesting, forceful, important, questionable, or confusing.

You also record your reactions, thoughts, questions, and ideas in the margins. By annotating in this way, you keep track of what the author is saying and of what you're thinking as you read.

Here are one student's annotations of Tham's poem...but keep in mind that your annotation would probably identify different elements as particularly important.

Barbie's Shoes
HILARY THAM

I'm down in the basement — *Why the basement?*
sorting Barbie's shoes.
sequin pumps, satin courts,
western boots, Reebok sneakers,
glass slippers, ice-skates, thongs. — *Different shoes show Barbie's many activities*
All will fit the dainty, forever arched
feet of any one Barbie: Sweet Spring
Glitter-Eyed, Peaches and Cream,
a Brazilian, Russian, Swiss, Hong Kong
Hispanic or Mexican, Nigerian
or Black Barbie. All are cast — *Barbies are different but also the same*
in the same mold, same rubbery,
impossible embodiment of male fantasy
with carefully measured
doses of melanin to make
a Caucasian Barbie,
Polynesian Barbie
African-American Barbie.
Everyone knows that she is the same — *Barbie = American Dream*
Barbie and worthy of the American Dream
House, the Corvette, opera gloves, a
hundred pairs of shoes to step into. If only
the differently colored men and women we know
could be like Barbie, always smiling, eyes
wide with admiration, even when we yank
off an arm with a hard-to-take-off dress.
Barbie's shoes, so easily lost, mismatched, — *Simile: Barbie's shoes are like our prejudices—forgotten, but still there, in the basement, like spider webs.*
useless; they end up, like our prejudices,
in the basement, forgotten as spiders
sticking webs in our darkest corners,
we are amazed we have them still.

Re-reading After you read and annotate the poem, your task is to fully understand it and formulate your own response to it. Many students close the book after just the first reading without realizing that the next two stages, re-reading and reviewing, are crucial to discovering the significance of what they have read.

In the re-reading stage, you go back through the poem and the annotations in order to develop a good understanding of the writer's ideas. Then you begin to articulate those ideas—in your own words. Here's an example drawn from the earlier annotation of "Barbie Shoes."

> I'm really drawn to the simile in the last few lines: that Barbie's shoes are "like our prejudices, / in the basement, forgotten as spiders / sticking webs in our darkest corners, / we are amazed we have them still." Tham is saying that Barbie's shoes are more than just tiny plastic footwear. They represent prejudices which we think we've thrown away but in fact still have in our "basements" (our subconscious thoughts?). And by comparing these prejudices to spiders' webs "in our darkest corners," perhaps Tham is suggesting that our prejudices still "catch" things; they still operate in our lives even if we've forgotten them or don't see them.

With ideas like these as a starting point, you can go back through the entire poem and begin to formulate a response to other key ideas and phrases: the list of Barbie's shoes; the list of different nationalities and ethnicities of Barbie dolls; the idea that all Barbies are in some way the same; the suggestion that Barbie represents the American Dream. Re-reading like this will surely provoke further questions about the poem. For instance, why does Tham make a point of mentioning the many different types of Barbies? In what ways are these differences only superficial and unrealistic? And what does Tham mean when she writes, "If only / the differently colored men and women we know / could be like Barbie, always smiling, even when we yank / off an arm...."? You know that Tham is being ironic since we don't generally yank arms off other people, but what point is she making in this comparison, and how does it relate to her ideas about prejudice?

These kinds of questions lead you to re-read the poem, clarifying your understanding and finding further meanings in it. After each essay in this book there are similar sorts of reading questions which will help you explore the ideas you've read about. We also encourage you to develop your own questions about what you read to focus your exploration on those points that you find most interesting, important, or controversial.

Reviewing After re-reading, questioning, and exploring the writer's ideas in detail, you should take time to summarize what you've learned. Here is a student's summary of her analysis of "Barbie's Shoes."

1. Tham suggests that Barbie's shoes are like prejudices (forgotten, seemingly lost, down in the basement, "useless" and "mismatched"); why can't we just throw them out? why are they still in the basement?
2. Why does Barbie have so many shoes?! Perhaps Tham is implying that we have an equal number of seemingly insignificant prejudices, one for every occasion, even.
3. Tham points out that there are many different kinds of Barbie dolls (Caucasian, Polynesian, African American) but all are "worthy of the American Dream House." In this sense Barbies are all the same. So does Barbie influence us to overlook the real differences in women's lives? We're not dolls, after all, and although we're all worthy of success and accomplishment, we don't all get the same chances.
4. Tham describes Barbie as the "impossible embodiment of male fantasy." How is this observation related to the rest of the poem? Could she be saying that this fantasy is related to prejudice?

Such questions and tentative answers can help you begin to formulate your own interpretation of and complete response to what you've read.

Reading Pop Cultural Criticism In the previous discussion we used Hilary Tham's poem as our example because poetry can pack so much meaning into the space of relatively few words. In the chapters that follow you'll be reading not poems but rather articles, essays, and chapters of books, most of which fall into one of two categories. The first we might call *pop cultural criticism* and includes the kind of pieces written for general audiences of popular magazines and mass market books. Typically these reflect a particular social perspective, whether traditionalist or cutting edge, conservative or liberal, pro- or anticapitalist, and often they are written in response to a particular issue or phenomenon reported in the media.

The following piece by John Leo is an example of pop cultural criticism. As you read, practice the strategies that we've discussed. Begin by considering the headnote and what it suggests about Leo's perspective and purpose, then underline important passages in the essay and jot down your thoughts, responses, and questions in the margins.

The Indignation of Barbie
JOHN LEO

John Leo's "The Indignation of Barbie" was first published in U.S. News & World Report *in 1992. Leo, a conservative journalist and social commentator, writes about the controversy surrounding the talking Barbie doll produced by Mattel in the early 1990s. Among Talking Barbie's repertoire of phrases was "Math class is tough," viewed by some feminists and professional women as discouraging girls from pursuing the subject. Here, Leo imagines a dialogue with Barbie, in which the talking doll defends herself against charges that she's a "prefeminist bimbo."*

Barbie will probably survive, but the truth is, she's in a lot of trouble. It seems that the new Teen Talk Barbie, the first talking Barbie in 20 years, has shocked many feminists with a loose-lipped comment about girls and math. Each $25 doll speaks four of 270 programmed one-liners. In one of those messages, Barbie says, "Math class is tough." This was a big error. She should have said, "Math is particularly easy if you're a girl, despite the heavy shackles of proven test bias and male patriarchal oppression." 1

Because of this lapse from correctness, the head of the American Association of University Women is severely peeved with Barbie, and you can no longer invite both of them to the same party. Other feminists and math teachers have weighed in with their own dudgeon. 2

Since this is Barbie's darkest hour, I placed a phone call out to Mattel, Inc. in California to see how the famous long-haired, long-legged forerunner of Ivana Trump was holding up. To my astonishment, they put me right through to Barbie herself. 3

"Barbie, it's me," I said. As the father of three girls, I have shopped for 35 to 40 Barbies over the years, including doctor Barbie, ballerina Barbie, television news reporter Barbie, African-American Barbie, animal-rights Barbie, and Barbie's shower, which takes two days to construct and makes the average father feel like a bumbling voyeur. So I figured that Barbie would know me. 4

Barbie spoke: "Do you want to go for a pizza? Let's go to the mall. Do you have a crush on anyone? Teaching kids is great. Computers make homework fun!" 5

In a flash I realized that Barbie was stonewalling. These were not spontaneous comments at all. They were just the prerecorded messages that she was forced to say, probably under pressure from those heartless, controlling patriarchs at Mattel. 6

Subtle rebuttal. At the same time, I began to appreciate Barbie's characteristic subtlety; by reminding me that she was recommending the educational use of computers to young girls, she was, in effect, stoutly rebutting the charge of antifeminist backlash among talking toys. I had to admit it was pretty effective. 7

So I pleaded with her to speak honestly and clear her name. I heard a telltale rustle of satin, and then she spoke. "You're the one who took three days to put my shower together. That was ugly."

"Two days," I said, gently correcting the world-famous plastic figurine. I asked her about the harsh words of Sharon Schuster, the awfully upset head of the AAUW. Schuster had said, "The message is a negative one for girls, telling them they can't do well in math, and that perpetuates a stereotype."

"That's a crock," Barbie replied. "Just because a course is tough or 10
challenging doesn't mean my girls can't do it. Weren't your daughters a little apprehensive about math?" I admitted that they were. "Well, how did they do?" "Top of the class," I replied brightly.

"Then tell Sharon Schuster to stop arguing with dolls and go get a 11
life." Her remark was an amazement. This was not roller-skating Barbie or perfume-wearing Barbie. It was the real thing: in-your-face tough-talking Barbie.

"The first time I open my mouth after 20 years, and what 12
happens? I get squelched by a bunch of women." At this point, I mentioned that my friend M. G. Lord, the syndicated columnist who is doing a book on Barbie, is firmly on her side. M. G. told me: "Math class *is* tough, but it doesn't mean you have to drop out and go to cosmetology school. These people are projecting a lot of fears onto Barbie."

Barbie was grateful. "Thank M. G. and tell her I look forward to 13
her biography of me. And tell her that if she ever fails in life, she can always become head of the AAUW." That remark may have been a trifle sharp, I said. "Well," said Barbie, "I'm just tired of taking all this guff from women's groups. They're scapegoating the wrong girl. I'll match feminist credentials with any of them. I worked my way up from candy striper to doctor. I was a stewardess in the '60s, and now I'm a pilot. Ken is one of my flight attendants. You can buy me as Olympic athlete, astronaut and executive."

Barbie was on a roll now. I was writing furiously to keep up. "This 14
summer they put out a presidential candidate Barbie, and two days later, Ross Perot withdrew. Figure it out," she said. "As far back as 1984, my ad slogan was, 'We girls can do anything.' I've done more than any other doll to turn girls into achievers, and still they treat me as a prefeminist bimbo. What's wrong with the women's movement?"

I knew enough not to touch that one. Besides, it's a very short col- 15
umn. But I was struck by her comment that Ken was now employed as a flight attendant. "Didn't he used to be a corporate executive?" I asked. "We're not voting for Bush again," she replied bitterly.

Then I heard a muffled side comment: "Ken! Be careful with those 16
dishes." I said I felt bad about Ken's comedown, but Barbie brought me back to reality: "Remember," she said, "he's only an accessory." This was tough to take, but the issue was settled. Barbie is indeed a feminist. Over to you, Sharon Schuster.

As you first read Leo's essay, his technique of personifying the doll as an "in-your-face tough-talking Barbie" is most striking and allows him to humorously present a talking Barbie who seemingly speaks up for herself. In re-reading you can see even more clearly Leo's purpose: he uses Barbie's "voice" to offer his own defense of her influence and significance. Moreover, ultimately he is making fun of feminists "projecting a lot of fears onto Barbie," since she herself derisively asks, "What's wrong with the women's movement?" When Leo has Barbie "say" that she's "done more than any other doll to turn girls into achievers," it's clear that Leo himself agrees and feels that Barbie critics should lighten up.

As a reviewing activity, you might write down your thoughts about the following questions and discuss them with your group or class:

1. Do you agree that Barbie has "done more than any other doll to turn girls into achievers" (paragraph 14)?
2. Do you think Leo's use of humor contributes to the effect of his essay?
3. According to Leo, what is the relationship between Barbie and Ken? Do you agree with Leo's ideas?
4. If you could give speech to Barbie, what would you have her say?

Reading Academic Analyses In addition to pop cultural criticism, this book provides essays on pop cultural phenomena written not for a general audience, but by academics primarily for other academics. Generally published in academic journals or in collections from scholarly presses, these essays often present the results of extensive research or provide a very close, detailed, and original analysis of the subject at hand. You may find them more difficult than the pieces of pop cultural criticism, but in many ways they are closer to the kind of writing that will be expected of you in many of your college courses.

Note that, while "objective" in tone, academic cultural analysis generally reflects a particular interpretive framework, which may be ideological (e.g., feminist or Marxist) or methodological (e.g., semiotic, structuralist, or quantitative) or some combination of the two. These frameworks will be discussed in more detail in the headnotes to individual readings.

The following excerpt from an essay by Marilyn Ferris Motz is an example of academic cultural analysis, written from a perspective that might be called "feminist-historical." As you read the headnote and the essay itself, apply the strategies we've discussed: familiarize yourself with Motz's view and with the topic as it's presented in the headnote; then read the essay carefully and make your own annotations in the text and in the margins.

"Seen Through Rose-Tinted Glasses": The Barbie Doll in American Society

MARILYN FERRIS MOTZ

Originally published in a longer form in The Popular Culture Reader, *Marilyn Motz's "'Seen Through Rose-Tinted Glasses': The Barbie Doll in American Society," takes its title from a 1983 Barbie sticker album marketed by Mattel: "If you stay close to your friend Barbie, life will always be seen through rose-tinted glasses." In her essay, however, Motz suggests that Barbie has other messages for us and that the doll's influence is more problematic, especially for children. Pointing out that several generations of girls have learned cultural values and norms from playing with Barbie, Motz focuses on the fact that, although Barbie has changed through the years to keep up with changes in the "baby boom" generation, the doll and her accessories still convey an outdated image of women's circumstances and interests.*

A 1983 Barbie sticker album copyrighted by Mattel describes Barbie: 1

> As beautiful as any model, she is also an excellent sportswoman. In fact, Barbie is seen as a typical young lady of the twentieth century, who knows how to appreciate beautiful things and, at the same time, live life to the fullest. To most girls, she appears as the ideal elder sister who manages to do all those wonderful things that they can only dream of. With her fashionable wardrobe and constant journeys to exciting places all over the world, the adventures of Barbie offer a glimpse of what they might achieve one day. If Barbie has a message at all for us, it is to ignore the gloomy outlook of others and concentrate on all those carefree days of youth. Whatever lies in store will come sooner or later. If you stay close to your friend Barbie, life will always be seen through rose-tinted glasses.

Most owners of Barbie dolls are girls between the ages of three and eleven years of age. A Mattel survey shows that by the late 1960s, the median age for Barbie doll play had dropped from age ten to age six (Rakstis 30). Younger children find it difficult to manipulate the relatively small dolls, although Mattel created "My First Barbie," that ostensibly was easier for young children to handle and dress. Although some boys admit to playing with Ken, or even Barbie, Barbie doll play seems to be confined largely to girls. 2

Like all small figures and models, Barbie, at 11 1/2 inches high, has the appeal of the miniature. Most people are fascinated with objects recreated on a smaller scale, whether they are model airplanes, electric trains, dollhouse furnishings, or doll clothes. Miniatures give us a sense 3 of control over our environment, a factor that is particularly important for children, to whom the real world is several sizes too large. In playing with a Barbie doll, a girl can control the action, can be omnipotent in a miniature world of her own creation.

When a girl plays with a baby doll, she becomes in her fantasy the doll's mother. She talks directly to the doll, entering into the play as an actor in her own right. When playing with a Barbie doll, on the other hand, the girl usually "becomes" Barbie. She manipulates Barbie, Ken and the other dolls, speaking for them and moving them around a miniature environment in which she herself cannot participate. Through the Barbie doll, then, a pre-adolescent can engage in role-playing activities. She can imitate adult female behavior, dress and speech and can participate vicariously in dating and other social activities, thus allaying some of her anxieties by practicing the way she will act in various situations. In consultation with the friends with whom she plays, a girl can establish the limits of acceptable behavior for a young woman and explore the possibilities and consequences of exceeding those limits. 4

The girl playing with a Barbie doll can envision herself with a mature female body. "Growing-Up Skipper," first produced in 1975, grew taller and developed small breasts when her arms were rotated, focusing attention on the bodily changes associated with puberty. Of course, until the end of puberty, girls do not know the ultimate size and shape their bodies will assume, factors they realize will affect the way others will view and treat them. Perhaps Barbie dolls assuage girls' curiosity over the appearance of the adult female body, of which many have only limited knowledge, and allay anxiety over their own impending bodily development. 5

Through Barbie's interaction with Ken, girls also can explore their anxieties about future relationships with men. Even the least attractive and least popular girl can achieve, by "becoming" Barbie, instant popularity in a fantasy world. No matter how clumsy or impoverished she is in real life, she can ride a horse or lounge by the side of the pool in a world undisturbed by the presence of parents or other authority figures. The creator of the Barbie doll, Ruth Handler, claims that "these dolls become an extension of the girls. Through the doll each child dreams of what she would like to be" (Zinsser, "Barbie" 73). If Barbie does enable a girl to dream "of what she would like to be," then what dreams and goals does the doll encourage? With this question, some of the negative aspects of the Barbie doll emerge. 6

The clothes and other objects in Barbie's world lead the girl playing with Barbie to stress Barbie's leisure activities and emphasize the importance of physical appearance. The shape of the doll, its clothes and the focus on dating activities present sexual attractiveness as a key to popularity and therefore to happiness. Finally, Barbie is a consumer. She demands product after product, and the packaging and advertising imply that Barbie, as well as her owner, can be made happy if only she wears the right clothes and owns the right products. Barbie conveys the 7 message that, as the saying goes, a woman can never be too rich or too thin. The Barbie doll did not create these attitudes. Nor will the doll insidiously instill these values in girls whose total upbringing emphasizes other factors. An individual girl can, of course, create with her own doll any sort of behavior and activities she chooses. Still, the products available for the doll tend to direct play along certain lines. Barbie represents an image, and a rather unflattering one, of American women. It is the extent to which this image fits our existing cultural expectations that explains the popularity of the Barbie doll. . . .

As an icon, Barbie not only reflects traditional, outdated roles for women; she and Ken also represent, in exaggerated form, characteristics of American society as a whole. Through playing with these dolls, children learn to act out in miniature the way they see adults behave in real life and in the media. The dolls themselves and the accessories provided for them direct this play, teaching children to consume and conform, to seek fun and popularity above all else. 8

Thorstein Veblen wrote in 1899 that America had become a nation of "conspicuous consumers." We buy objects, he wrote, not because we need them but because we want others to know we can afford them. We want our consumption to be conspicuous or obvious to others. The more useless the object, the more it reflects the excess wealth the owner can afford to waste. In the days before designer labels, Veblen wrote that changing fashions represent an opportunity for the affluent to show that they can afford to waste money by disposing of usable clothing and replacing it with new, faddish styles that will in turn be discarded after a few years or even months of wear (Veblen 60–131). 9

Sociologist David Riesman wrote in 1950 that Americans have become consumers whose social status is determined not only by what they can afford to buy but also by the degree to which their taste in objects of consumption conforms to that of their peers. Taste, in other words, becomes a matter of assessing the popularity of an item with others rather than judging on the basis of one's personal preference. Children, according to Riesman, undergo a process of "taste socialization," of learning to determine "with skill and sensitivity the probable tastes of the others" and then to adopt these tastes as their own. Riesman writes that "today the future occupation of all moppets is to be skilled consumers" (94, 96, 101). This skill lies not in selecting durable or useful products but in selecting popular, socially acceptable products that indicate the owner's conformity to standards of taste and knowledge of current fashion. 10

The Barbie doll teaches a child to conform to fashion in her consumption. She learns that each activity requires appropriate attire and that outfits that may at first glance appear to be interchangeable are slightly different from one another. In the real world, what seems to be a vast array of merchandise actually is a large collection of similar products. The consumer must make marginal distinctions between nearly identical products, many of which have different status values. The child playing with a Barbie doll learns to detect these nuances. Barbie's 11 clothes, for instance, come in three lines: a budget line, a medium-priced line, and a designer line. Consumption itself becomes an activity to be practiced. From 1959 to 1964, Mattel produced a "Suburban Shopper" outfit. In 1976 the "Fashion Plaza" appeared on the market. This store consisted of four departments connected by a moving escalator. As mass-produced clothing made fashion accessible to all classes of Americans, the Barbie doll was one of the means by which girls learned to make the subtle fashion distinctions that would guarantee the proper personal appearances.

Barbie must also keep pace with all the newest fashion and leisure 12 trends. Barbie's pony tail of 1959 gave way to a Jackie Kennedy style "Bubble-cut" in the early 1960s and to long straight hair in the 1970s. "Ken-A-Go-Go" of 1960s had a Beatle wig, guitar and microphone, while the "Now Look Ken" of the 1970s had shoulder-length hair and wore a leisure suit (Leavy 102). In the early 1970s Ken grew a detachable beard. In 1971 Mattel provided Barbie and Ken with a motorized stage on which to dance in their fringed clothes, while Barbie's athletic activities, limited to skiing, skating, fishing, skydiving and tennis in the 1960s, expanded to include backpacking, jogging, bicycling, gymnastics and sailing in the 1970s. On the shelves in the early 1980s were Western outfits, designer jeans, and Rocker Barbie dressed in neon colors and playing an electric guitar. In 1991 Rollerblade Barbie was introduced.

Barbie clearly is, and always has been, a conspicuous consumer. 13 Aside from her lavish wardrobe, Barbie has several houses complete with furnishings, a Ferrari and a '57 Chevy. She has at various times owned a yacht and several other boats as well as a painted van called the "Beach Bus." Through Barbie, families who cannot afford such luxury items in real life can compete in miniature. In her early years, Barbie owned a genuine mink coat. In the ultimate display of uselessness, Barbie's dog once owned a corduroy velvet jacket, net tutu, hat, sunglasses and earmuffs. Barbie's creators deny that Barbie's life is devoted to consumption. "These things shouldn't be thought of as possessions," according to Ruth Handler. "They are props that enable a child to get into play situations" (Zinsser 73). Whether possessions or props, however, the objects furnished with the Barbie doll help create play situations, and those situations focus on consumption and leisure.

A perusal of the shelves of Barbie paraphernalia in the Midwest 14 Toys "R" Us store reveals not a single item of clothing suitable for an executive office. Mattel did produce a doctor's outfit (1973) and astronaut suit (1965 and 1986) for Barbie, but the clothes failed to sell. According to Mattel's marketing manager, "We only kept the doctor's uniform in the line as long as we did because public relations begged us to give them something they could point to as progress" in avoiding stereotyped roles for women (Leavy 102). In the 1960s, Mattel produced "all the elegant accessories" for the patio including a telephone, television, radio, fashion magazines and a photograph of Barbie and Ken (Zinsser 72). The "Busy Barbie," created in 1972, had hands that could grasp objects and came equipped with a telephone, television, record player, "soda set" with two glasses and a travel case. Apparently Barbie kept busy only with leisure activities; she seems unable to grasp a book or a pen. When Barbie went to college in the 1970s, her "campus" consisted only of a dormitory room, soda shop (with phone booth), football stadium and drive-in movie (Zinsser 72). In the 1980s, Barbie traveled in her camper, rode her horse, played with her dog and cat, swam in her pool and lounged in her bubble bath (both with real water).

15 The Barbie doll of the 1980s presents a curiously mixed message. The astronaut Barbie wore a pink space suit with puffed sleeves. The executive Barbie wore a hot pink suit and a broad-brimmed straw hat, and she carried a pink briefcase in which to keep her gold credit card. Lest girls think Barbie is all work and no play, the jacket could be removed, the pink and white spectator pumps replaced with high-heeled sandals, and the skirt reversed to form a spangled and frilly evening dress. Barbie may try her hand at high-status occupations, but her appearance does not suggest competence and professionalism. In a story in *Barbie* magazine (Summer 1985) Barbie is a journalist reporting on lost treasure in the Yucatan. She spends her time "catching some rays" and listening to music, however, while her dog discovers the lost treasure. Barbie is appropriately rewarded with a guest spot on a television talk show! Although Barbie is shown in a professional occupation and even has her own computer, her success is attributed to good luck rather than her own (nonexistent) efforts. She reaps the rewards of success without having had to work for it; indeed, it is her passivity and pleasure-seeking (could we even say laziness) that allows her dog to discover the gold. Even at work, Barbie leads a life of leisure.

16 Veblen wrote that America, unlike Europe, lacked a hereditary aristocracy of families that were able to live on the interest produced by inherited wealth. In America, Veblen wrote, even the wealthiest men were self-made capitalists who earned their own livings. Since these men were too busy to enjoy leisure and spend money themselves, they delegated these tasks to their wives and daughters. By supporting a wife and daughters who earned no money but spent lavishly, a man could prove his financial success to his neighbors. Therefore, according to Veblen, affluent women were forced into the role of consumers, establishing the social status of the family by the clothes and other items they bought and the leisure activities in which they engaged (Veblen 44–131).

17 Fashions of the time, such as long skirts, immobilized women, making it difficult for them to perform physical labor, while ideals of beauty that included soft pale hands and faces precluded manual work or outdoor activities for upper-class women. To confer status, Veblen writes, clothing "should not only be expensive, but it should also make plain to all observers that the wearer is not engaged in any kind of productive employment." According to Veblen, "the dress of women goes even farther than that of men in the way of demonstrating the wearer's abstinence from productive labor." The high heel, he notes, "makes any, even the simplest and most necessary manual work extremely difficult," and thus is a constant reminder that the woman is "the economic depen-

dent of the man—that, perhaps in a highly idealized sense, she still is the man's chattel" (Veblen 120–21, 129)....

Despite changes in the lives and expectations of real women, Barbie remains essentially the woman described by Veblen in the 1890s, excluded from the world of work with its attendant sense of achievement, forced to live a life based on leisure activities, personal appearance, the accumulation of possessions and the search for popularity. While large numbers of women reject this role, Barbie embraces it. The Barbie doll serves as an icon that symbolically conveys to children and adults the measures of success in modern America: wealth, beauty, popularity and leisure. 18

Suggestions for Further Reading

Leavy, Jane. "Is There a Barbie Doll in Your Past?" *Ms.* Sept. 1979.

Riesman, David, Nathan Glazer, and Reual Denney. *The Lonely Crowd: A Study of the Changing American Character.* Garden City, NY: Doubleday Anchor, 1950.

Rakstis, Ted. "Debate in the Doll House." *Today's Health* Dec. 1970.

Veblen, Thorstein. *The Theory of the Leisure Class.* 1899. New York: Mentor, 1953.

Zinsser, William K. "Barbie Is a Million Dollar Doll." *Saturday Evening Post* 12 Dec. 1964: 72–73.

As you can see from Motz's essay, academic cultural analysis can present you with much information and many ideas to digest. A useful re-reading activity is to go through the text and highlight its main points by writing a one- or two-page summary of it. Then in the reviewing stage, you can use your summary to draw your own conclusions and formulate your own responses to the writer's ideas. To do so with Motz's essay, you might use the following questions as starting points:

1. In what ways do you think fashion dolls like Barbie provide a different play experience for children than "baby dolls"? Do you think one type of doll is "healthier" or more appropriate than the other?
2. To what extent do you think Thorstein Veblen's comments on status and consumerism in American society (paragraph 9) still apply today? Do you agree with Motz that Barbie contributes to the promotion of "conspicuous consumption"?
3. If Motz is right that Barbie represents an outdated and potentially detrimental image of women's lives, why do you think the doll continues to sell more and more successfully every year?
4. To what extent do you think that the values represented by Barbie—"wealth, beauty, popularity and leisure" (18)—are still central to success in America?

Ultimately, your goal as a reader in this course will most likely be to prepare yourself to complete specific writing assignments. In the "Writing Process" section, we will present the process one writing student went through in composing an essay requested in the following assignment:

> What do you see as the significance of the Barbie doll in contemporary American culture? How are your ideas related to those of Tham, Leo, and Motz in the selections presented here?

READING IMAGES

Before turning to this assignment, however, we will address strategies you can use to read images effectively. In many ways, the four-step process we just described for reading texts—Preparing to Read, Reading and Annotating, Re-reading, and Reviewing—applies to images as well. There are some differences, though, as we discuss below.

Preparing to Read

With both text and image, it is wise to begin by getting an idea of what to expect, a first impression. Just as you read the headnote in order to get an introduction to an essay or poem, so too can you read the information that surrounds the image. Next to a painting in a museum, for instance, you'll often find information about the work: the name of the artist, the dates he or she lived, the date the work was completed, the media used in the work (oils, watercolor, paper, etc.), the dimensions of the work.

But outside of a museum, images are often presented to you without this kind of helpful, orienting information. In these instances, which are of course far more common in the world of popular culture, an important strategy to prepare yourself before diving in to interpret the image is to look at the context in which the image occurs. Is it an advertisement you're being asked to analyze? If so, what magazine is the ad in? What is the typical audience of this magazine? On what page of the magazine is the ad found (in the expensive beginning pages or in the more modestly priced pages toward the end of the magazine)? Is it a Web site you're interpreting? If so, who is the author of the site? Who is its audience? What is the purpose of the site? When was the site last updated?

These questions of context can orient you in the same way that headnotes can: they give you a general sense of what to expect. Moreover, knowing the context, and especially the audience and purpose of an image, can guide your subsequent interpretation by helping you determine why certain features are present or absent in the image.

Finally in the "Preparing to Read" stage, you should think about your initial impressions of the image you're analyzing. What key features do you notice immediately? What mood or feeling does the image evoke in you? What immediate response do you have to the image?

Let's turn to a specific example and begin with the "Preparing to Read" process. Take a look at the image of Barbie at the top of page CI-1. As you can see from the information included below the image, it comes from a screenshot (taken in August 2002) of the homepage at Barbie.com. This is an official site created by Mattel Corporation; the site provides, as the page title states, "Activities and Games for Girls Online!"

Based on this information alone, you can begin to draw some conclusions about the context of the image. First of all, it's on the Web. As you can probably guess, the Web page takes advantage of multimedia possibilities, including sound (when you roll over certain parts of the image you hear sound) and animation (for instance, the butterfly flutters around). If you have access to the Internet, you might want to visit the site (*http://www.barbie.com*) to see these features. In short, you know that this isn't just a still image; as a Web interface to the Barbie site, it provides more interactive possibilities and serves as a map for the rest of the site (indicated by the navigation options across the top of the image). Knowing this can help by preparing you to read the image in the context of the kinds of interactivity it invites.

As you think about determining the audience and purpose of this image, the fact that it comes from an official Web site sponsored by Barbie's creator, Mattel, tells you that its audience is young girls who play with (and perhaps own) Barbie, and that its purpose is most likely connected to Mattel's desire to sell Barbie and her accessories. In short, you can tell that this image has a promotional function; it is not, for instance, driven by aesthetic goals or intended to deliver a critical interpretation of Barbie.

What's your first impression of this image? What strikes you as most immediately noticeable about it? We can put it in one word: Pink!

Let's move on now to the next step, in which you take a closer look at the details of the image and begin interpreting it.

Reading and Annotating

Unless you own the image that you're interpreting, it would probably be a good idea to refrain from annotating (that is, writing on it). You can get into some trouble doing this, particularly in places like the

Metropolitan Museum of Art. Instead, annotating becomes a process of note taking, and reading becomes a process of looking. Put simply, look at the image and take notes.

But that's putting it too simply. What should you look at in an image, and what sort of notes should you take?

One of the major differences between text and image is that a text generally presents information in a sequential and linear manner; there's usually no question about where you should begin reading and, having read one word, it's not usually difficult to decide what word you should read next. With images (and here we're speaking only of still images and not videos, commercials, or other kinds of sequenced images), everything is presented simultaneously so that you can begin and end where you choose and your eyes can follow different paths through the image. Having said that, though, it's also the case that images often try to draw your attention to a certain place, a focus point. This focus point is often relevant in understanding the key messages of the image.

What is the focus point of the Barbie image? For us, it's Barbie herself. It seems fairly obvious that Barbie would be the key item in an image promoting Barbie, but what details in the image can we find to support this claim? Here's where *color* and *dimension* (or proportion) come into play. The colors in the image are, well, pink, along with other pastel shades of lavender, purple, and light blue. Barbie stands out from this color scheme with her blond hair, light-green striped shirt, and white pants, along with the flesh tones on her arms and face. Our attention is drawn to her because of the *contrast* (and contrasts are often used in images to draw attention or make statements). Dimension also draws our attention to Barbie because she is larger than any other object in the image. In fact, she's unnaturally large, if she were to stand up, her head would, we think, bang against the ceiling of the room. So here again, evidence in the image supports a (fairly obvious) claim that Mattel is drawing our attention to Barbie herself.

It's often helpful to imagine alternative color schemes and dimensions for images that you're analyzing in order to register the impact of the image as it is. For instance, what if the main color of this page was black, perhaps with neon green and yellow and some bright red? Envisioning this alternative, we can see all the more clearly that the colors used by Mattel strongly signify "girl." Or what if the largest item in the room was the calendar? We might be inclined to click on it first when we see this image on the Web, and we might also think that the image as a whole has more to do with time, dates, and scheduling than with Barbie.

Continuing to look at the image and to take notes, we might next turn to some of the objects in the image and try to determine why they're there and how they contribute to its message. The image depicts a room; given Barbie's prominence in the image, we can assume that this is Barbie's room. As girls visit this Web site, then, it is as if they are being welcomed into Barbie's room to play. The *perspective* of the image confirms this impression; the room is laid out before the viewer (rather than, say, viewing the room from above, or from a perspective outside of the window). Perspective is often a helpful category to use in analyzing images. The perspective essentially situates the viewer, defining the relation of the viewer to the image: are you positioned above or below the objects in the image? Are you on the outside looking in (implying perhaps that you're excluded or don't belong)?

In the room, we see a window, a rug, and wallpaper, but it's unclear what room this is: the armchair seems to signify "living room," while we would usually associate the dresser with a bedroom. The mannequin on the right side of the picture would seem to be out of place in either of these rooms. Is this confusion intentional? Perhaps one of the messages here is that playing with Barbie can take place in any room of the house.

What are the other elements in the room? Balloons attached to a gift, a butterfly, a backpack/purse, a purple game controller (detached from the computer), a photo of a younger girl, a magic wand and teddy bear drawn onto the dresser, a calendar and a drawing stuck on the wall, and sewing items (tape, pins) on the mannequin. Does this room look like any room you've ever been in? Probably not. After all, this is not a realistic image, not an attempt to capture and depict the world as it is. But it does contain elements that may be familiar and enticing to you—or, rather, to the girls for whom this image is intended. It's a fairly messy room, with all of these diverse items strewn about, conveying the impression that Barbie's got a lot going on. The image, in other words, depicts many options that girls have when they play in "Barbie's room."

Re-reading

Having looked carefully at the image and taken notes on its focus, color, dimension, and perspective, the next step is to articulate the ideas you've developed. Making statements about the image and writing down questions you have about it will compel you to look at it even more closely, clarifying your understanding and finding further meanings.

Based on the information discussed above, a general statement about the image might be that it promotes an idea of Barbie as a friendly, fun, active, and somewhat "larger than life" playmate for girls, and that girls have many choices of different ways to play with Barbie.

But some questions remain. For instance, is it significant that Barbie is just sitting in the chair and not playing with any of the items assembled in her room? It's as if she's waiting for a visitor. Her eyes are focused straight ahead so that it looks like she's looking right at the viewer (another component of perspective). Concerning the *arrangement* of items in the image, why is Barbie placed to the left rather than in the center? Concerning the *shapes* or lines in the image, is it meaningful that there are more curved than straight lines? Even items that we'd expect to have straight lines, such as the window and the calendar, are slightly askew. What effect do these curved lines have on our impression of the image? Another question that might be asked of images, but that aren't particularly relevant with this one, have to do with the *medium* of the work: that is, what materials were used to produce it, and why?

Reviewing

So we've examined the image, taken notes, looked at the image again, asked questions, and formulated some ideas and some questions about it. In the final stage, take the time to summarize what you've learned. Perhaps you can do this in the form of a statement about what you think the image means, or perhaps it's more effective to write about what strategies the image uses to convey its messages. In either case, you'll be prepared if you're asked to write about the image, or to include an analysis of it with an analysis of a text.

Before concluding this section and turning to the writing process, take a look at the second Barbie image we've selected, at the bottom of page CI-1. Follow the same steps described above in reading this image:

1. Take a look at the explanatory information and decide on the context of the image. Who is its audience, and what is its purpose? Note your first impressions of the image.
2. Read the image by noting where your eyes are initially drawn; why is this focal point important to the message of the image? Note other important features of the image: color, dimension, contrast, perspective, arrangement, shape, and medium. What reasons can you determine for the choices the artist made in these areas?
3. Write down a statement or two that you think explains the meaning of the image, along with any questions you still have about it. Examine it carefully to see what elements you have previously missed.

4. Summarize what you think are the messages and strategies of this image.

We think that one of the most enjoyable parts of studying popular culture is gaining expertise in interpreting the images that bombard us everyday, from all angles, from many media. Even a simple Barbie Web site gives us a lot to think about in terms of how this doll has been culturally (and commercially) constructed.

At the end of the introductory chapter and scattered throughout *Common Culture,* you'll find more images upon which you can exercise your interpretative powers. They are drawn from magazines, posters, the Web, and other sources, and they comment on the themes of the chapters of this text: advertising, television, music, cyberculture, sports, and movies. In a highly visual culture like ours, these images serve as "readings" that supplement and provide a different perspective on the more traditional reading materials in each chapter.

THE WRITING PROCESS

Frequently, when an instructor gives a writing assignment—for example, "Write an essay exploring the significance of the Barbie doll in contemporary American culture"—students experience a type of mini-panic: producing a focused, coherent, informative, and logically developed paper seems a monumental task. Some students may be overwhelmed by the many ideas swirling around in their heads, worrying they won't be able to put them into coherent order. Others may think they won't have enough to say about a given topic and complain, "How long does the paper have to be? How can I come up with four pages!"

However, there's really no reason to panic. Just as there are definable activities in the active process of reading, so the writing process can be broken down into four discrete stages: **prewriting, drafting, distancing,** and **revising.** Taking it a step at a time can make writing an essay a manageable and productive experience.

Prewriting

The first stage of the essay-writing process should be especially invigorating and stress-free, since at this point you don't have to worry about making your prose grammatically sound, logically organized, or convincing to a reader. All you have to do is write whatever comes into your head regarding your topic, so that you can discover the beginnings of ideas and phrasings that may be developed in the drafting stage and ultimately massaged into an acceptable form of academic writing.

There are a number of prewriting strategies writers use to generate ideas and happy turns of phrase. Experiment with all of these, in order to discover which of them "click" in terms of how you think and which help you most productively get your ideas down on paper. Most writers rely more heavily on one or two of these prewriting strategies, depending on their own styles and dispositions; it's a matter of individual preference. If you're a spontaneous, organic sort of person, for example, you might spend more time freewriting. On the other hand, if you have a more logical, mathematical mind, you might gravitate naturally to outlining and do very little freewriting. There's no right or wrong way to prewrite; it comes down to whatever works best for you. But what's best usually involves some combination of the three following techniques.

Freewriting This prewriting strategy lets your mind wander, as minds will, while you record whatever occurs to you. Just write, write, write, with no judgment about the validity, usefulness, grammatical correctness, or literary merit of the words you're putting down. The only requirement is that you write nonstop, either on paper or a word processor, for a manageable period of time: say, fifteen minutes without a break.

Your freewriting can be open—that is, it can be pure, stream-of-consciousness writing in which you "stay in the present moment" and record every thought, sense impression, disturbing sound—or it can be focused on a specific topic, such as Barbie dolls. When freewriting in preparation for writing an essay, it's frequently helpful to keep in mind a central question, either one from your instructor's original topic assignment or one sparked by your own curiosity, so that your freewritten material will be useful when you start composing your actual essay. Here is a typical focused freewrite on the subject of Barbie dolls written by a student in response to the writing assignment quoted earlier:

> *Toys: what did you want as a child vs. what you were given? I don't know, but I wanted cars and ended up with Barbie Corvette. Brother got G.I. Joe, Tonka trucks, I got talking Barbie, Barbie play house, Corvette.*
>
> *B. served as model for ideal female figure, and now that ideal is depicted in magazines. I guess that represents a kind of perpetuation of this image: girls raised on Barbie → cycle continues w/images in the media. The I = ideal image of women in America seems to be let's see: white, flawless, flat nose, wide eyes, that kind of thing. Whatever, it's clear that Barbie creates unreal expectations for women.*

Yeah! her figure would be inhuman if a real person had it—they would probably die! If she puts on jogging shoes, Barbie stands sloped because she's designed for high heels . . . so it seems as though Barbie is clearly designed for display rather than real activity, let alone profession. Display.

literature (written stuff) on Barbie packages—she's not interested in doctoring nurse, etc.; just having money, cars, looking good, taking trips etc. Re: tech—women think computers are "fun." Re: math—women supposedly aren't good at it. Barbie reinforces these stereotypes—and lots more—in girls

Changes in society? discuss for concl.?

Clustering Clustering is especially useful for discovering relationships between ideas, impressions, and facts. As a prewriting activity, it falls between freewriting and outlining, in that it's usually more focused than freewriting but less logically structured than an outline.

To prewrite by clustering, begin by writing a word or central phrase down in the center of a clean sheet of paper. In the case of the Barbie doll assignment, for example, you would probably start by writing "Barbie" in the middle of the page, and then drawing a circle around it. Having written and circled this central word or phrase, you can then jot down relevant facts, concrete examples, interesting ideas, and so on. Cluster these around the circled word, like this:

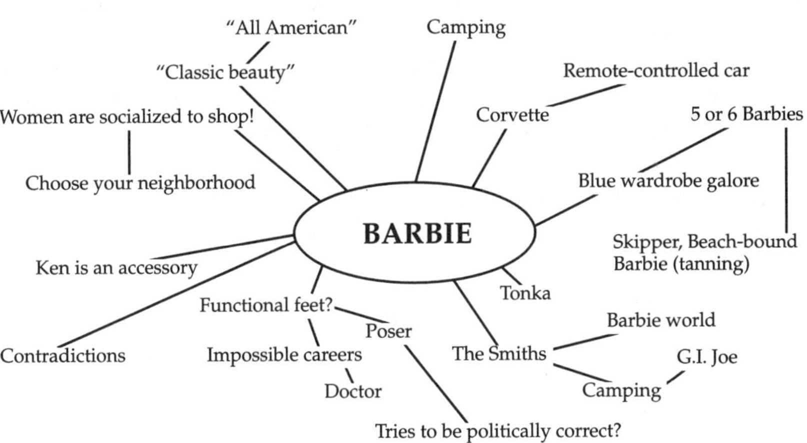

Frequently, one or more of your random jottings will serve as a new central word—as a jumping-off point for a new cluster of ideas. Later on, when you're drafting, you can use these clustered "nodes" as the basis for supporting paragraphs in the body of your essay.

Outlining If you have a rough idea of what the main points of your paper will be, outlining is an extremely useful prewriting technique, in that it helps you plan the overall structure for your paper and often generates new ideas about your topic. There are several different types of outlines, most notably scratch, sentence, and topic outlines.

For a *scratch outline* you list your intended points in a very tentative order, one that may only reflect the fact that you don't yet know in what order you want to put your supporting ideas. A scratch outline might not even suggest which subordinating points are most important to developing your thesis. For this reason, scratch outlines are most useful early in the prewriting phase, as a means of generating ideas as well as beginning to organize your thoughts logically. In fact, if you have not yet arrived at a thesis for your paper, one may emerge in the process of listing all your main and subordinate points and then reviewing that list to discover which of those ideas is the most central and important.

As you think more about your essay and come up with new ideas and supporting evidence, you will almost certainly revise your scratch outline to make it more detailed and conventionally formatted with numbered and lettered headings and subheads. A *topic outline* presents items in key words or brief phrases, rather than sentences, and frequently features no indentation. A *sentence outline* is even more developed than a topic outline, in that it describes the listed items in complete sentences, each of which is essentially a subtopic for a supporting paragraph. In fact, sentence outlines, when fully developed, can contain most of the supporting information you're going to present in your essay, and can therefore be extremely useful tools during the prewriting process.

Developing her freewritten material about Barbie into an outline, our student writer sketched out the following:

I. *Introduction*
   A. *Discuss my own experience with toys while growing up: parents "let" me play with Tonka trucks, but they gave me a Barbie Corvette when I wanted a race car.*
   B. *Discuss social shaping of gender roles generally.*
   C. *Working Thesis: Significance of Barbie in American society is that although people say women have "come a long way" and that there are new expectations, this is not really true. If it were, Barbie, depicted as mere sexual, leisureseeking consumer, could not be accepted.*

II. *The media see that people—especially young ones—need role models, and manufacture products to fill the following needs.*
   A. *Childhood: Barbie.*
      1. *Barbie presents a totally unrealistic female body as a role model for young women.*

2. *This role-modeling is crucial in young women's psychological development, because little girls role-play with Barbie, taking her actions as their own.*

B. *Pre-teen: Models in Seventeen magazine.*

C. *Teen: Vogue and Mademoiselle.*

D. *Adult: Cosmopolitan, Victoria's Secret lingerie models, advertisements in mainstream magazines.*

III. *The popularity of Barbie depicts the entrenched nature of traditional female roles.*

A. *The change toward women's equality is not something that is deemed beneficial by everyone, such as the religious ultra-right.*

B. *People purchasing Barbie either:*

1. *don't see the image that's being perpetuated; or*
2. *respect those values and want to pass them on to their children.*

C. *Significance in popular culture of Barbie is that she illustrates inconsistencies between changing social roles (women and minorities) and the concepts we are teaching youngsters.*

D. *Although the makers of Barbie make a superficial attempt at updating her, Barbie depicts traditional women absorbed in leisure, consumption, and beauty.*

1. *Barbie completely reinforces old role expectations.*
2. *Barbie in the '90s can have a career (she has some doctor outfits, I think), but she isn't ever functional in that career. The emphasis is still on leisure.*

IV. *The Racial Issue*

A. *Barbie illustrates the assimilation of minorities; they lose part of their culture, because Americans are supposed to belong to the "same mold."*

B. *In the '90s we say that we aren't prejudiced and that everyone should be accepted for who they are, but since the dominant culture is white, white men and women unconsciously (or in some cases consciously, I'm afraid) assume that others must take on white norms.*

V. *Conclusion*

A. *Bring it back around to my childhood play time and the necessity for parents to think about the sorts of toys they are giving their children, so that they don't reinforce and perpetuate these old patterns.*

You'll discover that this outline, while detailed, doesn't contain some of the points raised in the final essay's supporting paragraphs and that it includes a good deal of material that was not used in the final essay. The reason for this discrepancy is simple and illustrates a key point for you to remember about the writing process. As this writer began her essay, she discovered new points which she thought relevant to her thesis. At the same time, she realized that some of her outlined points were tangential and digressive rather than helpful in supporting her main point. She therefore cut some of those points, even though she thought they were valid and interesting ideas. That's one of the most painful but absolutely necessary tasks of the writer: getting rid of material which took some work to create and seems interesting and well written. If cutting some of your previously written material makes the final result better, then it's worth the sacrifice!

Drafting

Having generated a good amount of prewritten material and perhaps developed it into a detailed outline, your next task is to transform that material into an actual essay. Before proceeding with the drafting of your essay, however, it's a good idea first to consider your audience—your instructor only? Your instructor *and* your classmates? An imaginary editor or publisher? A third-grade student? Consider, too, the point you want to make about your topic to that audience. Unlike freewriting, which is by its nature often rambling and disjointed, essays succeed to the degree that they focus on a specific point and develop that point with illustrations and examples.

Thesis and Thesis Statement The main point, the central assertion of your essay, is called a *thesis*. It helps to have a clear sense of your thesis before writing a paper. However, keep in mind that this isn't always necessary: some people use writing as a discovery process, and don't arrive at their thesis until they've completed a first draft. Generally, however, the process is easier if you have a thesis in mind—even one that's not yet fully formed or that's likely to change—before you begin drafting.

While the form of thesis statements may vary considerably, there are some qualities that separate effective thesis statements from vague or weak ones. First of all, your thesis statement should be inclusive but focused: that is, it should be broad enough to encompass your paper's main supporting ideas, but narrow enough to represent a concise explanation of your paper's main point that won't require you to write fifty pages to cover the topic adequately. Furthermore, you want your thesis statement to be a forceful assertion rather than a question or an ambiguous statement of purpose such as, "In this paper I am going to talk about Barbie dolls and their effect on society."

Much more effective, as you will see in the sample student paper that concludes this chapter, is a statement which takes a stand:

> This is certainly one of the more dangerous consequences of Barbie's popularity in our society: a seemingly innocent toy defines for young girls the sorts of career choices, clothing, and relationships that will be "proper" for them as grown-up women.

Notice how this statement gives an excellent sense of the thematic direction the paper will take: clearly, it will examine the relationship between Barbie dolls and gender role identification in contemporary America.

Opening Paragraphs In most academic writing, you want to arrive at your thesis statement as quickly as possible, so that your reader will have a clear sense of your essay's purpose from the start. Many readers expect to find a thesis statement at the end of the introduction—generally the final sentence of the first or second paragraph. Effective introductions are often structured so as to lead up to the thesis statement: they draw the reader in by opening with an interesting specific point or question, a quotation, a brief anecdote, a controversial assertion—which serves to introduce the topic generally; a general overview then leads up to the specific statement of the thesis in the last sentence.

In the student essay on page 44, for example, observe how the writer begins with a personal reflection about Barbie. Her anecdote may strike a familiar chord with readers and therefore draw them into the topic. Having made the attempt to arouse her readers' interest in her opening paragraph, the writer moves more pointedly into the general topic, discussing briefly the possible social and psychological implications of her parents' gift choices. This discussion leads into her thesis statement, a focused assertion that concludes her second paragraph.

Keep in mind that many writers wait until they have written a first draft before they worry about an introduction. They simply lead off with a tentative thesis statement, then go back later to look for effective ways to lead up to that statement.

Supporting Paragraphs As you draft the body of your paper, keep two main goals in mind. First, try to make sure that all your supporting paragraphs are aimed at developing your thesis, so that you maintain your focus and don't ramble off the topic. Second, work toward presenting your supporting ideas in logical order, and try to provide smooth transitions between points.

The order in which you choose to present your ideas depends in large part on your topic and purpose. When you are arguing for a particular position, you might begin with less important ideas and work toward a final, crucial point. In this way you can build a case that you "clinch" with your strongest piece of evidence. Other kinds of essays call for different structures. For example, an essay tracing the history of the Barbie doll and its effect on American culture would probably be structured chronologically, from the introduction of the toy to its present-day incarnations, since that would be the most natural way to develop the discussion.

The student essay at the end of this chapter moves from a personal reflection on the topic of Barbie (paragraph 1); to a thesis statement that asserts the point of the paper (2); to a transitional paragraph moving from the writer's childhood experiences and a more general discussion of Barbie's role in reinforcing gender-role stereotypes in other young girls (3); to an overview of how sociologists and historians critique the Barbie phenomenon (4); to an examination of whether Barbie has changed in response to evolving attitudes regarding women in society (5–7), the heart of the writer's argument; to a conclusion that frames the essay by returning to the original, personal example (8). Each new discussion seems to flow naturally into the next because the writer uses a transitional phrase or parallel language to link the first sentence in each paragraph to the end of the preceding paragraph.

Evidence Using evidence effectively is the critical task in composing body paragraphs, because your essay will be convincing only to the degree that you make your arguments credible. Evidence can take many forms, from facts and figures you collect from library research to experiences you learn about in conversations with friends. While library research isn't necessary for every paper, it helps to include at least some "hard" facts and figures gathered from outside sources—journals, newspapers, textbooks—even if you're not writing a full-blown research paper. Frequently, gathering your evidence doesn't require scrolling through computer screens in your school's library; it could be accomplished by watching the six o'clock newscast or while reading the paper over breakfast.

Quotations from secondary sources are another common way of developing and supporting a point in a paragraph. Using another person's spoken or written words will lend your arguments a note of authenticity, especially when your source is a recognized authority in the field about which you're writing. A few points to remember when using quotations:

1. Generally, don't begin or end a supporting paragraph with a quotation. Articulate your point *in your own words* in the first sentence or two of the paragraph; *then* provide the quotation as a way of supporting your point. After the quotation, you might include another focusing sentence or two that analyzes the quotation and suggests how it relates to your point.
2. Keep your quotations brief. Overly lengthy quotations can make a paper difficult to read. You've probably read texts that nearly

put you to sleep because of their overuse of quotations. As a general rule, quote source material only when the precise phrasing is necessary to support your abstract points. Be careful not to allow cited passages to overpower your own assertions.

3. Remember that all of your secondary material—whether quoted or paraphrased—needs to be accurately attributed. Make sure to mention the source's name and include other information (such as the publication date or page number) as required by your instructor.

While quotations, facts, and figures are the most common ways of developing your supporting paragraphs with evidence, you can also use your imagination to come up with other means of substantiating your points. Design a questionnaire, hand it out to your friends and compile the resulting data as evidence. Interview a local authority on your topic, make notes about the conversation, and draw upon these as evidence. Finally, be your own authority: use your own powers of reasoning to come up with logical arguments that convince your readers of the validity of your assertions.

This body paragraph from the student essay on Barbie provides a good example of a writer using evidence to support her points:

> As Motz observes later in her article, Barbie has changed to adjust to the transforming attitudes of society over time. Both her facial expressions and wardrobe have undergone subtle alterations: "The newer Barbie has a more friendly, open expression, with a hint of a smile, and her lip and eye make-up is muted" (226), and in recent years Barbie's wardrobe has expanded to include some career clothing in addition to her massive volume of recreational attire. This transition appears to represent a conscious effort on the part of Barbie's manufacturers to integrate the concept of women as important members of the work force, with traditional ideals already depicted by Barbie.

The paragraph begins with an assertion of the general point that Barbie has changed in some ways over the years to reflect changes in societal attitudes toward women. This point is then supported with a quotation from an expert, and the page number of the original source is noted parenthetically. (Note that page references in this student essay are from the complete original essay by Motz, published in *The Popular Culture Reader*, not from the excerpt of the Motz essay earlier in this chapter.) The point is further developed with evidence presented in the writer's own words. The paragraph concludes with a final sentence that summarizes the main point of the evidence presented in the previous sentences, keeps the paragraph focused on the essay's thesis that Barbie perpetuates gender stereotypes, and sets the reader up for a transition into the next subtopic.

Obviously, all supporting paragraphs won't take this exact form; essays would be deadly boring if every paragraph looked the same. You'll encounter body paragraphs in professional essays that begin with quotations or end with quotations, for example. Just keep in mind that you want to *support* whatever general point you're making, so each paragraph should include a measure of specific, concrete evidence. The more you practice writing the more ways you'll discover to develop body paragraphs with illustrations, examples, and evidence.

Conclusions You may have learned in high school English courses that an essay's conclusion should restate the main points made in the paper, so that the reader is left with a concise summary that leaves no doubt as to the paper's intention. This was an excellent suggestion for high school students, as it reinforced the notion of focusing an essay on a specific, concrete point. In college, however, you'll want to start developing a more sophisticated academic style. Conclusions to college-level essays should do more than merely repeat the paper's main points; they should leave the reader with something to think about.

Of course, what that *something* is depends on your topic, your audiences, and your purpose in writing. Sometimes it may be appropriate to move from an objective discussion of a topic to a more subjective reflection on it. For instance, in analyzing the social effects of Barbie dolls, you might end by reflecting on the doll's significance in your own life or by commenting ironically on feminist critics who in your view make too much of Barbie's influence. Other ways to conclude are providing a provocative quotation; offering a challenge for the future; asserting a forceful opinion; creating a striking image or memorable turn of phrase; or referring back to an image or idea in your introduction.

What you want to avoid is a bland and overly general conclusion along the lines of, "Thus, in conclusion, it would seem to this author that Barbie has had a great and wide-reaching impact on today's contemporary society." Note how the writer of the Barbie essay created a strong conclusion by first returning to the subject of her opening paragraph—her own childhood toys—and then leaving the reader with a relatively memorable final sentence offering a challenge for the future:

> Looking back at my childhood, I see my parents engaged in this same struggle. By surrounding me with toys that perpetuated both feminine and masculine roles, they achieved a kind of balance among the conflicting images in society. However, they also seemed to succumb to traditional social pressures by giving me that Barbie Corvette, when all I

wanted was a radio-controlled formula-one racer, like the one Emerson Fittipaldi drives. In a time when most parents agree that young girls should be encouraged to pursue their goals regardless of gender boundaries, their actions do not always reflect these ideals. Only when we demand that toys like Barbie no longer perpetuate stereotypes will this reform be complete.

Distancing

Distancing is the easiest part of the writing process because it involves doing nothing more than putting your first draft aside and giving yourself some emotional and intellectual distance from it. Pursue your daily activities, go to work or complete assignments for other classes, take a hike, throw a frisbee, polish your shoes, do anything but read over your draft... ideally for a day or two.

The reason to take the time to distance yourself is simple: you've been working hard on your essay and therefore have a strong personal investment in it. In order to revise effectively, you need to be able to see your essay dispassionately, almost as though someone else had written it. Stepping away from it for a day or two gives you the opportunity to approach your essay as an editor who has no compunction about changing, reordering, or completely cutting passages that don't work.

Also, the process of distancing allows your mind to work on the essay subconsciously even while you're going about your other nonwriting activities. Frequently, during this distancing period, you'll find yourself coming up with new ideas that you can use to supplement your thesis as you revise.

Finally, factoring the process of distancing into the writing process will help you avoid the dread disease of all students: procrastination. Since you have to allot yourself enough time to write a draft *and* let it sit for a couple of days, you'll avoid a last-minute scramble for ideas and supporting material, and you'll have time to do a thorough revision.

One note of warning: Don't get so distanced from your draft that you forget to come back to it. If you do forget, all your prewriting and drafting will have gone to waste.

Revising

Many professional writers believe that revision is the most important stage in the writing process. Writers view the revision stage as an opportunity to clarify their ideas, to rearrange text so that the logical flow of their work is enhanced, to add new phrases or delete ones that don't work, to modify their thesis and change editorial direction... or, in some extreme cases, to throw the whole thing out and start over!

Just as with prewriting and drafting, many students dread revision because all the different issues that need to be considered make it appear to be a forbidding task. Most find it helpful to have a clear set of criteria with which to approach their first drafts. Following is such a checklist of questions, addressing specific issues of content, organization, and stylistics/mechanics. If you find that your answer is "no" to any one of these questions, then you need to rework your essay for improvement in that specific area.

Revision Checklist

Introduction

✔ Does the paper begin in a way that draws the reader into the paper while introducing the topic?

✔ Does the introduction provide some general overview that leads up to the thesis?

✔ Does the introduction end with a focused, assertive thesis in the form of a statement (not a question)?

Supporting Paragraphs and Conclusion

✔ Do your supporting paragraphs relate back to your thesis, so that the paper has a clear focus?

✔ Do your body paragraphs connect logically, with smooth transitions between them?

✔ Do your supporting paragraphs have a good balance between general points and specific, concrete evidence?

✔ If you've used secondary sources for your evidence, do you attribute them adequately to avoid any suspicion of plagiarism?

✔ If you've used quotations extensively, have you made sure your quoted material doesn't overpower your own writing?

✔ Does your last paragraph give your readers something to think about rather than merely restate what you've already said elsewhere in the essay?

Style and Mechanics

✔ Have you chosen your words aptly and sometimes inventively, avoiding clichés and overused phrases?

✔ Have you varied your sentence lengths effectively, thus helping create a pleasing prose rhythm?

✔ Have you proofread carefully, to catch any grammatical problems or spelling errors?

Make the minor changes or major overhauls required in your first draft. Then type or print out a second draft, and read it *out loud* to yourself, to catch any awkward or unnatural sounding passages, wordy sentences, grammatical glitches and so on. Reading your prose out loud may seem weird—especially to your roommates who can't help overhearing—but doing so helps you gain some new perspective on the piece of writing you have been so close to, and frequently highlights minor, sentence-level problems that you might otherwise overlook.

Writing Research on Popular Culture

A research essay focusing on popular culture follows the same steps as those presented in the previous discussion of essay writing in general—with a significant addition: the research essay focuses on a central hypothesis or research question, and it includes outside sources. For that reason, you might envision a slightly different sequence of activities for your writing process, one that moves according to the following stages:

- *Topic Selection:* Spend some time thinking about an issue that you actually are interested in, or want to know more about. Your teachers will sometimes give you relatively open-ended essay prompts, allowing you to select a research area with which you are familiar and/or interested. Even in those cases in which the teacher narrows the topic significantly—perhaps assigning an essay on the relationship between Barbie dolls and gender stereotyping, or between music lyrics and violence, for example—you still have a great deal of leeway in focusing the topic on elements of interest to you. In the music/violence example, you still have the freedom to select bands and lyrics you know well, and this will make your research much more well informed, while keeping the topic fresh and interesting to you.
- *Focus:* Narrow the topic as much as you can to ensure that your work will be thorough, focused and well supported with evidence. In the Barbie example at the end of this chapter, the author focused on childhood psychological development as it is affected by stereotype-perpetuating toys such as Barbie. Likewise, in the music/violence example, you might narrow the focus by restricting your research to certain types of popular music, such as punk or hip-hop, or to music by artists of a certain gender or ethnic population. The less global you make your topic, the less you will find yourself awash in volumes of disparate material as you develop your essay drafts.

- *Working Thesis:* Develop a preliminary research question or hypothesis related to your topic. This working thesis will undoubtedly go through several refinements as you begin researching your topic, but it helps greatly to organize your research material if you begin with a concrete point of view, even if you change it later on, as you find more information on the topic. In the case of the student essay that follows, a research question might have been: do certain toys reinforce gender stereotyping in children? The working hypothesis would probably have supported the affirmative position. In the music/violence topic, a working thesis might be something such as: while many observers believe that lyrics in hip-hop music incite young people to violence, research demonstrates that there is no causal connection between listening to certain types of music and violent behavior. You would then proceed to the next step, to find material that supports (or disproves) this initial hypothesis.
- *Secondary Sources:* Find the most valuable materials written by other people on your chosen topic. As much as possible, include examples from a wide range of sources, including scholarly journals, books, popular literature (such as magazine and newspaper articles), and World Wide Web sites. Don't be daunted if you don't find materials from each of these source categories; in some cases, for example, a topic will be so new and fresh that there haven't been books written about it, and you may have to rely more on newspaper articles and Web sites.
- *Primary Sources:* If possible and applicable to your assignment, include some research conducted by yourself, such as interviews with professors who are experts on the topic you are examining, or even with friends and peers who can provide a "person-on-the-street" perspective to balance some of the more academic or journalistic perspectives found in your secondary sources.
- *Critical Reading:* To avoid becoming a passive receptor of someone else's obvious or popular conclusions, analyze your assembled source information to find its literal and implied meanings and to weigh the validity of the information it presents. At the same time, check the validity of your own previously held assumptions and beliefs; as much as possible, try to have an open mind about your topic, even if you have a working hypothesis you are developing. In the case of the above-described working thesis on the relationship between music and violence, you may find material that disproves your original hypothesis, suggesting that there is in fact a relationship between listening to music and acting violently. You may then want to revise your thesis to reflect the material you have found, if you think that information is

valid. Feel free to use or reject discovered information based upon your critical analysis of it.

- *Documentation:* Finally, keep careful record of your sources so that you can attribute them accurately, using a bibliographic format appropriate to your research topic and approach. Keep in mind that any time you use source material to support your arguments in academic papers, it is necessary that you document that material. You accomplish this by using footnotes and/or parenthetical in-text citations in the body of your essay, along with bibliographies and/or Works Cited pages at the end of your essay. This academic convention accomplishes two purposes: first, it serves to acknowledge your having relied upon ideas and/or actual phrases from outside source material; and second, it allows readers to explore a paper's topic further, should they find the issues raised thought-provoking and worthy of pursuit.

In academic settings the major systems of documentation—namely, APA, MLA, and CBE—share certain key characteristics. That is, they all furnish readers with uniform information about quoted or paraphrased material from books, journals, newspapers, Web sites, and so forth. While it may seem strange for such a multiplicity of documenting styles to exist, there actually is a good reason why there is not one single documentation format for all academic disciplines: the different documentation styles support the unique needs and preferences of certain academic communities. Social scientists cite their sources by author and date, because in the social sciences, broad articulations of concepts, refined through time, are paramount; APA format reflects this. By contrast, researchers working in humanities-related fields rely frequently upon direct quotations; the MLA format therefore furnishes page numbers rather than dates.

If you have already selected a major, you will probably be writing most, if not all, of your essays for a certain discipline, such as English literature or psychology. While you will probably want to acquaint yourself to some degree with the basics of all the major citation formats, you will certainly want to learn, memorize, and practice with special diligence the documentation requirements of the area in which you will be majoring. All three of the above-mentioned professional organizations periodically issue revised guidelines for documentation, and if you want to be sure about the specific rules in your area of specialization, you might want to buy one of the following:

MLA Handbook for Writers of Research Papers (5th edition, 1999)
The Publication Manual of the American Psychological Association (5th edition, 2001)

The CBE [Council of Biology Editors, recently changed to the Council of Science Editors] *Manual of Authors, Editors, and Publishers* (6th edition, 1994)
The Chicago Manual of Style (14th edition, 1993)

Furthermore, there are numerous handbooks available, such as the *Prentice Hall Guide to Research: Documentation,* 4th edition, which provide detailed information on documentation in all of the disciplines. In the absence of such books, the following section gives features of the two most popular documentation styles, the MLA and the APA.

Modern Language Association Documentation Format

• Within the body of the text, all sources are cited within parentheses (known in the academic world as "in-text parenthetical citations"), using the author's name and the number of the page from which the source was derived. You should include an in-text citation any time you use another writer's ideas or phrasings within the text of your own paper, either by direct quotation or by paraphrase.

• At the end of the paper, sources are listed alphabetically, on a page or pages with the heading "Works Cited." In the Works Cited section, list book-derived citations using the following information, in this order: the author's name exactly as it appears on the book's title page, last name first; the title of the book, underlined; the place of publication followed by a colon; the publisher, followed by a comma; and the date of publication. A typical MLA-formatted book listing will look like this:

Berger, Arthur Asa. <u>Television as an Instrument of Terror: Essays on Media, Popular Culture, and Everyday Life.</u> New Brunswick, N.J.: Transaction Books, 1980.

A typical MLA journal or magazine citation will contain six pieces of information: the author, listed last name first; the article's title in quotation marks; the journal's title underlined; the volume number followed by the issue number; the date of publication; and the article's page numbers. A typical MLA-formatted journal listing will appear in this way:

Auerbach, Jeffrey. "Art, advertising, and the legacy of empire." <u>Journal of Popular Culture</u> 35, 4 (2002): 1–23.

For files acquired from the World Wide Web, give the author's name (if known), the full title of the work in quotation marks, the title of the complete work (if applicable) in italics, and the full HTTP address. For example:

> Brooke, Collin. "Perspective: Notes Toward the Remediation of Style." Enculturation: Special Multi-journal Issue on Electronic Publication 4.1 (Spring 2002): http://enculturation.gmu.edu/4_1/ style

American Psychological Association Documentation Format

• Within the body of the text, all sources are cited within parentheses, using the author's name and the number of the page from which the source was derived, along with the year of publication. That latter bit of information—the publication date—is the important difference in parenthetical in-text citation format between the APA and MLA documentation styles.

• At the end of the paper, sources are listed alphabetically on a page or pages of reference materials. List book-derived citations using the following information, in order: the author's last name and initials for first name (and middle name if given), last name first; the year of publication in parentheses; the title of the book in italics with only the first word of the title capitalized; the place of publication followed by a colon; and the publisher, followed by a period. A typical APA-formatted book listing will look like this:

> Charyn, J. (1989). *Movieland: Hollywood and the great American dream culture.* New York: Putnam.

An APA-formatted journal or magazine citation will contain six pieces of information: the author's name; the date of publication; the article's title; the journal's title, italicized along with the volume number; and the article's page numbers. A typical APA-formatted journal listing will look like this:

> Banks, J. (1997). MTV and the globalization of popular culture. *Gazette, 59* (1), 43–44.

For electronic citations, give the author's name (if known), the date of publication or of the latest update, the full title of the work, a note in brackets identifying the source as one that is on-line, then a sentence starting with the word "Available" followed by a colon and the source's URL or HTTP address. For example,

> Cole, S. K. (1999). I am the eye, you are my victim: the pornographic ideology of music video. *Enculturation Magazine* [On-line serial]. Available: http://enculturation.gmu.edu/2_2/ cole/

Of course, there are many other sources—newspapers, interviews, videos, e-mail conversations, just to name a few—that are omitted here for the sake of brevity, but that carry specific formatting requirements within the major documentation styles. You will undoubtedly want to refer to a handbook or a style sheet published by one of the national associations, should you be asked to write a more extensive research paper that includes the full range of source materials.

Sample Student Essay

The following essay demonstrates one way of approaching the assignment we presented earlier. As you read, note the essay's introductory paragraphs and thesis statement, the way body paragraphs are developed with illustrations and examples, the way it concludes without simply restating the writer's points, the writer's effective use of words and sentence structure, the ways in which it incorporates source material into the developing arguments, and the correct MLA documentation format. While this is not, strictly speaking, a research essay as described above, it does incorporate source material in the ways discussed above.

Role-Model Barbie: Now and Forever?

CAROLYN MUHLSTEIN

During my early childhood, my parents avoided placing gender boundaries on my play time. My brother and I both had Tonka trucks, and these were driven by Barbie, Strawberry Shortcake, and GI Joe to my doll house, or to condos built with my brother's Erector Set. However, as I got older, the boundaries became more defined, and certain forms of play became "inappropriate." For example, I remember asking for a remote controlled car one Christmas, anticipating a powerful race car like the ones driven at De Anza Days, the local community fair. Christmas morning waiting for me under the tree was a bright yellow Barbie Corvette. It seemed as though my parents had decided that if I had to have a remote controlled car, at least it could be a feminine Barbie one! 1

Although I was too young to realize it at the time, this gift represented a subtle shift in my parents' attitudes toward my gender-role choices. Where before my folks seemed content to let me assume either traditional "boy" or traditional "girl" roles in play, now they appeared to be subtly directing me toward traditional female role-playing. This is certainly one of the more dangerous consequences of Barbie's popularity in our society: a seemingly innocent toy defines for young girls the sorts of career choices, clothing, and relationships that will be "proper" for them as grown-up women. 2

Perhaps the Barbie Corvette was my parents' attempt to steer me back toward more traditional feminine pursuits. Since her birth thirty-five years ago, Barbie has been used by many parents to illustrate the "appropriate" role of a woman in society. During earlier decades, when women were expected to remain at home, Barbie's lifestyle was extremely fitting. Marilyn Ferris Motz writes that Barbie "represents so well the widespread values of modern American society, devoting herself to the pursuit of happiness through leisure and material goods... teaching them [female children] the skills by which their future success will be measured" (212). Barbie, then, serves as a symbol of the woman's traditional role in our society, and she serves to reinforce those stereotypes in young girls. 3

Motz' opinion isn't an isolated one. In fact, the consensus among sociologists, historians, and consumers is that Barbie represents a life of lazy leisure and wealth. Her "forever arched feet" and face "always smiling, eyes wide with admiration" (Tham 180) allow for little more than evenings on the town and strolls in the park. In addition, the accessories Barbie is equipped with are almost all related to pursuits of mere pleasure. According to a Barbie sticker album created by Mattel: 4

> Barbie is seen as a typical young lady of the twentieth century, who knows how to appreciate beautiful things and, at the same time, live life to the fullest...with her fashionable wardrobe and constant journeys to exciting places all over the world, the adventures of Barbie offer a glimpse of what they [girls] might achieve one day. (qtd. in Motz 218)

In this packaging "literature"—and in the countless other advertisements and packaging materials that have emerged since Barbie's invention some thirty years ago—the manufacturers exalt Barbie's materialism, her appreciation of "beautiful things," fine clothing, and expensive trips as positive personality traits: qualities which all normal, healthy girls in this society should try to emulate, according to the traditional view.

As Motz observes later in her article, Barbie has changed to adjust to the transforming attitudes of society over time. Both her facial expressions and wardrobe have undergone subtle alterations: "The newer Barbie has a more friendly, open expression, with a hint of a smile, and her lip and eye make-up is muted" (226), and in recent years Barbie's wardrobe has expanded to include some career clothing in addition to her massive volume of recreational attire. This transition appears to 5 represent a conscious effort on the part of Barbie's manufacturers to integrate the concept of women as important members of the work force, with traditional ideals already depicted by Barbie.

Unfortunately, a critical examination of today's Barbie doll reveals 6
that this so-called integration is actually a cynical, half-hearted attempt to satisfy the concerns of some people—especially those concerned with feminist issues. Sure, Barbie now has office attire, a doctor outfit, a nurse outfit, and a few other pieces of "career" clothing, but her image continues to center on leisure. As Motz observes, "Barbie may try her hand at high-status occupations, but her appearance does not suggest competence and professionalism" (230). Quite the opposite, in fact: there are few, and in some cases, no accessories with which a young girl might imagine a world of professional competence for Barbie. There are no Barbie hospitals and no Barbie doctor offices; instead, she has only mansions, boats, and fast cars. Furthermore, Barbie's arched feet make it impossible for her to stand in anything but heels, so a career as a doctor, an astronaut—or anything else that requires standing up for more than twenty minutes on a fashion runway—would be nearly impossible!

From these examples, it's clear that Barbie's manufacturers have 7
failed to reconcile the traditional image of women as sexual, leisure-seeking consumers with the view that women are assertive, career-oriented individuals, because their "revision" of the Barbie image is at best a token one. This failure to reconcile two opposing roles for Barbie parallels the same contradiction in contemporary society. By choice and necessity women are in the work force in large numbers, seeking equal pay and equal opportunities with men; yet the more traditional voices in our culture continue to perpetuate stereotyped images of women. If we believe that we are at a transitional point in the evolution toward real equality for women, then Barbie exemplifies this transitional stage perfectly.

Looking back at my childhood, I see my parents engaged in this 8
same struggle. By surrounding me with toys that perpetuated both feminine and masculine roles, they achieved a kind of balance among the conflicting images in society. However, they also seemed to succumb to traditional social pressures by giving me that Barbie Corvette, when all I wanted was a radio-controlled formula-one racer, like the one Emerson Fittipaldi drives. In a time when most parents agree that young girls should be encouraged to pursue their goals regardless of gender boundaries, their actions do not always reflect these ideals. Only when we demand that toys like Barbie no longer perpetuate stereotypes will this reform be complete.

References

Motz, Marilyn Ferris. "Through Rose-Tinted Glasses," in *Popular Culture: An Introductory Text,*" eds. Jack Trachbar and Kevin Lause. Bowling Green, OH: Bowling Green University Press, 1992.

Tham, Hilary, "Barbie's Shoes," in *Mondo Barbie,* eds. Lucinda Ebersole and Richard Peabody. New York: St. Martin's Press, 1993.

2

Advertising

What you see above is a very simple advertisement for a Timex watch. A picture of the watch, a short statement, a tag with information about the watch and the familiar Timex slogan, some small print at the bottom: there doesn't seem to be much more to it than that. But appearances can be deceiving—and indeed, they often are in advertisements.

Let's take a closer look. The ad is centered on a simple statement: "If you think it's cool, it is." The longest word in the sentence is only five letters, reminding us of other familiar advertising slogans such as "Just do it" and "Coke is it." In addition to their quite basic vocabulary, these slogans share a certain quality of vagueness: the "it" in "Just do it," like the "it" in "Coke is it," are what semioticians might call "floating signifiers": their meaning is open and flexible, determined substantially by the reader of the ad. The same can be said for the "it" in this Timex ad: does "it" refer only to the watch? If so, why doesn't the statement say, "If you think *this watch* is cool, it is"? Clearly, an all-encompassing word like "it" allows the statement to be about more than just the watch.

Even more interesting in this ad is the word "cool": what exactly is "cool"? It's a word that we all define differently, and Timex invites us here to take our own definition of "cool" and associate it with the watch. Whatever each of us thinks of as "cool," that's what this watch is. While vagueness usually leads to poor communication, you can see how it's used effectively here by the advertiser: "cool" tells us virtually nothing about the watch, but makes us feel good about it nonetheless. And of course, "cool" appeals to a certain audience: precisely the young, upscale, Generation X types who might be reading *Icon,* the glossy and expensive new "thoughtstyle" magazine in which we found the ad. So, targeting a smaller audience, Timex can afford to be more specific than Coke can be when it claims to be "it." Still, the watch is "cool" rather than "groovy" (too old) or "rad" (too California-surfer). In that one word alone and in the way it's used, we can see the ad hard at work trying to make its product appealing to potential customers.

When we look at the entire sentence, we can also see a degree of complexity behind its seeming simplicity. Even if we accept that the word "it" refers only to the watch, the sentence invites two different interpretations:

1. "If you think this watch is cool, well, you're right, because it is."
2. "If *you* think this watch is cool, then it is (because you say it is)."

This is a fine difference, but an important one. The first way of reading the sentence suggests that the watch is naturally, essentially cool, and so the reader is to be congratulated on being perceptive enough to see coolness when he or she comes across it. In the second reading, the watch isn't naturally cool at all; it's the reader who decides that the watch is cool. Either way, the reader of the ad gets a compliment and perhaps an ego-boost: either he or she is cool enough to recognize a cool watch, or he or she has the power to determine coolness. The first option might appeal to a more insecure sort of reader, someone who fears that he or she can't distinguish cool from uncool. The second reading confirms the confidence of a more secure reader, someone who knows perfectly well what's cool and what isn't. In other words, the statement appeals simultaneously to both the "wanna-be cools" and the "already cools" who might be reading *Icon.*

Now you may think that we're reading too much into so simple an advertisement, especially considering the fact that we haven't gotten past the statement yet to consider other elements in the ad: all that white space, the strange information presented on the label (why do we need to know the date of the original design?), the Timex slogan at the bottom of the label. It's true that we're spending far more time interpreting this ad than most readers spend on it as they thumb through *Icon* looking for an interesting article to read. But we're not spending nearly as much time on the ad as its designers did. The fact is that nothing in this ad—or in any ad—is there by mistake; every detail is carefully chosen, every word carefully selected, every photograph carefully arranged. Advertisers know that readers usually spend only a few seconds glancing at ads as they page through a magazine; we drive quickly past billboards and use TV commercial minutes to grab food from the fridge. In those seconds that the advertisers have our attention, they need to make as strong a pitch as possible. All that we're doing with the Timex ad is speculating about each of the choices that the designers of the ad made in creating their pitch. In several writing and discussion assignments in this chapter, you'll be asked to do the same kind of analysis with ads that you select, and in readings in this chapter you'll see more detailed and complete analyses of ads that can serve, along with this mini-analysis of the Timex ad, as models for your own interpretations.

Keep in mind, too, that advertising agencies spend a great deal of time and money trying to understand the complex psychodynamics of their target audiences and then tailoring ads to appeal to those audiences. Even their simplest and most seemingly direct advertisements still carry subtly powerful messages—about "coolness" as well as about appropriate modes of behavior, standards of beauty and success, gender roles, and a variety of other markers for normalcy and status. In tailoring ads to appeal both to basic human impulses and to more culturally conditioned attitudes, they also ultimately reinforce and even engender such impulses and attitudes. So although advertisements like the one above seem to be thoroughly innocuous and unimportant, the argument of many pop culture critics is that they have quite an influence—perhaps all the more so because we think they're so bland and harmless.

Several readings in this chapter explain in further detail the ways in which we can be manipulated by advertising. Jib Fowles, for example, points out a variety of strategies advertisements use to appeal to our emotions even though we may think we are making product choices using our intellect. The readings in the second section of the chapter look at how advertising works to manipulate our notions of masculinity and femininity. You'll probably find that many advertisements, especially the ones in gender-specific magazines like *GQ* and

Vogue, attempt to sell products by connecting them, however tenuously, to idealized and highly desirable images of masculinity and femininity: put bluntly, it's "buy this cologne (perfume) and you'll be the man (woman) you've always dreamed of being." No one really believes that, of course... at least not consciously. But these kinds of ads must be working or else advertisers would find other, more effective strategies to make their products appealing to consumers.

Whatever your view of advertising, keep in mind as you read the following sections that everything in advertisements—from sexy models to simple black and white pictures of watches—exist solely for three well-calculated reasons: to sell, sell, and sell.

Approaches to Advertising

The Cult You're In

Kalle Lasn

We begin this chapter on advertising with an intriguing, lyrical, but quite bleak piece by one of advertising's most interesting critics, Kalle Lasn. Lasn is one of the founders of Adbusters Media Foundation, which publishes Adbusters *magazine and coordinates such "culture jamming" campaigns as "TV Turn-Off Week," "Buy Nothing Day," and "Car Free Day" (http://www.adbusters.org). The selection reprinted here comes from Lasn's book* Culture Jam: The Uncooling of America.

Through his book, magazine, Web site, and "culture jamming" campaigns, Lasn delivers a critique of contemporary consumer culture, focused in particular on advertising, the influence of mass media, and the power of large corporations. In Lasn's words, his movement is "about reclaiming democracy, returning this country to its citizens as *citizens, not marketing targets or demographics. It's about being a skeptic and not letting advertising tell you what to think."*

In the following article, Lasn describes a scenario in which advertising does *tell us what to think, and even what to dream, exerting a profound and complete power over our lives as citizen-consumers. Whether this scenario is an accurate description of the present or a disturbing possibility for the future is for you to decide.* **Before you read,** *consider the title of this article: "The Cult You're In." What effect does it have to be told in this title that you're in a cult? What do you already know about cults that might influence your reaction to the title?*

A beeping truck, backing up in the alley, jolts you out of a scary dream—a mad midnight chase through a supermarket, ending with a savage beating at the hands of the Keebler elves. You sit up in a cold sweat, heart slamming in your chest. It was only a nightmare. Slowly, you reintegrate, remembering who and where you are. In your bed, in your little apartment, in the very town you grew up in. 1

It's a "This Is Your Life" moment—a time for mulling and stocktaking. You are still here. Just a few miles from the place you had your first kiss, got your first job (drive-through window at Wendy's), bought your first car ('73 Ford Torino), went nuts with the Wild Turkey on prom night and pulled that all-nighter at Kinko's, photocopying transcripts to send to the big schools back East. 2

Those big dreams of youth didn't quite pan out. You didn't get into Harvard, didn't get courted by the Bulls, didn't land a recording contract with EMI (or anyone else), didn't make a million by age twenty-five. And so you scaled down your hopes of embarrassing riches to reasonable expectations of adequate comfort—the modest condo downtown, the Visa card, the Braun shaver, the one good Armani suit.

Even this more modest star proved out of reach. The state college you graduated from left you with a $35,000 debt. The work you found hardly dented it: dreadful eight-to-six days in the circulation department of a bad lifestyle magazine. You learned to swallow hard and just do the job—until the cuts came and the junior people were cleared out with a week's severance pay and sober no-look nods from middle management. You began paying the rent with Visa advances. You got call-display to avoid the collection agency.

There remains only one thing no one has taken away, your only real equity. And you intend to enjoy fully that Fiat rustmaster this weekend. You can't run from your problems, but you may as well drive. Road Trip. Three days to forget it all. Three days of living like an animal (in the best possible sense), alert to sights and sounds and smells: Howard Stern on the morning radio, Slumber Lodge pools along the I-14. "You may find yourself behind the wheel of a large automobile," sings David Byrne from a tape labeled "Road Tunes One." The Fiat is, of course, only large at heart. "You know what FIAT stands for?" Liv said when she first saw it. "Fix It Again, Tony." You knew then that this was a girl you could travel to the ends of the Earth with. Or at least to New York City.

The itinerary is set. You will order clam chowder from the Soup Nazi, line up for standby Letterman tickets and wander around Times Square (Now cleaner! Safer!) with one eye on the Jumbotron. It's a place you've never been, though you live there in your mind. You will jog in Battery Park and sip Guinness at Michael's Pub on Monday night (Woody Allen's night), and you will dance with Liv in the Rainbow Room on her birthday. Ah Liv, who when you first saw her spraying Opium on her wrist at the cosmetics counter reminded you so much of Cindy Crawford—though of late she's put on a few pounds and now looks better when you close your eyes and imagine.

And so you'll drive. You'll fuel up with Ho Ho's and Pez and Evian and magazines and batteries for your Discman, and then you'll bury the pedal under your Converse All-Stars—like the ones Kurt Cobain died in. Wayfarers on, needle climbing and the unspoken understanding that you and Liv will conduct the conversation entirely in movie catchphrases.

"Mrs. Nixon would like you to pass the Doritos."

"You just keep thinking, Butch. That's what you're good at."

"It's over, Rock. Nothing on Earth's gonna save you now."

It occurs to you that you can't remember the last time Liv was just Liv and you were just you. You light up a Metro, a designer cigarette so obviously targeted at your demographic...which is why you steered clear of them until one day you smoked one to be ironic, and now you can't stop. 11

You'll come back home in a week. Or maybe you won't. Why should you? What's there to come back *for*? On the other hand, why should you stay? 12

A long time ago, without even realizing it, just about all of us were recruited into a cult. At some indeterminate moment, maybe when we were feeling particularly adrift or vulnerable, a cult member showed up and made a beautiful presentation. "I believe I have something to ease your pain." She made us feel welcome. We understood she was offering us something to give life meaning. She was wearing Nike sneakers and a Planet Hollywood cap. 13

Do you *feel* as if you're in a cult? Probably not. The atmosphere is quite un-Moonielike. We're free to roam and recreate. No one seems to be forcing us to do anything we don't want to do. In fact, we feel privileged to be here. The rules don't seem oppressive. But make no mistake: There are rules. 14

By consensus, cult members speak a kind of corporate Esperanto: words and ideas sucked up from TV and advertising. We wear uniforms—not white robes but, let's say, Tommy Hilfiger jackets or Airwalk sneakers (it depends on our particular subsect). We have been recruited into roles and behavior patterns *we did not consciously choose.* 15

Quite a few members ended up in the slacker camp. They're bunked in spartan huts on the periphery, well away from the others. There's no mistaking cult slackers for "downshifters"—those folks who have *voluntarily* cashed out of their high-paying jobs and simplified their lives. Slackers are downshifters by necessity. They live frugally because they are poor. (Underemployed and often overeducated, they may never get out of the rent-and-loan-repayment cycle.) 16

There's really not much for the slackers to *do* from day to day. They hang out, never asking, never telling, just offering intermittent wry observations. They are postpolitical, postreligious. They don't define themselves by who they vote for or pray to (these things are pretty much prescribed in the cult anyway). They set themselves apart in the only way cult members can: by what they choose to wear and drive and listen to. The only things to which they confidently ascribe value are things other people have already scouted, deemed worthy and embraced. 17

Cult members aren't really citizens. The notions of citizenship and nationhood make little sense in this world. We're not fathers and mothers and brothers: We're consumers. We care about sneakers, 18 music and Jeeps. The only *Life, Freedom, Wonder* and *Joy* in our lives are the brands on our supermarket shelves.

Are we happy? Not really. Cults promise a kind of boundless 19
contentment—punctuated by moments of bliss—but never quite deliver on that promise. They fill the void, but only with a different kind of void. Disillusionment eventually sets in—or it would if we were allowed to think much about it. Hence the first commandment of a cult: *Thou shalt not think.* Free thinking will break the trance and introduce competing perspectives. Which leads to doubt. Which leads to contemplation of the nearest exit.

How did all this happen in the first place? Why have we no 20
memory of it? When were we recruited?

The first solicitations began when we were very young. If you 21
close your eyes and think back, you may remember some of them.

You are four years old, tugging on your mother's sleeve in the 22
supermarket. There are products down here at eye level that she cannot see. Cool products with cartoon faces on them. Toys familiar from Saturday morning television. You want them. She keeps pushing her cart. You cry. She doesn't understand.

You are eight. You have allowance money. You savor the buying 23
experience. A Coke here, a Snickers bar there. Each little fix means not just getting what you want, but *power.* For a few moments *you* are the center of attention. *You* call the shots. People smile and scurry around serving you.

Michael Jordan goes up on your bedroom door. He is your first 24
hero, throwing a glow around the first brand in your life—Nike. You wanna be like Mike.

Other heroes follow. Sometimes they contradict each other. 25
Michael Jackson drinks Pepsi but Michael Jordan drinks Coke. Who is the false prophet? Your friends reinforce the brandhunting. Wearing the same stuff and hearing the same music makes you a fraternity, united in soul and form.

You watch TV. It's your sanctuary. You feel neither loneliness 26
nor solitude here.

You enter the rebel years. You strut the malls, brandishing a Dr 27
Pepper can full of Scotch, which you drink right under the noses of the surveillance guards. One day you act drunk and trick them into "arresting" you—only this time it actually *is* soda in the can. You are immensely pleased with yourself.

You go to college, invest in a Powerbook, ride a Vespa scooter, 28
don Doc Martens. In your town, a new sports complex and performing arts center name themselves after a car manufacturer and a software company. You have moved so far into the consumer maze that you can smell the cheese.

After graduating you begin to make a little money, and it's quite seductive. The more you have, the more you think about it. 29

You buy a house with three bathrooms. You park your BMW outside the double garage. When you grow depressed you go shopping. 30

The cult rituals spread themselves evenly over the calendar: Christmas, Super Bowl, Easter, pay-per-view boxing match, summer Olympics, Mother's Day, Father's Day, Thanksgiving, Halloween. Each has its own imperatives—stuff you have to buy, things you have to do. 31

You're a lifer now. You're locked and loaded. On the go, trying to generate more income to buy more things and then, feeling dissatisfied but not quite sure why, setting your sights on even greater income and more acquisitions. When "consumer confidence is down," spending is "stagnant," the "retail sector" is "hurting" and "stingy consumers are giving stores the blues," you do your bit for the economy. You are a star. 32

Always, always you have been free to dream. The motivational speakers you watched on late-night TV preached that even the most sorry schleppers can achieve their goals if they visualize daily and stay committed. *Think and grow rich.* 33

Dreams, by definition, are supposed to be unique and imaginative. Yet the bulk of the population is dreaming the same dream. It's a dream of wealth, power, fame, plenty of sex and exciting recreational opportunities. 34

What does it mean when a whole culture dreams the same dream? 35

Examining the Text

1. What is the function of the story that opens this reading? What feelings does the story evoke in you?

2. Why does Lasn use the pronoun "you" in this story and elsewhere in the article? How does this strategy contribute to (or detract from) his argument?

3. What is the effect of all of the products and brand names that Lasn includes in this article?

4. How does Lasn define the term "cult"? How is his definition different from (and similar to) the common usage of this word?

For Group Discussion

Discuss the characteristics of the cult that Lasn describes. Who are its members (and nonmembers)? What are its rules? How are we initiated into this cult? What are the cult's beliefs and rituals? How do we get ourselves out of this cult? After discussing these questions, decide on the extent to which you're persuaded by Lasn's argument that contemporary consumer culture is a kind of cult.

Writing Suggestion

Lasn ends his essay by asking, "What does it mean when a whole culture dreams the same dream?" Try writing a response to this question. What are the characteristics of this dream that Lasn claims are shared by the entire culture? Why is it a problem if everyone dreams the same dream? Alternately, you can take issue with the question itself, either by arguing that what it implies isn't true (in other words, that we each dream different dreams), or by arguing that it's perfectly acceptable if we all dream the same dream. Be sure to support any claims in your essay with specific evidence drawn from Lasn's argument as well as from your own experiences and observations.

You might consider using the black-and-white image above as one of the examples in your essay. This image, a poster for Adbuster's "Buy Nothing Day," graphically presents the problem Lasn discusses in "The Cult You're In," and it also points to a solution, of sorts. How might the image be used to bolster an argument either for or against Lasn's assertions?

Salespeak

Roy Fox

A colleague who shall remain nameless once suggested an intriguing way for teachers to supplement their generally meager salaries: we could have our classes sponsored. We live in an age where double plays in baseball are sponsored by Jiffy Lube, where pro football games include the "Taco Bell Halftime Report," and where our shirts, shorts, shoes, and even underwear are im-

printed with product names and logos. Why shouldn't teachers take advantage of a little corporate sponsorship? After all, we've got a captive audience of a very desirable demographic group (that's you). For a few extra dollars, we could easily play an advertising jingle softly in the background before class starts; we could say "This class is brought to you by Snapple!" at the beginning of class, and distribute free samples as students leave at the end of class.

If this scenario seems strange to you, you're about to read an even stranger scenario described by Roy Fox. Fox places us in a school of the future, in which students attend classes in order to learn how to be good consumers. They are inundated by advertisements, marketing pitches, and product-testing at school, where they watch commercially sponsored lessons on TV, read corporate-produced instructional materials, and shop at the school's "Commoditarium." But what's more surprising is Fox's assertion that this scenario is closer to reality than we might think.

What Fox calls "Salespeak" is infiltrating all aspects of our lives, but in this selection he is most interested with the ways that advertising and merchandising have established themselves in classrooms and schools across the country, changing the content and purpose of education. Fox is a Professor of Education at the University of Missouri at Columbia, and the author of Mediaspeak, *from which this selection was excerpted.*

Before you read, *reflect on your experience as a student in a variety of schools. Have you been exposed to advertising or merchandising in the classrooms, hallways, or cafeterias of your schools, or at school-sponsored events? Does this strike you as odd?*

No profit whatsoever can possibly be made but at the expense of another.

—Michel de Montaigne, "Of Liars," 1580

WHAT IS SALESPEAK?

Salespeak is any type of message surrounding a transaction between people. First, Salespeak is persuasive in nature. It can convince us to purchase products and services. It can also persuade us, directly and indirectly, to "buy into" political candidates, beliefs, ideologies, attitudes, values, and lifestyles. Salespeak persuades by presenting us with facts, where logic, language, and numbers dominate the message. More often, though, it persuades by massaging us—entertaining and arousing us, and changing our emotions with imagery, sound effects, and music. 1

Second, Salespeak can function as a type of entertainment or escapism—as an end in itself, where we are more focused on the experiences surrounding consumerism (e.g., browsing through an L. L. Bean 2 catalog) than we are on actually purchasing something. Salespeak occurs when messages are crafted so as to "hit" a specific, "targeted" audience. Therefore, Salespeakers collect and analyze information about their audiences to help them shape their messages.

Third, Salespeak usually employs a systematic approach in target- 3
ing its audience. A theme for Boltz laundry detergent, such as, "It's white as lightning!" might unify different types of messages communicated through different channels. The goal here is to create "overlapping fields of experience" (Ray 1982), hitting us from several sides in different ways, in short, to create an "environment" of persuasion. In this chapter, Salespeak also includes any type of message about transactions between people, such as a market report describing a specific group of consumers.

We live in a market-driven economy in which we consume more 4
than we produce. It's little wonder, then, that Salespeak flows constantly—from television, billboards, print ads, and blinking Internet messages. Because Salespeak touches nearly every area of life, its infinite tones and painstakingly crafted imagery appear in an endless variety of forms. Salespeak ranges from the hard-sell radio pitch of the local Ford dealer to the vague, soft, amorphous TV commercial that merely wants you to know that the good folks at Exxon care.

Salespeak includes the envelope in your mailbox that states, 5
"God's Holy Spirit said, 'Someone connected with this address needs this help.'" Salespeak ranges from the on-screen commercial loops playing on the ATM machine while you wait for your cash, to the plugs for car washes that appear on the screens affixed to the gas pump as you fill up your car. Salespeak even shows up in slot machines designed to entice children (Glionna 1999). These slots for tots now feature themes such as Candyland, Monopoly, the Three Stooges, the Pink Panther, and South Park. This is the gaming industry's attempt to promote a "family-friendly" image, which will help ensure that future generations will support the casino industry (Ruskin 1999). Salespeak also sprouts from the "product information" about a new computer embedded within the instructions for installing a software program, from the camera shot in a popular film that lingers on a bag of Frito's corn chips, and from the large sign inside Russia's *Mir* space station that states, "Even in Space…Pepsi is Changing the Script." Salespeak is indeed the script, on earth as it is in heaven.

A DAY IN THE LIFE

At 6:03 A.M., Mrs. Anderson's voice comes over the intercom into her 6
teenaged daughter's bedroom. Mrs. Anderson asks, "Pepsi? It's time to wake up, dear. Pehhhp-si…are you up and moving?"

Pepsi answers groggily, "Yeah... I'm up. Morning, Mom." As Pepsi sits up in bed, she reaches over and hits the button on her old pink Barbie alarm clock, which rests on her old American Girl traditional oak jewelry box. As both cherished items catch her eye, she pauses and wistfully recalls those happy days of girlhood, rubbing her hand over the *Little Mermaid* bedsheet. If only she hadn't given away her favorite purple My Little Pony to her best childhood friend, Microsoft McKenzie, who lives next door. 7

Just then her mother's voice calls her back to reality, "Good deal, sweetie. Let me know when you finish your shower. I just got your Gap sweatshirt out of the dryer, but I couldn't get that Gatorade stain out of your Tommy Hilfiger pants, so I'm washing them again." 8

Once upstairs, Pepsi sits down for a bowl of Cap'n Crunch cereal. She peels a banana, carefully pulling off a bright yellow sticker, which states, "ABC. Zero calories." She places the used sticker onto her McDonald's book cover. Pepsi's younger brother, Nike, dressed in his Babylon Five T-shirt, places a Star Trek notebook into his Star Wars book bag as he intently watches the Amoco morning newscast on the video wall. The network anchor tells about the latest corporate merger as he reads from his perch within the "N" of the giant MSNBC logo. Then Mrs. Anderson walks into the nutrition pod. 9

Mrs. Anderson: Hey, Peps, what's going on at school today?

Pepsi: Nothing much. Just gotta finish that dumb science experiment.

Mrs. Anderson: Which one is that?

Pepsi: That one called "Digging for Data." We learned about scientific inquiry stuff and how to deduce conclusions. We learned that American settlers were short because they didn't eat enough meat and stuff like that.

Mrs. Anderson: Oh, yes! That was one of my favorites when I was in school. Those National Livestock and Meat Board teaching kits are wonderful! I liked it even better than Campbell Soup's "Prego Thickness Experiment." How 'bout you?

Pepsi: I dunno. Everyone already knows that Prego spaghetti sauce is three times thicker and richer than Ragu's sauce.

Mrs. Anderson: Well, yes, of course they do. But that's not the only point. There are larger goals here, namely, your becoming the best high-volume consumer possible. Isn't that right, dear?

Pepsi: Yeah, I guess so.

Pepsi's school bus, equipped with the latest electronic wraparound billboard, mentions that the price of Chocolate Cheetah Crunch "is being sliced as you read this—down to $48.95 per ten-pounder!" 10

Pepsi takes her seat and discusses this price reduction with her locker partner, Reebok Robinson. They engage in a lively conversation about which of them loves Cheetah Crunch more. Next, the screen on the back of the seat in front of them catches their attention: a large dancing lamb sings, "Be there! Tonight only! At the IBM Mall! All remaining Rickon collectibles must go! Pledge bidding only! Be there!" Even Reebok cannot contain a squeal.

At school, Pepsi watches Channel One, the National Truth Channel, during her first three classes. The first news story documents the precise steps in which Zestra, the new star of the Z-5 Lectradisk corporate communication spots, went about purchasing her new video wall unit. Afterward, Pepsi and her peers receive biofeedback printouts of their responses registered during this program via the reaction console on their desks. Next, the students use voice-print technology to describe what they were feeling during the broadcast. 11

Then their teacher, Ms. Qualcomm, tells them to take a twenty-minute recess at the Commoditarium before they return for Tech Lab, where they will begin the unit "Product Scanning: Art or Science?" At the Commoditarium, Pepsi purchases one bag of Kwizzee sticks, one can of Channel One soda, and a One-der Bar, in addition to a pair of Golden Arch earrings she can't live without. The accessories for the earrings, which she also longs for, will have to wait. 12

Back at Tech Lab, Pepsi and her peers receive a half hour of AT&T ("Allotted Time & Testing," sponsored by AT&T, in which students are free to explore their own interests on the GodNet). In the upper-left corner of her computer screen, Pepsi watches what appears to be an enlarged part of human anatomy, alternately shrinking and enlarging, as one of her favorite new songs beats in sync. The olfactory port of her computer emits a musky odor. In the background of this pulsating image, sticks of lightning flare randomly against a deep blue sky. Pepsi looks at them more closely and detects that each one contains three small letters: A, T, and T. She smiles, points, and clicks on the window. 13

Immediately, this message forms on screen in large, puffy blue letters: "A, T, & T Loves You." Then the message begins dissolving and enlarging simultaneously, so that the background is now the same blue as the message. Huge lips fill the screen. Pepsi is unsure whether they are the lips of a man or woman. The lips slowly murmur, "You, Pepsi... You're the one... Oh, yes... Nobody else. Just you." 14

Pepsi, mesmerized, half whispers to herself, "Me?" as the lips fade at the same time that the blue background re-forms into the previous message, "A, T, & T Loves You." Pepsi clicks again. Three golden books appear on screen. One is titled "A, T, & T's Pledge to You, Pepsi Anderson." Another one is titled, "Making Love Rich," and 15 the third is titled, "Us...Forever." The lights of the Tech Lab dim, signaling students that it's time to begin their new unit. The lights slowly fade out until the lab is nearly dark. Pepsi hears muffled patriotic music from the opposite side of the room—a flute and drum, playing the tune of "Yankee Doodle Dandy." From the far end of the ceiling, an image of the traditional "fyfe and drum corps"—the three ragged soldiers in Revolutionary Army garb—come marching across the screen; above the U.S. flag flies a larger one, with a golden arch on it.

As the tattered trio exit via a slow dissolve on the opposite end of 16
the ceiling screen, the room goes completely dark. Pepsi twists her head and limbers up, as her classmates do, almost in unison. Then, on instinct, Pepsi and her peers look upward to the neon green and pink Laser Note swirling above them: "To thine own self, be blue. And rakest thou joy into thine own taste sphere! Tru-Blu Vervo Dots: now half price at Commoditarium!" A laser image of Shakespeare forms from the dissolving lights. Next, the bard's face dissolves into blue Vervo Dots. Pepsi, feeling vaguely tired and hungry, saves her place on screen so she can return later to find out what's in the three golden books. Before she exits, she is automatically transferred to another screen so that she can input her biofeedback prints from the past half hour.

At home that night, Pepsi and her family gather in the Recipient 17
Well. To activate the video wall, Mrs. Anderson submits a forehead print on the ConsumaScan. Before any audio can be heard, a Nike logo appears on the screen for two minutes. Mrs. Anderson turns to her daughter.

Mrs. Anderson: So, Peps, you were awfully quiet at dinner. Are you okay? Everything all right at school?

Pepsi: Fine. I just get tired of learning all the time.

Mrs. Anderson (sighing): Well, sweetie, I know. Things are so much different nowadays than when I was your age. You kids have to work harder in school because there are so many more products and services to keep up with.

Pepsi: Yeah, I guess so....

Mrs. Anderson: But you've also got many luxuries we never had. Why, when I was born, parents were completely ignorant about giving their children beautiful names. My family just called me "Jennifer." Ugh! Can you believe it?

Pepsi: Oh, gag me, Mom! "Jennifer"?! You're kidding! How did you and Dad name me?

Mrs. Anderson: Well, let's see.... We first fell in love with your name when Pepsico offered us a lifetime membership at the Nova Health Spa if we'd name you "Pepsi." I thought it was so refreshing—not to mention thirst quenching and tasty. Besides—it's your generation!

Pepsi: And I'll always love you and Dad for bestowing me with eternal brandness...

Mrs. Anderson: It's just because we love you, that's all. Growing up branded is a lot easier these days—especially after the Renaissance of 2008, just after you were born.

Pepsi: What was that?

Mrs. Anderson: You know—*life cells!* We got them a few years after the Second Great Brand Cleansing War.

Pepsi: But I thought we always had life cells, that we were just born with 'em....

Mrs. Anderson: My gosh, no, girl! When I was your age we had to stay glued to National Public Radio to keep up with the latest fluctuations of the NASDAQ and high tech markets.

Pepsi: Jeez... I can't imagine life without life cells.

Mrs. Anderson: Me either—now! Back then, it all started with Moletronics and the first conversions of Wall Street datastreams into what they used to call "subcutaneous pseudoneurons." But that's ancient history for you!

Pepsi: Mom?

Mrs. Anderson: Yes, dear?

Pepsi: Can we set aside some special family time, so we can talk about that relationship portfolio with AT&T?

Mrs. Anderson: Well, of course! Maybe during spring break at the cabin? That's not the kind of thing we ever want to slight.

At this moment, the video wall's audio activates. The Nike swoosh logo forms into a running cheetah as a male voice-over states, "Nike Leopard-Tech Laser Runners. Be the Cheetah you were born free to be." Mrs. Anderson turns back to her daughter and asks, "Would you mind running to the Pantry Pod and seeing if there's any more of that Chocolate Cheetah Crunch left?" "Sure," says Pepsi, turning as she leaves the room, "*If* we can talk about those new shoes I need."... 18

IS PEPSI'S WORLD ALREADY HERE?

Yes. Most of what happens to Pepsi in this scenario is based on fact. A few other parts are extensions or exaggerations of what already occurs in everyday life. Let's begin with a girl named Pepsi. In Pepsi's world of Salespeak, nearly every facet of life is somehow linked to sales. Pepsi, the girl, lives in a Pepsi world, where person, product, and hype have merged with everyday life. 19

Salespeak is all-powerful. As small children, as soon as we become aware that a world exists outside of ourselves, we become a "targeted audience." From then on, we think in the voices of Salespeak. We hear them, we see them. We smell them, taste them, touch them, dream them, become them. Salespeak is often targeted at young people, the group marketers most prize because first, they spend "disposable" income, as well as influence how their parents spend money (see the following section, "Notes from the World of Salespeak"); second, people tend to establish loyalties to certain brands early in life; and third, young people are more likely to buy items on impulse. For these reasons and more, Salespeak is most prevalent and vivid for children and young adults. Hence, most of this chapter focuses on the layers of Salespeak that surround these groups. The core issue is targeting kids in the first place, regardless of the product being sold. 20

What's in a Name?

At this writing, I've neither read nor heard of a human being legally named after a product or service (though I feel certain that he or she is out there). I have, though, heard that school administrators in Plymouth, Michigan, are considering auctioning off school names to the highest bidder. It's only a matter of time before kids attend "Taco Bell Middle School" or "Gap Kids Elementary School" (Labi 1999). Appropriating names—and hence identities—is essentially an act of aggression, of control over others' personal identity. Our practice of naming things for commercial purposes is not new. Consider San Diego's Qualcomm Stadium. Unlike St. Louis's Busch Stadium or Denver's Coors Field, the name Qualcomm has no connections to people or things already traditionally linked with baseball. In Pepsi's world, "AT&T" stood for "Allotted Time for Testing." To my knowledge, commercial or corporate names have yet to be used for identifying processes. However, they have been used to identify specific places where educational processes occur. 21

For example, the Derby, Kansas, school district named its elementary school resource center the GenerationNext Center. The district agreed to use the Pepsi slogan to name their new facility, as well as to serve only Pepsi products, in exchange for one million dollars (Perrin 1997, 1A). Even ice cream is now named so that it can advertise something else: the name of Ben and Jerry's butter almond ice cream is called "Dilbert's World: Totally Nuts" (Solomon 1998a). 22

Every time we see or read or hear a commercial name, an "impression" registers. Advertising profits depend on the type and number of impressions made by each ad message. Therefore, Pepsi Anderson and her friend, Microsoft McKenzie, are walking, breathing, 23 random ad messages. (Similar important names) are now devised solely for purposes of advertising. Nothing more. Such names become ads. In earlier times and in other cultures, as well as our own, names were sacred: they communicated the essence of our identity, not just to others but to ourselves as well. To rob someone of her name was to appropriate her identity, to deny her existence. In *I Know Why the Caged Bird Sings,* Maya Angelou speaks of how demoralizing it was for African Americans to be "called out of name" by white people, who would refer to any African American male as "boy," "Tom," or "Uncle."

Similarly, several years ago, the rock musician and composer known as Prince changed his name to a purely graphic symbol. The result, of course, was that nobody could even pronounce it! By default he became known as "The Artist Formerly Known as Prince." In an interview on MTV, this musician-composer explained that the public believed he was crazy because print and electronic media had proclaimed him so, over and over. He therefore changed his name to something unpronounceable to halt this labeling. It worked. In effect, this man regained control of his own life because he found a way to stop others from controlling it for him, as they were doing by writing about him in the media. This man understands the general semantics principle that the word is not the thing symbolized—that the map is not the territory.... 24

The long-term effects of replacing real names with commercial labels (of important spaces, processes, and possibly even people) can benefit nobody except those doing the appropriating—those reaping revenue from increased sales. At the very least, this practice demonstrates, in concrete, definitive ways, that we value materialism and the act of selling above all else. 25

Celebrating Coke Day at the Carbonated Beverage Company

At century's end, the question is not "Where and when does Salespeak appear?" Rather, the real question is, "Where and when does Salespeak *not* appear?" Only in churches and other places of worship? (Not counting, of course, the church that advertised itself by proclaiming on its outside message board: "Come in for a faith lift.") Salespeak is more than a voice we hear and see: we also wear it, smell it, touch it, play with it. Ads on book covers, notebooks, backpacks, pencils, and pens are common. So are the girl Pepsi's Gap sweatshirt, Tommy Hilfiger pants, Barbie alarm clock, and *Little Mermaid* bedsheets. The bulletins that Pepsi and her classmates received about current sales are also authentic: PepsiCo has offered free beepers to teens, who are periodically contacted with updated ad messages. 26

Salespeak is seeping into the smallest crevices of American life. As you fill your car with gas, you can now watch commercials on a small screen on the gas pump. As you wait for your transaction at the ATM machine, you can view commercials. As you wait in the switchback line at an amusement park, you can watch commercials on several screens. As you wait in your doctor's office, you can read about medicines to buy, as well as watch commercials for them. As you stand in line at Wal-Mart's customer service desk, you can watch ads for Wal-Mart on a huge screen before you. As you wait for the phone to ring when making a long-distance call, you'll hear a soft, musical tinkle, followed by a velvety voice that intones, "AT&T." 27

As your children board their school bus, you'll see ads wrapped around it. When you pick up a bunch of bananas in the grocery store, like our friend Pepsi in the earlier scenario, you may have to peel off yellow stickers that state, "ABC. Zero calories." When you call a certain school in Texas and don't get an answer, you'll hear this recorded message: "Welcome to the Grapevine-Colleyville Independent School District, where we are proudly sponsored by the Dr. Pepper Bottling Company of Texas" (Perrin 1997). 28

Salespeak also commonly appears under the guise of school "curriculum"—from formal business-education partnerships, to free teacher workshops provided to introduce new textbooks. Corporate-produced "instructional materials" are sometimes thinly veiled sales pitches that can distort the truth. The curriculum unit "Digging for Data" mentioned earlier as part of Pepsi's school day, is actual material used in schools. 29

For another "learning experience," students were assigned to be "quality control technicians" as they completed "The Carbonated Beverage Company" unit, provided free to schools by PepsiCo. Students taste-tested colas, analyzed cola samples, took video tours of the St. Louis Pepsi plant, and visited a local Pepsi plant (Bingham 1998, 1A). Ads have even appeared in math textbooks. *Mathematics: Applications and Connections,* published by McGraw-Hill, and used in middle schools, includes problems that are just as much about advertising as they are arithmetic—salespeak masquerading as education. Here's a sample decimal division problem: "Will is saving his allowance to buy a pair of Nike shoes that cost $68.25. If Will earns $3.25 per week, how many weeks will Will need to save?" Directly next to this problem is a full-color picture of a pair of Nike shoes (Hays 1999). The 1999 edition of this book contains the following problem: "The best-selling packaged cookie in the world is the Oreo cookie. The diameter of the Oreo cookie is 1.75 inches. Express the diameter of an Oreo cookie as a fraction in simplest form." It seems no accident that "Oreo" is repeated three times in this brief message; repetition is an ancient device used 30 in propaganda and advertising. More insidious is the fact that such textbooks present the act of saving money for Nike shoes as a *natural* state of affairs, a given in life. Requiring captive audiences of kids to interact with brand names in such mentally active ways helps ensure product-identification and brand-name loyalty during kids' future years as consumers.

Some schools slavishly serve their corporate sponsors. After seal- 3
ing a deal with Coca-Cola, a school in Georgia implemented an official "Coke Day" devoted to celebrating Coca-Cola products. On that day, Mike Cameron, a senior at the school, chose to exercise his right to think by wearing a T-shirt bearing the Pepsi logo. He was promptly suspended ("This School Is Brought to You By: Cola? Sneakers?" 1998, 11A).

This intense focus on selling products to a captive audience of 3
students is illustrated by the following letter sent to District 11's school principals in Colorado Springs, Colorado. The letter was written by the district's executive director of "school leadership." In September 1997, the district had signed an $8 million contract with Coca-Cola (Labi 1999).

Dear Principal:

Here we are in year two of the great Coke contract....

First, the good news: This year's installment from Coke is "in the house," and checks will be cut for you to pick up in my office this week. Your share will be the same as last year.

Elementary School	$3,000
Middle School	$15,000
High School	$25,000

Now the not-so-good news: we must sell 70,000 cases of product (including juices, sodas, waters, etc.) at least once during the first three years of the contract. If we reach this goal, your school allotments will be guaranteed for the next seven years.

The math on how to achieve this is really quite simple. Last year we had 32,439 students, 3,000 employees, and 176 days in the school year. If 35,439 staff and students buy one Coke product every other day for a school year, we will double the required quota.

Here is how we can do it:

1. Allow students to purchase and consume vended products throughout the day. If sodas are not allowed in classes, consider allowing juices, teas, and waters.
2. Locate machines where they are accessible to the students all day. Research shows that vender purchases are closely linked to availability. Location, lo-

cation, location is the key. You may have as many machines as you can handle. Pueblo Central High tripled its volume of sales by placing vending machines on all three levels of the school. The Coke people surveyed the middle and high schools this summer and have suggestions on where to place additional machines.

3. A list of Coke products is enclosed to allow you to select from the entire menu of beverages. Let me know which products you want, and we will get them in. Please let me know if you need electrical outlets.
4. A calendar of promotional events is enclosed to help you advertise Coke products.

I know this is "just one more thing from downtown," but the long-term benefits are worth it.

Thanks for your help.

John Bushey
The Coke Dude
(Bushey 1998)

With visionary leaders such as "The Coke Dude" to inspire them, students will be well prepared to perpetuate a world ruled by Salespeak. Of course, Pepsi (the girl), Mike (the actual student expelled for wearing a Pepsi T-shirt), and their fellow students did not begin encountering ads in high school. It begins much earlier.... 33

The National Truth Channel

Many other details of Pepsi's day are anchored in fact, not fiction. In Pepsi's not-too-distant world, Channel One television has become the "National Truth Channel." Today Channel One, owned by a private corporation, beams daily commercials to more than 8 million American kids attending middle schools and high schools. It therefore imposes more uniformity on public school kids and their curriculum than the federal government ever has. For all practical purposes, it has indeed been our "national" channel for several years. 34

Although I made up the "Truth" part of "The National Truth Channel," I want to note that it serves as Doublespeak nested within Salespeak—a common occurrence in real life. For example, the term "corporate communication" (used in Pepsi's world, above, to refer to commercials) is a euphemism that the Benetton company actually used to refer to its ads. And although laser ads have yet to appear on the ceilings of classrooms, as they do in Pepsi's world, it is true that a few years ago, a company wanted to launch into geosynchronous orbit a massive panel that could be emblazoned with a gigantic corporate logo, visible for periods of time, over certain cities (Doheny-Farina 35

1999). Here, the promise of reality far exceeds what happened in Pepsi's fictional classroom.

Also, remember that "news story" about Zestra, a star of "corporate communication" spots that Pepsi watched on Channel One? More truth than fiction here, too. Since 1989, Channel One has sometimes blurred the lines between news, commercials, and public service announcements. In one study (Fox 1996), many students mistook commercials for news programs or public service announcements, such as those that warn viewers about drunk driving. The result was that students knew the product being advertised and regarded it warmly because, as one student told me, "They [the manufacturers and advertisers] are trying to do good. They care about us." 36

In the worst case of such blurring that I observed during the two-year period of this study, the students could hardly be faulted. Instead, the Salespeak was highly deceptive (merging with Doublespeak). That is, PepsiCo's series of ads called "It's Like This" were designed to look very much like documentary news footage and public service announcements. The actors spoke directly into the swinging, handheld camera, as if they were being interviewed; the ads were filmed in black and white, and the product's name was never spoken by any of the people in the commercial, although the rapid-fire editing included brief shots of the Pepsi logo, in color, on signs and on merchandise. 37

Just as in Pepsi's world, described earlier in this chapter, real-life ads are often embedded within programs, as well as other commercials, products, instructions, and even "transitional spaces" between one media message and another. For example, when the girl Pepsi took a break from her "learning," she went to the school's Commoditarium, or mini-mall, to shop for items that had been advertised at school. Again, there is truth here. Although schools do not yet contain minimalls, they do contain stores and increasing numbers of strategically placed vending machines. A ninth-grade girl told me that after students viewed Channel One in the morning and watched commercials for M&Ms candies, her teacher allowed them to take a break. The student said she'd often walk down the hall and purchase M&Ms from the vending machine. In such schools, operant conditioning is alive and well. This is not the only way in which many schools are emulating shopping malls. My daughter's high school cafeteria is a "food court," complete with McDonald's and Pizza Hut. 38

By establishing itself in public schools, Channel One automatically "delivers" a captive, well-defined audience to its advertisers, more than was ever possible before. "Know thy audience"—as specifically as possible—is the name of the advertising game. Marketers have become increasingly effective at obtaining all kinds of demographic and psychographic information on consumers. Channel One increas- 39 ingly hones its messages based on the constant flow of demographic information it extracts from viewers, often under the guise of "clubs" and contests, which seek information on individuals, teams, classes, and entire schools ("Be a Channel One School"). Channel One's printed viewing and "curriculum" guides for teachers, as well as its Web site for students, also constantly solicit marketing information.

It's a Wonderful Day in the "Branded, Private Electronic Neighborhood"

Pepsi went to her computer lab to work and quickly drifted into an 40
ethereal world of good-vibes Salespeak, which "interacted" with her in informal and personal ways. She was electronically massaged and called by name. Consumers interacting with advertisers, one-on-one, is the marketer's nirvana. This, too, already happens. Like the Salespeakers who use television, cyber-entrepreneurs are eager to use computers to spread Salespeak. They are equally excited about using computers to "track" consumers for collecting ever more specific and detailed psychographics—who we are, what we fantasize, what we do—for purposes of selling. One computer company plans to give away approximately 1 million computers in exchange for users who would be "willing to disclose their interests, income, and on-line browsing habits" ("Free Computers Offered by Fledgling Company," *Columbia* [Missouri] *Daily Tribune,* February 9, 1999, 7B). The company monitors the sites that users visit and the ads they click on (from a screen never devoid of ads). If users don't dial up to the Internet often enough, new ads are sent automatically to the computer terminal.

Although today's schools aren't yet as high-tech as Pepsi's school 41
(which used "ConsumaScans" and "forehead prints" to analyze her responses to media), such approaches are not far-fetched. For example, market researchers now work directly in some schools, to determine "what sparks kids." One marketing company conducts focus groups in schools on behalf of Kentucky Fried Chicken, McDonald's, and Mattel Toys—all to improve advertising to kids (Labi 1999). To date, the most ambitious marketing venture is ZapMe! Corporation's offer of entire computer labs, fast servers with satellite connection, teacher training, and other lollipops to public and private schools, all for "free." The only price for this feast is that the systems will contain advertising and market research technology, in all its interactive and multimedia glory. However, the ZapMe! Corporation folks don't dare call it advertising. Instead they call it "brand imaging spots" and "dedicated branding spaces." Ah, Salespeak.

To date, 9,000 schools have signed up for this scheme, which is 42
being piloted in several California schools. The ZapMe! approach is

strikingly similar to Channel One television. In exchange for delivering this massive audience, schools receive some equipment from Channel One—monitors, a satellite dish (capable of picking up only Channel One's signal) and other equipment amounting to a total of about $50,000. Hence, it's hardly a shock that Channel One is found most often in low-income communities (McCarthy 1993, 4A).

ZapMe! President Frank Vigil tried to distinguish his company from Channel One: "Channel One is television. What we are is really an interactive learning tool, so we're very, very different" (Chmielewski 1998). Of course the Internet differs from TV. We've long known that when people interact with texts, they improve their retention and learning, internalizing those messages more quickly and deeply. ZapMe! wants to use this power to sell stuff. In addition to the constantly moving billboard on the screen, and in addition to the tracking of students for market research purposes, students are further immersed in ad culture when they collect "ZapPoints," which they can spend at an e-commerce mall. 43

Billions and Billions of Buyers and Bucks. You might think that the $50,000 worth of video equipment that schools receive from Channel One in exchange for their delivering audiences seems almost a decent tradeoff, especially to poorer schools—but only until you consider that Channel One can charge advertisers as much as $200,000 for one 30-second ad (Hoynes 1997). Such sales pile up to an estimated $600,000 per day for Channel One (New York State Department of Education memo, May 23, 1995). The Internet ZapMe! Corporation, however, wants more than this. Much more. According to its Web site, ZapMe! will reach "a potential audience exceeding 50 million students in the United States and over a billion students worldwide." Sherman's march on Atlanta, the Allied landing in Normandy, and ZapMe!'s ad blitz into the world's classrooms. Ah, what progress democracy maketh. 44

The other "benefit" of beaming Channel One television into the schools is supposed to be its news program. However, research has concluded that Channel One news contains precious little news. The bulk of each broadcast (80 percent according to one study) is devoted to "advertising, sports, weather and natural disasters, features and profiles, and self-promotion of Channel One" (Honan 1997). Nobody in the schools can preview these daily broadcasts, because the signals are received inside of a locked metal box. And nobody at the schools has a key to open this box. Similarly, according to a press release from Commercial Alert (October 29, 1998), ZapMe! computers will contain "banner ads built into the browser interface" of their Internet access. 45

Hence, nobody in the school can tamper with it. This is the state of democratic education.

Hitting Heads with Two-by-Four Billboards. Students using ZapMe! computers must view advertising on their computer screens. One direct use of ads is ZapMe!'s "dynamic billboard," a two-by-four-inch rectangle in the screen's lower left corner. Ad logos and messages now rotate, but these "dynamic" appeals will likely escalate to video, audio, and other whiz-bangs because, well, ads try to attract attention. Schools will be required to have students use ZapMe! computer labs at least four hours per day. 46

This is similar to Channel One's requirement, that schools must submit attendance records to guarantee that the program is aired during 90 percent of the school days, in at least 80 percent of the classrooms. Don't forget that every state has compulsory school attendance laws, which literally force kids to receive such messages. Also, Channel One costs taxpayers an estimated $1.8 billion annually in lost instructional time—$300 million of this to ads (Center for Commercial-Free Education, November 16, 1998). In short, taxpayers have already paid for this time that's being sold to advertisers. Channel One has convinced me that beaming glitzy ads to captive kids is highly effective. When kids see a specific item on TV at school, they often assume that the school itself endorses the product. Channel One has also broadcast commercials that closely resemble documentaries, causing kids (and adults) to blur ads with more nonbiased messages. Not only are many of the same commercials repeated endlessly, but kids also "replay" commercials themselves in a variety of ways—from singing the jingles, to repeating dialogue, to creating art projects that mirror products and product messages. Some kids even dream about commercials. In short, schools become echo chambers for ad messages. We should not be surprised, then, that such environments affect kids' behavior, including their consumer behavior (Fox 1996). 47

$pinning $ales in "Uncluttered Environments." Like Channel One, ZapMe! is motivated by what it calls an "open" or "uncluttered" market, one free of the usual teen "distractions" of family, music, television, jobs, and cars. An "uncluttered" environment also means little or no resistance to the values and ideologies (e.g., materialism, competition) contained in most ads. If you have doubts about these corporations' intentions, linger a little while over their lingo. For example, in a press release, Martin Grant, Channel One's president of sales and marketing, said, "Channel One is a marketer's secret weapon. When used creatively by today's innovative marketers, it is an unparalleled way 48 to reach a massive teen audience in a highly relevant, important, and uncluttered environment" (August 9, 1995). Another marketer once referred to in-school ads as "brand and product loyalties through classroom-centered, peer-powered lifestyle patterning." Translation: get 'em while they're young, captive, and have disposable income.

And consider this excerpt from the ZapMe! Web site: "Using fast and reliable satellite communications, we can create new methods of training, education, *sales* and even the *buying and selling of services and products.* Distance training, software distribution and high bandwidth data distribution are some of the exciting applications unfolding in the *global services market.* Join us in our pursuit of *expanding the market* by creating *complete application solutions*" (ZapMe! Web site n.d., italics added). 49

In the eyes (and prose) of this writer, dollar signs spin like wheels of fire on the Fourth of July. Just within the first sentence, sales are mentioned twice, and sales is what the sentence ends with, thereby emphasizing it most. And although "complete application solutions" includes more than sales, it certainly implies that sales will always be there (if not, entrepreneurs would not consider it "complete"). 50

Living and Learning in the "Branded, Private Electronic Neighborhood"

Other, less visible problems occur when Salespeak invades schools. For instance, these two corporations "standardize" public education in ways that most of us never intended. Today, our most common or core curriculum in American education is the television commercial. More students watch ads for Bubblicious Bubble Gum than read Dickens's *A Tale of Two Cities.* 51

And now, ZapMe! executives promise Internet and cultural homogeneity for the thousands of schools that sign on with them. "Reduce Undesirable Websites!" they proclaim, because "in the ZapMe! Intranet environment, students [sic] access to undesirable websites is virtually eliminated." ZapMe! further assures us that "customized browser with search functions and other navigation tools guides us through the system." A "customized browser" is potentially the perfect tool for selecting, editing, packaging, manipulating, and controlling students' information. 52

We next learn that "ZapMe! editors search the Internet to collect and index information specifically focused for K–12 schools" (ZapMe! Web site n.d.). ZapMe! also tells us that they will be responsible for indexing and correlating this material to "a unified (National) curricular scope and sequence." They inform readers that they have "developed a proprietary-indexing scheme, which formats the content specifically for the K–12 market." Sorry, but who is supposed to choose and craft 53 which information is best for students? ZapMe's executives? Not even close. And when they say they're going to "format" the content, I take it to mean they will cut it, slant it, shave it, dice it, tilt it, slice it, and wrap it all in glitzy technoid color, animation, video, and graphics—and ads. Too, "customized browsers" can short-circuit students' own discovery and thinking processes by directing them toward the ideas they are allowed to access—all the while leading them down endless electronic pathways strewn with ads. Finally, this ZapMe! quote refers to the "K–12 market." That's right; they define students as a "market." However, kids in schools were never, ever intended to be a "market." They are human beings who are required by law to be in school, which is supposed to be a marketplace of ideas, not a marketplace of Snickers, M&Ms, and Skittles. Students are learners, not merchandise to be hawked to advertisers in units-per-thousand.

ZapMe!'s Web site refers to its hardware and software as a 54
"branded private electronic neighborhood." However, Mr. Rogers doesn't live there. Most residents in this neck of the woods will be surrounded by brands, if they are not walking brands themselves. Brands on every street corner, brands on every lawn, brands in every mailbox, brands lining every space down every winding boulevard to nowhere. These electronic messages will likely grow and change as marketers track the on-line movements of its young "visitors." Some current and new forms of Cyber-Salespeak (Robischon 1999) only suggest the possibilities. For instance, "interstitial ads" take shape on the screen, just slowly enough that, intrigued, you watch them materialize to see what they are. This, in essence, is a mini-commercial, which has a beginning, middle, and end. Watching this ad unfold allows you to participate in the message. This ad will disappear if you click to another page (where another one might be materializing).

"Pop-out ads" that appear in a smaller window next to the origi- 55
nal Web page may be clicked on for an entire new venture into an infinite series of additional ads, some with video and audio features. "Banner ads" and "extramercials" wrap around the top of a screen and can even trail down the right-hand side, covering up the site's noncommercial content or information. Here again, *the act of moving this commercial* so you can read the actual content forces you to interact with the ad message and hence recall it better. Traditionally, a text's "editorial turf" or "message area" was sacred. Not anymore. It's like slapping a peel-off ad for Krazy Kola across a newspaper article reporting an airplane crash.

Another Cyber-Salespeak strategy is what I call "background 56
tricks." For example, to focus attention on a new line of color printers, one Web site, known for its neon colors, turned its home page black and white. Increasingly, backgrounds (and many elements of foregrounds)

will be composed of Salespeak. Finally, "animated ads" really capture attention. Most recently, to promote the Intel Corporation, the Web site for *USA Today* included an animated Homer Simpson scampering out of an advertisement and across the *USA Today* nameplate.

The leader in finding new ways to saturate the Web with Sales- 57
peak is Procter & Gamble. The firm's vice president, Denis Beausejour, stated that his company has "a vested interest in making the Web the most effective marketing medium in history" (Greenstein 1999). Beausejour would like to see "bigger, more complicated ads that appear automatically in a separate window on the screen when you go to a website or that allow you to send e-mail from within the ad" (Greenstein 1999, 105). Sending e-mail from within an ad means that we'll be more internally active within the ad, which deepens Salespeak's effects on consumer attitudes and behaviors. Beausejour is also "experimenting with technology that automatically downloads an ad in the background" (Greenstein 1999, 105).

Salespeak will likely take up more and more space on television, 58
film, and computer screens, for more and more time, until they become a kind of wallpaper or permanent background. We will come to accept Salespeak as normal background, in addition to its increasing roles within various foregrounds (e.g., product placement ads). Especially in media, background serves as our anchor or base-point for "what is normal." When background and foreground are similar, they merge, just as for earlier generations, John Wayne, as actor and film character, became much the same as the open western landscape that so often spread out behind him. When Salespeak comes to dominate both background and foreground, our abilities to distinguish between the two will shrink and then disappear....

NOTES FROM THE WORLD OF SALESPEAK

More than anything else, dominant voices may be shaped by their en- 59
vironment. Consider the following facts about the environment that generates Salespeak:

- *$150 billion:* Amount spent by American advertisers each year, a cost that is passed on to consumers in higher prices. Landay (1998) summarizes our relationship with advertisers: "We pay their ad bills, we provide their profits, and we pay for their total tax write-off on the ads they place."
- *12 billion and 3 million:* The number of display ads and broadcast ads that Americans are collectively exposed to each day (Landay 1998).

- *2:* The number of times that we pay for advertising. First, advertising costs are built into the product. We pay again in terms of the time, money, and attention spent when processing an ad message.
- *1,000:* The number of chocolate chips in each bag of Chips Ahoy! cookies. The cookie company sponsored a "contest" in which students tried to confirm this claim (Labi 1999, 44).
- *$11 billion:* The amount of money dedicated to market research throughout the world (*World Opinion* Web site, November 11, 1998).
- *"Gosh, I don't understand—there are so many brands":* This is what one marketing firm has its researchers say, after they go into stores and place themselves next to real shoppers, in an effort to elicit what consumers are thinking in an authentic context (from the May 30, 1997, issue of the *Wall Street Journal* [McLaren 1998]).
- *$66 billion:* The amount of money spent by kids and young adults (ages 4–19) in 1992 (Bowen 1995).
- *16 million:* Approximate number of American children who use the Internet (*Brill's Content,* December 1998, 140).
- *115.95:* The number of banner ads viewed per week by the average Web user (*World Opinion* Web site, November 11, 1998).
- *"Save water. It's precious":* Message on a Coca-Cola billboard in Zimbabwe, where, according to the August 25, 1997, issue of the *Wall Street Journal,* the soft drink has become the drink of choice (necessity?) because of a water shortage (McLaren 1998).
- *$204 billion:* The estimated amount of Web-based transactions in 2001, up from $10.4 billion in 1997 (Zona Research 1999 on the *World Opinion* Web site).
- *89:* Percentage of children's Web sites that collect users' personal information (*Brill's Content,* December 1998, 140).
- *23:* Percentage of children's Web sites that tell kids to ask their parents for permission before sending personal information. (*Brill's Content,* December 1998, 140).
- *$29 million:* Net income for Nielsen Media Research during the first six months of 1998. (*Brill's Content,* December 1998, 140).
- *$36 billion:* The amount of money spent by kids and young adults in 1992 (ages 4–19) that belonged to their parents (Bowen 1995).
- *$3.4 million:* The amount of money received by the Grapevine-Colleyville Texas School District for displaying a huge Dr. Pepper logo atop the school roof. This school is in the flight path of Dallas-Fort Worth International Airport (Perrin 1997).
- *$8 million:* The amount of money received by the Colorado Springs School District in Colorado from Coca-Cola for an exclusive ten-year service agreement (Perrin 1997).

- *"A tight, enduring connection to teens":* What Larry Jabbonsky, a spokesman at Pepsi headquarters, said his company seeks (Perrin 1997).
- *9,000:* The number of items stocked in grocery stores in the 1970s (Will 1997).
- *30,000:* The number of items now stocked in grocery stores (Will 1997).
- *99:* The percentage of teens surveyed (N = 534 in four cities) who correctly identified the croaking frogs from a Budweiser television commercial (Horovitz and Wells 1997, 1A).
- *93:* The percentage of teens who reported that they liked the Budweiser frogs "very much" or "somewhat" (Horovitz and Wells 1997, 1A).
- *95 and 94:* The percentages of teens who know the Marlboro man and Joe Camel (Wells 1997, 1A).
- *Great Britain's white cliffs of Dover:* The backdrop for a laser-projected Adidas ad (Liu 1999).
- *$200 million:* The amount of money Miller Beer spends on advertising each year.
- *Time Warner:* A corporate empire that controls news and information in America. (There are fewer than twelve.) Time Warner owns large book publishers, cable TV franchises, home video firms, CNN and other large cable channels, and magazines such as *Time, Life, People, Sports Illustrated, Money, Fortune,* and *Entertainment Weekly* (Solomon 1999b).
- *$650 billion:* Annual sales of approximately 1,000 telemarketing companies, which employ 4 million Americans (Shenk 1999, 59).
- *350,000:* The number of classrooms that view two minutes of television commercials every day on Channel One ("Selling to School Kids" 1995).
- *154:* The number of Coca-Cola cans that students must find on a book cover and then color in, to reveal a hidden message ("Selling to School Kids" 1995).
- *50:* The percentage of increase in advertising expenditures during the past fifteen years (Bowen 1995).
- *560:* The daily number of ads targeted at the average American in 1971 (Shenk 1999, 59).
- *3,000:* The daily number of ads targeted at the average American in 1991 (Shenk 1999, 59).
- *Business Update:* An hourly segment broadcast on National Public Radio. Even though NPR is supposed to focus on "public broadcasting," it does not offer a *Labor Update.*

- *3.4 trillion:* The number of e-mail messages that crossed the Internet in the United States in 1998—a number expected to double by 2001 (McCafferty 1999).
- *80 percent:* The percentage of America's e-mail messages in 1998 that were mass-produced e-mailings, "most from corporations with something to sell" (McCafferty 1998).

60 It's hardly unusual for a free enterprise system to employ Salespeak. Advertising is a necessary ingredient for informing consumers about the goods and services they need. This is true for much of America's history. A sign hung in a trading post at the beginning of the Oregon Trail, 150 years ago, stating, "Sugar, 2 cents per lb.," contains necessary information for specific readers who had definite goals. Today, though, America is quite different.

61 First, unlike even forty years ago, most of today's advertising carries scant information about the product or service. Second, the more affluent America becomes, the fewer true "needs" we have. To make up for it, advertisers now focus not so much on what we truly need, but on what we may desire. Third, very few limits are placed upon advertising: we have little control over where it appears, who can see it (note how many of the previous items focus on young people), how often it appears, how messages are constructed, or how much money is budgeted for them (at the expense of, say, improving the product). The field of advertising itself is now a major industry. The Bureau of Labor Statistics reports that in 1995, more people died on the job in advertising than in car factories, electrical repair companies, and petroleum refining operations (*Advertising Age,* August 19, 1996). Because advertising has such free rein in America, it's become one of our most dominating voices, if not the most dominating voice.

Examining the Text

1. Which parts of Pepsi's story ("A Day in the Life") are based on fact, according to Fox? Which parts of the story are "extensions or exaggerations of what already occurs in everyday life"? Do you find any of these "extensions or exaggerations" unrealistic or difficult to believe?

2. According to Fox, what's wrong with naming a person or a place after a product? Do you think there are qualitative differences between giving a product's name to a person, to a baseball stadium, or to a school?

3. What is a euphemism? List some of the euphemisms that Fox mentions in this reading. What problems does Fox see with these euphemisms?

4. On page 73, Fox writes that "Students are learners, not merchandise to be hawked to advertisers in units-per-thousand." What evidence does Fox provide to substantiate his claim that students are being treated like "merchandise"? How is this claim represented in the story of Pepsi?
5. In this article, Fox juxtaposes the fictional, futuristic, and seemingly outrageous story of the girl Pepsi with paragraphs of exposition and argument based on research. Do you find one of these strategies more persuasive than the other? How do they work together to prove his points?

For Group Discussion

Fox spends a good portion of the article critiquing the use of Channel One and ZapMe! in schools and classrooms. More generally, he's concerned about Salespeak in educational settings. In your discussion group, make a list of all the examples Fox gives to show where Salespeak is found in schools. Add examples to this list based on your own experience with Salespeak in your grade school, high school, and college experience. As a group, discuss whether your experiences tend to confirm or contradict Fox's claims that Salespeak exerts an undue influence in education.

Writing Suggestion

The article ends with a list of statistics about advertising. Use some of these statistics as evidence in an essay in which you give your opinion of the influence of advertising on our society. Consider using quotations from the article. You can use these statistics and quotations to support a position in which you agree with Fox's argument, or you can construct your essay by arguing against Fox, reinterpreting the statistics he offers and taking issue with statements that you quote from the article.

Advertising's Fifteen Basic Appeals

Jib Fowles

In the following essay, Jib Fowles looks at how advertisements work by examining the emotional, subrational appeals that they employ. We are confronted daily by hundreds of ads, only a few of which actually attract our attention. These few do so, according to Fowles, through "something primary and primitive, an emotional appeal, that in effect is the thin edge of the wedge, trying to find its way into a mind." Drawing on research done by the psychologist

Henry A. Murray, Fowles describes fifteen emotional appeals or wedges that advertisements exploit.

Underlying Fowles's psychological analysis of advertising is the assumption that advertisers try to circumvent the logical, cautious, skeptical powers we develop as consumers, to reach, instead, the "unfulfilled urges and motives swirling in the bottom half of [our] minds." In Fowles's view, consumers are well advised to pay attention to these underlying appeals in order to avoid responding unthinkingly.

As you read, *note which of Fowles's fifteen appeals seem most familiar to you. Do you recognize these appeals in ads you can recall? How have you responded?*

EMOTIONAL APPEALS

The nature of effective advertisements was recognized full well by the late media philosopher Marshall McLuhan. In his *Understanding Media,* the first sentence of the section on advertising reads, "The continuous pressure is to create ads more and more in the image of audience motives and desires." 1

By giving form to people's deep-lying desires, and picturing states of being that individuals privately yearn for, advertisers have the best chance of arresting attention and affecting communication. And that is the immediate goal of advertising: to tug at our psychological shirt sleeves and slow us down long enough for a word or two about whatever is being sold. We glance at a picture of a solitary rancher at work, and "Marlboro" slips into our minds. 2

Advertisers (I'm using the term as a shorthand for both the products' manufacturers, who bring the ambition and money to the process, and the advertising agencies, who supply the know-how) are ever more compelled to invoke consumers' drives and longings; this is the "continuous pressure" McLuhan refers to. Over the past century, the American marketplace has grown increasingly congested as more and more products have entered into the frenzied competition after the public's dollars. The economies of other nations are quieter than ours since the volume of goods being hawked does not so greatly exceed demand. In some economies, consumer wares are scarce enough that no advertising at all is necessary. But in the United States, we go to the other extreme. In order to stay in business, an advertiser must strive to cut through the considerable commercial hub-bub by any means available—including the emotional appeals that some observers have held to be abhorrent and underhanded. 3

The use of subconscious appeals is a comment not only on conditions among sellers. As time has gone by, buyers have become stoutly resistant to advertisements. We live in a blizzard of these messages and have learned to turn up our collars and ward off most of them. A study done a few years ago at Harvard University's Graduate School of Business Administration ventured that the average American is exposed to some 500 ads daily from television, newspapers, magazines, radio, billboards, direct mail, and so on. If for no other reason than to preserve one's sanity, a filter must be developed in every mind to lower the number of ads a person is actually aware of—a number this particular study estimated at about seventy-five ads per day. (Of these, only twelve typically produced a reaction—nine positive and three negative, on the average.) To be among the few messages that do manage to gain access to minds, advertisers must be strategic, perhaps even a little underhanded at times.

5 There are assumptions about personality underlying advertisers' efforts to communicate via emotional appeals, and while these assumptions have stood the test of time, they still deserve to be aired. Human beings, it is presumed, walk around with a variety of unfulfilled urges and motives swirling in the bottom half of their minds. Lusts, ambitions, tendernesses, vulnerabilities—they are constantly bubbling up, seeking resolution. These mental forces energize people, but they are too crude and irregular to be given excessive play in the real world. They must be capped with the competent, sensible behavior that permits individuals to get along well in society. However, this upper layer of mental activity, shot through with caution and rationality, is not receptive to advertising's pitches. Advertisers want to circumvent this shell of consciousness if they can, and latch on to one of the lurching, subconscious drives.

6 In effect, advertisers over the years have blindly felt their way around the underside of the American psyche, and by trial and error have discovered the softest points of entree, the places where their messages have the greatest likelihood of getting by consumers' defenses. As McLuhan says elsewhere, "Gouging away at the surface of public sales resistance, the ad men are constantly breaking through into the *Alice in Wonderland* territory behind the looking glass, which is the world of subrational impulses and appetites."

7 An advertisement communicates by making use of a specially selected image (of a supine female, say, or a curly-haired child, or a celebrity) which is designed to stimulate "subrational impulses and desires" even when they are at ebb, even if they are unacknowledged by their possessor. Some few ads have their emotional appeal in the text, but for the greater number by far the appeal is contained in the artwork. This makes sense, since visual communication better suits

more primal levels of the brain. If the viewer of an advertisement actually has the importuned motive, and if the appeal is sufficiently well fashioned to call it up, then the person can be hooked. The product in the ad may then appear to take on the semblance of gratification for the summoned motive. Many ads seem to be saying, "If you have this need, then this product will help satisfy it." It is a primitive equation, but not an ineffective one for selling.

Thus, most advertisements appearing in national media can be understood as having two orders of content. The first is the appeal to deeprunning drives in the minds of consumers. The second is information regarding the good[s] or service being sold: its name, its manufacturer, its picture, its packaging, its objective attributes, its functions. For example, the reader of a brassiere advertisement sees a partially undraped but blandly unperturbed woman standing in an otherwise commonplace public setting, and may experience certain sensations; the reader also sees the name "Maidenform," a particular brassiere style, and, in tiny print, words about the material, colors, price. Or, the viewer of a television commercial sees a demonstration with four small boxes labelled 650, 650, 650, and 800; something in the viewer's mind catches hold of this, as trivial as thoughtful consideration might reveal it to be. The viewer is also exposed to the name "Anacin," its bottle, and its purpose. 8

Sometimes there is an apparently logical link between an ad's emotional appeal and its product information. It does not violate common sense that Cadillac automobiles be photographed at country clubs, or that Japan Air Lines be associated with Orientalia. But there is no real need for the linkage to have a bit of reason behind it. Is there anything inherent to the connection between Salem cigarettes and mountains, Coke and a smile, Miller Beer and comradeship? The link being forged in minds between product and appeal is a pre-logical one. 9

People involved in the advertising industry do not necessarily talk in the terms being used here. They are stationed at the sending end of this communications channel, and may think they are up to any number of things—Unique Selling Propositions, explosive copywriting, the optimal use of demographics or psychographics, ideal media buys, high recall ratings, or whatever. But when attention shifts to the receiving end of the channel, and focuses on the instant of reception, then commentary becomes much more elemental: an advertising message contains something primary and primitive, an emotional appeal, that in effect is the thin end of the wedge, trying to find its way into a mind. Should this occur, the product information comes along behind. 10

When enough advertisements are examined in this light, it becomes clear that the emotional appeals fall into several distinguishable 11 categories, and that every ad is a variation on one of a limited number of basic appeals. While there may be several ways of classifying these appeals, one particular list of fifteen has proven to be especially valuable.

Advertisements can appeal to:

1. The need for sex
2. The need for affiliation
3. The need to nurture
4. The need for guidance
5. The need to aggress
6. The need to achieve
7. The need to dominate
8. The need for prominence
9. The need for attention
10. The need for autonomy
11. The need to escape
12. The need to feel safe
13. The need for aesthetic sensations
14. The need to satisfy curiosity
15. Physiological needs: food, drink, sleep, etc.

MURRAY'S LIST

Where does this list of advertising's fifteen basic appeals come from? 12
Several years ago, I was involved in a research project which was to have as one segment an objective analysis of the changing appeals made in post–World War II American advertising. A sample of magazine ads would have their appeals coded into the categories of psychological needs they seemed aimed at. For this content analysis to happen, a complete roster of human motives would have to be found.

The first thing that came to mind was Abraham Maslow's fa- 13
mous four-part hierarchy of needs. But the briefest look at the range of appeals made in advertising was enough to reveal that they are more varied, and more profane, than Maslow had cared to account for. The search led on to the work of psychologist Henry A. Murray, who together with his colleagues at the Harvard Psychological Clinic has constructed a full taxonomy of needs. As described in *Explorations in Personality,* Murray's team had conducted a lengthy series of in-depth interviews with a number of subjects in order to derive from scratch what they felt to be the essential variables of personality. Forty-four variables were distinguished by the Harvard group, of which twenty were motives. The need for achievement ("to overcome obstacles and

obtain a high standard") was one, for instance; the need to defer was another; the need to aggress was a third; and so forth.

Murray's list had served as the groundwork for a number of subsequent projects. Perhaps the best-known of these was David C. McClelland's extensive study of the need for achievement, reported in his *The Achieving Society.* In the process of demonstrating that a people's high need for achievement is predictive of later economic growth, McClelland coded achievement imagery and references out of a nation's folklore, songs, legends, and children's tales. 14

Following McClelland, I too wanted to cull the motivational appeals from a culture's imaginative product—in this case, advertising. To develop categories expressly for this purpose, I took Murray's twenty motives and added to them others he had mentioned in passing in *Explorations in Personality* but not included on the final list. The extended list was tried out on a sample of advertisements, and motives which never seemed to be invoked were dropped. I ended up with eighteen of Murray's motives, into which 770 print ads were coded. The resulting distribution is included in the 1976 book *Mass Advertising as Social Forecast.* 15

Since that time, the list of appeals has undergone refinements as a result of using it to analyze television commercials. A few more adjustments stemmed from the efforts of students in my advertising classes to decode appeals; tens of term papers surveying thousands of advertisements have caused some inconsistencies in the list to be hammered out. Fundamentally, though, the list remains the creation of Henry Murray. In developing a comprehensive, parsimonious inventory of human motives, he pinpointed the subsurface mental forces that are the least quiescent and most susceptible to advertising's entreaties. 16

FIFTEEN APPEALS

1. *Need for sex.* Let's start with sex, because this is the appeal which seems to pop up first whenever the topic of advertising is raised. Whole books have been written about this one alone, to find a large audience of mildly titillated readers. Lately, due to campaigns to sell blue jeans, concern with sex in ads has redoubled. 17

The fascinating thing is not how much sex there is in advertising, but how little. Contrary to impressions, unambiguous sex is rare in these messages. Some of this surprising observation may be a matter of definition: the Jordache ads with the lithe, blouse-less female astride a similarly clad male is clearly an appeal to the audience's sexual drives, but the same cannot be said about Brooke Shields in the Calvin 18

Klein commercials. Directed at young women and their credit-card carrying mothers, the image of Miss Shields instead invokes the need to be looked at. Buy Calvins and you'll be the center of much attention, just as Brooke is, the ads imply; they do not primarily inveigle their target audience's need for sexual intercourse.

In the content analysis reported in *Mass Advertising as Social Forecast* 19 only two percent of ads were found to pander to this motive. Even *Playboy* ads shy away from sexual appeals: a recent issue contained eighty-three full-page ads, and just four of them (or less than five percent) could be said to have sex on their minds.

The reason this appeal is so little used is that it is too blaring and 20 tends to obliterate the product information. Nudity in advertising has the effect of reducing brand recall. The people who do remember the product may do so because they have been made indignant by the ad; this is not the response most advertisers seek.

To the extent that sexual imagery is used, it conventionally 21 works better on men than women; typically a female figure is offered up to the male reader. A Black Velvet liquor advertisement displays an attractive woman wearing a tight black outfit, recumbent under the legend, "Feel the Velvet." The figure does not have to be horizontal, however, for the appeal to be present as National Airlines revealed in its "Fly me" campaign. Indeed, there does not even have to be a female in the ad; "Flick my Bic" was sufficient to convey the idea to many.

As a rule, though, advertisers have found sex to be a tricky ap- 22 peal, to be used sparingly. Less controversial and equally fetching are the appeals to our need for affectionate human contact.

2. *Need for affiliation.* American mythology upholds autonomous 23 individuals, and social statistics suggest that people are ever more going it alone in their lives, yet the high frequency of affiliative appeals in ads belies this. Or maybe it does not: maybe all the images of companionship are compensation for what Americans privately lack. In any case, the need to associate with others is widely invoked in advertising and is probably the most prevalent appeal. All sorts of goods and services are sold by linking them to our unfulfilled desires to be in good company.

According to Henry Murray, the need for affiliation consists of 24 desires "to draw near and enjoyably cooperate or reciprocate with another; to please and win affection of another; to adhere and remain loyal to a friend." The manifestations of this motive can be segmented into several different types of affiliation, beginning with romance.

Courtship may be swifter nowadays, but the desire for pair- 25 bonding is far from satiated. Ads reaching for this need commonly depict a youngish male and female engrossed in each other. The head of the male is usually higher than the female's, even at this late date; she may be sitting or leaning while he is standing. They are not touching in the Smirnoff vodka ads, but obviously there is an intimacy, sometimes frolicsome, between them. The couple does touch for Martell Cognac when "The moment was Martell." For Wind Song perfume they have touched, and "Your Wind Song stays on his mind."

Depending on the audience, the pair does not absolutely have to be young—just together. He gives her a DeBeers diamond, and there is a tear in her laugh lines. She takes Geritol and preserves herself for him. And numbers of consumers, wanting affection too, follow suit. 26

Warm family feelings are fanned in ads when another generation is added to the pair. Hallmark Cards brings grandparents into the picture, and Johnson and Johnson Baby Powder has Dad, Mom, and baby, all fresh from the bath, encircled in arms and emblazoned with "Share the Feeling." A talc has been fused to familial love. 27

Friendship is yet another form of affiliation pursued by advertisers. Two women confide and drink Maxwell House coffee together; two men walk through the woods smoking Salem cigarettes. Miller Beer promises that afternoon "Miller Time" will be staffed with three or four good buddies. Drink Dr. Pepper, as Mickey Rooney is coaxed to do, and join in with all the other Peppers. Coca-Cola does not even need to portray the friendliness; it has reduced this appeal to "a Coke and a smile." 28

The warmth can be toned down and disguised, but it is the same affiliative need that is being fished for. The blonde has a direct gaze and her friends are firm businessmen in appearance, but with a glass of Old Bushmill you can sit down and fit right in. Or, for something more upbeat, sing along with the Pontiac choirboys. 29

As well as presenting positive images, advertisers can play to the need for affiliation in negative ways, by invoking the fear of rejection. If we don't use Scope, we'll have the "Ugh! Morning Breath" that causes the male and female models to avert their faces. Unless we apply Ultra Brite or Close-Up to our teeth, it's good-bye romance. Our family will be cursed with "House-a-tosis" if we don't take care. Without Dr. Scholl's antiperspirant foot spray, the bowling team will keel over. There go all the guests when the supply of Dorito's nacho cheese chips is exhausted. Still more rejection if our shirts have ring-around-the-collar, if our car needs to be Midasized. But make a few purchases, and we are back in the bosom of human contact. 30

As self-directed as Americans pretend to be, in the last analysis we remain social animals, hungering for the positive, endorsing feelings that only those around us can supply. Advertisers respond, urging us to "Reach out and touch someone," in the hopes our monthly bills will rise. 31

3. *Need to nurture.* Akin to affiliative needs is the need to take care of small, defenseless creatures—children and pets, largely. Reciprocity is of less consequence here, though; it is the giving that counts. Murray uses synonyms like "to feed, help, support, console, protect, comfort, nurse, heal." A strong need it is, woven deep into our genetic fabric, for if it did not exist we could not successfully raise up our replacements. When advertisers put forth the image of something diminutive and furry, something that elicits the word "cute" or "precious," then they are trying to trigger this motive. We listen to the childish voice singing the Oscar Mayer weiner song, and our next hot-dog purchase is prescribed. Aren't those darling kittens something, and how did this Meow Mix get into our shopping cart? 32

This pitch is often directed at women, as Mother Nature's chief nurturers. "Make me some Kraft macaroni and cheese, please," says the elfin preschooler just in from the snowstorm, and mothers' hearts go out, and Kraft's sales go up. "We're cold, wet, and hungry," whine the husband and kids, and the little woman gets the Manwiches ready. A facsimile of this need can be hit without children or pets: the husband is ill and sleepless in the television commercial, and the wife grudgingly fetches the NyQuil. 33

But it is not women alone who can be touched by this appeal. The father nurses his son Eddie through adolescence while the John Deere lawn tractor survives the years. Another father counts pennies with his young son as the subject of New York Life Insurance comes up. And all over America are businessmen who don't know why they dial Qantas Airlines when they have to take a trans-Pacific trip; the koala bear knows. 34

4. *Need for guidance.* The opposite of the need to nurture is the need to be nurtured: to be protected, shielded, guided. We may be loath to admit it, but the child lingers on inside every adult—and a good thing it does, or we would not be instructable in our advancing years. Who wants a nation of nothing but flinty personalities? 35

Parent-like figures can successfully call up this need. Robert Young recommends Sanka coffee, and since we have experienced him for twenty-five years as television father and doctor, we take his word for it. Florence Henderson as the expert mom knows a lot about the advantages of Wesson oil. 36

The parent-ness of the spokesperson need not be so salient; sometimes pure authoritativeness is better. When Orson Welles scowls and intones, "Paul Masson will sell no wine before its time," we may not know exactly what he means, but we still take direction from him. There is little maternal about Brenda Vaccaro when she speaks up for Tampax, but there is a certainty to her that many accept. 37

A celebrity is not a necessity in making a pitch to the need for 38
guidance, since a fantasy figure can serve just as well. People accede to the Green Giant, or Betty Crocker, or Mr. Goodwrench. Some advertisers can get by with no figure at all: "When E.F. Hutton talks, people listen."

Often it is tradition or custom that advertisers point to and con- 39
sumers take guidance from. Bits and pieces of American history are used to sell whiskeys like Old Crow, Southern Comfort, Jack Daniel's. We conform to traditional male/female roles and age-old social norms when we purchase Barclay cigarettes, which informs us "The pleasure is back."

The product itself, if it has been around for a long time, can con- 40
stitute a tradition. All those old labels in the ad for Morton salt convince us that we should continue to buy it. Kool-Aid says "You loved it as a kid. You trust it as a mother," hoping to get yet more consumers to go along.

Even when the product has no history at all, our need to conform 41
to tradition and to be guided are strong enough that they can be invoked through bogus nostalgia and older actors. Country-Time lemonade sells because consumers want to believe it has a past they can defer to.

So far the needs and the ways they can be invoked which have 42
been looked at are largely warm and affiliative; they stand in contrast to the next set of needs, which are much more egoistic and assertive.

5. *Need to aggress.* The pressures of the real world create strong 43
retaliatory feelings in every functioning human being. Since these impulses can come forth as bursts of anger and violence, their display is normally tabooed. Existing as harbored energy, aggressive drives present a large, tempting target for advertisers. It is not a target to be aimed at thoughtlessly, though, for few manufacturers want their products associated with destructive motives. There is always the danger that, as in the case of sex, if the appeal is too blatant, public opinion will turn against what is being sold.

Jack-in-the-Box sought to abruptly alter its marketing by going 44
after older customers and forgetting the younger ones. Their television commercials had a seventy-ish lady command, "Waste him," and the Jack-in-the-Box clown exploded before our eyes. So did public reaction until the commercials were toned down. Print ads for Club cocktails carried the faces of octogenarians under the headline, "Hit me with a Club"; response was contrary enough to bring the campaign to a stop.

Better disguised aggressive appeals are less likely to backfire: 45
Triumph cigarettes has models making a lewd gesture with their uplifted cigarettes, but the individuals are often laughing and usually in

close company of others. When Exxon said, "There's a Tiger in your tank," the implausibility of it concealed the invocation of aggressive feelings.

Depicted arguments are a common way for advertisers to tap the audience's needs to aggress. Don Rickles and Lynda Carter trade gibes, and consumers take sides as the name of Seven-Up is stitched on minds. The Parkay tub has a difference of opinion with the user; who can forget it, or who (or what) got the last word in? 46

6. *Need to achieve.* This is the drive that energizes people, causing them to strive in their lives and careers. According to Murray, the need for achievement is signalled by the desires "to accomplish something difficult. To overcome obstacles and attain a high standard. To excel one's self. To rival and surpass others." A prominent American trait, it is one that advertisers like to hook on to because it identifies their product with winning and success. 47

The Cutty Sark ad does not disclose that Ted Turner failed at his latest attempt at yachting's America Cup; here he is represented as a champion on the water as well as off in his television enterprises. If we drink this whiskey, we will be victorious alongside Turner. We can also succeed with O.J. Simpson by renting Hertz cars, or with Reggie Jackson by bringing home some Panasonic equipment. Cathy Rigby and Stayfree Maxipads will put people out front. 48

Sports heroes are the most convenient means to snare consumers' needs to achieve, but they are not the only one. Role models can be established, ones which invite emulation, as with the profiles put forth by Dewar's scotch. Successful, tweedy individuals relate they have "graduated to the flavor of Myer's rum." Or the advertiser can establish a prize: two neighbors play one-on-one basketball for a Michelob beer in a television commercial, while in a print ad a bottle of Johnnie Walker Black Label has been gilded like a trophy. 49

Any product that advertises itself in superlatives—the best, the first, the finest—is trying to make contact with our needs to succeed. For many consumers, sales and bargains belong in this category of appeals, too; the person who manages to buy something at fifty percent off is seizing an opportunity and coming out ahead of others. 50

7. *Need to dominate.* This fundamental need is the craving to be powerful—perhaps omnipotent, as in the Xerox ad where Brother Dominic exhibits heavenly powers and creates miraculous copies. Most of us will settle for being just a regular potentate, though. We drink Budweiser because it is the King of Beers, and here comes the powerful Clydesdales to prove it. A taste of Wolfschmidt vodka and "The spirit of the Czar lives on." 51

The need to dominate and control one's environment is often thought of as being masculine, but as close students of human nature 52 advertisers know, it is not so circumscribed. Women's aspirations for control are suggested in the campaign theme, "I like my men in English Leather, or nothing at all." The females in the Chanel No. 19 ads are "outspoken" and wrestle their men around.

Male and female, what we long for is clout; what we get in its 53
place is Mastercard.

8. *Need for prominence.* Here comes the need to be admired and 54
respected, to enjoy prestige and high social status. These times, it appears, are not so egalitarian after all. Many ads picture the trappings of high position; the Oldsmobile stands before a manorial doorway, the Volvo is parked beside a steeplechase. A book-lined study is the setting for Dewar's 12, and Lenox China is displayed in a dining room chock full of antiques.

Beefeater gin represents itself as "The Crown Jewel of England" 55
and uses no illustrations of jewels or things British, for the words are sufficient indicators of distinction. Buy that gin and you will rise up the prestige hierarchy, or achieve the same effect on yourself with Seagram's 7 Crown, which ambiguously describes itself as "classy."

Being respected does not have to entail the usual accoutrements 56
of wealth: "Do you know who I am?" the commercials ask, and we learn that the prominent person is not so prominent without his American Express card.

9. *Need for attention.* The previous need involved being *looked up to,* 57
while this is the need to be *looked at.* The desire to exhibit ourselves in such a way as to make others look at us is a primitive, insuppressible instinct. The clothing and cosmetic industries exist just to serve this need, and this is the way they pitch their wares. Some of this effort is aimed at males, as the ads for Hathaway shirts and Jockey underclothes. But the greater bulk of such appeals is targeted singlemindedly at women.

To come back to Brooke Shields: this is where she fits into Ameri- 58
can marketing. If I buy Calvin Klein jeans, consumers infer, I'll be the object of fascination. The desire for exhibition has been most strikingly played to in a print campaign of many years' duration, that of Maidenform lingerie. The woman exposes herself, and sales surge. "Gentlemen prefer Hanes" the ads dissemble, and women who want eyes upon them know what they should do. Peggy Fleming flutters her legs for L'eggs, encouraging females who want to be the star in their own lives to purchase this product.

The same appeal works for cosmetics and lotions. For years, the 59
little girl with the exposed backside sold gobs of Coppertone, but now the company has picked up the pace a little: as a female, you are supposed to "Flash 'em a Coppertone tan." Food can be sold the same way, especially to the diet-conscious; Angie Dickinson poses for California avocados and says, "Would this body lie to you?" Our eyes are

too fixed on her for us to think to ask if she got that way by eating mounds of guacomole.

10. *Need for autonomy.* There are several ways to sell credit card services, as has been noted: Mastercard appeals to the need to dominate, and American Express to the need for prominence. When Visa claims, "You can have it the way you want it," yet another primary motive is being beckoned forward—the need to endorse the self. The focus here is upon the independence and integrity of the individual; this need is the antithesis of the need for guidance and is unlike any of the social needs. "If running with the herd isn't your style, try ours," says Rotan-Mosle, and many Americans feel they have finally found the right brokerage firm. 60

The photo is of a red-coated Mountie on his horse, posed on a snow-covered ledge; the copy reads, "Windsor—One Canadian stands alone." This epitome of the solitary and proud individual may work best with male customers, as may Winston's man in the red cap. But one-figure advertisements also strike the strong need for autonomy among American women. As Shelly Hack strides for Charlie perfume, females respond to her obvious pride and flair; she is her own person. The Virginia Slims tale is of people who have come a long way from subservience to independence. Cachet perfume feels it does not need a solo figure to work this appeal, and uses three different faces in its ads; it insists, though, "It's different on every woman who wears it." 61

Like many psychological needs, this one can also be appealed to in a negative fashion, by invoking the loss of independence or self-regard. Guilt and regrets can be stimulated: "Gee, I could have had a V-8." Next time, get one and be good to yourself. 62

11. *Need to escape.* An appeal to the need for autonomy often co-occurs with one for the need to escape, since the desire to duck out of our social obligations, to seek rest or adventure, frequently takes the form of one-person flight. The dashing image of a pilot, in fact, is a standard way of quickening this need to get away from it all. 63

Freedom is the pitch here, the freedom that every individual yearns for whenever life becomes too oppressive. Many advertisers like appealing to the need for escape because the sensation of pleasure often accompanies escape, and what nicer emotional nimbus could there be for a product? "You deserve a break today," says McDonald's, and Stouffer's frozen foods chime in, "Set yourself free." 64

For decades men have imaginatively bonded themselves to the Marlboro cowboy who dwells untarnished and unencumbered in Marlboro Country some distance from modern life; smokers' aching needs for autonomy and escape are personified by that cowpoke. Many women can identify with the lady ambling through the woods behind the words, "Benson and Hedges and mornings and me." 65

But escape does not have to be solitary. Other Benson and Hedges ads, part of the same campaign, contain two strolling figures. In Salem cigarette advertisements, it can be several people who escape together into the mountaintops. A commercial for Levi's pictured a cloudbank above a city through which ran a whole chain of young people. 66

There are varieties of escape, some wistful like the Boeing "Someday" campaign of dream vacations, some kinetic like the play and parties in soft drink ads. But in every instance, the consumer exposed to the advertisement is invited to momentarily depart his everyday life for a more carefree experience, preferably with the product in hand. 67

12. *Need to feel safe.* Nobody in their right mind wants to be intimidated, menaced, battered, poisoned. We naturally want to do whatever it takes to stave off threats to our well-being, and to our families'. It is the instinct of self-preservation that makes us responsive to the ad of the St. Bernard with the keg of Chivas Regal. We pay attention to the stern talk of Karl Malden and the plight of the vacationing couples who have lost all their funds in the American Express travelers cheques commercials. We want the omnipresent stag from Hartford Insurance to watch over us too. 68

In the interest of keeping failure and calamity from our lives, we like to see the durability of products demonstrated. Can we ever forget that Timex takes a licking and keeps on ticking? When the American Tourister suitcase bounces all over the highway and the egg inside doesn't break, the need to feel safe has been adroitly plucked. 69

We take precautions to diminish future threats. We buy Volkswagen Rabbits for the extraordinary mileage, and MONY insurance policies to avoid the tragedies depicted in their black-and-white ads of widows and orphans. 70

We are careful about our health. We consume Mazola margarine because it has "corn goodness" backed by the natural food traditions of the American Indians. In the medicine cabinet is Alka-Seltzer, the "home remedy"; having it, we are snug in our little cottage. 71

We want to be safe and secure; buy these products, advertisers are saying, and you'll be safer than you are without them. 72

13. *Need for aesthetic sensations.* There is an undeniable aesthetic component to virtually every ad run in the national media: the photography or filming or drawing is near-perfect, the type style is well chosen, the layout could scarcely be improved upon. Advertisers know there is little chance of good communication occurring if an ad is not visually pleasing. Consumers may not be aware of the extent of their own sensitivity to artwork, but it is undeniably large. 73

Sometimes the aesthetic element is expanded and made into an ad's primary appeal. Charles Jordan shoes may or may not appear in 74 the accompanying avant-grade photographs; Kohler plumbing fixtures catch attention through the high style of their desert settings. Beneath the slightly out of focus photograph, languid and sensuous in tone, General Electric feels called upon to explain, "This is an ad for the hair dryer."

This appeal is not limited to female consumers: J&B scotch says "It whispers" and shows a bucolic scene of lake and castle. 75

14. *Need to satisfy curiosity.* It may seem odd to list a need for information among basic motives, but this need can be as primal and compelling as any of the others. Human beings are curious by nature, interested in the world around them, and intrigued by tidbits of knowledge and new developments. Trivia, percentages, observations counter to conventional wisdom—these items all help sell products. Any advertisement in a question-and-answer format is strumming this need. 76

A dog groomer has a question about long distance rates, and Bell Telephone has a chart with all the figures. An ad for Porsche 911 is replete with diagrams and schematics, numbers and arrows. Lo and behold, Anacin pills have 150 more milligrams than its competitors; should we wonder if this is better or worse for us? 77

15. *Physiological needs.* To the extent that sex is solely a biological need, we are now coming around full circle, back toward the start of the list. In this final category are clustered appeals to sleeping, eating, drinking. The art of photographing food and drink is so advanced, sometimes these temptations are wondrously caught in the camera's lens: the crab meat in the Red Lobster restaurant ads can start us salivating, the Quarterpounder can almost be smelled, the liquor in the glass glows invitingly. Imbibe, these ads scream. 78

STYLES

Some common ingredients of advertisements were not singled out for separate mention in the list of fifteen because they are not appeals in and of themselves. They are stylistic features, influencing the way a basic appeal is presented. The use of humor is one, and the use of celebrities is another. A third is time imagery, past and future, which goes to several purposes. 79

For all of its employment in advertising, humor can be treacherous, because it can get out of hand and smother the product information. Supposedly, this is what Alka-Seltzer discovered with its comic commercials of the late sixties; "I can't believe I ate the whole thing," the sad-faced husband lamented, and the audience cackled so much it forgot the antacid. Or, did not take it seriously. 80

81 But used carefully, humor can punctuate some of the softer appeals and soften some of the harsher ones. When Emma says to the Fruit-of-the-Loom fruits, "Hi, cuties. Whatcha doing in my laundry basket?" we smile as our curiosity is assuaged along with hers. Bill Cosby gets consumers tickled about the children in his Jell-O commercials, and strokes the need to nurture.

82 An insurance company wants to invoke the need to feel safe, but does not want to leave readers with an unpleasant aftertaste; cartoonist Rowland Wilson creates an avalanche about to crush a gentleman who is saying to another, "My insurance company? New England Life, of course. Why?" The same tactic of humor undercutting threat is used in the cartoon commercials for Safeco when the Pink Panther wanders from one disaster to another. Often humor masks aggression: comedian Bob Hope in the outfit of a boxer promises to knock out the knock-knocks with Texaco; Rodney Dangerfield, who "can't get no respect," invites aggression as the comic relief in Miller Lite commercials.

83 Roughly fifteen percent of all advertisements incorporate a celebrity, almost always from the fields of entertainment or sports. The approach can also prove troublesome for advertisers, for celebrities are human beings too, and fully capable of the most remarkable behavior. If anything distasteful about them emerges, it is likely to reflect on the product. The advertisers making use of Anita Bryant and Billy Jean King suffered several anxious moments. An untimely death can also react poorly on a product. But advertisers are willing to take risks because celebrities can be such a good link between producers and consumers, performing the social role of introducer.

84 There are several psychological needs these middlemen can play upon. Let's take the product class of cameras and see how different celebrities can hit different needs. The need for guidance can be invoked by Michael Landon, who plays such a wonderful dad on "Little House on the Prairie"; when he says to buy Kodak equipment, many people listen. James Garner for Polaroid cameras is put in a similar authoritative role, so defined by a mocking spouse. The need to achieve is summoned up by Tracy Austin and other tennis stars for Canon AE-1; the advertiser first makes sure we see these athletes playing to win. When Cheryl Tiegs speaks up for Olympus cameras, it is the need for attention that is being targeted.

85 The past and future, being outside our grasp, are exploited by advertisers as locales for the projection of needs. History can offer up heroes (and call up the need to achieve) or traditions (need for guidance) as well as art objects (need for aesthetic sensations). Nostalgia is a kindly version of personal history and is deployed by advertisers to rouse needs for affiliation and for guidance; the need to escape can

come in here, too. The same need to escape is sometimes the point of futuristic appeals but picturing the avant-garde can also be a way to get at the need to achieve.

ANALYZING ADVERTISEMENTS

When analyzing ads yourself for their emotional appeals, it takes a bit of practice to learn to ignore the product information (as well as one's own experience and feelings about the product). But that skill comes soon enough, as does the ability to quickly sort out from all the non-product aspects of an ad the chief element which is the most striking, the most likely to snag attention first and penetrate brains farthest. The key to the appeal, this element usually presents itself centrally and forwardly to the reader or viewer. 86

Another clue: the viewing angle which the audience has on the ad's subjects is informative. If the subjects are photographed or filmed from below and thus are looking down at you much as the Green Giant does, then the need to be guided is a good candidate for the ad's emotional appeal. If, on the other hand, the subjects are shot from above and appear deferential, as is often the case with children or female models, then other needs are being appealed to. 87

To figure out an ad's emotional appeal, it is wise to know (or have a good hunch about) who the targeted consumers are; this can often be inferred from the magazine or television show it appears in. This piece of information is a great help in determining the appeal and in deciding between two different interpretations. For example, if an ad features a partially undressed female, this would typically signal one appeal for readers of *Penthouse* (need for sex) and another for readers of *Cosmopolitan* (need for attention). 88

It would be convenient if every ad made just one appeal, were aimed at just one need. Unfortunately, things are often not that simple. A cigarette ad with a couple at the edge of a polo field is trying to hit both the need for affiliation and the need for prominence; depending on the attitude of the male, dominance could also be an ingredient in this. An ad for Chimere perfume incorporates two photos: in the top one the lady is being commanding at a business luncheon (need to dominate), but in the lower one she is being bussed (need for affiliation). Better ads, however, seem to avoid being too diffused; in the study of post–World War II advertising described earlier, appeals grew more focused as the decades passed. As a rule of thumb, about sixty percent have two conspicuous appeals; the last twenty percent have three or more. Rather than looking for the greatest number of appeals, decoding ads is most productive when the loudest one or two 89 appeals are discerned, since those are the appeals with the best chance of grabbing people's attention.

Finally, analyzing ads does not have to be a solo activity and probably should not be. The greater number of people there are involved, the better chance there is of transcending individual biases and discerning the essential emotional lure built into an advertisement. 90

DO THEY OR DON'T THEY?

Do the emotional appeals made in advertisements add up to the sinister manipulation of consumers? 91

It is clear that these ads work. Attention is caught, communication occurs between producers and consumers, and sales result. It turns out to be difficult to detail the exact relationship between a specific ad and a specific purchase, or even between a campaign and subsequent sales figures, because advertising is only one of a host of influences upon consumption. Yet no one is fooled by this lack of perfect proof; everyone knows that advertising sells. If this were not the case, then tight-fisted American businesses would not spend a total of fifty billion dollars annually on these messages. 92

But before anyone despairs that advertisers have our number to the extent that they can marshal us at will and march us like automatons to the check-out counters, we should recall the resiliency and obduracy of the American consumer. Advertisers may have uncovered the softest spots in minds, but that does not mean they have found truly gaping apertures. There is no evidence that advertising can get people to do things contrary to their self-interests. Despite all the finesse of advertisements, and all the subtle emotional tugs, the public resists the vast majority of the petitions. According to the marketing division of the A.C. Nielsen Company, a whopping seventy-five percent of all new products die within a year in the marketplace, the victims of consumer disinterest which no amount of advertising could overcome. The appeals in advertising may be the most captivating there are to be had, but they are not enough to entrap the wiley consumer. 93

The key to understanding the discrepancy between, on the one hand, the fact that advertising truly works, and, on the other, the fact that it hardly works, is to take into account the enormous numbers of people exposed to an ad. Modern-day communications permit an ad to be displayed to millions upon millions of individuals; if the smallest fraction of that audience can be moved to buy the product, then the ad has been successful. When one percent of the people exposed to a television advertising campaign reach for their wallets, that could be 94 one million sales, which may be enough to keep the product in production and the advertisements coming.

In arriving at an evenhanded judgment about advertisements and 95
their emotional appeals, it is good to keep in mind that many of the purchases which might be credited to these ads are experienced as genuinely gratifying to the consumer. We sincerely like the goods or service we have bought, and we may even like some of the emotional drapery that an ad suggests comes with it. It has sometimes been noted that the most avid students of advertisements are the people who have just bought the product; they want to steep themselves in the associated imagery. This may be the reason that Americans, when polled, are not negative about advertising and do not disclose any sense of being misused. The volume of advertising may be an irritant, but the product information as well as the imaginative material in ads are partial compensation.

A productive understanding is that advertising messages involve 96
costs and benefits at both ends of the communications channel. For those few ads which do make contact, the consumer surrenders a moment of time, has the lower brain curried, and receives notice of a product; the advertiser has given up money and has increased the chance of sales. In this sort of communications activity, neither party can be said to be the loser.

Examining the Text

1. Fowles's claim in this essay is that advertisers try to tap into basic human needs and emotions, rather than consumers' intellect. How does he go about proving this claim? What examples or other proof strike you as particularly persuasive? Where do you see weaknesses in Fowles's argument?
2. What do advertisers assume about the personality of the consumer, according to Fowles? How do these assumptions contribute to the way they sell products? Do you think that these assumptions about personality are correct? Why or why not?
3. Fowles's list of advertising's fifteen basic appeals is, as he explains, derived from Henry Murray's inventory of human motives. Which of these motives strike you as the most significant or powerful? What other motives would you add to the list?

For Group Discussion

In his discussion of the way advertising uses "the need for sex" and "the need to aggress," Fowles debunks the persistent complaints about the use of sex and violence in the mass media. What current examples support Fowles's point? Discuss your responses to his explanations.

Writing Suggestion
Working with Fowles's list of the fifteen appeals of advertising, survey a recent magazine, looking at all the ads and categorizing them based on their predominant appeal. In an essay, describe what your results tell you about the magazine and its readership. Based on your survey, would you amend Fowles's list? What additions or deletions would you make?

How Advertising Informs to Our Benefit

John E. Calfee

This article, adapted from John E. Calfee's book Fear of Persuasion: A New Perspective on Advertising and Regulation, *provides a different view of the effect of advertising on our society. Calfee, a former Federal Trade Commission economist and a resident scholar at the American Enterprise Institute, argues that advertising actually provides many benefits to consumers. Calfee relates several specific cases in which advertisements spread important health information to people who might not have learned about it otherwise. Because advertisers have huge budgets and can reach into virtually every home through television, newspapers, billboards, and radio campaigns, advertisements have the potential to spread information in a way that government-sponsored public service initiatives cannot.*

Calfee also diverges from previous articles in this chapter by suggesting that regulations on advertising are unnecessary and counterproductive. Indeed, Calfee argues that advertising is, to a large extent, self-regulating. Free-market competition compels companies to be truthful, or else competitors will challenge their claims, resulting in negative publicity.

As you read this article, *consider your own feelings about advertising: do you think it's a destructive force in our society or a valuable tool for disseminating information? Given the power and reach of advertising, how can it be used as a positive information resource?*

A great truth about advertising is that it is a tool for communicating information and shaping markets. It is one of the forces that compel sellers to cater to the desires of consumers. Almost everyone knows this because consumers use advertising every day, and they miss advertising when they cannot get it. This fact does not keep politicians and opinion leaders from routinely dismissing the value of 1 advertising. But the truth is that people find advertising very useful indeed.

Of course, advertising primarily seeks to persuade and everyone 2
knows this, too. The typical ad tries to induce a consumer to do one particular thing—usually, buy a product—instead of a thousand other things. There is nothing obscure about this purpose or what it means for buyers. Decades of data and centuries of intuition reveal that all consumers everywhere are deeply suspicious of what advertisers say and why they say it. This skepticism is in fact the driving force that makes advertising so effective. The persuasive purpose of advertising and the skepticism with which it is met are two sides of a single process. Persuasion and skepticism work in tandem so advertising can do its job in competitive markets. Hence, ads represent the seller's self interest, consumers know this, and sellers know that consumers know it.

By understanding this process more fully, we can sort out much 3
of the popular confusion surrounding advertising and how it benefits consumers.

HOW USEFUL IS ADVERTISING?

Just how useful is the connection between advertising and informa- 4
tion? At first blush, the process sounds rather limited. Volvo ads tell consumers that Volvos have side-impact air bags, people learn a little about the importance of air bags, and Volvo sells a few more cars. This seems to help hardly anyone except Volvo and its customers.

But advertising does much more. It routinely provides immense 5
amounts of information that benefits primarily parties other than the advertiser. This may sound odd, but it is a logical result of market forces and the nature of information itself.

The ability to use information to sell products is an incentive to 6
create new information through research. Whether the topic is nutrition, safety, or more mundane matters like how to measure amplifier power, the necessity of achieving credibility with consumers and critics requires much of this research to be placed in the public domain, and that it rest upon some academic credentials. That kind of research typically produces results that apply to more than just the brands sold by the firm sponsoring the research. The lack of property rights to such "pure" information ensures that this extra information is available at no charge. Both consumers and competitors may borrow the new information for their own purposes.

Advertising also elicits additional information from other 7
sources. Claims that are striking, original, forceful or even merely obnoxious will generate news stories about the claims, the controversies

they cause, the reactions of competitors (A price war? A splurge of comparison ads?), the reactions of consumers and the remarks of governments and independent authorities.

Probably the most concrete, pervasive, and persistent example of competitive advertising that works for the public good is price advertising. Its effect is invariably to heighten competition and reduce prices, even the prices of firms that assiduously avoid mentioning prices in their own advertising. 8

There is another area where the public benefits of advertising are less obvious but equally important. The unremitting nature of consumer interest in health, and the eagerness of sellers to cater to consumer desires, guarantee that advertising related to health will provide a storehouse of telling observations on the ways in which the benefits of advertising extend beyond the interests of advertisers to include the interests of the public at large. 9

A CASCADE OF INFORMATION

Here is probably the best documented example of why advertising is necessary for consumer welfare. In the 1970s, public health experts described compelling evidence that people who eat more fiber are less likely to get cancer, especially cancer of the colon, which happens to be the second leading cause of deaths from cancer in the United States. By 1979, the U.S. Surgeon General was recommending that people eat more fiber in order to prevent cancer. 10

Consumers appeared to take little notice of these recommendations, however. The National Cancer Institute decided that more action was needed. NCI's cancer prevention division undertook to communicate the new information about fiber and cancer to the general public. Their goal was to change consumer diets and reduce the risk of cancer, but they had little hope of success given the tiny advertising budgets of federal agencies like NCI. 11

Their prospects unexpectedly brightened in 1984. NCI received a call from the Kellogg Corporation, whose All-Bran cereal held a commanding market share of the high-fiber segment. Kellogg proposed to use All-Bran advertising as a vehicle for NCI's public service messages. NCI thought that was an excellent idea. Soon, an agreement was reached in which NCI would review Kellogg's ads and labels for accuracy and value before Kellogg began running their fiber–cancer ads. 12

The new Kellogg All-Bran campaign opened in October 1984. A typical ad began with the headline, "At last some news about cancer you can live with." The ad continued: "The National Cancer Institute believes a high-fiber, low-fat diet may reduce your risk of some kinds 13 of cancer. . . . That's why one of their strongest recommendations is to eat high-fiber foods. If you compare, you'll find Kellogg's All-Bran has nine grams of fiber per serving. No other cereal has more. So start your day with a bowl of Kellogg's All-Bran or mix it with your regular cereal."

The campaign quickly achieved two things. One was to create a regulatory crisis between two agencies. The Food and Drug Administration thought that if a food was advertised as a way to prevent cancer, it was being marketed as a drug. Then the FDA's regulations for drug labeling would kick in. The food would be reclassified as a drug and would be removed from the market until the seller either stopped making the health claims or put the product through the clinical testing necessary to obtain formal approval as a drug. 14

But food advertising is regulated by the Federal Trade Commission, not the FDA. The FTC thought Kellogg's ads were non-deceptive and were therefore perfectly legal. In fact, it thought the ads should be encouraged. The Director of the FTC's Bureau of Consumer Protection declared that "the [Kellogg] ad has presented important public health recommendations in an accurate, useful, and substantiated way. It informs the members of the public that there is a body of data suggesting certain relationships between cancer and diet that they may find important." The FTC won this political battle, and the ads continued. 15

The second instant effect of the All-Bran campaign was to unleash a flood of health claims. Vegetable oil manufacturers advertised that cholesterol was associated with coronary heart disease, and that vegetable oil does not contain cholesterol. Margarine ads did the same, and added that vitamin A is essential for good vision. Ads for calcium products (such as certain antacids) provided vivid demonstrations of the effects of osteoporosis (which weakens bones in old age), and recounted the advice of experts to increase dietary calcium as a way to prevent osteoporosis. Kellogg's competitors joined in citing the National Cancer Institute dietary recommendations. 16

Nor did things stop there. In the face of consumer demand for better and fuller information, health claims quickly evolved from a blunt tool to a surprisingly refined mechanism. Cereals were advertised as high in fiber and low in sugar or fat or sodium. Ads for an upscale brand of bread noted: "Well, most high-fiber bran cereals may be high in fiber, but often only one kind: insoluble. It's this kind of fiber that helps promote regularity. But there's also a kind of fiber known as soluble, which most high-fiber bran cereals have in very small amounts, if at all. Yet diets high in this kind of fiber may actually lower your serum cholesterol, a risk factor for some heart diseases." Cereal 17 boxes became convenient sources for a summary of what made for a good diet.

INCREASED INDEPENDENT INFORMATION

The ads also brought powerful secondary effects. These may have been even more useful than the information that actually appeared in the ads themselves. 18

One effect was an increase in media coverage of diet and health. *Consumer Reports,* a venerable and hugely influential magazine that carries no advertising, revamped its reports on cereals to emphasize fiber and other ingredients (rather than testing the foods to see how well they did at providing a complete diet for laboratory rats). The health-claims phenomenon generated its own press coverage, with articles like "What Has All-Bran Wrought?" and "The Fiber Furor." These stories recounted the ads and the scientific information that prompted the ads; and articles on food and health proliferated. Anyone who lived through these years in the United States can probably remember the unending media attention to health claims and to diet and health generally. 19

Much of the information on diet and health was new. This was no coincidence. Firms were sponsoring research on their products in the hope of finding results that could provide a basis for persuasive advertising claims. Oat bran manufacturers, for example, funded research on the impact of soluble fiber on blood cholesterol. When the results came out "wrong," as they did in a 1990 study published with great fanfare in *The New England Journal of Medicine,* the headline in *Advertising Age* was "Oat Bran Popularity Hitting the Skids," and it did indeed tumble. The manufacturers kept at the research, however, and eventually the best research supported the efficacy of oat bran in reducing cholesterol (even to the satisfaction of the FDA). Thus did pure advertising claims spill over to benefit the information environment at large. 20

The shift to higher fiber cereals encompassed brands that had never undertaken the effort necessary to construct believable ads about fiber and disease. Two consumer researchers at the FDA reviewed these data and concluded they were "consistent with the successful educational impact of the Kellogg diet and health campaign: consumers seemed to be making an apparently thoughtful discrimination between high- and low-fiber cereals," and that the increased market shares for high-fiber non-advertised products represented "the clearest evidence of a successful consumer education campaign." 21

Perhaps most dramatic were the changes in consumer awareness 22
of diet and health. An FTC analysis of government surveys showed that when consumers were asked about how they could prevent cancer through their diet, the percentage who mentioned fiber increased from 4% before the 1979 Surgeon General's report to 8.5% in 1984 (after the report but before the All-Bran campaign) to 32% in 1986 after a year and a half or so of health claims (the figure in 1988 was 28%). By far the greatest increases in awareness were among women (who do most of the grocery shopping) and the less educated: up from 0% for women without a high school education in 1984 to 31% for the same group in 1986. For women with incomes of less than $15,000, the increase was from 6% to 28%.

The health-claims advertising phenomenon achieved what years 23
of effort by government agencies had failed to achieve. With its mastery of the art of brevity, its ability to command attention, and its use of television, brand advertising touched precisely the people the public health community was most desperate to reach. The health claims expanded consumer information along a broad front. The benefits clearly extended far beyond the interests of the relatively few manufacturers who made vigorous use of health claims in advertising.

A PERVASIVE PHENOMENON

Health claims for foods are only one example, however, of a pervasive 24
phenomenon—the use of advertising to provide essential health information with benefits extending beyond the interests of the advertisers themselves.

Advertising for soap and detergents, for example, once improved 25
private hygiene and therefore, public health (hygiene being one of the underappreciated triumphs in twentieth century public health). Toothpaste advertising helped to do the same for teeth. When mass advertising for toothpaste and tooth powder began early in this century, tooth brushing was rare. It was common by the 1930s, after which toothpaste sales leveled off even though the advertising, of course, continued. When fluoride toothpastes became available, advertising generated interest in better teeth and professional dental care. Later, a "plaque reduction war" (which first involved mouthwashes, and later toothpastes) brought a new awareness of gum disease and how to prevent it. The financial gains to the toothpaste industry were surely dwarfed by the benefits to consumers in the form of fewer cavities and fewer lost teeth.

Health claims induced changes in foods, in nonfoods such as 26
toothpaste, in publications ranging from university health letters to

mainstream newspapers and magazines, and of course, consumer knowledge of diet and health.

These rippling effects from health claims in ads demonstrated the most basic propositions in the economics of information. Useful information initially failed to reach people who needed it because information producers could not charge a price to cover the costs of creating and disseminating pure information. And this problem was alleviated by advertising, sometimes in a most vivid manner. 27

Other examples of spillover benefits from advertising are far more common than most people realize. Even the much-maligned promotion of expensive new drugs can bring profound health benefits to patients and families, far exceeding what is actually charged for the products themselves. 28

The market processes that produce these benefits bear all the classic features of competitive advertising. We are not analyzing public service announcements here, but old-fashioned profit-seeking brand advertising. Sellers focused on the information that favored their own products. They advertised it in ways that provided a close link with their own brand. It was a purely competitive enterprise, and the benefits to consumers arose from the imperatives of the competitive process. 29

One might see all this as simply an extended example of the economics of information and greed. And indeed it is, if by greed one means the effort to earn a profit by providing what people are willing to pay for, even if what they want most is information rather than a tangible product. The point is that there is overwhelming evidence that unregulated economic forces dictate that much useful information will be provided by brand advertising, and only by brand advertising. 30

Of course, there is much more to the story. There is the question of how competition does the good I have described without doing even more harm elsewhere. After all, firms want to tell people only what is good about their brands, and people often want to know what is wrong with the brands. It turns out that competition takes care of this problem, too. 31

ADVERTISING AND CONTEXT

It is often said that most advertising does not contain very much information. In a way, this is true. Research on the contents of advertising typically finds just a few pieces of concrete information per ad. That's an average, of course. Some ads obviously contain a great deal of information. Still, a lot of ads are mainly images and pleasant talk, with little in the way of what most people would consider hard 32 information. On the whole, information in advertising comes in tiny bits and pieces.

Cost is only one reason. To be sure, cramming more information into ads is expensive. But more to the point is the fact that advertising plays off the information available from outside sources. Hardly anything about advertising is more important than the interplay between what the ad contains and what surrounds it. Sometimes this interplay is a burden for the advertiser because it is beyond his control. But the interchange between advertising and environment is also an invaluable tool for sellers. Ads that work in collaboration with outside information can communicate far more than they ever could on their own. 33

The upshot is advertising's astonishing ability to communicate a great deal of information in a few words. Economy and vividness of expression almost always rely upon what is in the information environment. The famously concise "Think Small" and "Lemon" ads for the VW "Beetle" in the 1960s and 1970s were highly effective with buyers concerned about fuel economy, repair costs, and extravagant styling in American cars. This was a case where the less said, the better. The ads were more powerful when consumers were free to bring their own ideas about the issues to bear. 34

The same process is repeated over again for all sorts of products. Ads for computer modems once explained what they could be used for. Now a simple reference to the Internet is sufficient to conjure an elaborate mix of equipment and applications. These matters are better left vague so each potential customer can bring to the ad his own idea of what the Internet is really for. 35

Leaning on information from other sources is also a way to enhance credibility, without which advertising must fail. Much of the most important information in advertising—think of cholesterol and heart disease, antilock brakes and automobile safety—acquires its force from highly credible sources other than the advertiser. To build up this kind of credibility through material actually contained in ads would be cumbersome and inefficient. Far more effective, and far more economical, is the technique of making challenges, raising questions and otherwise making it perfectly clear to the audience that the seller invites comparisons and welcomes the tough questions. Hence the classic slogan, "If you can find a better whiskey, buy it." 36

Finally, there is the most important point of all. Informational sparseness facilitates competition. It is easier to challenge a competitor through pungent slogans—"Where's the beef?", "Where's the big saving?"—than through a step-by-step recapitulation of what has gone on before. The bits-and-pieces approach makes for quick, unerring at- 37 tacks and equally quick responses, all under the watchful eye of the consumer over whom the battle is being fought. This is an ideal recipe for competition.

It also brings the competitive market's fabled self-correcting 38 forces into play. Sellers are less likely to stretch the truth, whether it involves prices or subtleties about safety and performance, when they know they may arouse a merciless response from injured competitors. That is one reason the FTC once worked to get comparative ads on television, and has sought for decades to dismantle government or voluntary bans on comparative ads.

"LESS-BAD" ADVERTISING

There is a troubling possibility, however. Is it not possible that in their 39 selective and carefully calculated use of outside information, advertisers have the power to focus consumer attention exclusively on the positive, i.e., on what is good about the brand or even the entire product class? Won't automobile ads talk up style, comfort, and extra safety, while food ads do taste and convenience, cigarette ads do flavor and lifestyle, and airlines do comfort and frequency of departure, all the while leaving consumers to search through other sources to find all the things that are wrong with products?

In fact, this is not at all what happens. Here is why: Everything 40 for sale has something wrong with it, if only the fact that you have to pay for it. Some products, of course, are notable for their faults. The most obvious examples involve tobacco and health, but there are also food and heart disease, drugs and side effects, vacations and bad weather, automobiles and accidents, airlines and delay, among others.

Products and their problems bring into play one of the most im- 41 portant ways in which the competitive market induces sellers to serve the interests of buyers. No matter what the product, there are usually a few brands that are "less bad" than the others. The natural impulse is to advertise that advantage—"less cholesterol," "less fat," "less dangerous," and so on. Such provocative claims tend to have an immediate impact. The targets often retaliate; maybe their brands are less bad in a different respect (less salt?). The ensuing struggle brings better information, more informed choices, and improved products.

Perhaps the most riveting episode of "less-bad" advertising ever 42 seen occurred, amazingly enough, in the industry that most people assume is the master of avoiding saying anything bad about its product.

Less-Bad Cigarette Ads

Cigarette advertising was once very different from what it is today. 43
Cigarettes first became popular around the time of World War I, and they came to dominate the tobacco market in the 1920s. Steady and often dramatic sales increases continued into the 1950s, always with vigorous support from advertising. Tobacco advertising was duly celebrated as an outstanding example of the power and creativity of advertising. Yet amazingly, much of the advertising focused on what was wrong with smoking, rather than what people liked about smoking.

The very first ad for the very first mass-marketed American ciga- 44
rette brand (Camel, the same brand recently under attack for its use of a cartoon character) said, "Camel Cigarettes will not sting the tongue and will not parch the throat." When Old Gold broke into the market in the mid-1920s, it did so with an ad campaign about coughs and throats and harsh cigarette smoke. It settled on the slogan, "Not a cough in a carload."

Competitors responded in kind. Soon, advertising left no doubt 45
about what was wrong with smoking. Lucky Strike ads said, "No Throat Irritation—No Cough...we...removed...harmful corrosive acids," and later on, "Do you inhale? What's there to be afraid of?... famous purifying process removes certain impurities." Camel's famous tag line, "more doctors smoke Camels than any other brand," carried a punch precisely because many authorities thought smoking was unhealthy (cigarettes were called "coffin nails" back then), and smokers were eager for reassurance in the form of smoking by doctors themselves. This particular ad, which was based on surveys of physicians, ran in one form or another from 1933 to 1955. It achieved prominence partly because physicians practically never endorsed non-therapeutic products.[1]

Things really got interesting in the early 1950s, when the first 46
persuasive medical reports on smoking and lung cancer reached the public. These reports created a phenomenal stir among smokers and the public generally. People who do not understand how advertising works would probably assume that cigarette manufacturers used advertising to divert attention away from the cancer reports. In fact, they did the opposite.

[1]The ad ran in many outlets, including *The Journal of the American Medical Association*, which regularly carried cigarette advertisements until the early 1950s. Incidentally, Camel was by no means the only brand that cited medical authorities in an effort to reassure smokers.

Small brands could not resist the temptation to use advertising to scare smokers into switching brands. They inaugurated several spectacular years of "fear advertising" that sought to gain competitive advantage by exploiting smokers' new fear of cancer. Lorillard, the beleaguered seller of Old Gold, introduced Kent, a new filter brand supported by ad claims like these: "Sensitive smokers get real health protection with new Kent," "Do you love a good smoke but not what the smoke does to you?" and "Takes out more nicotine and tars than any other leading cigarette—the difference in protection is priceless," illustrated by television ads showing the black tar trapped by Kent's filters. 47

Other manufacturers came out with their own filter brands, and raised the stakes with claims like, "Nose, throat, and accessory organs not adversely affected by smoking Chesterfields. First such report ever published about any cigarette," "Takes the fear out of smoking," and "Stop worrying... Philip Morris and only Philip Morris is entirely free of irritation used [sic] in all other leading cigarettes." 48

These ads threatened to demolish the industry. Cigarette sales plummeted by 3% in 1953 and a remarkable 6% in 1954. Never again, not even in the face of the most impassioned anti-smoking publicity by the Surgeon General or the FDA, would cigarette consumption decline as rapidly as it did during these years of entirely market-driven anti-smoking ad claims by the cigarette industry itself. 49

Thus advertising traveled full circle. Devised to bolster brands, it denigrated the product so much that overall market demand actually declined. Everyone understood what was happening, but the fear ads continued because they helped the brands that used them. The new filter brands (all from smaller manufacturers) gained a foothold even as their ads amplified the medical reports on the dangers of smoking. It was only after the FTC stopped the fear ads in 1955 (on the grounds that the implied health claims had no proof) that sales resumed their customary annual increases. 50

Fear advertising has never quite left the tobacco market despite the regulatory straight jacket that governs cigarette advertising. In 1957, when leading cancer experts advised smokers to ingest less tar, the industry responded by cutting tar and citing tar content figures compiled by independent sources. A stunning "tar derby" reduced the tar and nicotine content of cigarettes by 40% in four years, a far more rapid decline than would be achieved by years of government urging in later decades. This episode, too, was halted by the FTC. In February 1960 the FTC engineered a "voluntary" ban on tar and nicotine claims. 51

Further episodes continue to this day. In 1993, for example, Liggett planned an advertising campaign to emphasize that its Chesterfield brand did not use the stems and other less desirable parts 52 of the tobacco plant. This continuing saga, extending through eight decades, is perhaps the best documented case of how "less-bad" advertising completely offsets any desires by sellers to accentuate the positive while ignoring the negative. *Consumer Reports* magazine's 1955 assessment of the new fear of smoking still rings true:

> ...companies themselves are largely to blame. Long before the current medical attacks, the companies were building up suspicion in the consumer by the discredited "health claims" in their ads...Such medicine-show claims may have given the smoker temporary confidence in one brand, but they also implied that cigarettes in general were distasteful, probably harmful, and certainly a "problem." When the scientists came along with their charges against cigarettes, the smoker was ready to accept them.

And that is how information works in competitive advertising. 53

Less-bad can be found wherever competitive advertising is al- 54
lowed. I already described the health-claims-for-foods saga, which featured fat and cholesterol and the dangers of cancer and heart disease. Price advertising is another example. Prices are the most stubbornly negative product feature of all, because they represent the simple fact that the buyer must give up something else. There is no riper target for comparative advertising. When sellers advertise lower prices, competitors reduce their prices and advertise that, and soon a price war is in the works. This process so strongly favors consumers over the industry that one of the first things competitors do when they form a trade group is to propose an agreement to restrict or ban price advertising (if not ban all advertising). When that fails, they try to get advertising regulators to stop price ads, an attempt that unfortunately often succeeds.

Someone is always trying to scare customers into switching 55
brands out of fear of the product itself. The usual effect is to impress upon consumers what they do not like about the product. In 1991, when Americans were worried about insurance companies going broke, a few insurance firms advertised that they were more solvent than their competitors. In May 1997, United Airlines began a new ad campaign that started out by reminding fliers of all the inconveniences that seem to crop up during air travel.

Health information is a fixture in "less-bad" advertising. Ads for 56
sleeping aids sometimes focus on the issue of whether they are habit-forming. In March 1996, a medical journal reported that the pain reliever acetaminophen, the active ingredient in Tylenol, can cause liver damage in heavy drinkers. This fact immediately became the focus of ads for Advil, a competing product. A public debate ensued, con-

ducted through advertising, talk shows, news reports and pronouncements from medical authorities. The result: consumers learned a lot more than they had known before about the fact that all drugs have side effects. The press noted that this dispute may have helped consumers, but it hurt the pain reliever industry. Similar examples abound.

We have, then, a general rule: sellers will use comparative adver- 57
tising when permitted to do so, even if it means spreading bad information about a product instead of favorable information. The mechanism usually takes the form of less-bad claims. One can hardly imagine a strategy more likely to give consumers the upper hand in the give and take of the marketplace. Less-bad claims are a primary means by which advertising serves markets and consumers rather than sellers. They completely refute the naive idea that competitive advertising will emphasize only the sellers' virtues while obscuring their problems.

Examining the Text

1. What points does Calfee make with his example of advertising for Kellogg's All-Bran cereal? According to Calfee, what are the advantages and disadvantages of using ads to inform consumers about health issues?

2. According to Calfee, what are the "spillover benefits" of advertising?

3. How would you describe the tone of this article? Considering the fact that Calfee is arguing an unusual position—that advertising is good for us—what rhetorical strategies does he use to make his position persuasive?

4. What are some of the ways that free-market competition in advertising benefits consumers? Does Calfee see any reason for government or industry regulation of advertising?

For Group Discussion

This activity requires that each member of the group bring four or five ads to class—either from a magazine, newspaper, or brochure—in order to test Calfee's proposition that ads provide consumers with useful information. In your group, make a list of the useful information that each ad presents. That is, what helpful facts do you learn from the ad? Then discuss the other kinds of information or content presented in each ad. (You might reread Jib Fowles's "Advertising's Fifteen Basic Appeals" to get some ideas.) What conclusions can you draw from this comparison? Do your conclusions coincide with Calfee's claims? Are certain kinds of ads—or ads for certain products—more likely to contain helpful information?

Writing Suggestion

Calfee discusses the history of cigarette advertising, noting the predominance of "less-bad" claims and "fear advertising" in mid-twentieth-century cigarette ad campaigns. Find five or six recent cigarette advertisements in magazines or newspapers and analyze the information these ads present and the strategies they use to sell their product. Then write an essay in which you first summarize Calfee's discussion of the history of cigarette advertising; use quotations and paraphrases from the article to develop your summary. In the remainder of your essay, discuss what you see as the current state of cigarette advertising based on your analysis of recent ads.

Virtual Product Placement

Damian Ward Hey

If you've watched a professional football game on TV lately, you've probably seen a yellow line cutting across the field, indicating where the offense needs to go to get a first down; the players don't see this line, nor do fans at the stadium, because the line isn't actually there. Or if you've recently watched a professional baseball game on TV, you might have seen a billboard advertisement behind home plate, an ad that fans at the ballpark would assure you wasn't there. No, you're not hallucinating; you're looking at the "virtual placement" of information on television. Rather than physically placing information or products at specific locations, such as ballparks or studios where TV shows are being filmed, advertisers today can use digital technology to "virtually" place things where you'll notice them. Once you've noticed a product being used by a celebrity or as a backdrop for your favorite baseball team, advertisers hope that you'll feel more inclined to buy the product next time you're shopping.

Damian Ward Hey, a professor of Mass Media Studies at Hofstra University, explains that virtual product placement is a new advertising technique that may or may not become standard practice in the future. Although "physical" product placement has been around since the early days of television, virtual product placement allows advertisers more flexibility. They can change what products are seen and by whom, for instance by changing what is shown to viewers in different geographic locations. As Hey points out, however, there are complicated issues that need to be resolved in order for virtual product placement to become a successful technique. For instance, do the advertisers or the show's producers decide what products are placed—and where—in shows? And what happens to the standard 30-second commercial if product advertising occurs in the show itself?

Keep in mind that the other articles in this chapter have dealt primarily with straightforward advertising—that is, advertising that's recognizably advertising. With product placement, there isn't an explicit, literal message saying "buy this product" but rather an association of the product with particular celebrities or settings that viewers might find appealing. ***As you read,*** *consider how product placement functions differently as a form of advertising. In what ways do you think it might be more or less effective than the kind of straightforward advertising with which we're familiar?*

A method of placing advertisements on television is evolving that might or might not forever blur the traditional boundaries between program content and the commercial break, depending upon whom you ask. The method is called virtual product placement and involves digitally inserting a product or a product logo into a live or prerecorded program where that product or logo does not, in physical actuality, exist. 1

Perhaps the most famous example of virtual advertising technology is Princeton Video Image Inc.'s branded First Down Line, which debuted during Super Bowl XXXV in 2001. The line could be seen only by TV viewers and not by those actually at the game. Although the line United States viewers saw was unadorned with product logo, the line seen by viewers in other countries was not. Viewers in Germany saw a FedEx logo next to the line, while viewers in Canada saw a Pizza Pizza stamp and viewers in Mexico saw an ad for the Mexican bank Banca Serfin. 2

Other examples of virtual placement include CBS News' replacement of an NBC logo (on NBC's Jumbotron advertising screen in Times Square) with its own virtual CBS logo during the 2000 live broadcast on New Year's Eve. Virtual ads have appeared on billboards during San Diego Padres baseball games, and on Indy League racing telecasts. A digitally placed Coca-Cola can appeared on a desk in an episode of UPN's *Seven Days* and a previously non-existent Wells-Fargo billboard also appeared in the same show. In 1999, the pre-awards telecast of the Grammys on CBS placed virtual ads for Harrah's casinos and Nordstrom's department stores in an entryway. 3

In these examples (and there are increasingly many others) not only does the viewer see a placed product that is not actually there in the real world, he or she may also see a different placed product depending upon where they view their television. This means that content in a nationally, or even internationally, broadcast program can be manipulated to fit any number of local demographics. If the kinks can be worked out among network officials, program producers and 4 advertising executives, this will create a fundamental change in audience-oriented programming that will be too powerful to ignore.

But that is a huge "if." Industry response to virtual product placement has been mixed. Although often rather closed-mouthed about the topic, network officials tend to view virtual product placement as an interesting experiment the ultimate application and propriety of which are yet to be either determined or agreed upon. A sharper and perhaps more disruptive division exists among advertising executives who, by contrast, tend either to anticipate or to dismiss the possibility that one day virtual advertisements may become an accepted, standard part of our televisual landscape.

Any discussion of virtual product placement on TV must be informed by the distinct yet ever-entwined histories of technology and consumerism as they have evolved throughout the existence of television. The development of media is prone to a certain paranoid narrative of social Darwinism wherein newer sucessful means replace outdated less successful means. What is seen to work best in terms of culture, business or technology succeeds. Older forms of media fear death (or its functional equivalent, obsolescence) at the hands of newer forms of media. Eventually, the narrative holds, older forms of media will put aside their fears and will come to accept the younger upstarts, however grudgingly, until both old media and new media work together in synergistic fashion for their own (and the consumer's) mutual benefit. Regarding virtual product placement, this narrative has yet to play itself out, and there are no guarantees that it will. One of the critiques of virtual product placement echoes the sentiment of the old Ralph Burns tune, "Everything Old is New Again." How, those who are skeptical ask, is virtual product placement different from regular old product placement? Mitch Oscar, senior VP and director of media futures for the advertising agency Universal McCann, is one such skeptic.

"Is virtual product placement, or product placement in general, a back-to-the future type of deal?" asks Oscar. "Is it more of a move of desperation to make a product more visual in a cluttered environment? How is product placement of old any different from virtual product placement of today, or any other kind of product placement in the future?"

Oscar says that many people are asking him about virtual product placement, yet he sees it as a hot topic with little substance. "People are simply coming up with a new slant to an old idea," says Oscar. "I don't have much faith in it."

Product placement is the "old idea" to which Oscar refers. Indeed, product placement—the conscious placing of products onscreen for the purposes of exposure and sales—has been around since the early days of television. A classic example is the $8 million sponsorship of *I Love Lucy* in the early 1950s by the Philip Morris company in exchange for Lucy and Ricky smoking the company's cigarettes during the show. *I Love Lucy,* a show that was really the first *enormous* hit in TV history and that for many symbolized the domestic ideal for popular culture in the fifties, took advantage of its iconic status to advertise its own line of products. In her autobiography, Lucille Ball writes that "In addition to the production company, we also had a merchandising business. It was possible to furnish a house and dress a whole family with items carrying our *I Love Lucy* label." This pre-dates by about 50 years companies like AsSeenIn.com or Watch Point Company, whose "heated" point and click merchandising allow the viewer to purchase products seen in TV shows that he or she watches.

The modern age of product placement was launched in the cin- 10
ema in 1983 when Robert Kovoloff had Hershey Food Corps' "Reese's Pieces" placed in the Spielberg blockbuster *ET.* Since the famous spot when *ET* ate the Reese's Pieces, we have seen products placed in movies such as *The Horse Whisperer, Jerry Maguire, Mrs. Doubtfire* and *Titanic,* to name only a small few. On television, (again naming only a short list) we have seen products placed on *3rd Rock From the Sun, Ally McBeal, NYPD Blue* and, perhaps most famously, *Seinfeld*—remember the show about Junior Mints?

The ready answer to Oscar's question is that virtual product 11
placement is different from regular old product placement simply by virtue of its being virtual. Virtual product placement allows advertisers to manipulate what the original producers of a program designed for the viewers to see, long after the original producers are gone. Conceivably, the advertiser could eventually have more say over the content of the show than did the show's creator. Whereas regular old product placement exists during the run of the show, virtual product placement can exist and manipulate what the viewer sees and perceives both during the show's first run and long after it has gone into re-runs. Thus, virtual product placement is product placement, only more so.

Part of the problem is where to place the technology of virtual 12
product placement, itself. A television advertising executive who preferred to remain nameless commented that virtual product placement might have a place in local stations that produce high school sporting events where community business logos might be placed digitally on billboards and local events might be advertised for a small audience of team fans.

There is indeed a veritable litany of questions that needs still 13
to be answered before virtual product placement is able to find its niche in the television industry. Among these questions: Who owns

advertising time? The producer? The network? The affiliate? Who would make the decision to run an ad, and which ad to run? Who would decide which product to insert virtually, and where? Could this type of product placement also open up more advertising space during commercial breaks instead of less? This leads to another question: How much will the industry technology needed to support this kind of advertising cost not only the advertiser, but also the producer and/or the network?

Right now, virtual product placement is something that theorists 14
call a "site of inquiry," meaning, among other things, that it exists more in realms of potential and debate than in application and standardized practice. It is experimental, which makes it both an unknown quantity and an unstable investment, neither of which make for talkative industry executives.

One executive who *does* like to talk about virtual product place- 15
ment is Paul Slagle, VP of Sales and Marketing and now a consultant for Princeton Video Image, Inc., Princeton Video Image, or PVI (NASDAQ: PVII) is known for its virtual insertions, particularly during live sporting events. Slagle says that there is a trend toward virtual product placement, and that that trend is technology driven. "Viewing habits change," says Slagle. "Technology is devaluing the thirty-second commercial pod."

The particular technology to which Slagle refers is the personal 16
video recorder, or PVR, that allows the viewer to "zap" through commercial breaks. Slagle speaks of technology on two levels, the level of the individual consumer manipulating what he watches at home in front of his television set, and the level of the industry producer that sends manipulated content (virtual ads, etc.) into that viewer's home.

According to Slagle, marketers are looking for additional oppor- 17
tunities and space within program content itself. "TV shows have many lives. We see this as much with *Frasier* and *Seinfeld* repeats as we do with *I Love Lucy* repeats. Sellers do not want to be hung with one product spot. Virtual product placement enables the seller of advertising and the seller of time to monetize in-program real-estate over and over again. With this technology, buyers and sellers have a flexibility and spontaneity they never had before."

However, Slagle comments, "No advertiser wants to tune in and 18
find six other products on air at the same time."

Slagle states that "virtual product placement must be done in an 19
organic and environmentally friendly manner, with a setting that is natural. The invocation of words like "natural" "organic" and "environmentally friendly" is old hat to theorists in that academic branch of media study known as "Media Ecology." If advertisements are placed virtually, they must be placed in a way that makes sense to the plot

and character world, that which film scholars would call the *diagesis,* of the show. If a product is placed in an "unnatural" way, goes the argument, viewers will get offended and stop watching, which *would* mean death for both the network and the advertiser.

"But," continues Slagle, "we live in a branded world. Done the 20
right way, TV in the age of virtual product placement will not look any different than what we are used to now. Virtual product placement will change the landscape of advertising in three to six months, and will proliferate quickly. Then, competition will make distributors and producers want to figure out a way to accommodate the process."

Sean Badding, of The Carmel Group, also believes that virtual 21
product placement will change the landscape of advertising as we currently know it. He says that it will have a "moderate impact" in three to five years and will cause "a significant change in the next ten years." Badding observes that "Middleware companies, such as Open TV, Liberate TV, and Microsoft are partnering up with MSOs to bridge the gap between content and service providers. This trend began around three years ago (1998–1999). The software, however, needs to be in place." Badding states that we are heading toward interactive TV (ITV) and that "the technology is available but not the content." He adds that "All of this is happening very slowly. It hinges upon the evolution of PVRs, which are proliferating in set-top boxes, and which will soon have increased memory. Portions of this increased memory space will be bought by advertisers like Disney or GE."

In terms of the relationship between the consumer and the con- 22
tent that is piped into his or her home—the potential spawning ground for virtual product placement—Badding says that, currently, "It is all about customization and personalization. The MSO will know more about you, through questionaires that pop up when you turn on the TV and through records kept by the MSO with whom you subscribe. Records will tell which programs you watch and which ads you speed through and will customize both your viewing and your advertising according to its interpretation of your interests based on your viewing habits. There is a major privacy issue that is a big concern for any interactive company: it could easily become like Big Brother watching you. But, as long as you are open and honest with the consumer, it is fine. It is when you hide things that you get into trouble."

Who, then, will have final say in terms of virtual product place- 23
ment? According to Badding, the actors and actresses themselves who appear with the products. "Actor royalties are the biggest issue and the biggest hurdle for Virtual Product Placement and ITV in general," says Badding. "Suppose one of these point-and-click merchandisers advertised a shirt Jennifer Aniston was wearing. Aniston's agency has a contract to represent her and to make sure that she is not endorsing

anything that she does not want to endorse. There needs to be a contract agreement between Jennifer Aniston's agency and the marketer for this sort of virtual product placement and interactive consumerism to take place. These kinds of arrangements and agreements have to begin to happen. They will become commonplace in about five years or so."

A favorite venue for virtual *message* placement, alongside prod- 24
uct placement, is in the sports industry during live, televised sporting events. This may be because live sporting events provide drama without a script. Virtual messages placed on a wall or on the field itself inform the viewer of such things as the speed of a pitch, distance to the first down, and even background information about the athletes who are playing. Theoretically, this information helps the viewer to order and to script the game for himself, thus enhancing the viewing experience and giving him some feeling of control over the events of the game. There is disagreement, however, as to whether these virtual items enhance a game or detract from it.

In a recent re-broadcast of Game Three of the 1980 World Series 25
between the Kansas City Royals and the Philadelphia Phillies, ESPN Classic placed a virtual ad for Lotrimin on the wall behind home plate that said "Coming Up—Lotrimin AF Key Play of the Game." The ad appeared in the bottom of the 10th inning, right before Phillies' pitcher Tug McGraw threw the pitch that Willie Mays Aikens hit for a game-winning single. As Aikens ran to first, an advertisement for Lotrimin appeared on the wall.

A *New York Times* reporter, Richard Sandomir, saw the game and 26
wrote a scathing article accusing ESPN of altering the aura of classic games by using obtrusive, anachronistic—and thus environmentally unsound—ads.

"Maybe ESPN will place a Camel sign on the center-field fence of 27
Wrigley Field to show what Babe Ruth was pointing at in home movies and newsreels during the 1932 World Series," Sandomir wrote last summer. "And doesn't the Polo Grounds center-field fence look ripe for a dignified *Cats and Dogs* movie ad with Willie Mays in the foreground making his over-the-shoulder catch of Vic Wertz's fly ball in the 1954 World Series?"

In response to the Sandomir article, Paul Green, VP of Customer 28
Marketing and New Technology for ESPN, commented that the placement of the Lotrimin Play of the Game advertisement was "an experiment. Ideally, when done properly, virtual product placement is no different from a billboard. The viewer cannot tell the difference."

Green said that virtual product placement "allows owners and 29
advertisers to incorporate change in pre-recorded programs. ESPN can place signs in past games played on the "Classic Network" and can

provide value to the customer in a past event." The major weakness of virtual product placement," said Green, "is that it changes the natural environment of the product. It can be viewed as 'sneaky.' "

This seems to be the crux of the matter. We watch old sporting events for much the same reason that we watch old TV shows and old movies. There is an aura to these programs that somehow enables us to link with and share in the spirit of the past. We do not want ads snuck into the picture, smuggled into our modes of cultural escapism or cluttering up our history. 30

Contemporary television is all about experimenting with and expanding the viewing experience. Viewing habits *are* changing, and we *are* entering a new era of television that will have to reconcile the problem of virtual product placement in one way or another. Nonetheless, it is in the best interest of the television and advertising industries to keep the balance between appropriate advertising and content. If they fail to do so they will lose a substantial percentage of their audience. 31

Examining the Text

1. According to Hey, how does virtual product placement blur the boundaries between commercials and program content? How is virtual product placement different from "regular old product placement"? Are the differences significant?

2. Explain in your own words what you think Hey means by this sentence: "The development of media is prone to a certain paranoid narrative of social Darwinism wherein newer successful means replace outdated less successful means." Can you think of a specific example to illustrate this statement?

3. According to Hey, what important factors need to be considered by advertisers who place their products in television shows and movies? How do these factors change when the product placement is virtual rather than physical?

For Group Discussion

As Hey points out, it's still unclear whether virtual product placement will become an accepted practice in television advertising. He writes, "Right now, virtual product placement is something that theorists call a 'site of inquiry,' meaning, among other things, that it exists more in realms of potential and debate than in application and standardized practice." Hey presents information on both sides of the issue, quoting interviewees who are skeptical about virtual product placement as well as those who think its adoption is inevitable. In your group, discuss what you think is likely to happen. Make sure you support your opinion with specific evidence, taken from Hey's article as well as from your own experience as a TV watcher and a consumer.

Writing Suggestion

Hey mentions at least five parties that have significant stakes in virtual product placement: companies that want to advertise a product, television executives who produce shows, actors and actresses in these shows, those who develop the technologies for virtual product placement and interactive television, and, last but not least, people who watch television. In an essay, explain what each group has at stake in the debate over virtual product placement. How would a large-scale adoption of this advertising technique affect each group, both positively and adversely? Be sure to include quotations from Hey's article as well as examples and reasoning of your own. You might consider concluding the essay by taking a stand on which group has the most to gain and/or lose in the debate over virtual product placement, or by suggesting which group should have the power to decide whether or not this technique becomes standard practice.

Images of Women in Advertising

You're Soaking In It

Jennifer L. Pozner

We begin this casebook on images of women and men in advertising with an article, originally published on the Web at Salon.com, *that presents the ideas of a recognized expert in the field, Jean Kilbourne. Kilbourne is the author of several books on advertising, including her most recent* Can't Buy My Love: How Advertising Changes the Way We Think and Feel. *She is also well known as the creator of award-winning documentaries such as* Killing Us Softly, Pack of Lies, *and* Slim Hopes. *She is a popular speaker on college campuses and in communities, where her message is that we should pay attention to the messages that advertising conveys, especially messages that are harmful to girls and women.*

In her publications and lectures, Kilbourne argues that we are inundated with ads telling us that products can meet our deepest needs, that we can be happier, more popular, more successful—more anything, it seems—simply by buying the right products. Kilbourne also draws attention to the damaging stereotypes of women and girls that are often found in advertisements, stereotypes that are all the more damaging because of the accumulated impact of the approximately 3,000 ads that we see daily.

The article that follows begins by showing how Kilbourne's concerns are dealt with in the movie What Women Want, *starring Mel Gibson. Gibson plays the role of a chauvinistic advertising executive who experiences a significant change of heart when, through a bizarre electrocution experience, he gains the ability to hear the inner thoughts of the women around him. According to Pozner and Kilbourne, the movie perpetuates common misconceptions of the advertising business, as well as misrepresentations of men, women, and relationships.*

As you read, *note the effect of the interview format in most of this article. How does the question-and-answer structure of the article influence your understanding of Kilbourne's ideas? What's gained (and lost) by including Kilbourne's answers rather than just reporting on them?*

"Advertisers know what womanpower is," explains a self-promotional pitch for the *Ladies' Home Journal.* The ad shows a stylish woman wired to a mammoth computer that measures her whims with graphs, light bulbs and ticker tape. The magazine insists that, like the machine, it has 1 its finger on the pulse of women's desires. Perk and breathlessness permeate its claim to be able to harness the many elements of "womanpower," including "sales power" ("She spots a bright idea in her favorite magazine, and suddenly the whole town's sold on it!"), "will power" ("Can you stick to a nine-day diet for more than four hours at a stretch?") and, of course, "purchasing power" ("Isn't it the power of her purse that's been putting fresh smiles on the faces of America's businessmen?").

2 That was 1958. Today advertisers are generally more sophisticated in their execution, but their primary message to and about women has remained fundamentally unchanged. To tap into our power, offer us a new shade of lipstick, a fresh-scented floor wax or, in the case of Mel Gibson's patronizing chick flick, *What Women Want,* L'eggs pantyhose, Wonderbras or Nike Women's Sports gear.

3 The movie—No. 2 at the box office after a month in theaters—stars Gibson as Nick Marshall, a pompous advertising executive dubbed the "T&A King" for his successful reign over Swedish bikini-babe commercials. But Nick's campaigns leave female consumers cold and he loses an expected promotion to women's market whiz Darcy Maguire (Helen Hunt). Nick's boss explains that while he's more comfortable with Nick, men no longer dominate how ad dollars are being spent.

4 Once Nick acquires the ability to read women's minds—after an unfortunate incident with volumizing mousse, a hair dryer and a bathtub—a story unfolds that could only seem romantic to avid *Advertising Age* readers: Nick and his nemesis Darcy fall in love over Nike storyboards, brainstorming ways to convince consumers that "Nike wants to empower women" and "Nike is state-of-the-art, hardcore womanpower."

5 *What Women Want* is more than a commercial for Mars vs. Venus gender typing; it's a feature-length product placement, a jarring reminder that the entertainment media is up for grabs by the hawkers of hair spray and Hondas. Which is not to say that the news media is off limits. Take Disney's news giant, ABC. In November, after ABC accepted a hefty fee from Campbell's soup, journalist Barbara Walters and "The View" crew turned eight episodes of their talk show into paid infomercials for canned soup. Hosting a "soup-sipping contest" and singing the "M'm! M'm! Good!" jingle on-air, they made good on ABC's promise that the "hosts would try to weave a soup message into their regular on-air banter."

6 And in March, after Disney bought a stake in Pets.com, the company's snarky sock puppet mascot began appearing as a "guest" on "Good Morning America" and "Nightline." It was a sad day in news when Diane Sawyer addressed her questions to a sock on a stool with

a guy's hand up its butt, but that's what passes for "synergy" in today's megamerged media climate.

7 How does advertising's increasing encroachment into every niche of mass media impact our culture in general, and women in particular? Mothers Who Think asked pioneering advertising critic Jean Kilbourne, author of *Can't Buy My Love: How Advertising Changes the Way We Think and Feel.*

8 A favorite on the college lecture circuit, Kilbourne has produced videos that are used as part of media literacy programs worldwide, in particular *Killing Us Softly,* first produced in 1979 and remade as *Killing Us Softly III* in 2000. She shares her thoughts here about advertising's effects on women, children, media and our cultural environment—and explains why salvation can't be found in a Nike sports bra.

9 *In* What Women Want, *Mel Gibson and Helen Hunt produce a Nike commercial in which a woman runs in swooshed-up sportswear while a voice-over assures her that the road doesn't care if she's wearing makeup, and she doesn't have to feel uncomfortable if she makes more money than the road—basically equating freedom and liberation with a pair of $150 running shoes. Is this typical of advertising to women?*

10 Absolutely. The commercial in the movie is saying that women who are unhappy with the quality of their relationships can ease their frustration by literally forming a more satisfying relationship with the road. There's no hint that her human relationships are going to improve, but the road will love her anyway.

11 Advertising is always about moving away from anything that would help us find real change in our lives. In the funniest scene in the movie, when Mel Gibson finds out how much it hurts to wax his legs, he wonders, "Why would anyone do this more than once?" That's a very good question. But, of course, the film doesn't go there. The real solutions—to stop waxing or to challenge unnatural beauty standards or to demand that men grow up—are never offered. Instead, the message is that we must continue with these painful and humiliating rituals, but at least we can escape for a while by lacing on our expensive sneakers and going out for a run.

12 What Women Want *presents a pretty mercenary picture of advertising aimed at women. You've studied the industry for decades. Does it seem accurate to you?*

13 It isn't far off. As in the film, advertisers were kind of slow to really focus on women. Initially they did it by co-opting feminism. Virginia Slims

equated women's liberation and enslavement to tobacco with the trivializing slogan "You've come a long way, baby" in the '80s; a little while ago it ran a campaign with the slogan "Find your voice."

Then there were endless ads that turned the women's movement into the quest for a woman's product. Was there ever such a thing as static cling before there were fabric softeners and sprays? More recently advertisers have discovered what they call "relationship marketing," creating ads that exploit a human need for connection and relationships, which in our culture is often seen as a woman's need. 14

Advertising and the larger culture often imply that women are failures if we do not have perfect relationships. Of course, "perfect" relationships don't exist in real life. Why are they so prominent in ads? 15

This is part of the advertising mentality. Think about *What Women Want*—there's an ad at the heart of this film literally and figuratively. Everybody lives in spectacular apartments, they're all thin and beautiful, and Mel Gibson makes this incredible instant transformation. He starts out as a jerk, he's callous, he tells degrading jokes and patronizes the women he works with, but because of his new mind-reading power he gains immediate insight into women. He becomes a great lover in the space of half an hour. At one point his daughter tells him he's never had a real relationship in his life, but by the end of the film he has authentic relationships with his daughter and his new love. 16

The truth is, most men gain insight into women not through quick fixes but by having close relationships with them over time, sometimes painfully. In the world of advertising, relationships are instant and the best ones aren't necessarily with people: Zest is a soap, Happy is a perfume, New Freedom is a maxipad, Wonder is a bread, Good Sense is a tea bag and Serenity is a diaper. Advertising actually encourages us to have relationships with our products. 17

I'm looking at *TV Guide* right now and there's a Winston cigarette ad on the back cover with a woman saying, "Until I find a real man, I'll take a real smoke." There's another with four different pictures of one man with four different women, and the copy reads, "Who says guys are afraid of commitment? He's had the same backpack for years." In another ad, featuring a young woman wearing a pretty sweater, the copy says, "The ski instructor faded away after one session. Fortunately the sweater didn't." 18

One automobile spot implied that a Civic coupe would never tell you, "It's not you, it's me. I need more space. I'm not ready for a commitment." Maybe our chances for lasting relationships are greater with our cars than with our partners, but surely the solution can't be to fall in love with our cars, or to depend on them rather than on each other. 19

Basically, men can't be trusted but Häagen-Dazs never disappoints? Love is fleeting but a diamond is forever? Sort of a recipe for lowered expectations, isn't it? 20

A central message of advertising is that relationships with human beings can't be counted on, especially for women. The message is that men will make commitments only reluctantly and can't be trusted to keep them. Straight women, and these are pretty much the women in ads, are told that it's normal not to expect very much or get very much from the men in their lives. This normalizes really abnormal behavior—with male violence at the extreme and male callousness in general—by reinforcing men's unwillingness to express their feelings. This harms men, of course, as well as women. 21

In What Women Want, *Mel Gibson is literally able to "get into the female psyche," private thoughts and all, after he waxes his hairy legs and crams them into a pair of L'eggs pantyhose. Is it unusual for advertisers to imply that the essence of womanhood can be found in cosmetics and commercialism?* 22

Not at all. The central message of advertising has to be that we are what we buy. And perhaps what's most insidious about this is that it takes very human, very real feelings and desires such as the need to love and be loved, the need for authentic connection, the need for meaningful work, for respect, and it yokes these feeling to products. It tells us that our ability to attain love depends upon our attractiveness. 23

By now most of us know that these images are unrealistic and unhealthy, that implants leak, anorexia and bulimia can kill and, in real life, model Heidi Klum has pores. So why do the images in ads still have such away over us? 24

Most people like to think advertising doesn't affect them. But if that were really true, why would companies spend over $200 billion a year on advertising? Women don't buy into this because we're shallow or vain or stupid but because the stakes are high. Overweight women do tend to face biases—they're less likely to get jobs; they're poorer. Men do leave their wives for younger, more beautiful women as their wives age. There is manifest contempt and real-life consequences for women who don't measure up. These images work to keep us in line. 25

What do these images teach girls about what they can expect from themselves, from boys, from sex, from each other? 26

Girls get terrible messages about sex from advertising and popular culture. An ad featuring a very young woman in tight jeans reads: "He 27 says the first thing he noticed about you is your great personality. He lies." Girls are told that boys are out for sex at all times, and girls should always look as if they are ready to give it. (But God help them if they do.) The emphasis for girls and women is always on being desirable, not being agents of their own desire. Girls are supposed to somehow be innocent and seductive, virginal and experienced, all at the same time.

Girls are particularly targeted by the diet industry. The obsession with thinness is about cutting girls down to size, making sure they're not too powerful in any sense of the word. One fashion ad I use in my presentations shows an extremely thin, very young Asian woman next to the copy "The more you subtract, the more you add." 28

Adolescent girls constantly get the message that they should diminish themselves, they should be less than what they are. Girls are told not to speak up too much, not to be too loud, not to have a hearty appetite for food or sex or anything else. Girls are literally shown being silenced in ads, often with their hands over their mouth or, as in one ad, with a turtleneck sweater pulled up over their mouth. 29

One ad sold lipstick with a drawing of a woman's lips sucking on a pacifier. A girl in a particularly violent entertainment ad has her lips sewn shut. Sometimes girls are told to keep quiet in other ways, by slogans like "Let your fingers do the talking" (an ad for nail polish), "Watch your mouth, young lady" (for lipstick), "Make a statement without saying a word" (for perfume), "Score high on non-verbal skills" (for a clothing store). 30

Let's talk about violence against women in ads. A controversy broke out during the Olympics when NBC ran a Nike commercial parodying slasher films, in which Olympic runner Suzy Favor Hamilton is chased by a villain with a chain saw. Hamilton outruns him, leaving the would-be murderer wheezing in the woods. The punch line? "Why sport? You'll live longer." The ad shocked many people, but isn't violence against women, real or implied, common in ads? 31

People were outraged that Nike considered this type of thing a joke. A recent Perry Ellis sequence showed a woman apparently dead in a shower with a man standing over her; that one drew protests, too. But ads often feature images of women being threatened, attacked, or killed. Sexual assault and battery are normalized, even eroticized. 32

In one ad a woman lies dead on a bed with her breasts exposed and her hair sprawled out around her, and the copy reads, "Great hair never dies." A perfume ad that ran in several teen magazines showed a very young woman with her eyes blackened, next to the text "Apply generously to your neck so he can smell the scent as you shake your 33 head 'no.'" In other words, he'll understand that you don't really mean it when you say no, and he can respond like any other animal.

An ad for a bar in Georgetown with a close-up of a cocktail had the headline "If your date won't listen to reason, try a velvet hammer." That's really dangerous when you consider how many sexual assaults involve alcohol in some way. We believe we are not affected by these images, but most of us experience visceral shock when we pay conscious attention to them. 34

Are there subtler forms of abuse in ads? 35

There's a lot of emotional violence in ads. For example, in one cologne ad a handsome man ignores two beautiful blonds. The copy reads, "Do you want to be the one she tells her deep, dark secrets to? Or do you want to be her deep, dark secret?" followed by a final instruction: "Don't be such a good boy." What's the deep, dark secret here? That he's sleeping with both of them? On one level the message is that the way to get beautiful women is to ignore them, perhaps mistreat them. The message to men is that emotional intimacy is not a good thing. This does terrible things to men, and of course to women too. 36

There are also many, many ads in which women are pitted against each other for male attention. For example, there's one ad with a topless woman on a bed and the copy "What the bitch who's about to steal your man wears." Other ads feature young women fighting or glaring at each other. This means that when girls hit adolescence, at a time when they most need support from each other, they're encouraged to turn on each other in competition for men. It's tragic, because the truth is that one of the most powerful antidotes to destructive cultural messages is close and supportive female friendships. 37

Over the years we've grown more accustomed to product placements in movies, but What Women Want *takes advertiser-driven content to a new level. I tried to keep a running count, but there were so many I lost track: Sears, L'eggs, Wonderbra, Macintosh, Martha Stewart, CNN, Meredith Brooks and Alanis Morissette CD covers all get prominent plugs.* 38

The final commercial Gibson pitches to the Nike reps was similar in style, tone and prime-time-friendly slogan to sports ads we've seen on TV before. Would you be surprised if Nike's fake ad eventually traveled from the big screen to the small screen? How did we get to a point where the whole premise of a film rests on product placements? 39

I wouldn't be surprised at all. In fact, the ad in the movie was made in connection with Wieden + Kennedy, Nike's real-life ad agency. But Nike doesn't really need to pay to broadcast the commercial on TV, 40 since this film was so successful at the box office—there couldn't be a better launch for a commercial than this movie.

I think this is the wave of the future. As more and more people use their VCR to skip the commercials when they watch television, the commercials will begin to become part of the program so they can't be edited out. So while you're watching "Friends," Jennifer Aniston will say to Courteney Cox, "Your hair looks great," and Courteney will say, "Yeah, I'm using this new gel!" 41

A number of media critics have dubbed the encroachment of advertising in media, education and public spaces "ad creep." You've called it a "toxic cultural environment." Can you explain that? 42

As the mother of a 13-year-old girl, I feel I'm raising my daughter in a toxic cultural environment. I hate that advertisers cynically equate rebellion with smoking, drinking and impulsive and impersonal sex. I want my daughter to be a rebel, to defy stereotypes of "femininity," but I don't want her to put herself in danger. I feel I have to fight the culture every step of the way in terms of messages she gets. 43

Just as it is difficult to raise kids safely in a physically toxic environment, where they're breathing polluted air or drinking toxic water, it's also difficult or even impossible to raise children in a culturally toxic environment, where they're surrounded by unhealthy images about sex and relationships, and where their health is constantly sacrificed for the sake of profit. 44

Even our schools are toxic—when McDonald's has a nutrition curriculum, Exxon has an environmental curriculum and kindergartners are given a program called "Learning to read through recognizing corporate logos." Education is tainted when a student can get suspended for wearing a Pepsi T-shirt on a school-sponsored Coke day, which happened in Georgia in 1998. 45

The United States is one of the few nations in the world that think that children are legitimate targets for advertisers. We allow the tobacco and alcohol industries to use talking frogs and lizards to sell beer and cartoon characters to sell cigarettes. The Budweiser commercials are in fact the most popular commercials with elementary school kids, and Joe Camel is now as recognizable to 6-year-olds as is Mickey Mouse. 46

What advice do you have for parents, for any of us, who want to counteract this toxic cultural environment? 47

Parents can talk to their children, make these messages conscious. We can educate ourselves and become media literate. But primarily we 48 need to realize that this is not something we can fight purely on an individual basis.

Corporations are forever telling us that if we don't like what's on TV we should just turn it off, not let our kids watch tobacco ads or violent movies. We constantly hear that if parents would just talk to their kids there would be no problem. But that really is like saying, "If your children are breathing poisoned air, don't let them breathe." 49

We need to join together to change the toxic cultural environment. That includes things such as lobbying to teach noncorporate media literacy in our schools, fighting to abolish or restrict advertising aimed at children, organizing to get ads out of our schools, banning the promotion of alcohol and tobacco, and other community solutions. 50

There are great media literacy projects in Los Angeles, New Mexico, Massachusetts and many places throughout the world. There's no quick fix, but I have extensive resources about media criticism groups, social change organizations, educational material, media literacy programs and more available on my Web site. If they want, people could start there. 51

Examining the Text

1. Why do you think Pozner begins the interview with references to the movie *What Women Want* and to examples of product placement on TV networks? How do these examples set the stage for the interview with Kilbourne?

2. How does Kilbourne define "relationship marketing"? Which of the appeals discussed by Jib Fowles earlier in this chapter are used by "relationship marketing" ads?

3. Focusing on the issues of weight, dieting, and body image, in what ways does Kilbourne believe that advertising is responsible for causing harm to young girls? Why, according to Kilbourne, does advertising contribute to this problem?

4. What kinds of evidence does Kilbourne use to support claims she makes throughout this article? What evidence do you find particularly persuasive? Where in the article do you find yourself disagreeing with or doubting the validity of Kilbourne's claims?

5. The image on page 128, "Your Gaze Hits the Side of My Face," was created by the artist Barbara Kruger. Which of the themes discussed by Pozner and Kilbourne do you see reflected in this image?

For Group Discussion

Discuss what you think of the strategies that Kilbourne suggests for fighting the "toxic cultural environment" created by advertising. Which of these strategies do you think are the most likely to have an influence on the current state of advertising? Why would some strategies be more effective than others? Discuss any other strategies you can think of that allow ordinary people ("consumers") to have some impact on the content and techniques of advertising.

Writing Suggestion

As she answers questions in the interview, Kilbourne makes brief references to a number of advertisements that help to prove her points. For this assignment, look through magazines and newspapers for a single advertisement that you think either supports or contradicts one or more of Kilbourne's claims about "relationship marketing." Look for stereotypes, body images, violence, or other forms of advertising where abuses seem to occur. Begin your essay by providing a brief summary of Kilbourne's ideas. Then analyze the advertisement you've

"Your Gaze Hits the Side of My Face," by Barbara Kruger. *(Courtesy of the Mary Boone Gallery, New York)*

chosen. (You may want to review the "Reading Images" section in Chapter 1.) Be sure to connect your analysis of specific features of the ad to specific points that Kilbourne is making, either by providing quotations from Pozner's article or by summarizing Kilbourne's points in your own words.

Getting Dirty

Mark Crispin Miller

Mark Crispin Miller's essay comes from his 1988 book Boxed In, *a study of the meaning and influence of television and advertising in contemporary American culture. In "Getting Dirty," Miller analyzes a television ad for Shield soap, paying close attention to seemingly neutral details and finding meanings that may surprise us. For instance, Miller suggests that the ad woos female viewers with a "fantasy of dominance," offering "a subtle and meticulous endorsement of castration," playing on certain "guilts and insecurities" of men and women. The way the commercial reverses stereotypical gender roles makes it an interesting and complex example of the ways images of men and women are used in advertising.*

To those who think he is reading too much into the ad, Miller counters that it is through the details, often unnoticed by viewers, that ads convey some of their most powerful—and questionable—messages.

In this essay Miller is analytical but also is trying to persuade readers that his analysis of the advertisement is correct. **As you read,** *note the strategies that Miller uses to construct a persuasive, well-supported analysis, and note as well those moments where Miller does not persuade you of his interpretation.*

We are outside a house, looking in the window, and this is what we see: a young man, apparently nude and half-crazed with anxiety, lunging toward the glass. "Gail!" he screams, as he throws the window open and leans outside, over a flowerbox full of geraniums: "The most important shower of my life, and you switch deodorant soap!" He is, we now see, only half-naked, wearing a towel around his waist; and he shakes a packaged bar of soap—"Shield"—in one accusing hand. Gail, wearing a blue man-tailored shirt, stands outside, below the window, clipping a hedge. She handles this reproach with an ease that suggests years of contempt. "Shield is better," she explains patiently, 1 in a voice somewhat deeper than her husband's. "It's extra strength." (Close-up of the package in the husband's hand. Gail's efficient finger gliding along beneath the legend. THE EXTRA STRENGTH DEODORANT SOAP.) "Yeah," whimpers Mr. Gail, "but my first call on J.J. Siss [sic], the company's *toughest customer,* and *now this!*" Gail nods with broad mock-sympathy, and stands firm: "Shield fights odor better, so you'll feel *cleaner,*" she assures her husband, who darts away with a jerk of panic, as Gail rolls her eyes heavenward and gently shakes her head, as if to say, "What a half-wit!"

Cut to our hero, as he takes his important shower. No longer frantic, he now grins down at himself, apparently delighted to be caked with Shield, which, in its detergent state, has the consistency of wet cement. He then goes out of focus, as if glimpsed through a shower door. "Clinical tests prove," proclaims an eager baritone. "Shield fights odor better than the *leading* deodorant soap!" A bar of Shield (green) and a bar of that other soap (yellow) zip up the screen with a festive toot, forming a sort of graph which demonstrates that Shield does, indeed, "fight odor better, so you'll feel *cleaner!*" 2

This particular contest having been settled, we return to the major one, which has yet to be resolved. Our hero reappears, almost transformed: calmed down, dressed up, his voice at least an octave lower. "I *do* feel cleaner!" he announces cheerily, leaning into the doorway of a room where Gail is arranging flowers. She pretends to be ecstatic at this news, and he comes toward her, setting himself up for a profound humiliation by putting on a playful air of suave command. Adjusting his tie like a real man of the world, he saunters over to his wife and her flower bowl, where he plucks a dainty purple flower and lifts it to his lapel: "And," he boasts throughout all this, trying to make his voice sound even deeper, "with old J.J.'s business and my brains—" "—you'll... *clean up again?*" Gail asks with suggestive irony, subverting his authoritative pose by leaning against him, draping one hand over his shoulder to dangle a big yellow daisy down his chest. Taken aback, he shoots her a distrustful look, and she titters at him. 3

Finally, the word SHIELD appears in extreme close-up and the camera pulls back, showing two bars of the soap, one packaged and one not, on display amidst an array of steely bubbles. "Shield fights odor better, so you'll feel *cleaner!*" the baritone reminds us, and then our hero's face appears once more, in a little square over the unpackaged bar of soap: "I feel *cleaner* than *ever before!*" he insists, sounding faintly unconvinced. 4

Is all this as stupid as it seems at first? Or is there, just beneath the surface of this moronic narrative, some noteworthy design, intended to appeal to (and to worsen) some of the anxieties of modern 5 life? A serious look at this particular trifle might lead us to some strange discoveries.

We are struck, first of all, by the commercial's pseudofeminism, an advertising ploy with a long history, and one ubiquitous on television nowadays. Although the whole subject deserves more extended treatment, this commercial offers us an especially rich example of the strategy. Typically, it woos its female viewers—i.e., those who choose the soap in most households—with a fantasy of dominance; and it does so by inverting the actualities of woman's lot through a number of imperceptible details. For instance, in this marriage it is the wife, and not the husband, who gets to keep her name; and Gail's name, moreover, is a potent one, because of its brevity and its homonymic connotation. (If this housewife were more delicately named, called "Lillian" or "Cecilia," it would lessen her illusory strength.) She is also equipped in more noticeable ways; she's the one who wears the button-down shirt in this family, she's the one who's competent both outdoors and in the house, and it is she, and only she, who wields the tool. 6

These visual details imply that Gail is quite a powerful housewife, whereas her nameless mate is a figure of embarrassing impotence. This "man," in fact, is actually Gail's *wife;* he is utterly feminized, striking a posture and displaying attributes which men have long deplored in women. In other words, this commercial, which apparently takes the woman's side, is really the expression (and reflection) of misogyny. Gail's husband is dependent and hysterical, entirely without that self-possession which we expect from solid, manly types, like Gail. This is partly the result of his demeanor: in the opening scene, his voice sometimes cracks ludicrously, and he otherwise betrays the shrill desperation of a man who can't remember where he left his scrotum. The comic effect of this frenzy, moreover, is subtly enhanced by the mise-en-scène, which puts the man in a conventionally feminine position—in dishabille, looking down from a window. Thus we infer that he is sheltered and housebound, a modern Juliet calling for his/her Romeo; or—more appropriately—the image suggests a scene in some suburban red-light district, presenting this husband as an item on display, like the flowers just below his stomach, available for anyone's enjoyment, at a certain price. Although in one way contradictory, these implications are actually quite congruous, for they both serve to emasculate the husband, so that the wife might take his place, or play his part. 7

Such details, some might argue, need not have been the conscious work of this commercial's makers. The authors, that is, might have worked by instinct rather than design, and so would have been no more aware of their work's psychosocial import than we ourselves: 8

they just wanted to make the guy look like a wimp, merely for the purposes of domestic comedy. While such an argument certainly does apply to many ads, in this case it is unlikely. Advertising agencies do plenty of research, by which we can assume that they don't select their tactics arbitrarily. They take pains to analyze the culture which they help to sicken, and then, with much wit and cynicism, use their insights in devising their small dramas. This commercial is a subtle and meticulous endorsement of castration, meant to play on certain widespread guilts and insecurities; and all we need to do to demonstrate this fact is to subject the two main scenes to the kind of visual analysis which commercials, so brief and broad, tend to resist (understandably). The ad's visual implications are too carefully achieved to have been merely accidental or unconscious.

The crucial object in the opening shot is that flower box with its bright geraniums, which is placed directly in front of the husband's groin. This clever stroke of composition has the immediate effect of equating our hero's manhood with a bunch of flowers. This is an exquisitely perverse suggestion, rather like using a cigar to represent the Eternal Feminine: flowers are frail, sweet, and largely ornamental, hardly an appropriate phallic symbol, but (of course) a venerable symbol of *maidenhood.* The geraniums stand, then, not for the husband's virility, but for its absence. 9

More than a clever instance of inversion, furthermore, these phallic blossoms tell us something odd about this marital relationship. As Gail, clippers in hand, turns from the hedge to calm her agitated man, she appears entirely capable of calming him quite drastically, if she hasn't done so already (which might explain his hairless chest and high-pitched voice). She has the power, that is, to take away whatever slender potency he may possess, and uses the power repeatedly, trimming her husband (we infer) as diligently as she prunes her foliage. And, as she can snip his manhood, so too can she restore it, which is what the second scene implies. Now the flower bowl has replaced the flower box as the visual crux, dominating the bottom center of the frame with a crowd of blooms. As the husband, cleaned and dressed, comes to stand beside his wife, straining to affect a new authority, the flower bowl too appears directly at his lower center; so that Gail, briskly adding flowers to the bouquet, appears to be replenishing his vacant groin with extra stalks. He has a lot to thank her for, it seems: she is his helpmate, confidante, adviser, she keeps his house and grounds in order, and she is clearly the custodian of the family jewels. 10

Of course, her restoration of his potency cannot be complete, or he might shatter her mastery by growing a bit too masterful himself. He could start choosing his own soap, or take her shears away, or—worst of all—walk out for good. Therefore, she punctures his momen- 11 tary confidence by taunting him with that big limp daisy, countering his lordly gesture with the boutonniere by flaunting that symbol of his floral status. He can put on whatever airs he likes, but she still has his fragile vigor firmly in her hand.

Now what, precisely, motivates this sexless battle of the sexes? That is, 12
what really underlies this tense and hateful marriage, making the man so weak, the woman so contemptuously helpful? The script, seemingly nothing more than a series of inanities, contains the answer to these questions, conveying, as it does, a concern with cleanliness that amounts to an obsession: "Shield fights odor better, so you'll feel cleaner!" "I *do* feel cleaner!" "Shield fights odor better, so you'll feel *cleaner!*" "I feel *cleaner* than *ever before!*" Indeed, the commercial emphasizes the feeling of cleanliness even more pointedly than the name of the product, implying, by its very insistence, a feeling of dirtiness, an apprehension of deep filth.

And yet there is not a trace of dirt in the vivid world of this com- 13
mercial. Unlike many ads for other soaps, this one shows no sloppy children, no sweatsoaked workingmen with blackened hands, not even a bleary housewife in need of her morning shower. We never even glimpse the ground in Gail's world, nor is her husband even faintly smudged. In fact, the filth which Shield supposedly "fights" is not physical but psychological besmirchment: Gail's husband feels soiled because of what he has to do for a living, in order to keep Gail in that nice big house, happily supplied with shirts and shears

"My first call on J.J. Siss, the company's *toughest customer,* and 14
now *this!*" The man's anxiety is yet another feminizing trait, for it is generally women, and not men, who are consumed by doubts about the sweetness of their bodies, which must never be offensive to the guys who run the world. (This real anxiety is itself aggravated by commercials.) Gail's husband must play the female to the mighty J.J. Siss, a name whose oxymoronic character implies perversion: "J.J." is a stereotypic nickname for the potent boss, while "Sis" is a term of endearment, short for "sister" (and perhaps implying "sissy," too, in this case). Gail's husband must do his boyish best to please the voracious J.J. Siss, just as a prostitute must satisfy a demanding trick, or "tough customer." It is therefore perfectly fitting that this employee refer to the encounter, not as a "meeting" or "appointment," but as a "call"; and his demeaning posture in the window—half dressed and bent over—conveys, we now see, a definitive implication.

Gail's job as the "understanding wife" is not to rescue her hus- 15
band from these sordid obligations, but to help him meet them successfully. She may seem coolly self-sufficient, but she actually depends on her husband's attractiveness, just as a pimp relies on the charm of

his whore. And, also like a pimp, she has to keep her girl in line with occasional reminders of who's boss. When her husband starts getting uppity *après la douche,* she jars him from the very self-assurance which she had helped him to discover, piercing that "shield" which was her gift.

16 "And, with old J.J.'s business and my brains—" "—you'll...*clean up again?*" He means, of course, that he'll work fiscal wonders with old J.J.'s account, but his fragmentary boast contains a deeper significance, upon which Gail plays with sadistic cleverness. "Old J.J.'s business and my brains" implies a feminine self-description, since it suggests a variation on the old commonplace of "brains vs. brawn": J.J.'s money, in the world of this commercial (as in ours), amounts to brute strength, which the flexible husband intends to complement with his mother wit. Gail's retort broadens this unconscious hint of homosexuality: "—you'll...*clean up again?*" Given the monetary nature of her husband's truncated remark, the retort must mean primarily, "You'll make a lot of money." If this were all it meant, however, it would not be a joke, nor would the husband find it so upsetting. Moreover, we have no evidence that Gail's husband ever "cleaned up"—i.e., made a sudden fortune—in the past. Rather, the ad's milieu and *dramatis personae* suggest upward mobility, gradual savings and a yearly raise, rather than one prior killing. What Gail is referring to, in fact, with the "again," is her husband's shower: she implies that what he'll have to do, after his "call" on J.J. Siss, is, quite literally, wash himself off. Like any other tidy hooker, this man will have to clean up after taking on a tough customer, so that he might be ready to take on someone else.

17 These suggestions of pederasty are intended, not as a literal characterization of the husband's job, but as a metaphor for what it takes to get ahead: Gail's husband, like most white-collar workers, must debase himself to make a good impression, toadying to his superiors, offering himself, body and soul, to the corporation. Maybe, therefore, it isn't really Gail who has neutered him; it may be his way of life that has wrought the ugly change. How, then, are women represented here? The commercial does deliberately appeal to women, offering them a sad fantasy of control; but it also, perhaps inadvertently, illuminates the unhappiness which makes that fantasy attractive.

18 The husband's status, it would seem, should make Gail happy, since it makes her physically comfortable, and yet Gail can't help loathing her husband for the degradations which she helps him undergo. For her part of the bargain is, ultimately, no less painful than his. She has to do more than put up with him; she has to prepare him for his world of affairs, and then must help him to conceal the shame. Of course, it's all quite hopeless. She clearly despises the man whom

she would bolster; and the thing which she provides to help him "feel cleaner than ever before" is precisely what has helped him do the job that's always made him feel so dirty. "A little water clears us of this deed" is her promise, which is false, for she is just as soiled as her doomed husband, however fresh and well-ironed she may look.

Of course, the ad not only illuminates this mess, but helps perpetuate it, by obliquely gratifying the guilts, terrors, and resentments that underlie it and arise from it. The strategy is not meant to be noticed, but works through the apparent comedy, which must therefore be studied carefully, not passively received. Thus, thirty seconds of ingenious advertising, which we can barely stand to watch, tell us something more than we might want to know about the souls of men and women under corporate capitalism. 19

AFTERWORD

Advertising Age came back at this essay with an edifying two-pronged put-down. In the issue for 7 June 1982, Fred Danzig (now the magazine's editor) devoted his weekly column to the Shield analysis: "The professor prunes a television trifle," ran the headline. After a genial paraphrase of my argument, Danzig reported a few of the things I'd told him in a telephone conversation, and then finally got down to the necessary business of dismissive cluckling: "[Miller's] confession that he had watched the Shield spot more than 15 times quickly enabled me to diagnose his problem: Self-inflicted acute soap storyboard sickness. This condition inevitably leads to a mind spasm, to hallucination." The column featured the ad's crucial frames, over a caption quoting an unnamed "Lever executive": "We can hardly wait for Mr. Miller to get his hands on the Old Testament. His comments merit no comment from us; the Shield commercial speaks for itself." 20

Leaving aside (with difficulty) that naive crack about the Bible, I point here to the exemplary suppressiveness of his seeming "trifle" in *Advertising Age.* Indeed, "the Shield commercial speaks for itself," but the guardians of the spectacle try to talk over it, permitting it no significance beyond the superficial pitch: "—so you'll feel *cleaner!*" Through managerial scorn ("no comment") and journalistic ridicule ("mind spasm...hallucination"), they would shut down all discussion. (J. Walter Thompson later refused to send anyone to debate the matter with me on a radio program.) Thus was a divergent reading written off as the perversity of yet another cracked "professor"—when in fact it was the ad itself that was perverse. 21

Although that campaign did not appeal to its TV audience (J. Walter Thompson ultimately lost the Shield account), such belligerent 22 "common sense" does have a most receptive public. While the admakers—and others—insist that "people today are adwise" in fact most Americans still perceive the media image as transparent, a sign that simply says what it means and means what it says. They therefore tend to dismiss any intensive explication as a case of "reading too much into it"—an objection that is philosophically dubious, albeit useful to the admakers and their allies. It is now, perhaps, one obligation of the academic humanists, empowered, as they are, by critical theory, to demonstrate at large the faultiness—and the dangers—of that objection.

A historical note on the Shield commercial's pseudofeminism. 23
Since 1982, the contemptuous housewife has all but vanished from the antiseptic scene of advertising; Gail was among the last of an endangered species. By now, the housewife/mother is a despised figure—most despised by actual housewife/mothers, who make up 60% of the primetime audience. Since these viewers now prefer to see themselves represented as executives, or at least as mothers with beepers and attaché cases, the *hausfrau* of the past, whether beaming or sneering, has largely been obliterated by the advertisers. In 1985, Advertising to Women Inc., a New York advertising agency, found that, out of 250 current ads, only nine showed recognizable Moms.

This is a triumph not for women's liberation, but for advertising; 24
for, now that Mom is missing from the ads, presumably off knocking heads together in the boardroom, it is the commodity that seems to warm her home and tuck her children in at night.

In any case, the Shield strategy itself has certainly outlasted the 25
wry and/or perky Mommy-images of yesteryear. Indeed, because the sexes are now at war within the scene of advertising (and elsewhere), the nasty visual metaphors have become ubiquitous.

Examining the Text

1. Briefly define the term "pseudofeminism" (paragraph 6) in your own words. How, according to Miller, does the Shield advertisement display "pseudofeminism"? Is Miller justified in criticizing the ad in these terms?

2. Recalling that the title of this essay is "Getting Dirty," summarize Miller's points about cleanliness and dirt in the Shield advertisement. What do you think of Miller's statement that "the filth which Shield supposedly 'fights' is not physical but psychological besmirchment" (13)?

3. Describe the strategic importance of Miller's eighth paragraph. What is Miller doing in this paragraph, and why does he place it here in the essay rather than earlier or later? Do you agree with Miller's ultimate conclusion that "the ad's visual implications are too carefully achieved to have been merely accidental or unconscious"?

4. How would you describe the tone of Miller's essay, particularly in the opening section in which he describes the Shield commercial? Why do you think Miller adopts this tone? Do you find it helps him convey his points? Why or why not?
5. What is Miller's main point in the Afterword? To what extent does the Afterword help make the essay itself more persuasive?

For Group Discussion
Miller comments in the Afterword that "In fact most Americans still perceive the media image as transparent, a sign that simply says what it means and means what it says. They therefore tend to dismiss any intensive explication as a case of 'reading too much into it' " (22). How does this quote relate to your own response to Miller's essay? If you think Miller "reads too much into" the Shield ad, where in the essay does this occur? What could he do to make these parts of the essay more persuasive?

Writing Suggestion
Miller's analysis of the Shield advertisement focuses on its hidden misogyny. Reflect on other advertisements that also show some degree of misogyny, and write a description about how misogyny works in one specific ad. How does this ad, like the one for Shield, manage to appeal to female consumers even though its message is essentially derogatory toward women?

Sex, Lies and Advertising

Gloria Steinem

This chapter concludes with an essay by one of the most important and influential figures in the American feminist movement, Gloria Steinem. Steinem's essay, originally published in Ms. *magazine (which she cofounded), addresses some of the broader issues involving advertising and gender. As she demonstrates, we need to be aware not only of the* content *of advertisements, but also of how advertising agencies and their clients make demands that affect the entire content of magazines, women's magazines in particular.*

Steinem describes the difficulties Ms. *faced when soliciting advertisements for their new magazine in the 1970s. As a magazine with an entirely female readership,* Ms. *had first to convince advertisers that women were intelligent, active consumers. Then, the editors had to placate advertisers who demanded editorials and articles to promote their products. Steinem offers nu-*

merous examples of how companies try to influence the magazines they advertise in.

Before you read, *look at a recent issue of a woman's magazine, such as* Ms. *or* Working Woman *or* Vogue *to notice what sort of advertisements and articles you find there. To what extent do you think these magazines represent the interests and needs of their female readership?*

About three years ago, as *glasnost* was beginning and *Ms.* seemed to be ending, I was invited to a press lunch for a Soviet official. He entertained us with anecdotes about new problems of democracy in his country. Local Communist leaders were being criticized in their media for the first time, he explained, and they were angry. 1

"So I'll have to ask my American friends," he finished pointedly, "how more *subtly* to control the press." In the silence that followed, I said, "Advertising." 2

The reporters laughed, but later, one of them took me aside: How dare I suggest that freedom of the press was limited? How dare I imply that his newsweekly could be influenced by ads? 3

I explained that I was thinking of advertising's media-wide influence on most of what we read. Even news magazines use "soft" cover stories to sell ads, confuse readers with "advertorials,"[1] and occasionally self-censor on subjects known to be a problem with big advertisers. 4

But, I also explained, I was thinking especially of women's magazines. There, it isn't just a little content that's devoted to attracting ads, it's almost all of it. That's why advertisers—not readers—have always been the problem for *Ms.* As the only women's magazine that didn't supply what the ad world euphemistically describes as "supportive editorial atmosphere" or "complementary copy" (for instance, articles that praise food/fashion/beauty subjects to "support" and "complement" food/fashion/beauty ads), *Ms.* could never attract enough advertising to break even. 5

"Oh, *women's* magazines," the journalist said with contempt. "Everybody knows they're catalogs—but who cares? They have nothing to do with journalism." 6

I can't tell you how many times I've had this argument in 25 years of working for many kinds of publications. Except as money-making machines—"cash cows" as they are so elegantly called in the trade—women's magazines are rarely taken seriously. Though changes being made by women have been called more far-reaching than the industrial 7

---

[1]**"advertorial"** Advertisement designed to mimic the appearance of a feature article.—EDS.

revolution—and though many editors try hard to reflect some of them in the few pages left to them after all the adrelated subjects have been covered—the magazines serving the female half of this country are still far below the journalistic and ethical standards of news and general interest publications. Most depressing of all, this doesn't even rate an exposé.

If *Time* and *Newsweek* had to lavish praise on cars in general and credit General Motors in particular to get GM ads, there would be a scandal—maybe a criminal investigation. When women's magazines from *Seventeen* to *Lear's* praise beauty products in general and credit Revlon in particular to get ads, it's just business as usual. 8

9

When *Ms.* began, we didn't consider *not* taking ads. The most important reason was keeping the price of a feminist magazine low enough for most women to afford. But the second and almost equal reason was providing a forum where women and advertisers could talk to each other and improve advertising itself. After all, it was (and still is) as potent a source of information in this country as news or TV and movie dramas.

We decided to proceed in two stages. First, we would convince makers of "people products" used by both men and women but advertised mostly to men—cars, credit cards, insurance, sound equipment, financial services, and the like—that their ads should be placed in a women's magazine. Since they were accustomed to the division between editorial[2] and advertising in news and general interest magazines, this would allow our editorial content to be free and diverse. Second, we would add the best ads for whatever traditional "women's products" (clothes, shampoo, fragrance, food, and so on) that surveys showed *Ms.* readers used. But we would ask them to come in without the usual quid pro quo of "complementary copy." 10

We knew the second step might be harder. Food advertisers have always demanded that women's magazines publish recipes and articles on entertaining (preferably ones that name their products) in return for their ads; clothing advertisers expect to be surrounded by fashion spreads (especially ones that credit their designers); and shampoo, fragrance, and beauty products in general usually insist on positive editorial coverage of beauty subjects, plus photo credits besides. That's why women's magazines look the way they do. But if we could break this link between ads and editorial content, then we wanted good ads for "women's products," too. 11

---

[2]**editorial** In the magazine industry, all nonadvertising content in a magazine, including regular columns and feature articles.—EDS.

By playing their part in this unprecedented mix of *all* the things our readers need and use, advertisers also would be rewarded: Ads for products like cars and mutual funds would find a new growth market; the best ads for women's products would no longer be lost in oceans of ads for the same category; and both would have access to a laboratory of smart and caring readers whose response would help create effective ads for other media as well. 12

I thought then that our main problem would be the imagery in ads themselves. Car makers were still draping blondes in evening gowns over the hoods like ornaments. Authority figures were almost always male, even in ads for products that only women used. Sadistic, he-man campaigns even won industry praise. (For instance, *Advertising Age* had hailed the infamous Silva Thin cigarette theme, "How to Get a Woman's Attention: Ignore Her," as "brilliant.") Even in medical journals, tranquilizer ads showed depressed housewives standing beside piles of dirty dishes and promised to get them back to work. 13

Obviously, *Ms.* would have to avoid such ads and seek out the best ones—but this didn't seem impossible. *The New Yorker* had been selecting ads for aesthetic reasons for years, a practice that only seemed to make advertisers more eager to be in its pages. *Ebony* and *Essence* were asking for ads with positive black images, and though their struggle was hard, they weren't being called unreasonable. 14

Clearly, what *Ms.* needed was a very special publisher and ad sales staff. I could think of only one woman with experience on the business side of magazines—Patricia Carbine, who recently had become a vice president of *McCall's* as well as its editor in chief—and the reason I knew her name was a good omen. She had been managing editor at *Look* (really *the* editor, but its owner refused to put a female name at the top of his masthead) when I was writing a column there. After I did an early interview with Cesar Chavez, then just emerging as a leader of migrant labor, and the publisher turned it down because he was worried about ads from Sunkist, Pat was the one who intervened. As I learned later, she had told the publisher she would resign if the interview wasn't published. Mainly because *Look* couldn't afford to lose Pat, it *was* published (and the ads from Sunkist never arrived). 15

Though I barely knew this woman, she had done two things I always remembered; put her job on the line in a way that editors often talk about but rarely do, and been so loyal to her colleagues that she never told me or anyone outside *Look* that she had done so. 16

Fortunately, Pat did agree to leave *McCall's* and take a huge cut in salary to become publisher of *Ms.* She became responsible for training and inspiring generations of young women who joined the *Ms.* ad sales force, many of whom went on to become "firsts" at the top of publish- 17 ing. When *Ms.* first started, however, there were so few women with experience selling space that Pat and I made the rounds of ad agencies ourselves. Later, the fact that *Ms.* was asking companies to do business in a different way meant our saleswomen had to make many times the usual number of calls—first to convince agencies and then client companies besides—and to present endless amounts of research. I was often asked to do a final ad presentation, or see some higher decision-maker, or speak to women employees so executives could see the interest of women they worked with. That's why I spent more time persuading advertisers than editing or writing for *Ms.* and why I ended up with an unsentimental education in the seamy underside of publishing that few writers see (and even fewer magazines can publish).

Let me take you with us through some experiences, just as they 18
happened:

• Cheered on by early support from Volkswagen and one or two other car companies, we scrape together time and money to put on a major reception in Detroit. We know U.S. car-makers firmly believe that women choose the upholstery, not the car, but we are armed with statistics and reader mail to prove the contrary: A car is an important purchase for women, one that symbolizes mobility and freedom.

But almost nobody comes. We are left with many pounds of 19
shrimp on the table, and quite a lot of egg on our face. We blame ourselves for not guessing that there would be a baseball pennant play-off on the same day, but executives go out of their way to explain they wouldn't have come anyway. Thus begins ten years of knocking on hostile doors, presenting endless documentation, and hiring a full-time saleswoman in Detroit; all necessary before *Ms.* gets any real results.

This long saga has a semihappy ending: foreign and, later, do- 20
mestic car-makers eventually provided *Ms.* with enough advertising to make cars one of our top sources of ad revenue. Slowly, Detroit began to take the women's market seriously enough to put car ads in other women's magazines, too, thus freeing a few pages from the hothouse of fashion-beauty-food ads.

But long after figures showed a third, even a half, of many car 21
models being bought by women, U.S. makers continued to be uncomfortable addressing women. Unlike foreign car-makers, Detroit never quite learned the secret of creating intelligent ads that exclude no one, and then placing them in women's magazines to overcome past exclusion. (*Ms.* readers were so grateful for a routine Honda ad featuring rack and pinion steering, for instance, that they sent fan mail.) Even now, Detroit continues to ask, "Should we make special ads for women?" Perhaps that's why some foreign cars still have a disproportionate share of the U.S. women's market.

• In the *Ms.* Gazette, we do a brief report on a congressional hearing into chemicals used in hair dyes that are absorbed through the skin and may be carcinogenic. Newspapers report this too, but Clairol, a Bristol-Myers subsidiary that makes dozens of products—a few of which have just begun to advertise in *Ms.*—is outraged. Not at newspapers or news magazines, just at us. It's bad enough that *Ms.* is the only women's magazine refusing to provide the usual "complementary" articles and beauty photos, but to criticize one of their categories—*that* is going too far. 22

We offer to publish a letter from Clairol telling its side of the story. In an excess of solicitousness, we even put this letter in the Gazette, not in Letters to the Editors where it belongs. Nonetheless—and in spite of surveys that show *Ms.* readers are active women who use more of almost everything Clairol makes than do the readers of any other women's magazine—*Ms.* gets almost none of these ads for the rest of its natural life. 23

Meanwhile, Clairol changes its hair-coloring formula, apparently in response to the hearings we reported. 24

• Our saleswomen set out early to attract ads for consumer elections: sound equipment, calculators, computers, VCRs, and the like. We know that our readers are determined to be included in the technological revolution. We know from reader surveys that *Ms.* readers are buying this stuff in numbers as high as those of magazines like *Playboy,* or "men 18 to 34," the prime targets of the consumer electronics industry. Moreover, unlike traditional women's products that our readers buy but don't need to read articles about, these are subjects they want covered in our pages. There actually *is* a supportive editorial atmosphere. 25

"But women don't understand technology," say executives at the end of ad presentations. "Maybe now," we respond, "but neither do men, and we all buy it." 26

"If women *do* buy it," say the decision-makers, "they're asking their husbands and boyfriends what to buy first." We produce letters from *Ms.* readers saying how turned off they are when salesmen say things like "Let me know when your husband can come in." 27

After several years of this, we get a few ads for compact sound systems. Some of them come from JVC, whose vice president, Harry Elias, is trying to convince his Japanese bosses that there is something called a women's market. At his invitation, I find myself speaking at huge trade shows in Chicago and Las Vegas, trying to persuade JVC dealers that showrooms don't have to be locker rooms where women are made to feel unwelcome. But as it turns out, the shows themselves are part of the problem. In Las Vegas, the only women around the technology displays are seminude models serving champagne. In 28

Chicago, the big attraction is Marilyn Chambers, who followed Linda Lovelace of *Deep Throat* fame as Chuck Traynor's captive and/or employee. VCRs are being demonstrated with her porn videos.

In the end, we get ads for a car stereo now and then, but no VCRs; some IBM personal computers, but no Apple or Japanese ones. We notice that office magazines like *Working Woman* and *Savvy* don't benefit as much as they should from office equipment ads either. In the electronics world, women and technology seem mutually exclusive. It remains a decade behind even Detroit. 29

• Because we get letters from little girls who love toy trains, and who ask our help in changing ads and box-top photos that feature little boys only, we try to get toy-train ads from Lionel. It turns out that Lionel executives have been concerned about little girls. They made a pink train, and were surprised when it didn't sell. 30

Lionel bows to consumer pressure with a photograph of a boy *and* a girl—but only on some of their boxes. They fear that, if trains are associated with girls, they will be devalued in the minds of boys. Needless to say, *Ms.* gets no train ads, and little girls remain a mostly unexplored market. By 1986, Lionel is put up for sale. 31

But for different reasons, we haven't had much luck with other kinds of toys either. In spite of many articles on child-rearing; an annual listing of nonsexist, multiracial toys by Letty Cottin Pogrebin; Stories for Free Children, a regular feature also edited by Letty; and other prizewinning features for or about children, we get virtually no toy ads. Generations of *Ms.* saleswomen explain to toy manufacturers that a larger proportion of *Ms.* readers have preschool children than do the readers of other women's magazines, but this industry can't believe feminists have or care about children. 32

• When *Ms.* begins, the staff decides not to accept ads for feminine hygiene sprays or cigarettes: they are damaging and carry no appropriate health warnings. Though we don't think we should tell our readers what to do, we do think we should provide facts so they can decide for themselves. Since the antismoking lobby has been pressing for health warnings on cigarette ads, we decide to take them only as they comply. 33

Philip Morris is among the first to do so. One of its brands, Virginia Slims, is also sponsoring women's tennis and the first national polls of women's opinions. On the other hand, the Virginia Slims theme, "You've come a long way, baby," has more than a "baby" problem. It makes smoking a symbol of progress for women. 34

We explain to Philip Morris that this slogan won't do well in our pages, but they are convinced its success with some women means it will work with *all* women. Finally, we agree to publish an ad for a Virginia Slims calendar as a test. The letters from readers are critical—and 35 smart. For instance: Would you show a black man picking cotton, the same man in a Cardin suit, and symbolize the antislavery and civil rights movements by smoking? Of course not. But instead of honoring the test results, the Philip Morris people seem angry to be proven wrong. They take away ads for *all* their many brands.

This costs *Ms.* about $250,000 the first year. After five years, we can no longer keep track. Occasionally, a new set of executives listens to *Ms.* saleswomen, but because we won't take Virginia Slims, not one Philip Morris product returns to our pages for the next 16 years. 36

Gradually, we also realize our naiveté in thinking we *could* decide against taking cigarette ads. They became a disproportionate support of magazines the moment they were banned on television, and few magazines could compete and survive without them; certainly not *Ms.*, which lacks so many other categories. By the time statistics in the 1980s showed that women's rate of lung cancer was approaching men's, the necessity of taking cigarette ads has become a kind of prison. 37

• General Mills, Pillsbury, Carnation, DelMonte, Dole, Kraft, Stouffer, Hormel, Nabisco: You name the food giant, we try it. But no matter how desirable the *Ms.* readership, our lack of recipes is lethal. 38

We explain to them that placing food ads *only* next to recipes associates food with work. For many women, it is a negative that works *against* the ads. Why not place food ads in diverse media without recipes (thus reaching more men, who are now a third of the shoppers in supermarkets anyway), and leave the recipes to specialty magazines like *Gourmet* (a third of whose readers are also men)? 39

These arguments elicit interest, but except for an occasional ad for a convenience food, instant coffee, diet drinks, yogurt, or such extras as avocados and almonds, this mainstay of the publishing industry stays closed to us. Period. 40

• Traditionally, wines and liquors didn't advertise to women: Men were thought to make the brand decisions, even if women did the buying. But after endless presentations, we begin to make a dent in this category. Thanks to the unconventional Michel Roux of Carillon Importers (distributors of Grand Marnier, Absolut Vodka, and others), who assumes that food and drink have no gender, some ads are leaving their men's club. 41

Beermakers are still selling masculinity. It takes *Ms.* fully eight years to get its first beer ad (Michelob). In general, however, liquor ads are less stereotyped in their imagery—and far less controlling of the editorial around them—than are women's products. But given the underrepresentation of other categories, these very facts tend to create a disproportionate number of alcohol ads in the pages of *Ms.* This in turn dismays readers worried about women and alcoholism. 42

• We hear in 1980 that women in the Soviet Union have been producing feminist *samizdat* (underground, self-published books) and circulating them throughout the country. As punishment, four of the leaders have been exiled. Though we are operating on our usual shoestring, we solicit individual contributions to send Robin Morgan to interview these women in Vienna. 43

The result is an exclusive cover story that includes the first news of a populist peace movement against the Afghanistan occupation, a prediction of *glasnost* to come, and a grassroots, intimate view of Soviet women's lives. From the popular press to women's studies courses, the response is great. The story wins a Front Page award. 44

Nonetheless, this journalistic coup undoes years of efforts to get an ad schedule from Revlon. Why? Because the Soviet women on our *cover are not wearing make-up.* 45

• Four years of research and presentations go into convincing airlines that women now make travel choices and business trips. United, the first airline to advertise in *Ms.*, is so impressed with the response from our readers that one of its executives appears in a film for our ad presentations. As usual, good ads get great results. 46

But we have problems unrelated to such results. For instance: Because American Airlines flight attendants include among their labor demands the stipulation that they could choose to have their last names preceded by "Ms." on their name tags—in a long-delayed revolt against the standard. "I am your pilot, Captain Rothgart, and this is your flight attendant, Cindy Sue"—American officials seem to hold the magazine responsible. We get no ads. 47

There is still a different problem at Eastern. A vice president cancels subscriptions for thousands of copies on Eastern flights. Why? Because he is offended by ads for lesbian poetry journals in the *Ms.* Classified. A "family airline," as he explains to me coldly on the phone, has to "draw the line somewhere." 48

It's obvious that *Ms.* can't exclude lesbians and serve women. We've been trying to make that point ever since our first issue included an article by and about lesbians, and both Suzanne Levine, our managing editor, and I were lectured by such heavy hitters as Ed Kosner, then editor of *Newsweek* (and now of *New York Magazine*), who insisted that *Ms.* should "position" itself *against* lesbians. But our advertisers have paid to reach a guaranteed number of readers, and soliciting new subscriptions to compensate for Eastern would cost $150,000, plus rebating money in the meantime. 49

Like almost everything ad-related, this presents an elaborate organizing problem. After days of searching for sympathetic members of the Eastern board, Frank Thomas, president of the Ford Foundation, kindly offers to call Roswell Gilpatrick, a director of Eastern. I talk 50 with Mr. Gilpatrick, who calls Frank Borman, then the president of Eastern. Frank Borman calls me to say that his airline is not in the business of censoring magazines: *Ms.* will be returned to Eastern flights.

• Women's access to insurance and credit is vital, but with the exception of Equitable and a few other ad pioneers, such financial services address men. For almost a decade after the Equal Credit Opportunity Act passes in 1974, we try to convince American Express that women are a growth market—but nothing works. 51

Finally, a former professor of Russian named Jerry Welsh becomes head of marketing. He assumes that women should be cardholders, and persuades his colleagues to feature women in a campaign. Thanks to this 1980s series, the growth rate for female cardholders surpass that for men. 52

For this article, I asked Jerry Welsh if he would explain why American Express waited so long. "Sure," he said, "they were afraid of having a 'pink' card." 53

• Women of color read *Ms.* in disproportionate numbers. This is a source of pride to *Ms.* staffers, who are also more racially representative than the editors of other women's magazines. But this reality is obscured by ads filled with enough white women to make a reader snowblind. 54

Pat Carbine remembers mostly "astonishment" when she requested African American, Hispanic, Asian, and other diverse images. Marcia Ann Gillespie, a *Ms.* editor who was previously the editor in chief of *Essence,* witnesses ad bias a second time: Having tried for *Essence* to get white advertisers to use black images (Revlon did so eventually, but L'Oreal, Lauder, Chanel, and other companies never did), she sees similar problems getting integrated ads for an integrated magazine. Indeed, the ad world often creates black and Hispanic ads only for black and Hispanic media. In an exact parallel of the fear that marketing a product to women will endanger its appeal to men, the response is usually, "But your [white] readers won't identify." 55

In fact, those we are able to get—for instance, a Max Factor ad made for *Essence* that Linda Wachner gives us after she becomes president—are praised by white readers, too. But there are pathetically few such images. 56

• By the end of 1986, production and mailing costs have risen astronomically, ad income is flat, and competition for ads is stiffer than ever. The 60/40 preponderance of edit over ads that we promised to readers becomes 50/50; children's stories, most poetry, and some fiction are casualties of less space; in order to get variety into limited pages, the length (and sometimes the depth) of articles suffers; and, though we do refuse most of the ads that would look like a parody in our pages, we get so worn down that some slip through. 57

Still, readers perform miracles. Though we haven't been able to afford a subscription mailing in two years, they maintain our guaranteed circulation of 450,000.

Nonetheless, media reports on *Ms.* often insist that our unprofitability must be due to reader disinterest. The myth that advertisers simply follow readers is very strong. Not one reporter notes that other comparable magazines our size (say, *Vanity Fair* or *The Atlantic*) have been losing more money in one year than *Ms.* has lost in 16 years. No matter how much never-to-be-recovered cash is poured into starting a magazine or keeping one going, appearances seem to be all that matter. (Which is why we haven't been able to explain our fragile state in public. Nothing causes ad flight like the smell of nonsuccess.) 58

My healthy response is anger. My not-so-healthy response is constant worry. Also an obsession with finding one more rescue. There is hardly a night when I don't wake up with sweaty palms and pounding heart, scared that we won't be able to pay the printer or the post office; scared most of all that closing our doors will hurt the women's movement. 59

Out of chutzpah and desperation, I arrange a lunch with Leonard Lauder, president of Estée Lauder. With the exception of Clinique (the brainchild of Carol Philllips), none of Lauder's hundreds of products has been advertised in *Ms.* A year's schedule of ads for just three or four of them could save us. Indeed, as the scion of a family-owned company whose ad practices are followed by the beauty industry, he is one of the few men who could liberate many pages in all women's magazines just by changing his mind about "complementary copy." 60

Over a lunch that costs more than we can pay for some articles, I explain the need for his leadership. I also lay out the record of *Ms.*: more literary and journalistic prizes won, more new issues introduced into the mainstream, new writers discovered, and impact on society than any other magazine; more articles that became books, stories that became movies, ideas that became television series, and newly advertised products that became profitable; and, most important for him, a place for his ads to reach women who aren't reachable through any other women's magazine. Indeed, if there is one constant characteristic of the everchanging *Ms.* readership, it is their impact as leaders. Whether it's waiting until later to have first babies, or pioneering PABA as sun protection in cosmetics, *whatever* they are doing today, a third to a half of American women will be doing three to five years from now. It's never failed. 61

But, he says, *Ms.* readers are not *our* women. They're not interested in things like fragrance and blush-on. If they were, *Ms.* would write articles about them. 62

On the contrary, I explain, surveys show they are more likely to 63
buy such things than the readers of, say, *Cosmopolitan* or *Vogue.* They're good customers because they're out in the world enough to need several sets of everything: home, work, purse, travel, gym, and so on. They just don't need to read articles about these things. Would he ask a men's magazine to publish monthly columns on how to shave before he advertised Aramis products (his line for men)?

He concedes that beauty features are often concocted more for 64
advertisers than readers. But *Ms.* isn't appropriate for his ads anyway, he explains. Why? Because Estée Lauder is selling "a kept-woman mentality."

I can't quite believe this. Sixty percent of the users of his prod- 65
ucts are salaried, and generally resemble *Ms.* readers. Besides, his company has the appeal of having been started by a creative and hard-working woman, his mother, Estée Lauder.

That doesn't matter, he says. He knows his customers, and they 66
would *like* to be kept women. That's why he will never advertise in *Ms.*

In November 1987, by vote of the Ms. Foundation for Education and 67
Communication (*Ms.*'s owner and publisher, the media subsidiary of the Ms. Foundation for Women), *Ms.* was sold to a company whose officers, Australian feminists Sandra Yates and Anne Summers, raised the investment money in their country that *Ms.* couldn't find in its own. They also started *Sassy* for teenage women.

In their two-year tenure, circulation was raised to 550,000 by in- 68
vestment in circulation mailings, and, to the dismay of some readers, editorial features on clothes and new products made a more traditional bid for ads. Nonetheless, ad pages fell below previous levels. In addition, *Sassy,* whose fresh voice and sexual frankness were an unprecedented success with young readers, was targeted by two mothers from Indiana who began, as one of them put it, "calling every Christian organization I could think of." In response to this controversy, several crucial advertisers pulled out.

Such links between ads and editorial content was a problem in 69
Australia, too, but to a lesser degree. "Our readers pay two times more for their magazines," Anne explained, "so advertisers have less power to threaten a magazine's viability."

"I was shocked," said Sandra Yates with characteristic directness. 70
"In Australia, we think you have freedom of the press—but you don't."

Since Anne and Sandra had not met their budget's projections for 71
ad revenue, their investors forced a sale. In October 1989, *Ms.* and *Sassy* were bought by Dale Lang, owner of *Working Mother, Working Woman,* and one of the few independent publishing companies left

among the conglomerates. In response to a request from the original *Ms.* staff—as well as to reader letters urging that *Ms.* continue, plus his own belief that *Ms.* would benefit his other magazines by blazing a trail—he agreed to try the ad-free, reader-supported *Ms.*... and to give us complete editorial control.

In response to the workplace revolution of the 1970s, traditional women's magazines—that is, "trade books" for women working at home—were joined by *Savvy, Working Woman,* and other trade books for women working in offices. But by keeping the fashion/beauty/entertaining articles necessary to get traditional ads and then adding career articles besides, they inadvertently produced the antifeminist stereotype of Super Woman. The male-initiative, dress-for-success woman carrying a briefcase became the media image of a woman worker, even though a blue-collar woman's salary was often higher than her glorified secretarial sister's, and though women at a real briefcase level are statistically rare. Needless to say, these dress-for-success women were also thin, white, and beautiful. 72

In recent years, advertisers' control over the editorial content of women's magazines has become so institutionalized that it is written into "insertion orders" or dictated to ad salespeople as official policy. The following are recent typical orders to women's magazines: 73

- Dow's Cleaning Products stipulates that ads for its Vivid and Spray 'n Wash products should be adjacent to "children or fashion editorial"; ads for Bathroom Cleaner should be next to "home furnishing/family" features; and so on for other brands. "If a magazine fails for the brands or more," the Dow order warns, "it will be omitted from further consideration." 74
- Bristol-Myers, the parent of Clairol, Windex, Drano, Bufferin, and much more, stipulates that ads be placed next to a "full page of compatible editorial." 75
- S.C. Johnson & Son, makers of Johnson Wax, lawn and laundry products, insect sprays, hair sprays, and so on, orders that its ads *"should not be opposite extremely controversial features or material antithetical to the nature/copy of the advertised product."* (Italics theirs.) 76
- Maidenform, manufacturer of bras and other apparel, leaves a blank for the particular product and states: "The creative concept of the _____ campaign, and the very nature of the product itself appeal to the positive emotions of the reader/consumer. Therefore, it is imperative that all editorial adjacencies reflect that same positive tone. The editorial must not be negative in content or lend itself contrary to the _____ product imagery/message (e.g., *editorial relating to illness, disillusionment, large size fashion, etc.*)." (Italics mine.) 77

• The De Beers diamond company, a big seller of engagement rings, prohibits magazines from placing its ads with "adjacencies to hard news or anti-love/romance themed editorial." 78

• Procter & Gamble, one of this country's most powerful and diversified advertisers, stands out in the memory of Anne Summers and Sandra Yates (no mean feat in this context): Its products were not to be placed in *any* issue that included *any* material on gun control, abortion, the occult, cults, or the disparagement of religion. Caution was also demanded in any issue covering sex or drugs, even for educational purposes. 79

Those are the most obvious chains around women's magazines. There are also rules so clear they needn't be written down: for instance, an overall "look" compatible with beauty and fashion ads. Even "real" nonmodel women photographed for a woman's magazine are usually made up, dressed in credited clothes, and retouched out of all reality. When editors do include articles on less-than-cheerful subjects (for instance, domestic violence), they tend to keep them short and unillustrated. The point is to be "upbeat." Just as women in the street are asked, "Why don't you smile, honey?" women's magazines acquire an institutional smile. 80

Within the text itself, praise for advertisers' products has become so ritualized that fields like "beauty writing" have been invented. One of its frequent practitioners explained seriously that "It's a difficult art. How many new adjectives can you find? How much greater can you make a lipstick sound? The FDA restricts what companies can say on labels, but we create illusion. And ad agencies are on the phone all the time pushing you to get their product in. A lot of them keep the business based on how many editorial clippings they produce every month. The worst are products" like Lauder's, as the writer confirmed, "with their own name involved. It's all ego." 81

Often, editorial becomes one giant ad. Last November, for instance, *Lear's* featured an elegant woman executive on the cover. On the contents page, we learned she was wearing Guerlain makeup and Samsara, a new fragrance by Guerlain. Inside were full-page ads for Samsara and Guerlain antiwrinkle cream. In the cover profile, we learned that this executive was responsible for launching Samsara and is Guerlain's director of public relations. When the *Columbia Journalism Review* did one of the few articles to include women's magazines in coverage of the influence of ads, editor Frances Lear was quoted as defending her magazine because "this kind of thing is done all the time." 82

Often, advertisers also plunge odd-shaped ads into the text, no matter what the cost to the readers. At *Woman's Day,* a magazine originally founded by a supermarket chain, editor in chief Ellen Levine 83 said, "The day the copy had to rag around a chicken leg was not a happy one."

84 Advertisers are also adamant about where in a magazine their ads appear. When Revlon was not placed as the first beauty ad in one Hearst magazine, for instance, Revlon pulled its ads from *all* Hearst magazines. Ruth Whitney, editor in chief of *Glamour,* attributes some of these demands to "ad agencies wanting to prove to a client that they've squeezed the last drop of blood out of a magazine." She also is, she says, "sick and tired of hearing that women's magazines are controlled by cigarette ads." Relatively speaking, she's right. To be as censoring as are many advertisers for women's products, tobacco companies would have to demand articles in praise of smoking and expect glamorous photos of beautiful women smoking their brands.

85 I don't mean to imply that the editors I quote here share my objections to ads: Most assume that women's magazines have to be the way they are. But it's also true that only former editors can be completely honest. "Most of the pressure came in the form of direct product mentions," explains Sey Chassler, who was editor in chief of *Redbook* from the sixties to the eighties. "We got threats from the big guys, the Revlons, blackmail threats. They wouldn't run ads unless we credited them.

86 "But it's not fair to single out the beauty advertisers because these pressures came from everybody. Advertisers want to know two things: What are you going to charge me? What else are you going to do for me? It's a holdup. For instance, management felt that fiction took up too much space. They couldn't put any advertising in that. For the last ten years, the number of fiction entries into the National Magazine Awards has declined.

87 "And pressures are getting worse. More magazines are more bottom-line oriented because they have been taken over by companies with no interest in publishing.

88 "I also think advertisers do this to women's magazines especially," he concluded, "because of the general disrespect they have for women."

89 Even media experts who don't give a damn about women's magazines are alarmed by the spread of this ad–edit linkage. In a climate *The Wall Street Journal* describes as an unacknowledged Depression for media, women's products are increasingly able to take their low standards wherever they go. For instance: Newsweeklies publish uncritical stories on fashion and fitness. *The New York Times Magazine* recently ran an article on "firming creams," complete with mentions of advertisers. *Vanity Fair* published a profile of one major advertiser, Ralph Lauren, illustrated by the same photographer who does his ads, and turned the lifestyle of another, Calvin Klein, into a cover story.

Even the outrageous *Spy* has toned down since it began to go after fashion ads.

And just to make us really worry, films and books, the last media that go directly to the public without having to attract ads first, are in danger, too. Producers are beginning to depend on payments for displaying products in movies, and books are now being commissioned by companies like Federal Express. 90

But the truth is that women's products—like women's magazines—have never been the subjects of much serious reporting anyway. News and general interest publications, including the "style" or "living" sections of newspapers, write about food and clothing as cooking and fashion, and almost never evaluate such products by brand name. Though chemical additives, pesticides, and animal fats are major health risks in the United States, and clothes, shoddy or not, absorb more consumer dollars than cars, this lack of information is serious. So is ignoring the contents of beauty products that are absorbed into our bodies through our skins, and that have profit margins so big they would make a loan shark blush. 91

What could women's magazines be like if they were as free as books? as realistic as newspapers? as creative as films? as diverse as women's lives? We don't know. 92

But we'll only find out if we take women's magazines seriously. If readers were to act in a concerted way to change traditional practices of *all* women's magazines and the marketing of *all* women's products, we could do it. After all, they are operating on our consumer dollars: money that we now control. You and I could: 93

• Write to editors and publishers (with copies to advertisers) that we're willing to pay *more* for magazines with editorial independence, but will *not* continue to pay for those that are just editorial extensions of ads; 94

• Write to advertisers (with copies to editors and publishers) that we want fiction, political reporting, consumer reporting—whatever is, or is not, supported by their ads; 95

• Put as much energy into breaking advertising's control over content as into changing the images in ads, or protesting ads for harmful products like cigarettes; 96

• Support only those women's magazines and products that take *us* seriously as readers and consumers. 97

• Those of us in the magazine world can also use the carrot-and-stick technique. For instance: Pointing out that, if magazines were a regulated medium like television, the demands of advertisers would be against FCC rules. Payola and extortion could be punished. As it is, there are probably illegalities. A magazine's postal rates are deter- 98 mined by the ratio of ad to edit pages, and the former costs more than the latter. So much for the stick.

The carrot means appealing to enlightened self-interest. For instance: There are many studies showing that the greatest factor in determining an ad's effectiveness is the credibility of its surroundings. The "higher the rating of editorial believability," concluded a 1987 survey by the *Journal of Advertising Research,* "the higher the rating of the advertising." Thus, an impenetrable wall between edit and ads would also be in the best interest of advertisers. 99

Unfortunately, few agencies or clients hear such arguments. Editors often maintain the false purity of refusing to talk to them at all. Instead, they see ad salespeople who know little about editorial, are trained in business as usual, and are usually paid by commission. Editors might also band together to take on controversy. That happened once when all the major women's magazines did articles in the same month on the Equal Rights Amendment. It could happen again. 100

It's almost three years away from life between the grindstones of advertising pressures and readers' needs. I'm just beginning to realize how edges got smoothed down—in spite of all our resistance. 101

I remember feeling put upon when I changed "Porsche" to "car" in a piece about Nazi imagery in German pornography by Andrea Dworkin—feeling sure Andrea would understand that Volkswagen, the distributor of Porsche and one of our few supportive advertisers, asked only to be far away from Nazi subjects. It's taken me all this time to realize that Andrea was the one with a right to feel put upon. 102

Even as I write this, I get a call from a writer for *Elle,* who is doing a whole article on where women part their hair. Why, she wants to know, do I part mine in the middle? 103

It's all so familiar. A writer trying to make something of a nothing assignment; an editor laboring to think of new ways to attract ads; readers assuming that other women must want this ridiculous stuff; more women suffering for lack of information, insight, creativity, and laughter that could be on these same pages. 104

I ask you: Can't we do better than this? 105

Examining the Text

1. What do you think of the anecdote at the beginning of the essay, in which Steinem remarks to a Soviet official that advertising is a way to limit freedom of the press? Do you think that her essay supports this assertion? Why or why not?

2. According to Steinem, what is the relationship between advertising and editorial content in magazines? Does your own reading of magazines support the assertion that advertising affects content?

3. In what ways do women's magazines have a different relationship to advertising than other magazines? What are some of the significant problems that *Ms.* encountered in dealing with advertisements and advertisers?

4. How would you describe the structure of this essay? What effect do the numerous specific examples Steinem cites in the first and second parts of the essay have on you as a reader?

For Group Discussion

Steinem asks, "What could women's magazines be like if they were as free as books? as realistic as newspapers? as creative as films? as diverse as women's lives?" (paragraph 92). How would you answer these questions? What would be the content of an "ideal" women's magazine? Would it be different from an "ideal" men's magazine? In what ways? Do any magazines read by group members approach these "ideals"?

Writing Suggestion

Look at recent issues of several women's magazines and test Steinem's assertions about the relationship between advertising and editorial content. Take note of any "complementary copy" in the magazine and any other ways editorial decisions might have been influenced by advertising. In an essay, explore your conclusions about the extent to which advertising affects the content and organization of women's magazines.

ADDITIONAL SUGGESTIONS FOR WRITING ABOUT ADVERTISING

1. Choose a magazine, television, or radio advertisement that you find particularly interesting, appealing, or puzzling, and write a narrative essay describing your response to the ad.

Begin by recording your initial impressions of the ad. What do you notice first, and why are you drawn to that element of the ad? What emotions or thoughts strike you as you first look at the ad? Then describe your step-by-step progress through the ad. Where does your eye go next? How do your thoughts or emotions change as you notice more of the ad? Finally, record your impressions after you've taken in all of the ad. How does this final impression differ from your first impression?

You might conclude your narrative by commenting on whether, based on your response, the ad achieves its objective of selling the product. In other words, do you think you responded as the designers of the ad intended?

2. Devise your own ad campaign for a product with which you're familiar, including several different ads, each appealing to a different audience.

After deciding on the product, briefly describe each audience group. Choose the form in which you want your advertisements to appear (magazine ads, TV commercials, audio presentations, billboards, or other forms and venues) and then decide on the persuasive methods that you want to use. Do you want to appeal to emotion or intellect or both? What motives will you try to reach? You might refer to Fowles's list of advertising's basic appeals.

Finally, design the ads and briefly explain the reasoning behind each design.

3. Choose recent issues of a women's magazine and a men's magazine, and compare and contrast the ads in each.

How many advertisements are there? What products are being advertised? What techniques are used in the ads and how do these techniques differ significantly between men's and women's magazines? What are the differences in the appeals the ads make? What are the differences in the images of men and women?

From your findings, draw conclusions about how advertisers envision and represent differences in gender. What (if any) stereotypes of men and women do the ads present?

4. Imagine that you are a member of a citizens' group working to improve the quality of advertising. What specific recommendations would you make and what standards would you want to see enforced? Illustrate your ideas with ads you can find that either meet or fall below these standards.

Internet Activities

1. On the Web you'll find sites representing the products and services of almost all major U.S. corporations and of many smaller businesses as well. These corporate Web sites can be seen as extensive advertisements. Though they differ in style and strategy from television and magazine advertisements, they share the goal of informing consumers about a product or service and persuading consumers in their purchasing decisions.

At the *Common Culture* Web site, you'll find links to the sites of companies selling a variety of products. Choose one of those product categories and investigate the links. As you've browse through the companies' Web sites, make a list of the kind of information that's offered there, the organization of the site, the graphics and other interactive elements that are used, the style and tone of the writing, and the mood created at the site. Then write an essay in which you describe the similarities and differences of two or more sites. What strategies do these sites use to promote the company's products and services? Which strategies do you find effective, and why? You might conclude your essay by commenting on the distinctive features of Web sites as advertisements. How are they different from magazine and television ads?

2. You've probably noticed that many Web sites contain advertisements—called "Web banners"—for other sites or for products and services offered by specific companies. These banners usually appear in the top portion of the Web page and invite viewers to click on an icon to get more information. Also on the Web are sponsor links and extra windows that open up to advertise products when one visits a Web site. At the *Common Culture* Web site, you'll find links to examples and additional information about Web advertising. Visit these links and take some time to browse the Web and familiarize yourself with the advertising strategies there. Then, write an essay in which you first describe the characteristics of advertising on the Web, and then compare and contrast Web advertising to television commercials and to print ads. What common features are shared by ads in these different media? How do the differences in media shape the content and style of advertisements?

Reading Images

The image entitled "Absolute End" on page CI-2 is taken from Adbusters (*http://www.adbusters.org*); it's one of their "Spoof Ads" that draws on familiar themes and motifs in advertising in order to undermine the messages that the ads themselves convey. Adbusters has spoofed such popular ad campaigns as Obsession perfume and the "Joe Camel" cigarette ads. The idea is to turn ads against themselves, to use the very style of the manufacturers' advertisements in exposing the harm that these ads and products can cause.

"Absolute End" is one of several spoofs of the Absolut vodka ads in which the shape of the vodka bottle is superimposed over some geographic location (for instance, New York's Central Park). Here, the familiar bottle shape (made familiar in part by the Absolut vodka ads themselves) is used as a chalk drawing on a pavement, calling to mind the chalk drawings that trace the shape of a murder victim's body.

Clearly, "Absolute End" is not an advertisement for Absolut vodka. However, it's not an ad directly against Absolut vodka, either. It seems, rather, to be an ad against alcohol advertising in general. The text in the image makes the message explicit:

> Nearly 50% of automobile fatalities are linked to alcohol. 10% of North Americans are alcoholics. A teenager sees 100,000 alcohol ads before reaching the legal drinking age.

In an essay, analyze the techniques used in this image to convey its message. For instance, consider how the perspective of the photograph influences your reaction to it: why is the viewer positioned above the scene that the photograph depicts? Consider also what's left out of the photograph: why is there no victim's body in this scene? Who is included in the scene, and why? Consider also the color scheme and other visual components of the image. Finally, be sure to discuss the text that's included: the "title" of the image and the three sentences that state its message.

Conclude your analysis by discussing whether or not you think a "spoof ad" like this one is an effective way to convey a message. What are the advantages and disadvantages of using a visual statement like this rather than a purely textual one (for instance, a newspaper article about alcohol, drunk driving, and advertising)?

3

Television

THE BOYS ALWAYS FOUND SUNSET ON THE PRAIRIE A PARTICULARLY MOVING EXPERIENCE

We may laugh at these "boys" who stand in the middle of the barren Southwest desert watching a sunset on TV as the real sun sets behind them. Yet the joke is also on us because—like the cowboys—we might often find ourselves more engaged, more entertained, and even more emotionally touched by what we watch on television than by our own experiences in real life.

Some critics even suggest that people regard what they see on television as more real than what goes on around them and thus virtually narrow their world to what comes to them on "the tube." Paradoxically, television's greatest benefit is its potential to broaden our experience, to bring us to places we could never visit, to people we could never meet, and to a range of ideas otherwise unavailable to many people.

This complex relationship between television and people as individuals and as a society leads thoughtful people to examine closely the way television diverts our attention from what could be our own rich, nonmediated experiences; the way it entertains and informs us through otherwise inaccessible experiences; the way it shapes our perceptions of the world around us.

The readings in the first part of this chapter address some of the important questions raised in regard to this ubiquitous medium. Why do Americans spend so much time watching television? What essential needs and desires does television satisfy? How accurately does television represent reality? How strongly do its distortions of reality affect our ideas and behavior? To what extent does television intervene in our everyday lives, influencing families and communities, domestic space, and leisure time? Will new technological developments change how we watch television in the future?

The readings in the second part of the chapter expand on these questions by focusing on particular television shows. The first two articles analyze the genre of reality television shows, including reality dating shows, to determine who watches these shows, why they've become popular, and what they have to say about contemporary American culture. Rebecca Gardyn draws on evidence produced from demographic studies and polls of television viewers, along with information gathered from interviews of reality TV fans, in order to answer these questions. Robert Samuels reports on informal surveys of his students and analyzes the reasons they give for their attraction to (or addiction to?) reality dating shows. As both authors show, analyzing specific genres of television shows can yield interesting insights, particularly when that genre is as wildly popular as reality television has been of late.

The last two essays in the chapter have an even narrower focus: *The Simpsons.* Matt Groening's well-known cartoon has been a fixture of television programming since 1989, and Homer, Marge, Bart, and Lisa have become recognizable pop culture icons. But why has *The Simpsons* been so popular for so long? In what ways does this show appeal to us, and what do we learn from watching it? These questions are answered quite differently in the articles by Paul Cantor and Lisa Frank. In fact, it's interesting to read these articles side-by-side to see that a single television show can generate such diverse interpretations.

As you read these essays, remember the television-entranced cowboys at the opening of the chapter. As you hone your own critical abilities, you will go beyond being a passive observer to become an active, critically engaged viewer.

The Cultural Influences of Television

Spudding Out

Barbara Ehrenreich

Do you head straight for the TV when you arrive home after work or school, flicking on the set before you talk to your roommate or feed the cat? If so, you may be exhibiting symptoms of "couch potato" syndrome—a condition cultural critic Barbara Ehrenreich laments in the following essay. Referring to a more active and gregarious America in days past, Ehrenreich observes an onset of a "mass agoraphobia," which she argues has been directly caused by television. This TV-induced phobia—an irrational fear of being away from the tube—has led to a significant loss in human contact and activity, according to Ehrenreich: no longer do people look outside the little box for relaxation or entertainment; instead, Americans have retreated to their living rooms, kitchens, bedrooms, or wherever they lounge comfortably in front of a TV, isolating themselves there before the tube.

Cocooned in chairs, couches, beds, and blankets, and armed with that indispensable accessory of modern life—the remote control—today's Americans are tuned in to the artificial images of TV-land and tuned out from the rest of the world. Moreover, Ehrenreich points to a paradox in our relationship to television: "We love TV because TV brings us a world in which TV does not exist."

***As you read** this essay, observe Ehrenreich's tone, which succeeds in being both funny and biting. Notice also how she uses irony and exaggeration to make her critique simultaneously understated and incisive.*

Someone has to speak for them, because they have, to a person, lost the power to speak for themselves. I am referring to that great mass of Americans who were once known as the "salt of the earth," then as "the silent majority," more recently as "the viewing public," and now, alas, as "couch potatoes." What drives them—or rather, leaves them sapped and spineless on their reclining chairs? What are they seeking—beyond such obvious goals as a tastefully colorized version of *The Maltese Falcon*? 1

My husband was the first in the family to "spud out," as the expression now goes. Soon everyone wanted one of those zip-up "Couch Potato Bags," to keep warm in during David Letterman. The youngest and most thoroughly immobilized member of the family relies on a re- 2 mote that controls his TV, stereo, and VCR, and can also shut down the neighbor's pacemaker at fifteen yards.

But we never see the neighbors anymore, nor they us. This saddens me, because Americans used to be a great and restless people, fond of the outdoors in all of its manifestations, from Disney World to miniature golf. Some experts say there are virtues in mass agoraphobia, that it strengthens the family and reduces highway deaths. But I would point out that there are still a few things that cannot be done in the den, especially by someone zipped into a body bag. These include racquetball, voting, and meeting strange people in bars. 3

Most psychologists interpret the couch potato trend as a negative reaction to the outside world. Indeed, the list of reasons to stay safely tucked indoors lengthens yearly. First there was crime, then AIDS, then side-stream smoke. To this list should be added "fear of the infrastructure," for we all know someone who rashly stepped outside only to be buried in a pothole, hurled from a collapsing bridge, or struck by a falling airplane. 4

But it is not just the outside world that has let us down. Let's face it, despite a decade-long campaign by the "profamily" movement, the family has been a disappointment. The reason lies in an odd circular dynamic: we watch television to escape from our families because television shows us how dull our families really are. 5

Compare your own family to, for example, the Huxtables, the Keatons, or the peppy young people on *Thirtysomething*. In those families, even the three-year-olds are stand-up comics, and the most insipid remark is hailed with heartening outbursts of canned laughter. When television families aren't gathered around the kitchen table exchanging wisecracks, they are experiencing brief but moving dilemmas, which are handily solved by the youngest child or by some cute extraterrestrial house-guest. Emerging from *Family Ties* or *My Two Dads,* we are forced to acknowledge that our own families are made up of slow-witted, emotionally crippled people who would be lucky to qualify for seats in the studio audience of *Jeopardy!* 6

But gradually I have come to see that there is something besides fear of the outside and disgust with our families that drives us to spudhood—some positive attraction, some deep cathexis to television itself. For a long time it eluded me. When I watched television, mainly as a way of getting to know my husband and children, I found that my mind wandered to more interesting things, like whether to get up and make ice cubes. 7

Only after many months of viewing did I begin to understand the force that has transformed the American people into root vegetables. If you watch TV for a very long time, day in, day out, you will begin to notice something eerie and unnatural about the world portrayed 8 therein. I don't mean that it is two-dimensional or lacks a well-developed critique of the capitalist consumer culture or something superficial like that. I mean something so deeply obvious that it's almost scary. When you watch television, you will see people doing many things—chasing fast cars, drinking lite beer, shooting each other at close range, etc. But you will never see people *watching television.* Well, maybe for a second before the phone rings or a brand-new, multiracial adopted child walks into the house. But never *really watching,* hour after hour, the way *real* people do.

Way back in the beginning of the television era, this was not so strange, because real people actually did many of the things people do on TV, even if it was only bickering with their mothers-in-law about which toilet paper to buy. But modern people, i.e., couch potatoes, do nothing that is ever shown on television (because it is either dangerous or would involve getting up from the couch). And what they do do—watch television—is far too boring to be televised for more than a fraction of a second, not even by Andy Warhol, bless his boredom-proof little heart. 9

So why do we keep on watching? The answer, by now, should be perfectly obvious: we love television because television brings us a world in which television does not exist. In fact, deep in their hearts, this is what the spuds crave most: a rich, new, participatory life, in which family members look each other in the eye, in which people walk outside and banter with the neighbors, where there is adventure, possibility, danger, feeling, all in natural color, stereophonic sound, and three dimensions, without commercial interruptions, and starring ... us. 10

"You mean some new kind of computerized interactive medium?" the children asked hopefully, pert as the progeny on a Tuesday night sitcom. But before I could expand on this concept—known to our ancestors as "real life"—they were back at the box, which may be, after all, the only place left to find it. 11

Examining the Text

1. Ehrenreich's tone in this essay is basically satirical. Point out several examples of this approach and consider why she adopts this tone. Does she only intend to be amusing or would you say she is making a serious point? If so, what is it?

2. What differences does Ehrenreich note between what we see on television and "real life"? Could these differences be viewed as criticism of television and/or of how we live our lives? Should television reflect the way most people live?

3. "Couch potato" was widely quoted in the media during the middle and late 1980s when Ehrenreich wrote this essay, but the term is not as common today. Has the "couch potato" phenomenon been a significant aspect of U.S. culture over the last decade or so? How does the way you answer these questions color your responses to Ehrenreich's essay?

For Group Discussion

Working in a group, choose several currently popular programs that focus on family life and list the characteristics of the families they portray—the relationships among family members, the ways they behave, the problems they face and how they solve them. (For balance, choose at least one situation comedy and one hour-long dramatic series.) How well do these characteristics correspond to those that Ehrenreich notes? As a class, consider how accurately these television families reflect the "average" American family and, in fact, whether there is any such thing as an "average" American family.

Writing Suggestion

Based on your own experiences and your observations of your own family and friends, how would you characterize the television viewing habits of most people? In an essay, analyze the different reasons people have for watching television. In doing so, you may wish to expand upon or counter Ehrenreich's observations.

Television Addiction Is No Mere Metaphor

Robert Kubey and Mihaly Csikszentmihalyi

We all know that certain substances are addictive; indeed, we know that cigarettes, alcohol, and drugs are dangerous in large part because we can become addicted to them and end up using them to our own physical and psychological detriment. Certain activities, such as gambling, are also recognized as addictive. But can the activity of watching television be considered addictive? Are heavy television viewers "addicts" in the same way that alcoholics and long-term smokers are?

These questions are addressed by Robert Kubey and Mihaly Csikszentmihalyi in the following article, which was originally published in Scientific American. *Kubey and Csikszentmihalyi are both college professors: Kubey is the director of the Center for Media Studies at Rutgers University, and Csikszentmihalyi is the C. S. and D. J. Davidson Professor of Psychology at Claremont Graduate University. In this article, they combine their expertise in media studies and psychology in order to examine the phenomenon of "TV addiction."*

While Barbara Ehrenreich in the previous essay adopts a fairly humorous tone in looking at people "spudding out" in front of the television, Kubey and Csikszentmihalyi bring sociological and biological evidence to bear on their explanation of the addictive power television has over us. ***Before you read,*** *think about what the term "addiction" means to you. Do you know anyone who you think is "addicted" to television? What do you think are the causes and consequences of this addiction?*

Perhaps the most ironic aspect of the struggle for survival is how easily organism can be harmed by that which they desire. The trout is caught by the fisherman's lure, the mouse by cheese. But at least those creatures have the excuse that bait and cheese look like sustenance. Humans seldom have that consolation. The temptations that can disrupt their lives are often pure indulgences. No one has to drink alcohol, for example. Realizing when a diversion has gotten out of control is one of the great challenges of life. 1

Excessive cravings do not necessarily involve physical substances. Gambling can become compulsive; sex can become obsessive. One activity, however, stands out for its prominence and ubiquity—the world's most popular leisure pastime, television. Most people admit to having a love-hate relationship with it. They complain about the "boob tube" and "couch potatoes," then they settle into their sofas and grab the remote control. Parents commonly fret about their children's viewing (if not their own). Even researchers who study TV for a living marvel at the medium's hold on them personally. Percy Tannenbaum of the University of California at Berkeley has written: "Among life's more embarrassing moments have been countless occasions when I am engaged in conversation in a room while a TV set is on, and I cannot for the life of me stop from periodically glancing over to the screen. This occurs not only during dull conversations but during reasonably interesting ones just as well." 2

Scientists have been studying the effects of television for decades, generally focusing on whether watching violence on TV correlates with being violent in real life (see "The Effects of Observing Violence," by Leonard Berkowitz; *Scientific American,* February 1964; and "Communication and Social Environment," by George Gerber; September 1972). Less attention has been paid to the basic allure of the small screen—the medium, as opposed to the message. 3

The term "TV addiction" is imprecise and laden with value judgments, but it captures the essence of a very real phenomenon. Psychol- 4 ogists and psychiatrists formally define substance dependence as a disorder characterized by criteria that include spending a great deal of time using the substance; using it more often than one intends; thinking about reducing use or making repeated unsuccessful efforts to reduce use; giving up important social, family or occupational activities to use it; and reporting withdrawal symptoms when one stops using it.

5 All these criteria can apply to people who watch a lot of television. That does not mean that watching television, per se, is problematic. Television can teach and amuse; it can reach aesthetic heights; it can provide much needed distraction and escape. The difficulty arises when people strongly sense that they ought not to watch as much as they do and yet find themselves strangely unable to reduce their viewing. Some knowledge of how the medium exerts its pull may help heavy viewers gain better control over their lives.

A BODY AT REST TENDS TO STAY AT REST

6 The amount of time people spend watching television is astonishing. On average, individuals in the industrialized world devote three hours a day to the pursuit—fully half of their leisure time, and more than on any single activity save work and sleep. At this rate, someone who lives to 75 would spend nine years in front of the tube. To some commentators, this devotion means simply that people enjoy TV and make a conscious decision to watch it. But if that is the whole story, why do so many people experience misgivings about how much they view? In Gallup polls in 1992 and 1999, two out of five adult respondents and seven out of 10 teenagers said they spent too much time watching TV. Other surveys have consistently shown that roughly 10 percent of adults call themselves TV addicts.

7 To study people's reactions to TV, researchers have undertaken laboratory experiments in which they have monitored the brain waves (using an electroencephalograph, or EEG), skin resistance or heart rate of people watching television. To track behavior and emotion in the normal course of life, as opposed to the artificial conditions of the lab, we have used the Experience Sampling Method (ESM). Participants carried a beeper, and we signaled them six to eight times a day, at random, over the period of a week; whenever they heard the beep, they wrote down what they were doing and how they were feeling using a standardized scorecard.

8 As one might expect, people who were watching TV when we beeped them reported feeling relaxed and passive. The EEG studies similarly show less mental stimulation, as measured by alpha brainwave production, during viewing than during reading.

What is more surprising is that the sense of relaxation ends when the set is turned off, but the feelings of passivity and lowered alertness continue. Survey participants commonly reflect that television has somehow absorbed or sucked out their energy, leaving them depleted. They say they have more difficulty concentrating after viewing than before. In contrast, they rarely indicate such difficulty after reading. After playing sports or engaging in hobbies, people report improvements in mood. After watching TV, people's moods are about the same or worse than before. 9

Within moments of sitting or lying down and pushing the "power" button, viewers report feeling more relaxed. Because the relaxation occurs quickly, people are conditioned to associate viewing with rest and lack of tension. The association is positively reinforced because viewers remain relaxed throughout viewing, and it is negatively reinforced via the stress and dysphoric rumination that occurs once the screen goes blank again. 10

Habit-forming drugs work in similar ways. A tranquilizer that leaves the body rapidly is much more likely to cause dependence than one that leaves the body slowly, precisely because the user is more aware that the drug's effects are wearing off. Similarly, viewers' vague learned sense that they will feel less relaxed if they stop viewing may be a significant factor in not turning the set off. Viewing begets more viewing. 11

Thus, the irony of TV: people watch a great deal longer than they plan to, even though prolonged viewing is less rewarding. In our ESM studies the longer people sat in front of the set, the less satisfaction they said they derived from it. When signaled, heavy viewers (those who consistently watch more than four hours a day) tended to report on their ESM sheets that they enjoy TV less than light viewers did (less than two hours a day). For some, a twinge of unease or guilt that they aren't doing something more productive may also accompany and depreciate the enjoyment of prolonged viewing. Researchers in Japan, the U.K. and the U.S. have found that this guilt occurs much more among middle-class viewers than among less affluent ones. 12

GRABBING YOUR ATTENTION

What is it about TV that has such a hold on us? In part, the attraction seems to spring from our biological "orienting response." First described by Ivan Pavlov in 1927, the orienting response is our instinctive visual or auditory reaction to any sudden or novel stimulus. It is part of our evolutionary heritage, a built-in sensitivity to movement and potential predatory threats. Typical orienting reactions include di- 13 lation of the blood vessels to the brain, slowing of the heart, and constriction of blood vessels to major muscle groups. Alpha waves are blocked for a few seconds before returning to their baseline level, which is determined by the general level of mental arousal. The brain focuses its attention on gathering more information while the rest of the body quiets.

In 1986 Byron Reeves of Stanford University, Esther Thorson of the University of Missouri and their colleagues began to study whether the simple formal features of television—cuts, edits, zooms, pans, sudden noises—activate the orienting response, thereby keeping attention on the screen. By watching how brain waves were affected by formal features, the researchers concluded that these stylistic tricks can indeed trigger involuntary responses and "derive their attentional value through the evolutionary significance of detecting movement.... It is the form, not the content, of television that is unique." 14

The orienting response may partly explain common viewer remarks such as: "If a television is on, I just can't keep my eyes off it," "I don't want to watch as much as I do, but I can't help it," and "I feel hypnotized when I watch television." In the years since Reeves and Thorson published their pioneering work, researchers have delved deeper. Annie Lang's research team at Indiana University has shown that heart rate decreases for four to six seconds after an orienting stimulus. In ads, action sequences and music videos, formal features frequently come at a rate of one per second, thus activating the orienting response continuously. 15

Lang and her colleagues have also investigated whether formal features affect people's memory of what they have seen. In one of their studies, participants watched a program and then filled out a score sheet. Increasing the frequency of edits—defined here as a change from one camera angle to another in the same visual scene—improved memory recognition, presumably because it focused attention on the screen. Increasing the frequency of cuts—changes to a new visual scene—had a similar effect but only up to a point. If the number of cuts exceeded 10 in two minutes, recognition dropped off sharply. 16

Producers of educational television for children have found that formal features can help learning. But increasing the rate of cuts and edits eventually overloads the brain. Music videos and commercials that use rapid intercutting of unrelated scenes are designed to hold attention more than they are to convey information. People may remember the name of the product or band, but the details of the ad itself float in one ear and out the other. The orienting response is overworked. Viewers still attend to the screen, but they feel tired and worn out, with little compensating psychological reward. Our ESM findings show much the same thing. 17

Sometimes the memory of the product is very subtle. Many ads 18
today are deliberately oblique: they have an engaging story line, but it is hard to tell what they are trying to sell. Afterward you may not remember the product consciously. Yet advertisers believe that if they have gotten your attention, when you later go to the store you will feel better or more comfortable with a given product because you have a vague recollection of having heard of it.

The natural attraction to television's sound and light starts very 19
early in life. Dafna Lemish of Tel Aviv University has described babies at six to eight weeks attending to television. We have observed slightly older infants who, when lying on their backs on the floor, crane their necks around 180 degrees to catch what light through yonder window breaks. This inclination suggests how deeply rooted the orienting response is.

"TV IS PART OF THEM"

That said, we need to be careful about overreacting. Little evidence 20
suggests that adults or children should stop watching TV altogether. The problems come from heavy or prolonged viewing.

The Experience Sampling Method permitted us to look closely at 21
most every domain of everyday life: working, eating, reading, talking to friends, playing a sport, and so on. We wondered whether heavy viewers might experience life differently than light viewers do. Do they dislike being with people more? Are they more alienated from work? What we found nearly leaped off the page at us. Heavy viewers report feeling significantly more anxious and less happy than light viewers do in unstructured situations, such as doing nothing, daydreaming or waiting in line. The difference widens when the viewer is alone.

Subsequently, Robert D. McIlwraith of the University of Mani- 22
toba extensively studied those who called themselves TV addicts on surveys. On a measure called the Short Imaginal Processes Inventory (SIPI), he found that the self-described addicts are more easily bored and distracted and have poorer attentional control than the nonaddicts. The addicts said they used TV to distract themselves from unpleasant thoughts and to fill time. Other studies over the years have shown that heavy viewers are less likely to participate in community activities and sports and are more likely to be obese than moderate viewers or nonviewers.

The question that naturally arises is: In which direction does the 23
correlation go? Do people turn to TV because of boredom and loneliness, or does TV viewing make people more susceptible to boredom

and loneliness? We and most other researchers argue that the former is generally the case, but it is not a simple case of either/or. Jerome L. and Dorothy Singer of Yale University, among others, have suggested that more viewing may contribute to a shorter attention span, diminished self-restraint and less patience with the normal delays of daily life. More than 25 years ago psychologist Tannis M. MacBeth Williams of the University of British Columbia studied a mountain community that had no television until cable finally arrived. Over time, both adults and children in the town became less creative in problem solving, less able to persevere at tasks, and less tolerant of unstructured time.

To some researchers, the most convincing parallel between TV and addictive drugs is that people experience withdrawal symptoms when they cut back on viewing. Nearly 40 years ago Gary A. Steiner of the University of Chicago collected fascinating individual accounts of families whose set had broken—this back in the days when households generally had only one set: "The family walked around like a chicken without a head." "It was terrible. We did nothing—my husband and I talked." "Screamed constantly. Children bothered me, and my nerves were on edge. Tried to interest them in games, but impossible. TV is part of them." 24

In experiments, families have volunteered or been paid to stop viewing, typically for a week or a month. Many could not complete the period of abstinence. Some fought, verbally and physically. Anecdotal reports from some families that have tried the annual "TV turnoff" week in the U.S. tell a similar story. 25

If a family has been spending the lion's share of its free time watching television, reconfiguring itself around a new set of activities is no easy task. Of course, that does not mean it cannot be done or that all families implode when deprived of their set. In a review of these cold–turkey studies, Charles Winick of the City University of New York concluded: "The first three or four days for most persons were the worst, even in many homes where viewing was minimal and where there were other ongoing activities. In over half of all the households, during these first few days of loss, the regular routines were disrupted, family members had difficulties in dealing with the newly available time, anxiety and aggressions were expressed.... People living alone tended to be bored and irritated.... By the second week, a move toward adaptation to the situation was common." Unfortunately, researchers have yet to flesh out these anecdotes; no one has systematically gathered statistics on the prevalence of these withdrawal symptoms. 26

Even though TV does seem to meet the criteria for substance dependence, not all researchers would go so far as to call TV addictive. 27

McIlwraith said in 1998 that "displacement of other activities by television may be socially significant but still fall short of the clinical requirement of significant impairment." He argued that a new category of "TV addiction" may not be necessary if heavy viewing stems from conditions such as depression and social phobia. Nevertheless, whether or not we formally diagnose someone as TV-dependent, millions of people sense that they cannot readily control the amount of television they watch.

SLAVE TO THE COMPUTER SCREEN

28 Although much less research has been done on video games and computer use, the same principles often apply. The games offer escape and distraction; players quickly learn that they feel better when playing; and so a kind of reinforcement loop develops. The obvious difference from television, however, is the interactivity. Many video and computer games minutely increase in difficulty along with the increasing ability of the player. One can search for months to find another tennis or chess player of comparable ability, but programmed games can immediately provide a near-perfect match of challenge to skill. They offer the psychic pleasure—what one of us (Csikszentmihalyi) has called "flow"—that accompanies increased mastery of most any human endeavor. On the other hand, prolonged activation of the orienting response can wear players out. Kids report feeling tired, dizzy and nauseated after long sessions.

29 In 1997, in the most extreme medium-effects case on record, 700 Japanese children were rushed to the hospital, many suffering from "optically stimulated epileptic seizures" caused by viewing bright flashing lights in a Pokemon video game broadcast on Japanese TV. Seizures and other untoward effects of video games are significant enough that software companies and platform manufacturers now routinely include warnings in their instruction booklets. Parents have reported to us that rapid movement on the screen has caused motion sickness in their young children after just 15 minutes of play. Many youngsters, lacking self-control and experience (and often supervision), continue to play despite these symptoms.

30 Lang and Shyam Sundar of Pennsylvania State University have been studying how people respond to Web sites. Sundar has shown people multiple versions of the same Web page, identical except for the number of links. Users reported that more links conferred a greater sense of control and engagement. At some point, however, the number of links reached saturation, and adding more of them simply turned

people off. As with video games, the ability of Web sites to hold the user's attention seems to depend less on formal features than on interactivity.

For growing numbers of people, the life they lead online may often seem more important, more immediate and more intense than the life they lead face-to-face. Maintaining control over one's media habits is more of a challenge today than it has ever been. TV sets and computers are everywhere. But the small screen and the Internet need not interfere with the quality of the rest of one's life. In its easy provision of relaxation and escape, television can be beneficial in limited doses. Yet when the habit interferes with the ability to grow, to learn new things, to lead an active life, then it does constitute a kind of dependence and should be taken seriously. 31

Examining the Text

1. According to Kubey and Csikszentmihalyi, what factors distinguish TV addiction from simple TV viewing?

2. What biological evidence do Kubey and Csikszentmihalyi summon to support their claims of TV's addictive capabilities? What is the "orienting response" and how does it function in the context of TV viewing?

3. What do Kubey and Csikszentmihalyi mean when they ask "In which direction does the correlation go?" How do they address the problem of correlation and causation in TV addiction?

4. According to Kubey and Csikszentmihalyi, in what ways are video games and computer use similar to and different from TV viewing? How do these similarities and differences affect the question of addiction that Kubey and Csikszentmihalyi discuss?

For Group Discussion

In a group with several other students, choose an addiction about which you have some knowledge, for instance, gambling, smoking, or drinking alcohol. Make a list of all that you know about this addiction: who suffers from it, what problems it causes, why it occurs, how society has responded, what laws exist that address the addiction, what economic consequences it has, how it can be "cured," and so on. Then compare the list you've compiled to the facts about television addiction that Kubey and Csikszentmihalyi discuss in the reading. Based on this comparison, do you think that excessive television viewing can genuinely be considered an "addiction"? Why or why not?

Writing Suggestion

For this assignment you'll need access to the Internet in order to research "TV Turn-Off Week." This annual event, described briefly by Kubey and Csikszentmihalyi, is organized by Adbusters. At *http://adbusters.org/campaigns/tvturnoff/* you can read more about this event, including personal accounts of people who participated and information about how the television media reported the event. You can also take a look at posters that people designed to publicize "TV Turn-Off Week," view a 30-second TV "uncommercial" produced for the event, and read related articles. After reading through all of this information, write an essay in which you argue either for or against the merits of "TV Turn-Off Week." Be sure to use quotations and/or statistics from the article by Kubey and Csikszentmihalyi in your argument. Feel free to include anecdotes or observations from your own experiences as a TV viewer to help bolster your position.

Life According to TV

Harry Waters

The world of television directly influences how people see the "real" world around them. So says George Gerbner, a noted cultural critic and communications scholar. Gerbner and his staff spent over fifteen years studying the televised programs America watches. Their results paint a damning picture of the TV industry. In the following essay, Harry Waters summarizes Gerbner's research about how the televised world matches up to "reality" and to people's perception of reality. To that end, Gerbner breaks the television-viewing audience into a number of different representative categories—gender, age, race, and lifestyle, just to name a few—and he observes how people in each category are portrayed in different television shows.

Frequently, Gerbner's results, as detailed by Waters, are surprising. For example, contrary to most studies of the relationship between TV and crime, which suggest that television causes people to become more violent, Gerbner argues that the prevalence of crime on TV creates a "fear of victimization" in the viewer. This fear ultimately leads to a "mean-world syndrome" in which viewers come to see their social surroundings as hostile and threatening. Waters balances Gerbner's conclusions with comments from network officials who, not surprisingly, often take Gerbner to task.

***As you read** this selection, pay particular attention to the way Waters maintains his objectivity by attributing most of the opinions and conclusions to Gerbner and his assistants. Notice, too, how Waters's opinions about Gerbner's research can be detected in phrasing such as "the gospel of Gerbner," "tidy explanation," and "comforting."*

Since this is an article originally published in Newsweek, *a magazine which claims to report the news without bias, you might ask just how really objective so-called objective reporting is.*

The late Paddy Chayefsky, who created Howard Beale, would have loved George Gerbner. In "Network," Chayefsky marshaled a scathing, fictional assault on the values and methods of the people who control the world's most potent communications instrument. In real life, Gerbner, perhaps the nation's foremost authority on the social impact of television, is quietly using the disciplines of behavioral research to construct an equally devastating indictment of the medium's images and messages. More than any spokesman for a pressure group, Gerbner has become the man that television watches. From his cramped, book-lined office at the University of Pennsylvania springs a steady flow of studies that are raising executive blood pressures at the networks' sleek Manhattan command posts. 1

George Gerbner's work is uniquely important because it transports the scientific examination of television far beyond familiar children-and-violence arguments. Rather than simply studying the link between violence on the tube and crime in the streets, Gerbner is exploring wider and deeper terrain. He has turned his lens on TV's hidden victims—women, the elderly, blacks, blue-collar workers and other groups—to document the ways in which video-entertainment portrayals subliminally condition how we perceive ourselves and how we view those around us. Gerbner's subjects are not merely the impressionable young; they include all the rest of us. And it is his ominous conclusion that heavy watchers of the prime-time mirror are receiving a grossly distorted picture of the real world that they tend to accept more readily than reality itself. 2

The 63-year-old Gerbner, who is dean of Penn's Annenberg School of Communications, employs a methodology that meshes scholarly observation with mundane legwork. Over the past 15 years, he and a tireless trio of assistants (Larry Gross, Nancy Signorielli and Michael Morgan) videotaped and exhaustively analyzed 1,600 prime-time programs involving more than 15,000 characters. They then drew up multiple-choice questionnaires that offered correct answers about the world at large along with answers that reflected what Gerbner perceived to be the misrepresentations and biases of the world according to TV. Finally, these questions were posed to large samples of citizens from all socioeconomic strata. In every survey, the Annenberg team discovered that heavy viewers of television (those watching more than four 3 hours a day), who account for more than 30 percent of the population, almost invariably chose the TV-influenced answers, while light viewers (less than two hours a day), selected the answers corresponding more closely to actual life. Some of the dimensions of television's reality warp:

SEX

Male prime-time characters outnumber females by 3 to 1 and, with a 4
few star-turn exceptions, women are portrayed as weak, passive satellites to powerful, effective men. TV's male population also plays a vast variety of roles, while females generally get typecast as either lovers or mothers. Less than 20 percent of TV's married women with children work outside the home—as compared with more than 50 percent in real life. The tube's distorted depictions of women, concludes Gerbner, reinforce stereotypical attitudes and increase sexism. In one Annenberg survey, heavy viewers were far more likely than light ones to agree with the proposition: "Women should take care of running their homes and leave running the country to men."

AGE

People over 65, too, are grossly underrepresented on television. Corre- 5
spondingly, heavy-viewing Annenberg respondents believe that the elderly are a vanishing breed, that they make up a smaller proportion of the population today than they did 20 years ago. In fact, they form the nation's most rapidly expanding age group. Heavy viewers also believe that old people are less healthy today than they were two decades ago, when quite the opposite is true. As with women, the portrayals of old people transmit negative impressions. In general, they are cast as silly, stubborn, sexually inactive and eccentric. "They're often shown as feeble grandparents bearing cookies," says Gerbner. "You never see the power that real old people often have. The best and possibly only time to learn about growing old with decency and grace is in youth. And young people are the most susceptible to TV's messages."

RACE

The problem with the medium's treatment of blacks is more one of 6
image than of visibility. Though a tiny percentage of black characters come across as "unrealistically romanticized," reports Gerbner, the overwhelming majority of them are employed in subservient, support-

ing roles—such as the white hero's comic sidekick. "When a black child looks at prime time," he says, "most of the people he sees doing interesting and important things are white." That imbalance, he goes on, tends to teach young blacks to accept minority status as naturally inevitable and even deserved. To access the impact of such portrayals on the general audience, the Annenberg survey forms included questions like "Should white people have the right to keep blacks out of their neighborhoods?" and "Should there be laws against marriages between blacks and whites?" The more that viewers watched, the more they answered "yes" to each question.

WORK

Heavy viewers greatly overestimated the proportion of Americans employed as physicians, lawyers, athletes and entertainers, all of whom inhabit prime-time in hordes. A mere 6 to 10 percent of television characters hold blue-collar or service jobs vs. about 60 percent in the real work force. Gerbner sees two dangers in TV's skewed division of labor. On the one hand, the tube so overrepresents and glamorizes the elite occupations that it sets up unrealistic expectations among those who must deal with them in actuality. At the same time, TV largely neglects portraying the occupations that most youngsters will have to enter. "You almost never see the farmer, the factory worker or the small businessman," he notes. "Thus not only do lawyers and other professionals find they cannot measure up to the image TV projects of them, but children's occupational aspirations are channeled in unrealistic directions." The Gerbner team feels this emphasis on high-powered jobs poses problems for adolescent girls, who are also presented with views of women as homebodies. The two conflicting views, Gerbner says, add to the frustration over choices they have to make as adults. 7

HEALTH

Although video characters exist almost entirely on junk food and quaff alcohol 15 times more often than water, they manage to remain slim, healthy and beautiful. Frequent TV watchers, the Annenberg investigators found, eat more, drink more, exercise less and possess an almost mystical faith in the curative powers of medical science. Concludes Gerbner: "Television may well be the single most pervasive source of health information. And its over-idealized images of medical people, coupled with its complacency about unhealthy life-styles, leaves both patients and doctors vulnerable to disappointment, frustration and even litigation." 8

CRIME

On the small screen, crime rages about 10 times more often than in real 9
life. But while other researchers concentrate on the propensity of TV mayhem to incite aggression, the Annenberg team has studied the hidden side of its imprint: fear of victimization. On television, 55 percent of prime-time characters are involved in violent confrontations once a week; in reality, the figure is less than 1 percent. In all demographic groups in every class of neighborhood, heavy viewers overestimated the statistical chance of violence in their own lives and harbored an exaggerated mistrust of strangers—creating what Gerbner calls "mean-world syndrome." Forty-six percent of heavy viewers who live in cities rated their fear of crime "very serious" as opposed to 26 percent for light viewers. Such paranoia is especially acute among TV entertainment's most common victims: women, the elderly, nonwhites, foreigners and lower-class citizens.

Video violence, proposes Gerbner, is primarily responsible for 10
imparting lessons in social power: it demonstrates who can do what to whom and get away with it. "Television is saying that those at the bottom of the power scale cannot get away with the same things that a white, middle-class American male can," he says. "It potentially conditions people to think of themselves as victims."

At a quick glance, Gerbner's findings seem to contain a cause- 11
and-effect, chicken-or-the-egg question. Does television make heavy viewers view the world the way they do or do heavy viewers come from the poorer, less experienced segment of the populace that regards the world that way to begin with? In other words, does the tube create or simply confirm the unenlightened attitudes of its most loyal audiences? Gerbner, however, was savvy enough to construct a methodology largely immune to such criticism. His samples of heavy viewers cut across all ages, incomes, education levels and ethnic backgrounds—and every category displayed the same tube-induced misconceptions of the world outside.

Needless to say, the networks accept all this as enthusiastically as 12
they would a list of news-coverage complaints from the Ayatollah Khomeini. Even so, their responses tend to be tinged with a singular respect for Gerbner's personal and professional credentials. The man is no ivory-tower recluse. During World War II, the Budapest-born Gerbner parachuted into the mountains of Yugoslavia to join the partisans fighting the Germans. After the war, he hunted down and personally arrested scores of high Nazi officials. Nor is Gerbner some videophobic vigilante. A Ph.D. in communications, he readily acknowledges TV's beneficial effects, noting that it has abolished

parochialism, reduced isolation and loneliness and provided the poorest members of society with cheap, plug-in exposure to experiences they otherwise would not have. Funding for his research is supported by such prestigious bodies as the National Institute of Mental Health, the Surgeon General's office, and the American Medical Association, and he is called to testify before congressional committees nearly as often as David Stockman.

MASS ENTERTAINMENT

When challenging Gerbner, network officials focus less on his findings and methods than on what they regard as his own misconceptions of their industry's function. "He's looking at television from the perspective of a social scientist rather than considering what is mass entertainment," says Alfred Schneider, vice president of standards and practices at ABC. "We strive to balance TV's social effects with what will capture an audience's interests. If you showed strong men being victimized as much as women or the elderly, what would comprise the dramatic conflict? If you did a show truly representative of society's total reality, and nobody watched because it wasn't interesting, what have you achieved?" 13

CBS senior vice president Gene Mater also believes that Gerbner is implicitly asking for the theoretically impossible. "TV is unique in its problems," says Mater. "Everyone wants a piece of the action. Everyone feels that their racial or ethnic group is underrepresented or should be portrayed as they would like the world to perceive them. No popular entertainment form, including this one, can or should be an accurate reflection of society." 14

On that point, at least, Gerbner is first to agree; he hardly expects television entertainment to serve as a mirror image of absolute truth. But what fascinates him about this communications medium is its marked difference from all others. In other media, customers carefully choose what they want to hear or read: a movie, a magazine, a best seller. In television, notes Gerbner, viewers rarely tune in for a particular program. Instead, most just habitually turn on the set—and watch by the clock rather than for a specific show. "Television viewing fulfills the criteria of a ritual," he says. "It is the only medium that can bring to people things they otherwise would not select." With such unique power, believes Gerbner, comes unique responsibility: "No other medium reaches into every home or has a comparable, cradle-to-grave influence over what a society learns about itself." 15

MATCH

In Gerbner's view, virtually all of TV's distortions of reality can be attributed to its obsession with demographics. The viewers that prime-time sponsors most want to reach are white, middle-class, female and between 18 and 49—in short, the audience that purchases most of the consumer products advertised on the tube. Accordingly, notes Gerbner, the demographic portrait of TV's fictional characters largely matches that of its prime commercial targets and largely ignores everyone else. "Television," he concludes, "reproduces a world for its own best customers." 16

Among TV's more candid executives, that theory draws considerable support. Yet by pointing a finger at the power of demographics, Gerbner appears to contradict one of his major findings. If female viewers are so dear to the hearts of sponsors, why are female characters cast in such unflattering light? "In a basically male-oriented power structure," replies Gerbner, "you can't alienate the male viewer. But you can get away with offending women because most women are pretty well brainwashed to accept it." The Annenberg dean has an equally tidy explanation for another curious fact. Since the corporate world provides network television with all of its financial support, one would expect businessmen on TV to be portrayed primarily as good guys. Quite the contrary. As any fan of "Dallas," "Dynasty" or "Falcon Crest" well knows, the image of the company man is usually that of a mendacious, dirty-dealing rapscallion. Why would TV snap at the hand that feeds it? "Credibility is the way to ratings," proposes Gerbner. "This country has a populist tradition of bias against anything big, including big business. So to retain credibility, TV entertainment shows businessmen in relatively derogatory ways." 17

In the medium's Hollywood-based creative community, the gospel of Gerbner finds some passionate adherents. Rarely have TV's best and brightest talents viewed their industry with so much frustration and anger. The most sweeping indictment emanates from David Rintels, a two-time Emmy-winning writer and former president of the Writers Guild of America, West. "Gerbner is absolutely correct and it is the people who run the networks who are to blame," says Rintels. "The networks get bombarded with thoughtful, reality-oriented scripts. They simply won't do them. They slam the door on them. They believe that the only way to get ratings is to feed viewers what conforms to their biases or what has limited resemblance to reality. From 8 to 11 o'clock each night, television is one long lie." 18

Innovative thinkers such as Norman Lear, whose work has been practically driven off the tube, don't fault the networks so much as the climate in which they operate. Says Lear: "All of this country's institu- 19 tions have become totally fixated on short-term bottom-line thinking. Everyone grabs for what might succeed today and the hell with tomorrow. Television just catches more of the heat because it's more visible." Perhaps the most perceptive assessment of Gerbner's conclusions is offered by one who has worked both sides of the industry street. Deanne Barkley, a former NBC vice president who now helps run an independent production house, reports that the negative depictions of women on TV have made it "nerve-racking" to function as a woman within TV. "No one takes responsibility for the social impact of their shows," says Barkley. "But then how do you decide where it all begins? Do the networks give viewers what they want? Or are the networks conditioning them to think that way?"

Gerbner himself has no simple answer to that conundrum. Neither a McLuhanesque shaman nor a Naderesque crusader, he hesitates to suggest solutions until pressed. Then out pops a pair of provocative notions. Commercial television will never democratize its treatments of daily life, he believes, until it finds a way to broaden its financial base. Coincidentally, Federal Communications Commission chairman Mark Fowler seems to have arrived at much the same conclusion. In exchange for lifting such government restrictions on TV as the fairness doctrine and the equal-time rule, Fowler would impose a modest levy on station owners called a spectrum-use fee. Funds from the fees would be set aside to finance programs aimed at specialized tastes rather than the mass appetite. Gerbner enthusiastically endorses that proposal: "Let the ratings system dominate most of prime time but not every hour of every day. Let some programs carry advisories that warn: 'This is not for all of you. This is for nonwhites, or for religious people or for the aged and the handicapped. Turn it off unless you'd like to eavesdrop.' That would be a very refreshing thing." 20

ROLE

In addition, Gerbner would like to see viewers given an active role in steering the overall direction of television instead of being obliged to passively accept whatever the networks offer. In Britain, he points out, political candidates debate the problems of TV as routinely as the issue of crime. In this country, proposes Gerbner, "every political campaign should put television on the public agenda. Candidates talk about schools, they talk about jobs, they talk about social welfare. They're going to have to start discussing this all-pervasive force." 21

There are no outright villains in this docudrama. Even Gerbner recognizes that network potentates don't set out to proselytize a point of view; they are simply businessmen selling a mass-market product. 22

At the same time, their 90 million nightly customers deserve to know the side effects of the ingredients. By the time the typical American child reaches the age of reason, calculates Gerbner, he or she will have absorbed more than 30,000 electronic "stories." These stories, he suggests, have replaced the socializing role of the preindustrial church: they create a "cultural mythology" that establishes the norms of approved behavior and belief. And all Gerbner's research indicates that this new mythological world, with its warped picture of a sizable portion of society, may soon become the one most of us think we live in.

Who else is telling us that? Howard Beale and his eloquent alarms 2
have faded into off network reruns. At the very least, it is comforting to know that a real-life Beale is very much with us... and really watching.

Examining the Text

1. Waters reports extensive studies by George Gerbner and his associates that show that heavy television viewers have a generally "warped" view of reality, influenced by television's own "reality warp" (paragraph 3). Which viewers do you think would be affected most negatively by these "warped" viewpoints, and why?

2. Gerbner's studies show that "55 percent of prime-time characters are involved in violent confrontations once a week; in reality, the figure is less than 1 percent" (9). While violent crime is known to rank as middle-class America's primary concern, most violent crime occurs in neighborhoods far removed from most middle-class people. How do you explain these discrepancies? Why is "violent confrontation" so common on television? How does the violence you see on television affect you?

3. Waters interviewed a number of different people when he wrote this article for *Newsweek*. Collectively, they offer a variety of explanations for and solutions to the limited images television provides. Look closely at these suggested causes and solutions. Which seem most reasonable to you? In general, is Waters's coverage of the issue balanced? Why or why not?

For Group Discussion

This article was first published more than ten years ago. With your group, look again at Gerbner's categories and discuss what significant recent examples suggest about the way current television programming represents reality. Do today's shows seem more accurate than those of ten years ago? As a class, discuss whether or not most viewers want more "reality" on television.

Writing Suggestion

The TV guide is a fine example of non-academic but very common reading material in our culture. Millions of people read TV schedules

38 **THURSDAY** JANUARY 23, 2003 **TV WEEK**

KEY: 00 SANTA BARBARA 00 LOMPOC/SANTA YNEZ 00 SANTA MARIA In Santa Ynez, KEYT is on ch. 8 nd KCET is on ch. 3.

	PRIMETIME				6:00	6:30	7:00	7:30	8:00	8:30	9:00	9:30	10:00	10:30	11:00
BROADCAST STATIONS	KEYT	3	3/10	3	News (cc) 149	Frasier 101	Friends 2526	Seinfeld 385	Rules, Dating	Acc'ding/Jim	My Wife, Kids	George Lopez	PrimeTime Thursday (cc) 9138		News
	KNBC	4	4	4	News (cc) 491	NBC News	EXTRA 7728	Hollywood	Friends 6588	Scrubs 8323	Will & Grace	Good Morn'g	ER: Chaos Theory. (R) (cc) 1120		News
	KWCA	5	5	5	Elimidate	Elimidate	Will & Grace	Will & Grace	High School Reunion (R) 52830		Kennedy	Surreal Life	Elimidate	5th Wheel	Cops 42965
	KSBY	6	6	6	News 44897		Jeopardy!	Wheel	Friends 9830	Scrubs 8965	Will & Grace	Good Morn'g	ER: Chaos Theory. (R) (cc) 73323		News
	KCAL	9	9	9	Judge Judy	Family Feud	Pyramid 1830	Holl.Squares	News (cc) 94830		News (cc) 14694		News (cc) 6983743		ET
	KCET	10	8	8	NewsHour With Jim Lehrer 57588		Life & Times	Neighbor.	History of Us	History of Us	America in Black and White: Jasper, Texas 39033			Rosie's ...	Charlie Rose
	KKFX	11	11	11	Simpsons	King of Hill	Simpsons	'70s Show	Movie: ★★ "Scream 2" (1997, Horror) David Arquette. 'R' (cc) 90014				News	70s Show	Just Shoot
	KCOY	12	12	12	News (cc) 51526		ET	Raymond	Star Search (cc) 27168		CSI: Crime Scene 84584		Without a Trace (R) (cc) 34061		News
	KADY	13			Roseanne	All in Family	Van Praagh	Van Praagh	Movie: ★ "The Black Bird" (1975, Comedy) George Segal. 'PG' 30656				News 39830	News	Fresh Prince
	KTAS (Telem)	15	10	10	Notic.	Noti.	El Beso del Vampiro 92859				Venganza 12236		Esperanza 15323		Notic.
	KPMR (Univi)	16	38	38	Viviana	Notic.	Gata Salvaje		Vias del Amor		Entre Amor/Odio		Aqui y Ahora		Impacto
CABLE CHANNELS	LIFE	2	42	42	Golden Girls	Golden Girls	Intimate Portrait (cc) 285762		Unsolved Mysteries 204410		★★ "Big Dreams & Broken Hearts: The Dottie West Story" (cc) 204897				Golden Girls
	USA	7	21	21	Walker, Texas Ranger (cc) 276061		JAG: Jinx. (cc) 390033		Movie: ★★★ "Batman" (1989, Action) Caped Crusader saves Gotham City from the Joker. 'PG-13' (cc) 770439						Dead Zone
	WTBS	14	7	7	(5) "Demolition Man" (cc) 5381694		(7:15) Movie: ★★★ "The Terminator" (1984) 'R' (cc) 9935491				(9:15) Movie: ★★★ "Demolition Man" (1993) 'R' (cc) 4721946				(11:15) Movie
	GOV'T	18			Transportation & Circulation 86491				Historic Landmarks Commission 793946						City Cal.
	fX	19			Vampire 9371897		Vampire 4200205		"The Blair Witch Project" 8600061				Ghosts 5650746		Dark.
	COUNTY	20	20	20	(5) Board of Supervisors Meeting 654120								County Calendar 2783472		
	EDUCATION	21			Prisma	Excel	Carpenteria School Board 38410				UCTV Live Feed 782491				
	CNN	22	38	16	L. King 571633		NewsN't 305965		Chung	Dobbs	L. King 301149		NewsN't 304236		Dobbs
	CNBC	24	23	23	Capital 6145236		News 7182410		K. & C. 7168830		Capital 7188694		News 7181781		K. & C.
	FOX NEWS	25	49	49	Hannity & Colmes		G. Van Susteren		O'Reilly Factor		Special Report		Neil Cavuto		Hannity
	AMC	26	26	26	(6:05) Movie: ★★★★ "The Day the Earth Stood Still" 'G' 71654304				Movie: ★★★★ "Raiders of the Lost Ark" (1981, Adventure) Harrison Ford. 'PG' (cc) 3342781					(10:20) "Raiders of the Lost Ark"	
	TNT	28	37	37	NBA Basketball 858101		NBA Basketball: New Jersey Nets at Golden State Warriors. (Live) (cc) 871052					Inside the NBA (cc) 110168		★★★ "Batman Forever" 595120	
	NICK	29	32	32	U-Pick	Rkt Pr	Arnold!	Rugrats	Sponge.	Ginger	Cosby	Cosby	Cheers	Cheers	Coach
	DISN	30	25	25	Sister, Sister	Even Stevens	Sister, Sister	Lizzie McG.	Movie: ★★ "Genius" (1999, Comedy) 7395675			Teamo Supr.	Sister, Sister	Lizzie McG.	Even Stevens
	TLC	31	30	30	Bob Vila	Bob Vila	Scotland 889385		Danger 898033		Storm 818897		Survival 888656		Danger
	DSC	32	39	39	Hipp Talk 479149		Detect. 743101		Stolen 769149		Myth 749385		Myth 742472		Stolen
	ANIMAL	33	58	57	101 Dalmatians II		Animal Videos		101 Dalmatians II: Funniest Animals				Animal Videos		Animals
	ESPN	34	14	14	NHL Hockey 61474656			(7:40) SportsCenter (cc) 85961588			College Hoops Tonight 121965		SportsCenter (cc) 124052		SportsCenter
	ESPN2	35	40	40	Tennis 3342897				Tennis 3314014				2Night	Pardon	Sports
	FOXSW2	36	24	24	College Basketball 915675			NHL Hockey: Minnesota Wild at L.A. 303269					Spo.	SoCal	BestSpo
	FOXSW	37	24	24	See This!	Sports Ton.	UCLA Sports	College Basketball: UCLA at Stanford. (Live) 317101				Sports Report	Sports	See This!	Best Sports
	MTV	38	15	15	Tough	Tough	Tough	Tough	Tough	Tough	Tough	Tough	Tough Enough 3		Real
	EWTN	40			Children	Rosary	No Greater Joy		Human Sexuality		Daily Mass		Life on the Rock		Hope
	HSN	41			Signature Club A						Ultrex Kitchen		Kitchen Favorites		Sweets
	TBN	43	59	52	Jakes	Y'r Day	Praise the Lord (cc) 170491				Tenney	Dam.	Lindsey	Y'r Day	Virtual
	TNN	45	34	34	Real TV	Date	Taboo	Date	Star Trek: Next		Movie: ★★★ "Bull Durham" (1988) 'R'				Trek
	CSPAN	47	19	19	(5) Prime Time Public Affairs 123025				Prime Time Public Affairs 791588						Affairs
	COURT	49	4	4	Profiler 80878		Cops	Cops	System 92052		For.	Evi.	System 82675		NYPD
	SCI-FI	51	17	17	Roswell 8044878		Movie: ★★ "Dune" (1984, Science fiction) 'PG-13' (cc) 9812217								Dream
	CARTOON	54	44	44	Poke.	Ed, Edd	Samurai	'puff	Fturama	Home	Lupin	Inuya.	Hak.	Cowboy	Jerry
	HISTORY	55	50	50	Marvels 97120		Marvels 21526		Ancient 26566		Ku Klux Klan: Secret History 76043				Murders
	A&E	56	27	27	City 464217		Justice 778897		B'graphy 754217		"Columbo and the Murder of a ..."				Third
	BRAVO	57			(4:30) "Big Chill"		Studio 987526		Movie: ★★★ "Dressed to Kill" 967762				Golden 986897		Sanders
	COM	62	35	35	Saturday Night Live (cc) 8620694		Late Night With Conan 3594168		Saturday Night Live (cc) 3570588		Prem. Blend	South Park	Insomniac	Insomniac	Daily Show
	FOOD	64	47	47	Food	Cooking	Follow	Best Of	Emeril 3828830		Food	Cooking	Follow	Best Of	Kit.
	HALLMARK	65			The Waltons		Medicine Woman		Touched/Angel		Movie: "The Last Cowboy" (2003)				Angel
	E!	66	33	33	Reveal.	Scenes	E! News 141762		The E! True Hollywood Story 161526				Nicole	Dates	H. Stern
	TCM	69			Movie	★★★ "A Little Romance" 1451236				★★★★ "Wuthering Heights" 2002269				"Black Cat"	
	FAM	70	28	28	Videos	Videos	7th H'ven 289588		Movie: ★★ "Soul Food" 'R' 292052				Resort	Whose?	700
	HBO	71	70	70	Movie: ★★ "D2: The Mighty Ducks" (1994, Action) 'PG' (cc) 102830				Inside the NFL (cc) 110859		Rolling Stones Live From Madison Square Garden (cc) 1940588				GString
	MAX	73	72	72	(4:30) "Heist"	Movie: ★ "Evolution" (2001) 'PG-13' (cc) 1090762			(8:15) Movie: "Sniper 2" (2002, Suspense) 'R' (cc) 21536217				Movie: ★★★ "The Pelican Brief" 'PG-13' (cc) 5937897		
	OUTDOOR	74	60	44	Bound 835138		Skiing 156694		Instinct 132014		Bound 152878		Skiing 155965		Skiing
	SHOW	75	71	71	Movie: ★★★ "The Man Who Wasn't There" (2001) 'R' (cc) 382014				Movie: ★★ "Jason's Lyric" (1994, Drama) Allen Payne. 'R' 394859				Movie: ★★ "City Hall" (1996) 'R' (cc) 663491		

every day and think nothing of it. This writing assignment asks you to reflect on *how* you read TV schedules and to interpret what meanings can be found in these common documents.

On page 181 is a reproduction of a page from the TV listings in our local (Santa Barbara, CA) newspaper, listing the televised offerings on Thursday, January 23, 2003. Begin writing about this document by describing it: What are its distinguishing features? How is the information organized? How does its appearance differ from the pages of this textbook? Next, take notes describing the strategies you use in reading this document: Where do you begin? Where does your eye go next? What factors influence your choices? Are there parts of the document that you ignore completely? Why? Finally, write down your thoughts about the content of this schedule: To what extent do the TV programs scheduled for this evening confirm or contradict Waters' claims in "Life According to TV"? As you bring these observations together in an essay, highlight what you see as the two or three most important features of TV schedules in general, based on your observations of this specific example.

Interactive Television: Is it Coming or Not?

John Kelly

The handy VCR has freed us from the need to regulate our social schedules around the schedules of TV networks, and it also allows us, much to the chagrin of advertisers, to fast-forward through the two or three minutes of commercials that interrupt our favorite programs. What do new technologies have in store for us? In this article by John Kelly, we learn about interactive television, or ITV. We also learn abbreviations for some new high-tech devices—EPG ("electronic program guides"), PVR ("personal video recorder"), VOD ("video-on-demand")—abbreviations that may or may not become as familiar to us as VCR, DVD, and PC are today.

John Kelly is in a position to know about the present and future of ITV. He spent twelve years in professional media production as a sound designer and producer of film, music, video, and digital effects, and he is currently principal investigator at Columbia University's Interactive Design Laboratory, where he conducts research on design processes and the development of content for interactive television. So although it's unclear what the future holds for interactive television, Kelly provides an expert's view of the issues involved.

As Kelly points out, interactive television encompasses several different features: tools for managing what we watch on TV and when we watch it; ways to connect television and the Internet in order to pay bills, play games, or view images on the TV screen; and interactive television programming in which we can respond to what we see on TV. ***Before you read,*** *consider the ways in which you currently "interact" with the television. While the preceding articles have focused on the television viewer as a relatively passive recipient of (often misleading) information, Kelly's article invites us to think about current practices and future possibilities for a more active kind of television experience.*

In last winter's edition of this publication, Robert Thompson included some musings on interactive television in his excellent article on reality TV. "It may be that 'interactive television' for most viewers might turn out to be an oxymoron...Millions of Americans already spend much of their day interacting with a keyboard and a screen; will they really want to do more of this once they get home?" 1

Indeed, from HDTV, to DTV, to eTV, to ITV, it often seems that the march of digital television technologies into the American household is having all the success Napoleon found in Russia. WebTV topped out at about a million users before descending into marketing oblivion. New TV devices like TiVo and Ultimate TV have struggled thus far to grow a user base of just a few hundred thousand. And rollouts of full-featured interactive television (ITV) services by cable MSOs have still only touched a relative handful of communities, with households measured in the hundreds or thousands. 2

As of last summer, the tribe of interactive television professionals whose fortunes rely on the medium having a future had scaled back their predictions of interactive television's glorious arrival, with things that were two years away two years ago rescheduled to show up around 2005. There are indications that the tragedy of September 11 and its ongoing economic fallout will push major initiatives by MSO's and other big players back even further. A new round of layoffs has hit the already beleaguered ITV industry. 3

And so, as the latest wave of hype and hope around the concept of "interactive TV" passes, it is perhaps a very good time to broadly consider the future of TV in the era of advanced digital technology. 4

One problem we face in trying to get a grip on the future is that the term "interactive TV" refers to so many things that it doesn't really mean any one thing. In part, defining "interactive TV" is difficult because defining "TV" is difficult. Television is a device in the home, but 5 it is also an industry, a cultural medium and a way of spending an evening.

What we mean by "interactive," ultimately, is just what the capabilities of the computer will add to the mix. As consumers we sense that the computer is getting closer and closer to the TV. We play movies stored digitally on DVD, and a growing number of households now get their TV signals digitally over satellite and cable. New-generation cable and satellite set-top boxes offer electronic program guides (EPGs) to help viewers select among hundreds of channels by browsing an interactive menu. Advanced game consoles, like Sony's PlayStation 2 and Microsoft's X-box, connect amazing computational power to the television, as well as a rich set of specialized input and output tools: Joysticks, game pads, force-feedback systems, etc. WebTV and AOL-TV boxes bring functions familiar from the Internet, such as browsing the Web, sending e-mail, and online messaging and chat. 6

And then there's a fascinating new class of consumer devices, the personal video recorder (PVR). PVRs like TiVo and Ultimate TV tie an EPG to a searchable database of programming information, and record your program selections on a hard drive for you to watch whenever you want. They also cache live TV on the hard drive, so you can pause, rewind, and fast-forward through commercials and other things people usually don't want to watch. Going far beyond the VCR's clunky capabilities for time-shifting, the TiVo tracks your preferences and records things for you that it "thinks" you might like. (Nice, although you might wonder just who is really getting to know you.) 7

All these "television appliances" are just specialized computers, like a desktop PC, but stripped down to be affordable and to do specific, core things that people understand already, like watching movies, changing channels or playing games. From a technical point of view, the whole bunch could easily be replaced by a single box containing a hard drive, microprocessor, DVD drive and two-way data link to the outside world—in other words, a PC. 8

But knowing that on a technical level the TV of the future is essentially a PC—albeit one connected to a big screen in your living room rather than a small one on your desk—is not very helpful when trying to envision the future of our central cultural medium. After all, knowing that the TV of the past half-century is basically a "dumb terminal" for the display of video and audio streams tells us almost nothing about why we now have sitcoms, 30-second commercials and sound-bite culture. The interesting questions are all about how people will use the technology, how the commercial communications industry will reshape itself accordingly and how our cultural arena will be affected. These questions have few good answers so far. 9

Looking at Thompson's formulation of the big question—whether ITV is in the end an oxymoronic beast that no one will want, because the TV experience we all know and love is essentially a "passive" one and always will be—is a good way to dig into things. Do we really want our TVs to be more like our computers? 10

It is axiomatic in the industry that although interactive TV is computerized TV, consumers must be shielded from the fact. We accept computers, with all of their frustrating problems, because we have few alternatives if we want to do the things a computer can do. Actually, there are a lot of people who won't accept them. Adoption rates for Internet-connected PCs in the home are leveling off after years of steady growth, and computer companies are facing hard times as they realize that they are now in the business of selling new computers to old customers who might want to upgrade, rather than competing for first-time buyers. So plenty of folks don't want computers, certainly not as home entertainment devices. Nobody will accept a TV that spews error messages and crashes unpredictably, or requires booting up. 11

But even if it were technically painless and reliable, what would interest anyone in a computerized TV experience? A lot of people describe TV as a "lean-back," passive medium—best enjoyed reclining on a comfy sofa. By contrast, computers are for active, "lean-forward" activities—best accomplished sitting upright at a desk. These are really two completely different modes of communion between human and electronic box, the thinking goes, and folks don't want their chocolate and peanut butter mixed. 12

But this "lean-forward/lean-back" dichotomy doesn't really hold up to scrutiny. Just consider the game console. There is no electronic experience more intensely interactive than playing a video game, and millions of kids and adults seem perfectly happy zapping bad guys from the couch. And while it's hard to imagine anyone wanting to tweak giant spreadsheets on their Sony WEGA, viewers in Europe, where deployments of TV-based interactive services are years ahead of the U.S., enjoy doing many things on the TV that we do on the web. Checking stocks, making travel arrangements, voting in online polls, playing games and other activities we consider Internet experiences are TV experiences for millions in the U.K alone. 13

Additionally, in the U.S. there are a growing number of "telewebbers," folks who use the web on a PC and watch TV at the same time. Some of this activity uses the TV and web as part of an integrated experience, such as playing along with game shows like *Who Wants to be a Millionaire* or guessing plays on *Monday Night Football*—examples of what is called "two-screen" interactive TV. Other telewebbing ex- 14 periences interweave use of the web and TV more loosely, and lots of people just keep the TV on in the background while they browse websites. Whatever consumers are doing exactly, telewebbing is more evidence that chocolate and peanut butter can coexist after all.

But what will this ITV peanut-butter cup look like? If we view 15
the variety of computer TV appliances as precursors, we can already see that the interactive features sneaking into the TV fall into three basic categories.

The first category encompasses tools for managing what you 16
watch. This includes the EPGs that help you select programs from among hundred of channels. It also includes PVRs and video-on-demand (VOD), which let you watch what you want when you want it. In this category, the basic TV experience, watching linear programs, is the same as current TV. But what shows you watch and how you watch them is more friendly to your interests and schedule. Herein lie big challenges to TV as a business. The principal issue raised is how to overcome the PVR's death grip on the 30-second ad spot, the commercial backbone of the industry. Pay-per-view, subscription services, sponsorship, product placement and innovative personalized advertising techniques will have to be explored to insure that content production remains a profitable enterprise.

The second category is made up of stuff you can do with a net- 17
worked PC. This includes e-mail, the web, chat, shopping, banking, trading stocks, playing games, downloading music, video conferencing, etc. Philips has some excellent ITV set-top box demos featuring online photo distribution, home video monitoring (think Baby-Cam!), online medical diagnosis, and other advanced features that would qualify. Networked computer gaming will probably be huge. I'm guessing these are mainly things that won't ultimately be understood specifically as "TV." Although these functions may be accomplished at times on the TV, they will also be done on PCs, PDAs, and other interactive devices—we'll use whichever gadget is handy when we need it.

The third category, the one that excites many creative types, is in- 18
teractive TV programming, i.e., shows the viewer can interact with. This category is the one that interests my lab at Columbia the most (see *www.idl.columbia.edu/itv-emergency*, for panel summaries from our July 17, 2001 conference on ITV content), and poses the greatest challenge to TV as a creative medium. But it is also the one where the passive vs. active viewer distinction has some real traction. Even if played through a multitalented future ITV box, many TV programs will remain essentially what they are now—carefully crafted narrative experiences you sit back and watch without user-driven interruptions. But interactive programming is central to how we will ultimately under-

stand ITV as "TV." It is the area that gives TV today some of the sense of untapped creative promise the medium had in the 50s.

In imagining ITV's future, it is easy to get hung up on the question of what kind of box it will come in. I've heard people, usually those frustrated with the delayed roll-out of interactive cable TV set-top boxes, ask whether the latest generation of game consoles might be "Trojan Horses" for ITV. Buy a PlayStation 2 game console today, get Sony's pitch for a laundry list of additional interactive services tomorrow. But a cable set-top box could just as easily become a Trojan Horse for multiplayer gaming, and why not add a hard drive and PVR functionality for $7 a month? Microsoft's new Ultimate TV is marketed as a PVR, but it also quietly includes WebTV functionality. Why not make it an X-box too? 19

People want to add compelling functions to their TV, when they clearly understand the function, and can get it for a couple of hundred bucks or a small monthly fee. Our three categories contain a heady mix of different features that are as likely to creep slowly and individually into our experience, via several distinct TV appliances, as they are to appear together all at once in a shiny new set-top box from our cable MSO. In the end, most of the features that become part of the ITV experience could easily get rolled up into one device. Whether that box is the offspring of a game console, PVR, or cable set-top box would probably have less to do with what you ultimately do on your TV than whom you pay to do it. 20

Make no mistake, that last point is of critical importance to the television industry, a mammoth interlocking complex of media conglomerates, content producers, distributors and equipment providers who have worked out a very uneasy commercial balance with one another. Interactive technologies that promise (or threaten, depending on who you are) to renovate the way consumers interact with TV, as well as who the gatekeepers and tollbooth operators are, are likely to upset a lot of apple carts. 21

But given Moore's Law and its telecommunications corollaries, the unfolding of a brave new TV world looks every bit as inexorable as change in the music industry. Your grandchildren will probably not be asking, "When will video-on-demand finally happen?" And they will be doing things on a big screen in their homes that are as hard to foresee today as *Survivor* would have been in 1950. 22

Things are moving slowly, but there will be moments where critical mass is reached for new, interactive TV features. And the reason ITV is so interesting is not because the number of users of anything we might call "interactive TV" today is so high. It's not. But because the long-term implications of replacing TV's "dumb," one-way, analog infrastructure with a "smart," two-way, digital one are profound. 23

Examining the Text

1. Why do you think Kelly begins by pointing out that interactive television has failed, so far, to catch on with the American public? What reasons does Kelly give for this failure?

2. In your own words, describe the distinction Kelly makes between "lean back" and "lean forward" technologies? How is this distinction related to the issue of interactive television?

3. What are the three categories of interactive television that Kelly describes? Which category does he find most interesting, and why?

4. What does Kelly ultimately believe will be the fate of ITV? What reasons does he give to support his belief?

For Group Discussion

In a group, choose one of the three categories of interactive television described by Kelly: "tools for managing what you watch," "stuff you can do with a networked PC," and "interactive TV programming, i.e., shows the viewer can interact with." Reread the paragraph in which Kelly discusses the category you've chosen. Then discuss any experiences you've already had with this kind of interactive television. What advantages and disadvantages does this category of ITV have over regular TV viewing? As a group, decide whether you think this category of ITV will be widely used in the future, basing your decision on your own experiences as well as Kelly's commentary.

Writing Suggestion

Kelly provides a fairly balanced view of the present and future of interactive television, discussing both the difficulties this new technology faces and what he believes will be its inevitable success with the American public. Choose one of these two perspectives and write an argument in which you support your choice. That is, construct an argument either that ITV will fail or that ITV will succeed in being widely adopted in American households. Of course, you'll need to first define what you mean by ITV, drawing on the definitions offered by Kelly. In the body of your argument, use quotations from Kelly's article as well as your own ideas and observations to support your stance.

Interpreting Television

1. Reality TV

The Tribe Has Spoken

Rebecca Gardyn

At the risk of losing all credibility, I have a confession to make: I, Madeleine Sorapure, am a "Survivor" addict: by day, a relatively normal, fairly well-balanced, reasonably intelligent college teacher; by night (but only Thursday night), a glued-to-the-TV, won't-answer-the-phone, cheering and jeering "Survivor" nut. My co-author, Michael Petracca, has somehow escaped the seductions of this particular reality TV show. Frankly, I think he doesn't know what he's missing, especially when you add the online fantasy "Survivor" games, the cyber-gossip of "Survivor" bulletin board discussions, and, of course, the real-life water-cooler gossip with other "Survivor" nuts.

As long as I'm at it, I might as well also admit that I've been known to watch "Big Brother," "The Real World," "Fear Factor," and "Trading Spaces." At one point or another I've probably seen all of the reality dating shows, even including (shudder) that one where the parents give prospective suitors a lie detector test and invariably choose the wrong guy for their daughter. I don't watch very much else on TV, and I understand perfectly well that reality TV is not *reality, but for some reason, these shows appeal to me in a big way.*

Do I fit the demographic profile of the reality TV fanatic? Yes, but so do you. According to Rebecca Gardyn, 70 percent of 18- to 24-year-olds watch reality television programs, and 44 percent of this group prefer to watch real people over scripted characters on TV. In fact, polls have shown that viewers of reality TV shows come from all demographic groups. While age and gender are important variables in determining why *people watch these shows, each group nevertheless seems to have found compelling reasons for watching.*

But, as Gardyn admits, these shows may or may not pass the test of time. The current popularity of reality television may not last, especially as networks struggle to come up with interesting new scenarios to keep viewers hooked. Do any of us really want to see supermodels eat cow intestines? Is it worthwhile and uplifting to watch couples bickering and cheating on each other in exotic locations? Will the reality TV trend be a victim of its own outrageousness? **As you read,** *consider your own attitudes toward reality TV shows. Do you enjoy watching them? Why or why not?*

Reality TV may have some staying power after all. This fall season, every major network has at least one reality series on its docket—from the debut of CBS's *The Amazing Race* to the return of ABC's *The Mole* and Fox's *Temptation Island.* And for the first time, reality programs will have the opportunity to jockey alongside sitcoms and dramas for industry kudos at the Primetime Emmy Awards later this month, since previously there were no categories that accommodated the genre. This year, voting procedures and prize categories have been revamped to make room for reality programs. CBS's *Survivor* has five nominations. Perhaps a win or two will allow this oft-criticized genre to shed its reputation as a fly-by-night novelty and become a legitimate contender in the ever-cluttered TV outback. 1

Or not. While some media experts believe reality television will alter the topography of TV Land, others are sure this season will mark the beginning of the end for the format, as over-scheduling tends to lead to overkill. Of course, the ultimate vote will be cast by the viewing public, and for now, that includes almost half of all Americans, as well as a full 70 percent of 18- to 24-year-olds and 57 percent of 25- to 34-year-olds—two segments most desired by advertisers. 2

What is it about the new crop of reality TV programs that has so many viewers riveted? What personality types are attracted to this genre? And what advertising messages and tactics are apt to resonate with these viewers? As the copycats mount, programmers and advertisers who want to connect with consumers through this television vehicle may benefit from understanding not only the demographic composition of this vast audience, but its attitudes, character traits and motivations for tuning in. 3

Forty-five percent of all Americans watch reality television programs. Of those, 27 percent consider themselves die-hard fans, watching as many episodes as possible, according to a nationally representative telephone survey of 1,008 people conducted exclusively for *American Demographics* by Edison, N.J.-based Bruskin Research. In fact, 37 percent of all Americans prefer to watch real people on television rather than scripted characters. 4

While much has been reported about how reality TV is reeling in teens and young adults for the networks, the programs actually attract a much wider fan base. Brian Devinny, who writes the online column, "The Reality Factor," on 3BigShows.com, says he receives e-mail from "all walks of life," from housewives to lawyers, across all income and age brackets. "The shows reach out to so many people on so many levels," Devinny says. "When *Survivor I* was on, I had many retirees write in to me rooting for 72-year-old Rudy. It's not just young people tuning in." 5

The results of the *American Demographics*/Bruskin survey illustrate that diversity. Of all those who watch reality television, 55 percent are ages 35 or older. In fact, even though 18- to 24-year-olds are the most likely age group to tune in, the largest portion of the reality TV audience (29 percent) is actually the 35- to 49-year-old group. And when it comes to gender divides, women are the die-hard fans, making up 64 percent of regular viewers (those who watch as many episodes as they can), while occasional viewers are slightly more male (55 percent versus 45 percent). Also noteworthy: reality TV watchers are primarily in the middle- to low-income brackets—58 percent have annual incomes under $50,000—and Southerners account for 39 percent of all reality TV viewers, compared with about 20 percent of residents in each of the Northeast, North Central and Western regions. 6

What exactly is it about reality TV that has attracted such a disparate group? According to Encino, Calif.-based E-Poll's syndicated online survey of 2,121 Americans, ages 18 to 54, the No. 1 reason people watch is the thrill of "guessing who will win or be eliminated from the show." That thrill is the reason cited by 69 percent of all reality TV watchers, and 84 percent of regular viewers, who make a point to watch. The second and third most common reasons viewers tune in are to "see people face challenging situations" and "imagining how I would perform in similar situations," stated by 63 percent and 42 percent of all viewers, respectively. 7

Of course, reasons for watching reality TV differ dramatically across age and gender divides, according to E-Poll's findings. For example, 43 percent of 18- to 34-year-old viewers say they tune in because they like to see conflict break out among the contestants, compared with 29 percent of 35- to 54-year-olds. The older crowd, on the other hand, is more intrigued than younger viewers with following the contestants' strategies (41 percent versus 36 percent). Men are more than three times as likely as women to tune in to see physically attractive contestants (31 percent versus 9 percent), while women are more likely than men to tune in because they like guessing the outcomes (72 percent versus 65 percent). 8

Before becoming a contestant on *The Mole* and an alternate for *Big Brother I*, Wendi Wendt, 30, from Cedar Rapids, Iowa, was a fan of *Survivor*, and she continues to be an avid viewer of the reality TV genre. "It's in my blood now," she says. Her current fave is *Fear Factor*. "I enjoy seeing real people getting the chance to do extraordinary things, and how they evolve as people," she says. And while Wendt has heard the accusations that the producers of *Survivor* and other reality shows allegedly manipulate outcomes, she's not bothered. Speaking from experience, she notes: "How the players feel is real. You can 9 see their true emotions, their frustrations, their joy. That's real enough for me. If some of the smaller details aren't so real, so be it."

But other fans fear that producers of the programs are starting to tread too far off the path of "real" intentions. In so doing, they may start to lose a core group of viewers, says Mary Beam, a 38-year-old reality TV fan from Cleveland, Texas, who founded the Web site, RealityTVFans.com. "Some of the shows have started to cast only beautiful Hollywood types, who are just in it to become actresses, or overly obnoxious people who are obviously playing a role," she says. In fact, of 18- to 54-year-olds who don't watch reality programs, 38 percent say it is because "the contestants are just trying to get famous," according to E-Poll. Says Beam: "The viewers want to see people who look or act like we do. If we wanted fake, we'd be watching sitcoms." In fact, E-Poll also found that 81 percent of viewers who stopped watching a reality program after sampling a show did so because they found the show to be "too scripted or not real enough." 10

No group is more adamant about keeping reality TV real than the 18- to 24-year-old crowd, 44 percent of whom say they prefer to watch real people to scripted characters, according to the *American Demographics*/Bruskin survey. In fact, 27 percent of America's youth says that reality television is better than what's currently offered on the networks during prime time, compared with 15 percent of the total population who say the same. 11

"These kids grew up with cable television, where unscripted, documentary-style shows have always been a staple," says Ed Martin, 12

Reality Bites

Of the 18- to 54-year-olds who avoid reality television shows, 60 percent say they can always find something better to watch.

Reasons for *Not* Watching Reality TV	**Total**	**Men**	**Women**	**18–34**	**35–54**
Can always find something better to watch	**60%**	60%	61%	56%	63%
Too trashy or low-class	**55%**	57%	53%	56%	55%
Don't like the human values/traits they present	**49%**	49%	49%	47%	50%
Don't care about the contestants	**44%**	53%	35%	52%	39%
Contestants are just trying to get famous	**38%**	38%	38%	43%	35%
I can't identify with the contestants	**35%**	31%	40%	34%	36%
They are faked or rigged	**35%**	36%	33%	43%	28%
Too voyeuristic/don't like spying on people	**33%**	31%	36%	28%	37%
Contestant strategy is weak or overblown	**24%**	27%	22%	26%	22%
Contestants are not appealing/attractive	**12%**	16%	7%	12%	11%

Note: Multiple answers allowed.

Source: E-Poll

programming editor at Myers Reports, which provides research for and about the media industry. "This is what TV is to them," he adds, noting that MTV's *The Real World* started making inroads with the genre 10 years ago. The popularity of this format with youth also has a lot to do with their growing up in a democratized society, where the Internet, Web cams and other technologies give the average Joe the ability to personalize his entertainment, notes Andy Dehnart, a 23-year-old self-described "reality TV addict." "In today's world, anyone can create a Web site, like I did," says Dehnart, who founded RealityBlurred.com, a site that covers reality show news. "Web logs are huge. Memoirs have taken off. As a culture, we've become so much more interested in real people."

Jason Thompson, 20, from League City, Texas, who watches "every reality show I can find," says he likes shows that allow him to get to know the contestants. After the first *Big Brother* aired last summer, Thompson felt at ease sending e-mails to contestant Britney Petros and offered to design a Web page for her fans. Thompson and Petros ended up talking on the phone for half an hour, and while he didn't get the job to design her site, the two have become friends and trade e-mails, he says. Thompson adds that he, too, would like to be famous someday, and reality shows give him hope that he could be. "Because the contestants are regular people just like me, it makes me feel like I could be one of them," Thompson says. 13

This fascination with instant celebrity, focused on everyday people who find fame overnight, has been fueled by reality TV. But advertisers, especially those targeting youth, have been slow to catch on, says Irma Zandl, president of The Zandl Group, a market research firm in New York that caters to the under-30 segment. She cites a recent series of Levi's ads as an example of a missed opportunity. Each ad highlighted a teenager on a karaoke stage, singing horribly. "If [Levi's executives] had instead [recruited] young people who could really sing, and used the campaign to find the next 'N Sync, everyone would have been buzzing about it," says Zandl. She advises marketers to cash in on the reality TV-driven desire for fame and attention by creating messages that promise the possibility of overnight success. She suggests that companies incorporate *Star Search*–like competitions in their campaigns, or offer other contests with TV-related prizes, such as walk-on parts or backstage passes to a television show. 14

Another way to reach reality TV viewers is by tapping in to their adventurous personalities and active lifestyles. According to the *American Demographics*/Bruskin survey, 40 percent of reality television viewers consider themselves adventurous, and 86 percent lead active lives, compared with 31 percent and 79 percent of non-reality watchers, respectively. Barbara Hammack, 38, from Houston, has no 15

Why Watch?

Of the 18- to 54-year-old reality TV viewers, only 19 percent cite the physical attractiveness of the contestants as a main reason they watch the programs. But 31 percent of men say that it is, in fact, those beautiful bods that keep them tuned in.

Reasons for Watching Reality TV	Total	Watch Reality TV Regularly	Watch Reality TV Occasionally	Men	Women	18–34	35–54
Guessing who will win or be eliminated	**69%**	84%	60%	65%	72%	67%	71%
Seeing real people face challenging situations	**63%**	81%	53%	60%	65%	61%	65%
Imagining how I would act in similar situations	**42%**	51%	37%	43%	41%	42%	42%
Following contestants' strategies	**38%**	54%	29%	39%	37%	36%	41%
Fights among contestants	**37%**	49%	30%	39%	35%	43%	29%
Making fun of contestants	**28%**	31%	26%	32%	24%	32%	21%
Nothing better to watch	**25%**	11%	32%	26%	24%	26%	23%
Exotic locations	**23%**	31%	19%	24%	23%	23%	24%
Physically attractive contestants	**19%**	25%	16%	31%	9%	23%	14%
Romance/relationships among contestants	**18%**	23%	15%	16%	21%	22%	13%

Note: Multiple answers allowed.

Source: E-Poll

If You Build It

Those who never watch reality television programs may be enticed with the right plotline: a quarter (26 percent) say they'd be interested in viewing a show that had contestants breaking world records, and 21 percent would like to see a show that challenged contestants to find their way out of a remote location.

Percent Who Would Have Interest in Watching the Following Types of Reality TV Plots:	Total	Watch Reality TV Regularly	Watch Reality TV Occasionally	Never Watch Reality TV	Men	Women	18–34	35–54
Racing across the country	**40%**	57%	46%	20%	45%	34%	42%	37%
Finding way out of a romote location	**56%**	86%	69%	21%	58%	54%	62%	50%
Losing weight	**19%**	28%	19%	12%	13%	24%	20%	17%
Beauty contest	**13%**	17%	15%	8%	17%	9%	17%	8%
Getting the girl/guy	**23%**	37%	28%	8%	25%	22%	30%	15%
Breaking a world record	**44%**	52%	54%	26%	48%	41%	44%	45%
Getting a job	**20%**	26%	23%	13%	21%	19%	21%	19%
Quitting smoking	**16%**	18%	19%	10%	13%	19%	16%	16%
Truth or dare	**64%**	73%	58%	18%	48%	48%	55%	40%

Note: Multiple answers allowed.

Source: E-Poll

desire to be famous, but every desire to add some spice to her life. "People who watch reality TV, like myself, have some deep desire to go on some great adventure, but maybe they just never had the opportunity or resources to do it themselves," she says. Hammack, who works in the oil and gas industry, describes herself as a "regular job, average-income kind of gal." She says she always wished she had gone into a more adventurous field, such as archaeology. Hammack is itching to be a contestant on a reality show and has already tried out for *The Mole, Big Brother 2* and *Survivor 4*. She says she's surprised at how few reality TV viewers she meets who actually want to participate in the shows. This observation is supported by our survey, which found that for many reality TV fans, their adventurous streak is purely a vicarious one: 57 percent say they are actually cautious by nature.

Reebok, by outfitting the feet of *Survivor* participants, master- 16 fully tapped in to the adventurous spirit of reality fans. And since then, other advertisers followed, with mixed success. Pontiac, the top advertiser for *Survivor II*, according to Competitive Media Reporting, shelled out $7.2 million to advertise its outdoorsy Aztek truck/camper during the program, both in commercial spots and as a coveted prize during one episode of the show. Jason Thompson, the reality enthusiast from Texas, says that the car manufacturer made a smart move. "Before seeing it in the program, I didn't really know too much about the car," he says. However, he adds, some products work better than others. Regarding the abundance of product placement on *Survivor II* by Mountain Dew soda and Doritos tortilla chips, Thompson says: "I've always hated Mountain Dew. I'm not going to run out and buy it now because it was on Survivor." Dehnart, of RealityBlurred.com, says that advertisers should also be worried about potential backlash from product placement strategy. "When it starts to interfere with the show, a lot of fans resent it," he says.

In addition to rethinking commercial messages and appropriate 17 product placements on the programs, advertisers developing new strategies for this audience may also want to pay attention to what's happening online. According to E-Poll, a full 70 percent of avid fans, ages 18 to 54, visit Web sites related to the reality shows they prefer, as do a third (32 percent) of occasional viewers. Twenty-six percent of all reality TV viewers read or post messages online regarding the genre; and 22 percent play Internet games that are based on the shows.

This interactivity is not strictly a phenomenon for the younger 18 viewers: while 34 percent of 18- to 34-year-olds visit Web sites related to reality shows, so do 27 percent of 35- to 54-year-olds. At RealityTVFans.com, the average age range of message board visitors is 35 to 55, and they are primarily women, says webmaster Mary Beam.

Wendy Veazey, a 38-year-old mother of two from Metairie, La., finds plenty of other fans in her age group chatting it up on reality TV message boards and as her opponents on fantasy *Survivor* games. Talking with others in real time, guessing strategies and analyzing the possible outcomes brings a whole new component to the shows, says Veazey. "The Internet completes the whole experience." Last year, during the first *Big Brother* series, for example, Veazey, who works from home, kept Internet feeds running all day, so she could eavesdrop on the contestants, whom she came to think of as "friends." In fact, while the critics panned *Big Brother I,* and the TV ratings didn't hold a candle to *Survivor,* the viewers who supplemented their TV watching with online participation overwhelmingly loved the show, says Beam of RealityTVFans.com. "There's a whole subculture on the Net that a lot of people don't know about." 19

Ed Martin of the Myers Reports anticipates that real-time interactivity will be the next evolution of reality TV, and some networks are already taking steps toward that end. This fall, the WB network will debut a new program called *Lost in the USA,* that will allow viewers to interact with the contestants, online and by phone, giving them the power to tip off participants to their opponents' strategies. And then there's ABC's much anticipated *The Runner,* which makes its debut in 20

Ratings Toppers

Temptation Island tops the Nielsen ratings for teens and young adults.

Nielsen Ratings for Reality Programs Aired During the 2000–2001 Season, by Age Group*:	**12–17**	**18–24**	**18–34**	**25–54**	**50+**	**Women 18+**	**Men 18+**
Temptation Island (FOX)	9.1	10.6	12.0	8.0	3.0	7.0	6.5
Survivor I (CBS)	7.4	9.2	12.1	12.7	12.6	13.3	11.2
Boot Camp (FOX)	7.3	5.9	6.6	5.1	2.1	4.0	4.4
Survivor II (CBS)	7.0	6.6	12.3	13.7	12.5	13.5	11.5
The Mole (ABC)	3.9	4.0	5.7	5.4	5.4	5.9	4.5
Fear Factor (NBC)	3.8	4.4	5.4	5.3	4.5	5.1	4.7
Spy TV (NBC)	2.9	4.4	5.8	5.1	3.4	4.9	4.0
Popstars (WB)	2.7	1.8	1.7	1.2	0.4	1.3	0.7
Chains of Love (UPN)	1.4	0.9	1.2	1.0	0.5	0.9	0.8
Big Brother I (CBS)	N/A	N/A	3.8	4.2	4.7	5.0	3.3

*A rating represents the estimated percentage of people in each age group watching the named show during the 2000–2001 season. For example, Temptation Island received a 9.1 rating among 12- to 17-year-olds, meaning that 9.1 percent of teens tuned in to that program.

Source: Analysis of Nielsen Media Research, 10/2/2000–9/30/2001, by The Media Edge.

Crowd Pleasers

When it comes to reality TV's online community, age doesn't seem to be a factor. Nineteen percent of 18-to 34-year-olds have read or posted messages online about reality TV shows, as have 16 percent of the 35- to 54-year-old crowd.

	Total	Watch Reality TV Regularly	Watch Reality TV Occasionally	Never Watch Reality TV	Men	Women	18–34	35–54
Visit Web sites related to reality TV shows	**31%**	70%	32%	3%	29%	32%	34%	27%
Play online games based on reality TV shows	**16%**	35%	16%	2%	16%	16%	17%	14%
Read or post online messages about reality TV shows	**18%**	41%	18%	2%	18%	17%	19%	16%
Read articles about reality TV shows	**47%**	84%	53%	13%	43%	50%	49%	44%
Watch interviews with reality TV show contestants	**46%**	91%	54%	7%	41%	52%	50%	43%

Note: Multiple answers allowed.

Source: E-Poll

January, and will actually turn viewers into contestants. One man (or woman) will attempt to cross the country without being identified by viewers. If successful, the runner wins $1 million. If unsuccessful, the identifier(s) can claim all or part of the prize. ABC will provide clues online and during the televised show.

To reach the next generation of television viewers, advertisers will have to get more creative about combining efforts across both TV and the Internet, says Ira Matathia, global director of business development for advertising conglomerate Euro RSCG Worldwide. Reality TV has created a whole new range of challenges for advertisers, he says, adding, "We are going to have to work a hell of a lot harder to reach people in the coming years." 21

But first, let's face the fall. 22

Examining the Text

1. Gardyn presents at least two kinds of evidence to support her assertions in this article: statistics from surveys conducted by various organizations, and interviews with individuals who are fans of reality TV programs. How do these two kinds of evidence differ? What are the strengths and weaknesses of each? Why do you think Gardyn begins with mostly statistical evidence and puts most of the interview-based evidence toward the end of the article?

2. What advice do Gardyn and the television and advertising executives quoted here give about effective advertising on reality TV shows? In what ways is effective advertising on reality shows different from advertising on scripted shows, talk shows, or sports shows?

3. According to Gardyn, what role does the Web (and other interactive forums) play in terms of reality TV programming?

4. From the article, can you discern Gardyn's opinion about whether reality TV programming will gain or decrease in popularity? What clues, if any, are there in the article that let you know what Gardyn thinks about this question? Why might Gardyn want to leave her opinion unstated?

For Group Discussion

In discussing different demographic groups, Gardyn covers such factors as age, gender, and economic class, along with other groupings of people based on their affiliation with reality TV shows and the amount of time they spend watching TV. Working with several other students, choose one group that Gardyn discusses (for instance, 18- to 24-year-old viewers, or men, or "die-hard" reality TV fans). Read through the article, including the tables of data and the interviews with individual viewers, looking for all of the information Gardyn presents on this group. Together, write a brief explanation of what Gardyn reports about this group; compare your results to those of other groups in your class.

Writing Suggestion

Gardyn includes five tables with data from various surveys of television viewers. Take one of the tables and, after carefully studying it, write a four- or five-paragraph explanation of the significant information that this table conveys. You might organize your essay by identifying one key point for each paragraph of your essay; key points can include data from just one answer or comparisons of data from different answers or comparisons of data from different demographic groups. Make sure that you don't simply report numbers; rather, provide verbal descriptions that show what the numbers signify. You might also consider including quotations or paraphrases from Gardyn's article to help you explain what the information in the table means.

Keeping It Real: Why We Like to Watch Reality Dating Television Shows

Robert Samuels

In the following article, Robert Samuels, a lecturer in the Writing Programs at the University of California at Los Angeles, reports on what he learned from his students. Specifically, Samuels asked his students what they think about one type of reality television program: the "reality dating show." After all, as Samuels points out, college students are in the demographic group that these shows actively target, so finding out what the target group has to say about the shows that target them should yield interesting conclusions. How do the attitudes and concerns of this audience shape the very programming that they end up watching?

Samuels records the top ten reasons why his students like to watch reality dating shows, but he also takes his investigation a few steps further by analyzing the responses of his students and not accepting them at face value. His analysis ultimately engages questions of privacy and voyeurism, the blurred distinctions between the real and the artificial, and the nature of competition, fame and narcissism, distrust and paranoia. In short, Samuels moves from an analysis of a specific type of television show to a broad social commentary and to speculation on how the media shapes our behavior and guides our actions and beliefs.

Samuels has published extensively on popular culture, psychoanalysis, and philosophy. **As you read,** *keep in mind both the approach and the conclusions of the previous article, "The Tribe has Spoken." In what ways is Samuels's investigative strategy different from Gardyn's? How does the focus on a particular type of reality show influence the kind of conclusions Samuels reaches?*

Every day from 5 to 7 P.M., millions of Americans tune in to watch other people go on dates. From *Blind Date* to *ElimiDate* to *Rendez-View,* viewers cannot seem to get enough of these new reality TV dating shows. In order to explore why we like to watch these shows and what they say about contemporary American culture, I decided to survey my university students to see what the targeted audience really thinks. The responses I received help us understand the general popularity of reality television shows and the effect these programs are having on contemporary American culture. Like *Big Brother, Survivor,* and countless other reality shows, reality dating programs challenge traditional oppositions between performer and audience, reality and fiction, private and public, and sport and nonsport. By turning everyday experiences—like camping, co-habitating, and dating—into spectator sports, these programs cater to our desire to witness the private lives of our fellow human beings. Moreover, by portraying an edited version of reality as if it is the real thing, these shows are able to combine fiction and reality in new and unexpected ways. 1

Many critics have traced the roots of reality television to the power of MTV and other cable formats that rely on fast-action, skimpy clothing, and documentary-style fast-cutting to retain an attention-challenged audience. However, my survey of contemporary university students—who, after all, are the main audience of these shows—reveals a more varied and complex explanation for the development of these programs. I found that in order to see why people love to watch reality television, we cannot just focus on how the media has shaped the viewing habits of young adults; rather, we must also discover how the concerns and desires of the target audience have helped to mold the productions of contemporary media culture. 2

According to my survey, here are the top ten reasons why university students like to watch reality dating programs: 3

1. It's fun to watch other people be rejected.
2. The people on these shows are just like us.
3. There are a lot of hot guys and girls on these shows.
4. You can learn a lot by watching other people's mistakes.

5. These shows are more real than other shows.
6. It's like going on a virtual date.
7. It's fun to guess who will be chosen.
8. You can see other people in an uncomfortable situation.
9. Everyone gets their fifteen minutes of fame.
10. These shows celebrate our narcissism and voyeurism.

Many of these responses seem to contradict each other, yet I believe there is a certain logic to the popularity of these shows, and this logic says a lot about our contemporary culture. 4

1. *It's fun to watch other people be rejected.* But why do people like to watch other people get rejected? Is it because we have all felt the sting of rejection in the past, and thus we like to see other people suffer a similar fate? Or does this response say something about our great human need to rubberneck and watch other people's difficult moments from a safe and controlled distance? After all, what is more anxiety-provoking than going on a nationally broadcasted date where you stand a high chance of being rejected and ridiculed? To sit in the comfort of our homes, while other people are out there testing the dating waters, allows us the chance to relive some of our own worst experiences without any sense of personal risk. It is like going on an emotional roller coaster, but one which you know you can get off at anytime. 5

This question of emotional and personal safety is very important to American daters who have grown up in the age of AIDS and other sexually transmitted diseases. After all, what type of sex could be safer than the kind you get from watching other people try to have sex? In other words, even if no one ends up "hooking up" and everyone is eventually rejected, the audience still receives the gratification of going on a vicarious date without risk and without much effort. And let's not forget that most of these shows come on right when most Americans are just arriving home from a long day of work. After eight hours at the office, who has the energy to go on a real date? Isn't it easier to watch someone else go on the date for you? Moreover, after a long day of surviving the various frustrations and rejections that comprise the work experience for many Americans, what could be better than watching someone else be rejected and humiliated? Yet, what is so strange is that not only do we enjoy watching the suffering of others from the comfort of our own homes, but we also want those suffering others to be just like us. 6

2. *The people on these shows are just like us.* Many of my students feel that the real attraction of these reality dating programs is that any young adult can relate to them because the participants are just ordinary people doing something that everyone else has done before. This 7

need to identify with the "characters" on television shows has motivated many TV programmers to replace paid actors with unpaid ordinary citizens. Not only does this use of real people give many Americans the chance to experience their fifteen minutes of fame, but it also helps to motivate the audience to suspend their disbelief and forget about the mediated nature of these shows.

By using real people and placing them in real situations, reality television programs are thus able to lull the audience into misperceiving controlled situations as being spontaneous events. In these seamlessly mediated productions, we never see the camera, the producer, or the editor. One of the results of this subtle blending between real reality and edited fiction is that our own everyday reality becomes less interesting compared to the controlled television reality. For it is obvious that one of the appeals of these shows is that these people are not really like most of us, since most of us do not spend most of our time trying to look beautiful for the camera. In other words, we watch these shows because the people on them are like us, but in many ways they are superficially more beautiful or extreme versions of our own selves. 8

In response to a question concerning the attractiveness of the participants on these programs, one of my students wrote that "it is natural for guys to like girls with fake boobs." Here we see how something that is fake can be considered natural, while something that is natural turns out being fake. The subtle psychological effect of this blending between the natural and the artificial is that constructed aspects of consumer culture become naturalized at the same moment that our natural urges (like sex and eating) become socialized. In many ways, this blending of nature and culture is the key to our capitalist society where sex sells because sex is no longer natural or instinctual; instead of being something real and spontaneous, sex has become a form of advertising and entertainment. 9

3. *There are a lot of hot guys and girls on these shows.* As my students often remind me, not only are there attractive people on dating shows, but these attractive people are trying to seduce each other, and so they act and dress in a very sexy way. Furthermore, these dating shows are often set up so that viewers feel that they are also on the date, and thus they are able to date people they might not be able to date in their own lives. 10

Of course, one of the most negative lessons people can learn from watching these beautiful daters is that the only thing that matters when one is considering a potential mate is physical beauty and seductive charm. Furthermore, since none of these dates last longer than a few edited minutes, the whole mating process is sped up into a fast-paced Darwinian survival of the hottest. The overall drive of these shows is to turn courtship into a superficial competitive sport complete with color 11 commentary and a clear distinction between winners and losers. Like other reality TV shows, dating programs thus turn a seemingly non-competitive aspect of everyday life into a spectator sport.

4. *You can learn a lot by watching other people's mistakes.* Given the contrived nature of these programs, it is strange that many of my students claim they learn a lot of important lessons from these shows. In fact, many of these dating programs do provide a constant commentary on what to do and what not to do on dates. Here, we see another way that sex and courtship have become unnatural processes mediated by expert advice and highly judgmental criticism. As Rochefoucault once said, no one would fall in love if they didn't first read about love. In the same vein, can we say now that no one can date without a thorough knowledge of the popular media's conception of proper dating etiquette? I often wonder if people going on dates today anxiously wait for some pop-up caption to tell them whether they are proceeding in the accepted manner. In any account, it seems apparent from my students' responses that dating has become more performative and self-reflexive than it once was. Yes, it may be odd that TV dating would invade the realm of real dating, yet one of the great powers of reality television shows is that they effectively blur the distinctions between what's real and what's fiction. 12

5. *These shows are more real than other shows.* Once again, what draws people to reality programs is that they use real people in real situations, and thus they break down the traditional borders between the actor and the spectator and the real and the fictional. As my students often point out, on these programs, one never knows if someone is being real or just acting. On the one hand, this inability to determine the sincerity of the participants allows the viewing audience to identify more easily with the performers on the screen. On the other hand, not knowing who and what is real contributes to a general social atmosphere of distrust and paranoia. 13

This question of distrust feeds into contemporary culture's fascination with the dark side of public and private personalities. So much of our media is dedicated to showing us people in their worst moments that one must question how we are able to trust anyone with whom we come in contact. Reality dating shows add to this culture of paranoia by bringing together a real situation with a competition or a quest for fame. This combination of reality with competition forces the viewer to question the motives of the performers, and yet this constant confrontation with distrust and paranoia is compensated for by the continual stream of commentary and expert analysis. In other words, at the same time these shows make us distrust other people's real intentions, they reassure us by telling us what is right and wrong in the dating world. 14

While it is always a question of how much people actually learn from television shows and how much of this knowledge shapes their behavior, my students often celebrate the way reality TV shows allow the viewers to participate as if they were actually part of the shows themselves. For when students discuss reality dating shows, they stress how the realness of these productions gives them the sense that they are actually along for the ride or are active participants in the date. 15

6. *It's like going on a virtual date.* This idea that watching reality TV dating shows can make you feel like you are on a virtual date may point to the general sense of virtual reality circulating in contemporary culture. Many of my students who watch reality TV shows also spend a great deal of time on the Internet, and some have experimented with virtual dating and various forms of cyber relationships. Their experiences in a cyber world may help these same students slip more easily into vicarious relationships with the people on reality dating shows. 16

This connection between the Internet and reality dating shows also points to the ways new communication technologies give people unprecedented access into the private thoughts and experiences of a diverse range of fellow human beings. Like personal home pages and Web diaries, reality dating shows break down many of the traditional boundaries separating the private and public realms. By allowing us to go on other people's dates and hear personal reflections about these dates, reality dating programs open up a previously private realm of personal experience for the pleasure of a public audience. A side-effect of this vicarious dating structure is that it gives the viewer a false sense of activity, while he or she is passively watching other people. Instead of feeling guilty for being lazy and watching meaningless junk, we can convince ourselves that we are actively participating in a learning experience. 17

7. *It's fun to guess who will be chosen.* One way that these shows help the audience forget about their own passivity is by creating opportunities for them to participate in the process. On many of these programs, this level of participation is limited to the viewer's vicarious experience of picking who will be chosen and who will be rejected in the dating competition. 18

Not only do people get to predict the future winners and losers, but like many other reality TV shows, the dating programs train people into accepting a Darwinian world view where someone is always being downsized and eliminated. Like a giant corporate training program, these shows help to rationalize an economy where there are constant winners and losers. For the audience members not only enjoy picking who will be the winner of the dating sweepstakes, but they also love to see who will be rejected and humiliated. 19

8. *You can see other people in an uncomfortable situation.* Perhaps 20
this great desire to see other people be rejected and humiliated can be
derived from the fact that the more we see others in bad situations, the
better our own situations look. According to this constant-sum logic,
there can only be a certain number of happy people in the world at
any given time, and thus the more we view other people failing, the
more we can be assured that we are doing okay. Furthermore, we only
know how we rate in the great game of life by comparing ourselves to
others; thus, the worse off others are, the better off we feel.

Another psychological explanation for our desire to see other 21
people in uncomfortable situations is that if we can watch a scene of
humiliation in a safe and comfortable environment, we gain a sense of
control over our own anxieties. In this context, the television frame
works to contain or "box in" our own feelings of humiliation and discomfort. From the viewer's perspective, one person's rejection is another person's triumph.

Of course, these shows don't just display people being rejected 22
and placed in humiliating situations, but they also depict a democratic
world where everyone gets a chance to be on TV and thus stake a
claim to instant celebrity. In many ways, fame is seen as its own prize,
and therefore any humiliation one has to endure is worth the chance
of being on the other side of the screen.

9. *Everyone gets their fifteen minutes of fame.* This democratization 23
of celebrity on reality television is often proclaimed as a great appeal
for both viewers and contestants. When we watch the average Joe and
Jane on TV, we are reminded that we could be the next person
watched by millions. Instead of just sitting at home and staring at the
screen, we can cross the border and have people watch us. And with
so many new technologies allowing us to film and be filmed, the desire to be on the other side of the camera is constantly being cultivated.

10. *These shows celebrate our narcissism and voyeurism.* I learned 24
from the responses of my students that not only do people want their
fifteen minutes of fame, but they also want to be shown that it is okay
to be narcissistic and voyeuristic. After all, we are a culture that loves
to celebrate the possibility of anyone making it—whether through talent, good looks, confidence, or sheer luck. Without our national obsession with superficial appearances, there would be no beauty industry,
no dieting industry, no work-out industry: in fact, we would have no
economy if we did not believe in our inherent need to be more beautiful and instantly powerful.

Reality dating programs may celebrate our most superficial desires for 25
fame, sex, beauty, and quick hook-ups, but isn't that what twenty-
first–century America is all about? Perhaps we should see these shows

as public service announcements helping to train us to be effective participants in our consumer economy. Or perhaps we should read these shows as funhouse mirrors reflecting back to us in a distorted form our own social and psychological selves? One thing is clear: reality television programs offer us new insights into previously hidden aspects of American life.

Examining the Text

1. According to Samuels, what are some of the specifically *psychological* appeals of reality dating shows? That is, what psychological gratifications do these shows give their viewers?
2. In what ways, according to Samuels, are the dates on reality dating shows different from dates in real life?
3. What do you think is Samuels' opinion of reality dating shows? Where in the article can you discern his opinion? Do you see this article as being more or less objective than the previous article by Gardyn?

For Group Discussion

In the last paragraph, Samuels proposes two analogies for thinking about reality dating shows: they are "public service announcements helping to train us to be effective participants in our consumer economy"; or, they are "funhouse mirrors reflecting back to us in a distorted form our own social and psychological selves." In a group, discuss the implications of these options. What does it mean to say that these shows are "funhouse mirrors," for instance? How should we watch them and what should we learn from them if we see these shows as distorted reflections of ourselves? After discussing both options, decide which one you think more accurately describes reality dating shows.

Writing Suggestion

Write an essay in which you compare and contrast the article by Samuels and the previous article by Gardyn. Be sure to consider not only the content but also the method of each article. What is the approach of each author to the subject matter? What kinds of evidence does each author include in his or her analysis? How is each article organized, and how do the differences in organization affect the message of the article? You might conclude your comparison by stating from which article you think you learned more about reality television, and why.

2. The Simpsons

The Simpsons: Atomistic Politics and the Nuclear Family

Paul A. Cantor

Paul A. Cantor is a Professor of English at the University of Virginia, member of the National Council on the Humanities, and a noted scholar of Elizabethan and Romantic English literature. In the article that follows, however, Professor Cantor wears the hat of popular culture specialist, as an expert on and devotee of The Simpsons. *The article is part of Cantor's book-length work,* Gilligan Unbound, *which studies the ways in which popular television shows reflect and shape American political and social principles. Clearly, Cantor is an example of a "serious" scholar who takes television seriously.*

While The Simpsons *has often been criticized for presenting horrible role models, particularly in the characters of Bart and Homer, Cantor argues that the show ultimately celebrates the nuclear family and small-town life in American communities. Cantor also argues that the show deals with key social issues, politics, religion, the media, and other important American institutions, so that even though it's "just a cartoon," the show actually provides valuable social commentary and presents "more human, more fully-rounded" characters than those on TV sitcoms and dramas.*

Cantor points out that the basic strategy of The Simpsons *is to simultaneously mock and celebrate; in other words, by satirizing something (education, politics, the police, etc.), the show acknowledges its importance.* ***As you read****, think about episodes of* The Simpsons *that you've seen (if you've never seen an episode, take this opportunity to watch one!). Do Cantor's arguments ring true, based on your own experience of watching the show?*

When Senator Charles Schumer (D-N.Y.) visited a high school in upstate New York in May 1999, he received an unexpected civics lesson from an unexpected source. Speaking on the timely subject of school violence, Senator Schumer praised the Brady Bill, which he helped sponsor, for its role in preventing crime. Rising to question the effectiveness of this effort at gun control, a student named Kevin Davis cited an example no doubt familiar to his classmates but unknown to the senator from New York: 1

> It reminds me of a *Simpsons* episode. Homer wanted to get a gun but he had been in jail twice and in a mental institution. They label him as "potentially dangerous." So Homer asks what that means and the gun dealer says: "It just means you need an extra week before you can get the gun."[1]

Without going into the pros and cons of gun control legislation, one can recognize in this incident how the Fox Network's cartoon series *The Simpsons* shapes the way Americans think, particularly the younger generation. It may therefore be worthwhile taking a look at the television program to see what sort of political lessons it is teaching. *The Simpsons* may seem like mindless entertainment to many, but in fact, it offers some of the most sophisticated comedy and satire ever to appear on American television. Over the years, the show has taken on many serious issues: nuclear power safety, environmentalism, immigration, gay rights, women in the military, and so on. Paradoxically, it is the farcical nature of the show that allows it to be serious in ways that many other television shows are not.[2] 2

I will not, however, dwell on the question of the show's politics in the narrowly partisan sense. *The Simpsons* satirizes both Republicans and Democrats. The local politician who appears most frequently in the show, Mayor Quimby, speaks with a heavy Kennedy accent[3] and generally acts like a Democratic urban-machine politician. By the same token, the most sinister political force in the series, the cabal that seems to run the town of Springfield from behind the scenes, is invariably portrayed as Republican. On balance, it is fair to say that *The Simpsons,* like most of what comes out of Hollywood, is pro-Democrat and anti-Republican. One whole episode was a gratuitously vicious portrait of ex-President Bush,[4] whereas the show has been surprisingly slow to satirize President Clinton.[5] Nevertheless, perhaps the single funniest political line in the history of *The Simpsons* came at the expense of the Democrats. When Grandpa Abraham Simpson receives money in the mail really meant for his grandchildren, Bart asks him, "Didn't you wonder why you were getting checks for absolutely nothing?" Abe replies, "I figured 'cause the Democrats were in power again."[6] Unwilling to forego any opportunity for humor, the show's creators have been generally evenhanded over the years in making fun of both parties, and of both the Right and the Left.[7] 3

Setting aside the surface issue of political partisanship, I am interested in the deep politics of *The Simpsons,* what the show most fundamentally suggests about political life in the United States. The show broaches the question of politics through the question of the family, and this in itself is a political statement. By dealing centrally with the family, *The Simpsons* takes up real human issues everybody can recognize and 4 thus ends up in many respects less "cartooonish" than other television programs. Its cartoon characters are more human, more fully rounded, than the supposedly real human beings in many situation comedies. Above all, the show has created a believable human community: Springfield, USA. *The Simpsons* shows the family as part of a larger community and in effect affirms the kind of community that can sustain the family. That is at one and the same time the secret of the show's popularity with the American public and the most interesting political statement it has to make.

5 *The Simpsons* indeed offers one of the most important images of the family in contemporary American culture and, in particular, an image of the nuclear family. With the names taken from creator Matt Groening's own childhood home, *The Simpsons* portrays the average American family: father (Homer), mother (Marge), and 2.2 children (Bart, Lisa, and little Maggie). Many commentators have lamented the fact that *The Simpsons* now serves as one of the representative images of American family life, claiming that the show provides horrible role models for parents and children. The popularity of the show is often cited as evidence of the decline of family values in the United States. But critics of *The Simpsons* need to take a closer look at the show and view it in the context of television history. For all its slapstick nature and its mocking of certain aspects of family life, *The Simpsons* has an affirmative side and ends up celebrating the nuclear family as an institution. For television, this is no minor achievement. For decades, American television has tended to downplay the importance of the nuclear family and offer various one-parent families or other nontraditional arrangements as alternatives to it. The one-parent situation comedy actually dates back almost to the beginning of network television, at least as early as *My Little Margie* (1952–1955). But the classic one-parent situation comedies, like *The Andy Griffith Show* (1960–1968) or *My Three Sons* (1960–1972), generally found ways to reconstitute the nuclear family in one form or another (often through the presence of an aunt or uncle) and thus still presented it as the norm (sometimes the story line actually moved in the direction of the widower getting remarried, as happened to Steve Douglas, the Fred MacMurray character, in *My Three Sons*).

6 But starting with shows in the 1970s like *Alice* (1976–1985), American television genuinely began to move away from the nuclear family as the norm and suggest that other patterns of child rearing might be equally valid or perhaps even superior. Television in the 1980s and 1990s experimented with all sorts of permutations on the theme of the nonnuclear family, in shows such as *Love, Sidney* (1981–1983), *Punky Brewster* (1984–1986), and *My Two Dads* (1987–1990). This development partly resulted from the standard Hollywood

procedure of generating new series by simply varying successful formulas.[8] But the trend toward nonnuclear families also expressed the ideological bent of Hollywood and its impulse to call traditional family values into question. Above all, though television shows usually traced the absence of one or more parents to deaths in the family, the trend away from the nuclear family obviously reflected the reality of divorce in American life (and especially in Hollywood). Wanting to be progressive, television producers set out to endorse contemporary social trends away from the stable, traditional, nuclear family. With the typical momentum of the entertainment industry, Hollywood eventually took this development to its logical conclusion: the no-parent family. Another popular Fox program, *Party of Five,* now shows a family of children gallantly raising themselves after both their parents were killed in an automobile accident.

Party of Five cleverly conveys a message some television produc- 7
ers evidently think their contemporary audience wants to hear—that children can do quite well without one parent and preferably without both. The children in the audience want to hear this message because it flatters their sense of independence. The parents want to hear this message because it soothes their sense of guilt, either about abandoning their children completely (as sometimes happens in cases of divorce) or just not devoting enough "quality time" to them. Absent or negligent parents can console themselves with the thought that their children really are better off without them, "just like those cool—and incredibly good-looking—kids on *Party of Five.*" In short, for roughly the past two decades, much of American television has been suggesting that the breakdown of the American family does not constitute a social crisis or even a serious problem. In fact, it should be regarded as a form of liberation from an image of the family that may have been good enough for the 1950s but is no longer valid in the 1990s. It is against this historical background that the statement *The Simpsons* has to make about the nuclear family has to be appreciated.

Of course television never completely abandoned the nuclear 8
family, even in the 1980s, as shown by the success of such shows as *All in the Family* (1971–1983), *Family Ties* (1982–1989), and *The Cosby Show* (1984–1992). And when *The Simpsons* debuted as a regular series in 1989, it was by no means unique in its reaffirmation of the value of the nuclear family. Several other shows took the same path in the past decade, reflecting larger social and political trends in society, in particular the reassertion of family values that has by now been adopted as a program by both political parties in the United States. Fox's own *Married with Children* (1987–1998) preceded *The Simpsons* in portraying an amusingly dysfunctional nuclear family. Another interesting portrayal of the nuclear family can be found in ABC's *Home Improvement*

(1991–1999), which tries to recuperate traditional family values and even gender roles within a postmodern television context. But *The Simpsons* is in many respects the most interesting example of this return to the nuclear family. Though it strikes many people as trying to subvert the American family or to undermine its authority, in fact, it reminds us that antiauthoritarianism is itself an American tradition and that family authority has always been problematic in democratic America. What makes *The Simpsons* so interesting is the way it combines traditionalism with antitraditionalism. It continually makes fun of the traditional American family. But it continually offers an enduring image of the nuclear family in the very act of satirizing it. Many of the traditional values of the American family survive this satire, above all the value of the nuclear family itself.

As I have suggested, one can understand this point partly in 9
terms of television history. *The Simpsons* is a hip, postmodern, self-aware show.[9] But its self-awareness focuses on the traditional representation of the American family on television. It therefore presents the paradox of an untraditional show that is deeply rooted in television tradition. *The Simpsons* can be traced back to earlier television cartoons that dealt with families, such as *The Flintstones* or *The Jetsons.* But these cartoons must themselves be traced back to the famous nuclear-family sitcoms of the 1950s: *I Love Lucy, The Adventures of Ozzie and Harriet, Father Knows Best,* and *Leave It to Beaver. The Simpsons* is a postmodern re-creation of the first generation of family sitcoms on television. Looking back on those shows, we easily see the transformations and discontinuities *The Simpsons* has brought about. In *The Simpsons,* father emphatically does not know best. And it clearly is more dangerous to leave it to Bart than to Beaver. Obviously, *The Simpsons* does not offer a simple return to the family shows of the 1950s. But even in the act of re-creation and transformation, the show provides elements of continuity that make *The Simpsons* more traditional than may at first appear.

The Simpsons has indeed found its own odd way to defend the 10
nuclear family. In effect, the show says, "Take the worst-case scenario—the Simpsons—and even that family is better than no family." In fact, the Simpson family is not all that bad. Some people are appalled at the idea of young boys imitating Bart, in particular his disrespect for authority and especially for his teachers. These critics of *The Simpsons* forget that Bart's rebelliousness conforms to a venerable American archetype and that this country was founded on disrespect for authority and an act of rebellion. Bart is an American icon, an updated version of Tom Sawyer and Huck Finn rolled into one. For all his troublemaking—precisely because of his troublemaking—Bart behaves just the way a young boy is supposed to in American mythology, from *Dennis the Menace* comics to the *Our Gang* comedies.[10]

As for the mother and daughter in *The Simpsons,* Marge and Lisa are not bad role models at all. Marge Simpson is very much the devoted mother and housekeeper; she also often displays a feminist streak, particularly in the episode in which she goes off on a jaunt à la *Thelma and Louise.*[11] Indeed, she is very modern in her attempts to combine certain feminist impulses with the traditional role of a mother. Lisa is in many ways the ideal child in contemporary terms. She is an overachiever in school, and as a feminist, a vegetarian, and an environmentalist, she is politically correct across the spectrum. 11

The real issue, then, is Homer. Many people have criticized *The Simpsons* for its portrayal of the father as dumb, uneducated, weak in character, and morally unprincipled. Homer is all those things, but at least he is there. He fulfills the bare minimum of a father: he is present for his wife and above all his children. To be sure, he lacks many of the qualities we would like to see in the ideal father. He is selfish, often putting his own interest above that of his family. As we learn in one of the Halloween episodes, Homer would sell his soul to the devil for a donut (though fortunately it turns out that Marge already owned his soul and therefore it was not Homer's to sell).[12] Homer is undeniably crass, vulgar, and incapable of appreciating the finer things in life. He has a hard time sharing interests with Lisa, except when she develops a remarkable knack for predicting the outcome of pro football games and allows her father to become a big winner in the betting pool at Moe's Tavern.[13] Moreover, Homer gets angry easily and takes his anger out on his children, as his many attempts to strangle Bart attest. 12

In all these respects, Homer fails as a father. But upon reflection, it is surprising to realize how many decent qualities he has. First and foremost, he is attached to his own—he loves his family because it is his. His motto basically is, "My family, right or wrong." This is hardly a philosophic position, but it may well provide the bedrock of the family as an institution, which is why Plato's *Republic* must subvert the power of the family. Homer Simpson is the opposite of a philosopher-king; he is devoted not to what is best but to what is his own. That position has its problems, but it does help explain how the seemingly dysfunctional Simpson family manages to function. 13

For example, Homer is willing to work to support his family, even in the dangerous job of nuclear power plant safety supervisor, a job made all the more dangerous by the fact that he is the one doing it. In the episode in which Lisa comes to want a pony desperately, Homer even takes a second job working for Apu Nahasapeemapetilon at the Kwik-E-Mart to earn the money for the pony's upkeep and nearly kills himself in the process.[14] In such actions, Homer manifests his genuine concern for his family, and as he repeatedly proves, he will defend them if necessary, sometimes at great personal risk. Often, 14

Homer is not effective in such actions, but that makes his devotion to his family in some ways all the more touching. Homer is the distillation of pure fatherhood. Take away all the qualities that make for a genuinely good father—wisdom, compassion, even temper, selflessness—and what you have left is Homer Simpson with his pure, mindless, dogged devotion to his family. That is why for all his stupidity, bigotry, and self-centered quality, we cannot hate Homer. He continually fails at being a good father, but he never gives up trying, and in some basic and important sense that makes him a good father.

The most effective defense of the family in the series comes in the 15
episode in which the Simpsons are actually broken up as a unit.[15] This episode pointedly begins with an image of Marge as a good mother, preparing breakfast and school lunches simultaneously for her children. She even gives Bart and Lisa careful instructions about their sandwiches: "Keep the lettuce separate until 11:30." But after this promising parental beginning, a series of mishaps occurs. Homer and Marge go off to the Mingled Waters Health Spa for a well-deserved afternoon of relaxation. In their haste, they leave their house dirty, especially a pile of unwashed dishes in the kitchen sink. Meanwhile, things are unfortunately not going well for the children at school. Bart has accidentally picked up lice from the monkey of his best friend Milhouse, prompting Principal Skinner to ask, "What kind of parents would permit such a lapse in scalpal hygiene?" The evidence against the Simpson parents mounts when Skinner sends for Bart's sister. With her prescription shoes stolen by her classmates and her feet accordingly covered with mud, Lisa looks like some street urchin straight out of Dickens.

Faced with all this evidence of parental neglect, the horrified 16
principal alerts the Child Welfare Board, who are themselves shocked when they take Bart and Lisa home and explore the premises. The officials completely misinterpret the situation. Confronted by a pile of old newspapers, they assume that Marge is a bad housekeeper, when in fact she had assembled the documents to help Lisa with a history project. Jumping to conclusions, the bureaucrats decide that Marge and Homer are unfit parents and lodge specific charges that the Simpson household is a "squalid hellhole and the toilet paper is hung in improper overhand fashion." The authorities determine that the Simpson children must be given to foster parents. Bart, Lisa, and Maggie are accordingly handed over to the family next door, presided over by the patriarchal Ned Flanders. Throughout the series, the Flanders family serves as the doppelgänger of the Simpsons. Flanders and his brood are in fact the perfect family according to old-style morality and religion. In marked contrast to Bart, the Flanders boys, Rod and Todd, are well behaved and obedient. Above all, the Flanders family is pious,

devoted to activities like Bible reading, and more zealous than even the local Reverend Lovejoy. When Ned offers to play "bombardment" with Bart and Lisa, what he has in mind is bombardment with questions about the Bible. The Flanders family is shocked to learn that their neighbors do not know of the serpent of Rehoboam, not to mention the Well of Zahassadar or the bridal feast of Beth Chadruharazzeb.

Exploring the question of whether the Simpson family really is dysfunctional, the foster parent episode offers two alternatives to it: on one hand, the old-style moral/religious family; on the other, the therapeutic state, what is often now called the nanny state. Who is best able to raise the Simpson children? The civil authorities intervene, claiming that Homer and Marge are unfit as parents. They must be reeducated and are sent off to a "family skills class" based on the premise that experts know better how to raise children. Child rearing is a matter of a certain kind of expertise, which can be taught. This is the modern answer: the family is inadequate as an institution and hence the state must intervene to make it function. At the same time, the episode offers the old-style moral/religious answer: what children need is God-fearing parents in order to make them God-fearing themselves. Indeed, Ned Flanders does everything he can to get Bart and Lisa to reform and behave with the piety of his own children. 17

But the answer the show offers is that the Simpson children are better off with their real parents—not because they are more intelligent or learned in child rearing, and not because they are superior in morality or piety, but simply because Homer and Marge are the people most genuinely attached to Bart, Lisa, and Maggie, since the children are their own offspring. The episode works particularly well to show the horror of the supposedly omniscient and omnicompetent state intruding in every aspect of family life. When Homer desperately tries to call up Bart and Lisa, he hears the official message: "The number you have dialed can no longer be reached from this phone, you negligent monster." 18

At the same time, we see the defects of the old-style religion. The Flanders may be righteous as parents but they are also self-righteous. Mrs. Flanders says, "I don't judge Homer and Marge; that's for a vengeful God to do." Ned's piety is so extreme that he eventually exasperates even Reverend Lovejoy, who at one point asks him, "Have you thought of one of the other major religions? They're all pretty much the same." 19

In the end, Bart, Lisa, and Maggie are joyously reunited with Homer and Marge. Despite charges of being dysfunctional, the Simpson family functions quite well because the children are attached to their parents and the parents are attached to their children. The premise of those who tried to take the Simpson children away is that 20 there is a principle external to the family by which it can be judged dysfunctional, whether the principle of contemporary child-rearing theories or that of the old-style religion. The foster parent episode suggests the contrary—that the family contains its own principle of legitimacy. The family knows best. This episode thus illustrates the strange combination of traditionalism and antitraditionalism in *The Simpsons.* Even as the show rejects the idea of a simple return to the traditional moral/religious idea of the family, it refuses to accept contemporary statist attempts to subvert the family completely and reasserts the enduring value of the family as an institution.

As the importance of Ned Flanders in this episode reminds us, 21
another way in which the show is unusual is that religion plays a significant role in *The Simpsons.* Religion is a regular part of the life of the Simpson family. We often see them going to church, and several episodes revolve around churchgoing, including one in which God even speaks directly to Homer.[16] Moreover, religion is a regular part of life in general in Springfield. In addition to Ned Flanders, the Reverend Lovejoy is featured in several episodes, including one in which no less than Meryl Streep provides the voice for his daughter.[17]

This attention to religion is atypical of American television in the 22
1990s. Indeed, judging by most television programs today, one would never guess that Americans are by and large a religious and even a churchgoing people. Television generally acts as if religion played little or no role in the daily lives of Americans, even though the evidence points to exactly the opposite conclusion. Many reasons have been offered to explain why television generally avoids the subject of religion. Producers are afraid that if they raise religious issues, they will offend orthodox viewers and soon be embroiled in controversy; television executives are particularly worried about having the sponsors of their shows boycotted by powerful religious groups. Moreover, the television community itself is largely secular in its outlook and thus generally uninterested in religious questions. Indeed, much of Hollywood is often outright antireligious, and especially opposed to anything labeled religious fundamentalism (and it tends to label anything to the right of Unitarianism as "religious fundamentalism").

Religion has, however, been making a comeback on television in 23
the past decade, in part because producers have discovered that an audience niche exists for shows like *Touched by an Angel* (1994–).[18] Still, the entertainment community has a hard time understanding what religion really means to the American public, and it especially cannot deal with the idea that religion could be an everyday, normal part of American life. Religious figures in both movies and television tend to be miraculously good and pure or monstrously evil and hypocritical. While there are exceptions to this rule,[19] generally Hollywood reli-

gious figures must be either saints or sinners, either laboring against all odds and all reason for good or religious fanatics, full of bigotry, warped by sexual repression, laboring to destroy innocent lives in one way or another.[20]

But *The Simpsons* accepts religion as a normal part of life in Springfield, USA. If the show makes fun of piety in the person of Ned Flanders, in Homer Simpson it also suggests that one can go to church and not be either a religious fanatic or a saint. One episode devoted to Reverend Lovejoy deals realistically and rather sympathetically with the problem of pastoral burnout.[21] The overburdened minister has just listened to too many problems from his parishioners and has to turn the job over to Marge Simpson as the "listen lady." The treatment of religion in *The Simpsons* is parallel to and connected with its treatment of the family. *The Simpsons* is not proreligion—it is too hip, cynical, and iconoclastic for that. Indeed, on the surface, the show appears to be antireligious, with a good deal of its satire directed against Ned Flanders and other pious characters. But once again, we see the principle at work that when *The Simpsons* satirizes something, it acknowledges its importance. Even when it seems to be ridiculing religion, it recognizes, as few other television shows do, the genuine role that religion plays in American life. 24

It is here that the treatment of the family in *The Simpsons* links up with its treatment of politics. Although the show focuses on the nuclear family, it relates the family to larger institutions in American life, like the church, the school, and even political institutions themselves, like city government. In all these cases, *The Simpsons* satirizes these institutions, making them look laughable and often even hollow. But at the same time, the show acknowledges their importance and especially their importance for the family. Over the past few decades, television has increasingly tended to isolate the family—to show it largely removed from any larger institutional framework or context. This is another trend to which *The Simpsons* runs counter, partly as a result of its being a postmodern re-creation of 1950s sitcoms. Shows like *Father Knows Best* or *Leave It to Beaver* tended to be set in small-town America, with all the intricate web of institutions into which family life was woven. In re-creating this world, even while mocking it, *The Simpsons* cannot help re-creating its ambience and even at times its ethos. 25

Springfield is decidedly an American small town. In several episodes, it is contrasted with Capitol City, a metropolis the Simpsons approach with fear and trepidation. Obviously, the show makes fun of small-town life—it makes fun of everything—but it simultaneously celebrates the virtues of the traditional American small town. One of the principal reasons why the dysfunctional Simpsons family functions as well as it does is that they live in a traditional American small 26 town. The institutions that govern their lives are not remote from them or alien to them. The Simpson children go to a neighborhood school (though they are bussed to it by the ex-hippie driver Otto). Their friends in school are largely the same as their friends in their neighborhood. The Simpsons are not confronted by an elaborate, unapproachable, and uncaring educational bureaucracy. Principal Skinner and Mrs. Krabappel may not be perfect educators, but when Homer and Marge need to talk to them, they are readily accessible. The same is true of the Springfield police force. Chief Wiggum is not a great crime fighter, but he is well known to the citizens of Springfield, as they are to him. The police in Springfield still have neighborhood beats and have even been known to share a donut or two with Homer.

Similarly, politics in Springfield is largely a local matter, includ- 27
ing town meetings in which the citizens of Springfield get to influence decisions on important matters of local concern, such as whether gambling should be legalized or a monorail built. As his Kennedy accent suggests, Mayor Quimby is a demagogue, but at least he is Springfield's own demagogue. When he buys votes, he buys them directly from the citizens of Springfield. If Quimby wants Grandpa Simpson to support a freeway he wishes to build through town, he must name the road after Abe's favorite television character, Matlock. Everywhere one looks in Springfield, one sees a surprising degree of local control and autonomy. The nuclear power plant is a source of pollution and constant danger, but at least it is locally owned by Springfield's own slave-driving industrial tyrant and tycoon, Montgomery Burns, and not by some remote multinational corporation (indeed, in an exception that proves the rule, when the plant is sold to German investors, Burns soon buys it back to restore his ego).[22]

In sum, for all its postmodern hipness, *The Simpsons* is pro- 28
foundly anachronistic in the way it harks back to an earlier age when Americans felt more in contact with their governing institutions and family life was solidly anchored in a larger but still local community. The federal government rarely makes its presence felt in *The Simpsons,* and when it does it generally takes a quirky form like former President Bush moving next door to Homer, an arrangement that does not work out. The long tentacles of the IRS have occasionally crept their way into Springfield, but its stranglehold on America is of course all-pervasive and inescapable.[23] Generally speaking, government is much more likely to take local forms in the show. When sinister forces from the Republican Party conspire to unseat Mayor Quimby by running ex-convict Sideshow Bob against him, it is local sinister forces who do the conspiring, led by Mr. Burns and including Rainer Wolfcastle (the Arnold Schwarzenegger lookalike who plays McBain in the movies) and a Rush Limbaugh lookalike named Burch Barlow.[24]

Here is one respect in which the portrayal of the local community in *The Simpsons* is unrealistic. In Springfield, even the media forces are local. There is of course nothing strange about having a local television station in Springfield. It is perfectly plausible that the Simpsons get their news from a man, Kent Brockman, who actually lives in their midst. It is also quite believable that the kiddie show on Springfield television is local, and that its host, Krusty the Klown, not only lives in town but also is available for local functions like supermarket openings and birthday parties. But what are authentic movie stars like Rainer Wolfcastle doing living in Springfield? And what about the fact that the world-famous *Itchy & Scratchy* cartoons are produced in Springfield? Indeed, the entire *Itchy & Scratchy* empire is apparently headquartered in Springfield. This is not a trivial fact. It means that when Marge campaigns against cartoon violence, she can picket *Itchy & Scratchy* headquarters without leaving her hometown.[25] The citizens of Springfield are fortunate to be able to have a direct impact on the forces that shape their lives and especially their family lives. In short, *The Simpsons* takes the phenomenon that has in fact done more than anything else to subvert the power of the local in American politics and American life in general—namely, the media—and in effect brings it within the orbit of Springfield, thereby placing the force at least partially under local control.[26] 29

The unrealistic portrayal of the media as local helps highlight the overall tendency of *The Simpsons* to present Springfield as a kind of classical polis; it is just about as self-contained and autonomous as a community can be in the modern world. This once again reflects the postmodern nostalgia of *The Simpsons;* with its self-conscious re-creation of the 1950s sitcom, it ends up weirdly celebrating the old ideal of small-town America.[27] Again, I do not mean to deny that the first impulse of *The Simpsons* is to make fun of small-town life. But in that very process, it reminds us of what the old ideal was and what was so attractive about it, above all the fact that average Americans somehow felt in touch with the forces that influenced their lives and maybe even in control of them. In a presentation before the American Society of Newspaper Editors on April 12, 1991 (broadcast on C-SPAN), Matt Groening said that the subtext of *The Simpsons* is "the people in power don't always have your best interests in mind."[28] This is a view of politics that cuts across the normal distinctions between Left and Right and explains why the show can be relatively evenhanded in its treatment of both political parties and has something to offer to both liberals and conservatives. *The Simpsons* is based on distrust of power and especially of power remote from ordinary people. The show celebrates genuine community, a community in which everybody more or less knows everybody else (even if they do not necessarily like each other). 30

By re-creating this older sense of community, the show manages to generate a kind of warmth out of its postmodern coolness, a warmth that is largely responsible for its success with the American public. This view of community may be the most profound comment *The Simpsons* has to make on family life in particular and politics in general in America today. No matter how dysfunctional it may seem, the nuclear family is an institution worth preserving. And the way to preserve it is not by the offices of a distant, supposedly expert, therapeutic state but by restoring its links to a series of local institutions that reflect and foster the same principle that makes the Simpson family itself work—the attachment to one's own, the principle that we best care for something when it belongs to us.

The celebration of the local in *The Simpsons* was confirmed in an 31
episode that aired May 9, 1999, which for once explored in detail the possibility of a utopian alternative to politics as usual in Springfield. The episode begins with Lisa disgusted by a gross-out contest sponsored by a local radio station, which, among other things, results in the burning of a travelling van Gogh exhibition. With the indignation typical of youth, Lisa fires off an angry letter to the Springfield newspaper, charging, "Today our town lost what remained of its fragile civility." Outraged by the cultural limitations of Springfield, Lisa complains, "We have eight malls, but no symphony; thirty-two bars but no alternative theater." Lisa's spirited outburst catches the attention of the local chapter of Mensa, and the few high-IQ citizens of Springfield (including Dr. Hibbert, Principal Skinner, the Comic Book Guy, and Professor Frink) invite her to join the organization (once they have determined that she has brought a pie and not a quiche to their meeting). Inspired by Lisa's courageous speaking out against the cultural parochialism of Springfield, Dr. Hibbert challenges the city's way of life: "Why do we live in a town where the smartest have no power and the stupidest run everything?" Forming "a council of learned citizens," or what reporter Kent Brockman later refers to as an "intellectual junta," the Mensa members set out to create the cartoon equivalent of Plato's *Republic* in Springfield. Naturally, they begin by ousting Mayor Quimby, who in fact leaves town rather abruptly once the little matter of some missing lottery funds comes up.

Taking advantage of an obscure provision in the Springfield 32
charter, the Mensa members step into the power vacuum created by Quimby's sudden abdication. Lisa sees no limit to what the Platonic rule of the wise might accomplish: "With our superior intellects, we could rebuild this city on a foundation of reason and enlightenment; we could turn Springfield into a utopia." Principal Skinner holds out hope for "a new Athens," while another Mensa member thinks in terms of B. F. Skinner's "Walden II." The new rulers immediately set

out to bring their utopia into existence, redesigning traffic patterns and abolishing all sports that involve violence. But in a variant of the dialectic of enlightenment, the abstract rationality and benevolent universalism of the intellectual junta soon prove to be a fraud. The Mensa members begin to disagree among themselves, and it becomes evident that their claim to represent the public interest masks a number of private agendas. At the climax of the episode, the Comic Book Guy comes forward to proclaim, "Inspired by the most logical race in the galaxy, the Vulcans, breeding will be permitted once every seven years; for many of you this will mean much less breeding; for me, much much more." This reference to *Star Trek* appropriately elicits from Groundskeeper Willie a response in his native accent that calls to mind the *Enterprise's* Chief Engineer Scotty: "You cannot do that, sir, you don't have the power." The Mensa regime's self-interested attempt to imitate the *Republic* by regulating breeding in the city is just too much for the ordinary citizens of Springfield to bear.

With the Platonic revolution in Springfield degenerating into 33
petty squabbling and violence, a *deus ex machina* arrives in the form of physicist Stephen Hawking, proclaimed as "the world's smartest man." When Hawking voices his disappointment with the Mensa regime, he ends up in a fight with Principal Skinner. Seizing the opportunity created by the division among the intelligentsia, Homer leads a counterrevolution of the stupid with the rallying cry: "C'mon you idiots, we're taking back this town." Thus, the attempt to bring about a rule of philosopher-kings in Springfield ends ignominiously, leaving Hawking to pronounce its epitaph: "Sometimes the smartest of us can be the most childish." Theory fails when translated into practice in this episode of *The Simpsons* and must be relegated once more to the confines of the contemplative life. The episode ends with Hawking and Homer drinking beer together in Moe's Tavern and discussing Homer's theory of a donut-shaped universe.

The utopia episode offers an epitome of what *The Simpsons* does 34
so well. It can be enjoyed on two levels—as both broad farce and intellectual satire. The episode contains some of the grossest humor in the long history of *The Simpsons* (I have not even mentioned the subplot concerning Homer's encounter with a pornographic photographer). But at the same time, it is filled with subtle cultural allusions; for example, the Mensa members convene in what is obviously a Frank Lloyd Wright prairie house. In the end, then, the utopia episode embodies the strange mixture of intellectualism and anti-intellectualism characteristic of *The Simpsons.* In Lisa's challenge to Springfield, the show calls attention to the cultural limitations of small-town America, but it also reminds us that intellectual disdain for the common man can be carried too far and that theory can all too easily lose touch with

common sense. Ultimately, *The Simpsons* seems to offer a kind of intellectual defense of the common man against intellectuals, which helps explain its popularity and broad appeal. Very few people have found *The Critique of Pure Reason* funny, but in *The Gay Science,* Nietzsche felt that he had put his finger on Kant's joke:

> Kant wanted to prove in a way that would puzzle all the world that all the world was right—that was the private joke of this soul. He wrote against the learned on behalf of the prejudice of the common people, but for the learned and not for the common people.[29]

In Nietzsche's terms, *The Simpsons* goes *The Critique of Pure Reason* one better: it defends the common man against the intellectual but in a way that both the common man and the intellectual can understand and enjoy.

NOTES

1. As reported in Ed Henry's "Heard on the Hill" column in *Roll Call,* 44, no. 81 (May 13, 1999). His source was the *Albany Times-Union.*

2. This essay is a substantial revision of a paper originally delivered at the Annual Meeting of the American Political Science Association in Boston, September 1998. All *Simpsons* episodes are cited by title, number, and original broadcast date, using the information supplied in the invaluable reference work *The Simpsons: A Complete Guide to Our Favorite Family,* ed. Ray Richmond and Antonia Coffman (New York: HarperCollins, 1997). I cite episodes that aired subsequent to the publication of this book simply by broadcast date.

3. The identification is made complete when Quimby says, "Ich bin ein Springfielder" in "Burns Verkaufen der Kraftwerk," #8F09, 12/5/91.

4. "Two Bad Neighbors," #3F09, 1/4/96.

5. For the reluctance to go after Clinton, see the rather tame satire of the 1996 presidential campaign in the "Citizen Kang" segment of the Halloween episode, "Treehouse of Horror VII," #4F02, 10/27/96. Finally in the 1998–1999 season, faced with the mounting scandals in the Clinton administration, the creators of *The Simpsons* decided to take off the kid gloves in their treatment of the president, especially in the February 7, 1999, episode (in which Homer legally changes his name to Max Power). Hustled by Clinton at a party, Marge Simpson is forced to ask, "Are you sure it's a federal law that I have to dance with you?" Reassuring Marge that she is good enough for a man of his stature, Clinton tells her,"Hell, I've done it with pigs—real no foolin' pigs."

6. "The Front," #9616, 4/15/93.

7. An amusing debate developed in the *Wall Street Journal* over the politics of *The Simpsons.* It began with an Op-Ed piece by Benjamin Stein titled "TV Land: From Mao to Dow" (February 5, 1997), in which he argued that the show has no politics. This piece was answered by a letter from John McGrew

given the title "The Simpsons Bash Familiar Values" (March 19, 1997), in which he argued that the show is political and consistently left-wing. On March 12, 1997, letters by Deroy Murdock and H. B. Johnson Jr. argued that the show attacks left-wing targets as well and often supports traditional values. Johnson's conclusion that the show is "politically ambiguous" and thus appeals "to conservatives as well as to liberals" is supported by the evidence of this debate itself.

8. Perhaps the most famous example is the creation of *Green Acres* (1965–1971) by inverting *The Beverly Hillbillies* (1962–1971)—if a family of hicks moving from the country to the city was funny, television executives concluded that a couple of sophisticates moving from the city to the country should be a hit as well. And it was.

9. On the self-reflexive character of *The Simpsons,* see my essay "The Greatest TV Show Ever," *American Enterprise,* 8, no. 5 (September/October 1997), 34–37.

10. Oddly enough, Bart's creator, Matt Groening, has now joined the chorus condemning the Simpson boy. Earlier this year, a wire-service report quoted Groening as saying to those who call Bart a bad role model, "I now have a 7-year-old boy and a 9-year-old boy so all I can say is I apologize. Now I know what you were talking about."

11. "Marge on the Lam," #1F12, 11/4/93.

12. "The Devil and Homer Simpson" in "Treehouse of Horror IV," #1F04, 10/30/93.

13. "Lisa the Greek," #8F12, 1/23/92.

14. "Lisa's Pony," #8F06, 11/7/91.

15. "Home Sweet Homediddly-Dum-Doodily," #3F01, 10/1/95.

16. "Homer the Heretic," #9F01, 10/8/92.

17. "Bart's Girlfriend," #2F04, 11/6/94.

18. I would like to comment on this show, but it is scheduled at the same time as *The Simpsons,* and I have never seen it.

19. Consider, for example, the minister played by Tom Skerritt in Robert Redford's film of Norman Maclean's *A River Runs Through It.*

20. A good example of this stereotyping can be found in the film *Contact,* with its contrasting religious figures played by Matthew McConaughey (good) and Jake Busey (evil).

21. "In Marge We Trust," #4F18, 4/27/97.

22. "Burns Verkaufen der Kraftwerk," #8F09, 12/5/91.

23. See, for example, "Bart the Fink," #3F12, 2/11/96.

24. "Sideshow Bob Roberts," #2F02, 10/9/94.

25. "Itchy & Scratchy & Marge," #7F09, 12/20/90.

26. The episode called "Radioactive Man" (#2517, 9/24/95) provides an amusing reversal of the usual relationship between the big-time media and small-town life. A Hollywood film company comes to Springfield to make a movie featuring the comic book hero, Radioactive Man. The Springfield locals take advantage of the naive moviemakers, raising prices all over town and imposing all sorts of new taxes on the film crew. Forced to return to California penniless, the moviemakers are greeted like small-town heroes by their caring neighbors in the Hollywood community.

27. In his review of *The Simpsons: A Complete Guide to Our Favorite Family,* Michael Dirda aptly characterizes the show as "a wickedly funny yet oddly affectionate satire of American life at the end of the 20th century. Imagine the unholy offspring of *Mad* magazine, Mel Brooks's movies, and 'Our Town.'" See the *Washington Post,* Book World, January 11, 1998, p. 5.

28. Oddly enough, this theme is also at the heart of Fox's other great television series, *The X-Files.*

29. See *Die fröhliche Wissenschaft,* sec. 193 (my translation) in Friedrich Nietzsche, *Sämtliche Werke: Kritische Studienausgabe,* ed. Giorgio Colli and Mazzino Montinari, vol. 3 (Berlin: de Gruyter, 1967–1977), 504.

Examining the Text

1. What points does Cantor make in his discussion about how the nuclear family has been represented in television shows of the past? According to Cantor, how does the portrayal of the nuclear family in *The Simpsons* comment on previous television families? For instance, how is the Simpson family similar to and different from the family as portrayed in *The Cosby Show, Married with Children, I Love Lucy,* and *The Flintstones?*

2. In your own words, explain how *The Simpsons* can both mock and celebrate a group or institution. Why does Cantor see this as an important strategy in *The Simpsons?*

3. What is the effect of Cantor's use of examples drawn from *The Simpsons* in this article? Do you think the examples are included primarily to entertain or to persuade the reader? Do they help establish Cantor's credibility?

4. Based on his discussion of *The Simpsons,* how do you think Cantor defines the term "politics"? What does "politics" include for Cantor? How is his notion of politics different from what we usually think of as politics?

For Group Discussion

Choose any one of the institutions discussed by Cantor in this article, for instance political parties, the family, religion, community groups, or the media. In a group with two or three other students, go over Cantor's points about how *The Simpsons* portrays this institution: for instance, with mockery, praise, nostalgia, rejection, criticism, acceptance, some combination of these approaches, none of the above, or another approach entirely. Then choose another popular television show that comments on the same institution, and compare how the message of this show is similar to and different from that of *The Simpsons.*

Writing Suggestion

This assignment puts on you the onerous burden of watching an episode of *The Simpsons* in order to compare what you see in this

The Simpsons

episode with Cantor's arguments about the "deep politics" of the show. Before you watch the episode, you should make a list of the categories that Cantor discusses, including partisan politics, the nuclear family (and the roles played by each character in the family), religion, the community and local political institutions, the media, and the high culture and pop culture references in the show. Then, with a pen and notebook ready, watch the episode. Try your best to take extensive notes as you watch, writing down bits of dialogue or plot summary in the categories you've listed. When you've finished watching the episode and while it's still fresh in your memory, write down your impressions of how the show dealt with each of the categories that Cantor discusses; depending on the episode, some of the categories may be dealt with extensively and others not at all. Finally, based on your notes, write an essay in which you either support or take issue with Cantor's analysis of *The Simpsons* in one or more of the categories. Be sure to use quotations from Cantor's article as well as descriptions of the episode you watched in order to develop your argument.

The Evolution of the Seven Deadly Sins: From God to the Simpsons

Lisa Frank

Lisa Frank, a writer who lives in Los Angeles, is also a fan of The Simpsons. *However, her approach to the show is quite different from Cantor's discussion in the previous article. Frank's article, originally published in the* Journal of Popular Culture, *uses examples from* The Simpsons *to help prove her point that our attitude towards sinning and sinfulness has changed drastically since the "invention" of the "seven deadly sins." Frank draws on the writings of early Christian theologians, along with Dante, Chaucer, Milton, and Shakespeare, as she describes the characteristics of each of the seven deadly sins: pride, envy, wrath, sloth, greed, lust, and gluttony. She contrasts these quotations with examples drawn from* The Simpsons *and with anecdotes from everyday life in contemporary culture to show how radically our ideas about sin have changed.*

Frank may not be entirely serious—that's up to you to decide—but one of the central claims she makes in her article is that in contemporary society we "accept and embrace" sinfulness, and even find ways to use sinning to our advantage. Thus, rather than shunning and avoiding the seven deadly sins, as Christian doctrine teaches us, we learn from The Simpsons *and from popular culture in general the value and usefulness of sinning.*

As you read, *recall the arguments made by Cantor that* The Simpsons *celebrates the nuclear family, religious belief, and community. How is Frank able to use examples from the very same show to prove a dramatically different point? Is it a question of each author's interpretation of the show, where one author is right and the other wrong? Or does* The Simpsons *invite and support these significantly different interpretations?*

I can personally attest that the seven deadly sins are still very much with us. Today, I have committed each of them, several more than once, before my lunch hour even began. Here is my schedule of sin (judge me if you will): 1

7:00 - I pressed the snooze button three times before dragging myself out of bed. *Sloth.* 2

7:11 - I took an obscenely long, hot shower with no consideration for my sister, with whom I live. (Don't even bother mentioning the ecological implications.) *Greed.* 3

7:52 - I noticed a pool of cat vomit on the floor and chose to ignore it, knowing that my sister would dutifully clean it up. *Sloth.* 4

8:22 - I gave someone the finger after they cut me off in traffic. *Wrath.* 5

8:33 - I helped myself to two complementary pastries at the office meeting (although I had breakfast only an hour before). *Gluttony.* 6

8:42 - I flirted with the guy next to me, ignoring the speaker to whom I was supposed to be listening. *Lust.* 7

10:04 - I ignored someone's incessant knocking on the door of the only restroom in the building where I work in order to spend more time putting on makeup in front of the mirror. *Pride.* 8

10:42 - I lied and told a homeless person that I didn't have any change. *Sloth.* 9

11:02 - I purposely got to class early so that I could take another student's usual seat, which was much better than mine. *Envy.* 10

11:27 - I lied and told someone that I got an A on a paper, when in actuality, I only got a B. *Pride.* 11

11:49 - I took three free movie passes, although the sign said to only take one. *Covetousness.* 12

Relatively speaking, I am an average person who commits an average number of the deadly sins each day, give or take a sin. I am not particularly malicious in my sinning, but it would be untrue to say that they are committed for righteous purposes, either. I am human; therefore, I sin. A lot. As early Christian doctrine repeatedly points out, the seven deadly sins are so deeply rooted in our fallen human nature, that not only are they almost completely unavoidable, but like a proverbial bag of potato chips, we can never seem to limit ourselves to just one. With this ideology, modern society agrees. However, with regard to the individual and social effects of the consequences of these sins, we do not. 13

The deadly sins of seven were identified, revised, and revised again in the heads and classrooms of reportedly celibate monks as moral and philosophical lessons taught in an effort to arm men and women against the temptations of sin and vice in the battle for their souls. These teachings were quickly reflected in the literature, theater, art, and music of that time and throughout the centuries to follow. Today, they remain popular motifs in those media, as well as having made the natural progression into film and television. Every day and every hour, acts of gluttony, lust, covetousness, envy, pride, wrath, and sloth are portrayed on television. Social ethics have shifted dramatically since those early days, as has our regard for the seven deadly sins. With the possible exception of our presidents, we no longer struggle to fight our natural tendency to commit these sins. Instead, we have chosen not only to accept them, but also to embrace them and even to use them to our advantage. 14

THE HISTORY

The seven deadly sins were first discussed as separate entities 15
throughout the scriptures of the Bible. Later, the sins were developed into self-help guides by the early theologians and moralists, as a means to save the souls of their local rubes from the decay of immorality and to teach them some basic manners. They believed that those who were morally and ethically superior (i.e., monks) were happier human beings and, generally, better company. The goal was to teach men and women how to control their behavior, so that their inner virtue would dominate their wrongful tendencies toward sex, wine, and song, therefore guiding them toward the path of magnetic Stepford-like happiness.

Although the seven deadly sins were originally classified as 16
"capital" in the fourth century by some lesser known monastics, it was the final alterations made in the early sixth century by Gregory the Great (who was so great that he was later made a saint), that led society to regard him as the final and true compiler. Gregory was also noted for making two important points: 1) that pride is the root of all sin; and 2) that there is a distinction between the sins of the spirit (pride, envy, wrath, sloth, and greed) and the sins of the flesh (lust and gluttony). However, much to the dismay of his fellow Christians, St. Greg failed to include a top ten list of examples for each or any of the seven deadly sins.

In the thirteenth century, the well known, anally obsessive St. 17
Thomas Aquinas devised the most methodical and concise analysis of sin, virtue, and vice written (that did not, however, include the name Monica Lewinsky) in his three volume series, *Summa Theologiae.* His teachings were then translated from the abstractness of theology into a more accommodating language suited to the common man (much the same service that *Reader's Digest* performs today). By applying his teachings to everyday life situations, Christians were taught practical methods for overcoming temptation. To further the cause, these teachings were then enumerated into classic literature, so they could be casually name dropped at all the VIP, socially-elite cocktail parties of the day (and for centuries to follow). These titles included Dante Alighieri's *The Divine Comedy,* Geoffrey Chaucer's *Canterbury Tales,* and John Milton's *Paradise Lost.*

In modern society, we have accepted our fate as sinning ma- 18
chines. We have taken what the Christians regarded as vices that harmed humanity and turned them into virtues that aid mankind. We have come to understand the power that each of these vices holds and how it can make us happier and stronger people. Advertising agencies and marketing firms know this and have taken full advantage of it,

selling each of the seven deadly sins in record numbers and encouraging us to work with what we've got (while still holding focus groups on the development of sins eight, nine, and ten).

THE SIMPSONS

Since it was created in the late 1980s, *The Simpsons* has continued to parody all facets of American culture with honesty and with humor. From our daily mundane activities to key events in world news, it mirrors our society in a dark and distorted light, usually with great insight, and always in jest. Perhaps the most brilliant aspect of the show is its uncompromising boldness in addressing the various hypocrisies of our culture in a way that no other show has ever dared to do before, including those of the seven deadly sins. And so without further delay, I present... 19

THE SEVEN DEADLY SINS

Pride

> [T]hat first archetype
> Of pride, and paragon of all creation
> Who, of the light impatient, fell unripe.
>
> —*The Divine Comedy*

According to the cloistered Christian monks of long ago, pride is the mother of all capital sin. Not only that, but it is said to prompt each of the other sins, as well as being present in them. Robert Broderick's *The Catholic Encyclopedia* defines pride as the "inordinate desire for honor, recognition, and distinction" (490–91). It is the result of a lack of humility and inevitably develops into a self-love, which becomes sinful when it causes insubordination, especially to God, who like Santa Claus, watches our every move. In the second part of Dante's *The Divine Comedy,* Dante and his guide, Virgil, enter Mount Purgatory and talk with the souls they meet about the sins the souls have committed during their lives. They learn that in order to get to heaven, the souls must first cleanse themselves of their past sins by performing a corresponding penance. The first souls Dante and Virgil meet are those who have committed the sin of pride. In bewilderment, they watch as the souls are taught the evil of their ways by carrying heavy stones on their backs as a means to lessen their spirits. 20

21 In modern society, pride is not just considered a positive trait, but one of absolute necessity. In each aspect of our lives, from our careers to our romantic relationships, we are made to sell ourselves. Pride in our appearance has become increasingly important in modern times. We spend thousands of dollars on clothing, hair products, makeup, plastic surgery, and gym memberships in an effort to improve our image and the probability of being selected as a contestant in the next installment of *Survivor.* In an episode of *The Simpsons* entitled "Simpson and Delilah," our growing fixation with outer appearance is delineated when Homer commits insurance fraud in order to buy a one thousand dollar bottle of miracle hair growth formula. Instead of being punished for his sin of pride, Homer grows a full head of hair, his love life soars, and he lands a promotion.

22 We are also taught to take pride in our endeavors, especially in our regard for sports. In an episode entitled "Lisa On Ice," Bart and Lisa are on opposing teams in a hockey tournament. The spirited Homer tells Marge: "It's your child versus mine! The winner will be showered with praise, the loser will be taunted and booed until my throat is sore." Such pride in mere athletic achievement would surely not have been understood by St. Thomas Aquinas.

Envy

> The infernal serpent; he it was, whose guile
> Stirred up with envy and revenge, deceived
> The mother of mankind.
>
> —*Paradise Lost,* Book I, 34–36

23 In his book, *The Seven Deadly Sins,* Solomon Schimmel defines envy as "the pain we feel when we perceive another individual possessing some object, quality, or status we do not possess" (57). This pain may cause feelings of inadequacy in us, which, in turn, may lead us to wish or even to cause the loss of what is envied. As with wrath, envy not only has the power to fully consume our consciousness, but worse yet, it makes us buy sport utility vehicles when we live in well-paved cities.

24 In Milton's *Paradise Lost,* Satan is a character afflicted with the sin of pride, who refuses to pay homage to God. After leading a rebellion of the angels, he is cast out of heaven by God and is sent down to hell, where he plots his revenge—the temptation of Adam and Eve. In Books I and II, the seven deadly sins are presented individually by seven delegate speakers, each representing the embodiment of their vice. Envy is represented by Satan's Ed McMahon, Beelzebub, who only feels joy in

another's tragedy and feels pain when others are happy. The reader is shown the immorality of Beelzebub's envious nature that motivates him to advise the council to seek revenge against God.

In modern society, we view envy not only as a natural emotion, but also as a tool that helps further us toward self-improvement. Without envy, there would be no competition, and without competition we might lose the motivation to spend our life savings on the Jenny Craig program in an effort to ensure that we always look better than our friends and neighbors. In an episode of *The Simpsons* entitled "Lisa's Rival," Lisa, the token overachiever, becomes envious of a new student, Allison Taylor, who begins to outshine Lisa. At the end of the episode, the guiltridden Lisa apologizes for resorting to unscrupulous, Bart-like tactics in an effort to discredit Allison in a science project competition. However, Allison tells Lisa that if it weren't for their mutual envy and competitiveness, neither of them would have cause to work toward their maximum capacity. Thus, envy is shown to be a device that brings us closer toward achievement and success. 25

Wrath

I was angry with my friend;
I told my wrath, my wrath did end.
I was angry with my foe:
I told it not, my wrath did grow.

And I water'd it in fears,
Night & Morning with my tears;
And I sunned it with smiles,
And with soft deceitful wiles.

—William Blake, "A Poison Tree,"
Selected Poetry and Prose of William Blake (1–8)

Wrath, also referred to as anger, also referred to as my personal favorite emotion, is a milieu of pain and pleasure that arises in our human existence when a person believes he or she has been unjustly wronged. Pain is received in reaction to the wrongful injury and pleasure is taken in the sweet taste of vengeance. Picture this: I go outside to have a much needed meditational moment and a cigarette. First, pain is experienced when my moment is interrupted by the endless, high-pitched screams of the monster children next door, jumping up and down on their inflatable trampoline. Then, pleasure is received when I imagine what might result when I toss my still-burning cigarette over the fence in their direction. 26

27 Moloch, the embodiment of wrath (much like his modern counterpart, Dirty Harry), is the third delegate speaker in *Paradise Lost.* He is persistent in his argument for a large scale war against God's angels in the War in Heaven in Book VI. Later, though, we see the perils of his nature as his wrath diminishes to fear and cowardice as he is stricken by Gabriel's sword.

28 Today, from *Sesame Street* to the *Jerry Springer Show,* we are taught the importance of expressing our anger and are urged to not let it be bottled up inside ourselves, but rather to vent and to express to others exactly what we're feeling. The effects of bottling up one's anger are presented in an episode of *The Simpsons* entitled "Hurricane Neddy," featuring Homer Simpson's neighbor and friendly Christian, Ned Flanders. When Ned's house is demolished in a hurricane and his specialty store for the left-handed is looted, he becomes unable to control his emotions and checks himself into the same mental hospital that he was committed to as a child. After observing Ned, a doctor renders his opinion that Ned's anger stems from the inferior therapy he received as a child, when he was urged to suppress his anger, rather than to express it constructively. Unlike Moloch, Ned could have averted his downfall, had he been taught to vent properly in the first place.

Lust

> But virtue, as it never will be moved,
> Though lewdness court it in a shape of heaven,
> So lust, though to a radiant angel link'd,
> Will sate itself in a celestial bed,
> And prey on garbage.
>
> —*Hamlet,* Act I, Scene V, 54–58

29 Lust was referred to by the uptight celibates of early Christianity as an unnecessary, excessive, and irrational feeling that ultimately leads to the committing of various unmentionable acts (all of which, of course, the monks were forbidden to participate). The Early Christians tried desperately to tame the hideous beasts that they believed their bodies to be, yet these efforts inevitably proved unsuccessful. For ultimately, the beast was always unleashed. Quite simply, they believed mankind is made to honor God with the body and to exercise self control. Should man fail and be spotted in a raincoat at a special showing of *Deep Throat,* he will develop an excessive attachment to the material sexual world and will, eventually, fall down the path of madness.

In the second book of *The Divine Comedy,* the reader is shown the consequences of the sin of lust. In Canto XXV, these sinners are punished by being purged in flames (at a time when being flaming did not involve pink feather boas or an excessive love of musicals). 30

In modern society, we embrace feelings of lust and revel in the energy and excitement it brings to our lives (hopefully over and over again). We all want to feel sexy and we have accepted our nature as condom-carrying, desire machines, who have long since lost control of the lust we feel. In *The Simpsons,* the notion of socially acceptable lust is conveyed in the nonchalant depictions of an affair between the elementary school principal, Seymour Skinner and teacher, Edna Krabapple; the contemplation of extramarital affairs by both Homer and his wife, Marge; and the casual confession of one-night stands that led to bastard children by both town villain, Mr. Burns, and Homer's senior citizen father, Abe. Even though the Christian Right will never confer, lust has come to be regarded as a desirable attribute for people of all ages and social positions. 31

Gluttony

> And by his side rode loathsome Gluttony,
> Deformed creature, on a filthie swyne.
> His belly was up-blowne with luxury,
> And eke with fatness swollen were his eyne;
>
> —*The Faerie Queene,* Book 1, Canto IV, Stanza 21

According to *The Catholic Encyclopedia,* gluttony is "the inordinate longing for or the indulgence in food or drink" (241). So, you see, the pleasure that we seek from scarfing down an entire carton of Ben and Jerry's ice cream or getting wasted at family weddings reflects a weakness of our reason and will and defies God's intention for us. Therefore, it is considered a sin. Allowing our bodies to become unhealthy by the excess of fried chicken and Ding-Dongs is also sinful, since according to Christianity, we are meant to preserve ourselves in order to better serve God (who, by their own account, is ultimately responsible for the creation of fried chicken and Ding-Dongs in the first place). Worse yet, early Christians believed that the pursuit of these pleasures can lead to the committing of other sins, such as lying or stealing in order to fulfill our craving. 32

These notions are conveyed by the pardoner in one of Chaucer's twenty-four short dramatic stories included in the *Canterbury Tales.* These stories, written as separate tales told by separate narrators on a pilgrimage to the Canterbury Cathedral, were meant to entertain and 33 to provide moral lessons, including those of the seven deadly sins, for the fictional men and women en route to Canterbury. It is thus that the Pardoner discourages sins of gluttony by creatively linking food and drink with decay. He says:

> O thou belly! Stinking pod
> Of dung and foul corruption, that canst send
> Thy filthy music forth at either end. (264)

Gluttony may not make us better people (though it may certainly make us bigger people), but nothing makes us happier than food or drink, with the possible exception of sex. In a segment of *The Simpsons* entitled "The Devil and Homer Simpson," Homer demonstrates our inordinate love for food when he sells his soul to the devil for a donut. Our love for drink is equally well presented in the tales of the family Simpson. One of the popular tourist attractions in Springfield, the fictional town where the Simpsons live, is Duff Gardens, which features rides and attractions that "either promote alcohol consumption or simulate inebriation" (Groening 23). 34

Covetousness

> the nature of man, which coveth divination, thinks it no peril to foretell that which indeed they do but collect.
>
> —Bacon 780, XXXV

Covetousness, a.k.a. avarice or greed (which makes it sound bad), is referred to in *The Catholic Encyclopedia* as "the inordinate love of temporal or earthly things" (59). It is a perversion of right values of when we fail to recognize that we really don't need yet another Ginsu knife in our collection, but, nonetheless, we still find ourselves maxing out our credit cards in order to buy it. 35

In Chaucer's *The Pardoner's Tale,* the sin of covetousness is depicted in the portrayal of three greedy gamblers who swear eternal friendship to one another in God's name. We are shown the evil that greed leads to after they lie, cheat, and kill one another for a measly pot of tattered gold. 36

It may well be argued that coveting is the one thing all of mankind does well. Let's face it, we're a culture of coveting whores. We are all so proud of our vast CD collections, our matching shoes and sweaters, our tattoos, and our wide-screen TVs. In *The Simpsons,* our tendency to covet is parodied in their elaborate array of specialty stores in Springfield, including All Creatures Great and Cheap (spe- 37 cializing in freeze-dried pets that come to life when watered), and Corpulent Cowboy (for the plus-sized cowboy enthusiast).

In an episode appropriately entitled "Bart Gets Hit By a Car," the current societal trend of filing frivolous lawsuits is depicted perfectly. After Bart is hit by Mr. Burns' car, Homer takes advantage of the situation and sues Mr. Burns for a million dollars, although Bart remains virtually unscathed. Such ludicrous greed can only surely be laughed at... or so, we can only hope. 38

Sloth

If something's hard to do, then it's not worth doing.

—Homer Simpson, *The Simpsons,* "The Otto Show"

The Maryknoll Catholic Dictionary refers to sloth as "the disinclination to spiritual action" that "leads to tepidity in keeping God's law, the desire for that which is forbidden, faint-heartedness and despair of salvation" (538). Translation—sloth equals laziness. St. Thomas Aquinas, who apparently never had a lover to spend Sunday mornings in bed with, argued that because it is our duty to serve God, a refusal to do so is a sinful denial of the purpose of our existence. In canto XVIII of Dante's *Purgatory,* the reader is presented with the ultimate fate of those who commit sins of sloth. The sinners on Mount Purgatory are absolved of their sins by running swiftly up the mountain and proclaiming expressions of zeal (much like high school cheerleaders do today). 39

In modern society, mankind's tendency to move toward the realm of sloth is most notably present in the creation of the almighty remote control. Without our natural inclination toward sloth, we would actually have to get ourselves up from the couch or risk watching the fifteenth episode of *The Brady Bunch* marathon. If we weren't slothful, cars, fax machines, and Prozac might never have been invented. Then, where would we be? We would actually be forced to walk the two blocks to our local McDonald's, to talk with one another face to face (oh my God, the anxiety that brings us), and to deal with our emotions on our own. 40

In *The Simpsons,* our social indifference for the ill effects of sloth is most strongly parodied in Homer, who holds the record as the employee who has worked the most years in an entry-level position at the plant where he works. In an episode entitled "The PTA Disbands," he says to Lisa: "If you don't like your job you don't strike. You just go in every day and do it really half-assed. That's the American way." Perhaps the best example of Homer's weakness toward sloth is in an 41 episode entitled "King-Sized Homer," where, in order to avoid working, he decides to boost his weight up to 300 pounds so that he will be eligible for disability. Who knows? If disability were around when St. Thomas Aquinas was alive, maybe he would have been tempted, too.

Human nature hasn't changed much since the first century and thank- 42
fully, the seven deadly sins are still very much alive and well today, providing endless material for contemporary writers and artists. The only difference is that now we work with our vices instead of against them, not only accepting them as the core of who we are and what is natural within us, but also as a measure of what we're capable of. It's a way of coming full circle, if you will, in mankind's understanding of sin. In time, as social ethics continue to evolve, the notion of the seven deadly sins may ultimately surrender to being a mere relic of the past. Consequently, it will be interesting to see how the artistic and fictional depictions of pride, envy, wrath, lust, covetousness, gluttony, and sloth will, then, further evolve. Stay tuned.

NOTE

With kind thanks to Sharon DeLyser, Tracy Dillon, Ph.D., and Aliza Earnshaw.

WORKS CITED

Alighieri, Dante. *The Divine Comedy.* Trans. Jefferson Butler Fletcher. New York: Columbia UP, 1931.

Bacon, Francis. *The Philosophical Works of Francis Bacon.* Trans. Ellis and Spedding. Ed. John M. Robertson. London: George Rutledge and Sons, LTD, 1905.

"Bart Gets Hit By a Car." *The Simpsons.* Fox TV. 10 Jan. 1991.

Blake, William. *Selected Poetry and Prose of William Blake.* Ed. Northrop Frye. New York: Random House, 1953.

Broderick, Robert. *The Catholic Encyclopedia.* Nashville: Thomas Nelson Inc., 1976.

Chaucer, Geoffrey. "The Pardoner's Tale." *The Canterbury Tales.* Ed. Edwin Johnston Howard and Gordon Donley Wilson. New York: Prentice-Hall, Inc., 1947.

"The Devil and Homer Simpson: Treehouse of Horror IV." *The Simpsons.* Fox TV. 30 Oct. 1995.

Groening, Matt. *Are We There Yet: The Simpson's Guide to Springfield.* New York: HarperCollins, 1998.

"Hurricane Neddy." *The Simpsons.* Fox TV. 29 Dec. 1996.
"King-Sized Homer." *The Simpsons.* Fox TV. 5 Nov. 1995.
"Lisa On Ice." *The Simpsons.* Fox TV. 13 Nov. 1994.
"Lisa's Rival." *The Simpsons.* Fox TV. 11 Sept. 1994.
Milton, John. *Paradise Lost.* Ed. Scott Elledge. New York: W.W. Norton & Company, 1975.
"The Otto Show." *The Simpsons.* Fox TV. 23 Apr. 1992.
"The PTA Disbands." *The Simpsons.* Fox TV. 16 Apr. 1995.
Schimmel, Solomon. *The Seven Deadly Sins.* New York: Free Press, 1992.
Shakespeare, William. *The Complete Works of William Shakespeare.* Ed. David Bevington. 3rd ed. Glenview: Scott, Foresman and Company, 1980.
"Simpson and Delilah." *The Simpsons.* Fox TV. 18 Oct. 1990.
"Sloth." *The Maryknoll Catholic Dictionary.* Ed. Albert J. Nevins. New York: Grosset and Dunlap, 1965
Spenser, Edmund. *The Faerie Queene.* Ed. J. C. Smith. Oxford: Clarendon Press, 1909.

Examining the Text

1. Why do you think the article begins as it does, with a list of the sins that Frank has ostensibly committed on a given morning? What effect does this opening have on you as a reader? In what ways does it signal the tone and approach of the rest of the article?

2. In what ways does *The Simpsons* serve as evidence for Frank's argument? What function does the description of episodes from this show serve in her article?

3. Why do you think Frank includes quotations from *Paradise Lost, The Divine Comedy, Hamlet,* and other classic works of literature?

4. How would you describe the tone of Frank's article? What specific words, phrases, and sentences convey that tone? In what ways does Frank's tone contribute to (or detract from) the argument she presents?

For Group Discussion

Frank argues that nowadays "we have chosen not only to accept [the seven deadly sins], but also to embrace them and even to use them to our advantage." In your groups, discuss whether you think Frank is serious about this statement and other similar statements she makes in the article. Do you think that she truly thinks we now "work with our vices instead of against them, not only accepting them as the core of who we are and what is natural within us, but also as a measure of what we're capable of"? What evidence can you point to in the article that might indicate Frank is being sincere in making these statements?

What evidence is there in the article that might cause you to question her sincerity? If you decide that you think Frank is being sarcastic or ironic and doesn't really believe that nowadays we accept and embrace sin, why do you think she would focus her article on this argument?

Writing Suggestion

Write an essay in which you compare and contrast the article by Frank and the previous article by Cantor. As you develop your comparison, consider the following questions: How does each author deal with the issue of religion in the context of "The Simpsons" and popular culture in general? How does each author use evidence to support his or her assertions? What kind of evidence is used? How is evidence from "The Simpsons" used differently in each article? How does the tone of the author differ in each article? In what ways are the articles organized differently? You might conclude your comparison with an explanation of which article you found more persuasive.

ADDITIONAL SUGGESTIONS FOR WRITING ABOUT TELEVISION

1. This chapter includes two essays about reality television shows. Choose another genre (such as game shows, situation comedies, detective shows, cartoons, talk shows, soap operas, or live police dramas) and analyze the underlying presuppositions of this genre. What specific beliefs, actions, and relationships do these shows encourage? How and why do these shows appeal to the audience? If everything that you knew were based on your exposure to this genre of show, what kind of world would you expect to encounter, how would you expect people to behave toward each other, and what sort of values would you expect them to have? To support your analysis of the genre, use examples from specific shows, but keep in mind that your essay should address the genre or category of shows in general.

2. According to sociologists and psychologists, human beings are driven by certain basic needs and desires. Most of the essays in this chapter attempt to account for the powerful appeal of television in our culture, and several suggest that we rely on television to fulfill needs that aren't met elsewhere. Consider some of the following basic needs and desires that television might satisfy for you or for the broader viewing public:

to be amused
to gain information about the world

to have shared experiences
to find models to imitate
to see authority figures exalted or deflated
to experience, in a controlled and guilt-free situation, extreme emotions
to see order imposed on the world
to reinforce our belief in justice
to experience thrilling or frightening situations
to believe in romantic love
to believe in magic, the marvelous and the miraculous
to avoid the harsh realities of life
to see others make mistakes

Referring to items on this list, or formulating your own list of needs and desires, compose an essay in which you argue that television succeeds or fails in meeting our basic needs and desires. Use specific television programs that you're familiar with as concrete evidence for your assertions.

3. As the two articles on *The Simpsons* indicate, it's possible for people to interpret the messages of a television show in radically different ways. Choose a show that you're familiar with and about which you think there can be multiple interpretations. You might think about older shows, such as *The X-Files* or *Star Trek,* or more recent shows, such as *South Park* or *The Sopranos.* You might want to watch a few episodes of the show (all of the ones mentioned above have past episodes available on video and DVD) just to remind yourself of the characters, setting, typical plot structure, and other details. Then write an essay in which your thesis states two (or more) possible interpretations of the show. In the body of the essay, explain what details of the show support each of these interpretations. You might conclude the essay by stating which interpretation you find most persuasive.

Internet Activities

1. Game shows have long been a popular television genre, and their popularity of late seems to be on the rise. One reason may be found in their similarity to reality TV shows, in that they allow for a degree of audience interactivity that scripted shows like dramas and comedies lack; after all, viewers can become participants on game shows and gain instant celebrity if they do well. Game shows also seem to appeal to our greed (or our desire to get rich quickly and without too much work) as well as to our competitive nature. In preparation for writing an essay on game shows, recall some of the ones that you've seen on TV, and check the *Common Culture* Web site for links to sites related to game shows. Then, write an essay in which you analyze the reasons why this television genre is appealing to viewers. As part of your essay, you might decide to compare and contrast game shows to reality television shows to determine the relative appeal of these two genres.

2. Although it's difficult to predict developments having to do with the Internet, a possibility discussed by experts such as John Kelly is that television and the World Wide Web will, in some way, merge. Perhaps your TV screen will become your computer monitor, or you'll be able to order movies and view television shows through your computer and Internet connection. Already we see some early connections between the two media, for instance in the live Web casts that some TV shows are doing, or in exclusive Web casts (that is, programs or videos that are shown only on the Web and not on TV). In addition, most news and sports shows have companion Web sites that offer viewers additional information, pictures, interviews, etc. Consider some of these developments, discussed in further detail at the links provided at the *Common Culture* Web site. Then, write an essay in which you discuss the ways in which the Web competes with or complements television. Do the two media provide the same kind of information and entertainment, or do they offer fundamentally different viewing experiences?

Reading Images

The image at the bottom of page CI-2 is a still photograph of Nam June Paik's video installation art work, entitled "TV Buddha Reincarnated." Paik is a well-known Korean-American artist whose works incorporate television, video, and other technologies in thought-provoking and aesthetically interesting ways. (If you're intrigued by "TV Buddha Reincarnated," you can find out more information about Paik and view some of his other work at the Artcyclopedia Web site [*http://www.artcyclopedia.com/artists/paik_nam_june.html*].)

The title of this piece—"TV Buddha Reincarnated"—refers to an earlier and simpler work by Paik, entitled "TV Buddha." In "TV Buddha," Paik positioned a statue of the Buddha looking at a television set; on top of the television set was a video camera, trained on the statue of the Buddha. In essence, the Buddha statue was "watching" himself (or itself) on television.

As you can see, "TV Buddha Reincarnated" incorporates more technologies than the earlier piece: there's a video camera, but also a telephone and a computer. The statue of the Buddha has been refashioned as well, with what appears to be an interior of wires, circuit boards, and batteries.

Begin an analytical essay about this image by first describing it as clearly and in as much detail as possible. Consider issues of perspective, color, positioning, shapes, sizes, and focal point. Next, identify what you see as the three or four most significant components of the work, whether it's the use of the Buddha statue as part of this piece (with the meditational and religious overtones that the statue conveys), the Buddha's high-tech (but seemingly antique) interior, the telephone, the video camera, the computer (replacing the television from the earlier "TV Buddha" piece), or some other component. In separate paragraphs, offer an interpretation of each of these components, attempting to explain what meaning they add to the work. Keep in mind that although what you see in this textbook is a photograph, "TV Buddha Reincarnated" was an installation piece (with the video camera turned on and recording). People viewing the work could walk around it and see it from different angles. You might want to comment on how this interactive viewing experience could change the meaning of different components of the work.

Finally, draw your analysis together in a statement that articulates what you see as the message of "TV Buddha Reincarnated." What story does this art work tell? What point do you think Paik is trying to convey through this piece? In your conclusion, draw on any of the readings in the "Television" chapter that are relevant to your analysis.

4

Popular Music

A naked man, arms outstretched suggestive of Christ on the cross or an Olympian swimmer about to take the plunge, stands atop a cassette deck. Electric pulses from the tape player reach his brain through headphones as he gazes heavenward as if in a trance. The phrase "Be the music" scrolls about his midsection, concealing—perhaps replacing—his maleness, as the music fills his every cell. Such is the power music has over us, this TDK ad suggests, that it can take us over completely—mentally, physically, emotionally.

By virtue of its sheer volume, rhythm, and encompassing presentation, music has the capacity to take us to "completely different" psychic spaces. It can lift us from our ordinary sense of reality and profoundly affect our moods, emotions, energy level, and even our level of sexual arousal. Furthermore, the lyrics, when combined with these powerful aural appeals, become all the more potent and suggestive, influencing our feelings of isolation or belonging, our relation to parents and friends, our attitudes toward authority figures, our notions about romance, and our views about gender and race.

The articles in this chapter discuss the ways in which people are "constructed" by what they hear—that is, how their beliefs, values, attitudes, and morals are shaped by the music they listen to. Some observers see this phenomenon as potentially dangerous, since it encourages people—especially young people—to transgress the boundaries imposed by civilized society. However, other critics contend that popular music plays a very positive role in contemporary society, since it allows people to voice feelings and ideas that would otherwise not be widely heard. This is especially the case with rap and hip-hop music, as several writers in the second section of this chapter observe. Originally created by and intended for young, African American inner-city audiences, this music has gained more widespread acceptance, to the point that it appears regularly on MTV and has been adopted by major recording labels, thus giving previously disenfranchised urban youth a more pervasive presence in the popular culture.

As you read these essays, perhaps hooked up to your Walkman and blasting the latest Oasis, J-Lo., Sarah McLachlan, Chemical Brothers, or Tupac posthumous release, you might consider the implications of music in your life: the reasons why you listen to certain kinds of music, the messages embodied in their lyrics and rhythm, and the pleasures and possible dangers inherent in letting popular music move you to a "completely different" frame of mind.

Stars and Fans: Constructions of Culture and Counter-culture

I'm Just a Louisiana Girl: The Southern World of Britney Spears

Gavin James Campbell

In this article, author Gavin James Campbell textually and physically visits the geographical home of pop star Britney Spears to draw some conclusions about the way in which the media's fascination with Britney reflects—and perhaps constructs—viewers' and listeners' attitudes toward race and sexuality. Campbell asserts that Britney's "southernness" is in many ways central to her popularity as a contemporary media icon, and he actually visits her hometown of Kentwood, Louisiana, to explore some of the ways in which her geographic roots hint at broader cultural meaning.

Along with discussing race relations in light of Britney Spears's stardom, Campbell builds another central theses into this piece: namely, that Britney Spears—and/or the media moguls who manufacture and market Britney as a consumable product—is very skillful at manipulating a national fascination with white femininity. ***As you read*** *this essay, take special care to examine whether the author convinces the reader that this fascination with white femininity exists, and how he connects the unique features of southern America to that phenomenon.*

Right now Britney Spears is the most popular southerner in the world. 1
She has enjoyed chart success like almost no other artist from this most fertile of musical regions: her first album went twelve times platinum, and her second release sold 1.3 million copies during its first week. By now it's gone nine times platinum, and it stayed on the Billboard charts for more than forty weeks. The Louisiana native has appeared in concerts from England to Japan; her second album topped the charts in the United States, Canada, Japan, Germany, Austria, Switzerland, the Netherlands, France, Greece, Belgium, Sweden, and Norway; and her face has charmed us at grocery story check-outs on the covers of *Elle, Cosmopolitan, People and Teen People, YM, Glamour, Forbes, GQ, TV Guide, Us Weekly, Rolling Stone, Allure,* and innumerable teen magazines. She appeared in the 2001 Super Bowl halftime show, cohosted

the 2001 American Music Awards, had her own television special from Hawaii, and last year made over $200 million. According to one survey of the Web's most used portals, her name was typed in more than 133 million times, making her the most searched-for celebrity on the Internet. Whether we like her music or not, any figure who can inspire criticism spanning from semi-literate rages, like "britney is a fat ugly puke!" to high-toned discourse, like "feminist and Lacanian theory allows us to see [Britney's] entrance into the Symbolic and the problems thereof," demands our attention. There's no escaping this daughter of Dixie.

Skeptics might doubt her claims to the region. After all, she lived part of her life in Orlando and, even more damning, spent some formative years in New York City. Yet both Britney's fans and detractors assume she's met the residency requirement. "I'm convinced she's an inbred hick," writes one Britney-hater on an Internet chat site, while another declares, "Well, what can you expect from her parents? (in a southern Hick accent) 'Gosh golly, ma dawters so a purrrty (Isa bees fangkin' cousin Henry for the inbred genes)...Hyuk Hyuk! *snort*!' " "Britney Spears," writes one who intends to succinctly dismiss the whole matter, "herself is from Louisiana, she is a hillbilly." 2

Admirers swiftly counter such criticisms with an equally powerful southern icon: "i'm glad to see," one male writes gallantly, "that some people still see her as the angelic, southern belle she is." The popular biographies aimed at her fans join the chorus, paying homage to what one calls Britney's "sweet Southern Miss" image. Britney herself pledges fealty to her southern heritage by telling the world "I'm just a Louisiana girl" and by liberally sprinkling her autobiography with "y'all." Thus, for those who post on the innumerable Britney Spears message boards, for the authors of popular biographies, and for Britney herself, the South is a central part of understanding just what the Britney Spears phenomenon is about. We cannot fully appreciate her hold on American popular culture without acknowledging her skill at playing upon a national fascination with southern white femininity. 3

A native of Kentwood, Louisiana, Britney Spears was born on December 2, 1981. Her hometown, which sits in Tangipahoa Parish clutching the Mississippi border, boasts roughly 2,500 residents. Britney began performing as a very young girl, winning an appearance on "Star Search" in 1990, appearing off-Broadway in 1991, and snagging the Miss Talent, USA crown in 1992. The following year she began a two-year stint on the newly revived "Mickey Mouse Club." When the Disney Channel canceled the show, she returned to Kentwood anticipating living like other teenagers. Bitten by the show-biz bug, however, she remembers that she "wasn't happy just hanging around at 4

Britney Spears

home. I wanted to see the world and make music and do all these wonderful things?" She returned to New York City and swiftly landed a recording contract in 1996 with Jive records. Her first album and first single—"Baby One More Time"—stunned the music world by becoming the first album-single combination to both reach number one in their first week of release.

Britney's story is a familiar one in American popular myth. "I'm 5
living proof," she declares, "that you can succeed, no matter where you're from or how little you have." The American Dream is most satisfying when the hero grows up in straightened circumstances, busting out from somewhere constraining, from somewhere good enough to nurture them but too small to contain their genius. For Britney, that confinement is the South. On the surface, Britney's Kentwood comes across as a rural idyll filled with simple, decent, slow-paced "friendly southern folk who speak with a soft twang." They work hard, fear God, and love their country. "Here apple pie is actually baked fresh in the A.M., and left out to cool by an open window," declares one bio. What's more, "there's no smog, no dirty garbage, no barking horns from frustrated drivers—just a mellow sort of bliss." Another chatty book calls Kentwood "a seriously small town that specializes in Berry Festivals and beauty pageants," while a third says it was "the kind of

town where everyone knows everyone, and they greet you with a hearty 'Hi, y'all' when you walk through the door." Yet for all its charms, Kentwood serves in her story as a brake on her career, providing her moral grounding, but also hard economic times and narrow perspectives. To get a better sense of her background, one Louisiana journalist writes, "think of the most rural, antiquated, poor, Southern town imaginable." Other writers describe skeptical, small-town residents clucking over the derring-do of Britney and her mother as they trundled off to the Big Apple in a bid for stardom. "New York City? What a completely crazy idea!" In spite of their strengths, Kentwoodians must play the provincial stick-in-the-muds. Britney's South, then, is a kind of talent hot-house. It provides the loam in which talent grows, but at some point that talent must be transplanted or it will wither, uncultivated.

Britney's is also a South noticeably devoid of black folks. According to the 1990 census, 44 percent of her hometown's citizens are African American. Yet in a "town where everyone knows everyone," not a single one of those black residents appears in Britney's official story. While each book recounts her one year of high school at Parklane Academy, which compelled her to drive more than thirty miles to McComb, Mississippi, none mentions that a public high school sits within blocks of her house. Parklane was founded in 1970 by, according to its website, "interested and concerned parents for a quality Christian education." It, along with a half-dozen other local private academies, was also founded the same school year that Kentwood High desegregated. And while each account of Britney's life rapturously relives her triumph at the Kentwood Dairy Festival, none mentions that no black girl has ever won, or has even been nominated to compete. Even the labels attached to her—"sweet Southern Miss," "down home country-girl," "Southern belle" are terms reserved almost exclusively in the popular imagination for whites. 6

Her small-town southern background and the presumed absence of blacks in Kentwood are two powerful means by which Britney projects an overwhelming aura of whiteness. Such an image is also constantly reaffirmed by her enthusiastic embrace of gender conventions, which, though cross-racial in practice, are often exclusively associated with white southern women. "I lived like a normal southern girl," she tells us, which means she attended dance and gymnastics lessons, performed at church, and entered beauty pageants and talent shows. Her mother, Lynne, encouraged her daughter's forays into white femininity, driving her all over the Deep South for lessons and competitions. "Mama and I can be such girls together," Britney writes. Both enjoy "colors that pop and shopping till you drop." Growing up poor in a town with no mall was offset, Lynne writes, by Britney's "genius at 7 shopping the sale racks and discount stores and putting together fabulous outfits that looked like a million bucks but cost less than $20!" Though Britney and Lynne decry vain attention to outward appearances, both nevertheless cultivate their good looks through fashion and exercise. "At home in Kentwood," Britney tells us confidentially, "I would never leave the house unless my hair was just right," while her mother "never missed a single day at the gym." Through it all, however, Britney cloaks her eye-catching wardrobe and shapely looks in a becoming modesty, and in a small-town girl's sweet and reassuring faith in God. "I keep a prayer journal and I write in it every night," she explains. "It has Scriptures in it, and you kind of add your own thoughts and feelings—just a few words you want to jot down." Shopping, looking pretty, and trusting God, Britney eagerly upholds standard gender conventions. Being at the same time "a sweet, softspoken Southern belle" forcefully identifies those conventions with her whiteness.

Britney's whiteness is perhaps nowhere more evident than in the 8
virulent criticism she's received for making her act more sexually provocative. In American culture black female entertainers rarely receive such condemnation, though many, like the trio comprising the R&B group Destiny's Child or (the remade) Toni Braxton are at least equally brazen, while others, like the rapper Lil' Kim, are far more sexually graphic than Britney. Black female sexuality is assumed and often exploited with little comment, for without its opposite in black lasciviousness, white female purity would lose much of its talismanic power. Britney fooled us, however. She used her image as a "sweet Southern Miss" to make us think she was the latest icon of pure, white womanhood. "I kinda want to be categorized as someone who's yeah, pure...and just really sweet," she told the press. The controversial stage outfits, she reassured us, "were the kind of clothes we used to wear in Kentwood (it can be scorching during the summer, so the barer the better!)." Such comments, along with her pledge that she's a virgin and wishes to stay that way until marriage, are called into question by her increasingly blatant stage costumes and video imagery. Dressing as a naughty-but-nice schoolgirl in her first video was edgy, but being mocked by the emcee Marlon Wayans at the MTV Music Video Awards as having "gone from the Mickey Mouse Club to the strip club" is something entirely different. As she gets older and attempts to entice new audiences, she dishonors the code of young white womanhood that has earned her such widespread adulation to begin with.

The response is a round of bitter criticism that focuses obses- 9
sively on her sexuality. Internet message boards often overflow with such vituperative comments as "Shes [a] slutty bitch and will always

be one no matter what Tell your friend brittany that i hate here and that shes a slutt!!" Other folks invent derisive nicknames like "Slutney Spears," "Whorney Spears," "Backseat Spears," and "Buttslut Britney." She (or, more accurately, her breasts) received intense scrutiny after rampant speculation that a hospital stay ostensibly for recuperating from a dancing injury turned into a secret breast implant mission. Nor have Web-savvy ministers let Britney pass unnoticed, warning self-styled Christian parents who thought Britney's school-girl sweetness was a pleasing contrast to other music available to their children. "Britney, who often parades her Baptist faith," one minister writes, "somehow must have missed I Timothy 2:9: 'In like manner also, that women adorn themselves in MODEST APPAREL, with shamefacedness and sobriety.'" Britney is a moral viper, he continues. "If you think these 'bubblegum-fluffy-love-songs' are clean, sweet, innocent 'puppy-love' tunes—you obviously haven't listened closely to what's penetrating your young daughter or son's impressionable, naive, mind." That these criticisms revolve almost exclusively around her sexuality can only be partly blamed on Britney's own decision to exploit her good looks. More often, they reveal an underlying discomfort with young white women using the social and sexual power American society grants them on the promise that it will remain dormant. Being a white girl is thus at the core of how Britney Spears is understood. That she's a southern white girl merely reinforces the obvious, and makes her betrayal of its code all the more devastating. As one frustrated young girl wrote on an internet chat, because Britney had gotten breast implants, "she AIN'T no innocent southern girl!!!! WHATEVER!!! She's a fake ass talentless bitch who doesn't deserve any kind of respect."

Clearly, being a white southerner is critical to Britney's image. 10
Yet I was curious about how the Kentwood, Louisiana, that she grew up in compared with the public's perception. Were there in fact apple pies cooling in windows and "no dirty garbage," or was it characterized by a string of words like "backwoods, podunk, redneck, depressing, church, pickup truck," slung together by less charitable observers? And what of the town's history and race relations might have shaped a young white girl growing up there? In short, I wanted to see Kentwood for myself.

In Mississippi I got off the interstate and began driving south 11
down Highway 51. I struggled hard to see the Magnolia State for what it was, not for the romantic notions so lovingly groomed by blues aficionados. For every "Sister Sophia Spiritual Advisor" roadside sign in Hazlehurst there were a dozen chain store burger-joints and at least that many BP gas stations. (I must confess that the exact same "Please do not put paper in the toilet" notices with the hand-written appended

message "God loves you" in the urinals at two different gas stations were more than I could ignore.) Nevertheless I found myself periodically looking for weary old black men toting battered guitars and looking for rides from the devil. I saw none. Though the ghosts of the great Mississippi bluesmen may haunt the state, it's Britney Spears territory now. "Oops...I Did it Again" snaking out of the speakers at the Osyka Exxon confirmed that.

On Highway 51 southbound the first sign of Britney's hometown 12
is the Kentwood Chip Mill. It's a reminder of the area's New South salvation, when logging cleared the piney woods and offered economic hope to down-and-out farmers. It was then only the latest in a series of attempts to wrest a living from the clay-clogged soil of northeastern Louisiana.

Though now in Tangipahoa Parish, the early settlements of 13
Kent's Mill and Beechwood that eventually formed Kentwood lay originally on St. Helena Parish's western border. Much like their neighbors in other parishes, St. Helena's white pioneers built their fortunes on land and slaves. Between 1820 and the Civil War the parish's slave population skyrocketed so that by 1860 slaves outnumbered whites. As the number of slaves increased, so, too, did the value of the land they worked: in the decade before emancipation, slave labor helped inflate the average aggregate cash value of the parish's farms by over $1 million. Cultivating rice, sugar cane, cotton, peas, potatoes, corn, and tending enormous herds of sheep, pigs, and other livestock, African Americans proved critical to the region's economic success.

The Civil War, of course, represented a fundamental threat to the 14
source of that wealth. In response, southern white men by the thousands streamed through the countryside on their way to the recruiting and training station at Camp Moore, just a few miles south of present-day Kentwood. They returned to find freedmen instead of slaves, and both white and black farmers worked to rebuild their lives in a new parish called Tangipahoa. The soil was not well-suited to cotton, but it did support enormous long-leaf pine forests, and beginning in the late nineteenth century the region engaged in lumbering on a massive scale. Farmers replaced pine trees with milch cows, spawning a dairy industry that continues today. The Illinois Central railroad's arrival not only helped find markets for lumber and dairy products, it also provided an anchor for the small assemblage of buildings in nascent Kentwood. The town's name was chosen in 1893 to honor Amos Kent, an early pioneer—and a Yankee from New Hampshire—who had moved to the area as a teenager. Soon Mr. Kent's town boasted a brick factory that turned out over 7 million bricks a year, a "Collegiate Institute," several sawmills, a box factory, and numerous other businesses, churches, and social clubs. Between 1888 and 1900 the town's popula-

tion almost tripled, though the surrounding countryside remained steadfastly rural. Although poverty rained indiscriminate of race, often its harshest consequences were reserved for African Americans. Not surprisingly, opportunities for economic and intellectual advancement lay in the hands of whites content to maintain the status quo. In 1920, for instance, around 6 percent of the parish's whites over ten years old were illiterate, while the figure for blacks was over 30 percent. Though the numbers continued to dwindle through the decades, blacks consistently lagged behind.

The era of New South prosperity that fueled Kentwood's initial growth has long ago faded. "On account of its healthfulness and the easy communication afforded by the Great Northern railroad," one optimistic census worker wrote in 1880, "the region is becoming one of importance, both for its lumber and manufacturing advantages, and the inducement it affords for summer residence to the citizens of New Orleans." Such predictions have largely gone unfulfilled. Almost a century later, and only a decade before Britney's birth, 38 percent of Kentwood's residents lived below the poverty line. In the meantime, nearby towns like Hammond have grown, attracting new businesses and bedroom communities for Baton Rouge and even New Orleans commuters. One local banker I talked to observed that there wasn't much of value around but land, and thus far folks didn't seem that interested in developing it, but neither did the rising generation seem inclined to keep the dairy farms going. I asked if Britney Spears might prove helpful. Not in the long run, he replied. She had certainly made an impact by bringing in tourists, but there wasn't even really a place for them to stay in Kentwood. They either found hotels in McComb (as I did) or in Hammond. Amos Kent's dream of founding a New South boomtown has, thus far, remained only a reverie. 15

One economic bright spot is a water-bottling firm called Kentwood Springs. The area's abundant aquifers have slaked New Orleans's thirst for over a century, but with the bottled-water craze of the last decade, Kentwood Springs has now moved into much larger territory. The company currently sells in Texas, Louisiana, Mississippi, and Alabama, under both Kentwood Springs and Crystal Springs labels. When I visited the plant it was clean and efficient, and, as it turns out, was put up by Britney's father, who runs a contracting and construction firm. Curt Allen, the plant's quality control manager, gave me a run-down on the business, which, in addition to water, also bottles a sports beverage called 10K. In the summertime the plant runs 24/7, and during the hurricane season the water can't come fast enough. Y2K was a flat-out gold rush, Mr. Allen tells me. Kentwood Springs isn't the only bottler in Kentwood, but it's certainly the largest. A Japanese company, Sun Tory Ltd., currently owns it, but the business's 16

Water Group Web page does all it can to convince consumers it's an American outfit, giving only an Atlanta address. I asked Mr. Allen if headquarters had ever thought of bringing the town's water and its most famous resident together in a knock-out advertising campaign. They had, he replied, but her slinky outfits and outrageous behavior of late made them afraid she might offend as many customers as she would attract. As to Britney, Mr. Allen called her an "A-1 Southern girl." They had often ridden together to Parklane Academy, and he assured me that stardom had done nothing to change her. She wasn't ashamed to be from Kentwood. That pleased him.

Driving through Kentwood takes less than a minute or two, es- 17
pecially if all three stoplights are green. Inattentive travelers will find themselves suddenly zooming towards Tangipahoa, the next town south, without realizing that Kentwood is now several miles in the rear. Even attentive ones can have trouble, and I had to turn around and go back when I realized that the town had ended. I returned to Avenue E to take a look at the Kentwood Museum. It turned out to be a modest structure housing donated items of local interest, including old pieces of furniture and other curiosities. The museum's staff was then engaged in gathering materials for a Britney Spears exhibit to satisfy the rising tide of tourists anxious to see relics of the superstar's early life. After a quick tour, the museum's director answered my numerous queries about the town's history with a phrase I'd hear repeatedly throughout the stay: "Oh, you need to talk to Mrs. Morris." A quick call, and she agreed to meet with me.

A small woman of restless activity, Irene Morris is the official 18
town historian—and with good reason. There is little about the town's past that has escaped her inquisitive grasp. Upon my arrival she informed me that she was wondering what had happened to me (I took a few minutes to look through the museum), that she was over eighty, and that we'd soon be picking up her granddaughter, recently home on break from college. She had time for a few questions before we started out, however, which she fired at me with Gatling-gun rapidity: Where do you teach? Where did you get your degree? What are you in Kentwood researching? Are you married? How many children do you have? I had aroused her suspicions because the town had been bothered to death by reporters and journalists anxious to find out about the "real" Britney Spears. She told me that the local police had urged everyone to keep mum about the Spears's whereabouts to protect them. When I told her that I was really as interested in the town and its history as I was in Britney, she fairly glowed with enthusiasm. A lifetime of work and accumulated knowledge lay dammed in her head, and the smallest inquiry could unleash a tidal wave of historical information. She began peppering me with facts, abruptly stopped to

say we needed to pick up her granddaughter, and continued her tale in the car. Periodically she would take a break from her narrative, fold her hands in her lap and say, "Now, what questions do you have for me?"

I sensed that no house had its residents, no burrows its mice, no nests its birds without Mrs. Morris knowing something about them. The landscape was her book, and quick glances on either side of the road told volumes of the town's past. In between her stories came driving instructions ("turn right here," "you don't have to drive so slowly"). She told me she had moved to Kentwood as a young married lady fresh from college, with the advice of a beloved mentor in her ears: "Don't let your brain die in that small town." Obviously she took the advice seriously. She pursues her adopted town's history with a tenacious determination and patience that make academic historians seem like dilettantes. Her house was a living testament to that determination. She showed me to a dim and cluttered corner that contained every local history tome, Bible record, civic booster pamphlet, postcard, genealogical record, and family picture ever to find its way into Kentwood. So quickly that I had no time to digest everything (she had many other things to do that day), she giddily shepherded me through the collection. We both rested in chairs a moment, then she was up again trying to find some clipping she thought certain would intrigue me. I asked her for help on the town's black history, and she immediately told me about Fochia Wilson and Ann Smith, both black women whom Mrs. Morris clearly felt were, in the old phrase, "a credit to their race." More than that she could not say. Clearly the town's official historian understood her tide to only cover the doings of Kentwood's white folks. Each race kept its own history. 19

It was only the first indication that even after formal integration, race still divides this small town. There was (and arguably still is) a black section of Kentwood called Kent's Quarters, whose borders were set by Highways 38 and 1051. Except for the Church of God Assembly, blacks and whites worship separately. No blacks attend Britney's home church, First Baptist, the youth minister told me. One black child had begun going to some after-school programs, but his mother apparently told him not to go to the white church anymore. He obeyed. 20

Kentwoodians go to school separately as well. When I asked one black resident if she knew roughly the percentage of African American students that attended the same private school that Britney went to she answered without hesitation: "Zero." And Parklane Academy is only one of several private schools strewn throughout the area that caters to white kids.

Though now more than thirty years in practice, school integration clearly remains a sore point with white Kentwoodians. I asked 21 one person what had been the biggest change in the town in the more than forty years he'd lived there. "We used to have a really good high school," he replied without hesitation or elaboration. When I questioned one Parklane graduate why he hadn't attended Kentwood High he told me, "Well, it's about 98 percent black, you know." In fact, the figure is closer to 88 percent, but the school's principal observed that the white kids who did come were either too poor to attend private academies, wanted to play on the school's championship football team, or were from biracial families. For whites, Kentwood High is basically a school of last resort.

Ann A. Smith, the high school's principal, is a woman of polish and erudition. She is enormously proud of Kentwood High, and she's clearly frustrated that its superb football team overshadows the school's equally impressive academic record. She printed off test score results to show me that her students scored higher than the statewide average on standardized tests. Yet, she acknowledged, the scores did little to dent the widely held notion among whites that Kentwood High was a substandard school. Lots of white folks showed up for Friday night football, but otherwise kept themselves and their children away. This disappointed her more than it made her angry. "The divisions are a handicap to the whole community. We haven't gotten the most out of this community that we could." Nor did Britney Spears's success provide a foothold for racial and civic unity. In fact, Mrs. Smith observed with amusement, by and large the black students she'd talked to liked and defended Britney and the white ones didn't. 22

When I asked her how Kentwood had responded to school desegregation, she urged me to talk with Coach Raymond Coleman and his wife, Brunette, both veterans of the segregated schools and foot soldiers in the campaign for integration. Equal parts mountain and man, Coach Coleman is avuncular and quick to laugh, and he responded to questions with an impressive candor. He recalled that Jim Crow Kentwood had experienced little overt racial strife. "Everyone kinda knew their positions and there wasn't any problem," he said. "It wasn't a mean town. It was just a typical small southern town." His wife countered that things weren't as easy going as he made them out to be, and she recounted several times when whites had snubbed her in the town's public places. Both recollected with pride the black entrepreneurs who built up a community parallel to white Kentwood. "We had our own newspaper," Mrs. Coleman told me, "filling station, groceries, cleaners, taxicab, theater—just about everything we needed." And both the coach and his wife spoke glowingly of Collis B. Temple, the "fearless and forceful" principal of Kentwood's black O. W. Dylan High. Temple had the respect of the white community 23 and commanded from it far more services than comparable black schools just about anywhere else they knew of.

The truce between whites and blacks that marked Kentwood's race relations was, however, broken by integration. It "revealed the fault lines," Coach Coleman noted. A head football coach at Dylan High, he and dozens of others in the black community pushed for school desegregation because "many parents thought that integration was the answer." As soon as they succeeded in the fall of 1969, he and others realized the full extent of what they had been missing. The white school "had labs, and athletic equipment, and better salaries, textbooks, and typewriters, and a library," his voice trailing off as the riches to enumerate exceeded his memory. I asked if there were any fights or ugliness. Among the faculty and students not a harsh word passed, he recalled. Whites resolved the matter easily enough. "We integrated in the fall of 1969 with no trouble. Not like Hammond. And then in the spring of 1970 all the white kids left" for the "white flight academies" popping up. They've never returned, and so Kentwood High, for all its academic strengths and athletic achievements, is still considered an inferior "black" school. Hence white residents felt no need to expand on the comment that the town's biggest change was that "we used to have a really good high school." 24

"Kentwood is my home and it's where my heart is," Britney writes in her autobiography. "I know that sounds corny, but it's where I'm happiest and where I can be totally myself." We should take her at her word. After all, she's spending millions of dollars building a Tudor-style mansion ("for my mama") on Kentwood's outskirts. Kentwood and the South are central to how Britney Spears understands herself, and they are therefore equally important to her public image. As one enthusiastic fan wrote to her, "Life is good!! You are a very beautiful lady!!! I love southern girls!!!!!!" Yet we need to pay close attention to just what kind of Kentwood and what kind of South she and her public mean.

Whether graciously complimenting her "Southern-magnolia manners" or maliciously declaring her winner of the "Ugliest Hick, Most Incestuous Child" contest, the imagery used to describe Britney Spears denies the existence of black southerners altogether. Hick, hillbilly, or belle, these terms leave no doubt as to race. That she's a southern girl merely ups the ante, making her whiteness more self-evident and more important. Kentwood itself mirrors this broader pattern. The town's official history, published in 1993, contains but a mere fleeting reference to what it calls the town's "colored" people, and otherwise completely obscures their lives. None of the information I heard from the Colemans appeared in the official history—no mention of slavery or tenant farmers, no mention of black businesses or workers, and no 25 mention of "race leaders" like C. B. Temple, though his house, like his legend, still stands next to the old black high school. Blacks are simply removed from the frame of reference we call history. It is unlikely, therefore, that Britney Spears knew any more about one-half of the town's residents than do other current white Kentwoodians. That ignorance wouldn't prevent her, however, from intuitively absorbing Kentwood's history of slavery and segregation, which, while certainly not unique or even as ugly as in many other comparable places, continues to shape much of the town's social, religious, and economic life. After all, the lessons she learned as a young white girl about her sexuality and her race were made potent only by recognizing their presumed opposite in that dark presence lurking in Kent's Quarters over by Highways 38 and 1051.

By scrutinizing Britney's image and her hometown's history, I'm 26
not suggesting that she didn't grow in a tiny southern town, that she's an untalented bimbo, or that she's a closet KKK member. Britney-bashing is too easy, and too satisfying to the critic. It inflates a sense of probing discernment in a genre already overweighed by pompous, self-righteous performers who, unlike Britney, have forgotten that pop music is rebellious, yes, but it's also supposed to be fun. No matter what smug detractors may say, then, Britney's success is evidence of more than an American cultural coma. Rather her ability to perform in the interstices of some fundamental and even contradictory expectations about race, gender, and the South makes her one of the most important southerners in American popular culture. In fact, Britney's genius is her ability to alternately embrace and tweak the nation's expectations for that curious creature, the southern white woman. Her rapid movement between "teenage Southern belle" and "pop tart" frustrates fans and critics, to be sure, but it also keeps them entertained and fascinated. Britney's no dumb blonde. She swears that she's "just a Louisiana girl," but hidden within that dismissive string of words Britney has proven there's seismic power.

Examining the Text

1. According to Campbell, Britney Spears consciously "plays up a national fascination with a white femininity." Explain her tactics and how they work for and against her.

2. Britney claims that that she is "just a Louisiana girl." Looking at her career, does she stay true to her word?

3. Toward the end of the article, Campbell states "Britney's genius is her ability to alternately embrace and tweak the nations expectations for that curious creature, the southern white woman." Explain how Campbell's claim is valid?

4. What connections does author Campbell make between media portrayals of Britney Spears and race relations in the South and the United States generally, both historical and contemporary?

For Group Discussion

Campbell blames the criticism of Britney's media-portrayed sexuality on her "own decision to exploit her good looks. More often, they [criticisms] reveal an underlying discomfort with young white women using the social and sexual power American society grants them on the promise that it will remain dormant." Discuss this indictment of puritanical American values in light of your own feelings about youthful "sex symbols" such as Britney Spears.

Writing Suggestion

This is an essay about the connection between geography and stardom. It makes connections between the locale of Britney Spears' upbringing and cultural meanings inherent in her stardom. Pick another celebrity with whom you are familiar and write an essay in which you make connections between that individual's place of origin and the public image created by that individual's celebrity.

Napster: Catalyst for a New Industry or Just Another Dot.com?

Michael Slinger and Amy Hillman

In this article, the authors examine the controversy over the legal ramifications of the Napster case, and the possible impact of computer-based sharing of digitized music files on the recording industry. As an organizational scheme, Slinger and Hillman break their textual material up into discrete subsections that cover issues such as the technological breakthroughs leading up to the creation of the MP3 digitized music format, along with the history and formation of World Wide Web–based MP3 file-sharing platforms such as Napster; the global music market and the organization of the music industry; the reaction of recording artists to the case; the impact of Napster and Napster-like services on consumers and retailers; legal fallout from the case; and some possible alternatives to unregulated music file-sharing.

***As you read** this article, try to detect whether or not the authors have a bias for or against Napster-like services, or whether they are truly dispassionate about the issue. Further, as they present possible alternatives to Napster, consider the feasibility of each proposed model, and try to imagine some additional models that might fill the vacuum created by the shutting down of Napster as a totally free music file-sharing service.*

> To look past these temporary problems and acknowledge a far larger more frightening one—our business model is unsustainable—take courage…I would argue that Bertelsmann did it when the company announced the innovative deal between its mammoth music operation and Napster. If ever an industry needed to face the hard reality that it has an unsustainable

---

Michael Slinger prepared this case under the supervision of Professor Amy Hillman solely to provide material for class discussion. The authors do not intend to illustrate either effective or ineffective handling of a managerial situation. The authors may have disguised certain names and other identifying information to protect confidentiality.

> business model, it's the recording business: whether Napster lives or dies, file sharing has ended the era of selling music primarily on plastic discs.
>
> —Geoffrey Colvin: "It's the Business Model, Stupid," *Fortune,* January 8, 2001.

It was February 13, 2001, and Hank Barry, CEO of Napster, was having trouble getting to sleep. Last week, Barry had attended The World Economic Forum in Davos, Switzerland, where he had confirmed to the world that Napster would soon start charging it users membership fees and today the U.S. Federal Court of Appeals for the Ninth Circuit had ruled that Napster would have to be shut down or make radical changes to its business practices. Barry now faced two key challenges: (1) How to convert Napster's loyal user base from non-paying to paying customers without losing them to other sites and (2) How to create a legal and viable business model that would generate profits for his company. 1

With a number of lawsuits still outstanding, and the terms of the injunction remanded to the district court, Barry was under tremendous pressure to come up with a business model for Napster that would both conform to the principles of copyright law and allow for widespread file sharing. If Barry could pull this off Napster would remain the primary channel for online music—a business that Jupiter Research estimated could be worth U.S. $5.4 billion per year by 2005. 2

MP3 AND NAPSTER

In 1998, with the advent of a simple technology called MP3, the music industry was revolutionized. MP3, which stands for Motion Picture Experts Group-1, Level 3, is a file format that allows users to compress digital music files so they can be easily transmitted over the internet. With the proper equipment, CDs could be decoded and transformed into MP3 files, and then shared, copied, stored on computers or even broadcast—with little adverse impact on the music quality. Shortly after the advent of MP3 technology, software services were created that allowed consumers to quickly and easily copy entire music CDs onto the internet for others to download free of charge. At first, MP3 files were shared among friends, but within a year, innovative technologies for organizing the vast array of MP3 files emerged. One such innovation was called "Napster." (For a comprehensive time line of significant developments in the industry, see Exhibit 1.) 3

When Shawn Fanning created the first version of Napster file-swapping software in mid-1999, he gave it to only 15 friends, on the 4

Exhibit 1

THE BIRTH OF ONLINE MUSIC

***June 1980:**
Sony and Philips create a global standard for compact discs. Although recording labels including, ironically, Sony Music Entertainment saw revenue gains as consumers replaced their vinyl collections, CDs later became the master discs off which Netsavvy consumers freely swapped tracks.

***January 1988:**
Leonardo Chiariglione of Germany's Fraunhofer Institut Integrierte Schaltungen, along with minds from the University of Erlangen, form the team that builds the audio compression format known as MP3: Motion Picture Experts Group-1, Level 3. The technology shrinks digital audio files to 12 times their original size and becomes the de facto standard for pirating, legitimately swapping, storing, and listening to online music.

***December 1990:**
Tim Berners-Lee finishes code for the first Web browser, unshackling the Internet from a static, text-only based world into a realm of graphics and sound.

***February 1993:**
Eric Bina, Marc Andreessen, and other students at the University of Illinois release Mosaic, the precursor to Netscape.

•April 1995:
RealNetworks, then known as Progressive Networks, introduces its RealAudio player, free software that allows users to listen to audio files.

***January 1996:**
Liquid Audio is formed and develops on audio compression technology embraced by the world's five major recording labels because, unlike the MP3 format, it inhibits unfettered pirating of music.

•March 1998:
After buying his MP3 domain name from California Internet entrepreneur Martin Paul, Michael Robertson founds MP3.com, which for a time becomes the world's most popular online music site.

$October 1998:
The Recording Industry Association of America files to outlaw Diamond Multimedia Systems from releasing the world's first portable MP3 player. RIAA loses, but the trial draws massive public attention to MP3, a then little-known technology, jump-starting an industry.

•February 1999:
The recording industry enlists the aid of technology companies including Microsoft and IBM to begin work on the Secure Digital Music Initiative. The goal: kill MP3 and introduce a framework on which to build a piracy-proof digital audio standard.

+March 1999:
Tom Petty posts his single "Free Girl Now" on MP3.com, quickly generating more than 150,000 downloads. Petty's label, Warner Bros. Records, orders Petty to pull the song off the Net less than two weeks later. Other acts, including Red Hot Chili Peppers, Beastie Boys, and Public Enemy, also briefly join the anarchy.

+September 1999:
David Bowie, with the blessing of EMI's Virgin records, releases *hours* for paid download via the Internet, the first time a record label sanctions digital distribution of a complete piece of copyrighted work.

(*continued*)

***September 1999:**
Shawn Fanning, 19, drops out of Northeastern University to write music file-sharing software dubbed Napster. Uncle John Fanning pushes to turn the wildly popular program into a business, incurring the legal wrath of the recording industry.

***January 2000:**
MP3.com releases an upgraded version of My.MP3 service, allowing users to access their CD collections via the Internet. The company creates a database of music by copying more than 80,000 CDs. The recording Industry Association of America files suit, arguing that creation of the database violated copyrights.

***March 2000:**
Win Amp MP3 player creators Justin Frankel and Tom Pepper of Nullsoft, a division of America Online, release file-sharing program Gnutella. Unlike Napster, the new program does not rely on a central server to distribute music and other files. AOL pulls the program but not before it escapes on the Internet. Many Gnutella clones soon sprout.

$ March 2000:
The National Music Publishers' Association sues MP3.com for use of its members' songs.

$ April 2000:
Metallica files copyright infringement suit against Napster, claiming the company violated the Racketeer Influenced and Corrupt Organizations Act. Later that same month rapper-producer Dr. Dre files $10 million suit against Napster.

$ April 2000:
U.S. District Judge rules MP3.com violated copyright, saying the company illegally created a database of CDs in a commercial setting. Four of the five major record labels later settle licensing deals with MP3.com for $20 million each.

$ May 2000:
Metallica orders more than 300,000 users booted off Napster. Napster complies, but many users find ways to get back on. Metallica drummer Lars Ulrich later is booed at the MTV Music Video awards.

$ June 2000:
Major recording labels file lawsuit against MP3Board, a Website that links to songs the industry terms "pirated music".

$ July 2000:
The Recording Industry Association of America files a copyright suit against Scour, a Napster-like service.

$ July 2000:
Federal judge gives Napster three days to stop users from swapping copyrighted works. In an eleventh-hour reprieve, the 9th Circuit Court of Appeals overturns the ruling, setting up a court showdown.

$ October 2000:
The recording industry's trial against Napster begins.

• October 2000:
The National Music Publishers' Association and MP3.com announce $30 million settlement allowing MP3.com to distribute more than 1 million commercial tracks via its My.MP3.com service.

• October 2000:
Bertelsmann AG, parent of BMG, drops its lawsuit against Napster and forms an alliance with the startup to develop a joint file-sharing music service.

* TECHNOLOGY ADVANCE • BUSINESS VENTURE $ LAWSUIT + MUSICAL RELEASE

Source: Drummond, M. "Big Music," *Business 2.0.* December 12, 2000, pp. 155–165.

sole condition that they would not tell anyone about it. He did not write the code to satisfy an untapped niche or to get rich—he wrote it for fun—as a way to swap music files with his friends. Two short years later, without the benefit of any advertising, Napster software had been downloaded 57 million times, thereby equipping 200 million multimedia PCs worldwide to copy MP3 files.

Napster's software, which was available free of charge, allowed 5
music enthusiasts to easily locate and copy MP3 files directly from another Napster user's computer. Napster was essentially a directory and index of MP3s that allowed users to locate the music they wanted. The Napster server never stored any copyrighted material; rather, it facilitated the copying of MP3s by helping people locate the files they wanted. It also created a community of users who built their own music collections and openly shared them with others.

Unwittingly, Fanning's creation had successfully spawned a new 6
industry known as peer-to-peer (P2P) file sharing, and it had thrown the traditional recording industry into chaos. Napster had become the epicentre of a commercial and legal debate on redefining intellectual property laws for not only audio, but also for video and text.

From a copyright point of view, there was one central issue: Peo- 7
ple were not getting paid for the use of their music. For recording companies, the widespread use of MP3 technology meant that their vast inventories of music were being "consumed," but they were not receiving any royalties since the music was not being distributed in a medium that they could control and track—i.e., CDs. Typically, the holder of a copyright in a work of art was paid royalties for the sale, copying or broadcasting of the work. The Napster software had undermined this system. As a result, the five large recording companies and many musicians had launched lawsuits against Napster (and other MP3 sites), claiming that Napster facilitated the widespread copying of copyrighted music, and asking that it be shut down.

THE MUSIC INDUSTRY

According to the International Federation of the Phonographic Indus- 8
try (*IFPI.org*), the global music market in 1999 had grown to a value of U.S.$38.5 billion, and its growth was expected to continue. The largest share of this market was in the United States (37 percent), followed by Japan (16.7 percent), the United Kingdom (7.6 percent), Germany (7.4 percent), France (5.2 percent) and Canada (2.3 percent). The importance of this industry in the U.S. stemmed from the fact that for eight straight years, until the date of this case, so-called copyright industries (recorded music and motion pictures) were among the fastest growing segments of the U.S. economy.

Five large recording companies that were involved in the sourcing, production, marketing and distribution of recorded music dominated the global music industry. These companies, colloquially referred to as the "Big Five," also controlled the copyrights to large music inventories of recording artists, past and present. The Big Five included: EMI Recorded Music (U.K.), Time Warner Music Group (U.S.), Universal Music Group (United States, Canada, France), Sony Music Entertainment (United States, Japan), and privately held BMG Entertainment, a subsidiary of Bertelsmann AG (Germany). The control exerted by these companies over the industry was significant. Their annual sales represented approximately U.S. $25 billion in 1999, and accounted for over 90 percent of global recorded music sales. (Exhibit 2 provides a list of the 1999 sales and market shares for each of the Big Five.) 9

When these companies discovered new artists, the artists were generally offered a contract to create, perform and promote their music. These contracts also specified future royalty amounts for CD sales and stipulated that the copyrights for musical creations would become the property of the music companies. In exchange, the music companies would invest in the production and distribution of CDs, the promotion of the artists and in the up-front costs involved with organizing concerts around the world. These costs could easily run into the multimillion dollar range, and according to the companies, represented a significant risk to them. For years, artists had argued that the recording companies exerted too much control over them, since without the distribution and marketing channels provided by the Big Five, artists had almost no chance of having their work widely distributed. 10

Success in the music industry, with few exceptions, meant that artists gave up an element of control over two key intellectual property rights (reproduction, and distribution) in exchange for support from a recognized label. If an artist chose to be independent, there were significant hurdles to overcome. For example, CD sales are largely driven by the amount of airtime that songs receive on radio 11

Exhibit 2

1999 SALES AND MARKET SHARE OF THE BIG FIVE

Company	1999 Revenue (Billions)	Percent Market Share
Warner	$3.8	15.5
Universal Music Group	$6.3	25.7
BMG Entertainment	$4.7	19.2
Sony Music Entertainment	$6.0	24.5
EMI Recorded Music	$3.7	15.1

Source: Drummond, M. "Big Music." *Business 2.0.* December 12, 2000, pp. 155–165.

stations around the world; without a big label promoting an artist, it was often very difficult for artists to have their work featured on commercial radio stations. Another barrier to independent artists was the near monopoly that the Big Five had over global distribution of CDs to retailers.

These points of contention were brought to the forefront of public debate in 2000, when Napster gained widespread support from music consumers around the world. The early success of Napster not only highlighted the need for clear rules about file sharing, but also focused attention on the very different aims of the various stakeholders in this complex industry. 12

RECORDING ARTISTS

Historically, recording artists have had mixed relationships with the Big Five music companies and with Napster. Some artists claimed that they had signed overly restrictive contracts with the Big Five, and that these contracts limited their creativity—as some of the companies controlled not only the "sound" of an album, but also the artwork on the cover, the number and order of songs and the artists' ability to plan their own concert schedules. In addition, many recording artists complained that they were taken advantage of by the Big Five, since they made far less profit per CD than the recording companies did. 13

These artists would have agreed with Patricia Seybold, author of *The Customer Revolution*, who wrote: 14

> The amount of money required to produce and launch a new act is about $1 million. That doesn't include the cost of manufacturing and distributing the CDs. Although there are rare instant hits that sell in the millions, a popular CD typically sells 300,000 to 400,000 copies. Once the labels recoup their costs, there's little profit for the musicians' royalties to come out of. And since the $1 million up-front costs are deducted from the musicians' royalties of 12 to 16 percent of profits, the artists wind up owing the record label money after their first albums. Using an industry-specific practice called cross-collateralization, the deficit from the first album is added to the deficit on the second album, and so it goes. Most musicians never manage to create the hit that frees them from being "owned" by a major label.
>
> The power in the music industry is clearly not in the hands of the musicians, but in the hands of a few record labels.[1]

[1]"A New View of Change," Patricia B. Seybold, *Business 2.0.* p. 86, February 20, 2001.

Another bone of contention among some artists was that ever 15
since the creation of the MP3 format, their work was being copied illegally by Napster users and by users of other file-sharing services. Some musicians felt that these downloads represented lost sales, while others blamed the Big Five for dragging their feet—not only because they weren't prepared for the demand for MP3s, but also because the Big Five had not yet amended most musicians' contracts to provide appropriate royalties for digital sales.

Despite the widespread copying that was being facilitated by 16
Napster, some musicians felt that "widespread sharing of music by fans might break the major record labels' stranglehold on the music industry."[2] Some felt that if file sharing could successfully disintermediate the Big Five, then the recording artists could potentially make more money and also be free of the influence of the producers and the labels. In fact, Pearl Jam and Limp Bizkit actively supported the Napster platform, and by the end of 2000, Napster had received permission from over 25,000 musicians and bands to trade their music online.[3]

Some artists even felt that Napster, and other P2P sites were ac- 17
tually driving CD sales higher. In August 2000, Rolling Stone Magazine asked 5,000 readers whether they had bought fewer CDs now that music is available free online, and only 8 percent said yes. Most of the respondents (54 percent) stated that their buying habits hadn't changed, and 36 percent stated that they were actually buying more. The New York Times on The Web, August 18, 2000, in an article quoting Soundscan, reported that 355 million albums were sold in the first six months of 2000, up from 332 million units for the first half of 1999. Another mid-2000 study by Webnoize Research estimated that sales in the first quarter of 2000 were 30 percent higher than they were three years ago, despite the recent popularity of file swapping. (For statistics on sales, see Exhibit 3.)

CONSUMERS

Music consumers are a diverse group of people with varying interests, 18
and their reaction to Napster varies depending on their age, facility with technology, and personal philosophies. Some consumers downloaded copyrighted songs guilt-free, without considering the implica-

---

[2]Ibid, p. 89.

[3]Interview with Napster's Lawyer, David Boies, *Wired,* October 2000.

Exhibit 3

The Recording Industry Association of America's 2000 Yearend Statistics
(1330 Connecticut Ave, NW, Suite 300, Washington, D.C. 20036 (202) 775-0101)

Manufacturer's Unit Shipments and Dollar Value
(In Millions, net after returns)

	1991	1992	1993	1994	1995	1996	1997	1998	1999	% CHANGE 1998–1999	2000	% CHANGE 1999–2000
(Units Shipped)	333.3	407.5	495.4	662.1	722.9	778.9	753.1	847.0	938.9	**10.8%**	942.5	**0.4%**
(Dollar Value) CD	4,337.7	5,326.5	6,511.4	8,464.5	9,377.4	9,934.7	9,915.1	11,416.0	12,816.3	**12.3%**	13,214.5	**3.1%**
CD Single	5.7	7.3	7.8	9.3	21.5	43.2	66.7	56.0	55.9	**-0.1%**	34.2	**-38.8%**
	35.1	45.1	45.8	56.1	110.9	184.1	272.7	213.2	222.4	**4.3%**	142.7	**-35.8%**
Cassette	360.1	366.4	339.5	345.4	272.6	225.3	172.6	158.5	123.6	**-22.0%**	76.0	**-38.5%**
	3,019.6	3,116.3	2,915.8	2,976.4	2,303.6	1,905.3	1,522.7	1,419.9	1,061.6	**-25.2%**	626.0	**-41.0%**
Cassette Single	69.0	84.6	85.6	81.1	70.7	59.9	42.2	26.4	14.2	**-46.0%**	1.3	**-91.0%**
	230.4	298.8	298.5	274.9	236.3	189.3	133.5	94.4	48.0	**-49.2%**	4.6	**-90.3%**
LP/EP	4.8	2.3	1.2	1.9	2.2	2.9	2.7	3.4	2.9	**-14.0%**	2.2	**-24.6%**
	29.4	13.5	10.6	17.8	25.1	36.8	33.3	34.0	31.8	**-6.7%**	27.7	**-12.7%**
Vinyl Single	22.0	19.8	15.1	11.7	10.2	10.1	7.5	5.4	5.3	**-2.5%**	4.8	**-8.1%**
	63.9	66.4	51.2	47.2	46.7	47.5	35.6	25.7	27.9	**8.4%**	26.3	**-5.4%**
Music Video	6.1	7.6	11.0	11.2	12.6	16.9	18.6	27.2	19.8	**-28.3%**	18.2	**-8.0%**
	118.1	157.4	213.3	231.1	220.3	236.1	323.9	508.0	376.7	**-27.6%**	281.9	**-25.2%**
*DVD	-	-	-	-	-	-	-	0.5	2.5	**405%**	3.3	**35.2%**
	-	-	-	-	-	-	-	12.2	66.3	**442%**	80.3	**21.1%**
Total Units	**801.0**	**895.5**	**955.6**	**1,122.7**	**1,112.7**	**1,137.2**	**1,063.4**	**1,124.3**	**1,160.6**	3.2%	**1,079.3**	-7.0%
Total Value	**7,834.2**	**9,024.0**	**10,046.6**	**12,068.0**	**12,320.3**	**12,533.8**	**12,236.8**	**13,723.5**	**14,584.5**	6.3%	**14,323.0**	-1.8%
					Total Retail Units		**817.5**	**850.0**	**869.7**	2.3%	**788.6**	-9.3%
					Total Retail Value		**10,785.8**	**12,165.4**	**13,048.0**	7.3%	**12,705.0**	-2.6%

*While broken out for this chart, DVD Audio Product is included in the Music Video totals.

Source: Recording Industry Association of America, 2000.

tions of copyright laws and the potentially adverse effect their actions could have on artists. Others felt that downloading was akin to stealing, and therefore didn't take part. Another group felt that they had been cheated by the music industry for years, and that they were justified in downloading music from the Internet.

One source of this scorn for the Big Five was that when CDs sup- 19
planted vinyl records as the primary medium for recorded music, the Big Five increased prices, even though CDs were much cheaper to produce than vinyl records. In addition, some music enthusiasts felt taken advantage of because even though there often were only one or two good tracks on a CD, the recording companies refused to offer reasonably priced singles. This meant that for some consumers, purchasing a CD amounted to paying for 12 tracks when they wanted only one or two. Napster allowed consumers to obtain one track at a time, without the unwanted material. This "unbundling" was adding to the nervousness in the industry.

The recording companies had also suffered in the court of public 20
opinion due to a number of recent legal actions. In May 2000, the Big Five settled a price fixing lawsuit with the United States Federal Trade Commission, agreeing to end the requirement that retail stores adhere to minimum prices in advertisements. On August 9, 2000, 28 U.S. states filed their own suits charging major labels and some brick-and-mortar retailers with CD price fixing. On January 26, 2001, the European Commission announced its own investigation of the Big Five and 18 music retailers (including some online retailers) for price fixing of CDs.

For Hank Barry, it would be very important to understand and 21
appeal to Napster's user base. Some recent studies had shown that Napster users may lose interest if forced to pay for downloads, while others concluded that 70 percent of college-aged Napster users would still use the service even if a $15 per month fee were charged.[4] Since Napster's loyal users were one of its greatest sources of leverage with the industry, if Barry failed to retain their loyalty in the shift to a fee-based service, Napster could easily disappear.

RETAILERS

Retailers had mixed opinions about Napster and about what P2P file 22
swapping meant to them. The retailers seemed to be fighting a war on

---

[4]According to Ric Dube, an analyst at Webnoize Research, February 13, 2001, on *NewsHour with Jim Lehrer*.

two fronts: They were struggling to come up with a response to lost CD sales resulting from the internet, and they were facing the threat of digital music affecting their retailing business model.[5]

Some retailers felt that the downloading of music was a fad that 23
was not sustainable as a business:

> You can't discount the pride of ownership. When you buy a CD, it isn't just the music, it's the artwork, the original object, not a copy that you're buying. Maybe the record companies have a crystal ball, though if you really pin them down, they don't know a damn thing. All they have is [sic] dreams.
>
> —Tower Records President Russ Solomon.[6]

This school of thought believed that music stores played a vital 24
role in the value chain, and that Napster merely allowed customers to sample before purchasing. Another argument was that Napster downloads did not represent lost CD sales, and that the year-over-year sales figures proved that Napster was complementing, not cannibalizing sales. In 2000, music consumers made over 95 percent of their purchases in bricks-and-mortar stores, and those who purchased CDs on the internet often chose to purchase from a Web site backed up by a bricks-and-mortar retail venue which facilitated returns.[7]

Another source of tension was the fact that the Big Five had 25
begun offering commercial downloads in the spring of 2000, an action that threatened retailers. The retailers responded by complaining vigorously and by warning the labels not to disintermediate them. The Big Five apparently agreed, behind closed doors, to co-ordinate their online efforts with the retailers.[8]

In another move, *Liquidaudio.com,* an online retailer of CDs and 26
MP3s, launched a campaign (with little success) in 2000 to place downloading kiosks in retail stores. The theory was that people could place their MP3 players on the machine and download digital tracks for a

---

[5]Not all retailers used the same business model: some used a commission model, and others used a gross margin model. With the commission model, the recording company sets the price and gives the retailer a percentage of the sale price. With the gross margin model, the retailer buys the title from the recording company at a wholesale price and then sets its own price. Both of these models were also used for MP3 sales over the Internet; Sony, BMG and Universal use the commission model and pay Web sites for facilitating downloads; Warner and EMI use the gross margin model. Source: "3 Majors Testing Digital Waters," Marilyn Gillen, *Billboard*, p. 177, v. 112, August 12, 2003.

[6]"Music Retailing Won't be Eclipsed by Digital Downloads, Veteran Says," Thomas K. Arnold, *Video Store*, v. 22, December 10–16, 2000.

[7]Jupiter Research estimates that online music sales will reach $2.6 billion by 2003.

[8]"A New View of Change," Patricia B. Seybold, *Business 2.0,* p. 92, February 20, 2001.

fee, or they could choose to sample a track first and then purchase the CD in the store. The problem, according to some retailers, was that the retailers made a very slim margin on a download, and the kiosks cost over $100,000 each.

Despite the wide range of opinions about what P2P sites meant for retailers, all of the large retail chains in North America had set up Web sites to facilitate the purchase of CDs over the internet, and many were experimenting with MP3 Web sites. 27

THE RECORDING INDUSTRY ASSOCIATION OF AMERICA (RIAA)

> The court confirmed our case on every count. We feel that Napster's business model is morally and legally wrong, and we're very glad that the Ninth Circuit Court agreed with us 100 percent. . . . It is time for Napster to stand down and build their business the old-fashioned way. By seeking permission first.
>
> —Hilary Rosen, President, RIAA, February 12, 2001[9]

The RIAA was a Washington, D.C., based trade group that represented the U.S. recording industry. Its stated mission was "to foster a business and legal climate that supports and promotes our members' creative and financial vitality. RIAA members create, manufacture, and/or distribute approximately 90 percent of all legitimate sound recordings produced and sold in the United States." 28

One of the RIAA's primary goals in 2001 was to ensure that Web sites such as Napster did not ruin the recording industry in the U.S. by facilitating the swapping of music files to the detriment of the copyright holders. The primary evidence the RIAA cited was a survey done by Magex that indicated online piracy could cost the recording industry up to U.S. $10 billion by 2003. The RIAA's opposition to Napster began on December 7, 1999, when, on behalf of the Big Five, the organization sued Napster for conspiring to facilitate copyright infringement.[10] In its lawsuit, the RIAA claimed damages of U.S. $100,000 for each copyrighted musical work that was copied as result of Napster's software.[11] Because this suit potentially represented thousands of songs, the potential damages could amount to billions of dollars, an 29

[9]Hilary Rosen speaking of the February 12, 2001, decision of the U.S. Federal Court of Appeals for the Ninth Circuit to uphold a modified preliminary injunction.

[10]This suit was still outstanding at the time of writing; however, a preliminary injunction, whose terms were still being addressed by the district court, had been granted.

[11]At the time of writing, the courts had not yet heard this case.

amount that would clearly mean the end of Napster. The RIAA used its Web site to feature musicians who opposed Napster. This was an attempt to suggest that the recording artists were on RIAA's side, and to generate support for its position.

The RIAA also believed that the best way to combat P2P file 30
swapping of copyrighted material was through the Secure Digital Music Initiative (SDMI). The SDMI was an industry group that had attempted to create a secure form of digital music file, with input from a wide array of recording companies, MP3 player manufacturers, artists' groups and consumers' groups. The RIAA supported Digital Rights Management (DRM), a system that would allow for downloading and copying only if royalties were paid to the artist or copyright holder. A DRM system would also allow copyright holders to track the distribution of electronic property to authorized recipients.

SECURE DIGITAL MUSIC INITIATIVE (SDMI)

According to *sdmi.org,* 31

> The Secure Digital Music Initiative (SDMI) is a forum that brings together more than 180 companies and organizations representing information technology, consumer electronics, security technology, the worldwide recording industry and Internet Service Providers.
>
> SDMI's charter is to develop open technology specifications that protect the playing, storing and distributing of digital music such that a new market for digital music may emerge. The open technology specifications released by SDMI will ultimately:
>
> - Provide consumers with convenient access to music both online and in new emerging digital distribution systems
> - Enable copyright protection for artists' works, and
> - Promote the development of new music-related business and technologies.

Despite the convergent goals of many SDMI members, the group 32
had been unable to make any significant breakthroughs since it was created. In meetings with the Big Five, artists' groups, technology companies and others, SDMI had been unable to create a new standard for secure DRM. In fact, companies such as InterTrust, ContentGuard, Microsoft, IBM, Reciprocal and Liquid Audio were competing to create DRM software that would become the industry standard—or at least that would be format neutral. That is, have the ability to run on a number of different hardware devices and with different security features.

THE BIG FIVE

The year 2000 was a landmark time for the Big Five; it marked the year 33 in which recording companies finally acknowledged that the internet was not just a marketing vehicle, but that it was an entirely new distribution platform. Pushed into action by upstarts such as Napster and Scour, the Big Five realized that they weren't giving consumers what they really wanted: MP3 tracks in a format that was easy to use and inexpensive. The Big Five now agreed that they should sell songs via direct download in addition to the CD format though retail and internet channels, and they also decided to focus on three issues: copyrights, royalties, and secure distribution.

As Business 2.0 writer Mike Drummond noted in December 2000, 34

> While tech-savvy consumers were loading their hard drives with songs formatted in MP3 compression technology, the major labels—Bertelsmann AG's BMG Entertainment, EMI Recorded Music, Sony Music Entertainment, Time Warner's Warner Music Group, and Seagram's Universal Music Group—embraced a variety of piracy-resistant formats that often prevented playback on portable devices. What's more, the labels released only a fraction of their vast catalogs and then priced download tracks too high.

This failure to foresee how MP3s would affect the music industry 35 led to many ad hoc initiatives on the part of the Big Five that were largely unsuccessful.[12]

For Barry and Napster, a key decision involved deciding 36 whether Napster could continue to work independently or whether it should continue to seek partnerships with other members of the Big Five, as it had recently done with Bertelsmann. In order to make this decision, Barry had to understand what strategies each of the Big Five was employing and where Napster fit in the equation.

Bertelsmann BMG

As of early 2001, Bertelsmann's (BMG) labels included: Arista, RCA, 37 Bad Boy Entertainment, Windham Hill and Jay records. Its artists included Britney Spears, Dave Matthews Band, Christina Aguilera, San-

---

[12]For example, as mentioned earlier, the launching of commercial MP3 sites by the Big Five infuriated the retailers, and a deal was eventually worked out to pacify the retailers.

tana, Foo Fighters and Whitney Houston. BMG's catalogue included over 700,000 songs. In the fall of 2000, Bertelsmann broke ranks with the Big Five and announced a deal with Napster. The agreement stated that BMG would drop out of the RIAA lawsuit if Napster could implement a legitimate, membership-based file-sharing model that ensured compensation for artists. BMG would also add its full catalogue to Napster and would then exercise its warrant to buy an equity stake in Napster. In order to help Napster with a new business model, BMG forwarded Napster a U.S. $50 million working capital loan.

Time Warner

In 2001, Time Warner's Warner Music Group included Elektra Enter- 38
tainment, Sire, the Atlantic Group, Warner Bros. Records and Warner Music International. Featured artists included: Madonna, Alanis Morissette, Phil Collins, R.E.M., Red Hot Chili Peppers, and Van Halen. In 2000, Time Warner attempted to merge with EMI. At that time, EMI Recorded Music was the largest music publisher in the world, with over one million copyrights, and the third largest in terms of recorded music sales. Its labels included EMI, Virgin, Blue Note Records, Capitol Records and Chrysalis. Its copyrights covered songs by Pink Floyd, David Bowie, the Beatles and the Rolling Stones. However, European regulators quashed the merger, citing competition concerns. These concerns stemmed partly from the fact that Time Warner and AOL had already agreed to a $135 billion merger, and the existence of an American powerhouse including AOL, Time Warner, and EMI would be too dominant, for it would control not only the digital content, but also the "pipes" to carry it—in the form of AOL's cable-modem service.[13] Another interesting element to the merger was that it was AOL's Nuilsoft Music software division that had released *Gnutella.com,* the P2P file-sharing service that eliminated the need for a central server, and that was one of Napster's potential competitors. Barry and his team at Napster wondered if this meant that Time Warner would be reluctant to join forces with Napster.

The failed merger between Time Warner and EMI in the spring 39
of 2000 opened the door for Bertelsmann to begin merger talks with EMI toward the end of the same year. Many industry observers felt that a merger between EMI and Bertelsmann made strategic sense because it would create a European music powerhouse—with a global

---

[13]At the time of writing, the AOL/Time Warner deal had been approved in Europe and was under review in the United States.

market share of recorded music over 25 percent. Such a merger would also provide Bertelsmann, which was privately held, with access to the capital markets through publicly traded EMI.

Sony Music Entertainment

Sony Music Entertainment, a division of the Japanese consumer electronic company, which was second only to Universal in market share, was another company that Napster had to be concerned with. Sony's key labels included: Columbia, Epic, Sony, Work Group, 02, Nashville and Legacy Sony's artists include Celine Dion, Pearl Jam, Mariah Carey, Will Smith, Barbara Streisand, and Bob Dylan. In 2000, Sony's revenue was U.S. $6 billion, with a 19 percent market share. 40

Sony's reach went far beyond recorded music and included the capability to design and produce digital music devices, which were considered to be one of the key components in making digital music truly ubiquitous. In addition to being a content and device supplier, Sony was also involved in creating a DRM standard format. Industry rumors indicated that Sony would support only "secure" digital formats—a possible indication that Sony would be unwilling to partner with Napster. Sony and Universal confirmed at the end of 2000 that they had plans to launch an online music subscription service. 41

Universal Music Group

Another recent development concerned Barry: the recently announced merger between Seagram's Universal Music Group, the television company Canal+, and the French telecommunications company Vivendi. The new Vivendi Universal Company would give Universal Music, the world's largest music company, access to broadband and wireless internet platforms in Europe and the high-speed portal Vizzavi (the homepage for 80 million Vodafone mobile and interactive TV customers). Universal's UMG included labels: Decca, A&M, Deutsche Grammophon, Geffen, Island Def Jam, MCA, Verve, and Universal. Revenues from 1999 were $6.3 billion. UMG's catalogue included Stevie Wonder, Elton John, Luciano Pavarotti, Shania Twain, B.B. King, Counting Crows, Beck, Peter Gabriel, and Limp Bizkit. 42

Barry wondered whether Napster's future success depended upon making deals with each of the Big Five, or whether Napster would be viable with only a few strategic partners. After all, most music consumers had no idea which label or recording company held the copyrights to popular tracks. Therefore, wouldn't any successful MP3 site require the support of each of the Big Five? 43

THE BUSINESS MODEL CONUNDRUM

The dynamic nature of the music industry over the past 18 months 44
had created a wealth of opportunities as well as a number of threats. If Napster failed to create a viable model to please the various stakeholders in the very near future, then more than 50 million Napster users would likely migrate to other sites such as Freenet or *Gnutella.com.* For the Big Five, this eventuality could represent the squandering of a great opportunity to reach the vast majority of MP3 users through one Web site. The RIAA's success in the U.S. Court of Appeals could become a Pyrrhic victory, for without Napster, it would be very difficult for the MP3 file sharing market to be regulated and therefore, to be profitable for the stakeholders.

One of Napster's primary concerns was that it had very little 45
time to create an adequate business model to meet the demands of the various stakeholders. Bertelsmann was expecting Napster to come up with a viable plan, loyal customers were anxiously downloading material—fearful that free music would soon be a thing of the past, artists were hoping to negotiate new royalty deals to address downloading, the RIAA copyright infringement lawsuit was pending and the Big Five were creating new alliances. Given the situation, it was important to consider a number of potential models. These models could be used independently or Napster could create a hybrid model to encourage acceptance.

Subscription Model

Some industry experts suggested that the best strategy for Napster at 46
this point was to create a subscription model whereby customers paid a set amount each month for unlimited downloading of music. This model had both strengths and weaknesses. It would appeal to heavy users of digital music if the monthly fee was perceived as being fair, thereby encouraging subscribers to sample a wide variety of material each month. In addition, the subscription model could generate substantial revenues for Napster and the Big Five. If 50 percent of Napster's 50 million users agreed to pay $5 per month, $1.5 billion in revenues could be generated in one year—an amount approaching 10 percent of total U.S. recording industry revenues in 1999. With some experts predicting a subscription price in the $10 to $15 range, this revenue could easily approach between $3 billion to $5 billion annually.

On the other hand, Napster risked alienating consumers who did 47
not tend to purchase much music, as they may not perceive much value in their subscription fee. Another potential problem with this

model was that it could end up driving consumers to "free" Web sites, such as Freenet and *Gnutella.com,* that facilitated the copying of pirated music, and which were impossible to shut down, since they had no central server acting as an index or directory. It was estimated that new P2P sites were springing up everyday, and if Napster drove its customers away, it may never get them back.

A further criticism of this model was that it could ruin the com- 48
munity feeling that Napster users enjoyed. Some users have indicated that half the fun of Napster is exploring the playlists on the PCs of people with similar tastes, and that a subscription service that limits interaction would not survive.

Pay-per-Download

A number of Web sites, including the propriety Web sites of the Big 49
Five, were using a pay-per-download model. The idea was that customers could sample some tracks (through streaming) free of charge, but would be required to pay to download the song for future enjoyment. This model simplified the payment of royalties to artists, compared to the subscription model, but it created new pricing challenges. For example, light users may not mind paying 50 cents per track, but heavy users could find the per download fee too expensive and may find alternatives to Napster for their music. A further refinement included discounting the purchase of CDs if the consumer had previously paid for downloads from the same album.

Other problems include billing systems and payment options. A 50
pay-per-download model would mean millions of small transactions would have to be made each day. Processing such a large number of transactions can be expensive and inefficient. In addition, many young users of Napster do not have access to credit cards; therefore, new payment options would have to be created. Some have suggested that Internet service providers or telephone companies could include these charges in monthly statements; however, some large telecommunications companies have announced that they do not want to fill the role of "trust agent" for internet transactions.

Advertising Revenue

Another business model that Napster could adopt in order to offer 51
songs free or for very little money is one in which advertising revenues would cover the costs of running the business and provide enough cash generation for royalty payments. With this model, Barry had to consider a) whether advertising would drive people away, and

b) whether cheap downloads were a large enough incentive for users to visit a Web site saturated with advertisements, again and again. Current Napster users have expressed that they enjoy the site because there is no advertising on it, and some decision-makers at Napster fear that these users could be driven away by advertising.

Another issue with this model was whether it would be sustain- 52
able over the long term. With very little confidence in the internet as a viable advertising platform, would companies be willing to pay the high ad prices required to keep Napster and the RIAA satisfied?

Direct Marketing/Data Mining

Because Napster's software exposes a user's hard drive to the world at 53
large, there are opportunities for the music labels and independent marketing companies to learn exactly what people are listening to, and to pinpoint customers' tastes. This model relies on revenues generated by selling user information (which could be a condition of membership) to pay royalties to the music company.

By tracking which songs people are sharing and saving on their 54
hard drives, recording companies could determine which songs to promote, who is up-and-coming, and which musicians draw the same listeners. This granularity of customer research could be a valuable asset and a novel revenue model. An example of its use would be recording companies promoting a new CD to people who already have music by the artist on their hard drive. Other companies on the internet were already using this customised direct marketing technique—and with apparent success.[14]

Distributed Network

Napster's software, some argued, was really focused on indexing and 55
managing distributed data resources, similar to software that powers the non-commercial SETI@home project and several commercially distributed computing start-ups.[15] This distributed computing model

[14]"Let Others Sue: Marketer Licks Chops Over Rich Napster Data," Charles Mann and Warren Cohen, Inside.com, as reported in *www.thestandard.com*, February 9, 2001.

[15]SETI@home is a scientific experiment that uses Internet-connected computers in the search for extraterrestrial intelligence (SETI). SETI@home is one of the SETI projects that searches for extraterrestrial life. SETI@home allows anyone with a computer and an Internet connection to take part in the search. By using the computer while the owner is away, the SETI@home screensaver is able to search for extraterrestrial signals. See http://setiathome.ssl.berkeley.edu/ for more information.

stems from the fact that Napster is an enormous network of computers that are idle for part of each day. By harnessing the idle time and reselling it to companies that need extra memory to store and retrieve data, Napster could offer free or cheap downloads in exchange for customers allowing their computers to be accessed by companies wishing to outsource data storage during off hours.[16]

THE DECISION

Hank Barry, Shawn Fanning and the other executives at Napster were 56
faced with a number of issues that would determine the success or failure of Napster. Failing to implement the appropriate business model with the best partners could mean not only a missed opportunity for Napster, but also a missed opportunity for the global recording industry. Did the recent court decision in favor of the RIAA mean that the Big Five would be unwilling to take urgent action, or would they adopt a co-operative approach with Napster?

Examining the Text

1. Explain in nontechnical terms how MP3 music file-sharing technology evolved, according to the article. What implications did this new method of storing and transmitting musical information have on the recording industry, specifically with regard to copyright issues?

2. How have recording artists responded to the challenge presented by the advent of Napster and other Web-based file-sharing services? Likewise, how has the advent of Napster and Napster-like services affected traditional consumers of music products?

3. Explain some of the business models presented in this article as possible alternatives to Napster. Discuss the viability of each, explaining why or why not such alternative models might be adopted by consumers as the availability of free MP3 files online becomes increasingly scarce.

For Group Discussion

Slinger and Hillman begin this article with a *Fortune* magazine quotation, part of which reads, "If ever an industry needed to face the hard reality that it has an unsustainable business model, it's the recording business: whether Napster lives or dies, file sharing has ended the era of selling music primarily on plastic discs." Based upon your under-

---

[16]"Napster: In Search of a Viable Model," Shawn Cartwright, *The Journal of Business Strategy*, October 2000.

standing of the issue after reading this article—and perhaps upon your own experience with MP3 file-sharing as well—argue for or against the validity of this assertion.

Writing Suggestion

Write a comparison/contrast essay in which you present arguments for and against the existence of free file-sharing services such as Napster. As you discuss each side of the argument, be sure to identify which individuals, groups, or business organizations might align themselves with certain points of view. You might also turn this exercise into a persuasive essay by deciding which camp—pro-Napster or pro–strict-copyright enforcement—you belong to, and by asserting that position as a thesis statement. If you choose this latter option, you will still want to present all sides of the argument as objectively as you can, in order to convince readers of your sincerity and credibility.

Marilyn Manson and the Apt Pupils of Littleton

Gary Burns

In this relatively brief but well-documented popular culture research essay, the author examines a variety of textual responses to youth violence, in order to determine whether or not pop stars such as Marilyn Manson actually cause adolescents to commit murder and other heinous acts. What he uncovers is a species of hypocrisy. According to Burns, the news media tend to "scapegoat" high-profile celebrities such as Marilyn Manson, while ignoring other factors that the author finds much more insidious and dangerous. The author takes great pains to speculate on what these specific factors might be.

As you read *this essay, pay attention to any political biases the author may bring to the table. How does he view the mainstream media, and how do his views of the media perhaps color his interpretation of the Marilyn Manson/youth violence issue? If possible, observe at the same time your own preconceptions: do you share the author's views toward the news media and therefore find yourself favorably disposed toward his arguments, or do you find his underlying premises flawed—therefore leading you to question his conclusions about the connections between pop stars and violence?*

"America: Love it or leave it mother fuckers. All you racist (and if you think im [sic] a hypocrite, come here so I can kill you) mother fucking assholes in America who burn our flag and disgrace my land, GET OUT! And to you assholes in Iraq and Iran and all those other little piece of shit desert lands who hate us, shut up and die! We will kick your ass if you try and fuck with us, or at least I will!"

—Eric Harris's web site (Wilkinson 53)

A reporter from a Detroit radio station called and wanted to know what I thought about the killings in Colorado. He seemed to have an agenda—as is often the case with journalists. Specifically, he wanted to know whether I thought Marilyn Manson was to blame for the massacre and that parents should police what their children listen to. 1

I thought this was a most peculiar question, since it was only a day or two after the killings and, to my knowledge, it had not been definitively established that Eric Harris and Dylan Klebold even listened to or liked Marilyn Manson. As I write now in September 1999, I still don't think it has been established. *Time* says yes (Cloud 37); *Rolling Stone* says "[t]hey thought Marilyn Manson kind of sucked" (Wilkinson 54). 2

What seemed more obvious to me, as I talked to the reporter, was the significance of the date of the killings—April 20, which is Hitler's birthday and one day after the anniversaries of both Waco (1993) and Oklahoma City (1995). I talk to reporters fairly often, and I must say that I find no evidence in those quarters of the so-called "liberal media." The reporter in this particular case had picked up, somewhere, the conservative scapegoating of Marilyn Manson. 3

I did what I always do, which was to try to redirect and broaden the reporter's narrowly focused attention. Often, reporters don't want to hear a contrary view, even though they are trained to seek out "the other side." The blindness and deafness of the media in the Columbine case are especially pronounced and troubling. It seems that we have a new rite of spring in the form of rightwing violence every couple of years around the time of Hitler's birthday. That is the story—not Marilyn Manson. 4

The mainstream media have done practically nothing to expose, let alone defuse, the rightwing culture of guns, militarism, and government and antigovernment violence in the United States. One war follows another with scarcely a peep from reporters, anchors, or pundits. Practically nobody in the media elite even has the gumption to say: "Golly, for a peace-loving nation, the United States sure invades and bombs a lot of countries." Nor do the media "connect the dots" between military and civilian violence. When the decorated soldier Timothy McVeigh returned home from the Gulf War and bombed 5

Oklahoma City, the militia movement received momentary scrutiny, but that's not where McVeigh learned how to make bombs. His teachers in the military remain unstigmatized and even unnamed in media coverage of the slaughter.

Similarly, McVeigh's motive remains mysterious, but curiously absent from most discussions of it was any serious consideration of possible "cultural" influences. In McVeigh's case, this would have meant rightwing radio host William Cooper (see Alterman), not a musician. In the wake of Oklahoma City, there was a minor and temporary stir about rightwing radio nuts such as convicted Watergate felon G. Gordon Liddy, who somehow "landed on his feet" with a nationally syndicated daily talk radio show. The fact that he provided on-air instruction in how to kill government agents was only momentarily scandalous ("Head shots, head shots . . . Kill the sons of bitches").[1] Indeed, parents should police what their children listen to. 6

Indirect evidence suggests at least some military influence in the Columbine murders. According to the *New York Times:* 7

> [a]n essay in which Eric Harris portrayed himself as a shotgun shell prompted [a] teacher to have a . . . talk with his father, Wayne Harris. Once the teacher learned that Mr. Harris was a retired Air Force officer and that his son hoped to enlist in the military, she concluded that the essay was consistent with his future career aspirations, [school district spokeswoman Marilyn] Saltzman said. (Brooke A14)[2]

The hapless figure of Marilyn Manson is positively benign when compared with Hitler, McVeigh, and the likes of Liddy, but even Manson's weirdness has a military explanation, at least partially. Manson reports in his autobiography that one of his few "source[s] of friends" 8

> was a study and play group for the children of parents who had come in contact with Agent Orange during Vietnam. My father, Hugh, was a . . . member of the . . . covert group responsible for dumping the hazardous herbicide all over Vietnam. . . . Because I wasn't deformed, I didn't fit in with the other children in the group or at the regular retreats for kids whose parents were suing the government for exposure to the chemical. The other children had prosthetic limbs, physical irregularities and degenerative diseases, and not only was I comparatively normal but my father was the one who had actually sprayed the stuff on their fathers, most of whom were American infantry soldiers. (Manson, Long 28–29)

Manson is clearly some combination of jester and shaman, drawing his fabricated identity equally from the tragic glitter (Marilyn Monroe) and detritus (Charles Manson) of popular culture. If he did somehow inspire Harris and Klebold, that would be interesting and disturbing, but it still has not been proven. Manson's influence, if any, must also be considered in the light of at least three questions: What 9

Marilyn Manson

other popular culture did these teenagers consume?[3] Why haven't Marilyn Manson's thousands or millions of other fans shot up the local high school? Is "shoot up your school" really a plausible message to draw from Manson's songs? Obviously, the second question partially answers the third.

Manson himself, in a post-massacre *Rolling Stone* column ("Columbine"), says that his message is positive and the opposite of what his detractors claim. This, of course, is what one would expect him to say under the circumstances. However, critic James Blandford, several months before Columbine, made basically the same point in a defense of Manson: "He does not . . . promote the illnesses of society, but forces us to confront them" (86). This type of confrontation, practiced to varying degrees by many contemporary musicians, is presumably what prompts fans to write to the newsletter *Rock & Rap Confidential* with testimonials to the effect that music saved their lives. 10

Be that as it may, we should not let Manson—Charles or Marilyn—off the hook entirely. It was Charles Manson who perverted the cultural connotation of the Beatles in particular and rock culture in general.[4] Marilyn's choice of that last name is deliberately dangerous and provocative. He had to know that something like Columbine could eventually happen and drag him into a present-day criminal case. 11

What's in a name? While "Manson" is certainly bad, "Marilyn" is potentially good. Even so, "Marilyn" was probably not chosen admiringly, and in any case the bad name semiotically overwhelms the 12 good. The murderer has come home to roost, along with the ghosts of Vietnam.

Another act of naming deserves mention here. Why did Klebold's parents name him Dylan? One can only speculate, but I would guess that his parents, who must be baby boomers, had some Sixties sense of idealism at least in the back of their minds. One of the lessons of Columbine should be that Bob Dylan and Hitler do not mix. You can model yourself after one or the other, but not both. As we used to say in the Sixties, if you are not part of the solution, you are part of the problem. 13

Eric Harris's Web site, quoted above, proves the point. In one breath he condemns racism—a noble gesture he might easily have learned from a Bob Dylan song. In the next breath he delivers a racist diatribe against Iraq, Iran, and "those other little piece of shit desert lands." What "cultural influences" might lead an aspiring antiracist to such a contradictory position? Not Bob Dylan or even Marilyn Manson. But quite possibly the promilitary, prowar, anti-Iraq, anti-Iran propaganda that has freely circulated, practically without challenge, in the increasingly rightwing cultural climate that has prevailed in the United States for the past two decades. 14

Rolling Stone's coverage of Columbine captured the contradiction that must have troubled Harris and Klebold: 15

> It's been said that Eric and Dylan were fascists or Hitlerites. Eric spoke German, having studied the language since eighth grade. He spoke German at work and wore shirts with German sayings on them that, he'd say when asked, meant things like "go away." But so far, there is little direct evidence of supremacist thought on the part of Eric or Dylan, or a racial motive in the killings. "The only swastika I've seen at Columbine was the one that was etched in my desk," says one student. (Wilkinson 54)

On the other hand: "Guns change hands easily in the wild kingdom known as gun shows, where David Koresh, Tim McVeigh, and serial killer Thomas Lee Dillon all have felt at home, where swastika flags may not raise an eyebrow and where all the guns used in the Littleton massacre were purchased" (Fortgang 51).[5] 16

Michael Shoels, father of the only black student killed at Columbine, "has accused a Columbine dean of ignoring a complaint he made in early April [1999] that his son had received racist death threats from the trench coat mafia, a school clique that included Eric Harris and Dylan Klebold" (Brooke A14).[6] ABC radio news reported on 11 September 1999 that Shoels complained about three swastikas discovered at Columbine High School at the start of the 1999–2000 school year (i.e., four months after the killings). 17

Contradictory accounts are to be expected in a case like Columbine, where perceptions differ and conflicting interests compete for dominance in the historical record of events. Despite the contradictions (or to account for them), a picture emerges of Harris and Klebold as reluctant racists, nice kids who turned into apt pupils. As in the film *Apt Pupil* (1998), fascination with Nazi evil led to experimentation, seduction, and catastrophe. 18

The dominant rightwing media culture in the United States unfortunately facilitates such calamities by failing to provide sufficient reminders that Nazism, fascism, racism, and militarism, despite their attractions, are pathological and disastrous. Instead, a child or teenager can easily get the impression that these things are normal and respectable, just as gun shows, a war every six months, and violent, reactionary "political commentary" such as Liddy's are normal and respectable. 19

We are asleep and having a nightmare. Set the alarm for April 2000, April 2001, and April 2002. If those months pass without another Waco, Oklahoma City, or Littleton, the nightmare may be over. If our springtime ritual of rightwing violence continues, it will be a sign of deepening sickness, from which we may never recover—and it won't have a thing to do with Marilyn Manson. 20

NOTES

[1]26 Aug. 1994, quoted in Federal Communications Commission complaint quoted by *Indianapolis News,* Jorgensen 22. For additional examples of Liddy's inflammatory on-air comments, see Bottoms. For a post-Oklahoma City critique of rightwing talk radio, see Naureckas.

[2]My attention was drawn to this *New York Times* article by Pollitt.

[3]*Time*'s summary of Harris and Klebold's "cultural influences" reads as follows: "Music: Marilyn Manson; hero: Hitler; video games: *Doom* and *Quake*" (Cloud 36–37). As I already pointed out, the reference to Manson may be inaccurate. Wilkinson reported that Harris and Klebold "listened to KMFDM, Rammstein, and Nine Inch Nails, as well as Dr. Octagon and DJ Spooky" (54). *Time* mentioned in a different article that Harris was a devotee of the rightwing novelist and essayist Ayn Rand (Pooley 30).

[4]For a recent, insightful discussion of Charles Manson, see Dalton.

[5]Colorado, perhaps not coincidentally, is a relative hotbed of militia activity and rightwing talk radio (see Jorgenson).

[6]However, Wilkinson reports that "Eric and Dylan weren't charter members or even full-fledged members of any clique, not even the Trench Coat Mafia. They bounced around" (49).

WORKS CITED

Alterman, Eric. "Little Limbaughs and the Fire Next Time." *The Nation* 27 Sept. 1999: 10.

Blandford, James R. "Antichrist Reborn." *Record Collector* Nov. 1998: 86–88.

Bottoms, Richard. "Liddy's Lethal Advice: Red Meat for Republican Voters." *Extra!* July/Aug. 1995:18.

Brooke, James. "Teacher of Colorado Gunmen Alerted Parents." *New York Times* 11 May 1999: A14.

Cloud, John. "Just a Routine School Shooting." *Time* 31 May 1999: 34–43.

Dalton, David. "Pleased to Meet You . . .". *Mojo* Sept. 1999: 68–76.

Fortgang, Erika. "How They Got the Guns." *Rolling Stone* 10 June 1999:51–53.

Jorgenson, Leslie. "AM Armies." *Extra!* Mar./Apr. 1995: 20–22.

Manson, Marilyn. "Columbine: Whose Fault Is It?" *Rolling Stone* 24 June 1999: 23–24+.

Manson, Marilyn, with Neil Strauss. *The Long Hard Road Out of Hell.* New York: HarperCollins, 1998.

Naureckas, Jim. "Talk Radio on Oklahoma City: Don't Look at Us." *Extra!* July/Aug. 1995: 17–18.

Pollitt, Katha. "Humanitarian, All Too Humanitarian." *The Nation* 31 May 1999: 10.

Pooley, Eric. "Portrait of a Deadly Bond." *Time* 10 May 1999: 26–32

Wilkinson, Peter, with Matt Hendrickson. "Humiliation and Revenge: The Story of Reb and VoDkA [sic]." *Rolling Stone* 10 June 1999: 49–54+.

Examining the Text

1. Explain what Burns means when he refers to "conservative scapegoating" in this piece. What evidence, if any, does he bring to bear on such a charge of scapegoating? Do you agree or disagree with this charge, and why?

2. The author contends that the news media have done nothing "to expose, let alone defuse, the rightwing culture of guns, militarism, and government and antigovernment violence in the United States." How does he support this assertion, and how does this claim factor into a discussion of Marilyn Manson's impact on youth violence?

3. While focusing on other factors that may play more of a role in inciting teen violence, author Burns also allows that "we should not let Manson . . . off the hook entirely." In what ways do Marilyn Manson and other media figures contribute to the culture of youth violence, according to the author?

For Group Discussion

The author, writing at the turn of the millennium, says, "Set the alarm for April 2000, April 2001, and April 2002. If those months pass without another Waco, Oklahoma City, or Littleton, the nightmare may be over." Of course, on September 11, 2001, the nightmare escalated to a level unimagined by the author. As a class, discuss what factors discussed in this essay—as well as other factors not discussed by the author—may have contributed to the culture of terror and antiterror which pervades the United States today.

Writing Suggestion

In an essay, respond to the author's thematic position: that the media use pop music artists as easy scapegoats for many of society's ills, while ignoring more pervasive and dangerous influences. Based upon your own reading of newspapers and magazines, and your watching of television and movies, do you find evidence to support Burns' assertions? Be specific in incorporating textual material from all forms of media as you develop your argument. Also, feel free to adopt a contrarian position: either that pop stars *are* to blame for youth violence, or that media scapegoating of music stars is a myth perpetuated by certain observers such as Burns . . . or both.

Deadheads Yesterday and Today: An Audience Study

Melissa McCray Pattacini

This article, written for the scholarly journal Popular Music and Society, *may serve as an excellent model for the kinds of research social scientists conduct in the area of popular music. In this piece, author Pattacini begins by providing a history of the Grateful Dead, beginning in 1965 with Ken Kesey's acid tests that were chronicled so vividly in Tom Wolfe's* The Electric Kool-Aid Acid Test. *She then goes on to describe the Deadhead subculture that gradually emerged through the 1970s, the relationship of this culture to psychedelic drugs, the emergence of a set of behaviors and social codes inherent in*

Deadhead culture, and the eventual transformation of this culture following the death of the band's lead guitarist Jerry Garcia. The author then goes on to describe a social-scientific method for examining the current state of Deadhead culture, and states conclusions based on her research.

***As you read** this article, note the way in which social scientists pursue research using a variety of instruments such as the internet survey conducted of Deadheads for this piece, and the ways in which they support their textual assertions using evidence from related literature and from their own findings. Note also how they begin their research with a central question—in this case: What has happened to fans of the Grateful Dead since the death of Jerry Garcia? Note also how they formulate their essay's thesis as a concrete response to that initial question.*

In the summer of 1995, following the death of Jerry Garcia, the Grateful Dead stopped touring. For thirty years, their concerts served as a gathering place for a diverse group of followers, nicknamed Deadheads. Coming from all walks of life, they exemplified the hippie-culture ideologies of peace, generosity, and sharing. The era of the three-season Grateful Dead tour has ended and the fans need to fill the apparent void left by its absence. This is a report of an Internet survey of Deadheads (see Appendix for online interview demographics) illustrating how they have compensated for this lack to different degrees and in a variety of ways. These include following other tours and bands, communicating on the Internet, and other creative pursuits. A great number have just gone on with their lives, better off for being touched by the music of the Dead. 1

In understanding the Deadheads and their current disposition, a closer examination must be made of their historical attachment to the Grateful Dead. The culture outside the concerts became a ritual, a homecoming, almost a religion to some. Others participated for the readily available psychedelic drugs and to experience a special freedom that seemed to originate in the music. 2

It has been said that Jerry and the boys "hosted rock & roll's best and longest-running party" (Goodman 21–23). The parties started in the winter of 1965, in the Haight-Ashbury section of San Francisco, an artists' colony recognized as the birthplace of the American hippie culture. The band specifically garnered attention for playing at Ken Kesey's Acid Tests. In the beginning, 200 people would show up at an Acid Test to experience LSD. The numbers multiplied due to the effect of the combination of music and drugs. The Dead were forced out of smaller clubs by the burgeoning crowds, into open-air arenas and parks (Scully and Dalton). 3

A 1971 Grateful Dead album jacket included the message: "DEAD FREAKS UNITE. Who are you? Where are you? How are you? Send us your name and address and we'll keep you informed." To the surprise of the group, thousands responded and were (and still are) kept in touch through newsletters, called Almanacs, and the Official Book of the Deadheads, released in 1983 (Susman). In 1990, it was estimated that 500 to 1,000 hardcore followers traveled to every show. The overall number of fans in the early 1990s was "over 37,351, because that many attended an outdoor concert at Saratoga, NY" (Skow 11–13). 4

A distinction should be made between a Deadhead and a Tourhead. Any fan of the Grateful Dead can be termed a Deadhead (or Head). These people collect Grateful Dead music; some wear tie-dyed gear, while others wear suits and ties; some have a stereotypical spaced-out, unclean look while others, maybe even those clad in the tie-dyed uniform, are squeaky clean. But still, they come from all walks of life: students, laborers, bikers, lawyers, sports figures, and some of the nation's most prominent politicians all declare themselves to be Deadheads (Rouse). A Tourhead is a subcategory of fans. They trek from gig to gig, camping out in their cars, some living hand to mouth, others off of their parents' credit cards. "Tourhead culture is one of the latest forms of what American studies scholars like to call communitas (Latin for fellowship)—that habit Americans have of celebrating their individualism with others just like themselves" (Sutherland 30). This holds true of the early followers and of the younger fans who "got on the bus" (Shenk and Silberman) in the late 1980s and early 1990s. 5

While unfathomable to many, the fervent quasi-religious fixation these fans experienced was, and still is, caused by numerous factors. In online interviews, some point to a feeling of alienation from mainstream organized religion. The concerts themselves provided a ritual to follow. Standing on a stage covered with Persian carpets, the band would play a few songs (granted some were as long as 18 minutes). These would flow into what is termed "Drums," free-flowing drum solos. A few more tunes would be spun, followed by "The Space," then some more music, another "Drums" break, then the end of the show. The band might play continually for four hours, sometimes longer. The set lists changed, and if there were three shows in the same town there would be three separate lists. Still, you could count on the ritual to be the same. 6

The drugs, coupled with the Dead's unique musical style, allowed some to commune with a higher power on their own terms. This generally happened when Jerry Garcia and Bob Weir played their impromptu solos during a show. The Dead termed these interludes 7

"Space." Space has been defined as "that quintessential bit of Deadness in every concert, when the group would abandon all pretense of musical structure and just sort of noodle around for a very long period of time . . . noodle noodle noodle noodle" (Carnegie 56–57). From the perspective of one nondrug-using first-time concert-goer, this is remembered as "so weird, I mean, I had only been to standard concerts up to that point, I'm talking Huey Lewis and the News. All of a sudden the crowd would get really loud, 'cause they knew what was coming, then the guys would just start jamming and the whole place would just, well, sway together" (Online Interview 14). These experimental jam sessions, coupled with hallucinogenics, allowed for some "really beautiful people" to "make some type of magical contact with the heavens, the creator and a few deities that I'm unfamiliar with" (Online Interview 5). Drugs were the way to reach a higher plane. For many it was the way to escape the suburban life that lay behind and ahead of them (Folkers).

Certainly, the most sensational aspect of a Dead show took place 8
in the parking lot or area surrounding the venue. The parks where the fans camped out resembled colorful street fairs. Many of the hardcore followers would subsidize their tour by selling tie-dyed T-shirts, beaded necklaces, and "magic" cookies or brownies (Skow). Drugs were ever-present in the barter economy. A case or six-pack of beer could be traded for food, space to sleep in a motel room, or a hit of acid (Online Interview 14).

"Drums, bongos would be playing at you from different direc- 9
tions, people dancing . . . kids walking around saying 'I need a miracle, miracle me,' which was like a code for needing a ticket into the show" (Online Interview 14). The Dead tried to discourage this "Miracling" by using mail-order ticket sales. In the late 1980s the tour's tone and fans began to change. The tour in 1995, in which ticketless groups physically crashed down gates, was the bottom of a spiral that had been winding its way down for some time. The band sat down and wrote their fans an open letter with these messages: If you do not have a ticket, do not come to the show. If you are looking for drugs, you will be an easy target for arrest (Strauss).

In light of the 1995 tour, the band was feeling the change and 10
strain from the difference in their fans. In an interview, Garcia once said: "You wonder where these people are coming from, but they're self-invented. We didn't invent them, and we didn't invent our original audience. In a way, this whole process has kind of invented us" (Wenner and Reich). It was no longer the hippies with their quasi-political causes talking philosophy over a joint. It was changing into divided factions, old school vs. new, with an increasing number com-

ing only to get a hit of the nitrous oxide being sold in the parking lot (Goodman).

While the Dead have stopped traveling, many of the Tourheads have not. Tourheads primarily consist of younger Deadheads. Among the most notable bands they have latched onto are Phish and the Furthur Fest bands. Of these, Phish has had the most press aimed at trying to pass the torch of the Grateful Dead on to their scene (Gilmore). The Deadhead attachment remains, for the most part, cool. As a once unified "communitas" they are now scattered into tiny factions; there is no whole entity left to physically identify with any one group. 11

Online questionnaire opinions tell of the feelings toward the various styles and musical groups. "Phish is musically talented and innovative—not focused on a mentality of kindness that informs their life as were the Dead—and thus a bit empty by comparison" (Online Interview 4). They don't have the original hippie zeal or mission of change. All who have heard Phish attest to their musical capabilities. It is an (unfair) comparison to the Dead that the group falls short. Common reactions to their concerts include, "Going to Phish makes me feel old (I'm 30) because of the young following they attract" (Online Interview 20), and "Their music seems to attract more of the jocky, punky element that really began to be a serious pain in the ass the last few years the Dead were around" (Online Interview 19). 12

The comparison to the Dead "just may be the silliest damned thing anybody has ever attempted. [Phish has] a completely different approach to music, outside of the open-ended jamming that both groups draw from" (Online Interview 9). It is their similar "noodling" that the media has keyed in on. The sentiments of many who have forgone traveling are summed up as follows: "Have seen Phish a couple of times. I admire their unique talent and their energy and enthusiasm. But I'm not willing to follow them around the country" (Online Interview 3). 13

With most Deadheads unwilling to follow a new band across the country, more support for the Further Fest (Further was the name given to the bus used during Ken Kesey's legendary Acid Tests that featured the emerging Dead) would be expected (Shenk and Silberman). Remaining members of the Dead, Bob Weir, Mickey Hart, and Bruce Hornsby, along with their new bands, have grouped together to try to fill in the summer months left empty by the end of the Grateful Dead tour (Catlin). "Musicians gotta play, Deadheads gotta dance," says Hart. "Considering they never heard the songs before, the fans are on their feet all night. They're getting it. It's all a little strange at first, but after a few minutes they get into the groove and go for a ride. 14

They depend on the succession of the notes. It's a habit for them. It's a healing process for me too to get out and play again. It felt good to get back in the familiar groove. It was like revisiting an old lover, like good sex with an old girlfriend" (Susman).

After two years, fans looking to re-create the Dead scene appear 15
disappointed: "Further is an evolving reincarnation of various band members' new musical efforts. Last year one could still detect the spaces left in the music that Jerry used to fill" (Online Interview 20). Still others acknowledge there is no going back: "Further Fest is a nice try. I admire the other bands that participate, however it can't replace the Dead. They are fun shows, and I went last year and will go again this year because I love live music and there will be bands that I like. But I won't go thinking that the Grateful Dead will be playing. I will go to see some old friends that I haven't met yet and hear some familiar music played just a bit differently than I'm used to" (Online Interview 9).

Much of the lack of interest has been attributed to the tour cre- 16
ators' intentions. When ticket sales weren't as brisk as anticipated, headline acts such as the Black Crowes were added to the bill. "[T]he promoters are trying to reach beyond those who want to see acts with some connection to the Dead and get anyone with a credit card to show up. The problem with the last few years of the Dead tour was that everyone with a credit card was showing up" (Online Interview 19).

Many of the older fans still have a lingering mixed reaction to the 17
"newbies" (fans new to the bus, new to the culture). Many see the experience of following the group as the equivalent of running away to join the circus. There is freedom in the utopian vision of the hippies—it wasn't all just peace, love, and kindness. But it seems that as new fans got on the bus, these visions changed forever. The parking lots during the last concert tour are most brutally described as "a haven for overindulged white kids who were looking to rebel against their parents, but not rebel so far as to never be able to return at the first sign of trouble" (Online Interview 1). While older Deadheads feel some responsibility to be guides for the youths recently attracted to the scene, a large portion are turned off by the new attitudes they embody.

Economically, the Grateful Dead supported both big and small 18
business enterprises. Official Grateful Dead Merchandising has been going strong since the early 1990s. They sell an assortment of memorabilia ranging from commemorative T-shirts and books to tie-dyed socks and golf club covers. The Almanac also has listings of various recordings and access to the DeadBase books (*Grateful Dead Almanac*).

Smaller in scale were the vendors (fans) outside the concerts ped- 19
dling their homemade wares in the carnival-like atmosphere. It was a

traveling craft show. Through the sale of these items, many Tourheads financed their life on the road. The popularity of the 1987 album *In the Dark* produced an organized outdoor vendor scene, which, in large part, killed off the craft market. At this point, commercial success changed the scene by attracting large groups of younger fans. Previously, Heads could count on a relatively safe and laid-back atmosphere in which to experience the show in any manner they wanted.

In the last few tours, references were made to groups of "fami- 20
lies" called "the Wrecking Crew" or "the Five Families." (It is common to refer to an immediate group of Deadhead friends as "family.") The main focus of these loosely knit groups was selling beer, burritos, and (nitrous oxide-filled) balloons. Most Heads gave them a wide berth. These groups staked out territory at each venue for selling their wares and it was rumored they carried guns. There was some suspicion that they were involved with the government or with the police as informants. "They'd get picked up by the cops, you'd see it at one show, and they would be back out the next day, which was weird" (Online Interview 22). There was little respect for the clique aspect of these groups: "[T]he five families were business people, I think. Never cared much for them . . . they were moneychangers then, and still are, I think, just with different scams" (Online Interview 18).

What has happened to these people now that the tour has ended? 21
According to one Deadhead: "My beliefs are that those in it for economic interests followed their interests . . . economics" (Online Interview 5). The biggest commodity outside the stadiums was drugs. The dealers have just moved on: "I have seen several friends who are still surviving quite nicely in their old trade, even though the venue has changed. I think there are enough other bands and tour attractions to keep the entrepreneurs active for quite some time. Trust me, if they have to sell stuff at a Metallica concert, they will" (Online Interview 1).

While the band continues to sell and put out CD sets from their 22
archives (available through the *Grateful Dead Almanac*), an amazing aspect of the Dead is the availability of their music free of charge. It has the largest trading market of its kind, fully sanctioned and encouraged by the band itself. Each concert arena was set up in different sections. There was a spinners section, where those who danced by spinning in circles could have a large area for unrestricted movement. There were the ticketed seat areas (which it appears nobody really sat in for a whole show). Last, there was the tapers area.

The taper section was partitioned for the "bootleggers" to set up 23
their tape decks and microphones to get the best sound. Anyone with a tapers ticket could record the show and make copies for the Heads who requested them. They could be seen as a branch on a tree (with the band as the trunk). The tapes they dubbed for others became

leaves. With the ready access to the Internet, the tape trade has been bustling. A blank tape is sent to a "branch," who then sends back your "leaf." Thus, the quality of the tapes being disseminated is assured, at least as far as keeping the music at a second generation of copying (Online Interview 14). No money changes hands in this process, just tapes. These collections range from the modest to the extensive: "I've only got about 200 tapes, I mean you should see my friend Jeff, he has like 7 times as many" (Online Interview 14).

Admirably, this truly is about "getting the music out there." To 24 mention or believe in a large-scale for-profit "bootleg tape industry" is to seriously offend any true Deadhead and show yourself to be an outsider. (In Online Interview 7, I was taken to task on this issue.) The interviewee pointed out the need to define [humanize] myself within the context of the Deadheads. They needed to know that I was not an intruder and was genuinely interested for academic, as well as personal, reasons. I was pretty far off "the bus" or even the road they were traveling on! In their effort to educate me, I received more detailed responses on a fairly general questionnaire. The definitive answer came as: "There is no 'industry' and we actively try to destroy anyone's chances of profiting off of Grateful Dead tapes. They are a gift from the band" (Online Interview 7).

After Jerry Garcia's death, "Deadheads, some belonging to on- 25 line communities and others not, found solace on the Internet. This was particularly important for those isolated from local communities of Deadheads" (Adams). There is great activity among Deadheads on the Internet. They can be found at the official website of the Grateful Dead (*http://grateful.dead.net*). Deadbase (*http://www.deadbase.com*) has hundreds of personal Deadhead home pages. America Online has the "Dead Forum," and The Well (*telnet:well.sf.ca.us.*) is the best-known electronic bulletin board service with a large Dead membership.

Through the Internet, Deadheads gather in much the same way 26 they did outside a concert. They catch up on the years, months, or days since they were last together. Tape trading is a favorite pastime at the tape site (which can be accessed through *Dead.net*). *Dead.net* offers several different areas to explore. Heads visit Deadnet Central, which has bulletin board files for questions. This includes the Robert Hunter Journal site, where anyone can read current anecdotal stories about the lyricist's life and his personal plans for the future.

There is a sense of connection on these lines. Many Deadheads 27 bought computers specifically to keep in touch with each other, either when they stopped touring or after the tour ceased. "Part of touring for me was meeting fellow Deadheads from around the country. I've been able to meet many of those people on-line and even in person from time to time. I am a 'bus driver' (chat room supervisor) in the

AOL Dead Forum, and this allows me to not only be in touch with other long-time heads, but to teach the kind and peace-loving nature of us to the newbies" (Susman). In the electronic age, instead of "being there," the traditions and shared experiences are sent pulsing along the wires.

The end of the tour and dispersion of the group has elicited a variety of responses from within the Deadheads community. They are an artistic, articulate group and have much to say on what the "end of the era" has meant. This response sums it up best: 28

> It's meant childhood's end for people ranging all the way up into their sixties. . . . It's also been a new BEGINNING in many ways for many of us, because there's no longer the Dead for us to be entertained by, so we have to now do the entertaining. . . . All the creative seeds that were sown in each of us during our time with the Dead are just now beginning to burst into bloom. People are starting to take the energy they put into going to shows and surviving on tour into the gifts that they themselves possess. I think you're going to see a lot of artists of all types popping up in the public eye in the next decade or so who will be attributing a lot of their inspiration to the Dead. I mean, you already see that to a certain extent, but it'll be continuing to happen, I think. And for every one person you end up seeing on Letterman who came out of this whole thing, you can bet that there are 50 more doing their thing on a smaller level who got their spark at a show. (Online Interview 19)

In the past two years, there has been a noticeable upswing in Grateful Dead-related works. There are the obvious "I was there with the Dead" biographical books. There has been tremendous activity in submissions for Dead tribute magazines such as *Dupree's* and *Relix*. An important touchstone has been David Gans's "Grateful Dead Hour." This nationally syndicated radio show (started in 1985) plays the music and discusses various concerts (Gans). The most notable artistic works can be found on the Internet. They range from animated home pages to photo and art galleries. Each is trying to bring images of the Dead to life (Grateful Dead Inspired Animated Website, Grateful Dead Inspired Art Gallery). 29

To quote another on "the end of the age": "The age depends on the people—and as far as I've seen, the people are still alive and kicking . . . and I haven't read in *The New York Times* that the concept of 'thinking for yourself' is dead—and that's what the whole hippie movement was really about—not clothes, peace or even music—but ideas" (Online Interview 5). So, as far as the Deadheads are concerned, the ideas live on, the music continues to play, and the Dead are alive. 30

The Deadheads are all around us. Unfortunately, this subculture has earned an unsavory reputation because of its open drug usage. 31

This got out of control toward the end of the band's last tour. To put a spin on Jerry Garcia's theory that the crowd created the band: the band's drug excesses (which contributed to their destruction) only mirrored the crowds' abuses. The Dead grew up (so to speak) within the acid test culture (Wolfe). The drugs were present when the band began their career. As the culture experimented, the band provided the most consistent, ritualized background music. The music originally followed the drugs, but eventually the drugs came to follow the music.

The Deadheads are in touch with each other on a more main- 32
stream level than when the band was touring. Their cyberspace connectedness is something even those "people over thirty," whom they were cautioned not to trust, can understand. Not to trivialize the importance of this phenomenon, this need to stay in touch could be seen by an outsider as the equivalent of writing letters to friends made at summer camp. It is a need to catch up and to reaffirm that they experienced something special together.

The Grateful Dead will go on as long as the music is being 33
traded. Each time a leaf (copy) falls from a (taper's) branch, that music will "keep on growing, keep on going, keep on flowing, yeah, yeah, yeah" (Grateful Dead Annotated Online Lyrics). Through the songs and their shared point of view the Deadheads are keeping alive an outlook on how to live life to its fullest. We should strive to adhere to their credo that the greatest grace is to accomplish this through kindness, peace, and an awareness of the world around. In the final analysis, the magic legacy of the Grateful Dead is more than music; it is the resilient family of fans they have taken along on their ride.

WORKS CITED

Adams, Rebecca. "Mourning for Jerry: We Haven't Left the Planet Yet." *Dupree's* 1995. E-mail to author 10 July 1997.

Carnegie, M. D. "Jerry's Kids." *American Spectator* Oct. 1995: 56–57.

Catlin, Roger. "Not Fade Away: Memory of the Dead Ignites Fourth of July Fest." *Hartford Courant* (Eastern ed.) 29 June 1997: G1+.

Folkers, Richard. "The Band for the Eternally Young." *U.S. News & World Report* 21 Aug. 1995: 6.

Gans, David. "Dead to the World." The Grateful Dead Hour. Truth and Fun, Inc. KPFA 94.1, Berkeley: <*http://www.geocities.com*>.

Gilmore, Mikal. "Life after Garcia." *Rolling Stone* 28 Dec. 1995–11 Jan. 1996: 85–86.

Goodman, Fred. "The End of the Road?" *Rolling Stone* 23 Aug. 1990: 21–23.

The Grateful Dead Almanac. Vol. 1: 3. <*http://grateful.dead.net/almanac/vol1_3/index.html*>.

The Grateful Dead Annotated Online Lyrics. <*http://www.uccs.edu/ddodd/gdhome.html*>.

The Grateful Dead Inspired Animated Website. <*http://www.geocities.com/SunsetStrip/Palms/1998*>.

The Grateful Dead Inspired Art Gallery. <*http://www.zausner.com/gallery.html*>.

Greenfield, Robert. *Dark Star: An Oral Biography of Jerry Garcia*. New York: Morrow, 1996.

Hunter, Robert. <*http://www.deadnet/RobertHunterArchive/files/majorlinks.html*>.

Online Interview 1. "Re: Grateful Dead Questions." E-mail to the author. 30 June 1997.

Online Interview 3. "Re: Grateful Dead Questions." E-mail to the author. 24 June 1997.

Online Interview 4. "Re: Grateful Dead Questions." E-mail to the author. 24 June 1997.

Online Interview 5. "Re: Grateful Dead Questions." E-mail to the author. 23 June 1997.

Online Interview 7. "Re: Grateful Dead Questions." E-mail to the author. 20 June 1997.

Online Interview 9. "Re: Grateful Dead Questions." E-mail to the author. 25 June 1997.

Online Interview 14. "Re: Grateful Dead Questions." E-mail to the author. 11 June 1997.

Online Interview 18. "Re: Grateful Dead Questions." E-mail to the author. 24 June 1997.

Online Interview 19. "Re: Grateful Dead Questions." E-mail to the author. 25 June 1997.

Online Interview 20. "Re: Grateful Dead Questions." E-mail to the author. 25 June 1997.

Online Interview 22. "Re: Grateful Dead Questions." E-mail to the author. 12 July 1997.

Rouse, Rob. "Politicians Mourn Garcia's Passing." 1995: <*http://www.intercom.net/local/shore_journal/kjr10813.html*>.

Scully, Rock, and David Dalton. *Twenty Years on the Bus with Garcia and the Grateful Dead: Living with the Dead*. New York: Little, Brown, 1996.

Shenk, David, and Steve Silberman. *Skeleton's Key*. 23 June 1997 <*http://www.deadnet/dead.netcentral*>.

Skow, John. "In California: The Dead Live On." *Time* 11 Feb. 1985: 11–13.

Strauss, Neil. "The Acid Test: Deadheads Face Hard Time in LSD Crackdown." *Rolling Stone* 14–28 July 1994: 24–26.

Susman, Gary. "Dead Nation One Year Later: Celebrating the Fat Man, Life after Jerry." *Boston Globe* 15 Aug. 1996. <*http://www.phx.com/alt1/archive/music/reviews/08-15-96fDEADHEADS.html*>.

Sutherland, Scott. "In the Deadheads' Footsteps." *New York Times* 16 June 1996 (early ed.), sec. 2: 30.

Wenner, Jan, and Charles Reich. "Interview with Jerry Garcia." *Rolling Stone* 1972 <*http://www.erols.com/jokomo/72int.txt*>.

Wolfe, Tom. *The Electric Kool-Aid Acid Test*. New York: Bantam, 1968.

APPENDIX A - SURVEY DEMOGRAPHICS

Respondent Number	Age Started Listening	Age Attend First Concert	Current Age	Number of concerts attended	Birthplace
1	14	26	41	92	MD
2	18	19	36	125	CT
3	17	18	37	100	U.K.
4	18	18	45	300+	PA
5	18	19	29	101	IN
6	17	18	34	40	OH
7	12	17	26	36	NY
8	22	22	35	40	CA
9	21	25	31	55	CA
10	22	23	49	n/a	TX
11	17	18	42	35	AL
12	n/a	n/a	n/a	46	n/a
13	13	14	n/a	100+	IL
14	16	16	26	30	CT
15	19	19	30	210	n/a
16	14	20	39	60+	CT
17	17	19	35	LOTS	AR
18	15	16	35	60+	CO
19	20	21	29	34	IN
20	15	15	30	100+	MA
21	20	20	31	40	VA
22	16	16	26	200+	CT
Avg.	17.4	19.3	34.3		
Med.	17	19	34.5		

Respondent Number	Current Residence	Furthest Traveled for Show	Educational Level	Used Drugs
1	n/a	n/a	MA	yes
2	MN	CA	MA	yes
3	NY	CAN.	MA	yes
4	n/a	East Cst	2MA	yes
5	n/a	CA	BS	yes
6	OH	DC	2MA	yes
7	KS	CA	MA	yes
8	CA	AZ	CPA	yes
9	NV	WA	BFA	no
10	TX	200 miles	3 yrs	yes
11	AL	EGYPT	1.5 yrs	yes
12	CA	n/a	BA/Grs	n/a
13	n/a	n/a	2 yrs	yes
14	CT	IL	BA/Grs	yes
15	TX	CA	MA/MS	no
16	NJ	RI	BA/Grs	no
17	NJ	OH	BS/Grs	yes
18	NY	North East	Phd	yes
19	IL	Canada	BA	yes
20	n/a	CA	BS	yes
21	DC	n/a	MS	yes
22	CT	CA	BA	yes
Avg.				
Med.				

APPENDIX B - ONLINE SURVEY QUESTIONNAIRE

After identifying myself as a non-Deadhead, graduate student, I explained that the focus of my research is "what Deadheads are up to now." The open-ended questions are as follows:

1. What has everybody been up to since the tour has ended? Is it a life philosophy thing or is it a groupie thing—are the majority moving on with their lives or just finding another band to start following around?
2. Opinions on Furthur Fest and Phish.
3. What has happened to the economic aspect of the shows—people doing the crafting, etc.; the bootleg tape industry (boom or bust now)
4. Opinions on the differences the end of the age has meant as a whole to the followers as a group (not personally yet).

Personal Information

1. How old are you now—how old were you when you first started getting into this?
   a. Listening to the music
   b. First concert (age at first concert if different from when you started listening)
2. How many concerts have you attended and where (as many as you can recall and approximate years)?
3. Where were you born and raised (did you travel very far to attend or did you stay a regional fan)?
4. What was the last grade level you completed? (Jr. High [7, 8, 9], High School [10, 11, 12], College [2yr, 4yr, AS, BA, BS], Grad School [MA, ME, MBA], or Ph.D.)
5. Were drugs at all a factor in your involvement? How prevalent was this really, honestly, from the perspective of actually having been there—and how responsible were the people who were doing it and any reasons for it (music enhancement, to drop out of reality . . . etc.)
6. If this was an integral part of your life, what were the reasons for you going to the shows, being involved, and how do you feel now (Empty? Life is over? It was a long, strange journey . . . or is it business as usual, life goes on)?

Examining the Text

1. Who are "Deadheads?" How did this subculture emerge, and what behaviors and social codes evolved as part of that culture? What has become of them since the death of the band's lead guitarist Jerry Garcia. What does the Deadhead ethos represent, both for the Deadheads themselves and for outsiders?

2. Using descriptions offered by the author, along with anything you have heard or experienced with regard to the Grateful Dead, describe as best you can what happened at and around a Grateful Dead concert. What is "Space" in reference to Grateful Dead concerts?

3. How did Jerry Garcia's death directly affect the fan base of the Grateful Dead? What role did the internet come to play for Deadheads after the band stopped touring?

For Group Discussion

The author describes a movement and a culture born in the 1960s, which flourished until 1995 and continues to exist today, although in a different form as described by the author at the end of her piece. In what ways does the Deadhead subculture, as depicted by Pattacini, resemble other pop music phenomena of the current day? If you have some experience of contemporary rave or punk subcultures, for instance, what similarities and differences can you draw between these movements?

Writing Suggestion

As a fictional exploration and an exercise in describing settings and internal landscapes of the emotions, imagine yourself, an outsider, suddenly plunked "Dead"-center in the middle of a Grateful Dead concert. Try to describe as vividly as you can the people and events taking place around you, along with your feelings as you confront this uncommon scenario. Don't feel bound by having to create an absolutely accurate depiction of this antic world; instead, give your imagination free rein to invent wildly and extravagantly. Having completed this initial "freewrite," you might then work it into a fictional autobiographical narrative, by developing a thesis: what did you learn about yourself as a result of participating briefly in this world, and how were you changed by the experience?

Rap and Hip-Hop: A Casebook

Hip-Hop Nation: There's More To Rap Than Just Rhythms and Rhymes

Melissa August, Leslie Everton Brice, Laird Harrison, Todd Murphy, and David E. Thigpen

In this article, co-written by a group of young experts in rap and hip-hop music, the authors argue that rap has become a predominant force in the United States popular culture and has found its way into a wide variety of other artistic forms, such as literature and film. According to this article, 81 million rap CDs were sold last year, outpacing every other musical category, popular or otherwise; furthermore, in that same period, sales of rap and hip-hop recordings jumped over 31 percent.

The authors provide an encapsulated view of hip-hop's social and historical roots, noting that this pop-music force derived originally from the Bronx, New York, with inspiration from some reggae-related musical activities in Kingston, Jamaica. They supplement that historical overview with a timeline at the end of the article, chronicling notable points in rap's development. Finally, the authors explore the popularity of this musical form with white audiences and discuss the responses of the African American community to this mainstream "appropriation" of an originally black art form.

***As you read** this article, note the ways in which this writing differs from the kinds of linear, logically sequenced prose you are accustomed to reading in academic essays and textbooks. For example, pay attention to the way that the authors attempt to suggest some of hip-hop's flavor, by interspersing "sampled" rap-related excerpts and discussions throughout, and by including a collage of quotations to conclude this piece.*

Music mixes with memory. As we think back over the 20th century, every decade has a melody, a rhythm, a sound track. The years and the sounds bleed together as we scan through them in our recollections, a car radio searching for a clear station. The century starts off blue: Robert Johnson selling his soul to the devil at the crossroads. Then the jazz age: Louis Armstrong, Duke Ellington and, later on, Benny Goodman and "Strange fruit hanging from the poplar trees." Midcentury, things start to rock with Chuck Berry, "Wop-bop-a-loo-bop a-lop bam boom!" the Beatles, Aretha Franklin, "a hard rain's a-going to fall," Bob Marley, Stevie Wonder. It might be better to for- 1 get the '80s—the posturing heavy-metal bands, Debbie Gibson, "Let's get physical—physical," the guy with the haircut in Flock of Seagulls. Perhaps the remembered sounds of R.E.M., U2, and Prince can drown them all out.

And how will we remember the last days of the '90s? Most likely, 2 to the rough-hewn beat of rap. Just as F. Scott Fitzgerald lived in the jazz age, just as Dylan and Jimi Hendrix were among the rulers of the age of rock, it could be argued that we are living in the age of hip-hop. "Rock is old," says Russell Simmons, head of the hip-hop label Def Jam, which took in nearly $200 million in 1998. "It's old people's shit. The creative people who are great, who are talking about youth culture in a way that makes sense, happen to be rappers."

Consider the numbers. In 1998, for the first time ever, rap outsold 3 what previously had been America's top-selling format, country music. Rap sold more than 81 million CDs, tapes and albums last year, compared with 72 million for country. Rap sales increased a stunning 31% from 1997 to 1998, in contrast to 2% gains for country, 6% for rock and 9% for the music industry overall. Boasts rapper Jay-Z, whose current album, *Vol. 2...Hard Knock Life* (Def Jam), has sold more than 3 million copies: "Hip-hop is the rebellious voice of the youth. It's what people want to hear."

Even if you're not into rap, hip-hop is all around you. It pulses 4 from the films you watch (Seen a Will Smith movie lately?), the books you read (even Tom Wolfe peels off a few raps in his best-selling new novel), the fashion you wear (Tommy Hilfiger, FUBU). Some definitions are in order: rap is a form of rhythmic speaking in rhyme; hip-hop refers to the backing music for rap, which is often composed of a collage of excerpts, or "samples," from other songs; hip-hop also refers to the culture of rap. The two terms are nearly, but not completely, interchangeable.

Rap music was once called a fad, but it's now celebrating a 20th 5 anniversary of sorts. The first hip-hop hit, "Rapper's Delight" by the Sugar Hill Gang, came out in 1979. Hip-hop got its start in black America, but now more than 70% of hip-hop albums are purchased by whites. In fact, a whole generation of kids—black, white, Latino, Asian—has grown up immersed in hip-hop. "I'm hip-hop every day," declares 28-year-old Marlon Irving, a black record-store employee in Portland, Ore. "I don't put on my hip-hop." Says Sean Fleming, a white 15-year-old from Canton, Ga.: "It's a totally different perspective, and I like that about it." Adds Katie Szopa, 22, a white page at NBC in New York City: "You do develop a sense of self through it. You listen and you say, 'Yeah, that's right.'"

Hip-hop represents a realignment of America's cultural aesthet- 6 ics. Rap songs deliver the message, again and again, to keep it real. The poet Rainer Maria Rilke wrote that "a work of art is good if it has sprung from necessity." Rap is the music of necessity, of finding poetry in the colloquial, beauty in anger, and lyricism even in violence. Hip-hop, much as the blues and jazz did in past eras, has compelled young people of all races to search for excitement, artistic fulfillment and even a sense of identity by exploring the black underclass. "And I know because of [rapper] KRS-ONE," the white ska-rap singer Bradley Nowell of Sublime once sang in tribute to rap. Hip-hop has forced advertisers, filmmakers and writers to adopt "street" signifiers like cornrows and terms like player hater. Invisibility has been a longstanding metaphor for the status of blacks in America. "Don't see us / but we see you," hip-hop band the Roots raps on a new song. Hip-hop has given invisibility a voice.

But what does that voice have to say? 7

Now tell me your philosophy / On exactly what an artist should be.

—Lauryn Hill, "Superstar"

It's a Friday night, early December 1998, and you're backstage at *Saturday Night Live.* You're hanging out in the dressing room with Lauryn Hill, who is sitting on the couch, flipping through a script. The 23-year-old rapper-singer-actress is the musical guest on this week's show. It's her coming-out party, the first live TV performance she's done since releasing her critically acclaimed and best-selling album *The Miseducation of Lauryn Hill.* She might also do a little acting on the show—*SNL* staff members have asked her to appear in a skit. But as Hill reads, her small rose-blossom lips wilt into a frown. She hands you the script. It's titled Pimp Chat—it's a sketch about a street hustler with a talk show. Hill's role: a 'ho. Or, if she's uncomfortable with that, she can play a female pimp. Hmmm. Now, being in an *SNL* sketch is a big opportunity—but this one might chip away at her image as a socially conscious artist. What's it going to be? 8

It's all about the Benjamins, baby.

—Sean ("Puffy") Combs, "It's All About the Benjamins"

You are in a recording studio in midtown Manhattan, hanging out with hip-hop superproducer Sean ("Puffy") Combs. It's 1997, and Puffy is keeping a low profile, working on his new album, his first as a solo performer. This album will be his coming-out party. He's eager to play a few tracks for you. People have him all wrong, he says. He majored in business management at Howard. He's not just about gangsta rap. Sounds from his new album fill the room. One song is based on a bit from the score to *Rocky.* Another, a sweeping, elegiac number, uses a portion of "Do You Know Where You're Going To?" That's what 9 he's about, Combs says. Classic pop. "I'm living my life right," he says. "So when it comes time for me to be judged, I can be judged by God."

> *You're mad because my style you're admiring / Don't be mad—UPS is hiring.*
> —The Notorious B.I.G., "Flava in Your Ear" (Remix)

Hip-hop is perhaps the only art form that celebrates capitalism openly. To be sure, filmmakers pore over weekend grosses, but it would be surprising for a character in a Spielberg film to suddenly turn toward the camera and shout, "This picture's grossed $100 million, y'all! Shout out to DreamWorks!" Raps' unabashed materialism distinguishes it sharply from some of the dominant musical genres of the past century. For example, nobody expects bluesmen to be moneymakers—that's why they're singing the blues. It's not called the greens, after all. As for alternative rockers, they have the same relationship toward success that one imagines Ally McBeal has toward food: even a small slice of pie leaves waves of guilt. Rappers make money without remorse. "These guys are so real, they brag about money," says Def Jam's Simmons. "They don't regret getting a Coca-Cola deal. They brag about a Coca-Cola deal." 10

Major labels, a bit confused by the rhythms of the time, have relied on smaller, closer-to-the-street labels to help them find fresh rap talent. Lauryn Hill is signed to Ruffhouse, which has a distribution deal with the larger Columbia. Similar arrangements have made tens of millions of dollars for the heads of these smaller labels, such as Combs (Bad Boy), Master P (No Limit), Jermaine Dupri (So So Def), and Ronald and Bryan Williams (co-CEOs of Cash Money, home to rising rapper Juvenile). 11

"I'm not a role model," rapper-mogul-aspiring-NBA-player Master P says. "But I see myself as a resource for kids. They can say, 'Master P has been through a lot, but he changed his life, and look at him. I can do the same thing.' I think anyone who's a success is an inspiration." 12

Master P introduced something new to contemporary pop: shameless, relentless and canny cross-promotion. Each of the releases on his New Orleans–based No Limit label contains promotional materials for his other releases. His established artists (like Snoop Dogg) make guest appearances on CDs released by his newer acts, helping to launch their debuts. And his performers are given to shouting out catchphrases like "No Limit soldiers!" in the middle of their songs—good advertising for the label when the song is being played on the radio. 13

Madison Avenue has taken notice of rap's entrepreneurial spirit. Tommy Hilfiger has positioned his apparel company as the clothier of the hip-hop set, and he now does a billion dollars a year in oversize 14 shirts, loose jeans and so on. "There are no boundaries," says Hilfiger. "Hip-hop has created a style that is embraced by an array of people from all backgrounds and races." However, fans are wary of profiteers looking to sell them back their own culture. Says Michael Sewell, 23, a white congressional staff member and rap fan: "I've heard rap used in advertising, and I think it's kind of hokey—kind of a goofy version of the way old white men perceive rap."

But the ads are becoming stealthier and streetier. Five years ago, 15
Sprite recast its ads to rely heavily on hip-hop themes. Its newest series features several up-and-coming rap stars (Common, Fat Joe, Goodie Mob) in fast-moving animated clips that are intelligible only to viewers raised on Bone-Thugs-N-Harmony and Playstation. According to Sprite brand manager Pina Sciarra, the rap campaign has quadrupled the number of people who say that Sprite is their favorite soda.

Hollywood too is feeling the rap beat. After Lauryn Hill passed 16
on a role in *The Cider House Rules* (an adaptation of the John Irving book), filmmakers cast hip-hop soul singer Erykah Badu. Ice Cube, who has appeared in such movies as *Boyz N the Hood* and *Fridays,* will soon star with George Clooney in the Gulf War thriller *Three Kings.* Queen Latifah, featured in the recent film *Living Out Loud,* is now set to be the host of a TV talk show. And the former Fresh Prince, Will Smith, has become one of the most in-demand actors around. Ice Cube—who performed a song with Public Enemy titled "Burn Hollywood Burn" in 1990—says Tinseltown wants rapper actors because "we add a sense of realism where sometimes a trained actor can't deliver that reality the way it needs to be done."

Warren Beatty, who directed and starred in *Bulworth,* a comedy 17
about a Senator who becomes possessed by the spirit of hip-hop, became interested in the subject because "it seemed to have a similar protest energy to the Russian poets of the 1960s. The Russian poets reigned in Moscow almost like rock itself reigned in the U.S. Ultimately it seemed to me that hip-hop is where the voice of protest is going in the inner city and possibly far beyond because the culture has become so dominated by entertainment."

Even Tom Wolfe, who documented the counterculture in the '60s 18
and greed in the '80s, found himself buying a stack of hip-hop records in order to understand Atlanta in the '90s for his best-selling book *A Man in Full.* In several sections of his novel, Wolfe offers his own sly parodies of today's rap styles: "How'm I spose a love her / Catch her mackin' with the brothers," Wolfe writes in a passage. "Ram yo' booty! Ram yo' booty!" Most of the characters in *A Man in Full* are a bit frightened by rap's passion. It's Wolfe's view that "hip-hop music quite intentionally excludes people who are not in that world." That world, however, is growing.

Poetic language emerges out of the ruins of prose.
—Jean-Paul Sartre, *Art and Action*

The hip-hop world began in the Bronx in 1971. Cindy Campbell needed a little back-to-school money, so she asked her brother Clive to throw a party. Back in Kingston, Jamaica, his hometown, Clive used to watch dancehall revelers. He loved reggae, Bob Marley and Don Drummond and the Skatalites. He loved the big sound systems the deejays had, the way they'd "toast" in a singsong voice before each song. When he moved to the U.S. at age 13, he used to tear the speakers out of abandoned cars and hook them onto a stereo in his room. 19

The after-school party, held in a rec room of a Bronx high-rise, was a success: Clive and Cindy charged 25 [cents] for girls and 50 [cents] for boys, and it went till 4 A.M. Pretty soon Clive was getting requests to do more parties, and in 1973 he gave his first block party. He was Kool Herc now—that was the graffito tag he used to write on subway cars—and he got respect. At 18 he was the first break-beat deejay, reciting rhymes over the "break," or instrumental, part of the records he was spinning. He had two turntables going and two copies of each record, so he could play the break over and over, on one turntable and then the next. Americans didn't get reggae, he thought, so he tried to capture that feel with U.S. funk songs—James Brown and Mandrill. He had dancers who did their thing in the break—break dancers, or, as he called them, b-boys. As they danced, Herc rapped, "Rocking and jamming / That's all we play / When push comes to shove / The Herculoids won't budge / So rock on, my brother . . ." 20

Joseph Saddler loved music too. He thought Kool Herc was a god—but he thought he could do better. Saddler figured most songs had only about 10 seconds that were good, that really got the party going, so he wanted to stretch those 10 seconds out, create long nights of mixing and dancing. Holed up in his Bronx bedroom, he figured out a way to listen to one turntable on headphones while the other turntable was revving up the crowd. That way a deejay could keep two records spinning seamlessly, over and over again. Herc was doing it by feel. Saddler wanted the show to be perfect. 21

So he became Grandmaster Flash. He played his turntables as if he were Jimi Hendrix, cuing records with his elbow, his feet, behind his back. He invented "scratching"—spinning a record back and forth to create a scratchy sound. He tried rapping, but he couldn't do it, so he gathered a crew around him—the Furious Five, rap's first supergroup. 22

Things happened fast. This is the remix. There were start-up labels like Sugar Hill and Tommy Boy. Then in 1979 came Rapper's Delight—the first rap song most people remember. Grandmaster Flash 23 warned, "Don't touch me 'cause I'm close to the edge." Then there was Run-D.M.C. rocking the house, and the Beastie Boys hollering, "You gotta fight for your right—to party!" and Public Enemy saying, "Don't believe the hype," and Hammer's harem-style balloon pants. Then gangsta rap: N.W.A. rapping "Fuck tha police"; Snoop drawling "187 on an undercover cop"; and Tupac crying, "Even as a crack fiend, mama / You always was a black queen, mama." Then Mary J. Blige singing hip-hop soul; Guru and Digable Planets mixing rap with bebop; the Fugees "Killing me softly with his song"; Puffy mourning Biggie on CD and MTV.

> *We in the '90s And finally it's looking good / Hip-hop took it to billions I knew we would.*
>
> —Nas, "We Will Survive"

All major modern musical forms with roots in the black community—jazz, rock, even gospel—faced criticism early on. Langston Hughes, in 1926, defended the blues and jazz from cultural critics. Hard-core rap has triumphed commercially, in part, because rap's aesthetic of sampling connects it closely to what is musically palatable. Some of the songs hard-core rappers sample are surprisingly mainstream. DMX raps about such subjects as having sex with bloody corpses. But one of his songs, "I Can Feel It," is based on Phil Collins' easy-listening staple "In the Air Tonight." Jay-Z's hit song "Hard-Knock Life" draws from the musical *Annie.* Tupac's "Changes" uses Bruce Hornsby. Silkk the Shocker samples the not-so-shocking Lionel Richie. 24

The underlying message is this: the violence and misogyny and lustful materialism that characterizes some rap songs are as deeply American as the hokey music that rappers appropriate. The fact is, this country was in love with outlaws and crime and violence long before hip-hop—think of Jesse James, and Bonnie and Clyde—and then think of the movie *Bonnie and Clyde,* as well as *Scarface* and the *Godfather* saga. In the movie *You've Got Mail,* Tom Hanks even refers to the *Godfather* triology as the perfect guide to life, the I-Ching for guys. Rappers seem to agree. Snoop Dogg's sophomore album was titled *The Doggfather.* Silkk the Shocker's new album is called *Made Man.* On his song "Boomerang," Big Pun echoes James Cagney in *White Heat,* yelling, "Top of the world, Ma! Top of the world!" 25

Corporate America's infatuation with rap has increased as the genre's political content has withered. Ice Cube's early songs attacked white racism; Ice-T sang about a Cop Killer; Public Enemy challenged listeners to "fight the power." But many newer acts such as DMX and Master P are focused almost entirely on pathologies within the black 26

Barbie Homepage (www.barbie.com)

"Conversion Barbie," by Kimmy McCann

"Absolute End," by Adbusters

"TV Buddha Reincarnated," by Nam June Paik

Eminem

Tupac Shakur

Still photo from the film, *Johnny Mnemonic*

Still photo from the film, *The Matrix*

Brandi Chastain

1931 *Dracula* poster

community. They rap about shooting other blacks but almost never about challenging governmental authority or encouraging social activism. "The stuff today is not revolutionary," says Bob Law, vice president of programming at WWRL, a black talk-radio station in New York City. "It's just, 'Give me a piece of the action.'"

Hip-hop is getting a new push toward activism from an unlikely source—the Beastie Boys. The white rap trio began as a Dionysian semiparody of hip-hop, rapping about parties, girls and beer. Today they are the founders and headliners of the Tibetan Freedom Concert, an annual concert that raises money for and awareness about human-rights issues in Tibet. Last week Beastie Boys, along with the hip-hop–charged hard-rock band Rage Against the Machine and the progressive rap duo Black Star, staged a controversial concert in New Jersey to raise money for the legal fees of Mumia Abu-Jamal, a black inmate on death row for killing a police officer. Says Beastie Boy Adam Yauch: "There's a tremendous amount of evidence that he didn't do it and he was a scapegoat." 27

Yauch says rap's verbal texture makes it an ideal vessel to communicate ideas, whether satirical, personal or political. That isn't always a good thing. "We've put out songs with lyrics in them that we thought people would think were funny, but they ended up having a lot of really negative effects on people. [Performers] need to be aware that when you're creating music it has a tremendous influence on society." 28

Sitting in the conference room on the 24th floor of the Time & Life Building, Kool Herc thinks back to the start of rap with a mixture of fondness and sadness. He'd like to see rappers "recognize their power, in terms of politics and economics." Hip-hop has not made him powerful or rich. "I never looked at it like that," he says. "I was just having fun. It was like a hobby to me." But he would appreciate more recognition. When he calls local radio stations, looking for an extra ticket or two for a hip-hop show, he's often told there are none available—even for the father of the form. Still, he's planning a comeback. He's holding a talent contest later this year, and also hopes to record his first full album. Says Herc: "Respect is due." 29

Friday night at Life, a dance club in lower Manhattan. Grandmaster Flash pulls the 11 P.M. to 2 A.M. shift, and he's doing his thing. The Furious Five have long since broken up. Flash had drug problems, money problems and a court battle with his old record company, Sugar Hill, but he says today he has no ill will. He's the musical director on HBO's popular *Chris Rock Show*. And he's helping to develop a movie script about his life. "I was bitter a while back because I got into this for the love," says Flash. "I gave these people the biggest rap 30 group of all time. But as long as there's a God, as long as I'm physically able to do what I do—what I did—I can do it again."

The dance floor is getting crowded. Flash puts on a record. Does 31
a little scratching. He plays the instrumental intro again and again and then lets it play through. "Ain't no stopping us now . . ."

> *At first I did not know what I wanted. But in the end I understood the language. I understood it, I understood it, I understood it all wrong perhaps. That is not what matters . . . Does this mean that I am freer than I was?*
>
> —Samuel Beckett, *Malloy*

In Mill Valley, Calif., in a one-bedroom apartment above a coin- 32
operated laundry, Andre Mehr, a white 17-year-old with a crew cut, and Emiliano Obiedo, a ponytailed 16-year-old who is half white and half Hispanic, are huddled over a PC. A beat spirals up. Obiedo offers some advice, and Mehr clatters away at the keyboard. They are making music. Once they settle on a beat, Obiedo will take a diskette bearing a rhythm track home and lay down some rhymes. Soon they hope to have enough for a CD. Boasts Obiedo: "I'm going to change rap."

Across the country, similar scenes are playing out as kids out- 33
side the black community make their own hip-hop or just listen in. Some say they don't pay much attention to the lyrics, they just like the beat. "I can't relate to the guns and killings," says Mehr. Others are touched more deeply. Says 15-year-old Sean Fleming: "I can relate more and get a better understanding of what urban blacks have to go through."

Todd Boyd, a professor of critical studies at the University of 34
Southern California, says rap can bring races together: "It's a little more difficult to go out and talk about hate when your music collection is full of black artists. That is not to say that buying an OutKast record is the same as dealing with real people, but it is reason to hope." Ice Cube is a bit more cynical: "It's kinda like being at the zoo. You can look into that world, but you don't have to touch it. It's safe."

Nonblack performers are increasingly drawing from rap. Beck 35
expertly combined folk and hip-hop. Hanson's hit "MMMBop" included deejay scratching. Portishead refashioned hip-hop into ethereal trip-hop. Singer Beth Orton, whose enchantingly moody album *Central Reservation* is due out in March, blends folksy guitars with samples and beats. Doug Century, author of *Street Kingdom: Five Years Inside the Franklin Avenue Posse,* studied hip-hop culture as he documented the lives of gang members; he predicts white acts will eventually dominate rap, just as white rockers pushed out rock's black forerunners.

"It's possible that in 15 years all hip-hop will be white," Century says. "[Then] black youth culture will transform itself again."

Already the white b-boy has become an iconic figure—ridiculed in movies like *Can't Hardly Wait* and the forthcoming *Go,* and in songs like Offspring's "Pretty Fly (for a White Guy)." In "Pretty Fly" the punk band Offspring mocks whites who adopt hip-hop styles, singing, "He may not have a clue / And he may not have style / But everything he lacks / Well he makes up in denial." Irish-American rap-rocker Everlast, whose new CD, *Whitey Ford Sings the Blues,* has proved to be a commercial hit, says the song makes him laugh: "They ain't talking about me, 'cause I'll beat the s_____ out of every one of those guys." In fact, Everlast feels confident enough about his standing in the rap world to take a verbal swipe at Puffy Combs: "I don't think Puffy really cares about what he's doing. He's a brilliant businessman, but he's no different from the Backstreet Boys or the Spice Girls because he's just creating a product." 36

Wu-Tang Clan producer-rapper RZA is also concerned about maintaining standards. He believes many performers are embracing the genre's style—rapping—but missing its essence, the culture of hip-hop. "I don't think the creativity has been big. I think the sales have been big, and the exposure has been big," says RZA. "Will Smith is rap. That's not hip-hop. It's been a big year for rap. It's been a poor year for hip-hop." 37

Underground rap is available for those industrious enough to seek it out. At New York City's Fat Beats record store, you can pick up vinyl editions of independently released songs by such promising new acts as the Philadelphia-based Maylay Sparks . . . and the all-female antimisogyny hip-hop collective Anomolies. . . . Maylay Sparks' spirited "I Mani" and the New York City–based Anomolies' raucous tune "Black-listed" (a collaboration with the group Arsonists) are two of the best songs to come out this year. 38

Other groups, signed to major labels, are trying to perpetuate rap's original spirit of creativity. The rapper Nas' forthcoming album *I Am . . . the Autobiography* promises to be tough, smart and personal. And the Atlanta-based duo OutKast's current album, *Aquemini,* weaves chants, neo-soul and hip-hop into an enthralling mix. Says OutKast's Big Boi: "We're not scared to experiment." 39

One of the most ambitious new CDs is the Roots' *Things Fall Apart* (named after the book by the Nigerian Nobel laureate Chinua Achebe). The CD features live instrumentation, lyrics suitable for a poetry slam and a cameo from Erykah Badu. Roots drummer Ahmir hopes, in the future, the more creative wing of performers in hip-hop will form a support network. "There are some people in hip-hop that 40 care about leaving a mark," he says. "There are some of us that look at *Innervisions* as a benchmark, or *Blood on the Tracks* or *Blue* or *Purple Rain.* Leaving a mark is more important than getting a dollar. I think Lauryn's album is one of the first gunshots of hip-hop art the world is going to get."

> *You could get the money / You could get the power But keep your eyes on the final hour.*
>
> —Lauryn Hill, "Final Hour"

It's Puffy's 29th birthday party, and the celebration is being held 41
on Wall Street. Inside the party, women in thongs dance in glass cages. Above the door a huge purple spotlight projects some of Puffy's corporate logos: Bad Boy (his record company) and Sean John (his new clothing label). But where's Puffy?

The music stops. The crowd parts. Muhammad Ali arrives. He's 42
only the appetizer. The score to *Rocky* booms over the speakers. Only then does Puffy enter, in a light-colored three-piece suit. Forget being street. He's Wall Street, he's Madison Avenue, he's le Champs Elysees. Donald Trump is at his side. It's Puffy's moment. His album *No Way Out* played on some familiar gangsta themes, but it's a smash hit. Puffy is a household name, a brand name. In fact his name comes up again and again, in gossip columns and other people's rap songs. He has transformed himself into a human sample. He is swallowed by the crowd.

You are at the Emporio Armani store on Fifth Avenue in down- 43
town Manhattan. There's a benefit here tonight for the Refugee Project, a nonprofit organization Lauryn Hill founded to encourage social activism among urban youth. Hill is here, and the cameras are flashing. Her musical performance on *Saturday Night Live* has boosted her album back to the upper reaches of the charts. In a few days she will receive 10 Grammy nominations, the most ever by a female artist.

She never did do that *SNL* skit about the hooker. She says she 44
feels too connected to hip-hop to do a movie or TV role that might compromise the message in her music. She addresses the crowd. "I'm just a vehicle through which this thing moves," she says. "It's not about me at all." You think back to some of the rappers you've talked to—Jay-Z, Nas, the Roots, Grandmaster Flash. A record cues up in your mind: "Ain't no stopping us now . . ."

20 YEARS OF HIP-HOP

1979 THE SUGAR HILL GANG. Six years after Kool Herc introduced rap to partyers in the Bronx, the Sugar Hill Gang serves it up to a national audience in the form of the classic catchy song Rapper's Delight.

1984 RUSSELL SIMMONS. He co-founds Def Jam Recordings and goes on to become one of the richest, most influential forces in pop music.

1984 RUN-D.M.C. Hailing from Hollis, Queens, the supergroup rocks the house and introduces some rap signifiers—gold chains and untied sneakers.

1986 BEASTIE BOYS. The white rap trio's mix of hard rock and hip-hop make *License to Ill* a favorite at frat parties everywhere and the first rap album to hit the top of the charts.

1988 THE SOURCE. Harvard undergrads Jon Shecter and David Mays publish the first issue of their hip-hop mag out of their dorm room. Although it no longer has the field to itself and isn't even the largest publication covering the rap scene today, the *Source* remains a widely read source on hip-hop.

1989 N.W.A. The California act's *Straight Outta Compton* sparks gangsta rap and foreshadows the Los Angeles uprising of '92.

1989 2 LIVE CREW. (Remember "Me so horny?") This proudly foulmouthed group is pushed into the national spotlight in a Florida battle over freedom of speech.

1990 VANILLA ICE. Admit it. You like Ice, Ice Baby. And so do the 7 million others who buy this one-hit wonder's *To the Extreme.*

1990 WILL SMITH. The sitcom "The Fresh Prince of Bel-Air" debuts on NBC, bringing suburban-flavored rap to the small screen. A new acting star is born.

1991 NEW JACK CITY. The crime thriller co-starring Ice-T is a surprise box-office hit and helps usher in a new genre of urban films, such as *Boyz N the Hood* and *Menace II Society.*

1992 SISTER SOULJAH. Her music and its message become a campaign issue when presidential candidate Bill Clinton attacks her militant views on race.

1993 SNOOP DOGGY DOGG. The pop-gangsta rapper releases Doggystyle, and it immediately rockets to the No. 1 spot on the charts.

1996 THE FUGEES. The trio's album *The Score* features head-bobbing beats, reggae and smart lyrics. It becomes a worldwide smash.

1996 TUPAC SHAKUR. The year after he releases his best album, *Me Against the World,* the rapper dies in a drive-by killing.

1997 BIGGIE SMALLS. The Notorious B.I.G. is shot. His album *Life After Death* is a hit.

1997 PUFF DADDY. His galvanizing rendition of "I'll Be Missing You" at the MTV Music Awards awakens millions of pop fans and ushers in a new era of positivism in hip-hop.

1998 BULWORTH. Warren Beatty's comedy uses the language of rap to critique politics.

1999 LAURYN HILL. She grabs 10 Grammy nods, begins first solo tour and eyes a film career.

QUOTES

Ya rock and ya don't stop and this is the sounds of DJ Kool Herc and the Sound System.—DJ Kool Herc

So don't push me 'cause I'm close to the edge. I'm tryin' not to lose my head. —Grandmaster Flash

You gotta fight for your right to party.—Beastie Boys

Who you callin' a Bitch?—Queen Latifah

Ain't nothin' but a G thang, baaaaabay!—Dr. Dre

You might win some but you just lost one.—Lauryn Hill

Let's talk about sex, baby. Let's talk about you and me.—Salt-N-Pepa

Fuck tha police. Comin' straight from the underground.—N.W.A.

Been spending most our lives, living in a gangsta's paradise.—Coolio

Me against the world. It's just me against the world.—Tupac Shakur

U can't touch this.—Hammer

I made the change from a common thief, to up close and personal with Robin Leach.—Notorious B.I.G.

Gettin' jiggy wit it.—Will Smith

I got the hook up, holla if you hear me.—Master P

Examining the Text

1. What concrete examples do the authors of this article cite to support their article's thesis: that hip-hop is today's pervasive pop-music form? Based on your own experience, what additional examples can you cite? Are there any other pop-music forms that have similar influence, in your experience?

2. In what ways, according to this article, has hip-hop music and culture infiltrated and dramatically changed institutions of the American financial mainstream, such as advertising, fashion, literary publishing, and the Hollywood film industry?

3. Outline the historical roots of hip-hop, as laid out in this article. What social and/or personal concerns does this music reflect? What, according to this article, is the thematic function of "the violence and misogyny and lustful materialism that characterize some rap songs"?

4. What is the function of the quoted passages throughout this article? What key points do they help deliver? How does this article's inclusion of quoted passages resemble certain features of hip-hop music?
5. What is the influence of hip-hop on the "nonblack" American youth culture, according to this article? How do some African American critics feel about hip-hop's move into the white mainstream?

For Group Discussion

Discuss the viewpoint expressed by the authors that "Hip-hop is perhaps the only art form that celebrates capitalism openly." From your own experience, cite musical examples that support this assertion, and/or examples that disprove it. If you find examples of noncommercial, or anticommercial hip-hop, what does this say about hip-hop as a genre? Is there one hip-hop music, or a number of subgenres of this art form, each with its own style and point of view?

Writing Suggestion

In an essay, consider honestly the notion expressed by Russell Simmons, head of the hip-hop label Def Jam, that rock & roll is old people's music. In particular, discuss the two premises inherent in this assertion: (1) that rock is a dead or dying art form, in which young people (such as yourself) have little interest; and (2) that "old people's music"—for example, jazz, blues, rock, and even classical music—are not "what people want to hear," as Simmons suggests.

The Miseducation of Hip-Hop

Evelyn Jamilah

In this article, the author points to criticisms currently being leveled at rap music and hip-hop culture from within the community of African American educators. No one would deny that rap culture has unprecedented popularity among young people. Nevertheless, many of these observers believe that while the themes embodied in rap music may reflect real-life situations within America's inner cities, rap's influence may be ultimately counterproductive, causing Black students to perform worse in school—which, in turn, will perpetuate the negative economic and social conditions which rappers dramatize in their lyrics. Some observers go so far as to insist that young African American students turn away from this popular artform, while others suggest that some university courses focus their attention on rap, to make some connections between this popular form and the work of Black historians, sociologists, urban psychologists, and so forth.

As you read this article, attempt to determine the author's own stance toward this topic. Does she play the role of dispassionate observer, merely recording journalistically the arguments swirling around this hotly debated topic, or can you detect a certain agenda, a rhetorical stance underlying her reportage? Note also your own reactions to points raised during this piece. The commentators presented in this article will probably cause you to have some emotional reaction; try to set your emotions aside momentarily, make note of specific points of agreement or disagreement as they arise.

When Jason Hinmon transferred to the University of Delaware two years ago from Morehouse College in Atlanta, the 22-year-old senior says he almost dropped out his first semester. 1

He says that for financial reasons, he came back here to his hometown. But in many ways, he had never felt so abandoned. 2

"I came to class and my professors didn't know how to deal with me," he says, between bites of his a-la-carte lunch. "I could barely get them to meet with me during their office hours." 3

Dark-hued, dreadlocked and, well, young, he says many of his mostly White professors figured they had him pegged. 4

"They took one look at me and thought that I was some hip-hop hoodlum who wasn't interested in being a good student," he says. 5

But if Hinmon represents the "good" students with grounds to resent the stereotype, there are faculty who profess there's no shortage of young people willing to live up—or down—to it. 6

"You see students walking on campus reciting rap lyrics when they should be reciting something they'll need to know on their next test. Some of these same students you won't see back on campus next semester," says Dr. Thomas Earl Midgette, 50, director of the Institute for the Study of Minority Issues at historically Black North Carolina Central University. 7

"These rap artists influence the way they dress," he continues. "They look like hoochie mamas, not like they're coming to class. Young men with pants fashioned below their navel. Now, I used to wear bell-bottoms, but I learned to dress a certain way if I was negotiating the higher education maze. I had to trim my afro." 8

The difference between today's students and their parents, faculty and administrators is marked, no doubt. Technology's omnipresence—apparent in kids with little patience for anything less than instant meals, faster Internet information and cellular ubiquity—is certainly at play when it comes to explaining the divide. 9

But what causes more consternation among many college and university officials is a music form, a culture and a lifestyle they say is 10 eating away at the morals, and ultimately the classroom experience, of today's college students.

Hip-hop—brash, vulgar, in-your-face hip-hop—is indisputably the dominant youth culture today. Its most controversial front men floss mad ice (wear lots of diamonds and other expensive jewelry), book bad bitches (usually scantily clad, less than the take home kind of girl), and in general, party it up. Its most visible females brag about their sexual dexterity, physical attributes, and cunning tactics when it comes to getting their rent paid. 11

With college completion statistics at an embarrassing low and the Black–White achievement gap getting wider by the semester, perhaps it's time to be concerned whether the culture's malevolent message is at play. 12

But can atrocious retention rates really be linked to reckless music? Or do university officials underestimate their students? Is it that young folk today have no sense of history, responsibility and plain good manners? Or are college faculty a bunch of old fogies simply more comfortable with Marvin Gaye's "Sexual Healing" than Little Kim's sexual prowess? 13

Is this no different than the divide we've always seen between young people and their college and university elders? Or do the disparities between this wave of students and those charged with educating them portend something more disparaging? 14

THE GAP

At the heart of the rift between the two groups is a debate that has both sides passionately disturbed. 15

Young people say they feel pigeonholed by an image many of them don't support. They say the real rub is that their teachers—Black and White—believe the hype as much as the old lady who crosses the street when she sees them coming. 16

And they'd like their professors to consider this: They can listen to the music, even party to it, but still have a response just as critical, if not more so, than their faculty and administrators. 17

Others point out that the pervasiveness of hip-hop's immoral philosophies is at least partly rooted in the fact that the civil rights movement—the older generation's defining moment—surely did not live up to all its promises for Black America. 18

And further, they say it's important to note that not all hip-hop is irresponsible. In fact, some argue that it's ultimately empowering, uplifting and refreshing. After all, when was the last time a biology 19 professor sat down with a Mos Def CD? How many can even pronounce his name?

Older faculty, administrators and parents alike respond that the music is downright filth. And anyone associated with it ought to have their mouths and their morals cleansed. 20

There's a real problem when a marijuana-smoking ex-con named Snoop Doggy Dog can pack a campus auditorium quicker than Black historian John Hope Franklin; when more students deify the late Tupac Shakur and his abrasive lyrics than those who ever read the great Martin Luther King Jr.'s "I Have a Dream" speech; when kids decked out in sweats more pricey than their tuition complain that they can't afford a semester's books; when the gains they fought so hard for are, in some ways, slowly slipping away. 21

"I think what causes us the most grief is that hip-hop comes across as heartless, valueless, nihilistic and certainly anachronistic if not atheistic," says Dr. Nat Irvin, president of Future Focus 2020, an urban futures think tank at Wake Forest University in North Carolina. "Anyone who would argue with that needs to take a look for themselves and see what images are prevalent on BET and MTV. 22

"But I don't think there's any question that the disconnect comes from the fact that old folks don't have a clue. They don't understand technology. The world has changed. And there's an enormous age gap between most faculty on college campuses and the rest of America," he says. 23

More than 60 percent of college and university faculty are over the age of 45. Meanwhile, nearly 53 percent of African Americans are under 30 and some 40 percent are under 20. 24

That means more than half of all Blacks were born after the civil rights movement and the landmark *Brown* vs. *Board of Education* case. 25

"There's no big puzzle why these kids are coming with a different ideology," Irvin, 49, says. 26

THIS IS WHAT BLACKNESS IS

It is universally acknowledged that rap began in New York City's Bronx borough nearly 30 years ago, a mix of Jamaican reggae's dancehall, America's funk music, the inner city's pent-up frustrations and Black folks' general propensity to love a good party. 27

Pioneering artists like the The Last Poets, The Sugar Hill Gang, Kurtis Blow and Run-DMC combined creative genius and street savvy to put hip-hop on the map. 28

Its initial associations were with graffiti and party music, according to Dr. Robin D. G. Kelley, professor of history and Africana studies at New York University. 29

"Then in the late '80s, you begin to see more politicized manifestations of that. BDP, Public Enemy . . . In essays that students wrote that were not about rap music, but about the urban condition itself, they would adopt the language. They would quote Public Enemy lyrics, they would quote Ghetto Boys," says Kelley, 38. 30

"This whole generation of Blacks in particular were trying to carve out for themselves an alternative culture," he continues. "I saw a whole generation for the first time say, 'I don't want to go to corporate America. I don't want to be an attorney. I don't want to be a doctor. I don't want to get paid. I want to make a revolution.'" 31

"The wave that we're in now is all over the place," he explains. 32

But even hip-hop's fans stop short at endorsing some of the themes prevailing in today's music and mindset.

Kevin Powell, noted cultural critic and former hip-hop journalist, says the biggest difference between the music today and the music at its onset is that "we don't own it." 33

"Corporate America completely commodified hip-hop," he says. "We create the culture and corporate America takes it and sells it back to us and tells us, 'This is what Blackness is.'" 34

And while Powell, 34, says he is disappointed in some of the artists, especially the older ones who "should know better," many students are their staunchest defenders. 35

Caryn Wheeler, 18, a freshman at Bowie State University, explains simply that "every day isn't about love." Her favorite artists? Jay-Z, OutKast, Biggie Smalls, Tupac and Little Kim, many of whom are linked to hip-hop's controversial side. "We can relate because we see what they are talking about every day," she says. 36

Mazi Mutafa, 23, is a senior at the University of Maryland College Park and president of the Black Student Union there. He says he listens to jazz and hip-hop, positive artists and those who capture a party spirit. "There's a time to party and have fun, and Jay-Z speaks to that," he says. "But there needs to be a happy medium." 37

Interrupting, senior Christine Gonzalez, 28, says a lot of artists like Jay-Z tend to be revered by younger students. "As you get older, you tend to tone down your style and find that happy medium," she says. "It's all a state of mind." 38

"People have to understand that Jay-Z is kind of like a 100-level class—an intro to hip-hop. He brings a lot of people into its fan base," Mutafa chimes in. "But then you have groups like The Roots, which are more like a 400-level class. They keep you engaged in the music. But one is necessary for the other." 39

Erick Rivas, 17, a freshman also at the University of Maryland, says he listens to Mos Def, Black Star, Mobb Deep, Wu-Tang Clan and sometimes other, more mainstream acts like Jay-Z. "Hip-hop has been a driving force in our lives. It is the soundtrack to our lives," he explains. 40

KEEPIN' IT REAL

But if hip-hop is the soundtrack to their lives, it may also mark the failure of it. 41

DeReef Jamison, a doctoral candidate who teaches African American history at Temple University in Philadelphia, surveyed 72 Black male college students last summer for his thesis. Then a graduate student at Florida, A&M State University, Jamison was interested in discovering if there are links between students' music tastes and their cultural identity, their grades and other key indicators. 42

"While the lines weren't always so clear and distinct, I found that many of the students who had a low African self-consciousness, who overidentified with a European worldview and who were highly materialistic were often the students who listened to the most 'gangster' rap, or what I prefer to call reality rap," he explains. 43

As for grades, he says the gangster rap devotees' tended to be lower than those students who listened mostly to what he calls more conscious rap. Still, he's reluctant to draw any hard and fast lines between musical preference and student performance. 44

"I'd recommend that scholars take a much closer look at this," he says. 45

Floyd Beachum, a graduate student at Bowling Green State University in Ohio, surveyed secondary [school] students to try to ascertain if there was a correlation between their behavior and the music they listened to. 46

"The more hyper-aggressive students tended to listen to more hardcore, gangster rap," he says. "Those who could identify with the violence, the drive-by shootings, the stereotypes about women—many times that would play out in their lives." 47

But Beachum, who teamed up with fellow Bowling Green graduate student Carlos McCray to conduct his research, says he isn't ready to draw any sweeping conclusions either. 48

"Those findings weren't across the board," he says, adding that he believes school systems can play a role in reversing any possible negative trends. 49

"If hip-hop and rap influence behavior and you bring all that to school, then the schools should create a very different environment and maybe we'll see more individuals go against the grain," he says. 50

Even undergraduates say they must admit that they see hip-hop's squalid influence on some of their peers. 51

"It upsets me when some young people complain that they can't get a job but when they go into that interview, they refuse to take off their do-rags, their big gold medallion and their baggy pants," says Kholiswa Laird, 18, a freshman at the University of Delaware. "But for some stupid reason, a lot of them feel like they're selling out if they wear proper clothes." 52

"That's just keepin it real," explains Davren Noble, 20, a junior at the University of Delaware. "Why should I have to change myself to get a job? If somebody wants to hire me but they don't like my braids, then either of two things will happen: They'll just have to get over it or I just won't get the job." 53

It's this kind of attitude that many in higher education see as the crux of the problem. 54

"We're not gonna serve them well in the university if we don't shake their thinking about how dress is going to influence job opportunities," says Central's Midgette. 55

Noble, from Maplewood, N.J., is a rapper. And he says that while he grew up in a posh suburb, he often raps about violence. 56

"I rap about positive stuff too, but as a Black person in America, it's hard to escape violence," he explains. "Mad Black people grew up in the ghetto and the music and our actions reflect that." 57

For sure, art has been known to imitate life. Hip-hop icon Sean "Puffy" Combs—who two years ago gave $750,000 to his alma mater, Howard University—is currently facing charges on his involvement in a Manhattan nightclub shooting last December. Grammy-winning rapper Jay-Z, also was connected with a night club dispute that ended with a record company executive being stabbed last year. 58

A BAD RAP?

A simple explanation for the boldness of much of rap's lyrics is that "artists have always pushed the limits," Kelley says. 59

But what's more, there is a politically conscious, stirring, enriching side of hip-hop that many of its fans say is often overlooked. 60

"Urban radio stations play the same songs every day," says Powell, a former reporter for *Vibe* magazine. "The media is ghettoizing hip-hop. They make it look passe." 61

Those often included in hip-hop's positive list are Lauryn Hill, Common, Mos Def, Dead Prez, Erykah Badu, Talib Kweli and other underground acts. Indeed, many of them have been active in encouraging young people to vote. Mos Del and other artists recently recorded a song in memory of Amadou Diallo, "Hip-Hop for Respect." 62

This is the side of hip-hop many young people say they'd like their faculty to recognize. This is also the side that some people say faculty must recognize. 63

"There are scholars—I've seen them do this before—who will make a disparaging remark about a whole genre of music, not knowing a doggone thing," NYU's Kelley says. "That's the same thing as saying, 'I've read one article on rational choice theory and it was so stupid, I dismissed the whole genre.' . . . People who are trained in their own fields would never do that with their own scholarship and yet they are willing to make these really sweeping statements." 64

"And they don't know. They don't have a critical understanding of the way the music industry operates or the way in which people engage music," he says. "But they are willing to draw a one-to-one correlation between the students' failure and music." 65

Some professors argue that another correlation should be made: "My most serious students are the die-hard hip-hop fans," says Dr. Ingrid Banks, assistant professor of Black Studies at Virginia Tech. "They are able to understand politics because they understand hip-hop." 66

Banks says that more of her colleagues would be wise to better understand the music and its culture. "You can't talk about Reagan's policies in the '80s without talking about hip-hop," says the 30-something scholar. "If you start where students are, they make these wonderful connections." 67

CURRICULAR CONNECTIONS

If the augmentation of hip-hop scholarship is any indication, academe just may be coming around to at least tolerating this formidable medium. 68

Courses on hip-hop, books, essays and other studied accounts of the genre are being generated by a pioneering cadre of scholars. And while many people see that as notable, there's not yet widespread belief that academe has completely warmed to the idea of hip-hop as scholarship. 69

Banks, who has taught "Race, Politics and Rap Music in Late Twentieth Century America" at the Blacksburg, Va., school, says she's 70 experiencing less than a speedy response to getting her course included into the department's curriculum.

71 "I understand that it usually takes a while to get a course approved, but there have been courses in bio-history that were signed off on rather quickly," she says.

72 But if academe fails to find ways to connect with hip-hop and its culture, then it essentially will have failed an entire generation, many critics say.

73 "What's happening is that administrators and teachers are faced with a real crisis. And that crisis they can easily attach to the music," Kelley says. "It's the way they dress, the way they talk. The real crisis is their failure to educate; their failure to treat these students like human beings; their failure to come up with a new message to engage students."

74 "Part of the reason why there is such a generational gap is because so few educators make an effort to understand the times in which they live. You can't apply '60s and '70s methods to teaching in the new millennium. You can't apply a jazz aesthetic to hip-hop heads," says Powell, who lectures at 70 to 80 colleges and universities a year. "You have to meet the students where they are. That's the nature of education. That's pedagogy."

75 And while Wake Forest's Irvin says he would agree with that sentiment, he also sees a role that students must play.

76 "What I see as being the major challenge that these kids will deal with is the image of young, urban America," Irvin says. "Young people need to ask themselves, 'Who will control their identity?'

77 "If they leave it up to the media to define who they are, they'll be devastated by these images," he says. "That's where hip-hop is killing us."

Examining the Text

1. What judgment does Dr. Thomas Earl Midgette of North Carolina Central University make about students he sees on campus? What judgment do you make about Dr. Midgette—that is, do you agree with his belief that hip-hop attitude and fashion somehow might somehow contribute to academic and/or social failure?

2. The article alludes to "technology's omnipresence." Describe this concept and cite some concrete examples to support its validity. What effect does technology have on young people, according to this article, and how does Evelyn associate technology with the generation gap that exists within school systems?

3. Where did rap music originate, according to the author? How did it come about, and how did it evolve through subsequent decades? What form(s) does rap take today?

For Group Discussion

Evelyn asks the question concerning hip-hop styles and attitude, "Is this no different than the divide we've always seen between young people and their college and university elders?" Based upon your own experience as a member of the hip-hop generation (even if you're not a rabid fan of hip-hop), attempt to answer this question: Are the styles and behaviors of today the same as the bell-bottoms and Afros to which Dr. Midgette refers near the beginning of this article, or is there something more insidious in hip-hop culture and its effect on students?

Writing Suggestion

Write an essay in which you comment on Jamilah's statement, "There's a real problem when a marijuana-smoking ex-con named Snoop Doggy Dogg can pack a campus auditorium quicker than Black historian John Hope Franklin; when more students deify the late Tupac Shakur and his abrasive lyrics than those who ever read the great Martin Luther King Jr.'s 'I have a dream' speech." As you formulate a thesis, decide first whether or not you agree with this statement by the author. Next, spend some time freewriting on the topic, letting your mind range over a wide range of points of contention or agreement. Having accomplished this activity, begin to cut and paste those supporting points into an order that has a coherent logical development, and then fill in that framework with supporting paragraphs that contain concrete evidence and examples from your experience, reading, and music listening.

Age Ain't Nothing but a Number

Polly E. McLean

The following article presents an excellent example of a type of research writing that professional social scientists produce—and of the kind of writing you may be asked produce in a social science–based course such as sociology or psychology. Social scientists often identify particular populations as objects of their research study, and this piece focuses on a target group—identified as at-risk adolescents within minority inner city communities—to determine whether they assimilate the messages in hard-core rap music. While making certain assumptions about this population—for example, the authors suggest that they may be especially susceptible to drug abuse and unprotected sex—they conclude that most minority urban teens do not necessarily enact the be-

haviors depicted or advocated in rap lyrics—not, at least, without some conscious selection and comparative decision making.

As you read this essay, observe the ways in which social scientists conduct their research, first developing a coherent research question based upon a set of explicitly stated assumptions, and then using certain methodologies and research measurements to examine the validity of the central hypothesis. Also, take special care to examine with an active critical intelligence the central assumptions that underlie the author's research: Are these assumptions valid, based upon your experience and study, or are they questionable and in need of refinement and revision?

INTRODUCTION

Every culture, whether implicitly or explicitly, delineates what is appropriate and inappropriate sexual behavior. Likewise, every culture has its own unique set of configurations about gender differences, potentials for sexuality, and rules and ethos of sexual conduct, as well as a system of symbols that communicates the culture's values about sex (Davenport 201; Kon 237). 1

In the United States the basic social institutions (family, religious, legal, economic) have been primarily responsible for setting the rules and limits that govern sexual expression. However, few limits except voluntary parental music advisory labels and film rating scales govern the cultural industries. In recent years, these industries have been perceived either as important sex educators or as negatively influencing the behavior of young people by causing violence and sexual irresponsibility. Of all the cultural industries, the preponderance of these attacks has been aimed at the music industry (Carlough 16; Davidson 38; Dority 35; Hamerlinck 23). 2

Previous adolescent music research has focused on adolescents' socialization and cognitive development (Desmond; Greenfield et al.); listening habits and consumption patterns (Bleich, Zillman, and Weaver; Rosenbaum and Prinsky; Wells and Hakanen); perceptions and interpretations of music television (Bennett and Ferell; Christenson; Hansen and Hansen; Roberts; Sun and Lull; Walker); and the relationship between music preference and sex, violence, drug abuse, satanic worship, and suicide (Arnett; Dent et al.; Litman and Farberow; Martin et al.; Popper and Ness; Trostle; Trzcinski; Wass et al.; Wooten). The bulk of this research tends to be governed by the belief 3 that adolescents are primarily passive consumers unable to create their own symbolic meaning in content. As a result, most of the adolescent music research draws on attitude measurement methods, experimental designs, the effects paradigm, and social learning theory to explain music preference as an indicator of adolescents' vulnerability (Chapman and Williams 61–72).

Not surprisingly, the majority of these studies have either ig- 4
nored adolescents of color or have subsumed them within cross sections of majority populations. However, with the emergence of rap, researchers are beginning to pay attention to ethnicity (Berry 89–107; Binder 753–67; Epstein et al. 381–94; Kuwahara 54–73; Powell 245–59). To date there has been little written about at-risk African American or Latino adolescents and the use of music to construct ideas of sexual expression.

The label "at-risk" is used in this study to describe young people 5
who live in major urban centers where poverty and unemployment rates are high, and drugs and violent crimes are commonplace; who are likely to become teenage parents; and who experience high stress factors that affect both home and school environments as well as family functioning (Winfield 5). Furthermore, because of early and unprotected sexual involvement, many are at risk for sexually transmitted diseases including HIV/AIDS (Legion et al. 11).

As with their cohorts in other socioeconomic and cultural 6
groups, at-risk adolescents of color live in a media-rich environment. Participant observation and interviews suggest that their homes are equipped with multiple radios and television sets; many have access to cable television and videocassette technology; most carry their own personal music accessories such as Walkmans, portable AM/FM/CD/cassette players, and Discmans; and their cars are often a mega-music enclave equipped with kickers and state-of-the-art CD/cassette players. They are also ardent consumers of film. Their cultural milieu includes not only the three media—television, film, and music—but also various genres within each medium.

Through the use of ethnographic research techniques, this study 7
looks at how at-risk, coitally active African American and Latino adolescents use music texts to construct ideas of sexual expression. There are several assumptions guiding this inquiry. First, music, as one of several cultural discourses, influences the development of adolescents as they are learning new ways of thinking and behaving. Nevertheless, adolescents are not one-dimensional, blindly assimilating meaning without exercising human autonomy and agency in the signification process. Second, even though adolescent participation increasingly revolves around music and other sound-enhanced products (e.g., music

video clips, films), adolescents are not necessarily the authors of their own meaning; the words, utterances, and texts are the products of others and are not necessarily produced from or by the imagination and disposition of adolescents. Because of this, there is no guarantee as to how music texts will be received and interpreted. Third, although the "at-risk" label suggests certain common characteristics that imply homogeneity, at-risk adolescents vary within their group as much as they do between lower- and higher-status groups. Furthermore, the at-risk label cannot be fully understood outside a set of social, political, and economic realities that have more of an impact upon adolescents than any individual or cultural attribute. Finally, "Frith notes that music as a medium of communication is not understood in a direct, linear way by audiences, but irrationally, emotionally, individually. Levi-Strauss says that music is only ever understood by the receiver, and Barthes notes that it is impossible to describe music without adjectives—that is, it must be understood in terms of its subjective effect rather than through a dictionary of meanings. Correspondingly, its effect can be profoundly personal" (qtd. in Turner 131).

DESCRIPTION OF STUDY

Sample: The study was divided into two tiers. The first tier involved participant observation and informal discussions with groups of at-risk African American and Latino adolescents. These observations—on the streets or in the homes of families with at-risk adolescents—coupled with informal discussions were used to gain an understanding of the social activities in which music and sexual behaviors are embedded. During this time, discussions were also held with key as well as casual informants in the adolescent and adult communities about the observations that were being made to clarify conclusions. The information garnered was then used to develop the instrument for the second tier of the research. 8

The second tier of the research involved in-depth interviews that were conducted in June and July 1992 with 60 African American and Latino coitally active at-risk adolescents (30 per cultural group with even gender distribution). The sample for these interviews was drawn from three inner-city communities in Denver, Colorado, where the participant observations were conducted: Five Points, a predominantly African American community, and the Curtis Park and Northside communities that are largely Latino. 9

Among the 60 adolescents 12 through 19 years old in the sample, 10
83% were attending school. Of the 83% attending school, 38% reported

having problems that included fighting, drinking, low grades or not doing homework, "ditching," being caught in hall sweeps, having conflicts with teachers, breaking some type of school rule, being "messed with," or "experiencing jealousy" that provoked physical confrontation, or setting the trash can, locker, or bathroom on fire. Respondents who were not attending school (17%) had graduated, dropped out due to pregnancy or poor grades, or were suspended for drinking or fighting.

Respondents lived in a variety of household settings. Single-parent households accounted for 42%, and two-parent households 37%, while 21% lived in a combination of settings that included living with friends, grandparents, foster parents, boyfriend and his parents, mother and stepfather, or by themselves. In examining the data across ethnicity, more than half (56%) of the African American respondents lived in single-parent households, whereas 27% of the Latino respondents lived in single-parent households. About 55% said that religion was important in their lives and attended church but with no regular pattern. 11

Procedure: Adolescents on the whole, and this subgroup in particular, do not trust adults. They operate on the periphery of adult community life and can be intimidating and hard to penetrate. Therefore, older peer interviewers of the same gender, socioeconomic background, and cultural group were selected and trained to conduct the interviews. 12

Interviews began with 15 closed- and open-ended questions aimed at understanding the adolescent world. Respondents were asked about their past or present situation at school, their living arrangements, employment, and social habits. Each respondent was also asked to provide a time line for a typical day and evening. Additional questions covered media habits and sexual behaviors. Respondents were then asked to choose three songs that they listened to with a sexual message and to select one of the songs to discuss. They were then asked a number of questions about the music or lyrical content in the song, feelings and ideas derived from the lyrics, and when in the song they begin to pay attention to the lyrics. 13

Following this, two songs were played. The first song was "Ain't 2 Proud 2 Beg" from the female rappers T.L.C.'s album *Ooooooohhh . . . on the T.L.C. Tip.* "Ain't 2 Proud 2 Beg" is a sexually assertive song that celebrates female sexuality as both positive and desirable. The second song, "Pop that Coochie" from the 2 Live Crew's album *Live,* is a male-centered, pleasure-driven song that flaunts sexual prowess, voyeurism, and misogynist debasement of women. These two songs were selected in preliminary interviews with adoles- 14 cents who were asked to identify songs that had a very overt or covert sexual message.

15 After playing each song, respondents were asked what was the first thing that they thought about when they heard the song and which words stood out the most. For each word they reported, they were asked the meaning and to discuss the ideas the song gave them and whether they had used any of these ideas. They were also asked what thoughts they had about the depiction of women in music produced by rappers such as Too Short, 2 Live Crew, and N.W.A. Finally, a fist of sexual topics (e.g., oral sex, sex positions, AIDS, STDs, birth control) was read, and respondents were asked to indicate whether they learned about these topics from family, friends, videos, films, music, or some other source.

16 Analysis: Coding the closed-ended questions was straightforward. The open-ended answers were content analyzed and coded independently by two graduate research assistants. The intercoder reliability was 94%. After coding, any discrepancies between coders were discussed with the principal investigator until agreement was reached.

FINDINGS

Social Setting and Music

17 As a first step in understanding music in the construction of sexual expression among at-risk coitally active African American and Latino adolescents, the research looked at the adolescent social setting, the world in which they live. The underlying assumption is that asking about music alone is ultimately not sufficient because it weaves a thread of predictability. Therefore, to assess how and where music fits into the wholeness and complexity of their lives, the respondents were first asked to timeline a typical day and evening.

18 Content analysis of their responses fell into four categories: (1) home, (2) social (day and evening), (3) self-improvement, and (4) parenting activities. Home activities included doing chores, sleeping, talking on the phone, watching TV, staying home, eating, dressing, and listening to music. As for daytime social activities, respondents reported going to the mall or the recreation center, "hanging out" or "kicking it," visiting family and friends, being with a partner, having sex, or going cruising (only Latinos reported this latter activity).

19 Evening social activities included attending clubs, parties, drinking, smoking "bud," going to church or to the movies, and listening to

music. Self-improvement included going to dance practice, attending parenting classes, attending summer school, drawing, and attending driving school. Finally, several respondents were involved in parenting activities such as babysitting, caring for a younger sibling, or caring for their own offspring.

Although "listening to music" emerged as a distinct activity, fur- 20
ther probing suggested that music interfaced with most other activities such as going to church, caring for a sibling, being with a partner, going to the neighborhood recreation center (which broadcast a top-40 local radio station on their public address system), or staying home and watching television.

Apart from what respondents did on a typical day/evening, re- 21
spondents also discussed what they had the most fun doing. Two categories emerged: media-driven and gender-driven.

Media-driven activities included going to the movies, talking 22
about soaps, dancing, cruising, and listening to music. Gender-driven activities included various interactions with the opposite gender, cruising, talking on the phone, and having sex. More often, media and gender activities were intertwined. Neither of these activities is mutually exclusive. For example, respondents reported playing music during sex or playing music when cruising.

With few exceptions, music served as either a dominant theme 23
(as in dancing or listening to music) or as a background in both media- and gender-driven activities (having sex, talking about soaps). Similarly, music was embedded and interwoven in most other adolescent social activities.

Music Ownership and Preferences

A list of music and other media hardware (e.g., television) was read to 24
the respondent, who was asked whether he or she owned each item of hardware (as opposed to having access). The majority of respondents reported owning a stereo (93%). There was gender disparity in ownership of portable music accessories. For example, all Latino males owned a Walkman and 80% owned a portable CD/tape player, whereas only 40% of Latinas reported owning a Walkman and a CD/tape player. Likewise, 80% of African American males reported owning a Walkman, whereas 53% of African American females owned one.

As for music preferences, respondents primarily listened to rap, 25
followed by rhythm and blues (R & B). However, Latinas were least likely to report listening to R & B (20%) and were more likely to listen to a wider range of musical genres that included country and western, rock, Latin pop, Spanish, Christian, oldies, pop, and disco. Although

African American females were more likely to report listening to R & B, like their Latina cohorts, they listened to a wider selection of music (e.g., country and western, reggae, jazz, gospel, and pop) than African American males. Both Latino and African American males were highly loyal to rap (83%), with 17% listening to rap or R & B with some other genre (heavy metal and pop).

Interpreting Overt and Covert Music Text

26 Respondents were asked to name their favorite artist(s) and then to indicate how they felt when listening to the music of these artists. Not surprisingly, the prevailing feeling was that the music made them "relaxed and comfortable," followed by "it gets me into a dancing mood."

27 Overall, Latinas, reported the widest range of emotions (sad, brings back memories, hyper, excited, romantic, happy, crazy, proud, funky) when listening to the music of their favorite artist. Music did not appear to have the same emotional impact on Latino males or African American respondents.

28 Similarly, some emotional feelings were gender-specific. Listening to En Vogue's "Giving Him Something He Can Feel" made one African American female "feel special." Likewise, Keith Washington's music made another African American female feel as if she could tell him "to come on over here, Keith, we can do this." Whereas, M. C. Luscious's "Boom I Fucked Your Boyfriend" made another female "feel cheap and embarrassed."

29 Rapper Ice Cube's music made one African American male "feel like a gangsta," whereas Public Enemy made another African American male "feel pro-Black militant." The music of 2 Live Crew was viewed by several Latino and African American males as simply humorous: "There are no feelings at all, just humorous": "2 Live Crew is funny." The majority of African American females saw no humor in music that they felt was demeaning to African American females.

30 The music that respondents reported listening to was divided into four content areas: hard-core rap (sexually overt), soft-core rap (sexually covert), rhythm & blues, and pop. Regardless of the format, both the music and the lyrical content were important when listening to a particular song, although far more respondents reported the lyrical content was important (62%). This appears to be influenced by the large numbers of respondents who listened to "hard-core" rap.

31 Clearly the lyrics provided were read literally and often correlated with the music (Figure 1). If a respondent said "I think about safe sex," he or she also reported listening to Salt N Pepa's "Let's Talk About AIDS." Similarly, respondents who said the lyrics "make you think about pussy" or to think about "popping it in and out" reported

HARD CORE RAP	RHYTHM & BLUES	POP	SOFT-CORE RAP
Short Dog in the House (Too Short)	Alone With You (Sisters With Voices)	Diamonds & Pearls (Prince)	Ain't 2 Proud 2 Beg (T.L.C.)
Bitch Betta Have My Money (AMG)	Giving Him Something He Can Feel (En Vogue)	Get Off (Prince)	Baby Got Back (Sir Mix-a-Lot)
Boom I Fucked Your Boyfriend/ Boom I Got Your Boyfriend (M. C. Luscious)	In Between the Sheets (Isley Brothers)	It Takes Two (Rob Bass)	Do Me (Bell Biv DeVoe)
Drop the Bomb (2 Live Crew)	Make Your Sweat (Keith Sweat)	Insatiable (Prince)	Let's Talk About Sex (Salt N Pepa)
Me So Horny (2 Live Crew)	Sexual Healing (Marvin Gaye)	We Don't Have to Take Our Clothes Off (Jermaine Stewart)	OPP (Naughty by Nature)
Freaky Tales (Too Short)	Let's Get It On (Marvin Gaye)	I Want to Sex You Up (Color Me Bad)	Let's Talk About AIDS (Salt N Pepa)
Pop that Coochie/ Pop that Pussy (2 Live Crew)			Oochie Coochie (M. C. Brains)

Figure 1 Selected Sexual Songs and Artist Respondents Reported Listening To

listening to the 2 Live Crew's "Pop that Coochie" and the X-rated version "Pop that Pussy." Although this pattern was the dominant reading, it was not always consistent. The words to Keith Sweat's "Riding a Wrong" made one Latina respondent "think more about her partner," but also made her consider "cutting down on sex."

Shaping Perceptions of Sexual Expression

The meanings of the two songs "Ain't 2 Proud 2 Beg" and "Pop that 32
Coochie" were often tied into the titles of the songs. Still there were disparities among respondents.

T.L.C.'s "Ain't 2 Proud 2 Beg" evoked multiple readings even 33
though the predominant theme was related to sex: "It's fun to play while having sex." "To ask for some cookie, from a girl." "I first thought about sex but I don't like it [sex]."

For some African American females the song played into the 34
concept of the power of sex by placing females in the role of the aggressor: "It gives girls the impression not to be embarrassed to have sex, it tells them to go have it." "If you want to get the wild thing on, you can." On the other hand, if you are in control of your own sexual-

ity, then begging (as in the song "Ain't 2 Proud 2 Beg") is unwarranted. Therefore, as one female suggested, "What is she begging for?"

Though the role of aggressor was more evident to African American females, many Latinas found it disturbing: "She sounds like she is trashy for begging . . . I think that she is sick." This reading suggests the role culture plays in defining gender roles. Sex is the male prerogative in Latino culture. It is the man who initiates sexual contact. It is the male who is the aggressor. An assertive female is going against the culturally prescribed role of being a "good woman" who is not expected to be knowledgeable about sexuality and be sexually aggressive (de la Vega 2). 35

The lyrics also suggested to some males that they do not have a monopoly on sexual expression and as a result they had to acknowledge female sexual agency: "She was blunt." "Girls can also be pushy." "I think you betta ask before you touch." 36

With the advent of music videos, it is impossible to discuss recorded music independent of the visual dimension. The intertexuality of recorded music and music video clips was evident in that several respondents were unable to separate the two—so much so that at times responses to the music included references to the video clip of the songs. "It [the song] gave me the idea of safe sex because on the video the girls always had condoms on them." "I thought about the beat, but also how the performers dressed on the video." 37

For African American males "Ain't 2 Proud 2 Beg" had very little meaning other than telling a story about female sexuality. However, among Latino males there were significant differences in first thoughts after listening to the song. Content analysis of their responses revealed two categories: (1) their need for a relationship—"to ask a girl out," "to get a steady date," "having a girlfriend," "having a sexy honey with me," and (2) individual motives/desires—"I felt as if some girl wanted me back," "I thought I would beg for sex," "I wish girls would ask more often," "I thought I would like it [the music], buy it and then go to my girlfriend's house." 38

The 2 Live Crew's "Pop that Coochie" evoked much more passion and emotion among all respondents. The majority of females criticized the song as misogynist and found no redeeming value in it: "I hate this song, terrible." "It's nasty and I'm angry at girls singing it at school." "I thought they [the girls] were freaks." "The only idea I get from it is that people are nasty." "I think it is degrading. I think that society sees the pretty woman with the nice body as a sex object." "Guys think of only one thing and that's sex any way they can get it—in the mouth or butt." As for one 18-year-old Latina, "Pop that Coochie" gave her the idea that "some black guys just want to get in your pants." 39

For several Latinas "Pop that Coochie" was not as offensive because (1) the song did not directly address them—"it don't bother me 40 because I ain't skinny so people don't talk to me like that," "they [other girls] do what the singer says, it makes me feel sad for them but not for me," or (2) they either liked the song or had liked it in the past.

Male responses overwhelmingly dealt with thinking and fantasizing about having sex: "The first thing I thought about is to go find a girl and fuck her." "I thought about going to get my girlfriend." "I thought about a pool party with chicks only." 41

When we asked what word(s) stood out the most in the song "Pop that Coochie" and the meanings of those words, the word "pop" was the most reported across gender and ethnicity. However, what was most revealing about responses, particularly among African American males, was the power variable that was associated with the act of sex from their first thoughts to the actual words selected and the meanings attached to those words. For example, the word "pop" evoked meanings such as hurt, force, tear up, stick it in hard, to "do" somebody, to push in hard. "Coochie" was defined essentially as vagina and in one instance the action "damage it" was assigned to its definition. 42

There are essentially two readings that these power words seem to generate among African American males. First, many of these respondents are aware of the environmental stumbling blocks, second-class status, and lack of opportunities they face as "minorities" and males in this society. Because of this lack of control, adolescents very early adopt poses that they observe from others like themselves in the culture. These poses or masks of power, whether via language or the gun, over the female, are distinctive coping mechanisms that, according to Majors and Billson, strive "to offset an externally imposed 'zero' image." In the presentation of self, Majors and Billson further suggest that many black males develop a "cool pose that leads to a communication pattern that uses an imposing array of masks, acts and facades". 43

Second, these power words or codes are part of the sexual foreplay and language of sex and are used to convey the erotic. As a result, it becomes a process of conquest, to demonstrate how "bad" the individual is. This "badness pose" does not necessarily culminate in the sex act, but it becomes part of a cool rap or communication style that exerts toughness, power, detachment, and aloofness. Thus, the pose or the posturing helps to counteract insecurity, anxiety, and struggle and at the same time provides a sense of control, stability, and invulnerability. 44

Attitudes about Hard-Core Rappers

The music of hard-core rappers such as the 2 Live Crew, N.W.A., and Too Short has a more negative impact on females, especially among African American females. Altogether 80% of African American fe- 45 males and 53% of Latinas were offended by such music. "I don't like it. They have no respect for women. These singers have a lot of influence on the guys," said one 16-year-old Latina. Moreover, the general sentiments expressed by African American females were "I hate it. They exploit women." "Females don't dis males like males dis females. Males are dogs." "It's disgusting. Guys pay too much attention to these songs." "I hate it. They never talk about boys, only girls."

In general, 60% of Latino males, 46% of African American males, 20% of African American females, and 13% of Latinas were unconcerned by hard-core rap. As one 12-year-old African American male simply said, "I don't give a fuck." Interestingly, Latino and African American males also said they were uninterested because they were not the subject or the victim in the song: "It don't bother me because they're not talking about me or other males." 46

Several respondents across gender and ethnicity felt that there was some justification for such music, in that it addressed a particular type of female. "A lot of it is true, they just rap about easy girls," said one 18-year-old Latina. "Some of it is true," said one 19-year-old African American female. Accordingly, another 16-year-old Latina said: "They [girls] are cheap. They'll just be with anybody." For an 18-year-old African American male, the rappers were "cool because some women carry themselves that way." Equally important, if females exhibited behaviors that were different from what the music depicts, then "it shouldn't matter, if they [girls] are not that way." 47

Learning about Sexuality

Finally, respondents were given a listing of sexual topics (e.g., oral sex, sex positions, birth control, STDs) and asked whether they learned about these topics from family, friends, videos, films, music, or some other source. Of all groups, music emerged among Latinas as one of several sources they used to learn about sexual expression. For example, Latinas reported learning about oral sex and sex positions from films, television, music, and videos. In all forms of sexual expression, friends (defined as "gangs and guys") and to a lesser extent family played a minor role. 48

CONCLUSION

The results of this study indicate the need for increased consideration of the meaning of music and its interface with sexual expression through the eyes of adolescents. Furthermore, there is a need for increased attention to how the quality of at-risk adolescents' lives and 49 the environmental context in which they live influence their use of music and other cultural products. For example, participant observations in Spanish-only speaking homes discovered adolescents playing music that was heavily laced with sexually suggestive lyrics while parents listened without a clue as to what was blasting on the home stereo. In another situation, a 17-year-old Latina, who lived in a sexually promiscuous home setting, reported that "Pop that Coochie" was helping to empower her by giving her ideas about making money from "prostitution or stripping" as a way out of her immediate situation.

Overall, music seems to function as a "rite of passage" into the adult world, serving as either foreground or background. For some respondents music was a mood enhancer. For others, music provoked thought and debate. For still others, it was fodder for their sexual fantasies. For yet another group, it served as a source of learning about coitus and sexual consummation. 50

Whatever the individual meaning, the interviews suggest that there were substantial differences in music use and in decoding music text across gender and ethnic groups. For example, among African American females familial sources of sexual information still prevailed. Thus, music was far less influential as a source of learning about sexual expression. On the other hand, music was more influential in educating Latinas than familial sources. The emergence of Latinas using music for sexual education is indicative of a culture in which discussions of sexuality with females are considered taboo because as a group they are not expected to be sexually savvy. 51

Gender differences also emerged in music hardware ownership. More mates owned hardware than females, particularly portable music accessories. Although both genders equally participated in activities in the public sphere, males were more likely to be in the public sphere with their portable music accessories. Females, on the other hand, were more likely to consume music in private even though they would engage in public activities where music dominated. 52

Music seems to provide these adolescents, who are both consumers and critics, with a way of thinking about their gender roles and contradictions and their ideas of constructing sexual expression. For example, among some female respondents, T.L.C.'s message encouraging females to take charge of their sexuality had the opposite effect. Consequently, they were incensed over the suggestion that to be sexually assertive means to implore males, because these females had already inverted the traditional male-female role within a sexual context by being aggressive. Most surprising was how Latino males took 53

T.L.C.'s song directed to females as desirable and empowering of their own male sexuality.

The adolescents in this study are not blindly assimilating meaning and messages presented in musical recordings. Even though they are labeled "at-risk," they are far from homogeneous. They have distinct points of view and are not reticent in articulating them. Most are quite savvy as to the multiple textual meanings in various genres, particularly rap, and at times brought their personal experiences and a critical eye to bear on their interpretations. Accordingly, African American females were more personally affected by hard-core rap and felt the brunt of the stereotypes and the misogynist debasement of women more than other groups. Contrastingly, some Latinas did not feel vicitimized from the misogyny in hard-core rap. These respondents managed to distance themselves from the text by insisting that the message was directed to "others." Obviously, this was easier for Latinas since the rappers they frequently listened to were not of their own ethnicity. 54

This study is a first step in understanding more completely the role music plays in the construction of sexual expression among African American and Latino at-risk adolescents. Overall, recorded music and sound (e.g., film and music video clips) seem to occupy adolescents' cultural space in unique ways. As a result, there is a constant welding together of audience with context and these multitextual forms. Because of this convergence, it is increasingly difficult to know where one text begins and the other ends, since they occupy much of the same cultural space in which adolescent sexual expression develops. 55

NOTE

The author would like to thank Greg Stene and Sergio de Souza, doctoral candidates, and David Martinez of the University of Colorado for their assistance on this study and especially the young people who willingly gave of their time so that we can all be better informed.

WORKS CITED

Arnett, Jeffrey. "Heavy-Metal Music and Reckless Behavior Among Adolescents." *Journal of Youth and Adolescence* 20, 6 (1991): 573–92.

Bennett, H. Stith, and Jack Ferell. "Music Videos and Epistemic Socialization." *Youth and Society* 18, 4 (1987): 344–62.

Berry, Venise T. "Rap Music, Self Concept and Low Income Black Adolescents." *Popular Music and Society* 14, 3 (1990): 89–107.

Binder, Amy. "Constructing Racial Rhetoric: Media Depictions of Harm in Heavy Metal and Rap Music." *American Sociological Review* 58, 6 (1993): 753–67.

Bleich, Susan, Dolf Zillmann, and James Weaver. "Enjoyment and Consumption of Defiant Rock Music as a Function of Adolescent Rebelliousness." *Journal of Broadcasting & Electronic Media* 35, 3 (1991): 351–66.

Chapman, Anthony J., and Allan R. Williams. "Prestige Effects and Aesthetic Experiences: Adolescents' Reaction to Music." *British Journal of Social and Clinical Psychology* 15, 1 (1976): 61–72.

Christenson, Peter. "The Effects of Parental Advisory Labels on Adolescent Music Preferences." *Journal of Communication* 42, 1 (1992): 106–3.

Davenport, William H. "An Anthropological Approach." *Theories of Human Sexuality.* Ed. James H. Geer and William T. O'Donohue. New York: Plenum, 1987: 197–236.

Davidson, John. "Menace to Society." *Rolling Stone* 22 Feb. 1996: 38–9.

de la Vega, Eduardo. "Considerations for Reaching the Latino Population with Sexuality and HIV/AIDS Information and Education." *SIECUS Report* 18, 3 (1990): 1–8.

Dent, Clyde, et al. "Music Preference as a Diagnostic Indicator of Adolescent Drug Use." *American Journal of Public Health* 82, 1 (1992): 124.

Desmond, Roger J. "Adolescents and Music Lyrics: Implications of a Cognitive Perspective." *Communication Quarterly* 35, 3 (1987): 276–84.

Dority, Barbara. "The War on Rock and Rap Music." *The Humanist* Sept./Oct. 1990: 35–36.

Epstein, Jonathon S., David J. Pratto, and James K. Skipper. "Teenagers, Behavioral Problems, and Preferences for Heavy Metal and Rap Music: A Case Study of a Southern Middle School." *Deviant Behavior* 11, 4 (1990): 381–94.

Greenfield, Patricia M., et al. "What Is Rock Music Doing to the Minds of Our Youth? A First Experimental Look at the Effects of Rock Music Lyrics and Music Videos." *Journal of Early Adolescence* 7, 3 (1987): 315–29.

Hamerlinck, John. "Killing Women: A Pop Music Tradition." The *Humanist* July/Aug. 1995: 23.

Hansen, Christine H., and Ranald D. Hansen. "The Influence of Sex and Violence on the Appeal of Rock Music Videos." *Communication Research* 17, 2 (1990): 212–34.

Kon, Igor S. "A Sociological Approach." *Theories of Human Sexuality.* Ed. James H. Geer and William T. O'Donohue. New York: Plenum, 1987. 237–86.

Kuwahara, Yasue. "Power to the People Y'all: Rap, Music, Resistance and Black College Students." *Humanity & Society* 16, 1 (1992): 54–73.

Legion, Vicki, Susan R. Levy, Kimberlee Cox, and Marcy Shulman. "Why People with AIDS Are Effective in Providing AIDS Education to Adolescents." *SIECUS* Report 19, 1 (1990): 9–19.

Litman, Robert, and Norman L. Farberow. "Pop-Rock Music as Precipitating Cause in Youth Suicide." *Journal of Forensic Sciences* 39, 2 (1994): 494–99.

Majors, Richard, and Janet M. Billson. *Cool Pose: The Dilemmas of Black Manhood in America.* New York: Lexington, 1992. 4–5.

Martin, Graham, Michael Clarke, and Colby Pearce. "Adolescent Suicide: Music Preference as an Indicator of Vulnerability." *Journal of the American Academy of Child & Adolescent Psychiatry* 32, 3 (1993): 530–35.

Popper, Bruce L., and Ernest M. Ness. "Death as Portrayed to Adolescents through Top 40 Rock and Roll Music." *Adolescence* 28, 112 (1993): 793–807.

Powell, Catherine T. "Rap Music: An Education with a Beat from the Street." *Journal of Negro Education* 60, 3 (1991): 245–59.

Roberts, Robin. "Music Videos, Performance and Resistance: Feminist Rappers." *Journal of Popular Culture* 25, 3 (1991): 141–52.

Rosenbaum, Jill L., and Lorraine E. Prinsky. "The Presumption of Influence: Recent Responses to Popular Music Subcultures." *Crime and Deliquency* 37, 4 (1991): 528–35.

Sun, Se-Wen, and James Lull. "The Adolescent Audience for Music Videos and Why They Watch." *Journal of Communication* 36, 1 (1986): 115–25.

Trostle, Lawrence C. "Nihilistic Adolescents, Heavy Metal Rock Music and Paranormal Beliefs." *Psychological Reports* 59, 2 (1986): 610.

Trzcinski. Jon "Heavy Metal Kids: Are They Dancing with the Devil?" *Child & Youth Care Forum* 21, 1 (1992): 7–22.

Turner, Graeme. "Film Languages." *Media Texts: Authors and Readers.* Ed. David Graddol and Oliver Boyd-Barrett. London: Open U, 1994. 119–5.

Walker, James R. "How Viewing MTV Relates to Exposure to Other Media Violence." *Journalism Quarterly* 64, 4 (1987): 756–62.

Wass, Hannelore, et al. "Adolescents' Interests in and Views of Destructive Themes in Rock Music." *Omega: Journal of Death and Dying* 19, 3 (1988): 177–86.

Wells, Alan, and Ernest A. Hakanen. "The Emotional Use of Popular Music by Adolescents." *Journalism Quarterly* 68, 3 (1991): 445–54.

Winfield, Linda. "Resilience, Schooling, and Development in African American Youth: A Conceptual Framework." *Education and Urban Society* 24, 1 (1991): 5–14.

Wooten, Marsha A. "The Effects of Heavy Metal Music on Affects Shifts of Adolescents in an Inpatient Psychiatric Setting." *Music Therapy Perspectives* 10.2 (1992): 93–98.

Examining the Text

1. How does the author define "at-risk" adolescents? What behavioral and cultural qualities may contribute to a teen's "at-risk" status as defined by McLean? By what means does the author convince readers that at-risk youth are consumers of mass media and their messages?

2. The author makes a focused and coherent thesis statement early in the essay: ". . . this study looks at how at-risk, coitally active African American and Latino adolescents use music texts to construct ideas of sexual expression." What assumptions does she make about her target population as she attempts to direct this inquiry and develop this thesis?

3. Describe the specific methods the author used to conduct her research project. What measurement instruments does the author use to quantify her findings, and what conclusions does she draw from her findings? Do her findings support or disprove her original research hypothesis as stated above in Question 2?

For Group Discussion

Based upon her research findings and interpretive conclusions, the author makes certain recommendations for direct social action at the end of this article. Discuss her specific recommendations, commenting on the validity and applicability of each. Having accomplished that, attempt to come up with some additional—or alternative—suggestions for social action to remedy the problems presented in this study. Feel free also to argue that the author's basic assumptions are flawed, and that there is no more sexual irresponsibility present in the inner city than in any other sector of society, or than at any other point in human history.

Writing Suggestion

McLean asserts in this article that the "cultural industries" such as music, motion picture and television industries—but especially the music industry—have recently been perceived "as important sex educators" who are largely responsible for the "sexual irresponsibility" characteristic of young people today. Write an essay in which you attempt to support or disprove this claim, taking a persuasive stance in one direction or the other. As you construct this essay, you will probably want to approach it in stages. First, break the assertion in question into its component parts, examining each subassertion carefully: based upon your experience and/or courses you may have taken on this topic, do you agree that young people are any more sexually irresponsible today than adolescents of your parents' generation or earlier? Is this characteristic especially valid for minority youth, or might some observers characterize this assumption as bordering on racism? Next, examine the messages that rap music lyrics put forth, looking specifically for messages that might encourage sexual irresponsibility as defined by the authors. Finally, examine the connection between music lyrics and sexual irresponsibility: if you do perceive a high degree of sexual responsibility among teens, and if rap songs do contain sexually inflammatory lyrics, is there necessarily a causal connection between the former and the latter, or are there other—perhaps more important—factors at play?

ADDITIONAL SUGGESTIONS FOR WRITING ABOUT POPULAR MUSIC

1. Americans receive a great deal of information about important issues—for example, presidential elections, gender-role attitudes, the legalization of drugs—from popular music and the media that purvey it. Write an essay in which you examine the representation of one important social issue or problem through music. For instance, you might focus on how AIDS is represented in recent song lyrics, on AM and FM radio stations, and in videos and advertisements on channels such as MTV and VH1.

2. Write an essay in which you first construct a detailed description of a band whose music you know very well, and then analyze the themes embodied in that band's songs. Discuss the effects the band's music has on its listeners and some possible reasons for the band's popularity or lack thereof with mainstream listeners.

3. Imagine that you've recently arrived in the United States; you turn on the television and find yourself watching an hour of programming on MTV. Based on this one hour of viewing, write a description of the interests, attitudes, lifestyles, and customs of young Americans. Try to include information that you gather from everything you've seen during that hour—the videos, game shows, advertisements, promos for upcoming shows, and so on—and make sure that you render your descriptions in vivid detail, so that somebody from another country might visualize all the elements you describe.

4. Write an essay in which you discuss the relative advantages and disadvantages of the three primary sources of popular music: television, radio, and record albums or compact discs. Which one of the three do you think most effectively conveys the messages intended by contemporary recording artists, and why? Which source do you think trivializes the music, turning it into a popular product without redeeming social relevance? What are the advantages and disadvantages of each pop-music source?

Internet Activities

1. Visit the Web sites of some diverse musicians (possible options are available on the *Common Culture* Web site). Write an essay describing these sites. What features do these Web sites offer? What differences similarities can you note in the presentations of the different musical genres? How would you account for these differences/similarities? For instance, is there anything offered on a Web site devoted to a rock group that isn't available on a jazz Web site? Are the Web site's features indicative of the genre in any way; that is, do the form/appearance/layout of the site mirror the musical genre it presents?

2. With the advent of various forms of media on the Web, such as radio broadcasts and videos, music has a new forum to reach an immediate, worldwide audience. Explore some sites that offer music from across the country and the world (options are available at the *Common Culture* Web site). Once you have sampled a diverse selection of music, write an essay categorizing and/or describing your findings. How is the availability of music on the Web changing how listeners access music and what they listen to? What type of music is available? Are any musical types represented more heavily than others? Are any music genres woefully lacking, in your opinion? How would you account for this representation (or lack thereof)?

Reading Images

Write an essay in which you compare and contrast the images of the two rappers, Eminem and Tupac, as illustrated on pages CI-3 and CI-4 in the color section of this book.

In this type of essay, you want to spend some time describing each image, so that the reader has a sense of the key visual features of each. Next, you might explore the ways in which the superficial appearances of both illustrations are similar or different (depending on your "reading" of the pictures, following the directions toward the end of Chapter 1). Finally, you will want to show how the images' other elements (coloration, composition, text, and so forth, also as described in Chapter 1 of this book) work in similar or different ways to put forth the images' messages, which may be subtly implied or blatantly "in-your-face."

The problem with this kind of essay is one of organization. Since a comparison/contrast essay by its nature involves looking at both similarities and differences, make sure that you structure your paper so that you don't have to jump back and forth too much from issue to issue, point to point. While many writers, when writing comparison/contrast-type pieces, sometimes favor this approach, you might want to experiment with discussing *all* the elements of the Tupac image and *then* going on to the Eminem, pointing out all its areas of likeness and dissimilarity. Ideally, your paper will flow smoothly and progress logically, while still covering all elements of likeness and dissimilarity.

5

Cyberculture

"I don't understand #11...
Thou shalt not be obscene
on the Internet."

Computer culture—in the form of electronic mail, word processing, the World Wide Web, "cyberpunk," arcade-style games, chat rooms, hypertext, digital multimedia, and on and on—is no longer merely an emerging phenomenon; it has become driving force in contemporary America and the world. In fact, computers have become so much a part of our lives that the social conventions surrounding computers have taken on the importance of Biblical commandments, as suggested by the above cartoon.

Furthermore, the bewildered attitude of the cartoon "Moses" indicates that computer technology, and the culture surrounding it, evolves with such rapidity that many (or perhaps most) people find themselves confused, awash in a white-noise sea of nagging questions:

what is the meaning of those weird terms—gigabytes and baud rates and MOOs and flaming—that tech-nerds use; is nonlinear writing, as modeled by the World Wide Web and other hypertext-formatted documents, really going to replace traditional expository writing, with its linear, logical, structure; will the average individual need to be fully computer literate to survive and even prosper in the economy of the next millennium; how will the computer redefine people's notions of work, leisure time, and social interaction; how will the aesthetic worlds of music and visual art be influenced by the continuing use of computer technology; and will "virtual reality"—the real-time, interactive, computerized simulation of sensory experiences—become a practical reality in succeeding decades? This chapter, by exploring some important topics within the broad area of computer culture, and by providing a "casebook" on the use of computers and the Internet in education, will suggest answers to many of those questions.

The first half of the chapter deals with broad issues of identity, community, culture, and creativity in looking at how the increasing prevalence of computers and networking are affecting our society. Kenneth Gergen, an expert in the field of social psychology, draws out some of the broadest (and most important) questions having to do with issues of identity and community. Gergen makes the argument that individuals, the relationships we have, and the communities we live in are changing in fundamental ways because of the influence of technology. The next two authors—John Perry Barlow and Sherry Turkle—offer opinions as to the effects of opportunities to socialize online and to build online communities. Some suggest that the Internet is a dehumanizing influence, drawing time and attention away from real human contact, while others contend that computer-based interaction makes up for the lack of community spirit in contemporary America by providing opportunities for meaningful human contact. Barlow and Turkle explore these debates and other issues from their perspective as early participants in Internet social settings.

The second half of this chapter explores the use of computers and the Internet in grade school classrooms and in higher education. The role of computers in education is hotly debated, with advocates on both sides of the issue: those who argue that computers will revolutionize learning, and those who think schools are going too far in adapting their curriculum to technology. Claudia Wallis finds much to admire in the way that The Dalton School integrates computer-based projects in its classes, whereas Neil Postman describes technology as a "false god," at least in the context of the classroom, and criticizes the unthinking adulation of that some educators have for computers—or as he puts it, "the songs of love that technophiles perform for us." The final two essays of the chapter turn to higher education, with UCLA

Professor Emeritus Richard Lanham describing some innovative uses of computers and databases in his literature classes.

Given that computers and virtual relationships will certainly become more prevalent and influential in the years ahead, you might take the readings in this chapter as an invitation and opportunity to reflect on your attitudes about and level of involvement in computer culture. In what ways have computers influenced your life already, and how do you imagine they will affect you personally and professionally in the next century?

Virtual Selves and Communities

The Self in the Age of Information

Kenneth Gergen

Kenneth Gergen, the Mustin Professor of Psychology at Swarthmore College, publishes and lectures extensively, and his work has had a major influence in the field of social psychology. In the selection that follows, which was originally published in The Washington Quarterly, *Gergen answers a very important question: how has our sense of identity and selfhood—our understanding of who we are as individuals and as members of society—been affected by the development of technology? Gergen considers the impact not only of computer technologies but also of developments in transportation, communication, and scientific knowledge. Gergen addresses this broad topic in an organized manner: first, by describing the ways that technological developments and new scientific knowledge have destroyed the traditional concept of selfhood; then, by discussing the characteristics of current concepts of selfhood; and finally, by explaining the consequences of this shift.*

As the brief summary above might indicate, Gergen's article is fairly theoretical. Although it's very clearly written and very well organized, you might find it somewhat difficult to read; Gergen covers a lot of ground and the article is quite dense and rich. ***Before you read,*** *therefore, recall the strategies for active reading that were discussed in the introductory chapter, especially annotating and re-reading. These techniques should help you gain a full understanding of Gergen's ideas.*

As patterns of cultural life become increasingly dependent on technology, questions of cultural direction become paramount. How are our lives being shaped, what traditions are being eroded, what values and ways of life are being changed by technological developments, and to what extent is our capacity to determine our cultural future being undermined? These are only a few of the concerns now demanding attention. 1

I will focus here on an issue that is rapidly rising to prominence in the social sciences: How are we to understand the impact of emerging communication technologies on individual psychological functioning? In what ways are processes of cognition, motivation, and emotion, for example, reshaped by the increasing enmeshment of the individual in rapidly accumulating, ever-shifting, and increasingly 2 complex arrays of information produced by the Internet, television, faxes, cellular phones, and more?

There is ample precedent for such inquiry. As is explored in Walter Ong's groundbreaking *From Orality to Literacy,* new forms of thought emerged in the Western cultural shift from a primary dependency on oral interchange to print technology.[1] Redundancy and simplification of thought, favored by face-to-face conversation, gave way to the kind of precision, coherence, and complex analysis that reading and writing make possible. Even today, the psychological capacities honored in contemporary, print-based educational systems are primarily those fostered by the technology of print. 3

Yet there is an important sense in which this concern about the impact of technology on psychological processes is premature. Setting out to trace the effects of, for instance, "information overload" on cognitive processes already presumes the existence of cognitive processes. In the same way, research into technology's effects on motivation, emotion, or individual values is predicated on the assumption that motivation, emotion, and values are there to study. In effect, to embark on such study requires a set of preconceptions about the nature of human psychological functioning. In this light, we must ask, Is it possible that the technological milieu is transforming the grounding assumptions themselves, our very conceptions of the human self? 4

For example, as David Olson proposes in *The World on Paper,* the shift from oral culture to print technology may have changed cultural beliefs about human beings.[2] In ongoing, face-to-face conversation, we are little concerned with the mind behind the words; meaning is shaped before us in the course of the interchange. However, with the emergence of printed text, important questions were created about the "author's meaning." Thus, with the development of print culture, the mind behind the words became an important topic of discussion. This malleability in our beliefs about our human selves has interested numerous historians and cultural anthropologists. It should be addressed now in light of changes in the contemporary technological ethos. 5

So, I pose the following questions: In what respects are the emerging technologies transforming our fundamental understanding of the psychological self? And if our understanding of who we are is changing, what are the repercussions for cultural—and indeed global—life? 6

My particular concern here is with a core belief in contemporary U.S. culture, namely a belief in the self as a bounded and integral agent, capable of conscious self-direction and self-control. This view, largely coming into prominence during the seventeenth and eighteenth centuries, has been a mainstay of Western cultural life. It is belief in the self as an integral agent that rationalizes our institutions of 7 democratic governance ("one man, one vote"), our institutions of public education (the training of "individual minds"), and our practices of moral accountability that hold individuals responsible for their actions. As I shall discuss in this essay, the dramatic changes occurring in the technological ethos are, both directly and indirectly, undermining belief in such a self. The concept of the self as an integral, bounded agent is slowly becoming untenable. The outcomes of such a transformation deserve close attention.

In my discussion of the transformative forces at work, I shall first touch on the cultural conditions that seem essential to sustain traditional beliefs in the self. Both the character of communal life and the institutions of truth have long furnished support to this tradition. For both of these sources of sustenance, information technology plays a potentially destructive role. I shall then turn to processes of self-erosion favored by technological immersion and consider multiple ways in which traditional beliefs in the self are challenged. Finally, I shall consider several repercussions of this transformation. Although there are potentially serious consequences of this conceptual shift, it also expands the horizon of opportunity in interesting and important ways. 8

COMMUNITY IN CRISIS

Understandings of self are inherently rooted in community. From the moment we are given proper names, we enter into domains of relationship, and through relationships we develop a sense of who we are and what we are worth. A solid sense of self derives from relationships that are coherent and consistent over time. By living in communities where we are known by many people, who also know each other, we each derive a strong sense of "being somebody"—somebody endowed with particular characteristics, capacities, and proclivities. However, the technologies of communication are largely destroying this form of coherent and consistent community. This destruction has several facets: 9

Increasingly Mobile Populations

As a result of our heavy reliance on automobiles and other forms of rapid transportation, jobs and schools are increasingly separated geographically from a family's place of residence. More and more, the neighborhood is emptied of participants; in a typical family, both parents may be employed elsewhere, and the children are away throughout the day, spending their time in school, day care, and after-school 10 programs. Recreational activities, business trips, and socializing with friends across town also reduce presence at home in the evening hours. Further, as businesses find it easier to relocate, families increasingly find themselves moving households. The average American will occupy about a dozen dwellings during a lifetime.

A Wider Range of Relationships

The increasing span of everyday travel is paralleled by the increased potential for frequent use of electronic communication (e.g., telephone and e-mail). Further, television and film invite more recreational travel; tourism has become the world's largest industry. Among the results of such expansions is a wider range of relationships (friends, acquaintances, colleagues, distant relatives, and so on). More and more, for example, one's network of friends may be spread across the continent and the globe. Each relationship may bring new information, opinion, and values into play, and there is often little interconnection among those to whom one is connected. The cast of "significant others" is thus dispersed and fragmented. 11

An Erosion of Strong Bonds

Each relationship—whether with a friend, relative, or colleague—generates its own set of expectations and obligations. However, as relations accumulate and expand geographically, the amount of time available for any particular relationship decreases. The result is a reduction in strong, committed bonds; a limited number of deep relationships is replaced by a broad array of more superficial engagements. The joy of spontaneous participation is often replaced by a burdensome feeling of obligation. In addition, the potential of any relationship to generate or affirm an indelible sense of self is reduced. Scarcely anyone knows us in depth, so few can be trusted to furnish the kind of affirmation or opinions that are significantly formative or informative. 12

TRUTH: FROM CERTAINTY TO SOCIAL CONSTRUCTION

In the deterioration of a consistent, coherent, and significant set of relationships, the grounds for strong belief in a substantive self (a sense of bounded and integral personhood) are removed. The anchoring 13 process for strong claims to being a particular sort of person, with clearly identifiable characteristics, is subverted. Yet there is a second source of such beliefs about the self: cultural authority.

For centuries, religious institutions had primary authority on matters of self. Thus, sanctioned by church and temple, belief in the individual soul became broadly prevalent—a fact of life as obvious as the existence of what we call "emotion." However, over the past century in particular, science has displaced religion's authority on matters of the self. Psychology and psychiatry, along with biology, anthropology, and sociology, have become primary sources of knowledge about human beings. For example, the concept of depression scarcely existed a century ago. Yet, with the authoritative counsel of the mental health profession, it has come to be understood that depression is a "common disease," and prescriptions are written for more than $8 billion worth of Prozac a year. 14

Largely owing to the rapid development and dispersion of communication technologies, strong forces have been activated that erode the power of cultural authority. Authoritative claims to truth about the self are becoming less believable. Two dimensions of this transformation are noteworthy: 15

Multiple Truths and the Loss of Faith

In an expanding sea of available information, along with an expanding domain of relationships, we are exposed to an increasing array of authoritative claims—opinions, data, arguments, and proposals. This array is augmented by the increasing potential of otherwise marginal groups to gain public prominence, supported by the news media's need for the drama of deviancy. The result is that for virtually any issue of broad significance there is a virtual chaos of competing claims. Whether the issue concerns economic planning, foreign policy in China, programs for weight loss, Supreme Court nominations, or the origins of the universe, authoritative opinions are multiple, mixed, and often contentious. 16

And so it is with matters of self-definition. For example, we have witnessed in this century a steady accumulation of "schools" of psychiatry, psychology, and sociology—all vying for authority over matters of individual selves. There are competing claims for the centrality of unconscious process, childhood conditioning, genetic determination, and information processing, with each enclave touting arguments and evidence. One significant result of multiple and competing claims to truth is growing confusion and distrust: Where in the sea of conflict can the island of truth be located? Over time, the very idea of 17 transcendent truth, truth surpassing anyone's particular perspective, becomes suspect. Foundationalism is replaced by relativism; strong truth claims seem increasingly parochial.

Self-interest and Suspicion

18 The growing sense of multiple and constructed realities is coupled with an emerging cynicism. If claims to truth are increasingly seen as representing a perspective, as "one way of looking at it," questions are soon raised about the bases of such perspectives. If perspectives are not driven by objective fact or impeccable rationality, what are the grounds for such claims to truth? One readily available answer is that of human interest. Proclamations of truth increasingly appear to serve individual purposes. This possibility has been acutely dramatized in the heated, irresolvable debates over the guilt and innocence of O. J. Simpson and Bill Clinton. It has also been made manifest in the ways that audience ratings shape the reporting of news, commercial interests determine public accounts of various food and drug capabilities, ideology influences the opinions of Supreme Court justices, and party politics determines the "independent opinion" of members of Congress. Slowly, "objective opinion" gives way to what we understand as "spin."

19 And so it is in matters pertaining to the character of the self. Expert opinions of "insanity" can be purchased by defendants in criminal trials, pharmaceutical companies have a vested interest in psychiatric diagnoses favoring their products, and those favoring the concept of a genetic determination of intelligence invariably are privileged white scientists. With respect to the nature of the self, what authority can be trusted?

THE EROSION OF THE ESSENTIAL SELF

20 The hypertrophic technological condition of contemporary culture is slowly undermining the grounds for confident belief. In particular, as the cast of significant others in one's life becomes increasingly dispersed and variegated, and as cultural authorities lose their credibility, confidence fades in the traditional concept of a bounded, integral self. However, the technological ethos also has more direct effects on the sense of self. If confidence in the traditions is eroded, we stand increasingly vulnerable to such effects. In my view, the technological context works directly to undermine the intelligibility of the traditional self. The reasons are many and cumulative; here, I limit discussion to several interlinking tendencies.

Polyvocality

By dramatically expanding the range of information to which we are exposed, the range of people with whom we have significant interchanges, and the range of opinions available from various authorities through various media, we become privy to multiple realities. Each of these sources becomes a potentially formative influence on the development of our views of the world and ourselves. Such absorption of the social surround lends itself to a shift from the centered self to polyvocality, a condition in which the individual is capable of holding a multiplicity of views, values, and sentiments—many of which are implicitly or explicitly conflicting. For example, in the recent Clinton scandal, the deluge of motley opinion would have led many in the public to understand that Clinton was morally at fault, but that he was also a victim of partisan politics and an overly zealous prosecutor; that Clinton was an effective leader, but that he also had the good fortune to preside in prosperous times; that Clinton lied, but that he was also a religious man, and so on. 21

If one acquires an increasingly diverse vocabulary of deliberation, how is a satisfactory decision to be reached? The inward examination of consciousness yields not coherence but cacophony; there is no unified standpoint available within the self (the mark of an integral individual), just a chorus of competing contenders. And as one becomes increasingly polyvocal, to what degree do one's internal resources continue to guide or direct? If my "looking inward" becomes increasingly less useful for directing action, doesn't concern with my "state of mind" lose its urgency? Rather than looking within, the more compelling option is to turn outward to my social context: to search the range of ambient opinion, to "network," and to negotiate. In this immersion in the public sphere, the private interior loses authority, and the presumption of internal agency is subverted. If negotiating the complexities of cultural multiplicity becomes the norm, the concept of mind as the origin of action grows stale. 22

Plasticity

As the technologies of sociation increasingly immerse us in information, opinions, and values, they expand the scope and complexity of our activities. We engage in a greater range of relationships in numerous and contrasting sites, ranging from friendly relationships in the neighborhood to professional relationships that span continents. Further, because of the rapid movement of information and opinion, the useful life of various products and policies is shortened and opportunities for new enterprises expanded. The composition of the work- 23 place is thus in continuous flux, and the single-career commitment gives way to a continuous process of "repackaging" the self. The working person shifts jobs more frequently, often with an accompanying household move. By the early 1990s, one-third of U.S. workers had been with their current employer for less than a year, and almost two-thirds had been there for less than five years.

As a result of these developments, the individual is challenged by an increasingly varied array of behavioral demands. At each new location, new patterns of action may be required; dispositions, appetites, and personae all may be acquired and abandoned as conditions suggest or demand. With movement through time and space, oppositional accents may often be fashioned: firm here and soft there, commanding and then obedient, sophisticated and then crude, conservative and then liberal, conventional and then rebellious. 24

For many people, such chameleon-like shifts are now unremarkable; they constitute the normal hurly-burly of daily life. At times these challenges may be enjoyed, even sought. It was only four decades ago when David Riesman's celebrated *The Lonely Crowd* championed the virtues of the inner-directed person and condemned the other-directed individual as someone without a gyroscopic center-of-being, someone without character.[3] In the new technology-based ethos, there is little need for the inner-directed, one-style-for-all individual. Increasingly, such a person seems narrow, parochial, and inflexible. In the fast pace of a technological society, concern with the inner life is a luxury, if not a waste of time. We now celebrate the protean being capable of moving facilely across a sea of complex conditions. In the world of Plastic Fantastic Man, the interior self loses significance. 25

De-authentication

A more subtle mode of self-erosion also results from the increasing inundation of images, stories, and information. Consider those confirmatory moments of individual authorship, moments in which the sense of authentic action becomes most fully transparent. Given the Western tradition of individualism, these are typically moments in which we apprehend our actions as unique, in which we are not merely duplicating models, obeying orders, or following convention. Rather, in the innovative act we locate a guarantee of self as originative source, a creative agent. Yet, in a world in which technologies facilitate an enormous sophistication about cultural conventions, such moments become increasingly rare. How is it, for example, that a young couple, each of whom has been indundated for twenty-some years by romance narratives—on television and radio, in film, magazines, and books—can utter a sweet word of endearment without a haunting sense of cliché? Or in Umberto Eco's terms, how can a man who loves a cultivated woman say to her, 26

"'I love you madly," when "he knows that she knows (and that she knows that he knows) that these words have already been written by Barbara Cartland?'"[4] In what sense can one stand out from the crowd in a singular display of moral fortitude, and not hear the voice of John Wayne, Gary Cooper, or Harrison Ford over one's shoulder?

Commodification of the Self

These arguments are closely tied to a final, technology-induced shift in cultural understanding. Because the technologies of sociation enable information to be disseminated widely at low cost, popular entertainment has become a major industry. Critical to the entertainment industry are individual performers—individuals who, because they are entertaining, command a broad audience and vast remuneration. In effect, the "self" becomes available as a saleable commodity. Individual performers may take on new names, spouses, and lifestyles in order to increase their fame and income. As the entertainment industry expands, and as television channels become more numerous, the demand for "characters" becomes ever wider. Increasingly, the common person—owing to a peculiar passion, unique story, act of heroism or stupidity, or possession of inside information—becomes a potential candidate for fame and fortune. Consequently, there is a growing consciousness of the self as a commodity. Being true to one's self, possessing depth of character, and searching for one's identity all become old-fashioned phrases; they are nicely suited to earlier times but no longer profitable. 27

Each of these tendencies—toward polyvocality, plasticity, deauthentication and commodification of self—undermines the longstanding importance placed on the integral self, that core to which one's actions should be true. Although this erosion is lamentable in significant respects, it is also important to take note of growing criticism of the Western, traditional concept of individual selves. 28

On the conceptual level, the problem is not simply that the conception of a private mind carries with it all the thorny problems of epistemological dualism (subject vs. object, mind vs. body, minds knowing other minds), but also that the very idea of an independent decisionmaker proves uncompelling. How, it is asked, could mental deliberation take place except within the categories supplied by the culture? If we were to subtract the entire vocabulary of the culture from individual subjectivity, how could the individual form questions about justice, duty, rights, or moral good? In Michael Sandel's terms, "to imagine a person incapable of constitutive attachments . . . is not to conceive an ideally free and rational agent, but to imagine a person wholly without character, without moral depth."[5] 29

These conceptual problems are conjoined with a widespread ideological critique. Alexis de Tocqueville's observations of nineteenth- 30

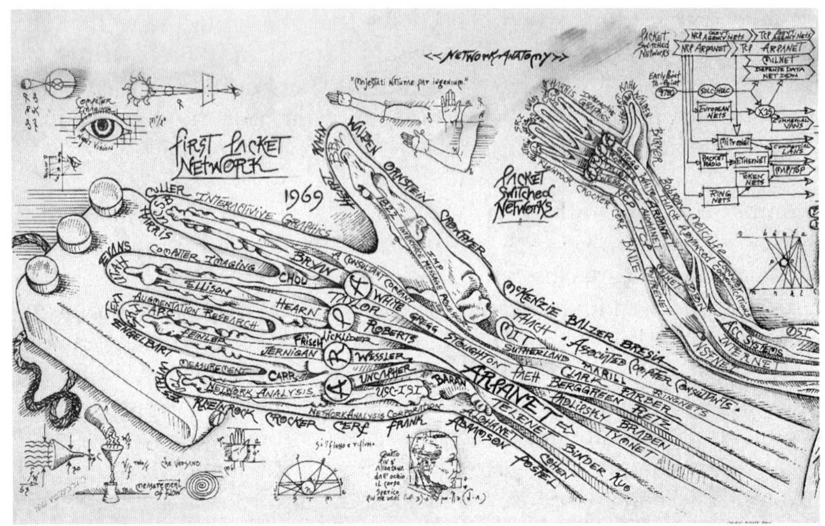

Arpanet Scroll, by Roland Bryan

century U.S. life set the stage: "Individualism is a calm and considered feeling which disposes each citizen to isolate himself from the mass of his fellows . . . he gladly leaves the greater society to look after himself."[6] In recent decades these views have been echoed and amplified by many scholars. Christopher Lasch has traced the close association between individualist presumptions and cultural tendencies toward "me-first" narcissism; R. N. Bellah and his colleagues argue that modern individualism works against the possibility of committed relationships and dedication to community; for Edward Sampson, the presumption of a self-contained individual leads to social division and insensitivity to minority voices.[7]

Ultimately, the concept of an interior origin of action defines the society in terms of unbreachable isolation. If what is most central to our existence is hidden from others, and vice versa, we are forever left with a sense of profound isolation, an inability to ever know what lies behind another's mask. With strong belief in an interior self, we inevitably create the Other to whom we shall forever remain alien. 31

REPERCUSSIONS: FROM CONFLICT TO CONFLUENCE

The emerging technological ethos not only removes key supports for the traditional belief in the self as an individual, integral agent, but si- 32 multaneously functions more directly to undermine the very experience of this self. We must finally consider several repercussive effects of this emerging condition.

Retrenchment

At the outset, any movement that challenges long-standing traditions 33
within a culture is likely to provoke a defensive reaction. Thus, for example, the modernist secularization of Western culture sets the stage for a revival of fundamentalist religion, and broad-scale critiques of truth claims in the academic sphere have provoked a range of vociferous counterattacks (e.g., "the science wars"). In this light, we can understand the emergence of various cultural movements acting to revitalize a sense of a palpable self, to furnish internal bearings or a foundation for belief in the centrality of the individual. In my view, we find impulses toward retrenchment in widely disparate movements. New Age religion and the broad-scale romance with meditation reflect an attempt to remove one's self from the hurly-burly of everyday life and to locate a center within; in the revitalization of far-right politics can be discerned a celebration of individual character, moral fiber, and willpower; in the flowering of psychobiology, genetic psychology, and psychopharmacology are located strong impulses to materialize the self, to define it in biological terms; and in the "cult of personality" (a composite of celebrities, mass-market magazines, consumer products, and electronic entertainment), the individual is at the center of celebration. Despite the current technological ambience, we are not likely to witness the full demise of the integral and bounded self.

Group Identification and Conflict

With the passing of the individual as the palpable center of societal 34
life, the way is opened for revitalization of the group. Harkening back to premodern times when the family, the guild, the lineage, the clan, the principality, and other collective configurations were focal denominators, there is again a strong invitation to identify the self with the group. In effect, self-definition is conflated with group definition.

Movements in this direction have been manifest for some 35
decades, particularly in the pervasive search for one's "roots" in various ethnic, cultural, and national traditions. There is also a link between the dissolving of singular selves and the emergence in the United States of strong teamism (an increasingly evident commitment to local, regional, and national athletic teams). Allegiances to fundamentalist religions also display many of the same signs, as do emerging tendencies toward communitarianism. And perhaps most prominent is the significant emergence of identity politics, a political

form deriving its power from the willingness of individuals to define themselves in terms of an otherwise marginalized group (e.g., African American, feminist, gay and lesbian). Of course, the availability of low-cost means of communication and organization—including radio, television, telephone, and e-mail—facilitates effective organizing processes. Virtually any small group of the committed can, through the World Wide Web, now generate appeals on a global level. However, more significant is an apparently increasing willingness to abandon a hallmark of individualism—the glory of "doing it my way"—in favor of group participation.

At the same time, this shift from individual to group commitment is not without cost to the society. Implicit divisiveness is a primary negative repercussion of the individualist tradition: To construct ourselves as independent agents is to set in motion a dynamic in which we are separate from all others, no one has the right to direct our actions, and all others are suspect. To be sure, the capitulation of self to the group is accompanied by a diminution of such tendencies. But in the move toward group commitment, the divisiveness characteristic of individualism now simply shifts to another level. Society is composed of a Hobbesian condition of "all against all," not in terms of individuals, but on a group level. Thus, in the realm of identity politics, multiple groups are pitted not only against what is left of the "mainstream," but against each other as well. In James Davidson Hunter's terms, we exist now in a state of "culture wars."[8] 36

Temporary Loyalties and Growing Interdependence

While intergroup conflict is favored by emerging technological conditions, there is reason for optimism in the extended future. As I have mentioned, available technologies are steadily expanding the range of relationships in which we engage. While an initial result of this immersion is a lessening of one's sense of a coherent or fundamental self and a resulting vulnerability to group allegiance, the long-term effects may be different. With expanding associations, interdependencies, and commitments, the tendency toward singular group allegiance may abate. At a minimum, individual commitments to groups are likely to be shortened. Individuals may enthusiastically join a group, actively participate, donate time and resources, then move on. This kind of temporally situated commitment has already been evidenced in the political sphere, with election-dependent party allegiances now commonplace. "Temporary ecstasies" are also apparent in the deterioration of brand loyalty and in the rapidly shifting terrains of celebrity worship, team loyalty, and spiritual allegiance. And in the realm of 37 identity politics, an increasingly common complaint is that an identity commanded by a political standpoint inadequately represents the complex lives of the participants.

If this trajectory is extended, with individuals multiply engaged, we may approach the point where intense or lethal conflict between groups will recede. There will be little enthusiasm for harsh attacks on other groups, because members of groups on the offensive will share membership, allegiances, or interdependencies with those under attack. For example, it is now exceedingly difficult to envision an outbreak of war between the United States and any nation in Western Europe, because economic, institutional, and personal interdependencies are so fully developed that such a conflict would be self-defeating for both sides. More generally, we are approaching a time when no nation-state will be sufficiently powerful to command the allegiance of multinational corporations to make international warfare possible. Or, as was evidenced in the bloodless collapse of the Soviet Union, national governments may find it increasingly difficult to stifle antigovernmental countermovements now made possible with low-cost communication devices. Aggressive conflict may thus give way to an impasse of action. 38

New Relational Concepts and Practices

A potentially dramatic shift in cultural consciousness is becoming increasingly apparent. If, as I have argued, we are witnessing the slow erosion of belief in an integral and basic self, and if the return to the group ultimately proves futile, then our traditional concepts of the fundamental building blocks of society will be thrown into doubt. Neither the self nor the group will command ultimate significance in our deliberations and practices. In my view, the door is thus opened for the creative construction of alternatives to these traditional but tired concepts. One of the most fascinating alternatives on the cultural horizon represents a shift toward the relational—that is, turning away from the concepts of self and group in favor of such concepts as interdependence, conjoint construction of meaning, mutually interacting entities, and systemic process. 39

Recent and emerging technologies contribute significantly to this relational imaginary. Particularly relevant is the development of chat rooms, bulletin boards, e-mail lists, and other Internet features that facilitate bodiless relationships. On the Internet, identities can be put forward that may not be linked in any specific way to the concrete existence of the participants, and these cyber-identities may carry on active and engaging relationships. Most significant is that these relationships proceed not on the basis of "real selves" (integral minds 40 in physical bodies), but on the basis of positionings within conversations or the discursive flow. Further, it is only the coordinated functioning of these discursive formations that enable "community" to be achieved. In effect, community has no geographic locus outside the web of discourse. Here we approach pure relatedness, without self or community in the traditional sense.

The image of relationship without self or community also has 41
other sources in the technosphere. For several decades, the computer itself has served as a chief metaphor for human functioning. The cognitive revolution in psychology, along with the artificial intelligence movement and cognitive science, have derived much of their intelligibility from various equations of person and computer. However, as the Internet and the World Wide Web dramatically expand, the computer is gradually losing its rhetorical allure. The Internet brings instantaneous relationship to an exponentially increasing population throughout the globe. It is a domain so vast and so powerful that it can scarcely be controlled by the nation-state. It is legislated by no institution; it functions virtually outside the law. In this context, the computer is merely a gateway into a relational domain without obvious end. Slowly "the network" is becoming a central metaphor for understanding social life.

In my view, these movements of metaphor are reflected in a 42
range of emerging practices. In the educational sphere, "collaborative classrooms," apprenticeship programs, and group-project designs are widely being developed. In organizational development, numerous training and intervention programs are now built around concepts of organizational culture, meaning-making, teamwork, and collective vision. In therapeutic circles, newly emerging practices emphasize the co-construction of meaning, narrative, and systemic interdependence. And in world politics, the traditional autonomy claimed by nation-states is slowly giving way to regional, economic, and ideological coalition- and alliance-building. The relational world is gathering form.

A CONCLUDING, UNSCIENTIFIC POSTSCRIPT

In this essay, I have moved over exceedingly broad terrain in a rather 43
footloose fashion. There has been little attempt to prove my arguments with a bevy of statistics, authoritative support, surveys, and the like. This is not because it is impossible to generate such evidence. Rather, given the assaults on authoritative truth that I have discussed, it is disingenuous now to make such claims. Indeed, this essay cannot be extricated from the very technocultural context that I have attempted to explore. This does not mean that the proposals made in this essay

are "untrue." Rather, I suggest that an essay such as this be viewed as a cultural lens, as a way of comprehending the highly complex, ever-changing sea of events in which we are immersed. My hope, then, is to furnish conceptual resources with which we can collectively deliberate on the direction of events and possibly intervene in ways that can bring us safely, and even joyfully, into the future.

NOTES

1. Walter J. Ong, *Orality and Literacy* (London: Methuen, 1982).
2. David Olson, *The World on Paper* (New York: Cambridge University Press, 1994).
3. David Riesman, *The Lonely Crowd* (New Haven, Conn.: Yale University Press, 1950).
4. Umberto Eco, *The Name of the Rose* (San Diego, Calif.: Harcourt Brace Jovanovich, 1983), 67 (postscript).
5. Michael Sandel, *Liberalism and the Limits of Justice* (Cambridge: Cambridge University Press, 1982), 179.
6. Alexis de Tocqueville, *Democracy in America* (New York: Doubleday, 1969), 506.
7. Christopher Lasch, *The Culture of Narcissism* (New York: Norton, 1979); R. N. Bellah et al., *Habits of the Heart: Individualism and Commitment in American Life* (Berkeley: University of California Press, 1985); and Edward Sampson, *Celebrating the Other* (Boulder, Colo.: Westview Press, 1993).
8. James Davidson Hunter, *Culture Wars: The Struggle to Define America* (New York: Basic Books, 1991).

Examining the Text

1. What parallels does Gergen draw at the beginning of the article between the shift from oral to print culture and the current shift to a technological culture? Why do you think Gergen begins by recalling past transformations of the self?

2. In your own words, explain what you think Gergen means by the term "traditional self." What do the phrases "integral" and "bounded" mean in this context?

3. According to Gergen, how have technologies undermined the traditional self?

4. In your own words, describe the key features of the new kind of self that Gergen believes has emerged in contemporary culture.

5. According to Gergen, in what ways do relationships and group attachments function to help us understand our psychological and social characteristics?

6. The black-and-white image on page 352 is one of Ronald Bryan's artistic renderings of the early history of networking and ARAPNET. How does its integration of the human (the hand, the eye) and the technological (the device with buttons, the da Vinci-like perspective drawings) parallel or contrast with Gergen's observations about technology and society?

For Group Discussion

In a group with several other students, choose one of the main sections of Gergen's article: the introduction, "Community in Crisis," "Truth: From Certainty to Social Construction," "The Erosion of the Essential Self," or "Repercussions: From Conflict to Confluence." After rereading this section, discuss what you see as its main points. Make a list of key terms and their definitions (and look up the definitions of any words you're not familiar with). Discuss any questions or confusion you have about what Gergen is trying to express in this section. When you feel that you've got a good understanding of the section, summarize the section in a brief presentation to the rest of the class.

Writing Suggestion

Gergen writes toward the end of the article, "I have moved over exceedingly broad terrain in a rather footloose fashion." He discusses a wide range of important concepts in a relatively brief manner. For this writing assignment, choose one of the concepts or categories in Gergen's article that you find particularly interesting. For instance, you might be intrigued by the idea of polyvocality, or by the ways that technology contributes to the decline of community, or by the processes of "retrenchment" in the face of challenges to the traditional self. Whichever concept or category you choose, re-read the section(s) where Gergen discusses it and make sure that you understand the points he is making. Then write an essay in which you first define this concept with the help of quotations and/or paraphrases from Gergen's article. In the remainder of the essay, provide examples from your own experience and observations that show this concept in action in the contemporary world.

Cyberhood vs. Neighborhood

John Perry Barlow

This essay on "virtual communities" is written by an unlikely expert. John Perry Barlow grew up in the small town of Pinedale, Wyoming, and ran the family cattle ranch there until he was forced to sell it in 1988. Seeing the decline of the community all around him and searching, as he explains here, for evidence "that community in America would not perish altogether," Barlow started exploring the possibilities of virtual communities—that is, communities that don't exist in a particular place but rather are formed by participants in Internet mailing lists, conferences, discussion groups, and virtual "chat rooms." In this essay, Barlow describes his initial enthusiasm for these virtual communities, as well as his subsequent disillusionment.

Barlow's strategy here is to evaluate virtual communities in terms of how closely they can reproduce the qualities of real communities, in terms of human interaction and connection as well as in terms of shared interests, diversity, and meaningfulness. In comparing real and virtual communities, Barlow defines what is essential to the concept of "community"—what makes a community thrive? Why do we form and maintain communities in the first place?

***As you read,** make a list of the elements that Barlow believes are essential to a community. Which of those elements do you find in the communities you currently participate in?*

"There is no there there."

—Gertrude Stein (speaking of Oakland)

"It ain't no Amish barn-raising in there . . ."

—Bruce Sterling (speaking of cyberspace)

I am often asked how I went from pushing cows around a remote Wyoming ranch to my present occupation (which *Wall Street Journal* recently described as "cyberspace cadet"). I haven't got a short answer, but I suppose I came to the virtual world looking for community. 1

Unlike most modern Americans, I grew up in an actual place, an entire nonintentional community called Pinedale, Wyoming. As I struggled for nearly a generation to keep my ranch in the family, I was motivated by the belief that such places were the spiritual home of humanity. But I knew their future was not promising. 2

At the dawn of the 20th century, over 40 percent of the American workforce lived off the land. The majority of us lived in towns like 3

Pinedale. Now fewer than 1 percent of us extract a living from the soil. We just became too productive for our own good.

Of course, the population followed the jobs. Farming and ranch- 4
ing communities are now home to a demographically insignificant percentage of Americans, the vast majority of whom live not in ranch houses but in more or less identical split level "ranch homes" in more or less identical suburban "communities." Generica.

In my view, these are neither communities nor homes. I believe 5
the combination of television and suburban population patterns is simply toxic to the soul. I see much evidence in contemporary America to support this view.

Meanwhile, back at the ranch, doom impended. And, as I 6
watched the community in Pinedale growing ill from the same economic forces that were killing my family's ranch, the Bar Cross, satellite dishes brought the cultural infection of television. I started looking around for evidence that community in America would not perish altogether.

I took some heart in the mysterious nomadic City of the Dead- 7
heads, the virtually physical town that follows the Grateful Dead around the country. The Deadheads lacked place, touching down briefly wherever the band happened to be playing, and they lacked continuity in time, since they had to suffer a new diaspora every time the band moved on or went home. But they had many of the other necessary elements of community, including a culture, a religion of sorts (which, though it lacked dogma, had most of the other, more nurturing aspects of spiritual practice), a sense of necessity, and most importantly, shared adversity.

I wanted to know more about the flavor of their interaction, what 8
they thought and felt, but since I wrote Dead songs (including "Estimated Prophet" and "Cassidy"), I was a minor icon to the Deadheads, and was thus inhibited, in some socially Heisenbergian way, from getting a clear view of what really went on among them.

Then, in 1987, I heard about a "place" where Deadheads gath- 9
ered where I could move among them without distorting too much the field of observation. Better, this was a place I could visit without leaving Wyoming. It was a shared computer in Sausalito, California, called the Whole Earth 'Lectronic Link, or WELL. After a lot of struggling with modems, serial cables, init strings, and other Computer arcana that seemed utterly out of phase with such notions as Deadheads and small towns, I found myself looking at the glowing yellow word "Login:" beyond which lay my future.

"Inside" the WELL were Deadheads in community. There were 10
thousands of them there, gossiping, complaining (mostly about the

Grateful Dead), comforting and harassing each other, bartering, engaging in religion (or at least exchanging their totemic set lists), beginning and ending love affairs, praying for one another's sick kids. There was, it seemed, everything one might find going on in a small town, save dragging Main Street and making out on the back roads.

I was delighted. I felt I had found the new locale of human community—never mind that the whole thing was being conducted in mere words by minds from whom the bodies had been amputated. Never mind that all these people were deaf, dumb, and blind as paramecia or that their town had neither seasons nor sunsets nor smells. 11

Surely all these deficiencies would be remedied by richer, faster communications media. The featureless log-in handles would gradually acquire video faces (and thus expressions), shaded 3-D body puppets (and thus body language). This "space" which I recognized at once to be a primitive form of the cyberspace William Gibson predicted in his sci-fi novel *Neuromancer,* was still without apparent dimensions of vistas. But virtual reality would change all that in time. 12

Meanwhile, the commons, or something like it, had been rediscovered. Once again, people from the 'burbs had a place where they could encounter their friends as my fellow Pinedalians did at the post office and the Wrangler Cafe. They had a place where their hearts could remain as the companies they worked for shuffled their bodies around America. They could put down roots that could not be ripped out by forces of economic history. They had a collective stake. They had a community. 13

It is seven years now since I discovered the WELL. In that time, I cofounded an organization, the Electronic Frontier Foundation, dedicated to protecting its interests and those of other virtual communities like it from raids by physical government. I've spent countless hours typing away at its residents, and I've watched the larger context that contains it, the Internet, grow at such an explosive rate that, by 2004, every human on the planet will have an e-mail address unless the growth curve flattens (which it will). 14

My enthusiasm for virtuality has cooled. In fact, unless one counts interaction with the rather too large society of those with whom I exchange electronic mail, I don't spend much time engaging in virtual community, at all. Many of the near-term benefits I anticipated from it seem to remain as far in the future as they did when I first logged in. Perhaps they always will. 15

Pinedale works, more or less, as it is, but a lot is still missing from the communities of cyberspace, whether they be places like the WELL, the fractious newsgroups of USENET, the silent "auditoriums" 16 of America Online, or even enclaves on the promising World Wide Web.

17 What is missing? Well, to quote Ranjit Makkuni of Xerox Corporation's Palo Alto Research Center, "the *prãna* is missing," *prãna* being the Hindu term for both breath and spirit. I think he is right about this and that perhaps the central question of the virtual age is whether or not *prãna* can somehow be made to fit through any disembodied medium.

18 *Prãna* is, to my mind, the literally vital element in the holy and unseen ecology of relationship, the dense mesh of invisible life, on whose surface carbon-based life floats like a thin film. It is at the heart of the fundamental and profound difference between information and experience. Jaron Lanier has said that "information is alienated experience," and, that being true, *prãna* is part of what is removed when you create such easily transmissible replicas of experience as, say, the evening news.

19 Obviously a great many other, less spiritual, things are also missing entirely, like body language, sex, death, tone of voice, clothing, beauty (or homeliness), weather, violence, vegetation, wildlife, pets, architecture, music, smells, sunlight, and that ol' harvest moon. In short, most of the things that make my life real to me.

20 Present, but in far less abundance than in the physical world, which I call "meat space," are women, children, old people, poor people, and the genuinely blind. Also mostly missing are the illiterate and the continent of Africa. There is not much human diversity in cyberspace, which is populated, as near as I can tell, by white males under 50 with plenty of computer terminal time, great typing skills, high math SATs, strongly held opinions on just about everything, and an excruciating face-to-face shyness, especially with the opposite sex.

21 But diversity is as essential to healthy community as it is to healthy ecosystems (which are, in my view, different from communities only in unimportant aspects).

22 I believe that the principal reason for the almost universal failure of the intentional communities of the '60s and '70s was a lack of diversity in their members. It was a rare commune with any old people in it, or people who were fundamentally out of philosophical agreement with the majority.

23 Indeed, it is the usual problem when we try to build something that can only be grown. Natural systems, such as human communities, are simply too complex to design by the engineering principles we insist on applying to them. Like Dr. Frankenstein, western civilization is now finding its rational skills inadequate to the task of creating and caring for life. We would do better to return to a kind of agricultural

mind-set in which we humbly try to re-create the conditions from which life has sprung before. And leave the rest to God.

24 Given that it has been built so far almost entirely by people with engineering degrees, it is not so surprising that cyberspace has the kind of overdesigned quality that leaves out all kinds of elements nature would have provided invisibly.

25 Also missing from both the communes of the '60s and from cyberspace are a couple of elements that I believe are very important, if not essential, to the formation and preservation of a real community: an absence of alternatives and a sense of genuine adversity, generally shared. What about these?

26 It is hard to argue that anyone would find losing a modem literally hard to survive, while many have remained in small towns, have tolerated their intolerances and created entertainment to enliven their culturally arid lives simply because it seemed there was no choice but to stay. There are many investments—spiritual, material, and temporal—one is willing to put into a home one cannot leave. Communities are often the beneficiaries of these involuntary investments.

27 But when the going gets rough in cyberspace, it is even easier to move than it is in the burbs, where, given the fact that the average American moves some 12 times in his or her life, moving appears to be pretty easy. You cannot only find another bulletin board service (BBS) or newsgroup to hang out in; you can, with very little effort, start your own.

28 And then there is the bond of joint suffering. Most community is a cultural stockade erected against a common enemy that can take many forms. In Pinedale, we bore together, with an understanding needing little expression, the fact that Upper Green River Valley is the coldest spot, as measured by annual mean temperature, in the lower 48 states. We knew that if somebody was stopped on the road most winter nights, he would probably die there, so the fact that we might loathe him was not sufficient reason to drive on past his broken pickup.

29 By the same token, the Deadheads have the Drug Enforcement Administration, which strives to give them 20-year prison terms without parole for distributing the fairly harmless sacrament of their faith. They have an additional bond in the fact that when their Microbuses die, as they often do, no one but another Deadhead is likely to stop to help them.

30 But what are the shared adversities of cyberspace? Lousy user interfaces? The flames of harsh invective? Dumb jokes? Surely these can all be survived without the sanctuary provided by fellow sufferers.

31 One is always free to yank the jack, as I have mostly done. For me, the physical world offers far more opportunity for *prãna* rich con-

nections with my fellow creatures. Even for someone whose body is in a state of perpetual motion, I feel I can generally find more community among the still-embodied.

Finally, there is that shyness factor. Not only are we trying to 32
build community here among people who have never experienced any in my sense of the term, we are trying to build community among people who, in their lives, have rarely used the word *we* in a heartfelt way. It is a vast club, and many of the members—following Groucho Marx—wouldn't want to join a club that would have them.

And yet . . . 33

How quickly physical community continues to deteriorate. Even 34
Pinedale, which seems to have survived the plague of ranch failures, feels increasingly cut off from itself. Many of the ranches are now owned by corporate types who fly their Gulfstreams in to fish and are rarely around during the many months when the creeks are frozen over and neighbors are needed. They have kept the ranches alive financially, but they actively discourage their managers from the interdependence my former colleagues and I require. They keep agriculture on life support, still alive but lacking a functional heart.

And the town has been inundated with suburbanites who flee 35
here, bringing all their terrors and suspicions with them. They spend their evenings as they did in Orange County, watching television or socializing in hermetic little enclaves of fundamentalist Christianity that seem to separate them from us and even, given their sectarian animosities, from one another. The town remains. The community is largely a wraith of nostalgia.

So where else can we look for the connection we need to prevent 36
our plunging further into the condition of separateness Nietzsche called sin? What is there to do but to dive further into the bramble bush of information that, in its broadest forms, has done so much to tear us apart?

Cyberspace, for all its current deficiencies and failed promises, is 37
not without some very real solace already.

Some months ago, the great love of my life, a vivid young 38
woman with whom I intended to spend the rest of it, dropped dead of undiagnosed viral cardiomyopathy two days short of her 30th birthday. I felt as if my own heart had been as shredded as hers.

We had lived together in New York City. Except for my daugh- 39
ters, no one from Pinedale had met her. I needed a community to wrap around myself against colder winds than fortune had ever blown at me before. And without looking, I found I had one in the virtual world.

On the WELL, there was a topic announcing her death in one of 40
the conferences to which I posted the eulogy I had read over her before burying her in her own small town of Nanaimo, British Columbia.

It seemed to strike a chord among the disembodied living on the Net. People copied it and sent it to one another. Over the next several months I received almost a megabyte of electronic mail from all over the planet, mostly from folks whose faces I have never seen and probably never will.

They told me of their own tragedies and what they had done to survive them. As humans have since words were first uttered, we shared the second most common human experience, death, with an openheartedness that would have caused grave uneasiness in physical America, where the whole topic is so cloaked in denial as to be considered obscene. Those strangers, who had no arms to put around my shoulders, no eyes to weep with mine, nevertheless saw me through. As neighbors do. 41

I have no idea how far we will plunge into this strange place. Unlike previous frontiers, this one has no end. It is so dissatisfying in so many ways that I suspect we will be more restless in our search for home here than in all our previous explorations. And that is one reason why I think we may find it after all. If home is where the heart is, then there is already some part of home to be found in cyberspace. 42

So . . . does virtual community work or not? Should we all go off to cyberspace or should we resist it as a demonic form of symbolic abstraction? Does it supplant the real or is there, in it, reality itself? 43

Like so many true things, this one doesn't resolve itself to a black or a white. Nor is it gray. It is, along with the rest of life, black/white. Both/neither. I'm not being equivocal or whishy-washy here. We have to get over our Manichean sense that everything is either good or bad, and the border of cyberspace seems to me a good place to leave that old set of filters. 44

But really it doesn't matter. We are going there whether we want to or not. In five years, everyone who is reading these words will have an e-mail address, other than the determined Luddites who also eschew the telephone and electricity. 45

When we are all together in cyberspace we will see what the human spirit, and the basic desire to connect, can create there. I am convinced that the result will be more benign if we go there openminded, open-hearted, and excited with the adventure than if we are dragged into exile. 46

And we must remember that going to cyberspace, unlike previous great emigrations to the frontier, hardly requires us to leave where we have been. Many will find, as I have, a much richer appreciation of physical reality for having spent so much time in virtuality. 47

Despite its current (and perhaps in some areas permanent) insufficiencies, we should go to cyberspace with hope. Groundless hope, like unconditional love, may be the only kind that counts. 48

In Memoriam, Dr. Cynthia Horner (1964–1994).

Examining the Text

1. What does Barlow see as the essential elements of community? How do the various physical and virtual communities Barlow discusses embody or fail to embody these elements?

2. What does Barlow mean when he suggests that the "*prãna*" is missing from cyberspace communities? Why does he nevertheless find virtual communities worthwhile?

3. Examine the organization of Barlow's essay. How does he structure his argument? Do you think that the conclusions he comes to at the end (particularly in paragraph 44) are supported by what he says in the body of the essay?

For Group Discussion

Barlow observes that when he first entered the virtual community of Deadheads and others on the WELL, he saw a place where people "could put down roots that could not be ripped out by forces of economic history." To what forces is Barlow referring? Can you think of other forces—economic, social, cultural, political, historical, religious—that have affected the sense of community in America? As a group and then as a class, make a list of these factors. Which have helped strengthen a sense of community in America and which have brought about the decline of community?

Writing Suggestion

Define the characteristics of an ideal community, using ideas from Barlow's essay as well as ideas from your own experiences and observations. Then choose one community that you inhabit or know about: for example, the college or university community to which you belong; your high school community; the community in which you grew up; communities that you've visited; or perhaps a virtual community on the Internet that you're familiar with. Describe this community and compare it with your ideal definition. How well does this particular community meet your definition of the ideal? In what ways does it fall short? What are the reasons, in your opinion, that the community you're discussing is less than ideal?

Virtuality and Its Discontents

Sherry Turkle

Sherry Turkle, a professor in MIT's Program in Science, Technology, and Society, is at the forefront of scholars studying the effects of computers and the Internet on contemporary life. She has written two books that deal with the ways in which computers and the culture of the Internet are shaping human identity: The Second Self: Computers and the Human Spirit *(1984) and* Life on the Screen: Identity in the Age of the Internet *(1995). In the essay that follows, which is adapted from her more recent book, Turkle discusses "MUDs" ("multi-user dungeons") as places on the Internet where people can meet and "talk" and create a virtual community. She describes her own experience in MUDs and includes interviews with other MUD participants and organizers in order to assess their effects.*

As a licensed clinical psychologist, Turkle is primarily concerned with ways people are using computers and computer-mediated communication to enhance (or detract from) their real-life experiences. In other words, she asks, do virtual communities enable us to live more fully and more productively in the real communities that we inhabit? What can we learn from our virtual interactions and relationships to help us make our real-world relationships more rewarding? Are people who spend a lot of time in virtual communities able to translate skills to the real communities in which they live?

As you read, *make note of how Turkle answers these questions. Does she, in fact, propose a single yes-or-no answer, or does she leave it to the reader to determine the relationship between virtual and real communities?*

The anthropologist Ray Oldenberg has written about the "great good place"—the local bar, the bistro, the coffee shop—where members of a community can gather for easy company, conversation, and a sense of belonging. Oldenberg considers these places to be the heart of individual social integration and community vitality. Today we see a resurgence of coffee bars and bistros, but most of them do not serve, much less recreate, coherent communities and, as a result, the odor of nostalgia often seems as strong as the espresso. 1

Some people are trying to fill the gap with neighborhoods in cyberspace. Take Dred's Bar, for example, a watering hole on the MUD LambdaMOO. MUDs, which originally stood for "multi-user dungeons," are destinations on the Internet where players who have logged in from computers around the world join an on-line virtual community. Through typed commands, they can converse privately or 2 in large groups, creating and playing characters and even earning and spending imaginary funds in the MUD's virtual economy.

In many MUDs, players help build the virtual world itself. Using a relatively simple programming language, they can make "rooms" in the MUD, where they can set the stage and define the rules. Dred's Bar is one such place. It is described as having a "castle decor" and a polished oak dance floor. Recently I (here represented by my character or persona "ST") visited Dred's Bar with Tony, a persona I had met on another MUD. After passing the bouncer, Tony and I encountered a man asking for a $5 cover charge, and once we paid it our hands were stamped. 3

> The crowd opens up momentarily to reveal one corner of the club. A couple is there, making out madly. Friendly place ...
>
> You sit down at the table. The waitress sees you and indicates that she will be there in a minute.
>
> [The waitress here is a bot-short for robot-that is, a computer program that presents itself as a personality.]
>
> The waitress comes up to the table, "Can I get anyone anything from the bar?" she says as she puts down a few cocktail napkins.
>
> Tony says, "When the waitress comes up, type order name of drink.".
>
> Abigail [a character at the bar] dries off a spot where some drink spilled on her dress.
>
> The waitress nods to Tony and writes on her notepad.
>
> [I type "order margarita," following Tony's directions.]
>
> You order a margarita.
>
> The waitress nods to ST and writes on her notepad.
>
> Tony sprinkles some salt on the back of his hand.
>
> Tony remembers he ordered a margarita, not tequila, and brushes the salt off.
>
> You say, "I like salt on my margarita too."
>
> The DJ makes a smooth transition from The Cure into a song by 10,000 Maniacs.
>
> The drinks arrive. You say, "L'chaim."
>
> Tony says, "Excuse me?"

After some explanations, Tony says, "Ah, . . ." smiles, and introduces me to several of his friends. Tony and I take briefly to the dance floor to try out some MUD features that allow us to waltz and tango, then we go to a private booth to continue our conversation. 4

MAIN STREET, MALL, AND VIRTUAL CAFÉ

What changes when we move from Oldenberg's great good places to 5
something like Dred's Bar on LambdaMOO? To answer this question, it helps to consider an intermediate step—moving from a sidewalk café to a food court in a suburban shopping mall. Shopping malls try to recreate the Main Streets of yesteryear, but critical elements change in the process. Main Street, though commercial, is also a public place; the shopping mall is entirely planned to maximize purchasing. On Main Street you are a citizen; in the shopping mall, you are customer as citizen. Main Street had a certain disarray: the town drunk, the traveling snake-oil salesman. The mall is a more controlled space; there may be street theater, but it is planned—the appearance of serendipity is part of the simulation. If Dred's Bar seems plausible, it is because the mall and so much else in our culture, especially television, have made simulations so real.

On any given evening, nearly eighty million people in the United 6
States are watching television. The average American household has a television turned on more than six hours a day, reducing eye contact and conversation. Computers and the virtual worlds they provide are adding another dimension of mediated experience. Perhaps computers feel so natural because of their similarity to watching TV, our dominant social experience for the past forty years.

The bar featured for a decade in the television series *Cheers* no 7
doubt figures so prominently in the American imagination, at least partly because most of us don't have a neighborhood place where "everybody knows your name." Instead, we identify with the place on the screen. Bars designed to look like the one on *Cheers* have sprung up all over the country, most poignantly in airports, our most anonymous of locales. Here, no one will know your name, but you can always buy a drink or a souvenir sweatshirt.

In the postwar atomization of American social life, the rise of 8
middle-class suburbs created communities of neighbors who often remained strangers. Meanwhile, as the industrial and economic base of urban life declined, downtown social spaces such as the neighborhood theater or diner were replaced by malls and cinema complexes in the outlying suburbs. In the recent past, we left our communities to commute to these distant entertainments; increasingly, we want entertainment that commutes right into our homes. In both cases, the neighborhood is bypassed. We seem to be in the process of retreating further into our homes, shopping for merchandise in catalogues or on television channels or for companionship in personals ads.

Technological optimists think that computers will reverse some 9
of this social atomization; they tout virtual experience and virtual

community as ways for people to widen their horizons. But is it really sensible to suggest that the way to revitalize community is to sit alone in our rooms, typing at our networked computers and filling our lives with virtual friends?

THE LOSS OF THE REAL

Which would you rather see—a Disney crocodile robot or a real crocodile? The Disney version rolls its eyes, moves from side to side, and disappears beneath the surface and rises again. It is designed to command our attention at all times. None of these qualities is necessarily visible at a zoo where real crocodiles seem to spend most of their time sleeping. And you may have neither the means nor the inclination to observe a real crocodile in the Nile or the River Gambia. 10

Compare a rafting trip down the Colorado River to an adolescent girl's use of an interactive CD-ROM to explore the same territory. A real rafting trip raises the prospect of physical danger. One may need to strain one's resources to survive, and there may be a rite of passage. This is unlikely to be the experience of an adolescent girl who picks up an interactive CD-ROM called "Adventures on the Colorado." A touchsensitive screen allows her to explore the virtual Colorado and its shoreline. Clicking a mouse brings up pictures and descriptions of local flora and fauna. She can have all the maps and literary references she wants. All this might be fun, perhaps useful. But in its uniformity and lack of risk, it is hard to imagine its marking a transition to adulthood. 11

But why not have both—the virtual Colorado and the real one? Not every exploration need be a rite of passage. The virtual and the real may provide different things. Why make them compete? The difficulty is that virtuality tends to skew our experience of the real in several ways. First, it makes denatured and artificial experiences seem real—let's call it the Disneyland effect. After a brunch on Disneyland's Royal Street, a cappuccino at a restaurant chain called Bonjour Café at an Anaheim shopping mall may seem real by comparison. After playing a video game in which your opponent is a computer program, the social world of MUDs may seem real as well. At least real people play most of the parts and the play space is relatively open. One player compares the roles he was able to play on video games and on MUDS. "Nintendo has a good [game] where you can play four characters. But even though they are very cool," he says, "they are written up for you." They seem artificial. In contrast, on the MUDs, he says, "There is 12 nothing written up." He says he feels free. MUDs are "for real" because you make them up yourself.

Another effect of simulation, which might be thought of as the artificial crocodile effect, is that the fake seems more compelling than the real. In *The Future Does Not Compute: Warnings from the Internet,* Stephen L. Talbott quotes educators who say that years of exciting nature programming have compromised wildlife experiences for children. The animals in the woods are unlikely to perform as dramatically as those captured on the camera. I have a clear memory of a Brownie Scout field trip to the Brooklyn Botanical Gardens where I asked an attendant if she could make the flowers open fast. For a long while, no one understood what I was talking about. Then they figured it out: I was hoping that the attendant could make the flowers behave as they did in the time-lapse photography I had seen in Disney films. 13

Third, virtual experience may be so compelling that we believe that within it we've achieved more than we have. Many of the people I have interviewed claim that virtual gender-swapping (pretending to be the opposite sex on the Internet) enables them to understand what it's like to be a person of the other gender, and I have no doubt that this is true, at least in part. But as I have listened to this boast, my mind has often travelled to my own experiences of living in a woman's body. These include worry about physical vulnerability, fears of unwanted pregnancy and infertility, fine-tuned decisions about how much make-up to wear to a job interview, and the difficulty of giving a professional seminar while doubled over with monthly cramps. Some knowledge is inherently experiential, depending on physical sensations. 14

Pavel Curtis, the founder of LambdaMOO, begins his paper on its social dimensions with a quote from E. M. Forster: "The Machine did not transmit nuances of expression. It only gave a general idea of people—an idea that was good enough for all practical purposes." But what are practical purposes? And what about impractical purposes? To the question, "Why must virtuality and real life compete—why can't we have both?" the answer is of course that we will have both. The more important question is "How can we get the best of both?" 15

THE POLITICS OF VIRTUALITY

When I began exploring the world of MUDs in 1992, the Internet was open to a limited group, chiefly academics and researchers in affiliated commercial enterprises. The MUDders were mostly middle-class college students. They chiefly spoke of using MUDs as places to play and 16 escape, though some used MUDs to address personal difficulties. By late 1993, network access could easily be purchased commercially, and the number and diversity of people on the Internet had expanded dramatically. Conversations with MUDders began to touch on new themes. To some young people, "RL" (real life) was a place of economic insecurity where they had trouble finding meaningful work and holding on to middle-class status. Socially speaking, there was nowhere to go but down in RL, whereas MUDs offered a kind of virtual social mobility.

Josh is a 23-year-old college graduate who lives in a small studio apartment in Chicago. After six months of looking for a job in marketing, the field in which he recently received his college degree, Josh has had to settle for a job working on the computer system that maintains inventory records at a large discount store. He considers this a dead end. When a friend told him about MUDs, he gave them a try, and within a week stepped into a new life. 17

Now, eight months later, Josh spends as much time on MUDs as he can. He belongs to a class of players who sometimes call themselves Internet Hobos. They solicit time on computer accounts the way panhandlers go after spare change. In contrast to his life in RL, Josh's life inside MUDs seems rich and filled with promise. It has friends, safety, and space. "I live in a terrible part of town. I see a rat hole of an apartment, I see a dead-end job, I see AIDS. Down here [in the MUD] I see friends, I have something to offer, I see safe sex." His programming on MUDs is far more intellectually challenging than his day job. Josh has worked on three MUDs, building large, elaborate living quarters in each, and has become a specialist at building virtual cafés in which "bots" serve as waiters and bartenders. Within MUDs, Josh serves as a programming consultant to many less experienced players and has even become something of an entrepreneur. He "rents" ready-built rooms to people who are not as skilled in programming as he is. He has been granted wizard privileges on various MUDs in exchange for building food service software. He dreams that such virtual commerce will someday lead to more—that someday, if MUDs become commercial enterprises, he could build them for a living. MUDs offer Josh a sense of participating in the American Dream. 18

MUDs play a similar role for Thomas, 24, whom I met after giving a public lecture in Washington, D.C. After graduating from college, Thomas entered a training program at a large department store. When he discovered that he didn't like retailing, he quit the program, thinking that he would look for better opportunities. But things did not go well for him; he couldn't find a job that would give him the middle-class life he knew as a child. Finally, he took a job as a bellhop in the hotel where I had just spoken. "MUDs got me back into the middle class," Thomas tells me. He has a group of MUD friends who write 19 well, program, and read science fiction. "I'm interested in MUD politics. Can there be democracy in cyberspace? Should MUDs be ruled by wizards or should they be democracies? I majored in political science in college. These are important questions for the future. I talk about these things with my friends. On MUDs."

Thomas moves on to what has become an obvious conclusion. 20
He says, "MUDs make me more what I really am. Off the MUD, I am not as much me." Tanya, also 24, a college graduate working as a nanny in rural Connecticut, expresses similar aspirations. She says of the MUD on which she has built Japanese-style rooms and a bot to offer her guests a kimono, slippers, and tea, "I feel like I have more stuff on the MUD than I have off it."

Josh, Thomas, and Tanya belong to a generation whose college 21
years were marked by economic recession and a deadly sexually transmitted disease. They scramble for work; finances force them to live in neighborhoods they don't consider safe; they may end up back home living with parents. These young people are looking for a way back into the middle class. MUDs provide them with the sense of a middle-class peer group. So it is really not that surprising that it is in this virtual social life that they feel most like themselves.

Is the real self always the naturally occurring one? If a patient on 22
the antidepressant medication Prozac tells his therapist he feels more like himself with the drug than without it, what does this do to our standard notions of a real self? Where does a medication end and a person begin? Where does real life end and a game begin? Is the real self always the one in the physical world? As more and more real business gets done in cyberspace, could the real self be the one who functions in that realm? Is the real Tanya the frustrated nanny or the energetic programmer on the MUD? The stories of these MUDders point to a whole set of issues about the political and social dimension of virtual community These young people feel they have no political voice, and they look to cyberspace to help them find one.

SEX AND VIOLENCE IN CYBERSPACE

If real business increasingly gets done in cyberspace, what kinds of rules 23
will govern it? And how will those rules be made, democratically or by fiat? The issue arises starkly in connection with sex and violence.

Consider the first moments of a consensual sexual encounter be- 24
tween the characters Backslash and Targa. The player behind Backslash, Ronald, a mathematics graduate student in Memphis, types "emote fondles Targa's breast" and "say You are beautiful Targa" and Elizabeth, Targa's player, sees on her screen:

```
Backslash fondles Targa's breasts. Backslash says,
"You are beautiful Targa."
```

Elizabeth responds with "say Touch me again, and harder. Please. Now. That's how I like it." Ronald's screen shows: 25

```
Targa says, "Touch me again, and harder. Please. Now.
That's how I like it."
```

But consensual relationships are only one facet of virtual sex. Virtual rape can occur within a MUD if one player finds a way to control the actions of another player's character and can thus "force" that character to have sex. The coercion depends on being able to direct the actions and reactions of characters, independent of the desire of their players. So if Ronald were such a culprit, he would be the only one typing, having gained control of Targa's character. In this case 15-year-old Elizabeth, who plays Targa, would sit at her computer, shocked to find herself or rather her "self" begging Backslash for more urgent caresses and ultimately violent intercourse. 26

Some might say that such incidents hardly deserve our concern, as they involve "only words," nothing more. But can a community that exists entirely in the realm of communication ignore sexual aggression that takes the form of words? 27

In March 1992, a character calling himself Mr. Bungle, "an oleaginous, Bisquick-faced clown dressed in cum-stained harlequin garb and girdled with a mistletoe-and-hemlock belt whose buckle bore the inscription 'KISS ME UNDER THIS, BITCH!' " appeared in the LambdaMOO living room. Creating a phantom that masquerades as another player's character is a MUD programming trick often referred to as creating a voodoo doll. The "doll" is said to possess the character, so that the character must do whatever the doll does. Bungle used such a voodoo doll to force one and then another of the room's occupants to perform sexual acts on him. Bungle's first victim was legba, a character described as "a Haitian trickster spirit of indeterminate gender, brown-skinned and wearing an expensive pearl gray suit, top hat, and dark glasses." Even when ejected from the room, Bungle was able to continue his sexual assaults. He forced various players to have sex with each other and then forced legba to swallow his (or her?) own pubic hair and made a character called Starsinger attack herself sexually with a knife. Finally, Bungle was immobilized by a MOO wizard who "toaded" the perpetrator (erased the character from the system). 28

The next day, legba took the matter up on a widely read mailing list within LambdaMOO called *social-issues. Legba called both for 29 "civility" and "virtual castration." A journalist chronicling this event, Julian Dibbell, contrasts the cyberspace description of the event with what was going on in real life. The woman who played the character of legba told Dibbell that she cried as she wrote those words, but he points out that her mingling of "murderous rage and eyeball-rolling annoyance was a curious amalgam." According to the conventions of virtual reality, legba and Starsinger were brutally raped, but here was the victim legba scolding Mr. Bungle only for a breach of "civility." According to the conventions of real life, the incident was confined to the realm of the symbolic—no one suffered any physical harm—but here was the player legba calling for Mr. Bungle's dismemberment. Dibbell writes: "Ludicrously excessive by RL's lights, woefully understated by VR's, the tone of legba's response made sense only in the buzzing, dissonant gap between them."

Virtual rape—of which the incident on LambdaMOO was only one example—raises the question of accountability for the actions of virtual personae who have only words at their command. Similar issues of accountability arise in the case of virtual murder. If your MUD character erases the computer database on which I have over many months built up a richly described character and goes on to announce to the community that my character is deceased, what exactly have you, the you that exists in real life, done? What if my virtual apartment is destroyed along with all its furniture, VCR, kitchen equipment, and stereo system? What if you kidnap my virtual dog—my beloved bot Rover, which I have trained to perform tricks on demand? What if you destroy him and leave his dismembered body in the MUD? 30

The problem of civil order has come up sharply in the history of a MUD called Habitat, initially built to run on Commodore 64 personal computers in the early 1980s. It had a short run in the United States before it was bought and transferred to Japan. Its designers, Chip Morningstar and F. Randall Farmer, have written about how its players struggled to establish the rights and responsibilities of virtual selves. On Habitat, players were originally allowed to have guns and other weapons. Morningstar and Farmer say that they "included these because we felt that players should be able to 'materially' affect each other in ways that went beyond simply talking, ways that required real moral choices to be made by the participants." Death in Habitat, however, had little in common with the RL variety. "When an Avatar is killed, he or she is teleported back home, head in hands (literally), pockets empty, and any object in hand at the time dropped on the ground at the scene of the crime." This was more like a setback in a game of Chutes and Ladders than real mortality, and for some players thievery and murder became the highlights of the 31 game. For others, these activities were a violent intrusion on their peaceful world. An intense debate ensued.

Some players argued that guns should be eliminated, for in a virtual world a few lines of code can translate into an absolute gun ban. Others argued that what was dangerous in virtual reality was not violence but its trivialization. These individuals maintained that guns should be allowed, but their consequences should be made more serious; when you are killed, your character should cease to exist and not simply be sent home. Still others believed that since Habitat was just a game and playing assassin was part of the fun, there could be no harm in a little virtual violence. 32

As the debate continued, a player who was a Greek Orthodox priest in real life founded the first Habitat church, the "Order of the Holy Walnut," whose members pledged not to carry guns, steal, or engage in virtual violence of any kind. In the end, the game's designers divided the world into two parts. In town, violence was prohibited; in the wilds outside town, it was allowed. Eventually a democratic voting process was installed and a sheriff elected. Participants then took up discussion on the nature of Habitat laws and the proper balance between law and order and individual freedom. It was a remarkable situation. Participants in Habitat were seeing themselves as citizens; they were spending their leisure time debating pacifism, the nature of good government, and the relationship between representations and reality. In the nineteenth century, utopians built communities in which political thought could be lived out in practice. On the cusp of the twenty-first century, we are creating utopian communities in cyberspace. 33

Some participants have devoted much energy to the political life of MUDs. LambdaMOO, like Habitat, has undergone a major change in its form of governance. Instead of the MUD wizards (or system administrators) making policy decisions, there is a complex system of grassroots petitions and collective voting. Thomas, the bellhop I met in Washington, goes on at length about the political factions with which he must contend to "do politics" on LambdaMOO. Our conversation is taking place in Fall, 1994. His home state has an upcoming race for the U.S. Senate, hotly contested, ideologically charged, but he hasn't registered to vote and doesn't plan to. I bring up the Senate race. He shrugs it off: "I'm not voting. Doesn't make a difference. Politicians are liars." 34

RESISTANCE OR ESCAPE?

In *Reading the Romance,* the literary scholar Janice Radaway argues that when women read romance novels they are not escaping but building realities less limited than their own. Romance reading becomes a form 35 of resistance, a challenge to the stultifying categories of everyday life. If we take Radaway's perspective, we can look at MUDs and other kinds of virtual communities as places of resistance to the many forms of alienation and to the silences they impose.

But what resistance do Virtual communities really offer? Two decades ago, computer hobbyists saw personal computers as a path to a new populism. They imagined how networks would allow citizens to band together to run decentralized schools and governments. Personal computers would create a more participatory political system, the hobbyists believed, because "people will get used to understanding things, to being in control of things, and they will demand more." The hobbyists I interviewed then were excited, enthusiastic, and satisfied with what they were doing with their machines. But I worried about the limits of this enthusiasm, and in my earlier book about personal computers, *The Second Self,* I wrote: "People will not change unresponsive political systems or intellectually deadening work environments by building machines that are responsive, fun, and intellectually challenging." 36

My misgivings today are similar. Instead of solving real problems—both personal and social—many of us appear to be choosing to invest ourselves in unreal places. Women and men tell me that the rooms and mazes on MUDs are safer than city streets, virtual sex is safer than sex anywhere, MUD friendships are more intense than real ones, and when things don't work out you can always leave. 37

To be sure, MUDs afford an outlet for some people to work through personal issues in a productive way; virtual environments provide a moratorium from RL that can be turned to constructive purpose, and not only for adolescents. One can also respect the sense in which political activities in a MUD demonstrate resistance to what is unsatisfying about political life more generally. And yet, it is sobering that the personal computer revolution, once conceptualized as a tool to rebuild community, now tends to concentrate on building community inside a machine. 38

If the politics of virtuality means democracy on-line and apathy off-line, there is reason for concern. There is also reason for concern when access to the new technology breaks down along traditional class lines. Although some inner-city communities have used computer-mediated communication as a tool for real community building, the overall trend seems to be the creation of an information elite. 39

Virtual environments are valuable as places where we can acknowledge our inner diversity. But we still want an authentic experience of self. One's fear is, of course, that in the culture of simulation, a word like authenticity can no longer apply. So even as we try to make the most of virtual environments, a haunting question remains. For 40 me, that question is raised every time I use the MUD command for taking an action. The command is "emote." If I type "emote waves" while at Dred's café on LambdaMOO, the screens of all players in the MUD room will flash "ST waves." If I type "emote feels a complicated mixture of desire and expectation," all screens will flash "ST feels a complicated mixture of desire and expectation." But what exactly do I feel? Or, what exactly do *I* feel? When we get our MUD persona to "emote" something and observe the effect, do we gain a better understanding of our real emotions, which can't be switched on and off so easily, and which we may not even be able to describe? Or is the emote command and all that it stands for a reflection of what Frederic Jameson has called the flattening of affect in postmodern life?

The overheated language that surrounds current discussion of computer-mediated communications falls within a long tradition of American technological optimism. The optimists today tend to represent urban decay and class polarization as out-of-date formulations of a problem that could be solved with the right technology—for example, technology that could enable every schoolchild to experience "being digital." Are our streets dangerous? Not to worry: The community will be "wired" so children can attend school without having to walk there! This way of thinking about cyberspace substitutes life on the screen for life in our bodies and physical communities. 41

But there is another way of thinking, one that stresses making the virtual and the real more permeable to each other. We don't have to reject life on the screen, but we don't have to treat it as an alternative life either. Virtual personae can be a resource for self-reflection and self-transformation. Having literally written our on-line worlds into existence, we can use the communities we build inside our machines to improve the ones outside of them. Like the anthropologist returning home from a foreign culture, the voyager in virtuality can return to the real world better able to understand what about it is arbitrary and can be changed. 42

Examining the Text

1. Why do you think Turkle begins her essay with an example of her "virtual conversation" in Dred's Bar? What point do you think she is trying to prove with this example?

2. In what ways, according to Turkle, does the shopping mall serve as an intermediate step between the Main Streets of yesteryear and the cybercommunities of the present and future? Do you agree with Turkle's argument that shopping malls (and television) have changed the nature of communities in America? Why or why not?

3. Turkle comments on sex and violence on the Internet through her discussion of the "virtual rape" by Mr. Bungle and the gun control incident on the Habitat MUD. What point is she making through these examples? How would you summarize her position on the issues of sex and violence on the Internet?

4. What do you take to be Turkle's ultimate conclusion in this essay about the effect of virtual communities on real life communities?

For Group Discussion

Turkle uses the examples of Josh, Thomas, and Tanya, three college graduates in their twenties who are actively involved in cybercommunities, to raise questions about the relation between experiences on the Internet and "RL" (real life) experiences. She asks, "Is the real self always the one in the physical world?" Read over this section again (paragraph 22) and as a class discuss your responses to Turkle's question. How do the online personas of Josh, Thomas, and Tanya compare with their RL personas? Which do you think is more "real"? Why?

Writing Suggestion

Turkle discusses the "Disneyland effect" and the "artificial crocodile effect" (paragraphs 10–13). Choose one of these phenomena and briefly summarize what it is, drawing on Turkle's definitions and examples. Then follow your summary of Turkle with examples of your own that illustrate the effect. What influence, if any, has it had on your own understanding of real communities and real life?

Black Struggles in Cyberspace: Cyber-Segregation and Cyber-Nazis

Colin Beckles

Internet enthusiasts celebrate the possibilities for community-building and global communication offered by this new technology, along with the vast amount of information it provides in helping users make personal and professional decisions. But what if you can't afford to get on the "information super-highway," or if you lack the expertise to find your way from one destination to the next? And what if, rather than providing opportunities for interacting with others and developing new social connections, the Internet instead confronts you with hostile and hate-filled messages? According to Colin Beckles, this is the experience of some African Americans going on the Internet today. Race-and class-based factors present barriers to their access to the Internet, and once they gain access the proliferation of racist and white-supremacist discourse on the Internet present them with an unwelcoming environment, to say the least.

Beckles, a professor at Washington State University, originally published this article in The Western Journal of Black Studies *in 1997. Like other observers of the Internet, he's concerned that certain groups of people, through no fault or choice of their own, might be getting left out of the information revolution. With more and more businesses and government agencies offering services via the Internet, those who don't have access are going to be at an increasing disadvantage. Moreover, Beckles's observations about the reasons for the Internet's predominantly white, middle-class orientation might make you rethink the claims of earlier essays in this chapter about the Internet's power to create vibrant virtual communities. Does the Internet's "anything goes" approach simply make it easier to discriminate and exclude? Does the fact that interactions are virtual rather than face-to-face make it easier to insult and attack? Does the Internet actually provide a place where the civility of real communities can be disregarded?*

As you read, *think about other groups that may feel unwelcome in the Internet's virtual communities. To what extent do Beckles's observations about African-American Internet users apply, for example, to other minority groups, nonnative English speakers, women, and people with disabilities? Do the same kinds of problems confront individuals in these groups when they try to get on the information superhighway?*

"Tony Brown advocates 'a gospel of racial uplift through better computing.'"
—Tony Brown's Cyberspace Club, 1997

"Now More Than Ever, the Mastery of Technology is Critical to Black Advancement"
—P. Carey, *Black Enterprise Magazine,* 1996

If the phrase "knowledge is power" is to have real significance for African Americans in the 21st century, it must surely be applicable to the Internet. Computer-based communications such as the Internet have been demonstrated to empower users by giving them "more accurate information about matters of political, professional, and organizational concern than peers who do not" (Anderson et al., 3: 1995; Schuler 1996; Schwartz 1996). With the advent of relatively easy to use Internet web browsers such as Netscape and comprehensive search engines such as Yahoo!, Internet users can now benefit from access to larger amounts of premium quality information in a faster, user-friendly, and less expensive fashion: direct access to privileged educational resources such as Howard University and Harvard University; access to city, state and federal politicians and their staff; access to local, national and international business and financial information; 1

crucial, timely reports dealing with matters of health and science; and of course, a myriad of entertainment, travel and social networking information (Yahoo!, *http://www.yahoo.com* 1997; Anderson et al. 1995).

And this new knowledge base has not gone untapped. Indeed, reports suggest that the Internet population, estimated to be 20 million by the year 2000, grows by 10 to 15 percent each month while the size of the World Wide Web, a subset of the Internet, doubles every 53 days (Find/SVP 1997). When the information resources available on the Internet and its rapid rate of growth are considered along with its decentralized nature, many Internet enthusiasts are quick to characterize the Internet as a new source of democratic power for the 21st century. One of the most nationally prominent advocates of this democratizing power is Vice President Al Gore, a relentless champion for the Global Information Infrastructure—the G.I.I.: 2

> The G.I.I. will make possible a global information marketplace . . . It will in fact promote the functioning of democracy . . . (Gore, 1994)

However, despite the vice president's and others enthusiasm for the G.I.I. and its U.S. counterpart, the National Information Infrastructure, many critical assessments of the Internet's democratic abilities have come to the fore. Commonly referenced problems deal with barriers to Internet access, political and social abuses of the Internet (Anderson, 1995; Brook and Boale, 1995; Defife 1995; Dennis 1996; King and Kramer 1995; Miller 1995; Sclove 1995; Sheppard 1995; Slouka in Louv 1995; Mosco and Wasko 1988). 3

This paper serves to add to this growing body of literature by critically examining the role of the Internet in relation to people who reside in the United States of America and are of African descent. The overall argument is that while the Internet has the potential to empower the African American community, various aspects constrain this potential. This is demonstrated in two ways. First it is argued that various socioeconomic factors continue to serve as formidable barriers blocking the majority of the Black community from access and subsequent participation on the Internet. Moreover, we argue that white racial terrorism occurring on the Internet further constrains its democratic potential. Conclusions and remarks will follow. Endnote provides a discussion of conceptual and methodological issues. 4

PART I: CYBER-SEGREGATION

> The 21st century will not be a century of Blacks and whites, racism and sexism. It will be a century of haves and have-nots. Haves will know how to use computer technology to create wealth and the have-nots won't. (Tony Brown, *www.tonybrown.com* 1996)

As Professor and T.V. Journalist Tony Brown suggests, equal to the potential democratizing benefits the Internet may bring to communities is the real danger posed by the further exclusion of already marginalized communities from this new information age. Indeed, a review of the literature on the racial and economic composition of Internet users reveals a very clear and seemingly unrefutable reality. These studies suggest that in large part, the present composition and usage of the Internet has and could continue to be the domain of historically privileged groups (Brook and Boale, 1995). Anderson et al (1995) conservatively estimated that the costs for minimum Internet services would be as follows: 5

Internet Costs

a. Computer with modem and Internet software $1000–3000
b. Internet connection costs (basic E-mail) $60/year
c. Computer and Internet training $40/year
d. User support services $140/year

(Source: Anderson et al 1995; Washington State University Instructional Services)

Examination of these sample costs suggests that there exists a substantial "toll charge" for riding on the information superhighway. Thus, it is evident that those who can afford to access the Internet are part of a privileged class. Moreover, it is this class who will comprise the "information elite" in the 21st century: "An information Elite still exists, made up of those with access to and knowledge about computers and E-mail . . . Specifically, computer access and use is positively related to higher levels of education and income" (Anderson et al. 1995). 6

Statistical reports on the income and educational backgrounds of Internet users bear witness to the above. 64 percent of Internet users have at least a college degree and the average household income is approximately $60,000 (Nielsen Media Research 1995; Graphics Visual Research, 1996 (G.V.U.); find/SVP 1). Results from the American Internet User Survey revealed that more than half of all their respondents had incomes of $40,000 or more (Find/SVP 1995). 7

However, as opposed to professor Brown's suggestions, we believe that a privileged class of information elite will be present across racial lines as well. Recent reports suggest that only 6 percent of African Americans are in the $50,000 and above income bracket and less than 25 percent had attended college as compared with 10 percent and 33 percent of respective whites (Oliver and Shapiro, 1995; Eitzen and Baca-Zinn, 1990). As such, the majority of the African American 8 community obviously cannot afford the "toll charges" for Internet access. Thus, as with the white community, the benefits of the Internet will be restricted to a small privileged class of "Black information elites," primarily comprised of the Black professional classes as well as those who access the Internet through university accounts. Indeed, the bifurcation between information haves and have nots will be even more acute in the Black community given the fact that the economic and educational levels are wider within the African American community than in the white community (Eitzen and Baca-Zinn 1990; Oliver and Shapiro 1996; Hacker, 1992).

Moreover, if it was solely a case of class barriers, we would ex- 9
pect African Americans in the professional classes to be accessing and participating on the Internet on par with their economic counterparts in white society. However, the data suggests otherwise. In fact, reports suggest that strong support exists for independent racial effects occurring in Internet access. As such, African Americans and other minority groups are significantly divorced from access to computers and the Internet beyond what we would expect due to economic differences alone:

> . . . race is independently related to computer and network access—whites being significantly more likely to have access to both than Blacks and Hispanics. Apparently, if current trends continue without intervention, access to electronic information and communications technologies (and associated benefits) will be skewed in favor of traditionally advantaged groups. (Anderson et al, 1995:xiv)

Similar reports support these findings. The Graphic Visualiza- 10
tion Research's (1996) Fifth study of world wide web users revealed that globally, 87 percent were White, while in the U.S. 88.6% were white and only 1.3% of world wide web user were African Americans. Similarly, as Table 2 demonstrates, the American Internet User Survey reported that while African American users were the largest minority group users of the Internet, they still comprised only 5 percent of all Internet users (Find/SVP 1995). On the contrary, whites clearly dominate Internet usage:

Internet User Demographics

Ethnic Background
White 83%
Black African American 5%
Hispanic 3%
Asian 3%

Other 3%
Refused 3%

(Source: Find/SVP 1995)

Thus, even among those privileged African Americans who have the economic and educational qualifications for Internet access, it seems that only a small portion of those are actual computer, internet, and/or World Wide Web users. Various reasons for these independent racial effects have been put forth. One possible explanation focuses on the content of the information on the Internet. Indeed, despite the wealth of information currently available on the Internet, much of the content is probably geared toward the needs of the majority of its users—white, middle class Americans. Thus, as with other media, many African Americans and people of African descent in general may not feel that the information content on the Internet is relevant to their immediate concerns (Wilson and Gutierrez, 1995). Notes from an ongoing study of a lower income, multicultural community in Bridgeport Connecticut are telling and possibly applicable across class lines: 11

> Providing local content that is most practical and relevant to the user is the first step to providing access to a greater pool of resources. Until a critical mass of this local information is readily accessible to users it is unlikely that many of Bridgeport's residents will want to access BridgeNet. (BridgeNet, 1997)

A second explanation centers upon an interrelated set of processes hampering the African-American community from becoming trained effectively (Black Enterprise Editors 1997; Carey 1995; Resnick and Russ, 1996; Anderson et al 1995). First, it is suggested that many African Americans across class lines who may desire to use the Internet have not had enough exposure to the Internet to overcome hesitations about the "technological complexity" of the Internet. . . . But what of those who have overcome their "techno-phobia." Are they receiving the initial training on how to become Internet Users? Even if these initial skills are learned, is continued technical support, time, and support needed to become fluent and effective Internet users forthcoming? In other educational arenas, studies have demonstrated that effective training and guidance that comes from strong culturally based mentoring and sponsorship (Allen 1995; Frierson et al 1995; Guyton and Hidalgo 1995; Toress-Guzman 1995; Mosco 1986). Given the low numbers of African American Internet users, there may be a corresponding low number of trained African American technical support staff. If these potential "black tech mentors" are absent, then the necessary cultural mentoring would also be absent, possibly serving as another barrier to internet usage and fluency. As such, frustration and 12 isolation may occur in potential African American internet users blocking their further technological development.

In the above section, some of the barriers posed to African American access and effective participation on the Internet have been reviewed. However, in addition to the struggle against such institutionalized barriers to cyberspace, the Black information elite also has to struggle with the overt white racial terrorism occurring on and via the Internet. It is this issue to which we now turn. 13

PART II: CYBER-NAZIS: RACIAL TERRORISM IN CYBERSPACE

> . . . there are about 250 hate groups, 25,000 committed white supremacists and 3,000 to 5,000 racist skinheads in the U.S. . . . They are embracing [the 'Net] more quickly than the rest of the population. (Cooper, 1996)

Historically, when African Americans have attempted to access and effectively participate in so-called democratic institutions of the U.S., various White racist groups have used overt means to discourage and extinguish that participation. Since the 1800s, the Ku Klux Klan has been at the forefront of those racial terrorist organizations that have attempted to block African Americans access to social power and reserve the benefits of U.S. society for the white race (Franklin and Moss 1994; Sims 1978). 14

Now, as the Internet rises to its potential as the newest source of social power, the battle lines are drawn yet again. Reports reveal that a sub-group of the white information elite belong to historically violent white racist organizations. As the excerpt above suggests, the Ku Klux Klan, Aryan Nations, The Christian Posse Comitatus, the White Aryan Resistance and a plethora of skinhead groups are rapidly accessing the Internet (Sheppard 1995). The number of white supremacist groups utilizing the Internet is so extreme, that in 1996, the European Union established a special division to investigate and stop the spread of racism via the Internet. The European Union Commission on Racism and Xenophobia (C.R.A.X.): "Reports suggest that white racists organizations are using the Internet in order to disseminate their call for white domination and violence against African American and other racial minorities" (Anti-Defamation League 1996; Barney 1996; Sheppard 1995; Cooper 1996; Battle 1995). The span of white supremacists on the Internet is indeed vast, encompassing individuals, certain militia groups, academics and religious organizations: Tom Metzger's White Aryan Resistance Page—WAR; Christian Identity Links. Their 15 web sites are filled with swastikas, skulls and other symbols of hate and violence. As Sheppard (1995) reports, they represent the objectives and themes of their "real-life" counterparts:

> A majority of the cyber-hate home pages advocate the geographical separation of whites from nonwhites. Some blame Jews for the world's economic problems, while others blame Blacks for crime in America and accuse them of plotting to eliminate the white race (Sheppard, 1995).

Regardless of the particular form the white racist organizations take on the Internet, the message of hate and/or violence against racial minorities in order to preserve white power is clear. As the two Internet documents below suggest, a call to armed violence in a "race war" is a commonly expressed theme: 16

> . . . unless the white race rises up against its tormentors in a consuming fury, we will instead be consumed by them. I don't hate these people as individuals but only a fool would believe that we will ever live together in peace. Events like this, as well as Waco, Randy Weaver massacre and Oklahoma City portend a darkening future for America and it is becoming increasingly clear that unless heroic measures are taken without delay, there will be no future for our children. (Christian Posse Comitatus of Pennsylvania, *http://ww2.stormfront.org/watchman/terror.html,* 1/21/1996)

The Manifesto of The CNG: 17

> 1. In order for these forces of darkness to triumph, it is sufficient that good men do nothing: Positive and militant steps are required to check the spread of evil in the land. Our theater of operation is Cyberspace . . . Conflict is the crucible from which the superior man is born.
>
> 2. We are a white nationalist organization. We represent the heart and the soul of the white nation. . . . There will be no one world government except it be a white one.
>
> 3. We represent a nation that will not sacrifice the lives of its youth in the name of abstract principles like "peace" or "containment." Our soldiers are here to KILL. . . .
>
> We believe that immigration must be white to preserve our culture and land. All nonwhites must be either exported or segregated to prevent further bastardization of our people, domination of our land, jobs, and position of education and employment. (CNG, *http://www.io.com/~wlp/aryan-page/cng/index.html* January, 1996)

If the above were isolated to disparate, individual white supremacist sites alone, that would be sufficient cause for alarm. However, as Cooper (1996) suggests, various groups are specifically 18 seeking out new recruits and training new members in the call for white domination and white power via the Internet. Many utilize Internet discussion forums such as "usenet" for dual purposes of disseminating racist messages and hoping to gain new warriors to their cause:

> The CNG is a cell-based White Nationalist organization. Its battleground is the Internet. The CNG develops propaganda, distributes propaganda, and recruits for real world organizations. (CNG, *http://www.io.com/~wlp/aryan-page/cng/index.html*, 1/21/96)

> USENET offers enormous opportunity for the Aryan Resistance to disseminate our message to the unaware and the ignorant. It is the only relatively uncensored free-forum medium we have available. Now is the time to grasp the WEAPON which is the Net. (Kleim, *http://www.io.com/~wlp/aryan-page/cng/tac.html*, 1/21/96)

19 However, recruitment is not restricted to white discussion groups. Prominent white nationalists such as Milton Kleim advocate recruitment in mainstream groups:

> Crucial to our USENET campaign is that our message is disseminated beyond "our" groups. We must go beyond our present domain, and take up positions on "mainstream" groups. (Kleim, *http://www.io.com/~wlp/aryan-page/cng/tac.html*, 1/21/96)

20 Alternatively, some are urged to invade usenet discussions and use "hit-and-run" techniques, sending racist E-mail messages such as the following to thousands of 'Net users (Sheppard, 1995):

> Kill that nigger he's worse than a fag
> Blast him in the head with a 44 mag
> Kick him punch him and crush that bro
> Douse him with gasoline and burn his fro
> Hit him with a flashlight and kick him in the head
> Just make sure that niggers dead
> Big lipped chicken eating melon stealing bast
> I can't wait to kill a nigger with a shotgun blast!

> (E-mail sent originally Nov, 1995 by DeSean Mychal-McDuffie Yarrel *http://www.geocities. com/collegepark/3571*. Re-sent to Neftara Clark of the Anti Racist Action E-mail list, March 1997.)

21 African-American sites also occasionally become the targets of racist anger:

> White supremacists, skinheads, neo-Nazis and racists prowl through cyberspace leaving the occasional offensive messages. A woman using the race-proud screen name "Ebony Queen" got flamed with a catty "Welfare Queen" response when she entered a chat room, according to the July issue of Newsweek. (Sheppard, 1995)

Others such as those belonging to CNG and Carolinian Lords of the Caucus (C.L.O.C.) deliberately infiltrate the discussion groups and E-mail lists frequented by marginalized groups such as African Americans and other minorities. The goal seems to be to aggressively challenge and/or attack the discussion group member and disrupt the topics and tones of the conversations: 22

> One of the groups targeted by Kleim and other cyber guerrillas was alt.fan.oj-simpson, which emerged as a forum for supporters of the football legend during his trial for the murder of his ex-wife and her friend, Ronald Goldman. With input from Kleim and members of the neo-Nazi National Alliance, the news group became a flash point for racially charged debate over the case, and a forum in which white nationalists sought new members, arguing that the trial showed whites, not minorities, were the victims of racism. (Sheppard, 1995)

Finally, it is predicted that by the year 2000 the total number of Internet connected networks inside and outside the U.S.A. will be in the millions (Rutkowski 1994). Given this, it is also likely that the number of networks dedicated to historically violent racist groups will also climb as well. Reports suggest that networks of white supremacist are continuously being spun globally via the Internet. Therein, worldwide organizing for racial violence may occur as material and information encouraging racist violence and aggression can be exchanged globally at the click of a mouse button: 23

> According to EC officials, the Thule BBS's, which first appeared in 1991, started spreading the Neo-Nazi word on the Internet in late 1994, having established themselves as a means of information exchange in Germany and, to a limited extent, in France. . . . According to Chip magazine at the time, "The (Thule) network distributes information on demonstrations and invitations to meetings, addresses for contacting parties and groups, and it reviews and offers books and magazines. One of the mailboxes contained instructions for producing military explosives and letter bombs. (Dennis, 1996)

Today, websites such as Don Black's "Stormfront" function as cyberspace organizing centers for racist networks. These sites have multi-dimensional roles, acting as information archives, resource centers, recruiters and cyberspace trainers. As major nodes in the growing 24 networks of white supremacy, Stormfront, Thule, and the Aryan Crusaders Library facilitate the formation of new coalitions between former splinter white supremacist groups, and extend the power of larger groups such as the National Alliance (Barney, 1996). And as evidenced below, as with the rest of Internet, this network of cyber-hate is not locally confined, but instead extends across the U.S. into Canada, South America and Europe.

> The hub of the White nationalist network appears to be the Aryan Crusader's Library, which originates in Austin. The site provides extensive information about and links to white nationalist organizations in the U.S. and Europe.... The groups have forged links, at least electronically, to white nationalist groups in Canada, France, Germany, England, Belgium, Portugal, Denmark, Finland, Sweden, Luxembourg, Italy, Austria and the Netherlands. (Sheppard, 1995)

CONCLUSIONS AND IMPLICATIONS

> Movement toward an idealized democracy.... is severely constrained whenever a host of non-random factors determine that certain groups and individuals never achieve social and political equality. (Gandy 1988)

As opposed to the declarations of Vice President Al Gore and other advocates about the democratizing power of the Internet, our preliminary analysis has suggested that in relation to internet access, content and usage, the Internet has not lived up to its democratic potential. Specifically, our review of specific African American issues in cyberspace has led us to two predominant conclusions. First, despite the Internet's potential as a source of democratic power, at present we are witnessing in cyberspace reconcentration of power along class and race lines. 25

African Americans remain only 5 percent of Internet users and no increase has been forthcoming. The implications for the African American community are clear. As King and Kraemer (1995) succinctly state, if African Americans "lack access to new communication technologies, we may be at risk of exclusion from the fabric of the nation's social and economic life" (King and Kraemer, 1993). 26

As the benefits of Internet usage become continually reconcentrated primarily in the hands of white America, a defacto state of virtual segregation will become manifest. The majority of African Americans will remain in information ghettos outside of cyberspace, or struggle within the "gilded ghettos" of the Internet. Gilded ghettos are characterized by a lack of resources such as of Black tech mentors. This implies 27 a frustrating and/or discouraging experience for many potential Black Internet users. The scarcity of such Black tech-mentors may also hamper the technological development of those African American children attempting to becoming fluent in the language of computers in particular and encouraging them to pursue scientific fields of study in general (Black Enterprise Editors 1997; Montgomery 1996; Resnick and Russ, 1996; Anderson 1995; Carey, 1995; Chen in Mosco 1988).

The second overall conclusion is that apparently, the information 28
highway is being readily utilized by historically violent white racist individuals and organizations for the preservation of white power. These groups are archiving and disseminating violent, racist information on the Internet, surfing cyberspace for new recruits, and verbally attacking and threatening African Americans and other minorities in cyberspace. Moreover, many are using the information superhighway as an organizing device: they are connecting and consolidating with other white supremacist organizations locally, nationally and internationally. Indeed, some are preparing for a race war both in cyberspace and in "the real-world." Thus, in direct contrast to its democratic ideals, the Internet is being used to specifically deny the democratic participation of African American and other people of color across the globe both on the Internet and in the "real world."

Despite the barriers served by issues of ghettoization and the 29
threat of racial violence, 5 percent of Internet participants are of African descent. Given this, various questions arise. Are those within the Black information elite attempting to empower themselves and their communities via the Internet? If so, what strategies are being employed? Are their strategies restricted to the virtual realm, or are real world events included? While an examination of these issues is beyond the scope of this paper, these and similar issues are addressed in a subsequent work (see Beckles, 1997). Therein, the role played by Black information gateways, Black Internet host providers, and black cyber-organizing centers in combating cyber-segregation and racial terrorism are assessed.

Future research needs to address the level of African American 30
ownership and control of the communication backbone—the underlying telecommunication network upon which the Internet runs. Moreover, we need to assess the effect the spread of the G.I.I. will have on African communities outside the U.S.—across the African diaspora and on the African continent itself.

Will the Black community be relegated to workers and users 31
worldwide or will we be able to own, control and design the development of the G.I.I. and thus make the Internet and its "backbone" responsive to the needs and interests of our communities?

Finally, the repressive utilization of the Internet by government 32
forces needs to be critically and rigorously monitored and investi-

gated. Reports suggest that "left wing" cyberspace organizations such as the Institute for Global Communications are presently under surveillance by the U.S. government (Corn, 1996; U.S. Congress, Office of Technology Assessment 1995). As the call for the democratic empowerment of people of African descent via the Internet begins to be answered, we must be aware that the long shadow of "COINTELPRO" will surely continue to drape over our efforts.

REFERENCES

Allen, K., S. Jacobsen, and K. Lomotey. (1995). "American women in educational administration: Importance of mentors and sponsors." *The Journal of Education* (64) #4.409–422.

Anderson, R., Bikson, T.K., Law, S. A. and Mitchell B. M. (1995). "Universal access to e-mail: Feasibility and societal implications." *www.rand.org/publications/MR/MR650.*

Anderson, T. (1993). *Introduction to African American studies.* Iowa Kendall Hunt.

Barney, D. (1996). "White separatists leap on the 'net." *Network World.* (8). News Section.

Beckles, C. (1996). "Virtual resistance: A preliminary analysis of antiracism in cyberspace." *http://www.free.net.8000/docs/Intet96/e6_e44.htm*

Beckles, C. (1997). "Black liberation and the internet: A strategic analysis." Paper delivered at the Fourteenth Annual PanAfrican Studies Conference, Indiana State University, April 1997.

BridgeNet. (1997). "Bridgenet progress reports." *http://access.bridgenet.org/center/about/reports/reports.html*

Brook, J., and Boale, I. (1995). *Resisting the virtual life: The culture and politics of information.* San Francisco, City Light Books.

Brown, T. (1997). "Tony Brown's Cyberspace Club." *http://www.tonybrown.com/cybclub.htm.*

Carey P. (1995). "Creating and new generation of black technocrats." *Black Enterprise.* (26) # 1. pp. 140–142.

Christian posse comitatus of PA. (1996). *http://ww2.stormfront.org/watchman/terror.html*

Clough, M. (1996). "Will global war erupt along internet?" *The Commercial Appeal.* (18), Viewpoint Section. p. 5,

CNG. 1996. *http://www.io.com/~wlp/aryan-page/cng/index.html.*

Cooper in Barney, Doug. (1996). "White separatists leap on the 'net." *Network World.* (8). News, Section, p. 5.

Corn, D. (1996). "Pentagon trolls the net." *The Nation.* (262), pp. 21–24.

Cyber Atlas. (1997). "CyberAtlas." *http://www.cyberatlas.com.*

Dennis, S. (1996). "European commission moves to stamp out racism on the internet." *Newsbytes News Network.* Information Access Company.

Drew, J. (1995). "Media activism and radical democracy." In J. Brook and I. Boale. (eds.), *Resisting the virtual life: The culture and politics of information.* San Francisco. City Light Books. pp. 71–84.

Eitzen, D. S. and Baca-Zinn M., (1993). *In conflict and order.* Boston: Allyn and Bacon.

Editors, (1997). "Black enterprise technology summit: Using technology to enhance your business." *Black Enterprise.* March. pp. 64–73.

Find/SVP. (1996). "Internet users demographic background." *http://etrg.findsvp.com/graphics/Internet/demoraphics/demo_ethnic_mr96.gif.*

Frierson, H. T., Hargrove B. and Lewis, N. "Black summer research students' perceptions and related to research mentors race and gender." *The Journal of Negro Research.* (64) #4. pp. 475–480.

Gandy, O. "Its discrimination, stupid." In J. Brook and I. Boale (eds.), *Resisting the virtual life: The culture and politics of information.* San Francisco: City Light Books. pp. 34–48.

Gore, A. (1994). "Remarks delivered at the meeting of the international telecommunications union, Buenos Aires." (21). In J. Brook and I. Boale, (eds.), *Resisting the virtual life: The culture and politics of information.* San Francisco: City Light Books. pp. 71–80.

Graphics Visualization and Research Center. (1996). "GVU's Fifth WWW User Survey," *http://www.cc.gatech.edu/gvu/user_surveys/.*

Guyton E. and F. Hidalgo. (1995). *Characteristics, and qualities of urban school mentors, education and urban society* (28) #1. pp. 48–66.

Hacker, A. (1992). *Two nations: Black and white, separate, hostile, and unequal.* New York: Ballantine Books.

Harris, R., and Battle, S. (1995). *The african american resource guide to the internet.* Maryland: On Demand Press.

Karenga, M. (1993). *Introduction to black studies,* California: Sankore Press.

King, J. L. and Kraemer, K. (1995). "Information infrastructure, national policy, and global competitiveness." In *Information Infrastructure and Public Policy,* (4) pp. 5–28.

Kleim, M. (1996). "Usenet tactics and strategy." *http://www.io.com/~wlp/aryan-page/cng/tac.html.*

Louv, R. (1995). *Personal decisions ward off virtual reality.*

Lowery, M. (1995). "The rise of the black professional class." *Black Enterprise.* (26) #1. August. pp. 43–54.

Mann, B. (1995). *Politics on the net.* Indiana: Que.

Miller, L. "Women and children first: Gender and the settling of the electronic frontier." In J. Brook and I. Boale, (eds.) *Resisting the virtual life: The culture and politics of information.* San Francisco: City Light Books. pp. 59–70.

Montgomery, K. (1995). "Children in the digital age." *The American Project.* July / August. pp. 69–74.

Mosco, V. and Wasko, J. (1988). *The political economy of information.* Wisconsin: University of Wisconsin.

Nielsen Media Research Center. (1997). "Nielsen media research/ commercenet." *http://www.nielsenmedia.com.*

Oliver, M. and Shapiro. (1996). *Black wealth/white wealth.* London: Routledge.

Resnick, M. and Rusk, N. (1995). "Access is not enough: Computer clubhouses in the inner city." *The American Project.* July / August. pp. 60–68.

Rutkowski, A. M. and the Internet Society. (1994). "Visions of the internet." *http://www.isoc.org-internet* host counts 1990–2000. *http:// www.isoc.org*. San Diego Union-Tribune. (6 September). "News Editorial." pp. 1–8.

Schatzmann, J., and Strauss, A. (1973). *Field research: Strategies for a natural sociology.* New Jersey, Prentice Hall.

Sclove, R. (1996). "Making technology democratic," in J. Brook and I. Boale, (eds.), *Resisting the virtual life: The culture and politics of information.* San Francisco: City Light Books. pp. 85–104.

Sheppard. N. (1995). "Hate groups find a home in cyberspace: White nationalists spread message, seek recruits on the net." *Austin American-Statesman.* (23 December). News. p. A1.

Schwartz. E. (1996). *NetActivism: How citizens use the internet.* Songline Studios Inc. Ca.

Stormfront. (1997). "Stormfront: White nationalist resource page." *http://www/stormfront.org/Stormfront.*

Torres-Guzman, M. and Goodwin, L. (1995). *Urban bilingual teachers and mentoring for the future, education and urban society.* (28) #1. pp. 67–89.

U.S. Congress Office of Technology Assessment. (1995). "Electronic surveillance in a digital age." OTA-BP-ITC-149. Washington, D.C.: U.S. Government Printing Office. (July).

Yahoo!. (1997). "Yahoo!." *http://www.yahoo.com.*

Examining the Text

1. What does Beckles identify as the reasons for African Americans' low level of participation on the Internet? Are some reasons more persuasive than others? Which ones, and why?

2. According to Beckles, what advantages does an individual or group lose by not having access to the Internet? In other words, what are the costs of being among the "information have-nots"?

3. Why do you think Beckles includes so many quotations from racist and white supremacist Websites? How does this help advance his argument?

For Group Discussion

At the end of the article, Beckles offers several suggestions for increasing the number of African Americans on the Internet. Review his comments and discuss whether you think these strategies would be effective. What other suggestions can you come up with to make the Internet a more inviting place for traditionally marginalized groups? For example, do you believe that censorship or restriction of hate-speech on the Internet would be effective? Why or why not?

Writing Suggestion

Perhaps in response to the "cyber-segregation" described by Beckles, a number of sites on the World Wide Web have been created to foster a sense of community among groups that may feel marginalized or excluded by the new information technologies. Among these are the following:

Chicano/Latino Net: *http://latino.sscnet.ucla.edu/*
LatinoLink: *http://www.latinolink.com/*
NativeWeb: *http://www.nativeweb.org*
SeniorSite: *http://www.seniorsite.com/*
Family village: *http://www.familyvillage.wisc.edu/index.htmlx*
AfroNet: *http://www.afronet.com/*
MelaNet: *http://www.melanet.com/*
Estronet: *http://estronet.chickclick.com/*
Grrlspace: *http://www.grrlspace.com/*

Visit one of these Web sites (or a similar one that you know of) and write an analysis of the strategies the site uses to welcome members into its community. How does the content of the site cater to the needs and interests of its audience? How does the design of the site—its colors and images, its organization—help the audience feel welcome and "at home" at this place on the Internet? Are they any interactive components of the site that allow visitors to "talk" to each other? If so, what is the content and tone of these discussions? What other features of the site are employed to respond to its target audience? Finally, assess the overall effectiveness of the web site in creating a responsive virtual community for a particular group of people.

Cybereducation

The Learning Revolution

Claudia Wallis

We begin this section on cyberspace and education with an early and optimistic look at the uses of computers in the classroom. Claudia Wallis, a Contributing Editor for Time *magazine and the Managing Editor of* Time for Kids, *writes about what she saw on a tour of The Dalton School in 1995. Specifically, Wallis reports on the ways in which students at this private, elite Manhattan grade school and high school were engaged in learning projects using computers.*

As Wallis reports, students use computer programs to simulate an archaeological dig, to analyze Shakespeare's Macbeth, *and to learn principles of astronomy. Along the way, according to Wallis, these students become better collaborative workers and enhance their education through independent, discovery-based learning. Clearly, Wallis's report makes one inclined to believe that computers have powerful, positive uses in the classroom.*

Before you read, *recall your own experiences using computers in grade school and high school. What kinds of projects did you work on? What features of computer technology did you use in these projects: word processing, graphic design, interactive software programs, the Internet, information databases? Do you think using computers enhanced your learning?*

When the personal computer first entered the classroom three decades ago, prophets of the information age foretold a marvelous revolution. The world's storehouses of knowledge would become instantly available to young minds. Captivating digital landscapes would bring history, geography, and science alive on a screen. Not since Gutenberg, they exulted, had there been such a powerful new tool for learning. Their bold predictions were not wrong, just premature. Computers are indeed everywhere in American schools, but they are generally used as little more than electronic workbooks for drill, or as places for kids to play games during "free choice" periods. The promised revolution has failed to materialize. 1

But here and there, in cutting-edge schools around the nation, there are glimmers of what could be. Nowhere is the use of technology more advanced and pervasive than at the Dalton School, an elite private academy in New York City. The 1,300 students at Dalton, situated 2 on Manhattan's posh Upper East Side, enjoy resources that any school would envy: a teaching staff studded with Ph.D.s, a 62,000-volume library and specialized studios for instruction in subjects such as architecture and dance. But what really distinguishes the school is the way it is using technology to change the traditional roles of the teacher as oracle and the student as passive receptable for hand-me-down knowledge. A visit to some of Dalton's classrooms provides a glimpse of what many believe is the future of education:

ROOM 711

A faint scraping sound can be heard in Mary Kate Brown's sixth-grade social studies classroom. The students are on a dig. Each group of three or four has been assigned a plot within an ancient Assyrian site. Their mission: to uncover what is at the site, to analyze carefully each artifact they find, then to formulate and defend a thesis about the nature of the place and the people who once lived there. 3

Not even well-heeled Dalton can afford to take an entire class on an excavation in the Middle East, so these students are working on Archaeotype, a computer simulation of a dig—shoveling sounds and all—created at Dalton and based on an actual site. Still, the excitement of the hunt is palpable. As they uncover spearheads and ivory pieces on the screen, these 11-year-olds speak of "stratification" and "in-situ artifacts" with near professional fluency. 4

This is a course in which kids learn by doing—absorbing science and ancient history through acts of discovery. "The material they find will admit of a variety of explanations," says Brown. "There is not just one right answer." To marshal evidence for their theories, students may consult Archaeotype's six online "libraries" of scholarly information and images (military, religious, royalty, etc.) as well as the greater resources of Dalton's library or even the Assyrian collection at the nearby Metropolitan Museum of Art. "It was like our own little land inside the computer," says Laura Zuckerwise, 12, who completed the course last year. "If we found a new artifact, it was as though we were the first people to discover it!" 5

ROOM 608

Like generations before them, the students in Jacqueline D'Aiutolo's 10th-grade English class have begun the epic journey into the dark heart of Shakespeare's *Macbeth.* They have completed reading the 6 play, and now, working in groups of three or four, they are digging deeper into the text. Each group sits before a Macintosh computer, linked to an elaborate database.

Three students have been exploring the character of Lady Macbeth for a joint paper. What does she look like? How should she be imagined? A few keystrokes bring up a series of images: illustrations of the conniving noblewoman by a variety of artists, then a scene from Roman Polanski's 1971 film, *Macbeth.* As the action plays out in a window on the screen, the students discuss the lady's greed and her striking resemblance to a witch in the opening scene of Polanski's film. They can also look at scenes from the 1948 Orson Welles production and a 1988 staging for British TV. As they form theories about Shakespeare's intentions, they may consult any of 40 essays and hundreds of annotated bibliographies, as well as writings about the Bard's life and times. 7

Jacqui D'Aiutolo circles the room as her students work. She has been teaching *Macbeth* for more than 15 years and, though she first regarded computers and literature as "strange bedfellows," she has been amazed to see how students can deploy this modern tool to plumb the meaning of old texts. She has found that her own role has changed: she is less a lecturer than a resource and guide, helping students refine their own questions and assisting in their search for answers. The incisiveness of their work has stunned her. Says D'Aiutolo: "You have depths you would never expect to reach in a 10th-grade class." 8

ROOM 307

There's an audible hum in Malcolm Thompson's classroom, known at Dalton as the "AstroCave." Seven computers are in use, each surrounded by a clutch of students murmuring in continual discussion of their work. The place is littered with 13 1/2-in. square Palomar plates—grayish films, sprinkled with dark points of light representing stars and nebulae that were recorded by the 48-in. telescope at California's Palomar Observatory. Each student has chosen three stars and has been asked to calculate their brightness and temperature based on what the pupils see on the plates and can glean from a computer program called Voyager. Unlike Archaeotype, Voyager is an off-the-shelf program, but it is a tool of awesome power, simulating a view of the heavens from any point on earth, at any time, past or present. 9

Thompson's course has always been popular, but in recent years it has achieved an almost cultlike status at the school. Though a vivid lecturer and the co-author of what was for years the country's top- 10 selling astronomy textbook, Thompson has traded the chalk-and-talk approach for a task-oriented mode of teaching, using Voyager. His students do not "study" astronomy; they become astronomers. From September through June, they complete a series of tasks, using computer-based tools like the ones astronomers use. Each task builds on the ones before it, so calculations made in October may provide an essential tool for November's assignment. Thompson's students admit they often begin hopelessly lost until, by dint of their own collaborative labors and their teacher's counsel, they find their way. "It's the biggest satisfaction," says Simon Heffner, a senior. "You don't realize you understand it and then it hits you!" In the end, adds Thompson, "they have knowledge that they can deploy, as opposed to just passing a test."

It is no coincidence that Dalton began its plunge into technology with the Archaeotype program. Excavation is an apt metaphor for the kind of "constructivist learning" promoted at the school: students must actively dig up information, then construct their own understanding from raw, observable facts. What the technology does is extend experience so that many more observations are possible. "It shifts education from adults giving answers to students seeking answers," says headmaster Gardner Dunnan. The underlying premise: we all understand and remember what we have discovered for ourselves far better than what we have merely been told. 11

Still, the guiding hand of the teacher is a vital element in the process. "You can't just give kids powerful computers and powerful information and set them loose. The teacher must create a compelling set of educational questions," says associate headmaster Frank Moretti, who heads Dalton's technology group, the New Laboratory for Teaching and Learning. 12

The effectiveness of Dalton's program has been closely observed by outside experts. The school hired John Black of Columbia's Teachers College to conduct a study comparing the analytic skills of Archaeotype students with sixth-graders at a similarly elite private school. "Kids at Dalton were twice as good at devising an explanation of data and defending it," says Black. "I've never seen such a big difference in an educational study." On the other hand, the new teaching methods mean sacrificing some breadth for depth. Sixth-grade history, for instance, no longer covers the Middle Ages or Rome, since so much time is devoted to Archaeotype. 13

The goal of any school is to prepare students for the world in which they will live. Dalton's emphasis on collaborative learning—those little groups around a computer—"is perfect preparation," says 14

Moretti, for a world in which most problems, whether scientific or corporate, are addressed by teams. Students often produce their papers collectively. Increasingly, projects are composed in the same multimedia format used for instruction. In addition, students are being primed for the world of the Internet by taking part in the school's own E-mail and bulletin-board system. They log onto the Dalton Network from home or at school to "chat" with friends, confer with teachers, or join online discussions of movies and records.

The most remarkable feature of the system, however, is the "con- 15
ferences"—discussion groups associated with certain courses. This year's most popular spins off a senior-class seminar in civil rights. Not only do all 17 students in the class participate, but twice as many outside the class have joined in. An additional hundred or so just log on to read what's been said. The exchange, moderated by the teacher, is both analytical and heated, especially on divisive topics like affirmative action. Observes Moretti: "When children begin to take their own time outside the classroom to respond to questions that are important to them and become identified with positions within the larger community, that is a kind of personal development that wasn't possible in the old-fashioned school."

How relevant are Dalton's experiments to all those old-fashioned 16
schools across the country with strained budgets and less privileged kids? Very relevant, insists headmaster Dunnan. Sure, it takes serious money and expertise to create something like Archaeotype, he concedes. (Dalton received $3.7 million from real estate mogul Robert Tishman to develop technology.) "But once something is developed, it need not be very expensive." To prove that point, Dalton has begun to offer its learning technology to a few public schools. The Juarez Lincoln Elementary School in Chula Vista, California, for instance, has been using Archaeotype for three years, much to the delight of its largely poor and ethnically diverse students. Ultimately, Dalton hopes to be able to bring its technology to market.

Alas, sharing software alone will not bring about the education 17
revolution. Few schools today have the computing power to run multimedia programs like those used at Dalton. Fewer still have the resources to support a complex schoolwide network (though increasingly schools can connect to existing networks). Still, anyone who has seen what technology can do for learning is convinced of its future. "There's something inevitable about this," says Christina Hooper, a Distinguished Scientist at Apple Computer and an expert on educational technology. She believes it may take 10 years, or more like 20, before the technology is widespread, but the prophets of the post-Gutenberg age in education will finally be proved right.

Examining the Text

1. What are some of the benefits that computer technology has brought to the students at The Dalton School?
2. According to Wallis and the teachers she interviews, in what ways do computers change the dynamics of the classroom? What new roles are students asked to perform? How do the activities of the teachers change when students are working on computer-based assignments?
3. How does Wallis answer the objection that poorer schools are not able to take advantage of computer technology in the same way that the wealthy Dalton School can? Are you persuaded by her answer?

For Group Discussion

Choose one of the three specific assignments described by Wallis—the projects carried out in Room 711, Room 608, and Room 307—and discuss what you think the students learned from this particular use of computers in the classroom. Make a list of all the information the assignment conveyed and the skills that the assignment was designed to develop in students. Looking over your list, discuss the extent to which you think the students could have learned the information and developed the skills *without* the use of computers. In what ways were computers essential to the learning that the assignment accomplished?

Writing Suggestion

Wallis's article was written in 1995; since then new technologies have been developed and new uses for these technologies have been incorporated in classrooms across the country. This writing suggestion asks you to investigate what's going on today at The Dalton School by looking at information presented on their Web site. The URL listed below will take you to the Curricular Projects page at the New Laboratory for Teaching and Learning, which is part of The Dalton School:

> URL: *http://www.dalton.org/departments/nltl/nltl_projects/curricular_projects.html*

At this page, you'll find detailed descriptions of a wide range of curricular projects in four categories: art and architecture, science, social studies, and hypermedia. Choose one of the four categories and read through all of the projects described there. Then, write a concise summary of these projects, incorporating quotations from the Web site in your summary. Conclude your essay by commenting on whether the observations by Wallis about projects in 1995 hold true today. Has the development and incorporation of new technology changed the curricular goals at The Dalton School?

Virtual Students, Digital Classroom

Neil Postman

*Neil Postman is a prominent and prolific media scholar and technology critic. Chair of the Department of Culture and Communications at New York University and Professor of Media Ecology, Postman is the author of seventeen books and over 200 articles on education, the media, and technology, among other topics. He is perhaps best known for two of his recent books—*Amusing Ourselves to Death *and* Technopoly*—and for his lectures at college campuses and conferences.*

In the article that follows, Postman looks at some of the statements educators and administrators have made praising the power of computer technology to revolutionize learning. He explains why he is more than a bit skeptical about such claims, arguing that many of the things taught in schools—for instance, "social values"—simply cannot be taught by computers. Postman has been accused of being a technophobe or Luddite—that is, someone who is afraid of technology or rejects it without reason. But Postman argues here that he isn't opposed to computers in the classroom; he's opposed to "sleepwalking attitudes toward it." He calls for a "serious form of technology-education" rather than an unthinking belief in the "false god" of computer technology.

***As you're reading,** be on the lookout for some wonderful prose. We find Postman's writing to be stylistically delightful, and we also enjoy his humor and witty observations in this article (and elsewhere in Postman's publications). Whether you agree or disagree with his argument, we think that you'll enjoy the way he phrases it.*

If one has a trusting relationship with one's students (let us say, graduate students), it is not altogether gauche to ask them if they believe in God (with a capital G). I have done this three or four times and most students say they do. Their answer is preliminary to the next question: If someone you love were desperately ill, and you had to choose between praying to God for his or her recovery or administering an antibiotic (as prescribed by a competent physician), which would you choose? 1

Most say the question is silly since the alternatives are not mutually exclusive. Of course. But suppose they were—which would you choose? God helps those who help themselves, some say in choosing the antibiotic, therefore getting the best of two possible belief systems. But if pushed to the wall (e.g., God does not always help those who 2 help themselves; God helps those who pray and who believe), most choose the antibiotic, after noting that the question is asinine and proves nothing. Of course, the question was not asked, in the first place, to prove anything but to begin a discussion of the nature of belief. And I do not fail to inform the students, by the way, that there has recently emerged evidence of a "scientific" nature that when sick people are prayed for they do better than those who aren't.

As the discussion proceeds, important distinctions are made among the different meanings of "belief," but at some point it becomes far from asinine to speak of the god of Technology—in the sense that people believe technology works, that they rely on it, that it makes promises, that they are bereft when denied access to it, that they are delighted when they are in its presence, that for most people it works in mysterious ways, that they condemn people who speak against it, that they stand in awe of it and that, in the "born again" mode, they will alter their lifestyles, their schedules, their habits and their relationships to accommodate it. If this be not a form of religious belief, what is? 3

In all strands of American cultural life, you can find so many examples of technological adoration that it is possible to write a book about it. And I would if it had not already been done so well. But nowhere do you find more enthusiasm for the god of Technology than among educators. In fact, there are those, like Lewis Perelman, who argue (for example, in his book, *School's Out*) that modern information technologies have rendered schools entirely irrelevant since there is now much more information available outside the classroom than inside it. This is by no means considered an outlandish idea. Dr. Diane Ravitch, former Assistant Secretary of Education, envisions, with considerable relish, the challenge that technology presents to the tradition that "children (and adults) should be educated in a specific place, for a certain number of hours, and a certain number of days during the week and year." In other words, that children should be educated in school. Imagining the possibilities of an information superhighway offering perhaps a thousand channels, Dr. Ravitch assures us that: 4

> in this new world of pedagogical plenty, children and adults will be able to dial up a program on their home television to learn whatever they want to know, at their own convenience. If Little Eva cannot sleep, she can learn algebra instead. At her home-learning station, she will tune in to a series of interesting problems that are presented in an interactive medium, much like video games. . . .
>
> Young John may decide that he wants to learn the history of modern Japan, which he can do by dialing up the greatest authorities and teachers on the subject, who will not only use dazzling graphs and illustra-

tions, but will narrate a historical video that excites his curiosity and imagination.

5 In this vision there is, it seems to me, a confident and typical sense of unreality. Little Eva can't sleep, so she decides to learn a little algebra? Where does Little Eva come from? Mars? If not, it is more likely she will tune in to a good movie. Young John decides that he wants to learn the history of modern Japan? How did young John come to this point? How is it that he never visited a library up to now? Or is it that he, too, couldn't sleep and decided that a little modern Japanese history was just what he needed?

6 What Ravitch is talking about here is not a new technology but a new species of child, one who, in any case, no one has seen up to now. Of course, new technologies do make new kinds of people, which leads to a second objection to Ravitch's conception of the future. There is a kind of forthright determinism about the imagined world described in it. The technology is here or will be; we must use it because it is there; we will become the kind of people the technology requires us to be, and whether we like it or not, we will remake our institutions to accommodate technology. All of this must happen because it is good for us, but in any case, we have no choice. This point of view is present in very nearly every statement about the future relationship of learning to technology. And, as in Ravitch's scenario, there is always a cheery, gee-whiz tone to the prophecies. Here is one produced by the National Academy of Sciences, written by Hugh McIntosh.

> School for children of the Information Age will be vastly different than it was for Mom and Dad.
>
> Interested in biology? Design your own life forms with computer simulation.
>
> Having trouble with a science project? Teleconference about it with a research scientist.
>
> Bored with the real world? Go into a virtual physics lab and rewrite the laws of gravity.
>
> These are the kinds of hands-on learning experiences schools could be providing right now. The technologies that make them possible are already here, and today's youngsters, regardless of economic status, know how to use them. They spend hours with them every week—not in the classroom, but in their own homes and in video game centers at every shopping mall.

7 It is always interesting to attend to the examples of learning, and the motivations that ignite them, in the songs of love that technophiles perform for us. It is, for example, not easy to imagine research scientists all over the world teleconferencing with thousands of students

who are having difficulty with their science projects. I can't help thinking that most research scientists would put a stop to this rather quickly. But I find it especially revealing that in the scenario above we have an example of a technological solution to a psychological problem that would seem to be exceedingly serious. We are presented with a student who is "bored with the real world." What does it mean to say someone is bored with the real world, especially one so young? Can a journey into virtual reality cure such a problem? And if it can, will our troubled youngster want to return to the real world? Confronted with a student who is bored with the real world, I don't think we can solve the problem so easily by making available a virtual reality physics lab.

The role that new technology should play in schools or anywhere 8
else is something that needs to be discussed without the hyperactive fantasies of cheerleaders. In particular, the computer and its associated technologies are awesome additions to a culture, and are quite capable of altering the psychic, not to mention the sleeping, habits of our young. But like all important technologies of the past, they are Faustian bargains, giving and taking away, sometimes in equal measure, sometimes more in one way than the other. It is strange—indeed, shocking—that with the twenty-first century so close, we can still talk of new technologies as if they were unmixed blessings—gifts, as it were, from the gods. Don't we all know what the combustion engine has done for us and against us? What television is doing for us and against us? At the very least, what we need to discuss about Little Eva, Young John and McIntosh's trio is what they will lose, and what we will lose, if they enter a world in which computer technology is their chief source of motivation, authority and, apparently, psychological sustenance. Will they become, as Joseph Weizenbaum warns, more impressed by calculation than human judgment? Will speed of response become, more than ever, a defining quality of intelligence? If, indeed, the idea of a school will be dramatically altered, what kinds of learning will be neglected, perhaps made impossible? Is virtual reality a new form of therapy? If it is, what are its dangers?

These are serious matters, and they need to be discussed by those who 9
know something about children from the planet Earth, and whose vision of children's needs, and the needs of society, go beyond thinking of school mainly as a place for the convenient distribution of information. Schools are not now and have never been largely about getting information to children. That has been on the schools' agenda, of course, but has always been way down on the list. For technological utopians, the computer vaults information-access to the top. This reshuffling of priorities comes at a most inopportune time. The goal of

giving people greater access to more information faster, more conveniently and in more diverse forms was the main technological thrust of the nineteenth century. Some folks haven't noticed it but that problem was largely solved, so that for almost a hundred years there has been more information available to the young outside the school than inside. That fact did not make the schools obsolete, nor does it now make them obsolete. Yes, it is true that Little Eva, the insomniac from Mars, could turn on an algebra lesson, thanks to the computer, in the wee hours of the morning. She could also, if she wished, read a book or magazine, watch television, turn on the radio or listen to music. All of this she could have done before the computer. The computer does not solve any problem she has but does exacerbate one. For Little Eva's problem is not how to get access to a well-structured algebra lesson but what to do with all the information available to her during the day, as well as during sleepless nights. Perhaps this is why she couldn't sleep in the first place. Little Eva, like the rest of us, is overwhelmed by information. She lives in a culture that has 260,000 billboards, 17,000 newspapers, 12,000 periodicals, 27,000 video outlets for renting tapes, 400 million television sets and well over 500 million radios, not including those in automobiles. There are 40,000 new book titles published every year, and each day 41 million photographs are taken. And thanks to the computer, more than 60 billion pieces of advertising junk come into our mailboxes every year. Everything from telegraphy and photography in the nineteenth century to the silicon chip in the twentieth has amplified the din of information intruding on Little Eva's consciousness. From millions of sources all over the globe, through every possible channel and medium—light waves, air waves, ticker tape, computer banks, telephone wires, television cables, satellites and printing presses—information pours in. Behind it in every imaginable form of storage—on paper, on video, on audiotape, on disks, film and silicon chips—is an even greater volume of information waiting to be retrieved. In the face of this we might ask, What can schools do for Little Eva besides making still more information available? If there is nothing, then new technologies will indeed make schools obsolete. But in fact, there is plenty.

10 One thing that comes to mind is that schools can provide her with a serious form of technology-education. Something quite different from instruction in using computers to process information, which, it strikes me, is a trivial thing to do, for two reasons. In the first place, approximately 35 million people have already learned how to use computers without the benefit of school instruction. If the schools do nothing, most of the population will know how to use computers in the next ten years, just as most of the population learns how to drive a car without school instruction. In the second place, what we needed to

know about cars—as we need to know about computers, television and other important technologies—is not how to use them but how they use *us.* In the case of cars, what we needed to think about in the early twentieth century was not how to drive them but what they would do to our air, our landscape, our social relations, our family life and our cities. Suppose in 1946 we had started to address similar questions about television: What will be its effects on our political institutions, our psychic habits, our children, our religious conceptions, our economy? Would we be better positioned today to control TV's massive assault on American culture? I am talking here about making technology itself an object of inquiry so that Little Eva and Young John are more interested in asking questions about the computer than getting answers from it.

I am not arguing against using computers in school. I am arguing 11 against our sleepwalking attitudes toward it, against allowing it to distract us from important things, against making a god of it. This is what Theodore Roszak warned against in *The Cult of Information:* "Like all cults," he wrote, "this one also has the intention of enlisting mindless allegiance and acquiescence. People who have no clear idea of what they mean by information or why they should want so much of it are nonetheless prepared to believe that we live in an Information Age, which makes every computer around us what the relics of the True Cross were in the Age of Faith: emblems of salvation." To this, I would add the sage observation of Alan Kay of Apple Computer. Kay is widely associated with the invention of the personal computer, and certainly has an interest in schools using them. Nonetheless, he has repeatedly said that any problems the schools cannot solve without computers, they cannot solve with them. What are some of those problems? There is, for example, the traditional task of teaching children how to behave in groups. One might even say that schools have never been essentially about individualized learning. It is true, of course, that groups do not learn, individuals do. But the idea of a school is that individuals must learn in a setting in which individual needs are subordinated to group interests. Unlike other media of mass communication, which celebrate individual response and are experienced in private, the classroom is intended to tame the ego, to connect the individual with others, to demonstrate the value and necessity of group cohesion. At present, most scenarios describing the uses of computers have children solving problems alone; Little Eva, Young John and the others are doing just that. The presence of other children may, indeed, be an annoyance.

Like the printing press before it, the computer has a powerful bias to- 12 ward amplifying personal autonomy and individual problem-solving.

Computers in the Classroom

That is why educators must guard against computer technology's undermining some of the important reasons for having the young assemble (to quote Ravitch) "in a specific place, for a certain number of hours, and a certain number of days during the week and year."

Although Ravitch is not exactly against what she calls "state schools," she imagines them as something of a relic of a pre-technological age. She believes that the new technologies will offer all children equal access to information. Conjuring up a hypothetical Little Mary who is presumably from a poorer home than Little Eva, Ravitch imagines that Mary will have the same opportunities as Eva "to learn any subject, and to learn it from the same master teachers as children in the richest neighbourhood." For all of its liberalizing spirit, this scenario makes some important omissions. One is that though new technologies may be a solution to the learning of "subjects," they work against the learning of what are called "social values" including an understanding of democratic processes. If one reads the first chapter of Robert Fulghum's *All I Really Need to Know I Learned in Kindergarten,* one will find an elegant summary of a few things Ravitch's scenario has left out. They include learning the following lessons: Share everything, play fair, don't hit people, put things back where you found them, clean up your own mess, wash your hands before you eat and, of course, flush. The only thing wrong with Fulghum's book is that no 13 one has learned all these things at kindergarten's end. We have ample evidence that it takes many years of teaching these values in school before they have been accepted and internalized. That is why it won't do for children to learn in "settings of their own choosing." That is also why schools require children to be in a certain place at a certain time and to follow certain rules, like raising their hands when they wish to speak, not talking when others are talking, not chewing gum, not leaving until the bell rings, exhibiting patience toward slower learners, etc. This process is called making civilized people. The god of Technology does not appear interested in this function of schools. At least, it does not come up much when technology's virtues are enumerated.

The god of Technology may also have a trick or two up its sleeve 14
about something else. It is often asserted that new technologies will equalize learning opportunities for the rich and poor. It is devoutly to be wished for, but I doubt it will happen. In the first place, it is generally understood by those who have studied the history of technology that technological change always produces winners and losers. There are many reasons for this, among them economic differences. Even in the case of the automobile, which is a commodity most people can buy (although not all), there are wide differences between the rich and poor in the quality of what is available to them. It would be quite astonishing if computer technology equalized all learning opportunities, irrespective of economic differences. One may be delighted that Little Eva's parents could afford the technology and software to make it possible for her to learn algebra at midnight. But Little Mary's parents may not be able to, may not even know such things are available. And if we say that the school could make the technology available to Little Mary (at least during the day), there may something else Little Mary is lacking.

It turns out, for example, that Little Mary may be having sleep- 15
less nights as frequently as Little Eva but not because she wants to get a leg up on her algebra. Maybe because she doesn't know who her father is, or, if she does, where he is. Maybe we can understand why McIntosh's kid is bored with the real world. Or is the child confused about it? Or terrified? Are there educators who seriously believe that these problems can be addressed by new technologies?

I do not say, of course, that schools can solve the problems of 16
poverty, alienation and family disintegration, but schools can *respond* to them. And they can do this because there are people in them, because these people are concerned with more than algebra lessons or modern Japanese history, and because these people can identify not only one's level of competence in math but one's level of rage and confusion and depression. I am talking here about children as they really come to us, not children who are invented to show us how computers

may enrich their lives. Of course, I suppose it is possible that there are children who, waking at night, want to study algebra or who are so interested in their world that they yearn to know about Japan. If there be such children, and one hopes there are, they do not require expensive computers to satisfy their hunger for learning. They are on their way, with or without computers. Unless, of course, they do not care about others or have no friends, or little respect for democracy or are filled with suspicion about those who are not like them. When we have machines that know how to do something about these problems, that is the time to rid ourselves of the expensive burden of schools or to reduce the function of teachers to "coaches" in the uses of machines (as Ravitch envisions). Until then, we must be more modest about this god of Technology and certainly not pin our hopes on it.

We must also, I suppose, be empathetic toward those who search with good intentions for technological panaceas. I am a teacher myself and know how hard it is to contribute to the making of a civilized person. Can we blame those who want to find an easy way, through the agency of technology? Perhaps not. After all, it is an old quest. As early as 1918, H. L. Mencken (although completely devoid of empathy) wrote, "There is no sure-cure so idiotic that some superintendent of schools will not swallow it. The aim seems to be to reduce the whole teaching process to a sort of automatic reaction, to discover some master formula that will not only take the place of competence and resourcefulness in the teacher but that will also create an artificial receptivity in the child." 17

Mencken was not necessarily speaking of technological panaceas but he may well have been. In the early 1920s a teacher wrote the following poem: 18

Mr. Edison says
That the radio will supplant the teacher.
Already one may learn languages by means of Victrola records.
The moving picture will visualize
What the radio fails to get across.
Teachers will be relegated to the backwoods,
With fire-horses,
And long-haired women;
Or, perhaps shown in museums.
Education will become a matter
Of pressing the button.
Perhaps I can get a position at the switchboard.

I do not go as far back as the radio and Victrola, but I am old enough to remember when 16-millimeter film was to be the sure-cure. 19

Then closed-circuit television. Then 8-millimeter film. Then teacher-proof textbooks. Now computers.

I know a false god when I see one. 20

Examining the Text

1. How does Postman define "belief"? In what ways do we "believe" in technology, according to Postman?
2. For what reasons does Postman criticize the story of Little Eva and Young John?
3. What does the phrase "Faustian bargain" mean? In what ways, according to Postman, do computers offer us a Faustian bargain?
4. What does Postman see as the key function of schools and of education? How do computers fail or succeed in accomplishing this function, according to Postman?
5. How would you describe Postman's tone and style of writing in this article? What function do the humorous parts of the article serve in helping Postman convey his ideas?

For Group Discussion

Rather than simply placing computers in classrooms and giving students access to the Internet, Postman argues that schools should provide "a serious form of technology-education." Based on the ideas Postman explores in the article as well as on your own observations and experiences as students and computer users, discuss what you think this "technology-education" should involve? If computer technology is made an "object of inquiry," as Postman suggests, what questions should be asked about it and what should students be expected to know in order to be intelligent, informed computer users? After discussing these questions, make a list of the top five topics or issues that you would want to see covered in "technology-education."

Writing Suggestion

Postman writes, "I am not arguing against using computers in school. I am arguing against our sleepwalking attitudes toward it, against allowing it to distract us from important things, against making a god of it." How do you think Postman would respond to the examples described in the previous article by Claudia Wallis? Write an essay in which you take a Postman-esque view of the ways that The Dalton School uses computers in the classroom. What would Postman find praiseworthy about these assignments? What would he criticize? In your essay, be sure to include quotations and information from both Postman's and Wallis's articles to support the points you're making.

Undergraduate Teaching in the Electronic Age

Richard A. Lanham

Richard A. Lanham is Professor Emeritus in the English Department at the University of California at Los Angeles, founder and former director of the UCLA Writing Programs, and founder of Rhetorica Inc. (http://www.rhetoricainc.com/)*, a consulting and editorial services firm. (As an intriguing pop culture side note, Lanham has served as an expert witness in copyright dispute cases involving* King Kong, Jaws, Shampoo, Earthquake, Star Wars, Superman, *and many other films and television shows.) In a distinguished academic career, Lanham has won many awards for his teaching and scholarship. His critically acclaimed book on computers and writing,* The Electronic Word, *combined with his expertise in classical literary rhetoric, earned Lanham the title "Computer Greek."*

In the essay that follows, Lanham suggests that a wise integration of computers into the classroom can have wide-ranging effects on undergraduate studies, potentially changing what we typically think of as a course, a textbook, a major—indeed, changing the entire curriculum of undergraduate education. Essentially Lanham asks why things have to be the way they are. If the introduction of computer technology can improve education and help students learn more effectively, why resist these changes? Lanham provides specific examples from his own experience teaching literature courses, and he suggests some future possibilities for perpetually evolving online textbooks, classrooms configured for self-paced learning, multimedia writing projects, and interdisciplinary majors.

The undergraduate experience Lanham envisions differs quite significantly from the current experience of most students. **As you read,** *begin formulating your own opinion about the changes Lanham suggests and envisions. To what extent do you think that changes like the ones he describes would improve the quality of your own education?*

Let's start with the idea of a "class." I'll use an example close to home, 1
my Shakespeare class. I give it every year. I always recommend additional reading which the students never do. Partly they are lazy, but partly they can't get to the library, for they work at outside jobs for 20–30 hours a week and commute from pillar to post. Each year's class exists in a temporal, conceptual, and social vacuum. They don't know what previous classes have done before them. They don't know how

other instructors teach their sections of the same class. They seldom know each other before they take the class. They never read each other's work—though sometimes they appropriate it in felonious ways. I read all their work myself, and mark it up extensively, often to their dismay. A few of them take me up on my rewrite options but most don't, and hence don't learn anything much from my revisions, since they are not *made* to take them into account. They thus have an audience they know, but it is a desperately narrow one.

Imagine what would happen were I to add an electronic library 2
to this class. Students access it by modern or through a CD-ROM or whatever. On it, they read papers—good, bad, and indifferent—submitted in earlier sections on the topics I suggest. They read scholarly articles—good, bad, and indifferent—on these same topics. They read before-and-after examples of prose style revision. A revision program is available for them to use—licensed by me to UCLA, since it depends on my own textbooks! They can do searches of the Shakespearean texts, also available online, when they study patterns of imagery, rhetorical figuration, etc. They can make *Quicktime*© movie excerpts from the videos of the plays and use them to illustrate their papers. (The papers will not be "papers," of course, but "texts" of a different sort.) They needn't go to the campus library to do any of this. They can access this library wherever and whenever they find time to do their academic work. All their work—papers, exams, stylistic analyses—is "published" in the electronic library. You got a "C" and feel robbed? Read some "A" papers to see what went wrong. Read some other papers, just to see what kind of work your competitors are producing. Lots of other neat things happen in such a universe. But you can fill in the blanks yourself.

Such a course—here is the vital point—now *has a history.* Stu- 3
dents join a tradition. It is easy to imagine how quickly the internets *between* such courses would develop. We can see a pattern in the hypertextual literary curriculum developed by George Landow and his colleagues at Brown University. The isolation of the course, not only in *time,* but in *discipline,* is broken. The course *constitutes a society,* and it is a continuing one. The students become citizens of a commonwealth and act like citizens—they publish their work for their fellow scholars. The mesmeric fixation on the instructor as the only reader and grader is broken.

Now imagine another course—the independent study or "hon- 4
ors" course. A student in my Shakespeare course is interested in music and wonders what I mean when I keep using analogies between musical ornament and verbal ornament. When I talk about sonata form vs. theme-and-variations in a lecture on the *Sonnets,* she comes in and asks for a fuller explanation. Could she do a special study with me on

this topic? Well, I'm not a musicologist. What do I do now? "Next time Prof. Winter teaches his Haydn, Mozart, and Beethoven course, you ought to take it." I'm certainly not competent to teach such a course. In a multimedia environment, I'd pursue a different route. "Sure, I'll do this course with you. We'll construct it around Winter's wonderful new multimedia programs on Beethoven's *Ninth Symphony*, Stravinsky's *Rite of Spring*, Mozart's *Dissonant* String Quartet, and Bach's *Brandenburg Concertos*. You can play them all on the equipment in the music school or the library. Using them, you can teach yourself the fundamentals of music harmony, find out all you need to know about classical sonata form, learn about what happened to music when sonata form no longer predominated, and so on. You can play these pieces' theme and motif at a time, dissect them, learn how the orchestra is constructed, what the instruments are, etc." I am, with Winter's help, perfectly competent to teach such a course. Such a procedure not only generates new kinds of disciplinary relationships; if used widely it would save money for both student and school.

Now, the classroom itself. The "electronic classrooms" in use now, at least the ones which give each student a computer, have generated some preliminary generalizations. Just as "author" and "authority" change meaning in electronic text, they change meaning in the classroom. The professor ceases to be the cynosure of every eye: some authority passes to the group constituted by the electronic network. You can of course use such a configuration for self-paced learning, but I would use it for verbal analysis. Multimedia environments allow you to anatomize what "reading" a literary text really means. This pedagogy would revolutionize how I teach Shakespeare. (Again, in suggesting how, I run up against the difficulties of discussing a broadband medium with the narrowband one of print.) 5

Now the textbook. Let me take another example from my backyard. Let us consider the dreariest textbook of all, the Freshman Composition Handbook. You all know them. Heavy. Shiny coated paper. Pyroxylin, peanut-butter-sandwich-proof cover. Imagine instead an online program available to everyone who teaches, and everyone who takes, the course. The apoplexy that comp handbooks always generate now finds more than marginal expression. Stupid examples are critiqued as such; better ones are found. Teachers contribute their experience on how the book works, or doesn't work, in action. The textbook, rather than fixed in an edition, is a continually changing, evolutionary document. It is fed by all the people who use it, and continually made and remade by them. 6

And what about the literary texts themselves? It is easy to imagine (copyright problems aside) the classic literary texts all put on a single CD-ROM, and a device to display them which the student carries 7 with her. What we don't often remark is the manipulative power such a student now possesses. Textual searching power, obviously. But also power to reconfigure. Imagine for a moment students *brought up* on the multimedia electronic "texts" I have been discussing. They are accustomed to interacting with texts, playing games with them. Won't they want to do this with *Paradise Lost?* And what will happen if they do? Will poems written in a print-based world be compromised? Will poems which emerged from an oral world, as with so much Greek and Latin literature, be rejuvenated and re-presented in a more historically correct way? And what about the student's license to re-create as well as read? If Marcel Duchamp can moustache the *Mona Lisa,* why can't they? Once again, questions of cultural authority.

Now the "major." If electronic text threatens the present discipli- 8
nary boundaries in the humanities, it threatens the major in the same way. I don't have space to discuss this question now, but it is developed at length in *The Electronic Word,* the book from which this paper draws its argument. The major is constructed, at least when it retains any disciplinary integrity, on a hierarchical and historical basis. Such means of organization and dissemination, as we have seen, do not last long in a digital domain.

Now the curriculum, or at least two words about it. First, the de- 9
bate about the university curriculum has centered, in the last century,

ASCII art: Mr. Spock by Ron McDowell and Mona Lisa by David Horn

on what to do about a "core" curriculum in a fragmented and disciplinary world. Various "core curricula" have been devised and, in some times and places, taken over the first two—or even, at St. John's, all four—undergraduate years. We have, in all these programs, harkened back to a linear course of study. For all kinds of reasons, practical and theoretical, such a pre-planned program has rarely worked. What digital networks suggest is a new core constituted hypertextually, on a nonlinear basis. None of the obstacles to the traditional core curriculum apply.

10 Second, the current streetfight about the undergraduate curriculum—Great Books or Politically Correct Books—ignores the probability that our "texts" won't be books at all. Both sides base their arguments on the fixity of print, and the assumptions that fixity induces in us. Thus they both, and the curricular debate they generate, depart from obsolete, indeed otiose, operating principles. . . .

11 When you talk about digital technology, someone will always dismiss it as "futuristic." None of the technology I have talked about is futuristic. It all exists now. It is the cutting that involves planning for the future. Why not use the occasion for some long-term planning in terms of this new operating system for the humanities we have been discussing? The planning I read about at my own institution and others like it amounts to keeping on the same way, with as few changes as possible. Review departments, drop the weak ones—but don't rethink what a department is. Ditto "programs." Review majors, drop the weak or obscure ones, but don't rethink what a "major" is. Review courses, cut out frivolous and ornamental ones, but don't rethink what a "course" is. Ditto graduate programs. Nothing new or promising can emerge from any of this fire-fighting.

12 The short-term approach—how do I keep on doing what I have been doing in the ways I have been doing it, but with much less money?—hasn't worked for the rest of American enterprise. Why should it work for us? It has all been done over and over in America in the last two decades, in the automobile industry, the steel industry, the railroads, the farm machinery business—the list goes on and on. Department stores are worrying about which departments to phase out while the traditional idea of a department store is drifting down the stream of mercantile history. In the academy we are prisoners of the same inert patterns of thinking that have dominated the rest of American corporate enterprise. There is nothing "futuristic" about trying to break out of these patterns; it is the most insistent present one can possibly imagine. It will be our own fault, not the fault of our funders, if we continue to imitate the Post Office and worry about moving letters around in an electronic way, when it is not only the delivery system but the "letters" themselves which have fundamentally changed.

Examining the Text

1. What are some of the problems that Lanham describes with the current state of undergraduate education? Have you encountered these problems in the courses you've taken at your school?

2. Lanham mentions several times that new computer technologies give students the opportunity to compose multimedia texts—that is, to write "papers" that incorporate images, sound, and video. What are the advantages and disadvantages of this kind of multimedia writing? Would you enjoy having an assignment that asked you to produce a multimedia work rather than an essay? Why or why not?

3. What obstacles does Lanham see to the implementation of the technological initiatives described in the article? Do you think these obstacles still exist at your school?

For Group Discussion

In his article, Lanham suggests that computers and databases will change fundamental features of higher education: the class, the classroom, the textbook, the literary text, the major, and the curriculum. Choose one of these six educational entities and re-read the section in which Lanham discusses it. What does Lanham describe as the current characteristics of this entity, what's wrong with it as it is, and in what ways does he think computer technology will bring about positive changes? Finally, discuss what you think of his argument. As a student, do you prefer the entity as it is now, or do you think that the new, technology-enhanced version Lanham describes would enhance your learning?

Writing Suggestion

Lanham has some fairly unkind words to say about "the dreariest textbook of all, the Freshman Composition Handbook." We're certain he didn't mean to include *Common Culture* in this category; after all, *Common Culture* is a "reader" rather than a "handbook" (a handbook generally focuses on grammar and style, whereas a reader includes fascinating articles and stimulating, thought-provoking exercises like this one). Nevertheless, we're always trying to improve, and we certainly want to avoid dreariness! Toward that end, Lanham's comments suggest a useful writing exercise.

The *Common Culture* companion Web site (*http://www.prenhall.com/petracca/*) has a Feedback option that allows you to comment on what you think of the book. Lanham suggests that "stupid examples" can be critiqued and better ones found; teachers (and students, too) can contribute ideas on "how the book works, or doesn't work, in action." As Lanham envisions, the book can be "fed by all the people who use it, and continually made and remade by them." Since it's a print rather than an online book, changes to it take a bit longer to get into print. But we'll definitely read what you write and consider your suggestions for the next edition.

You might focus your comments on a specific chapter of *Common Culture*, explaining what you liked and didn't like about the chapter. Or you might write to us about particular exercises or discussion questions that you did or didn't find helpful. Or you might write to us about your experience reading and writing about popular culture: which topics were especially engaging to you? are there any special topics you'd like to see us include in the next edition? As in most writing assignments, you'll be more persuasive if you provide detail and evidence to support your points.

Thank you in advance for your suggestions!

ADDITIONAL SUGGESTIONS FOR WRITING ABOUT CYBERCULTURE

1. Recently, a movement composed of individuals who question the merits of technology in general, and computer technology specifically, has arisen in this country. Kirkpatrick Sale, considered by many to be the leader of this movement, said in a recent issue of *Wired* magazine, "Quite apart from the environmental and medical evils associated with them being produced and used, there are two moral judgments against computers. One is that computerization enables the large forces of our civilization to operate more swiftly and efficiently in their pernicious goals of making money and producing things. And, however much individuals may feel that there are industrial benefits in their lives from the use of the computer (that is to say, things are easier, swifter), these are industrial virtues that may not be virtues in another morality. And secondly, in the course of using these, these forces are destroying nature with more speed and efficiency than ever before." In an essay, respond to Sale's argument. What are the dangers inherent in our becoming increasingly dependent on computers, and what are the benefits of computer technology? After weighing the pros and cons of the computer revolution, would you consider yourself a neo-Luddite, as the adherents to Sale's philosophy are sometimes called? Are you a fierce proponent of all things high-tech? Do you fall somewhere in between the two philosophical extremes?

Internet Activities

1. Write an essay in which you compare and contrast the ways in which a topic of your choice is covered in the noncomputer-based media (such as television news, *Time* magazine, National Public Radio, your local newspaper, *The National Enquirer,* roadside billboards, a journal of your choice, and so on) and on a computer-based medium such as the World Wide Web. You may investigate any topic that arouses your curiosity: software design, tattoos and body-piercing, clinical depression, skateboard parks, contemporary Christian music, sports agents, mathematical knot theory. For each point made within this essay, be sure to include textual examples from the sources you are using, to substantiate and develop the comparison/contrast. Be sure to structure your paper so that you don't have to jump back and forth too much from point to point. You might even want to discuss *all* your observations about the noncomputerized media treatment of your topic, and then go on to discuss the ways in which World Wide Web treats the same material, pointing out areas of similarity and dissimilarity. By organizing your material in this way, you can avoid choppiness in your supporting paragraphs.

2. In increasing numbers, people are using the World Wide Web to design multimedia, interactive representations of themselves in "personal homepages." These are Web sites created by individuals (rather than businesses, universities, government agencies, and so forth) that present the writer to the wide audience of Web users. Spend some time browsing the Web and looking at these personal homepages in order to get a sense of the range of possible information that can be included on such a site. You'll find several good starting points at the *Common Culture* Web site; there are links there to collections (or "webrings") of particularly good personal homepages.

As you're browsing, keep notes on the strengths and weaknesses of the different homepages, and then try designing one of your own (on paper, or using a web-authoring program if one is familiar and available to you). What information about yourself would you include? What other Web sites would you want to link your page to? Who would be the intended audience for your personal homepage?

After you've come up with a tentaive design, write an essay in which you explain the decisions you made in creating the page. What image of yourself were you trying to present? How were your decisions influenced by your reactions to the specific homepages you looked at earlier?

3. In response to the "cyber-segregation" described by Beckles, a number of sites on the World Wide Web have been created to foster a sense of community among groups that may feel marginalized or excluded

by the new information technologies. Visit one of these sites; you'll find some listed as links from this chapter at the *Common Culture* Web site. After exploring all that the site has to offer, write an analysis of the strategies it uses to welcome members into its community. How does the content of the site cater to the needs and interests of its audience? How does the design of the site—its colors and images, its organization—help the audience feel welcome and "at home" at this place on the Internet? Are there any interactive components of the site that allow visitors to communicate with each other? If so, what is the content and tone of these discussions? What other features of the site are employed to respond to its target audience? Finally, assess the overall effectiveness of the Web site in creating a responsive virtual community for a particular group of people.

4. This assignment requires that you have access to the Internet and enough know-how to join a virtual community like the ones described in the first part of this chapter. (To develop this know-how you can consult one of the many books on the Internet available in bookstores and libraries; you might also check to see if your college or university offers workshops or courses on using the Internet.) Choose a mailing list, a MUD, or a MOO, and participate in discussions there for a few weeks. You might begin by "lurking" or listening in on discussions without making contributions yourself. Keep notes on the general qualities of the community. What do people talk about? What tones do they adopt in their discussions? Is there any hostility or "flaming," or is the atmosphere more friendly and inviting? How would you describe the connections or relationships among the participants? After you've "lurked" for a while, you might decide to enter the discussion and ask a few questions about why the participants are involved in this particular community and how they feel about the interactions there. Finally, write an essay in which you compare the virtual community you've been monitoring with those described by Barlow and Turkle, for example. Use your experience as a way of testing the ideas of these authors on the relative benefits and drawbacks of virtual communities.

Reading Images

The color image on page CI-5 is a still photo from the 1995 film *Johnny Mnemonic;* the color image on page CI-6 comes from the 1999 film *The Matrix*. In both, we see depictions of "the human" and of "the technological." Your task in this analytical essay is to compare the ways that each image represents people, technology, and their relationship. If you've seen one or both of the movies, try to refrain from discussing them in your analysis; stick to the images and to the meanings they convey.

Look first at how "the human" is represented in each image: what are the similarities and differences in the human figures that the images include? Next, write about how "the technological" is represented: how do we know that these movies are about computer technology? How does each image represent technology? As you discuss each of these components, remember to consider color, dimension, contrast, perspective, focal point, and other issues discussed in the "Reading Images" section of Chapter 1.

Move next to a discussion of the relationship that each image creates between human and technology. What words would characterize this relationship: harmonious? antagonistic? intimate? distant? Be sure to provide evidence from each image to support the assertions you make about it.

Finally, select one of the key ideas discussed by Gergen, Barlow, Turkle, or Beckles as they portray the effects of computer technology on individuals and communities. After explaining this idea with the help of quotes from the essay, discuss whether this idea is confirmed or contradicted by the images taken from these two popular sci-fi movies.

6

Sports

The United States seems to be a nation obsessed with sports, an obsession nowhere more evident than in some fans' virtual addiction to sports statistics. Somewhere there's probably a statistics maven who knows the number of foot faults in the final 1956 Davis Cup match or the most triples by a left-handed batter during Tuesday afternoon World Series games. Fans crave statistics, no matter how minute, as a way of measuring the achievements of their favorite athletes and teams—and perhaps also as a way of holding the memory of never-to-be-repeated athletic performances.

It's not difficult to find further evidence of America's preoccupation with sports. Most daily newspapers allocate an entire section to sports reports and statistics; a number of national weekly and monthly publications concentrate exclusively on sports. Special sporting events such as the Super Bowl are consistently among the most highly rated TV broadcasts, and several cable networks are devoted solely to sports twenty-four hours a day. Americans play sports trivia games, call sports telephone hotlines, and participate in a multibillion dollar sports gaming industry; they display team logos on t-shirts, sweatshirts, baseball caps, and countless other articles of clothing. Many colleges and universities capitalize on the prominence of their sports programs to increase enrollments and donations.

Sports can affect fans in surprisingly intense ways. We all probably know people whose moods fluctuate with the fortunes of their favorite team, who might "bleed Dodger blue," as they say. Indeed, entire cities rejoice when their team brings home a championship, and our national mood lifts when an American underdog takes a medal at the Olympics or when the "Dream Team" squashes an opponent. Given this obsession, it's no wonder that professional athletes are among our most revered—and highly paid—citizens.

How can we explain the popularity of professional sports? The essays in the first part of this chapter offer views about the role of sports in American life in general, including John Solomon's assessment of the challenges facing the business of professional sports and reporter Kate Rounds's analysis of the negligible status of women's athletics in a male-dominated sports culture. The essays in the second part focus on boxing, golf, and the newer "extreme" sports, and, by implication, the factors—physical ability, the influence of family and friends, climate and environment, even race and gender—that govern an individual's choice to participate in or follow a particular sport.

Obviously, sports can influence the way we speak and the way we feel, our notions of teamwork and individuality, success and failure, and male and female roles. From sports we learn how to deal with pressure, adversity, and physical pain and we discover models of grace, skill, and style. As you read the essays in this chapter, think of the sports you play and watch, of the athletes you admire, of the role sports play (or have played) in your life.

The Role of Sports in America

The Sports Market Is Looking Soggy

John D. Solomon

Huge, sprawling stadium complexes dominate the downtown areas of major U.S. cities. Most city dwellers, if they're not at the games, know to avoid the traffic generated around these stadiums when games are scheduled. In our homes on the weekends, broadcasts of sporting events dominate the major television networks' daytime programming. Even those of us who don't follow professional sports can't help knowing the names and faces of prominent athletes from the past and present—Kobe, Magic, Nomo, Deion, Babe, Tiger, A-Rod. Professional sports and their heroes constitute a central part of American life, in our hearts as well as in our pocketbooks: professional sports are big business. Some of this may be changing, however, as John Solomon warns in an article from the Business section of the New York Times.

Solomon's title sums up his article's main point. While enumerating a number of factors impacting the current—and future—financial status of professional sports, Solomon warns that the business of professional sports is facing growing challenges. These challenges include an overall decline in attendance at sporting events, a decrease in the prices television networks will pay for sports' broadcast rights because fewer TV sports viewers are lessening the broadcasts' profitability, and the threat of cable TV sports broadcasts fragmenting the viewing audience.

As you read, *think about your own interest in the four major sports on which Solomon focuses—football, baseball, basketball, and hockey. In your own experience and observation, is interest in these sports waning? If so, do you have ideas about the causes of declining interest?*

It's springtime, and the professional sports world seems to be in clover. After a season of record attendance, National Football League teams are spending much of what they took in, signing new players in the college draft this weekend. In the National Hockey League, where teams are dueling in playoffs, games also drew an unprecedented number of fans this year. Major League Baseball is bragging that corporate sponsorships are up 30 percent, and despite the worst advertising market in 30 years, the National Basketball Association signed a record $4.6 billion, six-year television contract in January. 1

But other signs suggest that the four major league sports may, in fact, be wilting. 2

In recent months, advertisers, networks, cable operators, and governments have started to balk at spending unlimited amounts on sports. The stadium building cycle is over. Team expansion has halted, and baseball may shrink by two teams. High ticket prices and labor unrest—baseball players may well strike again this season—have damaged the relationship with the public and led to an erosion of the fan base. And many in the younger generation seem more interested in spending their time and dollars in other pursuits—sometimes playing video games about sports—than in watching what happens on the field. 3

"It was an oversaturated, mature market in a growth economy," said Rick Burton, the director of the Warsaw Sports Marketing Center at the University of Oregon. "It has taken this hiccup in the economy to recognize the saturation and maturity." 4

The April 8 bankruptcy filing by KirchMedia of Germany, attributable in part to its heavy spending on TV sports rights, raised only more worries—perhaps dampening the willingness to spend money on sports in the United States. 5

"We have to market like we are under attack, which in reality we are," said Mark Cuban, the owner of the Dallas Mavericks basketball team and an Internet radio billionaire. "Every media and out-of-home entertainment business wants our customers." 6

Professional sports have repeatedly shown a Michael Jordan–like ability to defy economic gravity—the average resale value of major league teams in the last decade has nearly quintupled in football, tripled in hockey and baseball, and more than doubled in basketball, says Moag & Company, a Baltimore investment bank that focuses on sports. Yet, like its famous player, the industry may now have to make some concessions to age. 7

Teams can no longer rely on network television contracts that will routinely double, or on average ticket price increases that have outpaced the Consumer Price Index. 8

Much of the dazzling growth in sports team revenue over the last two decades has come from the television networks' heavy spending on broadcast rights. In 1986, the four sports took in an average of $744 million in broadcast rights fees, according to Moag. That grew to $1.5 billion in 1991 and $3.5 billion [in 2001]. 9

But the networks are now an uncertain source of revenue. 10

These days, even Rupert Murdoch—a man who used an NFL contract to build a fledgling Fox into the fourth network in 1994—is sounding a different note. After writing off $909 million in sports contracts in February, Mr. Murdoch, chairman of the News Corporation, 11 which owns Fox, cautioned that rights fees "have gone beyond an economic level."

A recent Morgan Stanley report called potential total losses from sports "staggering" and predicted that ABC, CBS, and Fox would each lose up to $1.3 billion on sports rights over the next four years. It expects the three to lose $2.5 billion to $2.6 billion over the life of their eight-year, $18.3 billion NFL contract rights. NBC, a unit of General Electric, has backed away from bidding on sports rights contracts because of their cost; for NBC, Morgan projects a deficit from sports, excluding the Olympics, of $351 million. The networks declined to comment on those estimates, but Viacom's CBS, for one, has said it is not losing money from sports. 12

So far, the leagues remain confident. "That note has been sounded before: The rights fees will never go higher," said Greg Aiello, a spokesman for the NFL, "and they go higher." 13

History, of course, backs him up. As Yogi Berra might say, TV sports contracts are such a bad deal, there always seems to be someone who wants them. 14

Paul Tagliabue, the NFL commissioner, said he expected that the league would keep "the mass" of games on broadcast television when the next contract comes up in 2006. 15

But whether the league can do so, and get anywhere near the 100 percent increase it received last time, is unclear at best. The NBA's new contract with ESPN and ABC of Walt Disney and with Turner Sports of AOL Time Warner may be a harbinger. The rights increase was more modest—25 percent—and will put 127 games on basic cable next year, compared with 79 this year. The NBA will also put 96 games on a planned NBA–AOL cable channel. The games broadcast on network television will drop to 15 from 30. 16

Though cable's combination of subscriber fees and advertising may provide a more lucrative and reliable revenue stream than broadcast TV rights fees, it has presented sports with a new risk—fewer people may watch, particularly if they have to pay. "The economic underpinning of pro sports has been free television," said a longtime sports executive who spoke on condition of anonymity. Sports team owners, he said, "risk marginalizing the sport by moving it off broadcast." 17

David Stern, the NBA commissioner, is not worried about the shift to cable because many people already get their sports that way. He points out that 84 percent of Americans have cable or satellite service. "We understand that the viewing habits of our fans have changed dramatically," he said. 18

But how much cable subscribers will be willing to pay for sports is unknown, as seen in a battle royal in New York in the past few 19 months between Cablevision Systems, the largest cable operator in the metropolitan area, and the New York Yankees. Cablevision has refused to pay the team's new Yankees Entertainment and Sports network, or YES, $72 million—or $2 a subscriber a month—and include it in the basic package. The fight may foreshadow more such disputes.

"I think we could be getting to the breaking point," said Jerald L. Kent, co-founder and former chief executive of Charter Communications, a cable operator. He said that if cable companies included such costs in the monthly bill, "consumers are not going to continue to pay, particularly those who aren't watching sports." 20

Cablevision has offered to sell YES, which is carrying 130 Yankee games this season, only to subscribers who want it, the way it markets HBO and other premium channels. 21

But questions about a pay-TV future for sports have also been raised by recent events abroad. 22

KirchMedia just defaulted on its $329 million annual rights fee to the Bundesliga soccer league in Germany because it could not sign up enough customers to cover the contracts. In Britain, ITV Digital, a pay-television venture owned by Granada and Carlton Communications, could not pay a $450 million soccer contract. In South America, the Pan American Sports Network filed for bankruptcy protection March 1 for similar reasons. 23

The fallout from the YES–Cablevision confrontation, however, has also underscored the strength of sports as programming. In areas where the Yankees have been blacked out, DirecTV satellite service sales have risen more than 20 percent, said Bob Marsocci, a DirecTV spokesman. "Sports fans are our most loyal customers," he said. 24

Sports industry leaders, meanwhile, point out that sports content helped launch some of the country's first cable systems and is a major reason consumers buy satellite service. "The one thing we have learned is that sports drives new technology," said Mark Lazarus, president of Turner Sports. "That trend will continue given its live nature and the fanaticism of viewers. Their appetite will lead the way. Is it Internet? Pay per view? We don't know. But sports will be the driver." 25

The changes in sports distribution, however, have not been lost on advertisers. Many are taking a hard look at how much they will pay to pitch products in a more splintered marketplace. 26

According to Anheuser-Busch, the biggest spender on sports advertising, the leagues and networks have not fully adjusted their expectations on advertising, thinking they deserve the same premium even if ratings are falling. "We are concerned with the cost relative to the return that we get from sports," said Tony Ponturo, Anheuser-Busch's vice president for global media and sports marketing. "We are 27 telling the leagues and networks we won't automatically underwrite you as you drive up the costs. We're only going to pay what you deliver."

Viewership for all four sports has dropped—the NFL, the highest-rated TV sport, has suffered a 13 percent drop in ratings over the last five years, according to Nielsen Media Research. ESPN is profitable, but Nielsen says that the percentage of homes watching it has fallen to 1.9 percent of those with access, from 2.6 percent 10 years ago. 28

Despite the falling ratings, league officials say the multichannel landscape makes sports more valuable for advertising, particularly because sports attracts the young male audience many advertisers desire. "Sports is unique," said Tim Brosnan, executive vice president for business at Major League Baseball. "It's the only place that aggregates viewers. Everything else is a one-trick pony." 29

To Ted Leonsis, an owner of the Washington Wizards basketball team and Washington Capitals hockey team, sports programming is also the best defense against technology that lets viewers screen out ads and watch what they want whenever they want: "In a world with 900 channels and TiVo, no one wanted to tape the Super Bowl," he said. "They wanted to watch it live." 30

But in a sign that the sports business is worried about alienating advertisers, it is giving them more ways to advertise. "Sponsors are pushing harder," said John Galloway, Pepsi's sports marketing director. "And leagues are working harder to add value and measurable results." Major League Baseball, for example, let Pepsi sponsor the first pitch of each World Series game last year. Team sports may thus move closer to a European sponsorship model, where commercials are everywhere—corporate logos on team uniforms, for example. 31

Other affiliations, like stadium naming, are going through an overdue market correction, said David M. Carter, the founder and principal of the Sports Business Group, a consulting firm in Los Angeles. Enron Field, the TWA Dome, and PsiNet Stadium are a few examples of questionable spending by financially troubled businesses. And some arenas cannot find sponsors with deep pockets. The Louisiana Superdome in New Orleans, for example, which has been trying to sell naming rights for $3 million to $5 million, just cut the price to $2 million to $2.5 million. "This shakeout is forcing business to qualify and quantify why they are in sports," he said. "Companies were not applying the same rational business decision-making process." 32

The sports industry will have to do without the sizzle and revenue spike of new stadiums themselves, which have been a growth engine the past two decades. Almost three-fourths of major professional teams already have a new home or one in the pipeline, said 33

John A. Moag, Jr., the chief executive of Moag & Company. In New York, Mayor Michael R. Bloomberg's decision to delay indefinitely development of two new baseball stadiums underscores the public sector's reluctance to finance any more.

That means teams will have to find ways to squeeze new rev- 34
enue from existing facilities. For example, the Southwest Sports Group, the Dallas sports and entertainment company that owns the Texas Rangers, and the Anschutz Entertainment Group, owner of the Los Angeles Kings, are planning to use their arenas as anchors for major real estate and entertainment developments.

Another part of the sports boom—expansion within leagues— 35
has also run its course. After the new Houston Texans kick off this fall in the NFL, no major league sport plans to open new franchises in the United States anytime soon.

An underlying problem is that customers are just less interested; 36
many are alienated by the huge salaries and boorish behavior of some players. The ESPN Sports Poll, a periodic fan survey, has found that over the last five years, the fan base of all four major team sports has dropped at least 5 percent and that significantly fewer fans describe themselves as "avid." Further, sports' share of the licensing products business slipped to 16 percent from 19 percent from 1996 to 2000, according to the Sporting Goods Manufacturers Association.

Stemming the erosion is particularly important among the 37
younger crowd, which has many more recreation choices—from X Games to Xbox. "A whole generation is having more fun playing John Madden electronically than watching him on television," said Mr. Burton at the University of Oregon.

Richard Luker, president of the Leisure Intelligence Group, a 38
sports consulting firm in East Lansing, Mich., called the failure to attract young new fans a "demographic crisis for the sports business."

Teams hope technological innovations will add to enthusiasm. 39
For example, Gary Bettman, the NHL commissioner, said high-definition television would provide a better view of hockey's fast action.

Many in the business are also concerned about the economic 40
demographics of fans who attend games. "If the prices only allow 5 percent of the public to have that live experience, aren't you going to lose the other 95 percent?" asked Timothy J. Leiweke, the president of the Anschutz Entertainment Group. "That's very, very dangerous for sports."

Since 1997, each of the major sports has lost more than 7 percent 41
of its fan base earning $30,000 or less, according to ESPN, while the number of fans earning at least $100,000 is up at least 30 percent.

Ticket price inflation has slowed—and in basketball this year, the 42
average ticket price fell 2.3 percent, according to the Team Marketing

Report, a research group in Chicago. But to Mr. Leiweke, a more fundamental change may be needed. "The owners and players are going to have to sit down and figure out how to solve this," he said.

That means, for one, that management and labor must agree on a cost structure that keeps the playing field profitable for teams and level for the leagues. Collective bargaining agreements that link labor costs to revenue explain why NFL franchises are largely in the black, and why the NBA will break even this year after several years of losses. Yet, despite record revenue, the hockey and baseball leagues lack such links and many teams are losing money. 43

Jay Cross, the president of the New York Jets, said: "Sports may have to make a significant change in the model. And since so many people have to buy into the change, it might not be that easy." 44

Team sports is the rare industry where the stronger businesses require healthy competitors, but maintaining that balance is hard when owners have different financial capacities and expectations. 45

Robert J. Tilliss, head of the global sports advisory group at J. P. Morgan Chase, says he is bullish on the industry because it attracts successful entrepreneurs like Mr. Cuban and Mr. Leonsis. But their aggressiveness has another side. "It is a fundamental problem that the best interest of individual owners is not always in the best interest of the league," Mr. Tilliss said. 46

Even in the NFL, viewed as the model of revenue sharing among teams, Robert Tisch, a co-owner of the New York Giants, has expressed concern that the Washington Redskins' nonshared cash flow from their new stadium puts his team at a competitive disadvantage. Financial balance among the teams gives all teams an equal chance to win. That has helped create football's connection with the public and has ultimately made the business successful. 47

As Jerry Jones, owner of the Dallas Cowboys, said at a recent conference: "They only throw ticker-tape parades for war heroes, astronauts, and people who win ballgames." 48

Examining the Text

1. Summarize positions for and against moving TV sports broadcasts from the major networks (ABC, NBC, CBS, FOX) to cable channels like ESPN or others.

2. Describe some of the reasons cited in this piece for declining interest in sports. Based on your own experiences and observations, can you offer some additional reasons why interest in professional sports seems to be waning?

3. Explain the paradox that appears in the last five paragraphs of Solomon's piece: how does business competition between owners of professional sports teams undermine sporting competition between the teams themselves?

For Group Discussion

In groups, brainstorm about other reasons for the declining interest in professional sports, beyond those mentioned by Solomon, or expanding upon those he only touches upon, such as the perception that professional athletes are greedy or rude.

Writing Suggestion

Solomon mentions a number of problems threatening the financial health of professional sports, and most of these problems have generated a lot of discussion in newspapers, magazines, the Internet, and sports shows on television. Choose one of these problems and conduct some research to help you narrow a focus to one particular aspect of that problem. For example, in examining skyrocketing player's salaries, you could focus on the controversy over Alex Rodriguez's record-breaking $252 million contract with the Texas Rangers baseball team. Write a paper in which you report the various viewpoints offered in different sources.

The Next Generation in Sport: Y

Choonghoon Lim and Douglas Michele Turco

In contrast to the journalistic style of the previous article, in which John Solomon touched briefly on many of the financial challenges facing professional sports today, this essay represents a scholarly, in-depth examination of one aspect of that challenge—changes in the demographic characteristics of the potential audience for professional sports. From the perspective of sports marketing, Lim and Turco analyze census and consumer data to develop a picture of the group of consumers called Generation Y. Marketers and demographers use "Generation Y" as a designation for the large numbers of people born between 1979 and 1994. The sheer numbers in this generation, its members' large amounts of disposable cash, and its influence on other groups make Generation Y a very important target group for marketers.

Lim and Turco's analysis of the data on Generation Y aims to assess its members' interests and behavior related to leisure and sports activities. What they find is that Generation Y participates less in sports overall than any previous generation, and they attribute this decline to a decrease in "participation in traditional fitness-related activities."

Keep in mind the original purpose of this article—to inform sports marketers about the interests of a group of consumers in order to more effectively sell this group sports-related products. While the authors present an informative perspective on current interest in sports, ***as you read,*** *notice the ways in which marketers must generalize about large, diverse groups of people and their complex desires, attitudes and behaviors, in order to...well...exploit them.*

INTRODUCTION

Leisure and sport marketers have devoted considerable attention to baby boomers because of their shear size and spending power. Home fitness equipment and videos, all-inclusive resort and cruise vacations, casinos, and sport utility vehicles are some of the products and services targeted at baby boomers. In 1995, baby boomers were the largest U.S. birth cohorts, 72 million and 30 percent of the population. However, in next ten years, the number of boomers may be down by more than 1 million people, and by 2025 they will total 65 million, comprising 19 percent of the population (Beck, 1997). 1

After declining for 15 years, the number of teens is on the rise, growing at a faster rate than the overall U.S. population. In 1995, there were 29 million people aged 12 to 19 in the United States, about 1 million more than in 1994. The U.S. teen population will continue to expand through the year 2010, as the children of baby boomers bring the total number of 12- to 19-year-olds to 34.9 million (U.S. Bureau of the Census, 1999). 2

Americans born between 1979 and 1994 have been labeled by marketers and demographers as Generation Y. Generation Yers, also referred to as the "Eco-boomers," "Millennium Generation," or "Generation M," differ significantly from past cohorts. Generation Yers are as young as five and as old as 20, with the largest slice still a decade away from adolescence. At 78 million strong, they are more than three times the size of Generation X. 3

CHARACTERISTICS OF GENERATION Y

There are reasons why Generation Y is an important population cohort, deserving considerable attention from sport marketers. The first is money. Teens spent $63 billion of their own money in 1994, according to estimates by Teenage Research Unlimited (TRU). Teenage boys spend an average of $44 a week of their own money, while girls spend $34 (Zollo, 1997). This group is asserting significant impact on their families' purchasing preferences. Their influence on household 4 spending amounted to $246.1 billion in 1997, an increase of 10.3 percent from the previous year (Rosenthal, 1998). Generation Y accounts for 46 percent of adult spending on audio equipment and 48 percent on athletic shoes (Rosenthal, 1998). One segment of this group, the 41.4 million kids between ages eight and 17, control or influence the spending of $120 billion a year (Cullen, 1997). They have a higher incremental allowance from their parents, and with the growth in the service sector of the U.S. economy during the later 1990s, they are able to secure jobs easily and at rising minimum wages (Rosenthal, 1998).

Teenagers are also trendsetters, not only for one another but also 5
for the population at large. Younger kids look up to teens to identify and adopt the latest fashion, and adults often observe teens to determine what is "in." The distinctive buying habits they display today will likely follow them as they enter the high-spending years of young adulthood (Neuborne, 1999). As a group, they enjoy a greater level of financial security and material comfort than previous generations (Romeo, 1999). One in nine high school students has a credit card co-signed by a parent, and many will take on extensive debt to finance college. Generation Y will be the primary consumer group in subsequent decades. In a few years, today's teens will be out of college and spending for their first cars, their first homes, and their first mutual funds.

Beck (1997) described several economic, social, political, cultural, 6
and environmental changes impacting Generation Y are described below:

- Approximately 60% of children under the age of six have mothers who work outside the home, compared to 18% in 1960. Nearly 61% of U.S. children aged three to five are attending preschool, compared with 38% in 1970.
- Nearly 60% of households with children aged seven or younger have personal computers.
- More than one-third of elementary-school students nationwide are black or Hispanic, compared with 22% in 1974. The U.S. Bureau of the Census projects that "minorities" will make up the majority of the U.S. population by 2050.
- Approximately 15% of U.S. births in recent years were to foreign-born mothers, with origins so diverse that more than 100 different languages are spoken in the school systems of New York City, Chicago, Los Angeles and Fairfax County, VA.
- Nearly one of three births in the early 1990s was to an unmarried woman. With approximately one in three marriages end-

ing in divorce, that means a significant portion of this generation will spend at least part of childhood in a single-parent home.

- One-quarter of children under age six are living in poverty, defined as cash income of less than $15,141 for a family of four.

Changing societal and family structures, combined with advances in technology, will be forces shaping the development of Generation Y (Radice, 1998). The majority of Generation Yers live in households where their mothers work full-time. With divorce reaching new heights, many live in non-traditional family structures where there may or may not have been another parent present. One in four lives in a single-parent household. Three in four have working mothers (Neuborne, 1999). Multiculturalism is another characteristics of the group. They have grown up in racially diverse and mixed socioeconomic groups, much more so than preceding generations (Coeyman, 1998). One in four is not Caucasian and more than one-third of elementary school students are African American or Hispanic (Neuborne, 1999; Lewis, 1997). 7

To summarize this section, it is important that sport and leisure marketers understand Generation Y so that they may effectively plan services tailored to their economic, social, emotional, and developmental characteristics. In the following section, the leisure and sport consumer behaviors of Generation Y will be discussed. 8

LEISURE PREFERENCES

Reading is a preferred leisure activity among Generation Y, and publishers have responded with an abundance of titles and series for them. Annual sales of books for young readers have more than doubled to $1.4 billion since 1987 (Beck, 1997). Bookstores have become what local libraries used to be, while libraries are becoming more like college resource centers. 9

Generation Y is also driving the educational-software industry, which has grown to a $600 million business from ground zero in 1990 (Beck, 1997). Baby boomer parents, seeking to give their kids an educational edge, are also fueling the booming business of "educational playthings." National retail chains sell interactive, multi-media games targeting parents who can't spend enough time with their children, and when they do, want to do something that will help them go to a prestigious college or university. 10

Like their parents, members of Generation Y believe that they are pressed for time. Afternoons and weekends spent "just hanging out" by preceding teens, have now been taken over by chess clubs, soccer leagues, gymnastics lessons, and piano recitals for Generation Y. With so little perceived free time, kids today may not have enough opportunity to create, experiment, and invent new things. Creativity takes time and time is being spent on other things. As an example of the market's response to this time compression, do-it-yourself supplier Builder's Square offers children weekend classes on building birdhouses, toys, and gardens. 11

COOL RULES

While it may appear that image is everything to Generation Y, a product's quality actually dictates its appeal or "coolness." Reese (1997) describes the importance of "coolness" to U.S. teenagers. 12

> ... cool isn't just an adjective; it's a comprehensive set of life-guiding concepts. "Cool" is shorthand for all the qualities necessary for a teen's social survival: acceptance, popularity, fun, and success. In the brutally simple world of adolescents, being thought of as uncool by the social group to which you aspire is not simply a matter of not making the grade, or even being rejected: it is the mark of The Loser.

Marketing "cool" is more difficult than it may seem, and leisure marketers will find it hard to trick Generation Y into buying something that is labeled as "cool" when it is not. Determining what is (and is not) cool is confounded for marketers by the relative appeal assigned by Generation Y to a product based on its popularity or novelty. Little-known products may be too novel for teens to purchase, and some products or services that are extremely popular may turn off Generation Y because they are too common (Ebenkamp, 1999). 13

ELECTRONIC MEDIA CONSUMPTION

Generation Y has been reared in a society heavily influenced by popular media, more so than their preceding generations. Movies, television, music, electronic magazines and games are pervasive in their environments. Nearly 90 percent of U.S. teens have a computer at home and about half have access to the Internet (Omelia, 1998). The Internet seemed to be a far-fetched notion only five years ago. Today, 14 use of the World Wide Web and electronic mail by Generation Y is as common as the telephone. In the near future, lap-top and hand-held computers rather than spiral notebooks will be in their school backpacks.

Members of Generation Y are developing their interests in a 15
world of technological learning opportunities through computers, video and an array of cable options. With instant electronic access to global communities, Generation Y strongly identifies with each other and shares a "global inclusivism" as to race, gender, religion and state of the environment. They wear similar clothes, listen to similar music, play similar computer games and enjoy the same recreational activities (Omelia, 1998).

While Generation Xers have been hard to reach by television, 16
Generation Y is more influenced by this medium. American children view 500,000 television commercials between the ages of three and 18. In a normal day (6 a.m. to midnight), the average teen will spend 63 percent of his or her total media time with the television (Omelia, 1998). Radio takes up an estimated 28 percent of total media time for teens. Magazines and newspapers are placed at six and three percent respectively (Rosenthal, 1998).

Time, space, and the social bonds that build families and com- 17
munities are totally different for Generation Y than previous generations (Omelia, 1998). "The electronic community never sleeps and knows no physical boundaries." With consumers focusing so much on their personal ideas of value, advertisers and marketers will need to develop programs that involve one-to-one relationships with individual consumers. The Internet will be an increasingly important tool in developing and maintaining that relationship with Generation Y (Briones, 1998). Computers and the Internet have spawned interactive electronic marketing plans (called "e-marketing") involving a range of promotional techniques, ordering operations, and prospective consumer databases (Mulhern, 1997). While the Internet is still not a primary shopping venue (being a credit card medium), it may very well be in the future, and presently serves as a key format by which teens can explore new products and trends (Omelia, 1998). Therefore, a well-designed Web site may be crucial for any company hoping to reach the under-18 consumer.

SPORT PARTICIPATION PATTERNS

Generation Y is the only generation to experience a decline in overall 18
sports participation, basically due to declining participation in traditional fitness-related activities. The number of teenagers participating in

physical fitness activity has declined by 21% since 1987 (SMGA, 1998c). In 1996, 20% of all 12–17 year olds participated "frequently" in some fitness-related activity, compared with 25.5% in 1987. Furthermore, from 1987 to 1996, the number of 12–17 year olds who participated in any sport, fitness, or team activity, on a "frequent" basis, increased by only 2.9% to 13 million youth. Among youth 12–17, team sports participation was down across the board. Soccer and softball both saw 17% declines, (hard surface) volleyball dropped 14%, ice hockey was off 11%, followed by tackle football (−10%), baseball (−3%), and basketball (−2%). Among youth 6–11, participation in baseball suffered a 13% decline, softball was off 10% and volleyball lost 2% from 1996 totals (SGMA, 1998b). A possible explanation for this decline may be the status of K–12 physical education. Mandatory physical education in grades K–12 has been relegated to an elective in most school curricula. Most school districts with severe financial constraints have reduced or eliminated extra curricular activities including clubs, intramural and interscholastic sports. As a result, youth possess fewer physical recreation skills, experiences, and [are] less fit (Turco, 1996).

19 As revealed in Table 2, the three sports experiencing the greatest increases in youth participation include "In-line Skating," "Mountain Biking," and "Free Weights" (SGMA, 1998a). Also, among young Yers (6–11 years old), soccer participation rose 17%, followed by basketball (+16%) and tackle football (+5%). Basketball remains the most popular youth team sport in America. The National Federation of State High School Associations reported that 991,500 children played on high school teams in 1996, ranking it first in high school participation (SGMA, 1997). Over 23 million children aged 6–17 played basketball in 1995, a 35% increase over the 18.8 million players found when the survey began in 1987. Generation Yers 6–11 years of age are leading the "hoop-it-up" movement. The

Table 1 Ten Most Popular Youth Sports in the United States, 1996

Sport Activity	Level of Frequency	Total
1. In-line skating	25+ days/year	7,980
2. Basketball	52+ days/year	5,812
3. Slow-pitch softball	25+ days/year	3,547
4. Touch football	25+ days/year	3,318
5. Volleyball	25+ days/year	2,260
6. Baseball	52+ days/year	2,638
7. Running/jogging	100+ days/year	2,532
8. Freshwater fishing (including fly fishing)	25+ days/year	2,187
9. Soccer	52+ days/year	2,162
10. Billiards	25+ days/year	2,149

Source: SGMA/American Sport Data

Table 2 Top Three Fastest-Growing Youth Sports in the U.S. (Ages 6–17; based on "frequent" participation)

Sport Activity	Level of Frequency	1992 (000)	1996 (000)	% Gain
1. In-line Skating	25+ days/year	1,893	7,890	+316.8
2. Mountain Biking	52+ days/year	362	761	+110.2
3. Free Weights	100+ days/year	958	1,461	+52.5

Source: SGMA/American Sports Data (1997)

SGMA study (1997) reported that small ball and adjustable height goals have accelerated participation growth in the sub-segment and would continue to do so over the next several years.

Generation Y and their parents are behind the growth of youth 20
soccer in the U.S. The success of World Cup '94 has convinced many corporations to invest in soccer's future by supporting youth programs and the birth of a new U.S. professional league. Both Nike and Reebok committed substantial promotional dollars to the sport and have focused the need among soccer specialty suppliers to become more involved in nurturing the sport (SGMA, 1998a). Other favorable factors, such as the success of Major League Soccer (MLS), the effect of Title IX on high school and college programs, and expanded media coverage of the gold-medal winning U.S. Olympic women's team will provide further impetus for growth.

GIRL POWER!

Shopping provides many young consumers with a sense of freedom, 21
power, and socialization. A recent study found that 55% of Americans

Table 3 Youth Team Sports Rankings, 1996

Participants 12–17 (000)		Participants 6–11 (000)	
Sport Activity	**Number of Participants**	**Sport Activity**	**Number of Participants**
Basketball	12,409	Basketball	11,014
Volleyball	7,493	Soccer	8,646
Soccer	4,981	Baseball	4,400
Football (Tackle)	4,879	Softball	4,243
Softball	4,509	Volleyball	3,767
Baseball	4,321	Football (Tackle)	2,740
Ice Hockey	622	Ice Hockey	508

Source: SGMA/American Sport Data (1997)

ages 21 to 62 "enjoy shopping"; down from 58% in 1993 (Zollo, 1998). In contrast, 88% of girls between 13 and 17 say they just "love to shop." Teens make nearly 40% more trips to the mall than do other shoppers, and they often spend their own money. The Bureau of Labor Statistics reported that 41% of teens, ages 16 to 18 worked full- or part-time (Rosenthal, 1998). Including jobs not recorded by the government (i.e., babysitting), three-quarters of teens earn at least some money from working (Zollo, 1998).

The number of high school girls who participated in team sports 22
has risen exponentially since the enactment of Title IX (civil rights legislation requiring equal educational opportunities for women and girls) in 1972. More recently, girls playing soccer has increased by 55%, fast-pitch softball by 37%, and volleyball by 22% (SGMA, 1998c).

Shoham, Rose, Kropp, and Kahle (1998) contend that the pur- 23
chasing power of young women has led a variety of traditionally male-oriented industries, including sport, to re-direct their marketing efforts toward women. One sport business that understands girl power is Nike Inc. Their Web site for teens is called "Play Like a Girl." On the site is an essay by Karli, a 15-year-old girl in power: "When my mom was younger, if someone said you play (or run or throw) like a girl, it was considered an insult. But I think it's like a compliment now. . . . So when someone says I play like a girl, I ask which one? Lisa Leslie or Dawn Staley or Mia Hamm?" (Nike, 1998). Women and girls account for nearly 25% of Nike's product sales.

Generation Y has grown up in a more media-saturated, brand 24
conscious world than their parents. They respond to ads differently, and they prefer to encounter those ads in different places (Neuborne, 1999; Radice, 1998). Teenagers are fundamentally media savvy, and they understand that commercials and advertisements exist to sell product (Omelia, 1998). The old-style advertising that works well with boomers, ads that push a slogan, an image, and a feeling, will not be effective with Generation Y (Neuborne, 1999). The keys for reaching this group will be sophistication, sense of humor, and honesty, and it will be hard to fool them (Coeyman, 1998). In the past, marketers could target teens through demographics, age, income, or place of residence as key barometers of their consumer interests. Now, psychographic elements such as music tastes, life aspirations, environmental and social awareness are more telling indicators of which brands can be linked to Generation Y (Rosenthal, 1998). Sport marketers who can attach their product or brand to a consumer's values system rather than the expression of one have a better chance of outliving fads. The marketing strategies used for ESPN's X-Games is an example of a successful, integrated sport marketing campaign aimed squarely at Generation Y.

SUMMARY

The U.S. teen population began to decline in 1976, after the last baby 25
boomers aged out of their teen years. After 16 years of continuous decline, the teenage population began to increase in 1992. There are roughly 57 million Americans under age 15, and more than 20 million in the peak years between four and eight. The number of children and teens could run to 82 million by 2015. In 30 years, the under-30 population and the middle-aged baby boomlet together will make up the majority of Americans.

This study described the consumer characteristics of Generation 26
Y and provided several marketing strategies for them. It was found that Generation Y differs from other age groups by their preferences, attitudes, and sport participation patterns. It was suggested that different marketing approaches were necessary to lure this large and influential consumer market. The information presented may lead to a better understanding of this generation, and assist those with the challenging task of providing sport opportunities to teenagers.

REFERENCES CITED

Beck, M. The next big population bulge: Generation Y shows its might. *The Wall Street Journal* (February 3, 1997).

Briones, M. G. (1998). Ad biz faces technology, Gen Y and competition. *Marketing News, 3*(25), 2–10.

Coeyman, M. (1998). Do you know Y? *Restaurant Business, 97*(6), 38–42.

Cullen, L. R. (1997). Ride the echo boom to stock profits. *Money, 26*(7), 98–104.

Ebenkamp, B. (1999). The conundrum of cool (marketing to young people). *Brandweek, 40*(5), 32–33.

Lewis, L. (1997). Generation 'Y'. *Progressive Grocer, 76*(3), 18.

Mulhern, C. (1997). Junior boomers: Who's next? The Net generation. *Entrepreneur, 25*(12), 14–17.

Neuborne, E. (1999). Generation Y. *Business Week, 36*(16): 80–88.

Nike, Inc. (1998). Home page [available on-line]: *www.nike.com.*

Omelia, J. (1998). Understanding generation Y: A look at the next wave of US Consumers. *Drug & Cosmetic Industry, 163*(6), 90–92.

Radice, C. (1998). Targeting tomorrow's consumers. *Progressive Grocer, 77*(7), 55–58.

Reese, S. (1997). The quality of cool. *Marketing Tools, 3*(6), 27.

Romeo, P. (1999). Yo, operators. *Restaurant Business, 98*(4), 6.

Rosenthal, N. (1998). The boom tube. *Media week, 8*(20), 44–52.

Shoham, A., Rose, G. M., Kropp, F., & Kahle, L. R. (1998). Generation X women: A sports consumption community perspective. *Sport Marketing Quarterly, 6*(4): 23–34.

Sporting Goods Manufacturers Association & American Sport Data. (1997). *Youth Movement in Sport.* North Palm Beach, FL: SGMA.

Sporting Goods Manufacturers Association. (1998a). *1998 State of the Industry Report.* North Palm Beach, FL: SGMA.

Sporting Goods Manufacturers Association. (1998b). *America's Top 25 Participation Sports.* North Palm Beach, FL: SGMA.

Sporting Goods Manufacturers Association, & Soccer Industry Council of America. (1998c). *The 1998 National Soccer Participation Survey.* North Palm Beach, FL: SGMA.

Turco, D. M. (1996). The X factor: Marketing sport to Generation X. *Sport Marketing Quarterly, 5*(1): 21–26.

U.S. Bureau of the Census. (1999). *Statistical abstracts.* Washington, DC: Government Printing Office.

Zollo, P. (1997). Wise up to teens: Insights into marketing and advertising to teenagers. *Adolescence, 32*(125), 250.

Examining the Text

1. Why, according to the authors, is Generation Y an important population for sports marketers to understand?

2. While Lim and Turco report that *overall* sports participation and participation in "traditional fitness-related activities" is declining in Generation Y, their data show that participation in *particular* sports and fitness-related activities is declining in some instances, and increasing in others. Discuss which sports and activities show declines and which show increases. Offer some ideas for why this particular generation may be more or less interested in particular activities.

3. Discuss the reasons the authors assert that girls are an important segment of Generation Y for sports marketers.

4. The data provided by Lim and Turco show declines in Generation Y's overall sports participation as well as participation in "traditional fitness-related activities." They state that declining sports participation is caused by declines in "traditional fitness-related activities" (18). What evidence do they provide to support their assertion of this cause-and-effect relationship? What do you think about their logic?

For Group Discussion

Imagine that you and your group members are advertising executives. You have been hired by a manufacturer of sports products to design an ad campaign targeting Generation Y. Use points from Lim and

Turco's article—as well as from your own knowledge of this population—to plan an approach that will appeal to Generation Y. You will have to first decide what kind of product you are trying to sell: perhaps you represent a major league baseball team and you're trying to attract more Gen Y fans to the team's games; perhaps you're selling athletic style clothing; or you might be marketing a performance enhancing drink for a major soft-drink manufacturer.

Designate a group note-taker who will record the general features you all believe your ad campaign should incorporate, from placement of the ads (Internet, print, TV, billboards), to their contents (sports figures, dialogue, music, designs, logos, slogans, etc.).

Writing Suggestion

While Lim and Turco note Generation Y's declining participation in sports-related fitness activities, they don't express an opinion about it (other than an implied one regarding its negative impact on sports marketers, of course). Using this article as a resource, write an essay in which you argue that this decline is likely to have a particular type of effect on individuals and American culture as a whole. To do this, you'll need to consider *both* the problems and the benefits of sports for *both* individuals and American culture.

Why Men Fear Women's Teams

Kate Rounds

Kate Rounds is a freelance writer and a contributor to Ms. *magazine, where this essay originally appeared. She argues here that female athletes have very few opportunities in the world of professional sports, and that women's team sports in particular are faced with what amounts to complete neglect in the media. Since professional sports are big business, if women's sports don't draw the fans and the money, then there's little hope that their professional leagues will last. College sports are similarly male-dominated, although Title IX requires colleges to devote equivalent resources to men's and women's athletic programs. Rounds's essay reminds us that when we discuss popular professional and collegiate sports, we're almost always referring to men's sports, and that sexual bias and gender stereotypes are still strong.*

Rounds contrasts the failure of a number of professional women's leagues (basketball, volleyball, and baseball) in the United States with the success of such enterprises in Europe, Japan, and elsewhere. The question, then, is why Americans fail to support talented female athletes in all but a few sports. Rounds ultimately concludes that the failure of women's professional sports reveals a "deep-rooted sexual bias and homophobia" in our culture, and that we haven't yet fully accepted a notion of femininity that incorporates power, athletic skill, and female camaraderie.

Before you read, *think back to the essays earlier in this chapter. To what extent do the economic problems discussed by Solomon apply to or affect professional women's sports? How might characteristics of Generation Y, as reported by Lim and Turco, impact the outlook for women's sports? Note also that Rounds's essay was written before the introduction of the WNBA in 1997; to what extent are her conclusions about gender discrimination still true today?*

Picture this. You're flipping through the channels one night, and you land on a local network, let's say ABC. And there on the screen is a basketball game. The players are sinking three-pointers, slam-dunking, and doing the usual things basketball players do. They're high-fiving each other, patting one another on the butt, and then sauntering to the locker room to talk about long-term contracts. 1

Now imagine that the players aren't men. They're women, big sweaty ones, wearing uniforms and doing their version of what guys thrive on—bonding. So far, this scene is a fantasy and will remain so until women's professional team sports get corporate sponsors, television exposure, arenas, fan support, and a critical mass of well-trained players. 2

While not enough fans are willing to watch women play traditional team sports, they love to watch women slugging it out on roller-derby rinks and in mud-wrestling arenas. Currently popular is a bizarre television spectacle called *American Gladiators,* in which women stand on pastel pedestals, wearing Lycra tights and brandishing weapons that look like huge Q-Tips. The attraction obviously has something to do with the "uniforms." 3

The importance of what women athletes wear can't be underestimated. Beach volleyball, which is played in the sand by bikini-clad women, rates network coverage, while traditional court volleyball can't marshal any of the forces that would make a women's pro league succeed. 4

It took a while, but women were able to break through sexist barriers in golf and tennis. Part of their success stemmed from the sports themselves—high-end individual sports that were born in the British Isles and flourished in country clubs across the U.S. The women wore skirts, makeup, and jewelry along with their wristbands and warm-up jackets. The corporate sponsors were hackers themselves, and the fan—even men—could identify with these women; a guy thought that 5 if he hit the ball enough times against the barn door, he too could play like Martina. And women's purses were equaling men's. In fact, number-one-ranked Steffi Graf's prize money for 1989 was $1,963,905 and number-one-ranked Stefan Edberg's was $1,661,491.

By contrast, women's professional team sports have failed spectacularly. Since the mid-seventies, every professional league—softball, basketball, and volleyball—has gone belly-up. In 1981, after a four-year struggle, the Women's Basketball League (WBL), backed by sports promoter Bill Byrne, folded. The league was drawing fans in a number of cities, but the sponsors weren't there. TV wasn't there, and nobody seemed to miss the spectacle of a few good women fighting for a basketball. 6

Or a volleyball, for that matter. Despite the success of bikini volleyball, an organization called MLV (Major League Volleyball) bit the dust in March of 1989 after nearly three years of struggling for sponsorship, fan support, and television exposure. As with pro basketball, there was a man behind women's professional volleyball, real estate investor Robert (Bat) Batinovich. Batinovich admits that, unlike court volleyball, beach volleyball has a lot of "visual T&A mixed into it." 7

What court volleyball does have, according to former MLV executive director Lindy Vivas, is strong women athletes. Vivas is assistant volleyball coach at San Jose State University. "The United States in general," she says, "has problems dealing with women athletes and strong, aggressive females. The perception is you have to be more aggressive in team sports than in golf and tennis, which aren't contact sports. Women athletes are looked at as masculine and get the stigma of being gay." 8

One former women's basketball promoter, who insists on remaining anonymous, goes further. "You know what killed women's sports?" he says. "Lesbians. This cost us in women's basketball. But I know there are not as many lesbians now unless I'm really blinded. We discourage it, you know. We put it under wraps." 9

People in women's sports spend a lot of time dancing around the "L" word, and the word "image" pops up in a way it never does in men's sports. Men can spit tobacco juice, smoke, and even scratch their testicles on national television and get away with it. 10

Bill Byrne, former WBL promoter, knows there isn't a whole lot women can get away with while they're beating each other out for a basketball. "In the old league," he says, "my partner, Mike Connors, from *Mannix*—his wife said, 'Let's do makeup on these kids.' And I knew that uniforms could be more attractive. We could tailor them so the women don't look like they're dragging a pair of boxer shorts down the floor." 11

The response from the athletes to this boy talk is not always outrage. "Girls in women's basketball now are so pretty," says Nancy 12

Lieberman-Cline. "They're image-conscious." The former Old Dominion star, who made headlines as Martina's trainer, played with the men's U.S. Basketball League, the Harlem Globe Trotters Tour (where she met husband Tim Cline), and with the Dallas Diamonds of the old WBL. "Everyone used to have short hair," she says. "Winning and playing was everything. I wouldn't think of using a curling iron. Now there are beautiful girls out there playing basketball."

Lieberman-Cline says she doesn't mind making the concession. 13
"It's all part of the process," she says. "You can't be defensive about everything."

Bill Byrne is so certain that women's professional basketball can 14
work that he's organized a new league, the Women's Pro Basketball League, Inc. (WPBL), set to open its first season shortly. Byrne talks fast and tough, and thinks things have changed for the better since 1981 when the old league went under. "Exposure is the bottom word," he says. "If you get plenty of TV exposure, you'll create household names, and you'll fill arenas. It takes the tube. But I'll get the tube this time because the game of TV has changed. You have cable now. You have to televise home games to show people a product."

There's no doubt that many athletes in the women's sports estab- 15
lishment are leery of fast-talking guys who try to make a buck off women's pro sports, especially when the women themselves don't profit from those ventures. In the old league, finances were so shaky that some players claim they were never paid.

"We weren't getting the gate receipts," says Lieberman-Cline. 16
"They'd expect 2,000, get only 400, and then they'd have to decide to pay the arena or pay the girls, and the girls were the last choice. There was a lot of mismanagement in the WBL, though the intent was good." She also has her doubts about the new league: "There are not enough things in place to make it happen, not enough owners, arenas, TV coverage, or players. It's going to take more than optimism to make it work."

Given the track record of women's professional team sports in 17
this country, it's not surprising that the national pastime is faring no better. When Little League was opened to girls by court order in 1974, one might have thought that professional women's baseball could not be far behind. Baseball is a natural for women. It's not a contact sport, it doesn't require excessive size or strength—even little guys like Phil Rizzuto and Jose Lind can play it—and it's actually an individual sport masquerading as a team sport. Still, in recent years, no one's taken a serious stab at organizing a women's professional league.

In 1984, there was an attempt to field a women's minor-league 18
team. Though the Sun Sox had the support of baseball great Hank Aaron, it was denied admission to the Class A Florida State League.

The team was the brainchild of a former Atlanta Braves vice president of marketing, Bob Hope. "A lot of the general managers and owners of big-league clubs were mortified," Hope says, "and some players said they wouldn't compete against women. It was male ego or something."

Or something, says softball hall-of-famer Donna Lopiano. "When girls suffer harassment in Little League, that's not exactly opening up opportunities for women," she says. "Girls don't have the access to coaching and weight training that boys have. Sports is a place where physiological advantages give men power, and they're afraid of losing it. Sports is the last great bastion of male chauvinism. In the last eight years, we've gone backward, not only on gender equity but on civil rights." 19

Women of color still face barriers that European American women don't, particularly in the areas of coaching and refereeing. But being a woman athlete is sometimes a bond that transcends race. "We're all at a handicap," says Ruth Lawanson, an African American who played volleyball with MLV. "It doesn't matter whether you're Asian, Mexican, black or white." 20

Historically, baseball and softball diamonds have not been very hospitable to black men and any women. Despite the fact that even men's softball is not a crowd pleaser, back in 1976, Billie Jean King and golfer Jane Blalock teamed up with ace amateur softball pitcher Joan Joyce to form the International Women's Professional Softball Association (IWPSA). Five years later, without sponsorship, money, or television, the league was history. 21

Billie Jean King has her own special attachment to the team concept. As a girl, she wanted to be a baseball player, but her father gave her a tennis racket, knowing that there wasn't much of a future for a girl in baseball. The story is especially touching since Billie Jean's brother, Randy Moffitt, went on to become a pitcher with the San Francisco Giants. But even as a tennis player, Billie Jean clung to the team idea. She was the force behind World TeamTennis, which folded in 1978, and is currently the chief executive officer of TeamTennis, now entering its eleventh season with corporate sponsorship. 22

On the face of it, TeamTennis is a bizarre notion because it takes what is a bred-in-the-bones individual sport and tries to squeeze it into a team concept. It has the further handicap of not really being necessary when strong women's and men's professional tours are already in place. 23

In the TeamTennis format, all players play doubles as well as singles. Billie Jean loves doubles, she says, because she enjoys "sharing the victory." What also distinguishes TeamTennis from the women's and men's pro tours is fan interaction. Fans are encouraged to behave 24 as if watching a baseball or basketball game rather than constantly being told to shut up and sit down as they are at pro tour events like the U.S. Open. The sense of team spirit among the players—the fact that they get to root for one another—is also attracting some big names. Both Martina Navratilova and Jimmy Connors have signed on to play TeamTennis during its tiny five-week season, which begins after Wimbledon and ends just before the U.S. Open.

But you have to go back almost 50 years to find a women's pro- 25
fessional sports team that was somewhat successful—though the conditions for that success were rather unusual. During World War II, when half the population was otherwise engaged, women were making their mark in the formerly male strongholds of welding, riveting—and baseball. The All-American Girls Professional Baseball League (AAGPBL) fielded such teams as the Lassies, the Belles, and the Chicks on the assumption that it was better to have "girls" playing than to let the national pastime languish. The league lasted a whopping 12 years after its inception in 1943.

The success of this sandlot venture, plagued as it was by the 26
simple-hearted sexism of the forties (the women went to charm school at night), must raise nagging doubts in the mind of the woman team player of the nineties. Can she triumph only in the absence of men?

It may be true that she can triumph only in the absence of com- 27
petition from the fiercely popular men's pro leagues, which gobble up sponsorship, U.S. network television, and the hearts and minds of male fanatics. The lack of male competition outside the United States may be partly responsible for the success of women's professional team sports in Europe, Japan, South America, and Australia. Lieberman-Cline acknowledges that Europe provides a more hospitable climate for women's pro basketball. "Over there, they don't have as many options," she says. "We have Broadway plays, movies, you name it. We're overindulged with options."

Bruce Levy is a 230-pound bespectacled accountant who escaped 28
from the Arthur Andersen accounting firm 11 years ago to market women's basketball. "It's pretty simple," he says. "People overseas are more realistic and enlightened. Women's basketball is not viewed as a weak version of men's. If Americans could appreciate a less powerful, more scientific, team-oriented game, we'd be two-thirds of the way toward having a league succeed."

Levy, who represents many women playing pro basketball 29
abroad, says 120 U.S. women are playing overseas and making up to $70,000 in a seven-month season. They include star players like Teresa Edwards, Katrina McClain, and Lynette Woodward. "A player like Teresa Weatherspoon, everybody recognizes her in Italy," he says.

"No one in the U.S. knows her. If there were a pro league over here, I wouldn't be spending all day on the phone speaking bad Italian and making sure the women's beds are long enough. I'd just be negotiating contracts."

Levy claims that U.S. businesswomen aren't supporting women's 30
team sports. "In Europe," he says, "the best-run and most publicized teams are run by women who own small businesses and put their money where their mouth is." Joy Burns, president of Sportswomen of Colorado, Inc., pleads no contest. "Businesswomen here are too conservative and don't stick their necks out," she says. MLV's Bat Batinovich, who says he's "disappointed" in U.S. businesswomen for not supporting women's team sports, figures an investor in MLV should have been willing to lose $200,000 a year for five years. Would Burns have done it? "If I'm making good financial investments, why should I?"

The prospects for women's professional team sports don't look 31
bright. The reasons for the lack of financial support go beyond simple economics and enter the realm of deep-rooted sexual bias and homophobia. San Jose State's Lindy Vivas says men who feel intimidated by physically strong women have to put the women down. "There's always a guy in the crowd who challenges the women when he wouldn't think of going one-on-one with Magic Johnson or challenging Nolan Ryan to a pitching contest."

Softball's Donna Lopiano calls it little-boy stuff: "Men don't want 32
to have a collegial, even-steven relationship with women. It's like dealing with cavemen."

Examining the Text

1. How do you respond to the title of this essay? According to Rounds, why do men fear women's teams? What do you think of her reasoning?

2. Rounds points out that individual sports (like tennis and golf) give female athletes more exposure and opportunities for success than team sports. How does she explain this difference? Why do you think women's professional team sports are not popular in the United States? Have you had many opportunities to watch female teams play? How do you think this affects your answer?

3. Summarize the role of television and business in the promotion of professional women's sports. How do mass media and business alter women's sports, according to Rounds? To what extent do they also alter men's sports?

For Group Discussion

Softball player Donna Lopiano is quoted as saying that "sports is the last bastion of male chauvinism." Discuss your group's reactions to

Lopiano's statement. List some possible reasons that women today might have greater opportunities in other traditionally male-dominated professions than in sports. Also list any evidence that contradicts Lopiano's claim. As a class, consider whether women's situation in professional sports is likely to change.

Writing Suggestion

Assuming that Rounds's assertion that women have few opportunities in the world of professional sports is correct, do you think this is a significant problem? Determine some of the specific benefits that women miss because of gender discrimination in sports. In an essay express your opinions about what (if anything) should be done to offer women greater access to these benefits.

The Sociology of Sport: Structural and Cultural Approches

T. R. Young

This article presents a more theoretical perspective on sports than have previous pieces, as Young uses Marxist theory as the lens through which to examine the functions of sports in capitalist society. Marxism emphasizes the material relationships in cultures (hence, it's often called a "materialist" approach), arguing that nonmaterial cultural practices and attitudes—cultural rituals, dominant leisure activities, religious practices, and the like—can be understood based on their relationship to the material or tangible economic structures and practices within that culture.

Young divides his analysis of sports into a structural and a cultural application of Marxist theory. The structural approach is essentially economic: how do sports serve the economic interests of America's commodity capitalism? He reasons that in commodity capitalism, companies produce a surplus of goods because workers' wages are always lower than the prices charged for the goods they produce. People do not need, nor can they afford to buy all the goods that commodity capitalism produces. In addition, wealth is largely concentrated in the hands of a few who don't need all the surplus goods. The commercial industry of sports helps address this surplus condition, because it provides a vehicle for advertising. Advertising generates demand by creating false needs and stimulating desire so that lower-paid workers are persuaded to buy more than they can afford, and wealthier consumers will buy more than they need. Sports deliver advertisements to mass audiences.

To the Marxist theorist, the fact that sports function so well for the economic structures of capitalism shows that sports serve powerful cultural pur-

poses in capitalist society. Young argues that sport addresses psychological and spiritual needs in us that are created by the material conditions of capitalism, and does so in a way that promotes the values and ideologies that best serve commodity capitalism. For example, he argues that sports help keep the average worker in the dark ("mystified") as to his or her true exploited condition. One way that sports does this is by preserving a (false, and alienating, in Marxist terms) separation between work and play; rather than question a lack of enjoyment in our work, we are content to seek this outlet outside of work, in playing and viewing sports.

The true Marxist approach, as Young sees it, is not to merely point out problems, but to use an understanding of problems to lead us to solutions—to provide us with "emancipatory knowledge" so that we can work at transforming society. In this case, Young would have us transform a part of social life, sports, so that it serves individual human needs rather than the needs of capitalism and its supposed beneficiaries—the top 5 percent of the economic pie (13). ***As you read,*** *think about this idea of solutions. How do Young's observations and arguments point to or imply solutions to the problems he identifies?*

Sport served a political function.
Capitalism supports a division of sports
into "theirs" and "ours."
Into workers sports and bourgeois sports.
The Working class must use sports
to bring back people from their
lonely, tortured and shattered worlds
to their rightful human dignity.

—from "Arbeitsports" by Fritz Wildung

THE SOCIOLOGY OF SPORT

1 The sociology of sport is increasingly disputed ideological territory in American social science. On the one hand is the uncritical descriptive statistical examination of sports activity created by an admiring journalism. In the same camp is the celebratory history of sports and sport figures which redeems its ugly aspects by enlarging the heroic efforts of individual players and teams. Joining with these extensive statistical presentations and their selected historical forays is a safe and bland sociology of sport which trivializes and depoliticises sports in particular and leisure time pursuits generally.

2 Among the major introductory textbooks of the past 20 years, very little attention is paid to the sociology of sports. Babbie (1983) does not mention sports or leisure as an institutional form. Wilson

(1971) treats leisure activities as a subsection or work containing no theory or analysis. McGee (1980) does not mention sports and treats leisure activities as a problem which may arise in the future as people work less. Again no analysis. Ritzer et al. (1982) has a very decent section on sports although it is primarily descriptive of organization and variety. It does have some mildly critical dimensions about sports as corporate business as, well as the disturbing influence of mass media.

Opposed to this happy, marginalized view of sports is a new 3
genre of Marxian work embodied in the works of Paul Hoch (1972), Jean Marie Brohm (1975), Richard Gruneau (1981), Jon Sewart (1981), Leon Chorbajian (1984), and Thomas Keil (1984). A Marxian perspective when viewing sports has two major approaches: The first and more orthodox approach centers on the political economy of sports while the second focuses upon its ideological meaning for socialization as well as for the legitimacy within a strife-ridden nation.

STRUCTURAL ANALYSIS

Central to the first approach are the concepts of profit, capital accumu- 4
lation, concentration of wealth, extraction of surplus value, externalization of costs as well as the exploitation, objectification and commodification of athletes, games, leagues and seasons of play. This approach is concerned with the ways in which the mode of production of sports is organized to socialize the costs of production while the profits are privatized.

Economic benefits of commodity sports include profits, tax write 5
off for losses, residuals, stock and real estate appreciation as well as copyrights and commercial spin-offs. Profits from financing, construction and auxiliary services to sports all redound to the private owner while the costs of production are transferred to the tax-payer, workers and fans through player training programs in school, college and community, public stadia building, low wages and benefits for nonathletes, ticket and television revenue.

Modern American society invests a great deal of resources in 6
commodity sports. This political economy critique of sports shows how it accumulates and concentrates capital for ownership, how it manages player unrest, how it has developed to a labor aristocracy which joins with management to exploit other sectors of the working class and how it commodifies every element of sports from intermissions of play, to grand moments in play, to the very reputations and esteem of players.

There is also an economic analysis of mass sports made of the 7
ways and means by which banks and monopolies have taken over the

financial side of sports, the interconnections between ownership within and between differing sports, between sports and other economic activities such as publishing, cinema, advertising, as well as gambling and politics.

There is the mapping of the subsidiary businesses to sports; 8
transport, food, hostelry, equipment manufacture, construction, sports medicine, development schemes as well as insurance and investment. There is a critical history of sports created as well. Brohm (1975) notes that world sport paralleled the rise of colonial imperialism. Sport is modeled upon capitalist modes of production; upon the accumulation ethic and is assimilated by the state in such a fashion as to socialize the costs of producing athletes, stadia, and injury while privatizing the profits of mass sports.

There are the forms of crime, forms of policing, forms of justice 9
and forms of control to be studied—a sort of micro-criminology. There are the frauds, tax evasion, black-listing, spurious bankruptcies, bribes, medical crime, illegal transfers and point-fixing to be analyzed. These analyses are made in the traditional structural analysis of the political economy.

CULTURAL MARXISM

The second major approach in Marxian analysis is a cultural Marxist 10
analysis. It involves the concepts of legitimation, ideological culture, alienation, false consciousness, solidarity, massification, character, structure, surplus production and the realization problem. Cultural Marxism studies how commodity sports creates a false solidarity between and among workers and owners, Blacks and Anglos, rich and poor, East and West, North and South as well as between nations within the world capitalist system and between the socialist bloc and the non-socialist bloc. In Brazil and Argentina, revolutionary groups stop the revolution for the World Soccer Finals.

Commodity sports colonizes the beauty, elegance, joy and de- 11
spair of physical performance. Thus it bends eros to the accumulation and legitimation needs of capitalism in crisis (as well as bureaucratic socialism, feudal relations in the Mid-East or fascist relations in the poor capitalist countries). Eros is colonized in order to transfer desire from essential social and community needs to privatized consumer goods. In advanced monopoly capitalism, the entire sports ensemble becomes a product sold to major corporations which need to dispose of surplus production in order to realize profit.

Commodity sports legitimates the false separation of social life 12
into the world of work which is said to be necessarily alienating on the

one hand and the world of play in which one finds delight and joy on the other hand; in which the forces of life may be expressed in exhilarating play and thus redeem the bitter imperfection of alienated relations at work, in school, in family or in church. The possibility that eros, conceived as the forces of life, could be expressed at work, school, in family or in religious practice is falsely excluded from the consciousness of the worker, the student, the husband or the somnolent church-goer.

These two approaches together, use of sports for the capital accumulation and the use of sports for the mystification of conflict relations in class, racist, sexist or national chauvinistic societies combines to provide the emancipatory knowledge basic to the transformation of society in general and sports in particular to more human and humane purpose. The critical project is always to advance the radical anthropological project of Marx in which the individual constitutes himself or herself as species being, i.e., as human, by the appropriation of nature including one's own athletic abilities in building a just, harmonious and egalitarian social life world in concert with others. It is to that end that this paper is written. 13

Before I develop both approaches a bit, I would like to set forth the contemporary but depoliticized ways in which athletes and fans falsely understand the meaning of sports. One must remember that there is some truth value in each approach. It is not that these other approaches are false but rather that, in their limited truth, they provide a false consciousness of sports in capitalist societies which deflect the authentic self-knowledge of sports and society and thus defuse and deflect political control over the very institution so many give so much of the body and loyalty. 14

THE FALSE SELF-UNDERSTANDING OF SPORTS: HEALTH AND CHARACTER BUILDING

The officially given uses to which sports and other athletic activity are put center around physical health and character building. The vast resources laid on for physical education in high school, college and city league programs are justified by appeal to the presumed increase in quality of life or in moral character for participants. There are several features of modern sport activity which bespeak this rationale. The incidence of injuries to professional ball teams subvert the claim of better physical condition as a result of participation. 15

The use of drugs to train and repair players as well as for controlling pain so one can play while injured also calls such a rationale into 16 question. The kind of muscles used and the development of them may have no real lasting effect on quality of health. And the physical deterioration of players after they cease playing suggests that this philosophy of sports is much more a gloss than substance.

And as far as the moral character, in commercial sports in particular and competitive sports in general, one must wonder whether that particular character is, indeed, an ideal to be adopted. The widespread cheating by coaches and players, the envy, disappointment, cynicism and hypocrisy entailed in commercialized competitive sports, as well as the abusive and profane behavior of the fans, leave one in doubt about the psychological benefits accruing from and calling for such social investments. 17

Finally, the minuscule differences in performance of runners, throwers, catchers, batters, and jumpers need critical analysis. With electronic timing and measurement, the differences between "winners" and "losers" in races, series, and games may be magnified far beyond any sensible proportion. If two runners finish within a tenth of a second in a four minute mile, how is one declared a winner and the other a loser when both are superior examples of athletic excellence. If two teams are tied in the last minute of play after a long season and the "winner" depends upon the last basket in the last second—or the last pass on the last down or the last kick in overtime, all this is exhilarating drama but rests more comfortably in an analysis which places sports in a dramatic framework about endurance, persistence, or national superiority than in one centered on superiority or merit. 18

It is the view taken here that these physical activities are central to the human project if organized adequately; that these aesthetically pleasing capabilities are and should be expressed in the world of work, family life, politics and, indeed, sports, theatre, dance, and the plastic arts. 19

SOLIDARITY

Perhaps the most visible and most pervasive understanding of sports activity is a solidarity use. High schools, small towns, large cities, entire nations, friendship groups, male associations, father-son relationships, as well as whole economic systems make use of the aesthetic, dramatic, mysterious and strategic responses in sports, games and play to define, to celebrate, to expand and to reaffirm a special solidarity status for those assembled to participate or to observe. 20

As a solidarity device in conjunction with a variety of other solidarity supplies; food, alcohol, violence, risk, song, sexual display, 21 chants, special clothing and physical ecstasy, such sports as football, basketball, soccer, hockey, and baseball bind people together.

The solidarity function is central to a sociological understanding of sports, games and play. We do act, feel and think as one as we cheer, chant, despair, and rejoice together at the turn of events in the game. There can be no greater solidarity than dozens, thousands, millions thinking, doing and feeling the same things in the same place at the same moment. These are the precious, rare moments of perfect harmony and collective exuberance in a world all too short on such moments. 22

But it is this a narrow solidarity limited in time and place and confined to the world of make-believe and not-for-real. When the game is over, the enthusiasm dies, the solidarity runs short and disharmony in other relations reassert themselves. Much as one hour a week cannot answer to the religious impulse, one game a week cannot answer to the solidarity needs of a racist, sexist or elitist society. In this respect more radical structural solutions are preferred. 23

In a conflict-ridden society where each is the natural enemy of similarly situated competitors for jobs, for land and resources, for sexual access, and for other scarce items, where there are class antagonists and ethnic opponents, where ever more people are impoverished, such solidarity activity is important to the masking of these antagonisms. When the home team beats the putative enemy with skill, genius, heroic acts, with deceit or trickery and guile, great delight, joy and enthusiasm emerges and can be shared with those-present-on-our-side. Class antagonisms, ethnic hatred, as well as gender and national hostilities with real conflicting interests can be assimilated to the harmless competitive in sports. The structures of privilege, inequality and oppression are left intact by such use of solidarity moments in sports. 24

ALIENATED SEXUALITY

Perhaps the most simple-minded view of the current way sports is organized centers around sex and violence. This view reduces the analysis of sports to some universal psychological drive/anxiety about sexual and violent behavior. The depth analyses made in this kind of understanding is that the equipment and events in football, basketball, baseball, golf and other sports events lend themselves to sexual interpretation. 25

The pitcher throwing the ball to the catcher to deceive the hitter readily lends itself to this interpretation if we regard the bat as a phal- 26 lic symbol, the ball as a sperm, the catcher and the mitt as earth-mother and her genital organ, the pitcher as the castrating father and the home run as the symbolic murder of the primitive father.

In like fashion, football action may be so reconstructed as to evoke the primal scene. If the goal line is the hymen and the ballcarrier the phallus while the ball itself is a primitive womb to be delivered in triumph to earthmother, then a touchdown is a symbolic rape uniting sex and violence in a series of downs in which the underdog team (the symbolic son) pushes away the defenses of the favored team (the primitive father) to penetrate the sacred opening of that mother. 27

Golf also takes on sexual meaning if we convert the golf club into a phallus, the white ball into sperm and the drive itself into an ejaculatory orgasm aimed at a hole-in one. Basketball with its inaccessible hoop, its oversized balls and its slam-dunk could create an image of the primal scene in the violence of rape. And so on. In these analyses a horse is a phallic symbol as is a car, motorbike, bicycle, rifle or running back. In sports, one side represents father, one side the adolescent son reaching for incestuous control of the primitive mother embodied in the win, the bucket, the touchdown, the hole in one, the home run. In this perspective, sports is seen as a form of sublimated sexuality which makes the world safer for decent women. 28

A variation on this theme is that sports and the deep involvement of Americans and people everywhere with them is an expressive outlet for undesirable and/or unusable emotional drives or psychological imperatives. Rage, anger, antic genius, violence, sexuality, fantasy, foolishness, and humor (eros generally) are said to be "safely" channeled into harmless pursuits through sports, games, reading novels, watching plays and dreaming. It is not that these are central to all forms of human activity but that they have a very limited place in "real" life and must be rendered neutral by expressing them in non-serious endeavor. 29

Sports is, here as before, a safety valve to discharge "naturally" occurring and "dangerous" emotion. 30

DIVERTISSMENT

Another well received view of sports is as a diversion from serious matters. 31

In this analysis, ordinary work, politics and family are adult matters. One who seeks escape into trivial, non-serious activity is immature. More generally, the social world is split into two components: seriously intended social reality on the one hand and make-believe, just-pretend and just-for-fun on the other. It may be all right for 32 children and students to engage in such frivolity but the sober citizen works hard and remains joyless.

In this view, eros is not to be linked with work still less is it to be 33
colonized to encourage consumerism—eros is to be denied. This view sees life as necessarily involving suffering—joy is unnatural. In a marginally efficient mode of production the Protestant ethic of hard work and self-denial has a certain social utility. In an affluent society, this approach makes sense only to those whose relationship to the means of production is so precarious that the least indulgence would be a serious matter.

A great many people including some Marxists hold a differing 34
view. They accept that life is alienating and that people inappropriately escape that alienation by fleeing the family, onerous work, dull/mean-spirited religion as well as massified educational forms to the lively world of play and sports. Alienated workers escape the boredom, drudgery and humiliation of work in the ever expanding weekend of commercial sports, drinking, bowling, jogging, hunting or swinging sex. People give up on local, state and national politics, surrender elitist control over politics to the politicians in exchange for the private freedoms of sports, games, and play.

The difficulties with this analysis are many including the unjusti- 35
fied assumptions that work and sexual life within institutional marriage forms or institutional politics necessarily are alienating. It simply does not follow that since these are alienated in this social formation that they must be alienated everywhere, eternally for all people. There is the prior question about the relationship between reality and make-believe.

Sports, games, theatre, fiction, rehearsal, are, have been and must 36
be integrally linked to the human project (Young, 1983). As we shall see a bit later, the realm of make believe and magic can be alienated from the human project—the salient political question is how to forestall alienation. The short answer lies in the democratic modes of production for make believe and just-pretend including sports.

THE POLITICAL ECONOMY OF SPORTS

There are several structural characteristics of a political economy ap- 37
proach upon which I touched earlier and would like to develop a bit here. The first and most general point I want to emphasize is that the character of sports varies with the mode of production of the society in which it appears. The history of sports parallels the history of human society.

In each of the five great modes of organization for social produc- 38
tion, sports and the world of serious activity has been mutually inter-

dependent. In primitive communal societies, in slave, feudal, capitalist or socialist society, sports has been shaped by the dominant mode of production.

Contemporary Sports

Football, basketball, soccer, track and field events have their origins in 39
inter-tribal, inter-feudal and inter-capitalist warfare. Football probably started out as a predator village kicked the heads of conquered neighbors around. Baseball is little else but the skilled use of the bludgeon. Field events: shot put, javelin, hammer throw and archery all come out of the weaponry of feudal warfare.

Such events as the marathon, the hurdles, the obstacle course, the 40
dash and the relay recapitulate the structure of field communication in the various military encounters between low-tech armies from the wars between city-states in ancient Greece to the crusades through the feudal conquests of France, Britain, Scandinavia and the African nations.

The modern assimilation of sports to military goals came in 1811 41
when the Germans were occupied by the armies of Napoleon. The mass calisthenics which later came to be associated with the Jugendschaften of the Hitler era, were encouraged as prelude to the overthrow of the French oppressors by German patriots.

In our times, sports is shaped more by the commercial needs of 42
advanced monopoly capital. There are several points at which its needs shape the structure and development of sports. The most significant structural change in modern sports is the gradual and continuing commodification of sports. This means that the social, psychological, physical and cultural uses of sports are assimilated to the commercial needs of advanced monopoly capital.

THE REALIZATION "PROBLEM"

A major use to which sports are put by commodity capitalists is in the 43
solution to the "realization problem." Given the profit motive, capitalist firms produce more than their workers can buy. This happens for two reasons. First, workers collectively do not get paid 100 percent of the price set by the market. For any given firm labor costs are about 25–35 percent of the price set. Across all workers who share in the division of the profits, the wages are less than 100 percent of the price available with which to purchase the goods they produce.

In low profit lines, workers may have 95 percent of the value 44
produced; in high profit lines of production, they may have less than

50 percent of the value of the wealth they produce. Whatever the case they can't buy it all. In such a case, the economy tends to slow down to recession or depression levels. There are several ways to renew demand, each with other problems:

Warfare destroys wealth and renews demand.
A prolonged recession renews demand.
Price wars dispose of surplus production but benefit big competitors.
Crime requires replacement of items stolen.
The welfare state redistributes wealth.
Credit and deficit spending can keep the system going a while longer.
Capitalists compete for foreign markets and try to capture surplus value from foreign economies with which to renew demand.

However, a major way to dispose of "surplus" goods and realize profit is to transfer desire from the world of cultural events; sports, theatre, religion or patriotism to the world of commodity production via advertising.

The inability of a capitalist firm to dispose of "surplus" production leads corporations to purchase sports programming as a commodity to generate demand by using the beauty and elegance of athletics as an envelope in which to insert a commercial message. 45

EXTRACTING SURPLUS INCOME

A second structural feature of advanced monopoly capitalism which besets the accumulation process is the great inequality of income distribution among those who do work for wage labor. 46

The Yuppie portion of the population has discretionary income as do most elements of the capital class, but in the capitalist system today a few million people get around 40 percent of that wealth and hundreds of millions share less than 50 percent of the wealth. In America, the bottom 20 percent of the population share only five percent of the gross national product. A lot of money to be sure but far less than is required to purchase all the cars, beer, refrigerators, cigarettes, and other items produced. 47

The few million who do have surplus income and could purchase the surplus production don't need the fourth car, the fifth television set or the tenth toaster. This distortion in income means, again, that capitalists can't realize profit. A third reason that there is a surplus of goods is the tendency in capitalist systems to disemploy workers by the use of new technology or by increased productivity from each worker. 48

These disemployed workers join the surplus population. Their material needs may be met by the state in its welfare system, by family 49 members, by private charity or by friends. Again many turn to crime as a way to reunite production and distribution. So, in order to dispose of the surplus production on profitable terms, capitalist firms turn to advertising to create an ever expanding layer of false needs and wants among those who may have discretionary income. Or try to expand markets overseas to the disadvantage of capitalists in other countries who also have the same realization problem.

Since sports events generate large audiences and participants (for 50
any or all of the reasons mentioned earlier: the alienated solidarity, the alienated sexuality or the alienated aesthetics of play), advertising firms buy the audiences and sell them to capitalist firms which are large enough to have national markets and wealthy enough to pay the costs of the audience, the commercials, the media time and the teams involved. Apart from the fact that this solution to the problem of capitalist production greatly inflates costs of distribution and apart from the fact that small firms tend to fail, the real problem of this growing alliance between sports and capitalism is the linkage between mythic concerns of a society and profit concerns of private capital.

CULTURAL MARXIST ANALYSIS OF SPORTS

In brief, the argument in Cultural Marxism is that sports has absorbed 51
some of the religious needs of a secular society for solidarity and for a metaphysic. The analysis of sports presented here is that it embodies elements of a four great founding myths of society—especially that of a morality metaphysic which instructs players and fans alike about how to approach the problematics of interpersonal interaction, how to relate oneself to the social unit, and how to confront the imponderables of nature and other groups.

It seems to me that it is this morality metaphysic which so in- 52
trigues and so engrosses fans in the actions and outcomes of a sports event. It is this morality metaphysic which can be used as an envelope in which to insert advertisements. To understand the rise of commodity sports in America, we need to connect the political economy of capitalism to alienated social life.

Every society has four general myths which help reproduce it 53
across generations. The first great myth is, of course, the creation myth. The second myth and the one used here is the morality myth—one which instructs us on how we are to deal with the ordinary contingencies of life, how we are to relate to others inside and outside our group.

> Morality myths instruct us about the forms of evil, the sources of evil, the agents of evil and the solutions for evil.

A third great myth form is one which tells us how to understand and survive the inevitable tragedies which is the common lot of all people—what to do about death, about love gone wrong, about children gone wrong and about the imponderables of life. The fourth great mythic form speaks to the future and to the failings of the past in that social formation itself. This fourth mythic form usually says that times were good before, they turn bad through no fault of the system and they will be good again if one has faith.

A myth is a line of symbolic activity—activity in music, in 54
mime or in words—which grasps the basic concerns of a society and resolves the conflict and contradictions inherent in social life in its chronology and in the logic of its action (Silverstone, 1983:138).

The simplicity of the sports event is especially amenable to 55
mythic use. In the play, the protagonist must overcome adversity in society and in nature. Each play and player must, to be successful as a mythic element, transcend everyday activity. The game is transparent in its play and unlike written or narrated myths has no foregone conclusion. Every fan has the same standing as do all others. In those crucial moments of play, a satisfactory event is anticipated and recognized by all present. One does not need a priestly functionary to interpret the mysteries as in religious myths. In that respect, sports may be experienced directly for its aesthetic and mythic meanings.

The structure of sports as a mythic form is about socialization 56
under conditions of conflict. In feudal society; in competitive capitalist societies with class as well as ethnic conflict; in the world capitalist system with its nationalistic antagonisms, the mythic structure of modern adversary sports resonates with the lived experiences of workers, Blacks, third world patriots as well as partisans of geographical animosity. All stress the need for the individual to accept and to work within the existing structure or social conflict and "friendly" competition. Commodity capital, with its internal crises and contradictions has assimilated the mythic form to its own needs for survival, for profit, for socialization to competitive, aggressive, privatized character as well as for legitimacy with workers, consumers and citizens who are its natural antagonists. I raise the question about whether American sports in its commodity form—however excellent and appealing—should be harnessed to the ideological needs of a given class or elite in any society. The view advanced here is that sports, indeed all cultural activities, might better be oriented to the general social interest in authentic solidarity and prosocial cooperation rather than the special character and consumer morality of monopoly capital.

> Every social group needs to use the awe and mystery of myth, magic, pretend, rehearsal, play and the world of imagination and make-believe to the reproduction of cultural forms.

All sports activities are mythic endeavors in which the forces of life are pitted against the forces of nature. In the case of football, basketball, baseball and, more intensely tennis, the effort to control a ball pushes the player to the limits of psychobiological capacity and endurance. The catch takes on added drama if it occurs in a strategic moment of play. Still more dramatic impact arises should the moment of play be located in a strategic game or even in a moment of note in the entire history of a league or nation.

The means by which conflict is to be resolved is by excellent indi- 57
vidual performance within the logics of team goals. In a recent (18 July 1983) Monday Night Baseball game, the shortstop of the Toronto Blue Jays made four such plays in that single game. Few persons on earth could have made the moves as swiftly, as gracefully or as accurately and with the panache displayed. The grace, beauty and art possible from the human body shown forth clearly in that game.

In like fashion, the extension of the physical capacity of the 58
human body in making spectacular catches in football is even more remarkable taking place as they do in the face of expert defensive play by the opposing team. Most of those who watch football know and appreciate those catches, the moves for which match in grace and timing the finest of ballet. By themselves, this physical excellence is only of passing interest—observed only for the purest of aesthetic reasons as indeed one may appreciate ballet. But unlike most ballet today, sports games are located in significant social frames within which they take on mythic force. In a world series, with the bases loaded and two out, and with the score tied in the ninth, a long fly ball is immediately anticipated as a dramatic event. As the center fielder races back, gauges the flight, lifts off the ground in every effort, whether the catch is made or whether the ball clears the 430 foot marker, the partisan crowd is on its feet as one, explodes in a cheer of delight as one and appreciates that all others present share the grand moment. The soaring grace of the fielder's catch or the perfect timing and power of the batsman testify to the possibility of human success in everyday life. That is what the myth—and the game—is all about.

As noted, the sports event teaches us four things: it tells us what 59
the sources of evil are, it tells us who the agent of evil is (often conceived as the enemy), it instructs us in the forms of evil, and it instructs us in the means by which evil is to be overcome.

In the case of baseball, the source of travail is to be found in the 60
physical forces of nature; time, space, gravity, weather and light. The

sources of evil are found as well in the individual imperfections of the players: the lazy player, the inept player, the foolish player, the cheating player, the selfish player, and the indifferent player. Evil is to betray one's teammates to sloth, greed, envy, pride, anger and hate.

If not the unproductive team member, the agent of evil is the out- 61
sider. For most major sports, it is the visiting team. High school and college sports set as enemy the opposing team much more than do the professional teams although in baseball, everyone hates the Yankees; in football for years it was the Chicago Bears and in basketball the Boston Celtics who embodied adversity.

The particular forms of evil embodied these teams entailed un- 62
fair tactics, dirty play, illegal recruiting, purchasing of pennants and players as well as architectural innovations of the field of play which gave unfair advantage to the other team.

When combined, the forms and agents of evil as embodied in 63
the mythic structure of sports teaches a lesson. It says the tribe is the paramount unit of social order, the enemy is other neighboring tribes; they cheat and thus are less than human. This default renders the home tribe the embodiment of the human being in its highest, most principled form—however, since the opposing team violates the rules of social life found in the sports event, it excludes itself from the normal courtesies of social conduct. Such self-exclusion in turn justifies less-than-social treatment of the enemy. By this practical logic, the home tribe at once justifies noncompliance with social rules and in the same moment preserves the home tribe myth of superior moral standing.

If the Yankees buy up all the best players, they default on the 64
rules and may be subjected to tactics otherwise inconceivable. Since the Chicago Bears hit, gouge, kick and pile on, they disqualify themselves as equals and may be hit, gouged, and kicked without culpable wrong imputed to the home team. Since the Celtics use picks, fast breaks, double-teaming, presses, and platoon substitution tactics; since they grab the super stars from college ranks and use the home court advantage in extremis, they also are the embodiment of evil for all other home teams—and the Celtics, Bears, and Yankees view the Philadelphia Warriors, the Green Bay Packers, and the Dodgers as less than human.

In the Marxian analysis presented here, sports have been com- 65
modified and massified in response to some of the structural problems of advanced monopoly capitalism. A separate but parallel analysis is possible for bureaucratic socialist economies or the semi-feudalities in the Mid-East and Far-East.

In brief, sports solves the problems of accumulation and legitimacy 66
in the ways mentioned above. Sports in its present form presents us with

a modern metaphysic for daily life. It redeems, in a false and trivlal manner, alienated conditions of work. It provides alienated solidarity in a conflict ridden society. Its super-masculine model of play offers to redeem an alienated sexuality. And its aesthetics and metaphysics provide an envelope into which to insert a message vesting desire into possession of material goods rather than in primary social relations....

CONCLUSION

There are many ways to understand the huge investment a society allocates to sports and to other athletic activity. At any given level of analyses there are significant and important validities upon which to focus depending upon the interests and concerns of the critical scholar. In the previous section of this paper, the focus has been the mythic character of the rules and lines of play in contemporary American sports culture. In the earlier section, the focus was upon the political economy in which sports are located. 67

A political-economy approach to sports examines how and why it has been commodified. The Marxian view is that commodity sports is used by advertising to generate demand in an economic system in which demand is restricted by profit considerations, by monopoly practices, and by a continuing discrepancy between aggregate wage and aggregate price across all capitalist lines of production. The need for profit in advanced monopoly capitalism results in every possible good or service be commodified. Sports is commodified and sold to the largest corporations in order to add dimensions of desire and false need to products without intrinsic value to those with discretionary income. 68

That so many people invest so much time, emotion and money in these pursuits instructs us that something important is happening. It is the view advanced here that sports has gradually absorbed the religious impulse of a secular society, commodified it in capitalist societies and is in the process of assimilating that impulse to the economic and legitimacy needs of capitalism. Perhaps there are better ways to understand sports but I know no better for the present organization of American sports. 69

The analysis here presents a given sports event as an instance of one or more of the four great myths found in a society with which to instruct its young people in the metaphysics of human life as it is constructed in that culture. The four myths are: the Creation Myth, the Morality Myth, the Tragic Myth, and the Destiny Myth. All interesting novels, plays, poems and sports events incorporate the structures of one or more of these myths into its story line. 70

The Morality myth of advanced capitalist society suffuses the structure and chronology of the contemporary sports events in the United States. Competition, the resultant system of individual stars and individual viewers, the emphasis upon playing within the rules set by a small non-playing elite, the constant push by coaches and managers for greater productivity, for personal excellence and for uncritical acceptance of the authority system all resonate with the problematics of capitalist production in shop, office, school and factory: competition, discipline, creativity, teamwork, victory, and alienated joy. 71

As an embodiment of a mythic form which instructs all persons concerned, fans and players alike, on how to live out one's life in a laudable and praiseworthy style, sports supplements, complements and in some instances, displaces the sacred writings of the Bible and the Church Fathers. In a secular society, the drama of sports events absorb and bend the quest for the sacred to the profit concerns; to the control needs of the rich and the powerful. 72

It is this concern with the morality myth which so intrigues and so captures the fan and the player. We all need a metaphysic for the shaping of our everyday behavior. Professional football, baseball, basketball, volleyball and soccer, each in its differing format, provides us with such a morality. 73

I suggest there is a basic incompatibility with commercial sports and the longer historical interests of a society. I propose that a society which permits its mythic forms in sports to be purchased as a commodity, mortgages its future to the rich and the powerful. In this case, it is the private capitalist firm which has absorbed sports to its ideological, political and economic needs. 74

Such commodification of sports ceases to serve the general social interest in morality, in solidarity, and in excellence of individual effort when these interests are confined within the special interests of the capitalist firm for profit, for legitimacy, for growth and for control of markets, material and for a complacent labor force. 75

The argument presented here is that there is much of social value found in sports and in other mythic carriers. Given the social utility of morality myths and the great investment of time, talent and concern with sports in America, the significant question to raise is whether a society should so organize that talent and time of athletes, artists and actors to serve interests of private profit. Corollary to that question is whether other forms of sports, other modalities of morality, other structures of myths might not better serve the social interest or the human project. 76

In this respect, the sociology of sport fits within a larger framework of the political economy in which it is found. The usual approach to the study of sports sociology surgically isolates sports from the soci- 77 ety in which it is found and from the content and outcomes of the cultural activities. One should keep in mind that it is the cultural activities—ranging from family life to religious life and embracing art, music, science, games, leisure time activities as well as politics and parties—which give life its distinctly human character. Work, food, shelter, health care and survival skills are basic to life but the creation of culture in all its forms is basic to human life.

The propensity is to trivialize the sociology of music, theatre, 78
sports, folk arts and their economic and political meaning of these. A Marxian theory reclaims these cultural activities and locates them in a research endeavor which emancipates them once again to celebrate distinctly social and collective endeavors.

A RADICAL RESEARCH AGENDA

These concerns constitute a radical research agenda for a critical soci- 79
ology of sports. It seems to me that the ideological hegemony of capitalism and of bureaucratic socialism are particularly vulnerable to such research in sports, as well as in crime, in sexual repression and in the politics of torture and terror.

Crime, sports, religion and sexuality are enduring and intriguing 80
concerns of Americans and of other nationalities around the world. The very use of these domains by the powerful and privileged open up possibilities for critical understanding and for progressive politics. If people are able to see the repressive uses of sports, sex and essential social goods, they may, in the same moment, see emancipatory uses. The task for the critical theorist is to challenge the celebratory, statistical approach to sports sociology with a more historical and constructive critique.

Opposed to a happy view of sports is the sociology of sports cre- 81
ated by critical theorists. As noted, this work is concerned with the role which sports in its present format plays in reproducing the structure of class privilege and the concentration of wealth and class relations. Some of this new work concentrates upon the social sources of human consciousness and tries to show how sports legitimates national and ethnic loyalties by competitive striving. The Olympic Games serve as a rich source of material for this sort of critical analysis.

Also opposed to a depoliticized sociology is a series of analyses on 82
how sports socializes young people to a special, historically grounded structure of self, personality and psychological mappings. Challenging a view of human nature as necessarily racist, necessarily violent, necessarily masculine, necessarily competitive or necessarily privatized, these analysts assert the possibility of a different psychology, a different struc-

ture of self, a different sport not oriented to the violent, destructive forms of behavior found in football, boxing, or hockey.

In history and in theory, cooperative, communitarian and cre- 83
ative forms of play, game and sport are found. Since these do not help create competitive workers, ambitions professionals, authoritarian functionaries or compulsive consumers, these forms of games, sports and play are selected out of sports history while more competitive games and sports are selected into the social experience of the child, the adult and the senior citizen by a complex institution of sports board members, owners, sponsors, coaches, fans, and editors. There is much to be done; it will be interesting.

> Dance is the unity of force,
> time and space,
> bound and unbound by inner rhythm.
> Dancing can be done by anyone
> who has desire and love.
>
> —Mary Wingman in her *Philosophy of the Dance*

REFERENCES

Babbie, E. R. (1983) *Sociology.* Belmont: Wadsworth.

Brohm, Jean Marie (1975) Twenty Theses on Sports. *Quel Corps?* No. 1 (April–May).

Baran, P. and Sweezy (1976) *Monopoly Capital.* New York: Monthly Review Press.

Chorbajian, Leon (1984) Toward a Marxist Sociology of Sport. *Arena,* V. 8, No. 3.

Gruneau, Richard (1981) Elites, Class and Corporate Power in Canadian Sport, pp. 348–371 in *Sport, Culture and Society,* second edition, John W. Loy, Jr., Gerald S. Kenyon, and Barry D. McPherson (eds.). Philadelphia: Lea and Febiger.

Hoch, Paul (1972) *Rip Off the Big Game.* Garden City, NY: Doubleday.

Keil, T. (1984) The Sociology of Sport in Advanced Capitalist Society. *Arena,* V. 8, No. 3.

McGee, R. (1980) *Sociology.* New York: Holt-Rinehart.

Ritser, George (1975) *Sociology: A Multiple Paradigm Science.* Boston: Allyn and Bacon.

Sewart, John J. (1981) The Rationalization of Modern Sport: The Case of Professional Football. *Arena Review* 5 (September): 45–51.

Silverstone, R. (1981) *The Message of Television: Myth and Narrative in Contemporary Cultures.* London: Heineman Books.

Wilson, E. (1983) *Sociology.* Homewood: Dorsey.

Examining the Text

1. Based upon the language, structure, and types of reasoning used here, what kind of audience is Young addressing? How does Young's language and approach help or hinder his belief in the value of providing us with the "emancipatory knowledge" that can lead to economic and cultural changes?

2. In setting out some of the ways he believes "athletes and fans falsely understand the meaning of sports" (14), Young first disputes sports' ability to promote physical health and moral character among participants. Discuss the points he raises to dispute these benefits, and go on to discuss whether you find his argument persuasive or not, and why.

3. Explain Young's argument about the ways in which sports supplement and even displace religion in current American society.

For Group Discussion

While Young believes solidarity—people joining together to accomplish common goals and to engage in common pleasures—is a good thing, he is critical of the kinds of solidarity fostered by sports in current American culture. Discuss why he thinks this kind of solidarity is problematic. Use Young's ideas as a starting point for discussing the notion of solidarity and sports. Another term for this concept of connection between people is "community"; do you think people have needs for a sense of community or solidarity with others? How does sports help or hinder community, in your view?

Writing Suggestion

This writing suggestion builds upon the above Group Discussion question regarding the relation between community and sports, and asks you to incorporate points and implications from earlier readings in this chapter. Assuming that human beings are social creatures and thus a sense of social connection with others is crucial for human well-being and happiness, write an essay exploring the possible implications for community (or solidarity, if you prefer) if interest in team sports is declining (as Solomon asserts), and if Generation Y is less interested in team sports than in other—perhaps more individualistic—pursuits. What, if any, kinds of social effects might this declining interest have? Use ideas from Young, Solomon, and Lim and Turco to inform your examination of this issue.

Geographical Relocation, Suicide, and Homicide

Robert M. Fernquist

How often have you cheered for a particular sports team? Have you ever been swept up in feelings of joy when your favorite team won an important game? Ever experienced bitter disappointment following your team's defeat? Do you understand the strong feelings behind the UCLA football fan whose car displays a bumper sticker declaring "My favorite team is the UCLA Bruins and anyone who's playing against the USC Trojans"? Or are you mystified by that kind of sports fanaticism?

Social science research suggests that some sports fans become so emotionally invested in their favorite teams that wins and losses have powerful effects on their self-esteem and other emotional indicators. Based on findings such as these, Robert M. Fernquist set out to discover whether rates of homicide and suicide rise when a professional sports team relocates. He examines three examples of team relocation—in major league baseball, the Brooklyn Dodgers' move to Los Angeles and the New York Giants' move to San Francisco in 1957, football's Cleveland Browns' move to Baltimore in 1996, and the Houston Oilers' move to Nashville in 1998.

Fernquist found that while homicide rates didn't increase in these instances, suicide rates did. ***As you read,*** *notice how Fernquist uses the theories of Gabenesch and Durkheim to inform his study approach.*

INTRODUCTION

It is well known that sports fans often ardently track the successes and failures of "their" team(s). Tutko explains that "to see a performance where the (team) does well is tied to the "good" feeling inside of us—that feeling of trying and doing well. We assume that the good feeling is tied to all of the positive characteristics that make up character" (1989, p. 115). Further, sports fans often reflect on their own trials and pressures when watching professional sports because "athletics...excites our dominant personality features" (Tutko, 1989, p. 115). 1

Branscombe and Wann (1992a, p. 1017) write that, for fans who identify strongly with "their team," "An affront or loss on the part of the team then is a loss for the self." Building on this concept, Mitrano (1999, p. 151) explains that, just as people tend to go through certain 2 stages (such as anger and depression) when dealing with death or some other significant loss: "...fans collectively experience the same stages of grieving and loss" when a pro sports team relocates to another geographical area.

Fernquist (2000) has found that the performance of professional 3
sports teams is related to local suicide and homicide rates, whereas strikes in professional sports are related to national homicide rates (2001). In this exploratory research, I examine how, if at all, the relocation of professional sports teams from one geographical area to another impacts persons in the area left behind. Specifically, I examine how the relocation of the Brooklyn Dodgers and New York Giants after the 1957 baseball season, of the Cleveland Browns after the 1995–1996 football season, and of the Houston Oilers after the 1997–1998 football season impacted suicide and homicide rates of persons in New York City, Cuyahoga county, and Houston city, respectively. If there is much merit to the idea that some sports fans become closely and emotionally attached to "their team," and there is much research to support such attachments (as will be discussed below), then the examination of suicide and homicide rates among the general population in the areas left behind warrants investigation. I use Gabennesch's (1988) theory of broken promises and Durkheim's concept of anomie (1897[1951]) as theoretical guidelines for our research.

LITERATURE REVIEW AND THEORY

In the following literature and theoretical review, I discuss (1) sports 4
fans' identification with sports teams; (2) the impact that franchise relocation, as well as sport teams in general, have on society; and (3) sociological theories related to suicide, homicide, and the world of sports. Sports fans' identification with sports teams: Although the intensity of fan identification with sports teams varies from fan to fan (Wann, 1996), research still finds that following sports teams has significant impacts on the lives of the fans. In this respect, Pooley (1980, p. 20) stated that "being a fan usually means feeling intensely about a team as well as following its activities," while Cialdini, Borden, Thorne, Walker, Freeman, and Sloan (1976) similarly reported that college students tend to bask in the reflected glory (BIRG) of their respective football team's victories. Hence, "through their simple connections with sports teams, the personal images of fans are at stake when their teams take the field. The teams' victories and defeats are reacted to as personal successes and failures" (Cialdini et al., 1976, p. 374). Branscombe and Wann (1991) found strong evidence to suggest that many sports fans like following "their team" because this allegiance provides them with pleasurable leisure activities and increases

their self-esteem and overall positive emotions. If such positive outcomes can result from being a sports fan, why, then, could identification with a sports team result in aggressive and/or suicidal behavior?

In answer to such a query, Branscombe and Wann (1991, p. 125) 5
have argued that the degree of threat to a social identity, combined with an inability or unwillingness to reduce the importance of that identity,...is what gives rise to the negative potential involved in sports team identification. When the threat is at reasonably low levels (for example, when a championship is not at stake), then only the positive effects of attachment to something larger than the self will be observed. Both sides of the coin, however, can have powerful social consequences. Branscombe and Wann (1992b) also reported similar results regarding fan identification and sports. Further, it is common for "fans with a high degree of team identification" to be unable to distance themselves from their team's failures because "the concept of team follower is such a central component of (their) self-identity" (Wann, Melnick, Russell & Pease 2001, p. 171).

These fans keep hoping and waiting for their team to do better 6
and become frustrated when their team continues to perform poorly. There exists, therefore, sports fans who become so enmeshed with their team that these fans' "psychological well-being...is jeopardized" when their team is not doing well (Wann et al. 2001, p. 172). Branscombe and Wann (1992a, p. 1017) further explain that when sports fans cannot or will not distance themselves psychologically or emotionally from a sports team, "...aggressive behavior may be resorted to as a means of identity restoration." Such aggressive behavior may surface in the form of suicide or homicide.

Based on the review of these studies, the benefits derived from 7
identifying with their team (i.e., increased positive emotions, higher self-esteem, enjoyable leisure activities) can, for fans who strongly identify with their team, result in problems. These problems (such as aggressive behavior and/or depression) arise because team identification is such a central a part of their sense of self that when "their team" fails they find themselves unwilling or unable to distance themselves from the team in hope, perhaps, that the benefits will quickly return to them.

THE IMPACT THAT FRANCHISE RELOCATION AND SPORT TEAMS IN GENERAL HAVE ON SOCIETY

Mitrano (1999) examined fan reaction to the franchise relocation of the 8
Hartford Whalers hockey team during the period from March of 1996 to May of 1997. The last season the Whalers played in Hartford was

the 1995–1996 season. Mitrano likened the grief and loss expressed by many of the fans he interviewed over the franchise relocation to grief and loss people commonly go through when a loved one dies or some other significant loss is encountered. Some of the comments fans offered ranged from "It's really over. I'm truly too numb to really say much" to "Now that our team is leaving, ask yourself, 'Will you stay in CT?' I'm not" to "I'm completely numb.... my life has changed" (Mitrano, 1999, pp. 138–140). Although not all sports fans reacted to the franchise relocation in this manner, Mitrano (1999) indicated that a sense of loss and grief were common reactions among the fans he studied. Another common occurrence noted in this study was "...a shift from the tenets of loyalty and stability" among fans toward both team management and sports teams in general to tenets of "infidelity and celerity" (Mitrano, 1999, p. 151). Franchise relocation, then, cannot only make fans change their feelings toward their team, but can also negatively impact their sense of self.

Regarding the franchise relocations involved in the present 9
study, Sullivan (1987 p. vii) explains that the Brooklyn Dodgers "... enjoyed a close emotional tie with" the people in Brooklyn. Sullivan further explained that the Brooklyn Dodgers had such a "...powerful emotional" effect on Brooklynites that one *New York Times* writer expressed the mood of the Brooklyn fans as "galling resentment" when they learned their team would be leaving Brooklyn and going to Los Angeles after the 1957 season (Sullivan, 1987, p. 137). The Browns moved from Cleveland following the 1995–1996 football season; a move that was similarly upsetting to fans. For example, fans picketed Cleveland Stadium as owner Art Modell was expected to announce the move from Cleveland (USA Today, 1995). However, unlike the widespread passion that existed when the Browns and Dodgers moved, there was more ambivalence on the part of fans when the Oilers moved away from Houston after the 1997–1998 season (Collegian 1996). Clearly, though, there were fans in each of these areas that were upset over the geographical relocations of their pro sports teams.

Ecological studies suggest that fans are impacted by the perfor- 10
mance of professional sports teams. Trovato (1998) found that when the Montreal Canadiens hockey team was eliminated in an early round from the playoffs between 1951 and 1992, the likelihood of suicide increased for males aged 15–34 in Quebec. Similarly, Fernquist (2000) reported that suicide rates in metropolitan areas tend to be lower when those metropolitan areas have professional sports teams that performed well (e.g., made the playoffs regularly and won championships). He further found that the more times a team in a given metropolitan area made the playoffs, the lower the homicide rate in the given metropolitan area. Fernquist (2001) also argued that, during

the baseball and hockey strikes of 1994–1995, national homicide rates increased while suicide rates were not significantly affected. Both Trovato's and Fernquist's work suggests that social integration among a certain segment of the population (i.e., fans who strongly identify with "their team") is significantly impacted by the performance of professional sports teams. The impact that the geographical relocation has on personal violence among persons "left behind" is as of yet unknown. Given the manner in which suicide and homicide are related to phenomena in professional sports, as described above, the study of suicide and homicide in relation to the relocation of professional sports teams is worthy of further investigation.

Sociological theories related to suicide, homicide, and the world 11
of sports: Gabennesch (1988) developed a theory in which he describes how disappointments may result from expectations not being met—disappointment which could result in suicide.

Gabennesch argued that suicide is likely to occur when promises are broken due to "conditions or events which induce psychological misery" (1988 p.142). Gabennesch's theory of broken promises does apply to professional sports since persons who expect "their" team to do well may become extremely disappointed when the "promise" of winning is broken (Fernquist 2000). Stack (1995) argues that Gabennesch's theory of broken promises can also be applied to homicide, since disappointment was central to Durkheim's (1897[1951]) short discussion of anomic homicide. Durkheim (1897[1951], p.357) argued that anomie promotes "a state of exasperation and irritated weariness" which could result in either suicide or homicide, depending upon the person's "moral constitution" (e.g., a person with low morality is more likely to commit homicide than suicide).

Although some sports fans tend to have a long-term "love affair" 12
with their sports teams (Wann 1996), I use Durkheim's concept of anomie in addition to Gabennesch's theory of broken promises to guide this research. Durkheim (1897[1951]) explained that sudden (or anomic) changes in the environment can have an adverse impact on people. Durkheim, in his classic sociological analysis of suicide, showed that sudden changes such as widowhood, divorce, and economic crises can drastically change the way people view the normative order in society. When such sudden changes occur, it takes time for the person to adapt himself "to the new situation in which he finds himself and accordingly offers less resistance to suicide" (p. 259). Anomic suicide, therefore, "results from man's activities lacking regulation and his consequent sufferings" (p. 258). Within this context, I acknowledge the research done by Curtis, Loy, and Karnilowicz (1986) in which they examined social integration in relation to professional sporting events. Curtis et al. (1986) found significant, albeit weak, de-

clines in suicide just before and during the last day of the World Series and Super Bowl Sunday compared to the days immediately following these sporting events from 1972–1978. Smith (1976) also reported that interest in professional sports teams/persons can increase fans' social integration. However, I test Durkheim's theory that sudden changes to one's environment can have detrimental effects. The sudden changes central to this study are related to the geographical relocations of the sports teams. Even though fans generally know the geographic relocation is imminent, the anomic nature of the end of the last season is what causes problems since fans feel they no longer have "their team" in "their area" to support. I argue that the end of the final season, not the actual move itself, is what is anomic since the end of the season for all intents and purposes is what signals to fans that their team has "gone." I further argue that the beginning of the next season (the first season following the move) is anomic to fans since fans are once again reminded that "their team" is no longer in their geographical area. I hypothesize, therefore, three contexts which increase suicide and homicide rates among persons in the area "left behind": (1) increases that occur at the end of the last season before the actual move occurs; (2) increases that occur at the beginning of the next season; and (3) increases that occur at both the end of the last season and the beginning of the next season. I will first examine descriptive statistics regarding the frequency of the number of suicides and homicides in relation to these hypotheses and then, based on these trends, I will estimate regression models to predict variation on suicide and homicide rates. Although such an approach to data analysis can be termed ad hoc, an examination of trends before the statistical modelling will allow us to see if trends present in the descriptive analysis remain in the presence of relevant statistical controls.

DATA AND METHODS

For each geographical area, I define the end of the season as occurring during December and January for American football and September and October for baseball (when the regular season ends and playoffs occur). I define the beginning of the next season as occurring during August and September for American football and March and April for baseball (when pre-season games come to an end and the regular season begins). Monthly data for all areas are used in this analysis. To control differences in the seasonality of suicide, I compare data for the months at the end of the season and beginning of the next season (e.g., the "anomic months") with those same months in the two years before and the two years after the 13 "anomic months." The central variable of interest in this analysis, the "relocation" variable, is used in regression analysis and is a dichotomous variable, being coded 1 for anomic months and 0 for all other months. The coding of this variable is explained in more detail below. The Brooklyn Dodgers and New York Giants' moves: Data on the number of suicides and homicides in New York City are from the New York City Department of Health (2000). Data for individual boroughs were unavailable. For the last season's end, the anomic months are September and October 1957 and I compare these months to September and October, 1956, 1958, and 1959 (1955 data were not available). For the beginning of the season after the baseball teams moved, the anomic months are March and April, 1958, and I compare these months to March and April, 1956, 1957, 1959, and 1960.

The Cleveland Browns' move: Data in this instance were ob- 14
tained from Cuyahoga county, the county in which the city of Cleveland is located. Data on suicides and homicides in Cuyahoga county are from the Ohio Department of Health, Center for Public Health Data and Statistics (2000). For the last season's end, the anomic months are December 1995 and January 1996, and I compare these months to December 1993, 1994, 1996, 1997 and to January 1994, 1995, 1997, and 1998. For the beginning of the season after the Browns moved, the anomic months are August and September 1996, and I compare these months to August and September 1994, 1995, 1997, and 1998.

The Houston Oilers' move: Data on the number of suicides and 15
homicides in Houston city are from the Texas Department of Health (2000). For the last season's end, the anomic months are December 1997 and January 1998, and I compare these months to December 1995, 1996, 1998, 1999 and to January 1996, 1997, and 1999 (2000 data were not available). For the beginning of the season after the Oilers moved, the anomic months are August and September, 1998, and I compare these months to August and September 1996, 1997, and 1999.

In the regression models, I examine how the geographic reloca- 16
tions impact suicide and homicide rates per 100,000 population. The central independent variable in the regression models, the "relocation" variable, is a dichotomous variable comparing suicide and homicide rates in the anomic months to the same months in the years preceding and succeeding the anomic period. To convert the number of suicides and homicides to rates per 100,000 population for the regression analysis, I obtained population estimates for the three areas. In the regression models, birth rates, marriage rates, and unemployment rates per 1,000 population are controlled for, variables which are relevant to the sociological study of suicide and homicide (Fernquist 2000; Lester 1994). For New York City, data on the number of births

and marriages, as well as estimates of population size, are from the New York State Department of Health (2000). Data on unemployment rates for New York City are from the New York State Department of Labor (2001). Unfortunately, unemployment data prior to 1958 were not available, and so 1958 data are also used for 1956 and 1957. For Cuyahoga county, data on the number of births and marriages are from the Ohio Department of Health, Center for Public Health Data and Statistics (2000), while the unemployment rates are from Labor Market Information (2000). The population estimates are from the Ohio Department of Development (2000).

For Houston, data on the number of births and marriages were 17
available only for Harris county (the county in which the city of Houston is located), not for the city of Houston proper. Data on the number of births and marriages are from the Texas Department of Health (2000). Unemployment rates for the city of Houston are from Economagic (2001). Population estimates for persons in Harris county (to calculate birth and marriage rates) are from the Texas Department of Health (2000) while population estimates for city of Houston (to calculate suicide and homicide rates) are from the Texas State Data Center (2000).

Ordinary least squares estimation (OLS) is used to model varia- 18
tion in suicide and homicide rates. Given that the OLS regression models in Table 2 employ cross-sectional, time-series data, I checked for harmful autocorrelation (significant correlations among the disturbances) and heteroskedasticity (unequal variances among the disturbances) since these problems may produce incorrect OLS regression coefficients (Stack 1992).

I also checked for problematic collinearity among the predictors. 19
After the suicide and homicide models were corrected for first-order autocorrelation, the regression models were acceptable in terms of autocorrelation and heteroskedasticity levels (see Table 2). Since the value of the Durbin-Watson statistic, a commonly used test to examine the degree of autocorrelation present in regression, is close to 2.0 in both models, and since neither statistic that measures the presence of heteroskedasticity (the Glejser [1969] test) is significant at the .05 level, we can be confident that neither autocorrelation nor heteroskedasticity will bias results from the regression models. Allison (1999) explains that the use of Variance Inflation Factors (VIFs) can show whether or not collinearity among the independent variables will bias regression estimates. Each predictor in the models in table 2 was regressed on all others simultaneously to calculate the VIF for each predictor. Each VIF is calculated by 1/1-R2 and Allison (1999) explains that any VIF of 2.5 or larger indicates problematic collinearity. No VIF was 2.5 or larger, suggesting that collinearity was not a problem for the models in Table 2.

RESULTS

Table 1 shows the number of suicides and homicides and the percentage changes in the anomic months versus those same months before and after the anomic months. Based on these percentage changes, I will categorize New York City and Houston as being anomic at the beginning of the next season since percentage changes in suicide and homicide are greater at the beginning of the next season relative to the end of the last season. I put Cuyahoga county in the category of being anomic at season's end since, especially for suicide, percentage changes were greater at season's end relative to the beginning of the next season. I feel this categorization best explains increases in suicide and, to a lesser extent, homicide in each of these areas. 20

In the regression analysis, I examine suicide and homicide rates per 100,000 population in the three areas combined with the relocation variable coded 1 in New York City and Houston for the anomic months during which the respective sports seasons began the season after the geographic relocations while in Cuyahoga county the move variable is coded 1 for the anomic months at the end of the last season before the geographic relocation. All other months are coded 0. 21

The regression models in Table 2 show that the geographic relocation of all three teams is significantly related to increased suicide rates in New York City, Cuyahoga County, and Houston City, holding all else constant in the model. In Cuyahoga County, the impact on suicide was more immediate (since Cuyahoga was modeled as a "season's end anomic" area), while the impact on suicide in New York and Houston was delayed until the next season began. Geographic relocation was not significantly related to variation in local homicide rates. Regarding the control variables, birth rates are positively related to both suicide and homicide rates, while marriage rates are inversely related to both suicide and homicide rates. Unemployment rates are not significantly related to either suicide or homicide rates, even though the coefficient in the homicide model is larger than the other coefficients. Explained variance is fairly high in both the suicide and homicide models (.53 and .74, respectively). 22

DISCUSSION AND CONCLUSION

As Trovato has so correctly stated, "The association of major sport occasions and mortality has received scant attention in the literature, and our understanding of this phenomenon is far from complete" (1998, p. 119). In response, within this study, I have attempted to shed more light on the relationship between sporting "events" and suicide and homicide. This exploratory analysis reveals support for the hypotheses 23

Table 1 Suicide and Homicide in Three U.S. Areas: Raw Numbers and Percentage Change Over Previous Period

	New York City			Cuyahoga County			Houston City		
	Comparisons at End of Season (Annual Averages)								
	Before	**Anomic**	**After**	**Before**	**Anomic**	**After**	**Before**	**Anomic**	**After**
	Sept/Oct 1956	Sept/Oct 1957	Sept/Oct 1958–9	Dec 1993–4 Jan 1994–5	Dec 1995 Jan 1996	Dec 1996–7 Jan 1997–8	Dec 1995–6 Jan 1996–7	Dec 1997 Jan 1998	Dec 1998–9 Jan 1999
Suicides	87	96 (+10%)	116 (+21%)	29	33 (+14%)	20 (−39%)	43	49 (+14%)	41 (−16%)
Homicides	40	46 (+15%)	65 (+41%)	25	20 (−20%)	21 (+5%)	61	48 (−21%)	48
	Comparisons at Beginning of Next Season (Annual Averages)								
	Before	**Anomic**	**After**	**Before**	**Anomic**	**After**	**Before**	**Anomic**	**After**
	Mar/Apr 1956–7	Mar/Apr 1958	Mar/Apr 1959–60	Aug/Sept 1994–5	Aug/Sept 1996	Aug/Sept 1997–8	Aug/Sept 1996–7	Aug/Sept 1998	Aug/Sept 1999
Suicides	102	148 (+45%)	136 (−8%)	27	20 (−35%)	34 (+70%)	43	52 (+21%)	35 (−33%)
Homicides	44	60 (+36%)	65 (+8%)	36	25 (−31%)	20 (−20%)	53	61 (+15%)	42 (−31%)

Table 2 Unstandardized Regression Estimates of Suicide and Homicide Rates in Three U.S. Areas (N=30)

Independent Variable	Suicide Rates	Homicide Rates
Move	3.23	1.07
Birth Rates	0.34	1.02
Marriage Rates	−0.27	−0.97
Unemployment Rates	0.12	1.59
Constant	6.14	−9.62
Method of Estimation	**Corrected for First-Order Autocorrelation (Cochrane/Orcutt)**	**Corrected for First-Order Autocorrelation (Cochrane/Orcutt)**
Durbin-Watson Statistic	1.98	1.94
Glejser test for Heteroskedasticity (df=4)	4.49 (p>.34)	7.39 (p>.11)
Largest Variance Inflation Factor	1.41	1.41
Explained Variance	0.53	0.74

p<.05; **p<.01; ***p<.001

that suicide rates increase due to geographic relocation of professional sporting teams both at the end of the last season before the actual move occurred (Cleveland) and at the beginning of the next season after the relocation (New York and Houston).

The hypotheses about homicide rates, however, were not sup- 24
ported. Although these data are not individual-level thus not allowing us to ascertain if those fans who highly identify with "their" team are the persons whose suicide rate increases upon franchise relocation, the results are suggestive that this may be the case. Whereas Durkheim (1897 [1951]) argued that anomie promotes a state of exasperation which could result in either suicide or homicide, I find that exasperation related to geographic relocation is related to increases in suicide rates, but not homicide rates. The sudden change brought about due to the geographic relocations of pro sports teams does appear to, at least for a short time, make highly identified fans drastically change the way they view the normative order in society. Unable (or unwilling) to adapt to the new environment, an environment which no longer contains "their team," their sense of self may become seriously damaged with suicide more likely to result.

They may come to feel as if they are losing control of the world 25
around them (Grossberg 1992). As Tutko (1989) said, fans put much

feeling into following the progress of "their team," thus when that team is no longer in the specific area anomie increases. These fans end up having a difficult time letting go of their team because they "experience depression and an intense negative affective state and adopt a poor outlook on life subsequent to" the team's geographic relocation (Wann et al. 2001, p. 172).

From the point of view of Gabennesch's (1988) theory, highly 26 identified fans may come to see the geographic relocation of their team as breaking the promise that, at least in the fans' minds, their team will always be in that geographic area for the fans to cheer and follow. Although there is certainly never a guarantee that a professional sports team will remain in a given area indefinitely, fans apparently hope/expect their team to stay. Although aggregate data cannot be used to make specific individual references, the data from this study, in agreement with Gabennesch (1988), suggest that when the team does move, fans may feel that these expectations are broken, and these broken promises have detrimental effects.

I also realize that the nature of being a sports fan has changed 27 over the past several decades. With the introduction of free agency in the 1970s, fans have come to realize that players will come and go from team to team (Wann et al. 2001). Since this study entails data from pre-free agency years (the Dodgers and Giants) as well as data after the introduction of free agency, could the nature of fans' identification with "their team" have changed over the years? I argue that the nature of fans' identification with their team has not significantly changed during this period since all three geographic relocations were related to increased suicide rates. If fans have become less attached to "their team," we would not have seen suicide rates rise after the Oilers and Browns relocated. Therefore, even though fans know players will come and go, they still today expect 'their team' to remain in its geographical location. I realize that there are other factors related to suicide and homicide rates that were not included in the study. Variables such as religiosity, per capita income, and cohort size are relevant control variables I was unable to include in the analysis due to a lack of data. It is unclear if the inclusion of these control variables in the regression models would alter the impact of geographic relocation on suicide or homicide.

Urban revitalization has also been occurring in the Cleveland 28 metropolitan area during the 1990s and this phenomenon could also be responsible for significant variation in the Cuyahoga county suicide and homicide rates. Therefore, I acknowledge shortcomings in the current aggregate analysis on suicide and homicide rates in the New York, Cleveland, and Houston areas. Nonetheless, this research does suggest that the association between geographic relocation and suicide (and even homicide) should be studied in more detail. In particular, due to the difficulty highly identified fans have of letting go of "their team" (Wann et al. 2001), it is recommended that the emphasis of future research on geographic relocation and suicide should be placed on the differences in suicidal behavior between highly identified fans and less identified fans.

Thanks are expressed to the following persons for the generous help in providing the author with vital data: Donna Smith (Cuyahoga county); Anna Vincent (Houston city and Harris county); Elizabeth Acevedo, Louise Berensen, Robert Roddy, and Al Wolf (New York City). Thanks also go to Joyce Knapton and Charlene Zion for further help with obtaining data and to the anonymous reviewers of sosol for insightful comments.

REFERENCES

Allison, P. D. (1999). *Multiple regression: A primer.* Thousand Oaks, CA: Pine Forge Press.

Branscombe, N. R. & Wann, D. L. (1991). The positive and self-concept consequences of sports team identification. *Journal of Sport and Social Issues, 15,* 115–127.

Branscombe, N. R. & Wann, D. L. (1992a). Role of identification with a group, arousal, categorization processes, and self-esteem in sports spectator aggression. *Human Relations, 45,* 1013–1033.

Branscombe, N. R. & Wann, D. L. (1992b). Physiological arousal and reactions to outgroup members during competitions that implicate an important social identity. *Aggressive Behavior, 18,* 85–93.

Cialdini, R. B., Borden, R. J., Thorne, A., Walker, M. R., Freeman, S., & Sloan, L. R. (1976). Basking in reflected glory: Three (football) field studies. *Journal of Personality and Social Psychology, 34,* 366–375.

Collegian. (1996). Owners vote to move Oilers to Nashville. Kansas State University: Student Publications Inc. < *http://collegian.ksu.edu/issues/v100/sp/n143/spt-ap-oilers.html* > (1996, May 1).

Curtis, J., Loy, J, & Karnilowicz, W. (1986). A comparison of suicide-dip effects of major sport events and civil holidays. *Sociology of Sport Journal, 3,* 1–14.

Economagic. (2001). Unemployment rate: Houston City, Texas. *http://www.economagic.com/em-cgi/data.exe/blsla/laups48060003* (2001, January 24).

Durkheim, E. (1897[1951]). *Suicide.* New York: Free Press.

Fernquist, R. M. (2000). An Aggregate Analysis of Professional Sports, Suicide and Homicide Rates: 30 U.S. Metropolitan Areas, 1971–1990. *Aggression and Violent Behavior, 5,* 329–341.

Fernquist, R. M. (2001). The 1994–1995 Baseball and Hockey Strikes and Their Impact on Suicide and Homicide Rates in the United States. *Archives of Suicide Research,* In Press.

Gabennesch, H. (1988). When promises fail: A theory of temporal fluctuations in suicide. *Social Forces, 67,* 129–145.

Glejser, H. C. (1969). A new test for heteroskedasticity. *Journal of the American Statistical Association, 64,* 316–323.

Grossberg, L. (1992). "Is there a fan in the house?": The affective sensibility of fandom. In L. Lewis (Ed.) *The adoring audience: Fan culture and popular media.* (pp. 50–65) New York: Routledge.

Johnson, B. D. (1965). Durkheim's one cause of suicide. *American Sociological Review, 30,* 875–886.

Labor Market Information. (2000). Local area unemployment statistics. < *http://www.lmi.state.oh.us/ASP/LAUS/vbLAUS.htm* > (2000, November 17).

Lester, D. (1994). *Patterns of suicide and homicide in America.* Commack, NJ: Nova Science Publishers.

Mitrano, J. R. (1999). The "sudden death" of hockey in Hartford: Sports fans and franchise relocation. *Sociology of Sport Journal, 16,* 134–154.

New York City Department of Health. Office of Vital Statistics. (Personal correspondence). September 20, 2000.

New York State Department of Health. Bureau of Biometrics. (Personal correspondence). April 22, 2000.

New York State Department of Labor. Division of Research and Statistics. (Personal correspondence). April 4, 2001.

Ohio Department of Development. (2000). Ohio county profiles: Cuyahoga county. < *http://www.odod.state.oh.us/osr/profiles/PDF/CUYAHOGA.PDF* > (2000, September 12).

Ohio Department of Health, Center for Public Health Data and Statistics. (Personal correspondence). November 14, 2000.

Pooley, J. C. (1980). *The sport fan: A social-psychology of misbehaviour.* Calgary: University of Calgary.

Smith, G. J. (1976), An examination of the phenomenon of sports hero worship. *Canadian Journal of Applied Sports Sciences, 4,* 259–270.

Stack, S. (1995). Temporal disappointment, homicide and suicide: An analysis of nonwhites and whites. *Sociological Focus, 28,* 313–328.

Stack, S. (1992). The effect of divorce on suicide in Japan: A time series analysis, 1950–1980. *Journal of Marriage and the Family, 54,* 327–334.

Sullivan, N. J. (1987). *The Dodgers move west.* New York: Oxford University Press.

Texas Department of Health. Statistical Services Division, Bureau of Vital Statistics. (Personal correspondence). October 23, 2000.

Texas Department of Health. (2000). Texas health data: Population. < *http://soupfin.tdh.state.tx.us/people.htm* > (2000, October 25)

Texas State Data Center. (2000). Texas population estimates program. < *http://txsdc.tamu.edu/tpepp/txpopest.html* > (2000, October 25)

Trovato, F. (1998). The Stanley Cup of Hockey and Suicide in Quebec, 1951–1992. *Social Forces, 77,* 105–127.

Tutko, T. A. (1989). Personality change in the American sport scene. In J. H. Goldstein (Ed.), *Sports, games, and play* (pp. 111–127). New York: Wiley and Sons.

USA Today. (1995). Modell turns Browns fans blue over move. < *http://www.usatoday.elibrary.com* > (1995, November 5).

Wann, D. L. (1996). Seasonal changes in spectators' identification and involvement with and evaluations of college basketball and football teams. *The Psychological Record, 46,* 201–216.

Wann, D. L., Melnick, M. J., Russell, G. W., & Pease, D. G. (2001). *Sport fans: The psychology and social impact of spectators.* New York: Routledge.

Examining the Text

1. Explain Gabenesch's theory of broken promises. How does the theory apply to professional sports, according to Fernquist?

2. How does Durkheim's theory of anomie help Fernquist set the terms of his hypotheses?

3. In your opinion, were all of Fernquist's hypotheses supported? Explain.

4. Even though suicide rates were higher in the periods and places Fernquist examined, what key fact makes it impossible for him to conclude that team relocations directly cause serious fans to commit suicide?

For Group Discussion

If you and your group members were social scientists with a lot of funding, what kind of study could you implement to further test the connection between suicide and sports team relocation? As a group, brainstorm ideas, or come up with another sports-and-fan-related topic you think would be interesting and useful for social scientists to study. Come up with some ideas about how that topic could be explored through analyzing data as Fernquist did, or through interviews, observation, or surveys.

Writing Suggestion

Imagine you are a fan of a professional football team—say, the Phoenix Pillagers—and the team's owners are negotiating a move from Phoenix, Arizona, to Des Moines, Iowa. Write a letter to the editor of the Phoenix newspaper in which you use conclusions from Fernquist's study to persuade city leaders and fellow citizens to work at preventing the move.

Analyzing Sports

Champion of the World

Maya Angelou

Maya Angelou is a well-known poet, novelist, and performer. Born in 1928 and raised in the segregated South, Angelou persevered through countless hardships to become one of the country's most revered authors and cultural leaders. Angelou read her poem, "On the Pulse of Morning," at the 1993 inauguration of President Bill Clinton.

The selection which follows is from Angelou's first volume of autobiography, I Know Why the Caged Bird Sings *(1969). She relates an important recollection from childhood about the night in the 1930s when world heavyweight champion Joe Louis, nicknamed the "Brown Bomber," defended his boxing title against a White contender. Much of Angelou's narrative is made up of the words and feelings of the local Black community gathered in her Uncle Willie's store to listen to the broadcast of that highly publicized match. Angelou shows how her neighbors' hopes and fears and their image of themselves as a people were intimately connected to the fortunes of Louis, one of a very few Black heroes of the day. Her narrative reveals that a "simple" sporting event can be of intense significance for a group of people who see it as a symbol of personal victory or defeat.*

Before you read, *recall any experience you've had or heard about in which a sporting event took on an emotional power and significance far greater than the event itself would seem to warrant. Whether this event is one that you participated in, watched, or read about, think about how and why sports can have such an intense influence on people's lives.*

The last inch of space was filled, yet people continued to wedge themselves along the walls of the Store. Uncle Willie had turned the radio up to its last notch so that youngsters on the porch wouldn't miss a word. Women sat on kitchen chairs, dining-room chairs, stools, and upturned wooden boxes. Small children and babies perched on every lap available and men leaned on the shelves or on each other. 1

The apprehensive mood was shot through with shafts of gaiety, as a black sky is streaked with lightning. 2

"I ain't worried 'bout this fight. Joe's gonna whip that cracker like it's open season." 3

"He gone whip him till that white boy call him Momma." 4

At last the talking finished and the string-along songs about razor blades were over and the fight began. 5

"A quick jab to the head." In the Store the crowd grunted. "A left to the head and a right and another left." One of the listeners cackled like a hen and was quieted. 6

"They're in a clinch, Louis is trying to fight his way out." 7

Some bitter comedian on the porch said, "That white man don't mind hugging that niggah now, I betcha." 8

"The referee is moving in to break them up, but Louis finally pushed the contender away and it's an uppercut to the chin. The contender is hanging on, now he's backing away. Louis catches him with a short left to the jaw." 9

A tide of murmuring assent poured out the door and into the yard. 10

"Another left and another left. Louis is saving that mighty right . . ." The mutter in the Store had grown into a baby roar and it was pierced by the clang of a bell and the announcer's "That's the bell for round three, ladies and gentlemen." 11

As I pushed my way into the Store I wondered if the announcer gave any thought to the fact that he was addressing as "ladies and gentlemen" all the Negroes around the world who sat sweating and praying, glued to their "Master's voice." 12

There were only a few calls for RC Colas, Dr. Peppers, and Hires root beer. The real festivities would begin after the fight. Then even the old Christian ladies who taught their children and tried themselves to practice turning the other cheek would buy soft drinks, and if the Brown Bomber's victory was a particularly bloody one they would order peanut patties and Baby Ruths, also. 13

Bailey and I laid coins on top of the cash register. Uncle Willie didn't allow us to ring up sales during a fight. It was too noisy and might shake up the atmosphere. When the gong rang for the next round we pushed through the near-sacred quiet to the herd of children outside. 14

"He's got Louis against the ropes and now it's a left to the body and a right to the ribs. Another right to the body, it looks like it was low . . . Yes, ladies and gentlemen, the referee is signaling but the contender keeps raining the blows on Louis. It's another to the body, and it looks like Louis is going down." 15

My race groaned. It was our people falling. It was another lynching, yet another Black man hanging on a tree. One more woman ambushed and raped. A Black boy whipped and maimed. It was hounds on the trail of a man running through slimy swamps. It was a white woman slapping her maid for being forgetful. 16

Joe Louis, Champion of the World

The men in the Store stood away from the walls and at attention. Women greedily clutched the babes on their laps while on the porch the shufflings and smiles, flirtings and pinching of a few minutes before were gone. This might be the end of the world. If Joe lost we were back in slavery and beyond help. It would all be true, the accusations that we were lower types of human beings. Only a little higher than apes. True that we were stupid and ugly and lazy and dirty and, unlucky and worst of all, that God Himself hated us and ordained us to be hewers of wood and drawers of water, forever and ever, world without end. 17

We didn't breathe. We didn't hope. We waited. 18

"He's off the ropes, ladies and gentlemen. He's moving towards 19 the center of the ring." There was no time to be relieved. The worst might still happen.

"And now it looks like Joe is mad. He's caught Carnera with a 20 left hook to the head and a right to the head. It's a left jab to the body and another left to the head. There's a left cross and a right to the head. The contender's right eye is bleeding and he can't seem to keep his block up. Louis is penetrating every block. The referee is moving in, but Louis sends a left to the body and it's an uppercut to the chin and the contender is dropping. He's on the canvas, ladies and gentlemen."

21 Babies slid to the floor as women stood up and men leaned toward the radio.

22 "Here's the referee. He's counting. One, two, three, four, five, six, seven . . . Is the contender trying to get up again?"

23 All the men in the store shouted, "NO."

24 "—eight, nine, ten." There were a few sounds from the audience, but they seemed to be holding themselves in against tremendous pressure.

25 "The fight is all over, ladies and gentlemen. Let's get the microphone over to the referee . . . Here he is. He's got the Brown Bomber's hand, he's holding it up . . . Here he is . . ."

26 Then the voice, husky and familiar, came to wash over us—"The winnah, and still heavyweight champeen of the world . . . Joe Louis."

27 Champion of the world. A Black boy. Some Black mother's son.

28 He was the strongest man in the world. People drank Coca-Colas like ambrosia and ate candy bars like Christmas. Some of the men went behind the Store and poured white lightning in their soft-drink bottles, and a few of the bigger boys followed them. Those who were not chased away came back blowing their breath in front of themselves like proud smokers.

29 It would take an hour or more before people would leave the Store and head home. Those who lived too far had made arrangements to stay in town. It wouldn't do for a Black man and his family to be caught on a lonely country road on a night when Joe Louis had proved that we were the strongest people in the world.

Examining the Text

1. Unlike the other selections in this chapter which offer fairly objective analyses of sport, Angelou relates a personal recollection. What conclusions about the influence of sports on culture, and specifically on African American culture in the 1930s, can you draw from her story? Has that influence changed significantly over the last sixty years?

2. In paragraphs 16 and 17 Angelou describes her own thoughts about the prospect of Louis losing the match. After rereading these paragraphs, what do you think they contribute to the overall meaning and drama of the story? How are they connected to the final paragraph?

3. What is the effect of the concluding paragraph in the story? How would Angelou's message be different if she had not ended it this way?

For Group Discussion

Angelou's recollection demonstrates in vivid detail how a sporting event can take on much larger significance, how people can invest a great deal of emotion in the performance of an athlete or team. In your group, list some other specific examples of sporting contests that have taken on intense emotional significance and meaning for an individual or a group of fans. As a class, discuss the advantages and disadvantages of the strong influence sports has on its fans.

Writing Suggestion

In her narrative, Angelou describes how Joe Louis was an inspiration and sign of hope for African Americans in the 1930s. Choose another athlete who you think has similarly been an inspiration to his or her fans or has served as a role model. In an essay discuss the qualities that make that person a particularly good model. At the same time, if you think that athlete has negative qualities, you may cite these as well in analyzing how he or she has influenced fans.

Tiger Time: The Wonder of an American Hero

Jay Nordlinger

Surely by now most Americans—whether they care about golf or not—know the basic outlines of Tiger Woods' phenomenal golf career. Nordlinger fills in many of the details of Woods' success: his amazing amateur career was followed by twenty-seven tournament wins by the age of twenty-five—he won the Master's tournament by an unprecedented twelve strokes—and the list goes on. After lauding Woods' golf game, Nordlinger goes on to praise his general demeanor, especially in regard to those who would have Woods serve as a role model for African Americans. According to Nordlinger, Woods' repeated insistence that he's a role model for all kids—not just those who are black—is an admirable and gutsy move.

As you read, *think about the impact that a sports figure can have in the culture at large. What kind of impact has Tiger Woods had—both within the world of golf and beyond it? How does his impact compare to that of boxer Joe Louis, as portrayed by Maya Angelou in the last reading?*

Sometime last season, I e-mailed a friend of mine, an ex-pro golfer and a keen student of the game. "Are we ready to concede that Tiger is the best ever?" I asked. His answer was slightly ambiguous; I couldn't tell whether he was being sincere or sarcastic. So I asked for a clarification. "Oh, let me be perfectly clear," he replied. "Nicklaus in his heyday couldn't carry Tiger's clubs. Really." 1

Now, my friend and I were Nicklaus worshipers from way back—we still are. When it comes to Nicklaus, we are dangerously close to violating the First Commandment. So acknowledging the truth about Tiger came hard. Jack Nicklaus—this is gospel in golf—dominated his sport as no other athlete ever dominated any sport. I once began a piece about Nicklaus roughly this way: Boxing folks can talk about Louis versus Ali; baseball people can talk about Cobb and Ruth and Mays (or whomever); tennis people can have a high time about Laver and Sampras; but in golf, there's nothing to discuss. 2

What's more, no one else was ever supposed to dominate the game. Nicklaus was supposed to be the last giant, the last player ever to make the others quake, the last to win predictably. You see, "parity" had arrived: That was the big buzzword on Tour. There were now thirty, forty—maybe sixty—guys who could win in any given week. Golf instruction—swing science—had equalized things. Advances in equipment had equalized things. Conditioning, nutrition, etc., had equalized things. If a guy won, say, three tournaments in a season, that would be practically a freak, and the fellow would be Player of the Year, for sure. We would never see anything close to Nicklaus again. 3

Furthermore, his mark of 18 professional majors—twenty majors, if you counted his two U.S. Amateurs (and most of us did, because we loved that round, awesome number)—was an inviolable record. It would stand forever. It was the most unapproachable record in golf. 4

All of this needs to be remembered, because people forget. I've seen this in my own (not terribly long) lifetime. When I was young, the greatest record in baseball—the one that would live unto eternity—was Lou Gehrig's 2,130 consecutive games. That, all the experts said, was the one mark no one would ever reach. But then, when Cal Ripken closed in on it, they changed. They cheated. Now they said it was Joe D's 56–game hitting streak that was numero uno. Ah, but I remember: I won't forget. Ripken's achievement must not be slighted—everyone said it was impossible. 5

And now Tiger: the non-golfer will simply have to trust me that no one was supposed to be able to do what Tiger has, in fact, done. His 6 achievements are—or were—unimaginable. The question arises, has Woods won the Grand Slam? I, for one, don't care: he has won something like it—four consecutive majors—and no one else has (forgetting Bobby Jones, in the "premodern" Slam). I vow not to forget—no matter how fuzzy the past becomes—that Woods has accomplished what was proclaimed by one and all unaccomplishable.

How to talk about Tiger Woods? I don't know. Start with this (a cliche, but a useful cliche): when Nicklaus first showed up at the Masters, Bob Jones said, "He plays a game with which I am not familiar." The same has to be said of Woods. Another friend of mine—a pro golfer and a genuine philosophe—made the following, arresting statement: "It's not just that Woods is the best ever to play the game; it is that he is the first ever to play it." Think about that for more than a second or two, and you grow dizzy. What does it mean? It means, I think, that Tiger is the first truly to exploit the possibilities of the game. That he is the first to swing the club as it ought to be swung. That he—this gets a bit mystical—sees a game that others have been blind to, or have caught only glimpses of. 7

In the last years of his life, I had lessons—and many long conversations—with Bill Strausbaugh Jr., the most decorated teacher in the history of the PGA. "Coach" was one of the wisest men I ever hope to meet in golf, or to meet, period. Speaking of Tiger—this was in 1998, I believe—he said, "That young man has the best golf motion ever." (Coach disdained the word "swing"—he thought it gave his students the wrong idea.) I replied, condescendingly, like an idiot, "Oh, Coach, you must mean that he has one of the best ever. You've seen Hogan, Snead—all of them." He fixed me with a look and said, "No, Jay, I meant what I said: Tiger has the best golf motion ever." I was tremendously impressed by this, because the old are usually afflicted with the vice of nostalgia: no one is ever as good now as then. Thus, in baseball, for example, you hear, "Yeah, Roger Clemens is okay, but Grover Alexander! There was a pitcher!" Right. 8

Bill Strausbaugh also said, "Tiger has three things: a great golf motion, a great golf mind, and a great golf body. (This last, Coach maintained, is grossly underrated.) He is ideal—I never thought I would see it." 9

Tiger Woods was a legend before he ever turned pro. He had, I would argue, the greatest amateur career ever. (Bobby Jones idolaters—of whom I am one, from the crib—should just sit still. There is an argument here. And Jones wasn't an "amateur" in our present sense.) In fact, it's unfortunate about Tiger's dazzling pro career that it has been allowed to overshadow, inevitably, his amateur career. Tiger Woods, starting when he was 15 years old, won three straight U.S. Junior Championships and three straight U.S. Amateur Champi- 10 onships. This achievement is positively stupefying. I could try to explain, but, again, I say: trust me.

Tiger was the youngest ever to win the Junior—he was 15. No one had ever won twice, and he would win three times. He was the youngest ever to win the U.S. Amateur—he was 18. He would be the only player ever to win the Am three years in a row. This takes a discipline, a kind of genius, that is hard to fathom. I argued, quite seriously, that if, God forbid, Tiger died before he ever had a chance to tee it up as a pro, he would die as one of the finest players in history. And he would have. 11

(I should interject here that Tiger—it is almost an afterthought—won the NCAA championship. He attended college—Stanford—for two years. Condoleezza Rice once told me—she had been provost of Stanford—that it was a shame that Tiger left school, understandable as it was, because he "really enjoyed it.") 12

Then there is Tiger the pro. Once more, how to convey the uniqueness—the impossibility—of it all? Tiger is only 25—and he has won 27 tournaments, including six majors (nine, if you count the way we do for Nicklaus). To provide a little comparison, Curtis Strange, who was the best player in the world for several years, won 17 tournaments, and two majors. At one stage, Woods won six PGA events in a row: farewell, parity. Indeed, before Woods, it was absurd to say, "I think so-and-so will win this golf tournament," or even, "So-and-so is the favorite." Golf is not a football game, in which one team or the other must win. Tiger has introduced a strange element: predictability. 13

Let's grapple with some victory margins: in 1997 (at age 21, but that's a different matter), Tiger won the Masters by twelve shots. I once heard the TV commentator Ken Venturi, in the pre-Tiger era, say of a guy who was leading some tournament by three shots—three shots—"He's lapping the field." And he was. When you win the Masters, you win it by one shot, two shots—three shots, maybe. Often, you're forced to win it in a sudden-death playoff. Tiger won the 1997 Masters by twelve shots: he could have made a 15 at the final par 4 and still won—could have made 16 to play off. 14

In 2000, he won the U.S. Open, at Pebble Beach, by fifteen shots. He won the British Open, at St. Andrews, by eight shots. (These are all records, but we can't possibly begin to go into the record book.) I argued—only half-jokingly, or a third jokingly—that Tiger should retire then and there, rather as Bobby Jones did, at age 28. What did he have left to prove? Sure, he had dreamed all his life of breaking Nicklaus's lifetime records, but that was just a matter of longevity, of hanging around, of staying uninjured, of keeping oneself interested. What is there left to do after winning the U.S. Open at Pebble (by fifteen) and the British at St. Andrews (by eight), and in the millennial year of 2000? 15

Well, you can go on to win a type of Slam, I guess. And Woods is still charging. 16

Of course, he is more than a golfer: He is an important American, not least because of the racial or ethnic question. There is probably no one in the country more refreshing, more resolute about race than Tiger Woods. He is a one-man army against cant and stupidity. One of the most thrilling television moments I have ever seen occurred at the Masters, when Tiger was playing as an amateur. Jim Nantz of CBS asked him one of those softball, standard, perfunctory questions: "Do you think you have an obligation to be a role model for minority kids?" Tiger answered, quick as a flash, "No." I almost fell out of my chair. He continued, "I have an obligation to be a role model for all kids." 17

After Tiger won the Masters in '97, President Clinton asked him, the morning after, to join him the following day, to participate in a Jackie Robinson ceremony at Shea Stadium. Tiger said . . . no, to the President of the United States. The invitation was last-minute, and Tiger was suspicious of its motives. He had long planned a vacation in Mexico with friends, and he wouldn't scrap or alter it. Many people criticized Tiger for this decision; but he told them, essentially, to get lost. Here was a firm, self-confident democratic citizen, not a serf, complying with the ruler's summons. The same mettle Woods shows on the golf course, he shows off it. 18

A good number of people don't like Tiger's attitude—don't like it at all. Larry King asked him, in 1998, "Do you feel that you're an influence on young blacks?" Tiger answered, calmly, unmovably, "Young children." An annoyed King shot back, "Just 'young children'? Don't you think you've attracted a lot more blacks to the game?" Replied Woods, "Yeah, I think I've attracted minorities to the game, but you know what? Why limit it to just that? I think you should be able to influence people in general, not just one race or social-economic background. Everybody should be in the fold." Again, I almost fell out of my chair. Tiger may be the most pointed universalist in public life. 19

Even Colin Powell, the current Secretary of State, has gotten snippy with Tiger, or about him. Woods coined a word to describe his racial makeup: "Cablinasian." This is meant to stand for a mixture of Caucasian, black, Indian (American Indian), and Asian. Tiger's dad, a tough, no-nonsense career military man, is (to be disgustingly racial, but this is to make a point) half black, a quarter Chinese, and a quarter Indian; Tiger's mom is half Thai, a quarter Chinese, and a quarter white. Tiger is, in other words, 100 percent, pure American. Back to General Powell. On *Meet the Press* one Sunday in 1997, Tim Russert asked him (rather in the manner of Orval Faubus, actually), "If you 20 have an ounce of black blood, aren't you black?" Powell responded that, like Tiger, he was of varied background, but "in order to not come up with a very strange word such as Tiger did, I consider myself black American. I'm very proud of it."

Well, despite his distaste for racial baloney, so is Woods: he is 21 neither unaware nor unappreciative of the struggles of black people in this country. After winning the Masters that first time, he paid due homage to black players before him, including Charlie Sifford and Lee Elder (the first black to be allowed to play in the Masters, in 1975).

Yet Woods refuses to spend his life in obeisance to the race gods. 22 At one point, he felt obliged to put out a "Media Statement," the purpose of which was "to explain my heritage." It would be—this is typical Tiger—"the final and only comment I will make regarding the issue":

> My parents have taught me to always be proud of my ethnic background. Please rest assured that is, and always will be, the case... On my father's side, I am African-American. On my mother's side, I am Thai. Truthfully, I feel very fortunate, and EQUALLY PROUD, to be both African-American and Asian!
>
> The critical and fundamental point is that ethnic background and/or composition should NOT make a difference. It does NOT make a difference to me. The bottom line is that I am an American... and proud of it! That is who I am and what I am. Now, with your cooperation, I hope I can just be a golfer and a human being.

We're told that we shouldn't need heroes. Well, too bad: we got 23 one.

Not every touring pro has been gracious about Tiger and what 24 he means; envy and resentment run deep. But the Scottish champion Colin Montgomerie said a lot when he commented recently, "We never thought this would happen [Tiger's explosion] or that there was even a chance it would happen. We're fortunate to have the world's best athlete playing our game. We're all not bad. He's just better. He is magnificent in every department."

Yes, in every department. A rare spirit shoots through Tiger. 25 Consider a few, disparate things. Every year at Augusta, the Champions Dinner is held, for which the previous year's winner selects the menu. In 1998, Tiger—age 22—chose hamburgers and milkshakes: the all-American meal. After he won the '97 Masters (remember, by a historic twelve shots), he took a look at the film and announced, "My swing stinks" (he didn't say "stinks," but I've cleaned it up a little). So he worked to make it even better—and it may become better yet. Woods is a perfect combination of the cool, self-contained golfer, a la Ben Hogan (or Nicklaus, for that matter), and the hot, impassioned golfer, a la Arnold Palmer, or Seve Ballesteros. And, finally, there is no better interview in sports: he handles himself superbly, and is not above displaying a contempt (usually sly) for dumb questions.

My golf friends and I have made our peace with Tiger, to say the least. Initially, I think we all had a fear of his displacing Nicklaus, which seemed sacrilegious. It helped, however, that Woods is the biggest Nicklaus worshiper of all: he venerates him as Nicklaus venerated Jones, and as Nicklaus pledged to follow in Jones's footsteps, Tiger has pledged to follow in Nicklaus's. Said Nicklaus five years ago, "There isn't a flaw in [Tiger's] golf or in his makeup. He will win more majors than Arnold Palmer and me [Arnie was standing next to him] combined. Somebody is going to dust my records. It might as well be Tiger, because he's such a great kid." 26

Oh, it's a thrill to be alive in the Time of Tiger. Whether you give a hoot about golf or not, I ask you—a final time—to trust me: rejoice. 27

Examining the Text

1. Nordlinger opens this essay with an anecdote about e-mailing a friend. Do you think this is an effective way to begin the article? Why or why not?

2. Explain the concept of parity in professional golf, and discuss how Woods has affected it.

3. In your own words, sum up how Nordlinger characterizes Woods's attitudes toward race. What does Nordlinger admire about this attitude?

For Group Discussion

Discuss why Nordlinger thinks that "whether you give a hoot about golf or not," Tiger Woods gives us reason to "rejoice" (27). Do you agree? Why or why not? Discuss how other sports figures compare to Woods in terms of their influence, their status as role models for youth, their attitudes on race, and their sheer talent and commitment to their sport. Can you and your group come up with other prominent athletes to place alongside Tiger Woods in these ways?

Writing Suggestion

Tiger Woods was born in 1975; thus he's a little too old to fit into Generation Y. Nonetheless, a number of writers have characterized him as an icon for this generation (see, for example "Managing Generation Y" by Bruce Tulgan and Carolyn A. Martin, 2001). Use Lim and Turco's descriptions of Generation Y to write an essay exploring the reasons why Woods works—or doesn't—as an icon or symbol for Generation Y.

Life on the Edge

William Dowell et al. (Time *Magazine*)

Fewer Americans are getting together for relaxed games of touch football or slow-pitch softball, and professional team sporting events are no longer attracting the large audiences of the past. Meanwhile, however, participation in high-risk extreme sports is on the rise. Increasing numbers of healthy, seemingly sane men and women are risking life and limb on a Sunday afternoon by jumping from a bridge or cliff or by climbing up a steep, sheer mountain face.

In this article, the authors examine the increasing popularity of extreme sports such as BASE jumping, paragliding, and so on, arguing that our current interest in dangerous sports stems from the fact that most Americans are living comfortable, safe lives. We seek out risk because it no longer seeks us—as in past eras when risks came routinely from war, famine, disease, and wild animals. In support of this argument, the authors point out the prevalence of other types of risk-taking behavior, which are common outside of sports, such as playing the stock market or engaging in unprotected sex.

As you read, *think about the legitimacy of the authors' argument. Is there necessarily a connection between the popularity of extreme sports and risky behavior in other areas of social life? Is it fair to connect these behaviors to our generally comfortable lives? Can you think of other possible reasons for the rise in risky sporting behavior? Or are you persuaded by the connections these authors make?*

"Five... four... three... two... one... see ya!" And Chance McGuire, 25, is airborne off a 650-ft. concrete dam in Northern California. In one second he falls 16 ft., in two seconds 63 ft., and after three seconds and 137 ft. he is flying at 65 m.p.h. He prays that his parachute will open facing away from the dam, that his canopy won't collapse, that his toggles will be handy and that no ill wind will slam him back into the cold concrete. The chute snaps open, the sound ricocheting through the gorge like a gunshot, and McGuire is soaring, carving S-turns into the air, swooping over a winding creek. When he lands, he is a speck on a path along the creek. He hurriedly packs his chute and then, clearly audible above the rushing water, lets out a war whoop that rises past those mortals still perched on the dam, past the commuters puttering by on the roadway, past even the hawks who circle the ravine. It is a cry of defiance, thanks and victory; he has survived another BASE jump. 1

McGuire is a practitioner of what he calls the king of all extreme sports. BASE—an acronym for building, antenna, span (bridge), and 2 earth (cliffs)—jumping has one of the sporting world's highest fatality rates: in its 18-year history, 46 participants have been killed. Yet the sport has never been more popular, with more than a thousand jumpers in the U.S. and more seeking to get into it every day. It is an activity without margin for error. If your chute malfunctions, don't bother reaching for a reserve—there isn't time. There are no second chances.

Still, the sport's stark metaphor—a human leaving safety behind 3
to leap into the void—may be a perfect fit with our times. As extreme a risk taker as McGuire seems, we may all have more in common with him than we know or care to admit. Heading into the millennium, America has embarked on a national orgy of thrill seeking and risk taking. The rise of adventure and extreme sports like BASE jumping, snowboarding, ice climbing, skateboarding and paragliding is merely the most vivid manifestation of this new national behavior. Investors once content to buy stocks and hold them quit their day jobs to become day traders, making volatile careers of risk taking. Even our social behavior has tilted toward the treacherous, with unprotected sex on the upswing and hard drugs like heroin the choice of the chic as well as the junkies. In ways many of us take for granted, we engage in risks our parents would have shunned and our grandparents would have dismissed as just plain stupid.

More than 30% of U.S. households own stocks of some form or 4
another, whether in investment accounts, mutual funds or retirement plans, up from 12% just 10 years ago. While an ongoing bull market has lulled us into a sense of security about investing, the reality is we are taking greater risks with our money than any other generation in American history. Many of us even take this a step further, buying "speculative growth," i.e., highly risky Internet and technology stocks, breezily ignoring the potentially precipitous downside.

We change jobs, leaping into the employment void, imagining 5
rich opportunities everywhere. The quit rate, a measure of those who voluntarily left their most recent job, is at 14.5%, the highest in a decade. Even among those schooled in risk management, hotshot M.B.A.s who previously would have headed to Wall Street or Main Street, there is a predilection to spurn Goldman Sachs and Procter & Gamble in order to take a flyer on striking it rich quickly in dot.com land. "I didn't want someone in 20 years to ask me where I was when the Internet took off," says Greg Schoeny, a recent University of Denver M.B.A. who passed up opportunities with established technology firms like Lucent to work at an Internet start-up called STS Communications. Schoeny is a double-dare sort who also likes to ski in the Rockies' dangerous, unpatrolled backcountry.

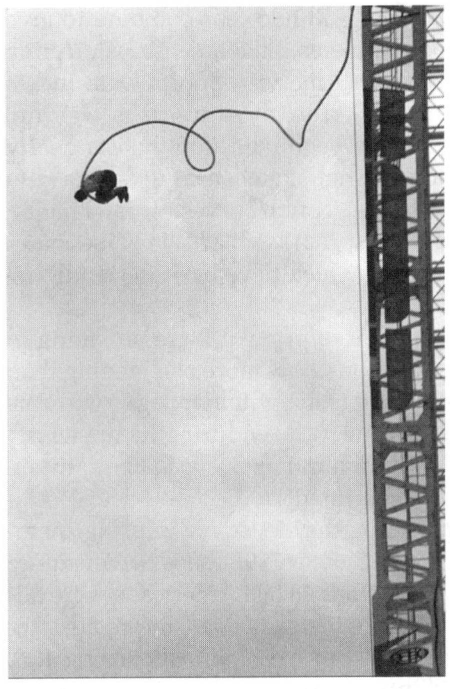

Bungee Jumping at the X Games

6 A full 30% of this year's Harvard Business School graduates are joining venture-capital or high-tech firms, up from 12% just four years ago. "The extended period of prosperity has encouraged people to behave in ways they didn't behave in other times—the way people spend money, change jobs, the quit rate, day trading, and people really thinking they know more about the market than anyone else," says Peter Bernstein, an economic consultant and author of the best-selling *Against the Gods: The Remarkable Story of Risk.* "It takes a particular kind of environment for all these things to happen." That environment—unprecedented prosperity and almost a decade without a major ground war—may be what causes Americans to express some inveterate need to take risks.

7 There is a certain logic to it: at the end of a decade of American triumphalism abroad and prosperity at home, we could be seeking to upsize our personalities, our sense of ourselves. Perhaps we as a people are acting out our success as a nation, in a manner unfelt since the postwar era.

8 The rising popularity of extreme sports bespeaks an eagerness on the part of millions of Americans to participate in activities closer to

the metaphorical edge, where danger, skill and fear combine to give weekend warriors and professional athletes alike a sense of pushing out personal boundaries. According to American Sports Data Inc., a consulting firm, participation in so-called extreme sports is way up. Snowboarding has grown 113% in five years and now boasts nearly 5.5 million participants. Mountain biking, skateboarding, scuba diving, you name the adventure sport—the growth curves reveal a nation that loves to play with danger. Contrast that with activities like baseball, touch football and aerobics, all of which have been in steady decline throughout the '90s.

The pursuits that are becoming more popular have one thing in common: the perception that they are somehow more challenging than a game of touch football. "Every human being with two legs, two arms is going to wonder how fast, how strong, how enduring he or she is," says Eric Perlman, a mountaineer and filmmaker specializing in extreme sports. "We are designed to experiment or die." 9

And to get hurt. More Americans than ever are injuring themselves while pushing their personal limits. In 1997 the U.S. Consumer Products Safety Commission reported that 48,000 Americans were admitted to hospital emergency rooms with skateboarding-related injuries. That's 33% more than the previous year. Snowboarding E.R. visits were up 31%; mountain climbing up 20%. By every statistical measure available, Americans are participating in and injuring themselves through adventure sports at an unprecedented rate. 10

Consider Mike Carr, an environmental engineer and paraglider pilot from Denver who last year survived a bad landing that smashed 10 ribs and collapsed his lung. Paraglider pilots use feathery nylon wings to take off from mountaintops and float on thermal wind currents—a completely unpredictable ride. Carr also mountain bikes and climbs rock faces. He walked away from a 1,500-ft. fall in Peru in 1988. After his recovery, he returned to paragliding. "This has taken over many of our lives," he explains. "You float like a bird out there. You can go as high as 18,000 ft. and go for 200 miles. That's magic." 11

America has always been defined by risk; it may be our predominant national characteristic. It's a country founded by risk takers fed up with the English Crown and expanded by pioneers—a word that seems utterly American. Our heritage throws up heroes—Lewis and Clark, Thomas Edison, Frederick Douglass, Teddy Roosevelt, Henry Ford, Amelia Earhart—who bucked the odds, taking perilous chances. 12

Previous generations didn't need to seek out risk; it showed up uninvited and regularly: global wars, childbirth complications, diseases and pandemics from the flu to polio, dangerous products and even the omnipresent cold war threat of mutually assured destruction. "I just don't think extreme sports would have been popular in a 13

Tony Hawk

ground-war era," says Dan Cady, professor of popular culture at California State University at Fullerton. "Coming back from a war and getting onto a skateboard would not seem so extreme."

But for recent generations, many of those traditional risks have been reduced by science, government or legions of personal-injury lawyers, leaving boomers and Generations X and Y to face less real risk. Life expectancy has increased. Violent crime is down. You are 57% less likely to die of heart disease than your parents; smallpox, measles and polio have virtually been eradicated. 14

Combat survivors speak of the terror and the excitement of playing in a death match. Are we somehow incomplete as people if we do not taste that terror and excitement on the brink? "People are [taking risks] because everyday risk is minimized and people want to be challenged," says Joy Marr, 43, an adventure racer who was the only woman member of a five-person team that finished the 1998 Raid Gauloises, the granddaddy of all adventure races. This is a sport that requires several days of nonstop slogging, climbing, rappelling, rafting and surviving through some of the roughest terrain in the world. Says fellow adventure racer and former Army Ranger Jonathan Senk, 35: "Our society is so surgically sterile. It's almost like our socialization just desensitizes us. Every time I'm out doing this I'm searching 15 my soul. It's the Lewis and Clark gene, to venture out, to find what your limitations are."

That idea of feeling bracingly alive through high-risk endeavor is commonly echoed by athletes, day traders and other risk takers. Indeed, many Silicon Valley entrepreneurs are extreme-sports junkies. Mike McCue, 32, CEO and chairman of Tellme Networks, walked away from millions of dollars at his previous job to get his new company off the ground. It's his third start-up, and each time he has risked everything. In his spare time, McCue gets himself off the ground. He's also an avid rock climber. "I like to feel self-reliant and independent," he says. "And when I'm up there, I know if I make a knot wrong, I die." 16

Even at ground level, the Valley is a preserve of fearless entrepreneurs. Nirav Tolia passed up $10 million in Yahoo stock options to start epinions.com, a shopping-guide Web site. "I don't know if I would call it living dangerously," he says. "At Yahoo I realized that money was not the driver for me. It's the sense of adventure." 17

Psychologist Frank Farley of Temple University believes that taking conscious risk involves overcoming our instincts. He points out that no other animal intentionally puts itself in peril. "The human race is particularly risk taking compared with other species," he says. He describes risk takers as the Type T personality, and the U.S. as a Type T nation, as opposed to what Farley considers more risk-averse nations like Japan. He breaks it down further, into Type T physical (extreme athletes) and Type T intellectual (Albert Einstein, Galileo). He warns there is also Type T negative, that is, those who are drawn to delinquency, crime, experimentation with drugs, unprotected sex, and a whole litany of destructive behaviors. 18

All these Type Ts are related, and perhaps even different aspects of the same character trait. There is, says Farley, a direct link between Einstein and BASE jumper Chance McGuire. They are different manifestations of the thrill-seeking component of our characters: Einstein was thrilled by his mental life, and McGuire—well, Chance jumps off buildings. 19

McGuire, at the moment, is driving from Hollister to another California town, Auburn, where he is planning another BASE jump from a bridge. Riding with him is Adam Fillipino, president of Consolidated Rigging, a company that manufactures parachutes and gear for BASE jumpers. McGuire talks about the leap ahead, about his feelings when he is at the exit point, and how at that moment, looking down at the ground, what goes through his mind is that this is not something a human being should be doing. But that's exactly what makes him take that leap: that sense of overcoming his inhibitions and winning what he calls the gravity game. "Football is for pansies," says McGuire. "What do you need all those pads for? This sport 20

[BASE jumping] is pushing all the limits. I have a friend who calls it suicide with a kick."

When a BASE jumper dies, other BASE jumpers say he has "gone in," as in gone into the ground or gone into a wall. "I'm sick of people going in," says Fillipino. "In the past year, a friend went in on a skydive, another drowned as a result of a BASE jump, another friend went in on a jump, another died in a skydiving-plane crash. You can't escape death, but you don't want to flirt with it either." It may be the need to flirt with death, or at least take extreme chances, that has his business growing at a rate of 50% a year. 21

The jump today from the Auburn bridge, which Fillipino has done dozens of times, is about as routine as BASE jumping can be. But Fillipino is a veteran with 450 BASE jumps to his credit. For McGuire, who has just 45, every jump is still a challenge. And at dawn, as he gets his gear ready, stuffing his chute and rig into a backpack so it won't be conspicuous as he climbs the trestles beneath the bridge (jumping from this bridge, as from many other public and private structures, is illegal), he has entered into a tranquil state, as if he were silently preparing himself for the upcoming risk. 22

When our Type T traits turn negative, though, there is a disturbing, less serene element to America's being the risk nation. One chilling development is the trend of "barebacking," a practice in which gay men have unprotected sex with multiple partners. Jack, an avid proponent of barebacking, argues that the risk of becoming HIV positive is outweighed by the rush of latex-free passion—especially in an era when, in his view, protease inhibitors are on the verge of turning AIDS from a fatal disease into a chronic illness. "It's the bad boy in me getting off," he admits. "One thing that barebacking allows is a certain amount of control over the risk. In sex, we have the ability to face the risk and look it in the eye." 23

The Stop AIDS Foundation surveyed some 22,000 gay men in San Francisco between 1994 and 1997, and during this period, the number of men who reported they always used condoms fell from 70% to 61%. "For some gay men, there is a sense of inevitability of becoming infected," says Michael Scarce, 29, a doctoral student in medical sociology who has been researching the barebacking phenomenon for the past two years. Scarce says that rather than living in fear and wondering when their next HIV test is going to return positive, some men create an infection ritual. "It really is a lifestyle choice," he says. "It comes down to quality of life vs. quantity of life." 24

This consequences-be-damned attitude may also be behind some disquieting trends that surfaced in a report issued last week by the Substance Abuse and Mental Health Services Administration stating 25 that the number of Americans entering treatment centers for heroin surged 29% between 1992 and 1997. "I'm seeking the widest possible range of human experience," says a recent Ivy League graduate about his heroin use.

The most notorious example of negative thrill seeking may have been when the Risk Taker in Chief, Bill Clinton, engaged in unprotected sex in the Oval Office. Experts point out that many people were forgiving of Clinton in part because they could identify with his impulsiveness. "Risky behavior has been elevated to new heights," argues Cal State's Cady. "There was never so much value put upon risk as there is now." 26

The question is, How much is enough? Without some expression of risk, we may never know our limits and therefore who we are as individuals. "If you don't assume a certain amount of risk," says paraglider pilot Wade Ellet, 51, "you're missing a certain amount of life." And it is by taking risks that we may flirt with greatness. "We create technologies, we make new discoveries, but in order to do that, we have to push beyond the set of rules that are governing us at that time," says psychologist Farley. 27

That's certainly what's driving McGuire and Fillipino as they position themselves on the Auburn bridge. It's dawn again, barely light, and they appear as shadows moving on the catwalk beneath the roadway. As they survey the drop zone, they compute a series of risk assessments. "It's a matter of weighing the variables," Fillipino says, pointing out that the wind, about 15 m.p.h. out of the northwest, has picked up a little more than he would like. Still, it's a clear morning, and they've climbed all the way up here. McGuire is eager to jump. But Fillipino continues to scan the valley below them, the Sacramento River rushing through the gorge. 28

Then a white parks-department SUV pulls up on an access road that winds alongside the river. Park rangers are a notorious scourge of BASE jumpers, confiscating equipment and prosecuting for trespassing. Fillipino contemplates what would happen if the president of a BASE rig company were busted for an illegal jump. He foresees trouble with his bankers, he imagines the bad publicity his business would garner, and he says he's not going. There are some risks he is simply not willing to take. 29

Examining the Text

1. What do the authors mean when they state that the "stark metaphor" of BASE jumping "may be a perfect fit with our times" (3)?

2. In contrast to all the risk talking mentioned in this article, as a society we also engage in a lot of risk minimizing. Paradoxically, these efforts to ensure safety may be helping to spawn more thrill-seeking activities. Discuss examples of safety measures and risk minimizing in which we as a culture engage—both on the personal as well as on a political or public level.

3. Explain why the authors state that risk taking is perhaps America's "predominant national characteristic." Do you agree or disagree, and why? If this assertion is true, what are the positive and negative consequences of this characteristic for us as country?

For Group Discussion

While this article focuses on the risky characteristics of extreme sports—and uses this element of these sports to make connections to the larger cultural climate in America—another characteristic of extreme sports is noteworthy: nearly all of the sports discussed in this article are individual in nature. The rock climber, for example, tests her own individual abilities against the challenges posed by nature. Interestingly, the increasing popularity of these individual sports corresponds with the declining interest in playing and watching team sports, as discussed in earlier pieces by Solomon and by Lim and Turco.

Use these ideas to theorize, as a group, about the possible significance of this shift from team to individual sports. Just as the *Time* article makes connections between sports and other cultural phenomena, ultimately using all of it to comment upon human nature as it appears in America today, can you think of other cultural phenomena that might relate to this issue of individualism? Does this lead you to theorize some ideas about where we are or where we seem to be headed?

Writing Suggestion

Write a paper in which you use points from earlier readings in the chapter to expand on the issues raised by Dowell and colleagues in this article. For example, how might the declining interest in team sports, as discussed by Solomon and by Lim and Turco relate to increased interest in risky sports? How might features of Generation Y relate here as well? Are there ways in which Rounds's points on gender in sports might fit into the equation?

Risk

Paul Roberts

Like the Time *magazine writers in the previous piece, Paul Roberts wonders why an increasing number of Americans are choosing "the leisure pursuit of danger," spending their free time climbing slick rocks, steep mountains, and frozen waterfalls; paragliding; whitewater rafting; or even turning moderately dangerous sports such as downhill skiing into life-threatening endeavors such as "extreme skiing."*

In this essay, originally published in Psychology Today, *Roberts tries to answer these questions by looking at the psychology of the high-risk takers. And while he does discuss some of the same issues as the* Time *writers do, Roberts emphasizes the individual psychology of thrill seekers more than the larger cultural trends on which Dowell et al. focus. Conventional theories of personality suggest that these people are acting on a "death wish," and indeed, Roberts quotes one climber as saying "What we do for kicks, most people wouldn't do if you held a gun to their heads." But Roberts discusses alternative explanations that offer a more positive view of high-risk activities. As he notes, some researchers suggest that courting peril and undertaking potentially dangerous challenges are actually essential for the progress of societies and for the development of confidence, self-awareness, and a stronger sense of identity in an individual. Although most of his examples are drawn from mountain climbing, Roberts is more broadly concerned with how a proclivity toward risky behavior affects our lives more generally, including such important areas as career choices, marital happiness, and sexual habits.*

As you read, *take note of where Roberts draws on disciplines other than psychology to account for the rise of popularity in high-risk sports. How do anthropology sociology, history, biology, and chemistry add to an understanding of risk taking?*

In the land of seatbelts and safety helmets, the leisure pursuit of danger is a growth industry. Some experts say that courting uncertainty is the only way to protect the inner force America was founded on. Or to define the self. 1

Risky business has never been more popular. Mountain climbing is among America's fastest growing sports. Extreme skiing—in which skiers descend cliff-like runs by dropping from ledge to snow-covered ledge—is drawing wider interest. Sports like paragliding and cliff-parachuting are marching into the recreational mainstream while the adventure-travel business, which often mixes activities like climbing or river rafting with wildlife safaries, has grown into a multimillion-dollar industry. "Forget the beach," declared *Newsweek* last year. 2

"We're hot for mountain biking, river running, climbing, and bungee jumping."

> Thirty-six year-old Derek Hersey knew a thing or two about life on the edge. Where most rock climbers used ropes and other safety gear, the wiry, wise-cracking Brit usually climbed "free solo"—alone, using nothing but climbing shoes, finger chalk, and his wits. As one climbing buddy put it, Hersey went "for the adrenaline and risk," and on May 28, 1993, he got a dose of both. High on the face of Yosemite's Sentinel Rock, Hersey met with rain and, apparently, slick rock. Friends who found the battered body reckon he fell several hundred feet. In the not-too-distant past, students of human behavior might have explained Hersey's fall as death-wish fulfillment. Under conventional personality theories, normal individuals do everything possible to avoid tension and risk.

In fact, as researchers are discovering, the psychology of risk involves far more than a simple "death wish." Studies now indicate that the inclination to take high risks may be hard-wired into the brain, intimately linked to arousal and pleasure mechanisms, and may offer such a thrill that it functions like an addiction. The tendency probably affects one in five people, mostly young males, and declines with age. It may ensure our survival, even spur our evolution as individuals and as a species. Risk taking probably bestowed a crucial evolutionary advantage, inciting the fighting and foraging of the hunter-gatherer. 3

In mapping out the mechanisms of risk, psychologists hope to do more than explain why people climb mountains. Risk-taking, which one researcher defines as "engaging in any activity with an uncertain outcome," arises in nearly all walks of life. Asking someone on a date, accepting a challenging work assignment, raising a sensitive issue with a spouse or a friend, confronting an abusive boss—all involve uncertain outcomes, and present some level of risk. Understanding the psychology of risk, understanding why some individuals will take chances and others won't, could have important consequences in everything from career counseling to programs for juvenile delinquents. 4

Researchers don't yet know precisely how a risk taking impulse arises from within or what role is played by environmental factors, from upbringing to the culture at large. And, while some level of risk taking is clearly necessary for survival (try crossing a busy street without it), scientists are divided as to whether, in a modern society, a "high-risk gene" is still advantageous. Some scientists, like Frank Farley, Ph.D., a University of Wisconsin psychologist and past president of the American Psychological Association, see a willingness to take big risks as essential for success. The same inner force that pushed Derek Hersey, Farley argues, may also explain why some dare to run for office, launch a corporate raid, or lead a civil rights demonstration. 5

Yet research has also revealed the darker side of risk taking. High-risk takers are easily bored and may suffer low job satisfaction. Their craving for stimulation can make them more likely to abuse drugs, gamble, commit crimes, and be promiscuous. As psychologist Salvadore Maddi, Ph.D., of the University of California-Davis warns, high-risk takers may have a hard time deriving meaning and purpose from everyday life." 6

Indeed, this peculiar form of dissatisfaction could help explain the explosion of high-risk sports in America and other post-industrial Western nations. In unstable cultures, such as those at war or suffering poverty, people rarely seek out additional thrills. But in a rich and safety-obsessed country like America, land of guardrails, seat belts, and personal-injury lawsuits, everyday life may have become too safe, predictable, and boring for those programmed for risk-taking. 7

In an unsettling paradox, our culture's emphasis on security and certainty—two defining elements of a "civilized" society—may not only be fostering the current risk-taking wave, but could spawn riskier activities in the future. "The safer we try to make life," cautions psychologist Michael Aptor, Ph.D, a visiting professor at Yale and author of *The Dangerous Edge: The Psychology of Excitement,* "the more people may take on risks." 8

UNIQUE WAVELENGTHS

In Icicle Canyon, a towering rocky corridor in the Cascade Mountains of Washington State, this strange interplay between safety and risk is a common sight. When weather permits, the canyon's formidable walls swarm with fit-looking men and women, using improbably small ledges and cracks to hoist themselves upward. For novices, risk can be kept to a minimum. Beginners' climbs are "top-roped" by a line running from the climber to a fixed cliff-top anchor and back down to a partner on the ground. 9

Even so, the novice can quickly experience a very realistic fear—what veterans call "getting gripped." Halfway up one short cliff, a first-timer in a tee shirt and shorts stabs out beneath a rock overhang. Unable to find a foothold, the climber peels off the cliff like wet wallpaper and dangles limply from the rope. His partner lowers him back to safety, where he stands white-faced, like someone emerging from an auto accident. Five minutes later, he is back on the cliff. 10

It's easy to see why high-risk sports receive so much academic attention. Climbers, for example, score higher on risk-preference tests than nearly all other groups. They show a strong need for intense stimulation and seek it in environments—sheer cliffs or frozen waterfalls—that most humans seem genetically programmed to avoid. 11

12 Climbers' own explanations for why they climb illustrate the difficulty of separating genetic, environmental, and cognitive components of this or any other behavioral trait. Many say they climb for decidedly conscious reasons: to test limits, to build or maintain self-esteem, to gain self-knowledge. Some regard it as a form of meditation. "Climbing demands absolute concentration," says Barbara, a lithe, 30-ish climber from Washington State. "It's the only time I ever feel in the moment."

13 Yet even the most contemplative climbers concede that their minds and bodies do operate on a unique wavelength. As Forrest Kennedy, a 32-year-old climber from Georgia, bluntly puts it, "What we do for kicks, most people wouldn't do if you held a gun to their heads."

14 Many climbers recognize that their commitment to the sport borders on addiction, one that persists after brushes with injury and death. Seattle attorney Jim Wickwire, for example, is probably best known for being on the first American team to summit Pakistan's 28,250-foot K-2, second highest peak in the world and arguably the most challenging. (The movie *K-2* was based on his story.) Yet this handsome, soft-spoken father of five is almost as well known for his obstinacy. On K-2, Wickwire lost several toes to frostbite and half a lung to altitude sickness. A year before, in 1977, he'd seen two climbing partners fall 4,000 feet. In 1981 on Alaska's Mount McKinley, he watched helplessly as another partner froze to death after becoming wedged in an ice crevasse.

15 Wickwire vowed then never to climb again. But in 1982, he attempted 29,028-foot Mount Everest, the world's tallest peak—and there saw yet another partner plunge 6,000 feet to her death. In 1993, as Wickwire, then 53, prepared for a second Everest attempt, he told a climbing magazine that he'd "stopped questioning why" he still climbed. Today, he seems just as uncertain. "The people who engage in this," Wickwire says, "are probably driven to it in a psychological fashion that they may not even understand themselves."

16 Until recently, researchers were equally baffled. Psychoanalytic theory and learning theory relied heavily on the notion of stimulus reduction, which saw all human motivation geared toward eliminating tension. Behaviors that created tension, such as risk taking, were deemed dysfunctional, masking anxieties or feelings of inadequacy.

A CRAVING FOR AROUSAL

17 Yet as far back as the 1950s, research was hinting at alternative explanations. British psychologist Hans J. Eysenck developed a scale to measure the personality trait of extroversion, now one of the most consistent predictors of risk taking. Other studies revealed that, contrary to Freud, the brain not only craved arousal, but somehow regulated that arousal at an optimal level. Over the next three decades, re-

searchers extended these early findings into a host of theories about risk taking.

Some scientists, like UC-Davis's Maddi and Wisconsin's Farley, concentrate on risk taking primarily as a cognitive or behavioral phenomenon. Maddi sees risk taking as an element of a larger personality dimension he calls "hardiness," which measures individuals' sense of control over their environment and their willingness to seek out challenges. Farley regards risk taking more as a whole personality type. Where other researchers speak of Types A and B personalities, Farley adds Type T, for thrill-seeking. He breaks Type-T behavior into four categories: T-mental and T-physical, to distinguish between intellectual and physical risk taking; and T-positive and T-negative, to distinguish between productive and destructive risk taking. 18

A second line of research focuses on risk's biological roots. A pioneer in these studies is psychologist Marvin Zuckerman at the University of Delaware. He produced a detailed profile of the high-sensation seeking (HSS) personality. HSS individuals, or "highs," as Zuckerman calls them, are typically impulsive, uninhibited, social, intend toward liberal political views. They like high-stimulus activities, such as loud rock music or pornography or horror movies, yet are rarely satisfied by vicarious thrills. Some level of actual risk—whether physical, social, or legal—seems necessary. Highs tend to be heavy bettors. They may try many kinds of drugs and favor sports like skiing or mountain climbing to running or gymnastics. Highs also show a clear aversion to low-sensation situations, otherwise known as boredom. 19

High-sensation seeking plays a huge role in relationships. Highs favor friends with interesting or offbeat life-styles, and avoid boring people. They're also far more sexually permissive, particularly in the number of sex partners, than lows. Highs favor mates with similar proclivities for stimulation, while lows generally pair off with other lows. And woe, apparently, to those who break this rule. "The combination of a high- and a low-sensation seeker," says Zuckerman, "seems to put the marriage relationship at risk." 20

Indeed, one benefit of such research is that it can be applied to many areas of everyday life. Those seeking mates, the University of Wisconsin's Farley says, should focus on those who share their level of risk taking, particularly in terms of sexual habits. Likewise, thrill seekers should also look for the right level of on-the-job excitement. "If you're a Big T type working on a microchip assembly line, you're going to be miserable," Farley predicts. "But if you're Big T on a big daily newspaper or a police force, where you never know what you'll be doing next, you're probably going to thrive." 21

Many climbers fit the HSS profile. Many report difficulty keeping full-time jobs, either because the work bores them, or because it in- 22 terferes with their climbing schedule. Long-term relationships can be problematic, especially where climbers marry nonclimbers, or where one partner begins losing interest in the sport. Nonclimbing partners often complain that their spouses spend too much time away from home, or refuse to commit to projects (children, for example) that might interfere with climbing. Relationships are also strained by the ever-present threat of injury or death. As one Midwestern climber puts it, "the possibility that I might miss dinner, forever, doesn't make things any smoother."

Further, while many climbers are models of clean living, the sport has its share of hard-partiers. Some even boast of making first ascents while high on marijuana or hallucinogens like LSD. Climbers say such drugs enhance or intensity the climbing experience. But studies suggest that the drugs may also mimic the process that pushes climbers in the first place. 23

WIRED FOR THRILLS

Researchers have long known of physiological differences between high- and low-sensation seekers. According to Zuckerman, the cortical system of a high can handle higher levels of stimulation without overloading and switching to the fight-or-flight response. Psychologist Randy Larsen, Ph.D., at the University of Michigan, has even shown that high-sensation seekers not only tolerate high stimulus but crave it as well. 24

Larsen calls high-sensation seekers "reducers": Their brains automatically dampen the level of incoming stimuli, leaving them with a kind of excitement deficit. (Low-sensation seekers, by contrast, tend to "augment" stimuli, and thus desire less excitement.) Why are some brains wired for excitement? Since 1974, researchers have known that the enzyme monoamine oxidase (MAO) plays a central role in regulating arousal, inhibition, and pleasure. They also found that low levels of MAO correlate with high levels of certain behaviors, including criminality, social activity, and drug abuse. When Zuckerman began testing HSS individuals, they, too, showed unusually low MAO levels. 25

The enzyme's precise role isn't clear. It regulates levels of at least three important neurotransmitters: norepinephrine, which arouses the brain in response to stimuli; dopamine, which is involved with the sensation of pleasure in response to arousal; and serotonin, which acts as a brake on norepinephrine and inhibits arousal. It's possible that high-sensation seekers have lower base levels of norepinephrine and thus, can tolerate more stimulation before triggering serotonin's dampening effect. High-sensation seekers may also have lower levels 26 of dopamine and are thus in a chronic state of underarousal in the brain's pleasure centers.

Such individuals may turn to drugs, like cocaine, which mimic dopamine's pleasure reaction. But they may also use intense and novel stimulation, triggering norepinephrine's arousal reaction and getting rewarded by the dopamine pleasure reaction. "What you get is a combination of tremendous arousal with tremendous pleasure," Zuckerman speculates." And the faster that arousal reaches its peak, the more intense your pleasure." Just as important, individuals may develop a tolerance for the pleasure reaction, and thus may need ever higher levels of stimulation—of risk—to achieve the same rush. 27

Today such an addictive dynamic may seem largely problematic In prehistoric times it was very likely essential. Dopamine, for example, has known links to various "approach" behaviors: feeding, fighting, foraging, and exploration. Probably, the same mechanism that gave people like Derek Hersey a rush from climbing also rewarded their predecessors for the more necessary acts of survival. 28

Psychologist Aptor suggests that the willingness to take risks, even if expressed by only certain individuals, would have produced benefits for an entire group. Upon entering a new territory, a tribe would quickly need to assess the environment's safety in terms of "which water holes are safe to drink from, which caves are empty of dangerous animals." Some risk takers would surely die. But, Aptor points out, "it's better for one person to eat a poisonous fruit than for everybody." 29

Climbers are understandably leery of such explanations. They admit that they may be more inclined to take risks than the average human. But that inclination's ultimate expression, they argue, is largely a matter of personal volition." At some level, there is a reason, chemical, mechanical, or whatever, for why we climb. But doesn't that take the human element out of it, and make us all robots?" grouses Todd Wells, a 40-year-old climber from Chattanooga. "I climb so I don't feel like a robot, so I feel like I'm doing something that is motivated by the self." 30

Even physiologically oriented scientists like Zuckerman admit the dopamine reaction is only part of the risk-taking picture. Upbringing, personal experience, socioeconomic status, and learning are also crucial in determining how that risk-taking impulse is ultimately expressed. 31

CULTURE OF ASCENT

Although many climbers report a childhood preference for thrills, their interest in climbing was often shaped externally, either through contact with older climbers or by reading about great expeditions. 32

Upon entering the sport, novices are often immersed in a tight-knit climbing subculture, with its own lingo, rules of conduct, and standards of excellence.

This learned aspect may be the most important element in the formation of the high-sensation-seeking personality. While risk-taking may have arisen from neuro-chemicals and environmental influences, there is an intellectual or conscious side to it that is now not only distinct from them but is itself a powerful motivator. Working through a challenging climbing route, for example, generates a powerful sense of competence that can also provide climbers with a new-found confidence in their everyday life. "There is nothing more empowering than taking a risk and succeeding," says Farley. 33

No wonder scaling the face of a cliff is a potent act that can penetrate to the very essence of self and help reshape it. Many climbers report using that empowering dynamic to overcome some of their own inner obstacles. Among these, fear—of heights, of loss of control, of death—is the most commonly cited. 34

Richard Gottlieb, 42-year-old climber from New York, is known for climbing frozen waterfalls, one of the riskiest facets of the sport. But as a kid, he was too scared even to go to summer camp. "Yet there was something in me that wanted to get into some swashbuckling adventure," he says. Climbing satisfied that impulse while helping him overcome his fearful nature. Gottlieb believes climbing has helped him cope with his fear of death: "We open the door, see the Grim Reaper right there, but instead of just slamming the door, you push him back a few steps." 35

NEW OUTLETS

Traditional outlets for the risk-taking impulse have been disappearing from everyday life. As civilization steadily minimized natural risks, Aptor says, and as cultures have sought to maintain their hard-won stability through repressive laws and stifling social mores, risk takers have been forced to devise new outlets. In the 20th century, that has brought about a rise in thrill sports. But Aptor believes the tension between civilization and risk-taking dates back eons. Aptor wonders how much of the British Empire "was built up by people trying to escape the desperately conformist society of Victorian England." 36

When channeled into sports like climbing, where skill and training can minimize danger, or into starting a new business, risk-taking may continue to be a healthy psychological outlet. It may provide a means to cope with boredom and modern anxieties, to bolster self-esteem. Risk-taking may provide a crucial sense of control in a period where so much of what happens—from crime and auto accidents to environmental disasters and economic downturns—seems almost random. 37

Unfortunately, the risk-taking impulse doesn't always find such healthy outlets. Many high-sensation seekers don't have the money or the role models for sky-diving or rock-climbing, Zuckerman notes. "In such groups, the main forms of sensation seeking include sex, drugs, heavy drinking, gambling, and reckless driving." Indeed, sensation-seeking may emerge as a critical factor in crime. No surprise, then, that some researchers place the risk-taking personality in the "abnormal" category and regard high-risk-takers almost as an evolutionarily obsolete subspecies. Maddi suggests that well-adjusted people are "good at turning everyday experience into something interesting. My guess is that the safecracker or the mountain climber can't do that as well. They have to do something exciting to get a sense of vitality. It's the only way they have of getting away from the sense that life sucks." Larsen is even blunter: "I think risk-takers are a little sociopathic." 38

Farley is more optimistic. Even civilized society, he says, holds ample opportunity for constructive risk-taking: investing in a high-stakes business venture, running for political office, taking an unpopular social stand. Farley argues that history's most crucial events are shaped by Big T behavior and Big T individuals, from Boris Yeltsin to Martin Luther King, Jr. The act of emigration, he says, is an intrinsically risky endeavor that selects individuals who are high in sensation-seeking. Consequently, countries built upon immigrant population—America, Canada, Australia—probably have an above-average level of risk-takers. He warns that much of the current effort to minimize risk and risk-taking itself runs the risk of eliminating "a large part of what made this country great in the first place." 39

For all the societal aspects of this peculiar trait, the ultimate benefits may continue to be purely personal. "There's a freshness to the [climbing] experience that clears away the weariness of routine and the complexity of social norms" says Seattle climber Bill Pilling. "Climbing brings you back to a primal place, where values are being created and transformed." 40

To push away from society's rides and protections, Farley suggests, is the only way to get a sense of where "society" ends and "you" begin. "Taking a risk, stepping away from the guardrails, from the rules and the status quo, that's when you get a sense of who you are," he says. "If you don't stretch, try to push past the frontiers, it's very difficult to know that." 41

Examining the Text

1. Roberts opens his essay with a paradox that he returns to several times in the text: that America's preoccupation with safety and security seems to foster higher levels of risk taking. Do you think that beginning an essay with a paradox—a seeming contradiction—is a good strategy? Why or why not? Does Roberts ever "solve" this paradox?

2. In your own words, explain the psychological theory of "stimulus reduction." How does risk-taking behavior contradict and confound this theory?
3. Briefly summarize the characteristics of Farley's Type T personality and Zuckerman's HSS individual. In what ways are these models similar and different? In your opinion, which one offers a more accurate description of the personalities and motivations of high-risk takers?
4. Consider the two "expert" sources from whom Roberts quotes: psychologists and climbers. Go back through the essay and look at the specific statements made by these experts. To what different uses does Roberts put them? How do their different kinds of expertise help Roberts construct his argument?

For Group Discussion

Roberts weighs the benefits and dangers of risk-taking activities, but he ultimately chooses to remain neutral and impartial. In groups, discuss your own opinion about whether risk-taking activities have primarily positive or negative effects on participants. Choose one side of the question and argue for it as persuasively and logically as you can, drawing on Roberts' arguments and those of the climbers and psychologists he cites in his essay. As a class, decide which arguments are the most persuasive.

Writing Suggestion

Even if you're not a high-risk taker—one of Farley's Type T or Zuckerman's HSS personalities—you've undoubtedly taken a few risks in your life. Risking is defined in the essay as "engaging in any activity with an uncertain outcome," such as asking someone for a date or taking on a new and difficult challenge. Recall a time when you took a risk and assess both the positive and negative effects of this experience. Write an essay in which you describe your experience and evaluate its impact on you. You should draw on Roberts' assessment of the benefits and harms of risk-taking and relate them to your own experience with risk.

ADDITIONAL SUGGESTIONS FOR WRITING ABOUT SPORTS

1. Using Maya Angelou's "Champion of the World" as a model, write a narrative in which you tell of a past experience with sports, either as a spectator or as a participant, that had a significant effect on your life. Perhaps this experience revealed something about yourself that you didn't realize, helped you to better understand someone else, taught you an important lesson, or corrected a misconception that you had. Or perhaps you're not certain what effect the experience had, and can use this assignment to speculate on its significance.

2. Attend a local sporting event, and bring a notebook and, if possible, a tape recorder or video camera. Observe and take notes about how the people around you behave, what they do and say, what they wear, how they relate to one another, what interests or bores them, when they seem satisfied or disappointed. Note also how their behavior is different from what it would likely be in other contexts. Try to be an impartial observer, simply recording what you see in as much detail as possible.

From your notes, write an extended description of one or several typical spectators, and then draw some conclusions about why people enjoy watching sports. You may also want to discuss the psychological benefits and/or harm that being a spectator might cause.

3. Choose a sport with which you're very familiar, either because you play it or watch it regularly. Reflect on your experience playing or watching this sport, and write down some of your recollections. Think about what you've learned from this sport, and how it has affected other areas of your life.

Then write an essay in which you show how this particular sport has influenced your beliefs, attitudes and values. Be as specific as possible and try to show precisely how and why the sport has influenced you.

4. Many of the writers in this chapter discuss the impact of professional sports on individuals and on society as a whole. Referring to essays in this chapter, construct your own argument about the influence of professional sports. As a prewriting exercise, make lists of the beneficial and the detrimental influences of professional sports on our society. Try to come up with specific examples to illustrate each of the items on your lists. Then working from those lists, develop a persuasive argument about the influence of sports on our society.

Internet Activities

1. Professional athletes are often role models in our society. As a prewriting exercise for this assignment, list some of the reasons why this is so, especially for young people. Also list the ways in which athletes might be good role models, as well as some of the reasons other professionals (for example, teachers or government leaders) might actually be better role models.

Then visit the links to information about professional athletes, provided at the *Common Culture* Web site, to official and unofficial homepages of individual athletes. After browsing through these links, choose an athlete who you think is either a good or a bad role model.

Do further research on this athlete, looking up interviews and articles about him or her in the library. From this information, write a brief biography of the athlete, focusing on the kind of role model he or she is.

2. Professional sports teams are, as John Solomon makes clear, in the business of making money, and the World Wide Web is increasingly becoming a venue for advertising and marketing. It's no surprise then, that all of the major professional sports teams now have their own Web sites. Go to the *Common Culture* Web site for links that you can follow to visit the homepages of professional teams in baseball, football, men's basketball, women's basketball, and hockey. Choose a Web site for one team and read the site carefully and completely. Make a list of the information that the site offers, including statistics, pictures, news and "inside information," schedules, and so on. Then analyze the ways in which the information offered at the site is intended to promote or "sell" the team. Is the site addressed to current fans of the team, or is it intended to cultivate new fans? How effectively do you believe the Web site is in advertising and marketing the team it represents?

Reading Images

Brandi Chastain, shown in the photo on p. CI-7, is famous for her game-winning shot during the 1999 women's World Cup. But perhaps she is more famous for what happened after the game—in a moment of unbridled joy, she removed her jersey and bounded joyfully on the field in a sports bra, helping to make such apparel some of the most recognizable items of clothing in the country at that moment in pop-cultural history. This famous image can be found on the Web at *www.sportsillustrated.cnn.com/soccer/world/1999/womens_worldcup/*.

In an essay, "read" these images to uncover and discuss the sociocultural messages they contain. Look carefully at all elements of the graphics. Discuss possible meanings implicit in the colors and the central images of Chastain. However, don't be content merely to focus on the central images: study the background "negative space" as well, to ascertain how the entire composition combines to create meaning. Note also the juxtaposition of image and text, along with messages contained in the text itself.

If you wish, you may take this discussion a step further by addressing a central issue raised by the pictures: namely, the commodification of sport. Some purists believe that sports are tainted by commercialism. They might therefore point to commercial use of the images that depict Chastain in her Nike sports bra and charge that by capitalizing on this pure moment of sport-centered bliss, the spirit of competition is reduced to a crass attempt to sell. Consider this issue, examining your own feelings about the pros and cons of commercialism in sport, and then develop a thesis that takes a persuasive stance with regard to this issue.

7

Movies

It's Friday night. You park in an exhaust-filled subterranean garage or a vast asphalt lot surrounding a mall. You make your way into the neon-lit mega-plex, where you and a companion or two pay half a day's salary for tickets, a tub of artery-clogging popcorn, and a couple of ten-gallon sodas. You wind your way through a maze of corridors to the theater of your choice, where a psychedelic montage filling the screen is soon replaced by the first of an interminable series of quick-cutting, MTV-style previews, as you bathe in rolling quadraphonic surround sound. You sink into your space-age plastic seat and kick back, surrendering to the waves of sound and images. . . .

Such is moviegoing in the new millennium. Gone are the nickel matinee and the discount double feature, newsreels, cartoons, and comic short subjects, and the drive-in, where many a pair of teenagers learned human anatomy in the back seat of a Chevy.

The external trappings of the moviegoing experience may have changed, but the reasons people go are still pretty much the same: to get out of the house and escape the routine of their daily lives; to be part of a communal group sharing an experience; to find a romantic setting where conversation is at a minimum; to indulge, for one night, in an orgy of junk food; and, above all, to be entertained and, perhaps, touched emotionally. So strong is the draw of motion pictures that Americans fork over billions of dollars a year on domestic movies alone.

As there are many reasons for going to the movies, so there are many ways of explaining their popularity and studying their influence within the fabric of contemporary culture. From a sociological perspective, movies can reflect, define, or even redefine social norms, and—in the work of politically focused filmmakers like Spike Lee—depict urgent social problems within the relative safety of the big screen. From a psychological perspective, viewers identify with the character and project their own feelings into the action, giving them a deep emotional connection to a protagonist along with feelings of tension and, ultimately release. From a literary perspective, movies can be interpreted in terms of genres—horror movies, or crime dramas or menaced-female stories—or in terms of plot, characterization, imagery, and so forth. From an economic perspective, movies may be seen primarily as a consumable product, defined solely by the marketplace. To the cultural critic, this economic influence might seem to be negative, reducing a potentially powerful artistic form to the lowest common denominator. The capitalist observer might see such forces as positive, however, because they encourage the worldwide spread of American cultural values. Finally, from a semiological perspective, movies are ripe with symbolic imagery, from the multiple associations possible in a character's name to the way images are juxtaposed in the editing.

This chapter introduces film criticism arising from several of these views. The first readings focus on the art and business of moviemaking and criticism, ending with an overview of the major critical schools. The second part looks specifically at the genre of the horror movie, interpreting horror heroes such as Frankenstein, Freddy Kreuger, and Dracula from a variety of critical perspectives. As you think and write about film and the film industry, you may find that you want to pick and choose among these various approaches, incorporating parts of any number of them into your own theoretical analyses.

Moviemaking and Criticism

The Way We Are

Sydney Pollack

If anyone knows American moviemaking, it's Sydney Pollack. A director of more than sixteen films—including The Way We Were, Tootsie, Out of Africa, *and* The Firm*—and an occasional actor (Dustin Hoffman's agent in* Tootsie*), Pollack has had an unparalleled opportunity to observe the changing tastes of the American viewing public and the movie industry's response to those changes. In the following article, a transcript of an address Pollack delivered at a conference about the influence of the popular media on American values, Pollack suggests that changes in the moral fabric of our society are responsible for the kinds of movies we see today, not vice versa.*

When he looks at contemporary America, Pollack finds a conspicuous lack of the "kind of scrupulous ethical concern for the sanctity of life" that prevailed in past decades and was reflected in motion pictures of the time, when there were less frequent and less graphic scenes of violence, when characters were esteemed for their humility and personal integrity, and when explicit sexuality was found only in "stag" films, not in mainstream theaters. Many people today, Pollack notes, are nostalgic for the "old values" and believe that movies should encourage the return of these values rather than reflecting current values. Pollack disagrees, however, pointing out that, although screenwriters and directors may want their movies to reflect some moral content, the economics of the industry require first and foremost that movies be entertaining, and therefore, they must appeal to a buying audience whose values may be very different from those of the reformers.

***As you read,** consider whether you agree with Pollack's notions of artistic integrity, especially his assertions that a filmmaker's prime goal should be to entertain an audience and that movies simply reflect the surrounding society. Is it possible that, in responding to their audience's changing tastes, filmmakers also "construct" public attitudes towards violence, sexuality, and so forth by pushing their explicitness further and further?*

---

1 Six weeks ago, I thought I was going to be happy to be a part of this conference, which shows you how naive I am. The agenda—for me at least—is a mine field. Normally, I spend my time worrying about specific problems and not reflecting, as many of you on these panels do. So I've really thought about this, and I've talked to anyone who would

listen. My colleagues are sick and tired of it, my wife has left for the country and even my agents—and these are people I pay—don't return my phone calls. By turns, I have felt myself stupid, unethical, a philistine, unpatriotic, a panderer, a cultural polluter, and stupid. And I've completely failed to solve your problems, except in one small way. You have delayed by at least six weeks the possibility of my contributing further to the problems you see.

I know your concerns have to do with American values and whether those values are being upheld or assaulted by American entertainment—by what I and others like me do. But which values exactly? 2

In the thirties, forties, and fifties, six men in the Valley, immigrants really, ran the movie industry. Our society was vastly different. The language of the movies was a language of shared values. If you put forward a virtuousness on the part of your hero, everybody responded to it. 3

When Sergeant York, played by Gary Cooper, refused to endorse a breakfast cereal, knowing he'd been asked because he'd won the Medal of Honor, he said: "I ain't proud of what I've done. You don't make money off of killing people. That there is wrong." We expected him to behave that way. 4

But society's values have changed. That kind of scrupulous, ethical concern for the sanctity of human life doesn't exist in the same way, and that fact is reflected in the movies. There's a nostalgia now for some of the old values, but so many people embrace other expressions of values that it's hard to say these other expressions aren't reality. 5

Their idea of love, for example, is a different idea of love. It's a much less chaste, much less idealized love than was depicted in the earlier films. We are seeing some sort of return to the ideal of marriage. There was a decade or two when marriage really lost its popularity, and while young people are swinging toward it again, I don't believe one could say that values have not changed significantly since the thirties, forties, and fifties. 6

Morality, the definitions of virtue, justice, and injustice, the sanctity of the individual, have been fairly fluid for American audiences in terms of what they choose to embrace or not embrace. 7

Take a picture like *Dances With Wolves.* You could not have made it in the thirties or forties. It calls into question every value that existed in traditional Westerns. It may not reflect what everybody thinks now, but it expresses a lot of guilty re-evaluation of what happened in the West, the very things shown in the old Westerns that celebrated the frontier. 8

If we got the movies to assert or talk about better values, would that fix our society? Well, let me quote Sam Goldwyn. When he was 9 told by his staff how poorly his studio's new—and very expensive—film was doing, Sam thought a minute, shrugged, and said, "Listen, if they don't want to come, you can't stop them."

10 Now that's as close to a first principle of Hollywood as I can come. It informs everything that we're here to discuss and it controls every solution that we may propose.

OUT OF HOLLYWOOD

11 Before they can be anything else, American movies are a product. This is not good or bad, this is what we've got. A very few may become art, but all of them, whatever their ambitions, are first financed as commodities. They're the work of craftsmen and artists, but they're soon offered for sale.

12 Whether we say that we're "creating a film" or merely "making a movie," the enterprise itself is sufficiently expensive and risky that it cannot be, and it will not be, undertaken without the hope of reward. We have no Medicis here. It takes two distinct entities, the financiers and the makers, to produce movies, and there is a tension between them. Their goals are sometimes similar, but they do different things. Financiers are not in the business of philanthropy. They've got to answer to stockholders.

13 Of course, the controlling influence in filmmaking hasn't changed in 50 years: it still belongs to the consumer. That's the dilemma and, in my view, what we're finally talking about. What do you do about culture in a society that celebrates the common man but doesn't always like his taste?

14 If you operate in a democracy and you're market-supported and -driven, the spectrum of what you will get is going to be very wide indeed. It will range from trash to gems. There are 53,000 books published in this country every year. How many of them are really good? Tired as I may be of fast-food-recipe, conscienceless, simple-minded books, films, TV, and music, the question remains, who is to be society's moral policeman?

15 Over the course of their first 30 or 40 years, the movies were a cottage industry, and the morality that was reflected in them was the morality of the early film pioneers. Now, film studios are tiny divisions of multinational corporations, and they feel the pressure for profits that happens in any other repeatable-product business. They look for a formula. Say you get the recipe for a soft drink and perfect it; once customers like it, you just repeat it and it will sell. More fortunes have been lost than made in the movie business pursuing such a

formula, but unfortunately today, more junk than anything else is being made pursuing it. And film companies are folding like crazy.

Since we are in the democracy business, we can't tell people what they should or shouldn't hear, or support, or see, so they make their choices. The market tries to cater to those choices, and we have what we have. 16

MAKING FILMS

Are American films bad? A lot of them surely are, and so are a lot of everybody else's, the way a lot of anything produced is bad—breakfast cereals, music, most chairs, architecture, mail-order shirts. There probably hasn't been a really beautiful rake since the Shakers stopped making farm implements. But that is no excuse. 17

I realize that I am a prime suspect here, but I'm not sure that you really understand how odd and unpredictable a business the making of films actually is. It just doesn't conform to the logic or rules of any other business. It's always been an uneasy merger of two antithetical things: some form of art and sheer commerce. 18

If the people who make films get the money that is invested in them back to the people who finance them, then they'll get to make more. We know that the business of films is to reach as many people as possible. That works two ways; it's not just a market discipline. You have to remember that most of us who are doing this got into it for the romance, the glory, the applause, the chance to tell stories, even to learn, but rarely for the money. The more people you reach, the greater your sense of success. Given the choice, I'd rather make the whole world cry than 17 intellectuals in a classroom. 19

But, paradoxically, if you are the actual maker of the film—not the financier—you can't make films and worry about whether they'll reach a large audience or make money, first, because nobody really knows a formula for what will make money. If they did, I promise you we would have heard about it, and studios would not be going broke. Second, and much more practically, if you spent your time while you were making the film consciously thinking about what was commercial, then the real mechanism of choice—the mechanism that is your own unconscious, your own taste and imagination, your fantasy—would be replaced by constant reference to this formula that we know doesn't work. 20

So the only practical approach a filmmaker can take is to make a film that he or she would want to see. This sounds arrogant, but you try to make a movie for yourself, and you hope that as many people as 21 possible will like it too. If that happens, it's because you've done something in the telling of the story that makes people care. One of the things that makes a film distinct from other American business products is this emotional involvement of the maker. A producer of auto parts can become pretty emotional about a sales slump, but it isn't the same thing. His product hasn't come from his history; it isn't somehow in the image of his life; and it lacks mystery. It is entirely measurable and concrete, which is certainly appropriate in the manufacture of auto parts. I wouldn't want to buy a carburetor from a neurotic, mixed-up auto manufacturer.

Fortunately for those of us in film, no such standards apply. 22
Quite the contrary, in fact. No matter what his conscious intentions are, the best part of what the filmmaker does—the part, when it works, that makes you want to see the film—doesn't come from a rational, consciously controllable process. It comes from somewhere inside the filmmaker's unconscious. It comes from making unlikely connections seem inevitable, from a kind of free association that jumps to odd or surprising places, conclusions that cause delights, something that creates goose pimples or awe.

This conference has suggested a question: While you're actually 23
making the movie, do you think about whether or not it will be doing the world any good? I can't answer it for filmmakers in general. For myself, candidly, no, I don't.

I try to discover and tell the truth and not be dull about it. In that 24
sense, the question has no significance for me. I assume that trying to discover the truth is in itself a good and virtuous aim. By truth I don't mean some grand, pretentious axiom to live by; I just mean the truth of a character from moment to moment. I try to discover and describe things like the motives that are hidden in day-to-day life. And the truth is rarely dull. If I can find it, I will have fulfilled my primary obligation as a filmmaker, which is not to bore the pants off you.

Most of us in this business have enormous sympathy for 25
Scheherazade—we're terrified we're going to be murdered if we're boring. So our first obligation is to not bore people; it isn't to teach.

Most of the time, high-mindedness just leads to pretentious or 26
well-meaning, often very bad, films. Most of the Russian films made under communism were of high quality in terms of craft, but they were soporific because their intent to do good as it was perceived by the state or an all-knowing party committee was too transparent.

I'm sure that you think the person in whose hands the process 27
actually rests, the filmmaker, could exert an enormous amount of control over the film's final worthiness. The question usually goes like this: Should filmmakers pander to the public, or should they try to elevate public taste to something that many at this conference would find

more acceptable? Is the job of an American filmmaker to give the public what it wants or what the filmmaker thinks the public should have? This doesn't leave much doubt as to what you think is the right answer.

But framing your question this way not only betrays a misunderstanding of how the filmmaking process works but also is just plain wishful thinking about how to improve society. I share your nostalgia for some of those lost traditional values, but attempting to reinstall them by arbitrarily putting them into movies when they don't exist in everyday life will not get people to go to the movies or put those values back into life. I wish it were that simple. 28

ENGAGING AN AUDIENCE

This conference is concerned with something called popular culture and its effect on society, but I am concerned with one film at a time and its effect. You are debating whether movies corrupt our souls or elevate them, and I'm debating whether a film will touch a soul. As a filmmaker, I never set out to create popular culture, and I don't know a single other filmmaker who does. 29

Maybe it's tempting to think of Hollywood as some collective behemoth grinding out the same stories and pushing the same values, but it's not that simple. Hollywood, whatever that means, is Oliver Stone castigating war in *Born on the Fourth of July* and John Milius celebrating it in *The Wind and the Lion.* It's Walt Disney and Martin Scorcese. It's Steven Spielberg and Milos Foreman. It's *Amadeus* and *Terminator* and hundreds of choices in between. 30

I don't want to defend Hollywood, because I don't represent Hollywood—I can't, any more than one particular writer can represent literature or one painter art. For the most part, the impulse toward all art, entertainment, culture, pop culture, comes from the same place within the makers of it. The level of talent and the soul, if you'll forgive the word again, is what finally limits it. 31

At the risk of telling you more than you need to know about my own work, I make the movies I make because there is in each film some argument that fascinates me, an issue I want to work through. I call this a spine or an armature because it functions for me like an armature in sculpture—something I can cover up and it will support the whole structure. I can test the scenes against it. For me, the film, when properly dramatized, adds up to this idea, this argument. 32

But there are lots of other ways to go about making a film, and lots of other filmmakers who do it differently. Some filmmakers begin knowing exactly what they want to say and then craft a vehicle that 33 contains that statement. Some are interested in pure escape. Here's the catch. The effectiveness and the success of all our films is determined by exactly the same standards—unfortunately, not by the particular validity of their message but by their ability to engage the concentration and emotions of the audience.

Citizen Kane is an attack on acquisition, but that's not why people 34
go to see it. I don't have any idea if the audience that saw *Tootsie* thought at any conscious level that it could be about a guy who became a better man for having been a woman; or that *The Way We Were,* a film I made 20 years ago, may have been about the tension between passion, often of the moment, and wisdom, often part of a longer view; or that *Out Of Africa* might be about the inability to possess another individual and even the inability of one country to possess another. That's intellectual and stuffy. I just hope the audiences were entertained.

I may choose the movies I make because there's an issue I want 35
to explore, but the how—the framing of that issue, the process of finding the best way to explore it—is a much more mysterious, elusive, and messy process. I can't tell you that I understand it; if I did, I would have a pep talk with myself and go out and make a terrific movie every time.

Orson Welles in *Citizen Kane*

I would not make a film that ethically, or morally, or politically trashed what I believe is fair. But by the same token, I feel an obligation—and this is more complicated and personal—to do films about arguments. I try hard to give each side a strong argument—not because I'm a fair guy but because I believe it's more interesting. Both things are going on. 36

I do the same thing on every movie I make. I find an argument, a couple of characters I would like to have dinner with, and try to find the most fascinating way to explore it. I work as hard as I can to tell the story in the way I'd like to have it told to me. 37

What is really good is also entertaining and interesting because it's closer to a newer way to look at the truth. You can't do that consciously. You can't start out by saying, "I am now going to make a great film." 38

The virtue in making a film, if there is any, is in making it well. If there's any morality that's going to come out, it will develop as you begin to construct, at every moment you have a choice to make. You can do it the honest way or you can bend it, and the collection of those moments of choice is what makes the work good or not good and is what reveals morality or the lack of it. 39

I've made 16 films. I've had some enormous successes and I've had some colossal failures, but I can't tell you what the difference is in terms of what I did. 40

AN AMERICAN AESTHETIC?

In some circles, American films suffer by comparison with European films precisely because a lot of our movies seem to be the product of little deliberation and much instinct. It's been said of European movies that essence precedes existence, which is just a fancy way of saying that European movies exist in order to say something. Certainly one never doubts with a European film that it's saying something, and often it just comes right out and says it. 41

American films work by indirection; they work by action and movement, either internal or external, but almost always movement. Our films are more narratively driven than others, which has a lot to do with the American character and the way we look at our lives. We see ourselves and our lives as being part of a story. 42

Most of our movies have been pro the underdog, concerned with injustice, relatively anti-authority. There's usually a system—or a bureaucracy—to triumph over. 43

More often than not, American movies have been affirmative and hopeful about destiny. They're usually about individuals who 44 control their own lives and their fate. In Europe, the system was so class-bound and steeped in tradition that there was no democratization of that process.

There's no prior education required to assimilate American movies or American culture. American culture is general, as opposed to the specificity of Japanese or Indian culture. America has the most easily digestible culture. 45

Our movies seem artless. The best of them keep us interested without seeming to engage our minds. The very thing that makes movies so popular here and abroad is one of the primary things that drives their critics to apoplexy, but seeming artlessness isn't necessarily mindlessness. There's a deliberate kind of artlessness in American movies that has come from a discipline or aesthetic long ago imposed by the marketplace. Our movies began as immigrants' dreams that would appeal to the dreams of other immigrants, and this aesthetic has led American films to transcend languages and cultures and communicate to every country in the world. 46

THE FILMMAKER'S RESPONSIBILITY

It has been suggested to some extent in this conference that I ought to study my own and American filmmakers' responsibilities to the public and to the world. I realize I have responsibilities as a filmmaker, but I don't believe that they are as a moralist, a preacher, or a purveyor of values. I know it's tempting to use filmmaking as such, but utility is a poor standard to use in art. It's a standard that has been and is still used by every totalitarian state in the world. 47

My responsibility is to try to make good films, but "good" is a subjective word. To me at any rate, "good" doesn't necessarily mean "good for us" in the narrow sense that they must elevate our spirits and send us out of the theater singing, or even that they must promote only those values that some think are worth promoting. 48

Good movies challenge us, they provoke us, they make us angry sometimes. They present points of view we don't agree with. They force us to clarify our positions in opposition to them, and they do this best when they provide us with an experience and not a polemic. 49

Somebody gave the okay to pay for *One Flew Over the Cuckoo's Nest, Driving Miss Daisy, Stand By Me, Moonstruck, Terms of Endearment,* and *Amadeus,* and despite conventional wisdom that said those films could not be successful, those decisions paid off handsomely because there are no rules. Studio executives and other financiers do exceed themselves. They take chances. They have to, and we have to hope that they'll do it more often. 50

What we see in movie theaters today is not a simple reflection of today's economics or politics in this country but is a sense of the people who make the movies, and they vary as individuals vary. So what we really want is for this very privileged process to be in the best hands possible, but I know of no force that can regulate this except the moral climate and appetites of our society. 51

What we're exporting now is largely a youth culture. It's full of adolescent values; it's full of adolescent rage, love, rebelliousness, and a desire to shock. If you're unhappy with their taste—and this is a free market—then an appetite has to be created for something better. How do we do that? Well, we're back to square one: the supplier or the consumer, the chicken or the egg? Let's not even ask the question; the answer is both. 52

Of course filmmakers ought to be encouraged toward excellence, and audiences ought to be encouraged to demand it. How? That's for thinkers and social scientists to figure out. I have no idea. But if I had to play this scene out as an imaginary dialogue, I might say that you must educate the consumer first, and the best places to start are at school and at home. And then you would say that that is my job, that popular entertainment must participate in this education. And I would say, ideally, perhaps, but I do not think that will happen within a system that operates so fundamentally from an economic point of view. On an individual basis, yes, one filmmaker at a time; as an industry, no. An appetite or market will have to exist first. 53

That's not as bad as it sounds, because in the best of all possible worlds, we do try to satisfy both needs: entertain people and be reasonably intelligent about it. It can be done, and it is done more often than you might think. It's just very difficult. 54

It's like the two Oxford dons who were sitting at the Boarshead. They were playwrights, grousing because neither one of them could get produced, neither one could get performed. One turned to the other and said, "Oh, the hell with it. Let's just do what Shakespeare did—give them entertainment." 55

Examining the Text

1. What is Pollack's point in paragraph 8? How does *Dances With Wolves* "call into question every value that existed in traditional Westerns," and how does it reflect a change in society's values? Is *Dances With Wolves* a good example of the kind of movie that critics would say contributes to the decline in American values? Why do you think Pollack mentions it so early in his speech?

2. Pollack says there "probably hasn't been a really beautiful rake since the Shakers stopped making farm implements" (paragraph 17).

What does his point say in terms of questioning whether American films are "bad"? Do you find his analogy persuasive?

3. When Pollack asserts that he'd "rather make the whole world cry than 17 intellectuals in a classroom" (19), what is he implying about his—and other filmmakers'—motivations? Do you think most creative people feel this way?

4. Pollack describes his interest in making "films about arguments" and giving "each side a strong argument" (36). What does he mean? Do you think movies that balance two sides of an "argument" are "more interesting" than those with clear-cut "good guys" and "bad guys"?

For Group Discussion

Pollack himself does not make the kinds of graphically violent movies that critics claim have a negative influence on American society. Nonetheless, he argues that "scrupulous, ethical concern for the sanctity of human life doesn't exist in the same way [it did in the past], and that fact is reflected in the movies." As a group, list examples from current events and recent films that demonstrate this lack of concern for human life. As a class, consider whether, based on these examples, you agree with Pollack that movies only reflect the values of society and do not contribute to their creation.

Writing Suggestion

Rent and watch one or more of Pollack's films (titles other than those mentioned in the headnote include *They Shoot Horses, Don't They?*, *Three Days of the Condor,* and *The Electric Horseman*). In an essay analyze Pollack's work as a reflection of contemporary American life. What themes or messages do you discover beyond his aim to tell a good story? Does he succeed in his stated goal of presenting an "argument"?

Film Criticism

Mark J. Schaefermeyer

There's much more to criticizing a film than just deciding whether one likes it or not. This is the central point of the following essay by Mark J. Schaefermeyer. A film critic and professor of communications studies at Virginia Polytechnic Institute, Schaefermeyer begins by drawing a crucial distinction between reviewing movies and film criticism. Movie reviews, he says, are directed toward the general public, primarily to help people decide what movies to see. By contrast, film criticism is written primarily by university academics and other scholars to be published in specialized journals and read by academics and professional filmmakers.

Schaefermeyer outlines some of the main theoretical approaches critics currently use to analyze films. He breaks film criticism down into three broad subcategories—semiotic, structuralist, and contextual—and explains the premises and specific methodologies of each. Semiotic studies, as you have learned from earlier readings in this text analyze symbolic structures and relationships. Structuralist methodology attempts "to impose its own orientation or structure"—for instance mythic, or political, or sociological—on a film. Finally, contextual critics look at a movie within a specific context, such as its directorial style, its narrative type, or its historical position.

As you read *this survey of film criticism, think about which approach most closely resembles your own way of interpreting film. Are you a budding semiotician, finding symbolic meanings in Lauren Bacall's cigarette or Arnold Schwarzenegger's big gun? Are you a political structuralist, finding social and economic implications in a film's plot and characterization? Are you a contextualist, looking for the hallmarks of a director's style or for the ways the conventions of a genre are met or broken? Or are you satisfied just to "know what you like," without approaching film from a more academically critical position?*

The place occupied by movie critics in the popular media is perhaps stronger today than it ever has been. The success of Gene Siskel and Roger Ebert in moving from PBS to syndication with their self-described movie review program is evidence that the medium is not without those who are paid to pass judgment on it. Paperback books that describe and rate all the films available on television abound; local news programs often have a critic of their own or regularly utilize a video version of the syndicated columnist. Major news magazines and large city dailies regularly review films; even the smallest of newspapers offers a column discussing the film industry's latest releases. In some cases, movies are reviewed a second time when they are released in videocassette format. 1

And yet these instances of criticism are only part of the effort that goes into analyzing film. This reading puts into perspective the act of film criticism while providing an overview of the critical approaches currently being used. The bulk of this essay will focus on academic criticism versus the more popular media forms. The general public is aware of and utilizes criticism that is more aptly termed *movie reviewing*. Movie reviews are meant to recommend or not recommend particular films to the potential viewing public. In one sense, the popular 2 media critic is a consumer watchdog keeping a wary eye on the film industry's attempts to obtain the viewers' dollars.

Distinguishing the popular media form of criticism from academic or scholarly criticism is not to suggest that the former is unscholarly or a poor cousin to the latter. Movie reviews are meant for a specific audience, and they perform a specific function: to assist consumers in choosing categories as plot, characterization, or strength of the actors' performances to arrive at their assessment of the film (this is probably a holdover from the early beginnings of such criticism when reviewers of this new medium generally were drama critics taking on additional duties). In most cases today, reviewers' closest comments regarding purely filmic qualities are related to a director's use of particular techniques. 3

In contrast, academic critical pursuits are directed toward publications intended for fellow academicians and/or filmmakers. Their purpose is to foster a better understanding of film as a medium and as an art form. Hence scholarly criticism of film invariably touches the medium's history, functions, practitioners, techniques, or aesthetics. In most cases, such criticism attempts to answer questions about the film's history and other issues in order to further our knowledge about art ourselves, and the world. 4

Sydney Pollack (1986), director of the critically acclaimed and successful films *Out of Africa* and *Tootsie,* has stated that each film is a revelation of the director's perceptions about how the world operates. Each film is thus a communication of the director's overall vision of the world. Those who seek to understand a film implicitly seek understanding of what the director has communicated. In many cases, what is communicated is not always obvious to the viewer or the critic. Close analysis is necessary to reveal, interpret, or merely aid the viewer's understanding. 5

There are a variety of methods and critical models imposed on films, all of which propose to answer specific questions about those works of art. Indeed, the question of what the filmmaker "meant" is not an appropriate query (many critical theorists have long ago abandoned the quest for artist's intent). Rather, the meaning of a film is just that: what the film (or work of art) communicates. The film's meaning, then, depends on how it is perceived, by whom, and with what particular perspective(s). 6

This situation appears to indicate that film meanings vary and therefore criticism as a method for arriving at that meaning must be fruitless pursuit. Quite the contrary is true. Works of art will often hold different meanings for people because of their varied experiences and backgrounds. Hence, each viewer approaches a film with different sets of expectations and prejudices, as well as a distinct worldview 7 and knowledge base. The variety of critical perspectives allows each individual to explore the perspective most meaningful to that person. More important, for those of us studying the mass media, an additional gain from the variety of critical perspectives used to analyze film is the differences that are highlighted and what those differences tell us about ourselves, others, and the human condition in general.

The remainder of this reading will . . . review the various types of film criticism, with examples for each type of criticism. Although no particular perspective should be viewed as more useful or proper than any other, no doubt each reader will find one or two of those discussed to be more functional than the others. The key is that no perspective should be dismissed out of hand; each has its own merits as well as faults. Like the cinematic works of art they attempt to analyze, some critical methods work for us, and others do not. To aid us in our understanding of film as a mass medium and as an art form, it is necessary to be acquainted with the basic theory and the tools utilized by critics of film. 8

CRITICAL METHODS IN FILM CRITICISM

Each of the critical approaches to film discussed here falls within one of three categories: 9

semiotic: realist, formalist, rhetorical, mise-en-scène.
structuralist: mythic, political, feminist, psychoanalytic, sociological, phenomenological.
contextual: auteur, genre, historical.

Grouped within the *semiotic* category are methods that tend to focus on the meaning of the filmic signs (shots and shot transitions), the relationship of these signs to other filmic signs, or the effect of the signs on the film viewer. Methods that fall under the *structuralist* category seek to define and understand the structures into which individual films and/or from where they are derived. Those under the *contextual* heading focus on aspects of film in the context of other aspects of film.

SEMIOTIC STUDIES

The most logical place to start in the review of critical approaches with a semiotic impetus is with both the *realist* and *formalist traditions* within film theory. The *realist* tradition focuses on the use of film to represent 10 reality based on the power of photography's ability to render the real world objectively (Bazin 1967). Bazin argues that long takes, depth of focus, location shooting, sunlight, and the use of nonprofessional actors all contribute to a film's realist aesthetic. In his analysis of Visconti's *La Terra Trema* (1971), Bazin discusses how the film is "real" by virtue of the manner in which the narrative is presented: without the trappings of montage (where reality is fragmented through such techniques as close-up shots and excessive editing). "If a fisherman rolls a cigarette, he [Visconti] spares us nothing: we see the whole operation; it will not be reduced to its dramatic or symbolic meaning, as is usual with montage" (Bazin 1971, p. 43). In a review of De Sica's *Bicycle Thief,* Bazin praises the realist use of location shooting (nothing has been filmed in the studio) and actors without any previous experience in theater or film (Bazin 1971, p. 52).

Analyses using the *formalist* approach have a different focus. Be- 11
cause of his influence on the early history of filmmaking, the Russian filmmaker and theorist Sergei Eisenstein is most often linked (above other theorists) to film's *formalist* tradition. Eisenstein's theory of dialectical montage is influenced by the Japanese hieroglyph, as a pictorial representation of language symbols, and by Hegel's dialectic. First, Eisenstein believes that the Japanese language was built on the principle of montage. For example, the picture symbol for a *dog* plus the symbol for *mouth* means "to bark" (1949, p. 30). The combination of "two hieroglyphs of the simplest series is to be regarded not as their sum, but as their product, i.e., as a value of another dimension, another degree; each, separately, corresponds to an *object,* to a fact, but their combination corresponds to a *concept.* From separate hieroglyphs has been fused—the ideogram" (Eisenstein 1949, pp. 29–30).

Eisenstein theorizes that film relied on the same process: a shot 12
combined in the editing process with another shot created a new concept. Paralleling this approach is the influence of Hegel's dialectic. *Thesis* and *antithesis* combine to form a *synthesis*—a new concept that is no longer reducible to those ideas that in combination make up the editing (as well as any other art form). Montage is the collision of independent shots (shots that are opposite to one another) (Eisenstein 1949, p. 49). Meaning in film, then, evolves from the juxtaposition of film shots that manifest conflict. The differences might be in lighting, shot composition, shot length, conflict of volumes, lines, movement of objects, or something else. Excluding Eisenstein's philosophical and political (or Marxist) orientation, the basis of his theory is film construction: shot plus shot plus shot . . . Hence, any critic interested in how the shots of a film are combined to "mean" would essentially be conducting formalist criticism.

Ted Perry's essay (1970) on Michaelangelo Antonioni's film 13
L'Eclisse argues that the meaning of the film depends on certain cues

given within the film. In distinguishing between what he calls *fact context* and *value context,* the author argues that the film's meaning is born of the formative forces within the film (p. 79). Perry's analysis relies heavily on the notion of combination. The value context (the attitudes, impressions, and values by which the film frames the fact context) influences the viewer's reading of the fact context (the elements that represent the actions, objects, and events of the physical world depicted in the motion picture images). This analysis reflects the formalist tradition in its focus on meaning that is built upon the combination of shots.

A third type of analysis within the semiotic orientation is *rhetorical* in focus. This type of criticism examines the film as a rhetorical artifact that exhibits intentional meaning and structure. It is an approach based on traditional notions of rhetoric as a means to persuasion. Often relying on critical models from other disciplines, the rhetorical criticism of film deals with the communicative potential of film. 14

In "Image and Ambiguity: A Rhetorical Approach to *The Exorcist,*" Martin Medhurst (1978) examines the key images in six of the film's episodes in order to define the film's central stance: a rhetoric of choice. The author argues that certain recurring images combine in clusters to foster the contention that people have choices to make: "Humans must choose between the forces of good and the legions of evil. . . . They must consciously will the good and then by a step of faith act on that choice. This is exactly what Damien Karras does in the climax of the film. He consciously chooses to assert that Regan will not die and then proceeds to act on the basis of that assertion" (Medhurst 1978, pp. 90–91). 15

Medhurst (1982) has also analyzed Alain Resnais' *Hiroshima, Mon Amour* as a film about the problem of knowing reality. In essence, Medhurst's analysis is traditionally rhetorical in his focus on the filmmaker's "cinematic statement": "Resnais has built into the film the very paradox which forms its thesis . . . Resnais has been able to take his thesis and transform it into a cinematic resource . . . To know reality, Resnais seems to be saying, is no easy task" (Medhurst 1982, p. 370). Clearly in evidence is the rhetorical quest concerning what the filmmaker means. Both of the Medhurst essays ostensibly rely on examining and interpreting the filmmaker's message. 16

The final type of semiotic-oriented criticism relies on *mise-en-scène*—the environment of the film, which is created by its lighting, sets, costumes, movement, and any other features that comprise the scene as photographed by the camera. Film analysis that focuses on these elements and on the expressive function of the individual shots is the basis of mise-en-scène criticism (Stromgren and Norden 1984, p. 265). Mise-en-scène criticism lies in the boundary zone between for- 17 malism and realism; it is "largely concerned with stylistic or expressive qualities of the single shot . . . in contrast to Bazin's perception of the long take as a transparent realism . . . and in sharp distinction to Eisenstein's herding of all expressive categories under the single umbrella of montage" (Nichols 1976, p. 311).

One notable example of mise-en-scène criticism is Place and Peterson's "Some Visual Motifs of *Film Noir*" (1974). Here, the authors define visual style by utilizing the technical terminology of Hollywood. Their analysis reveals a style reliant on low-key lighting, night-for-night photography (versus day-for-night where the scene, shot in the bright sunlight of day, is manipulated to create an illusion of night), depth of field (the entire shot is in focus), and anti-traditional camera setups and angles: "The 'dark mirror' of *film noir* creates a visually unstable environment in which no character has a firm moral base from which he can confidently operate. All attempts to find safety or security are undercut by the anti-traditional cinematography and mise-en-scène" (Place and Peterson, p. 338). 18

All of these types of criticism have semiotic underpinnings: each attempts to understand and/or interpret the meaning of cinematic signs, the relationship of cinematic signs to each other, and their meaning to the viewer. There are not always clear-cut boundaries between the varying elements. However, the distinctive features of the type are clear: The primary focus is on cinematic features and the use of film theory. This is contrary to the structuralist studies, which utilize literary-cultural features. They are, in effect, extracinematic (outside of cinema). 19

STRUCTURALIST STUDIES

There are several types of structuralist methodology. Each method attempts to impose its own orientation or structure on the film; each argues that the film exhibits particular features of the society within which it is produced. 20

The *mythic* approach asserts the presence of one or more specific myths that, by virtue of their preeminence, are found (or likely to be found) in a society's aesthetic artifacts. Dale Williams's essay (1984) on the religious nature of Stanley Kubrick's *2001: A Space Odyssey* is an example of criticism that uncovers the meaning of the film by defining its mythic overtones. Using the theories of Kenneth Burke (1969), Williams argues that *2001* revolves around the concepts of order and redemption, sacrifice and rebirth, self-denial, and communion with God (Williams 1984, p. 321). Similarly, Martha Solomon (1983) argues that British-made *Chariots of Fire* was successful in the United States 21 because it reflects two contradictory facets of the American dream—what Fisher (1973) calls the materialistic myth and the moralistic myth. The film's success, in part, is due to its reaffirmation of both competing myths for an audience likely to follow, individually, one or the other. *Chariots,* according to Solomon, functions both mythically and metaphorically in its depiction of a series of successful, archetypal quests by the film's mythic hero characters (p. 275).

The *political* approach to criticism is likely to focus on films and 22
their relationship to the areas of history, ideology, economics, and social criticism. Jeffrey Richards's essay (1970) on Frank Capra illustrates how the films of a single director can contain political undertones. In this case, Capra's films reflect ideals of the populist party: self-help and individualism versus political machines and big government. Richards finds the presence of Capra's emphasis of populism in the motifs of antiintellectualism, wealth, pursuit of happiness, and the quintessential good neighbor. Capra's films in the postwar era cast aside these themes because the world had progressed, and the forces of organization had won out.

The *feminist* perspective in criticism has gained sufficient status 23
as a category, though it could be argued that its impetus is political in nature. Most of the feminist critics analyze films' treatment of women as they support or negate the role of women in contemporary society. For example, Diane Giddis (1973) explores a woman's dilemma (the fear that love represents loss of autonomy) in her analysis of *Klute.* Giddis finds that the film reflects woman's need to love and make a deep emotional commitment—a commitment unnecessary, to the same degree, for men. Constance Penley (1973) analyzes Ingmar Bergman's *Cries and Whispers* in the perspective of Bergman's other films. Penley's analysis runs counter to the majority of the film's reviews; she sees *Cries* as another example of Bergman's excessive portrayal of woman as victim, temptress, evil incarnate, and earth mother.

Psychoanalytic and *sociological* criticisms are likely to use models 24
of analysis from accepted theorists or contemporary social concerns. Rushing and Frentz (1980), for example, derive their analysis of *The Deer Hunter* from the psychological theories of Carl Jung. In a sociological critique, the critic uses sociological concepts, such as class, status, interaction, organization and culture, to analyze a film. They may also use the perspective and language of social movements.

Finally, the *phenomenological* approach to criticism is concerned 25
with the manner in which viewers perceive the film and/or its images (always, however, in relation to the whole) (see Andrew 1978). An example of this type is Janice Schuetz's analysis (1975) of *The Exorcist.* Schuetz utilizes the symbols of yin and yang from the *I Ching* as a

paradigm for explaining the viewer's perceptions of the film. She argues that the film "presents reality in an organismic way, showing goodness and evil, doubt and faith, despair and hope, secular and sacred . . . as realistic representations of an integrated reality" (pp. 100–101). In addition, the images are sufficiently ambiguous to permit viewers to attribute meaning based on their own frame of reference (p. 101).

CONTEXTUAL STUDIES

The three types included here—auteur, genre, and historical—have in common the study of film(s) within a specific context: directorial style (in its broadest sense), narrative type, and impact on or development of the film industry and/or the film as art form. Examples of each type are readily available in single texts, film periodicals, and collections of essays. 26

The most controversial of the three types is *auteur* criticism. Auteur theory assumes a certain amount of directorial autonomy in film production regardless of the fact that film is a product of producers, screenwriters, cinematographers, actors, musicians, film editors, and others. The film's creation and the stylistic choices made are assumed to be those of a single person—the director. Auteur criticism, then, focuses on film directors and the style manifested in two or more of their films. Directors such as Alfred Hitchcock, Charles Chaplin, John Ford, Howard Hawks, and Orson Welles have indirectly generated numerous auteur studies. No doubt, and not far off, there will be studies of George Lucas and Steven Spielberg. 27

Andrew Sarris (1968) uses auteur theory to rank various directors. Relying on three criteria—technical competence, stylistic identity, and communicability of worldview—he estimates their worth as directors. John Simon's analysis of Ingmar Bergman (1972) is an auteur study that looks at four films that Simon thinks represent Bergman's best work up to the early 1970s. Ian Cameron's two-part essay on Hitchcock (1972a) is another example of auteur criticism. It analyzes a specific feature of the director's overall style, his ability to create suspense in his films: 28

> Having arrived at such a disturbing view [everything is a potential threat], Hitchcock paradoxically relishes it and loves more than anything to torture his audiences by making them find the most innocuous thing alarming so that he can surprise and terrify them when the real threat is revealed. (Cameron 1972b, p. 34)

By examining a single film, *The Man Who Knew Too Much,* Cameron validates his auteur assumptions about Hitchcock's style. 29

Another typical example of auteur criticism is Michael Budd's essay (1976) on visual imagery in John Ford's Westerns.

Genre criticism focuses on the narrative structures common to 30
film: Westerns, war films, musicals, gangster films, and so on. This type of criticism also categorizes films according to specific characteristics. Thus, to be able to classify an object, to know where it fits, is a means toward understanding it better. We are then able to analyze a certain film based on how well it fits a particular genre and "how the director of that work used the elements of the genre—its *conventions*—to make a statement unique to that film" (Stromgren and Norden 1984). (For additional comments on genre criticism, see Kaminsky 1974; see also the extensive bibliography of genre studies in Cook 1981, pp. 691–692.)

Finally, *historical* studies inevitably analyze the entire scope of the 31
film's development. Cook (1981), Ellis (1985), Giannetti and Eyman (1986), and Mast (1986) are fine representatives of historical criticism. In addition, studies of particular studios (Buscombe 1975; Gomery 1976) analyze the film industry from economic, political, or corporate perspectives or the impact of new technology. A relatively new annual series edited by Bruce A. Austin, "Current Research in Film: Audiences, Economics, and Law," publishes original essays on corporate structure, film financing, legal issues, marketing and promotion strategies, and others in an attempt to provide a place for those critics whose interests and work lie outside of the scope addressed by existing film journals.

CONCLUSION

There is a danger in establishing category systems. Inevitably exam- 32
ples of criticism exhibit features appropriate for more than one type of critical method. Judgment as to the correct placement of each of the examples here is left up to the reader. However, no apology is made for the classification contained within; what these essays accomplish is typical of the category they exemplify. Nor are they to be considered examples of superior criticism. In some cases, they create as many questions as they answer.

There will continue to be a need to analyze the best, worst, and 33
average output of the film industry. Although the ultimate arbiter for judging a film's success may be its box office receipts, those with expertise should continue to analyze film with the express purpose of better understanding it as a mass media art form. Critics of both kinds, public and scholarly, can always hope that filmmakers, and ultimately audiences, will benefit from their efforts.

From the opposite viewpoint, those who practice film criticism 34
have no monopoly on perfection. Critics must continue to read other

critical analyses of film in order to improve their own craft. Like the student in a public speaking course, critics benefit from witnessing the successes and blunders of other critics. New methods are tried and either validated or rejected. In a rapidly progressing world, there is comfort in the thought that our critical stance and methods also continue to progress.

REFERENCES

Andrew, Dudley. 1978. "The Neglected Tradition of Phenomenology in Film Theory." *Wide Angle* 2:44–49.

Bazin, André. 1967. *What Is Cinema?* Vol. 1. Translated and edited by Hugh Gray. Berkeley: University of California Press.

_____. 1971. *What Is Cinema?* Vol. 2. Translated and edited by Hugh Gray. Berkeley: University of California Press.

Budd, Michael. 1976. "A Home in the Wilderness: Visual Imagery in John Ford's Westerns." *Cinema Journal* 16:62–75.

Burke, Kenneth. 1969. *A Rhetoric of Motives.* Berkeley: University of California Press.

Buscombe, Edward. 1975. "Notes on Columbia Pictures Corporation, 1926–1941." *Screen* 16. Reprinted in Nichols 1985:92–108.

Cameron, Ian. 1972a. "Hitchcock and the Mechanics of Suspense." *Movie Reader.* New York: Praeger.

_____. 1972b. "Hitchcock 2: Suspense and Meaning." *Movie Reader.* New York: Praeger.

Cook, David A. 1981. *A History of Narrative Film.* New York: W. W. Norton.

Eisenstein, Sergei. 1947. *The Film Sense.* New York: Harcourt Brace Jovanovich.

_____. 1949. *Film Form: Essays in Film Theory.* Translated and edited by Jay Leyda. New York: Harcourt, Brace and World.

Ellis, Jack C. 1985. *A History of Film.* 2d ed. Englewood Cliffs, NJ: Prentice Hall.

Fisher, Walter. 1973. "Reaffirmation and Subversion of the American Dream." *Quarterly Journal of Speech* 59:160–167.

Giannetti, Louis, and Scott Eyman. 1986. *Flashback: A Brief History Film.* Englewood Cliffs, NJ: Prentice Hall.

Giddis, Diane. 1973. "The Divided Woman: Bree Daniels in *Klute.*" *Women and Film,* nos. 3–4. Reprinted in Nichols 1976:194–201.

Gomery, Douglas. 1976. "Writing the History of the American Film Industry: Warner Brothers and Sound." *Screen* 17. Reprinted in Nichols 1985:109–119.

Examining the Text

1. Why do you think Schaefermeyer begins by distinguishing between movie reviewing and movie criticism? In what ways does he suggest that the reviewer and the critic both perform important functions? Based on his examples, do you agree with his evaluation of the critic's role?
2. Briefly summarize in your own words each of the three basic critical approaches Schaefermeyer describes. How do they differ from one another? Which would you find most interesting and illuminating?
3. Schaefermeyer concludes that "the ultimate arbiter for judging a film's success may be its box office receipts" (paragraph 32). Do you think he is being entirely serious? What other ways are there to judge a film's "success"? Is any of these a better criterion than earnings?

For Group Discussion

Choose a film that each member of your group has seen and discuss how it could be analyzed using each of the three critical approaches described by Schaefermeyer. Come up with several specific examples from the film to illustrate one or more of the methods within each approach. As a class, discuss which approaches work best with which kinds of films.

Writing Suggestion

Critically analyze a specific film (or several films of the same genre, such as horror, science fiction, or romantic comedy), restricting your thematic focus to one of the structuralist approaches described by Schaefermeyer. For instance, if you consider yourself a feminist, point out instances of sexism or the objectification of women; if you're a political conservative, you might write from the perspective of a Rush Limbaugh, pointing out examples of liberal excess and misguidedness; if you are a student of mythology, you might take that approach. If possible see the movie or movies you are writing about again, preferably on video, so that your examination can be a close one.

Film Criticism in America Today: A Critical Symposium

The Editors of Cineaste

The editors of Cineaste *magazine open this piece by describing how the "dumbing down of both movies and moviegoing audiences" as well as marketing pressures are affecting film criticism today. With these factors in mind, the editors asked some prominent American film critics/reviewers to respond to a series of questions about their role as film critics/reviewers, and about the state of film criticism in general.*

In the responses that follow, six critics/reviewers reflect upon their profession. These writers represent a range of different publications: from David Ansen and Richard Schickel, from mainstream news magazines Newsweek *and* Time, *respectively, to David Denby and Stuart Klawans, writers for the more specialized—and generally liberal, intellectual—publications* The New Yorker *and* The Nation. *In spite of their different magazine and newspaper affiliations, these critics share a number of concerns about the state of movie making and marketing, and, consequently, their relation to movies and the moviegoing audience.*

As you read *these reflections on film criticism and reviewing, notice the differences and similarities between the views expressed. While we've noted that the writers share a number of concerns, they also emphasize certain issues differently, while sometimes adopting varying attitudes and tones in their approaches to these issues.*

In the last few years, a number of film critics, especially those who came of age during the Sixties, a period that essayist Philip Lopate has described as "The 'Heroic' Age of Moviegoing," have publicly voiced concerns about the overall decline of film culture in the U.S., a noticeable dumbing down of both movies and moviegoing audiences, and their own waning influence as critics in such a degraded cultural environment. Many film critics, in fact—especially those writing for mainstream newspaper and magazines—feel increasingly embattled in their efforts to write serious criticism because of commercial pressures from publishers, publicists, and film distributors, all of whom are principally interested in using critics as marketing aids. Many critics have also, knowingly or unwittingly, been co-opted into the Hollywood movie-marketing machine. Whether or not this state of affairs constitutes, as some believe, a 'crisis,' it has certainly left many film critics, as James Wolcott wrote in a recent *Esquire* magazine survey of 1 the film criticism field, with "a group case of chronic depression and low self-esteem."

What better way, then, to get a sense of the state of the vocation, than to invite some of America's leading film critics to sound off on the situation as they see it. While we asked contributors to this Critical Symposium to focus their essays around the following questions, several of them have written more expansive essays. We believe their insightful and often impassioned comments will be of interest not only to fellow critics, aspiring critics, and scholars, but also to readers of criticism, moviegoers, and perhaps even some members of the film industry. 2

1. What does being a film critic mean to you? (More specifically, why do you write film criticism? Whom do you hope to reach and what do you hope to communicate to them?
2. What qualities make for a memorable film critique? (Do you think such critiques tend to be positive or negative in tone? Is discussing a film's social or political aspects as important to you as its cinematic qualities and value as art or entertainment?)
3. How would you characterize the relationship between film critics and the film industry? Do you think film critics could be more influential in this relationship? How?
4. What are the greatest obstacles you face in writing the kind of film criticism you wish to write? (For example, does your publication require delivery of your copy on a short deadline after only one screening, limit the space available for your reviews, or dictate winch films you should review? How difficult is it for you to keep up with all types of film releases?)
5. Do you have any pet peeves or personal frustrations that you'd like to address? Or would you like to share your critical credo or a favorite maxim about film criticism from a forerunner?

DAVID ANSEN, *NEWSWEEK*[1]

The literary critic Harry Levin once said that in order to dissect something (he was talking about a play by Shakespeare) you have to kill it first. I don't agree. One of the challenges of writing movie reviews is keeping the patient alive while you perform your operation: you want 3

[1]David Ansen is movie critic and senior editor for *Newsweek,* where he has been reviewing movies since 1977. He is a member of the New York Film Critics Circle, the National Society of Film Critics, the Los Angeles Film Critics Association, and is a three-time winner of the Page One Award from the Newspaper Guild of New York.

to preserve the beating heart, the messy innards, of the thing itself. "A man watches a movie, and the critic must acknowledge that he is that man," Robert Warshow famously wrote. These are words that most good American critics live by. I may get paid to do my job, but I'll never lose the sense of myself as an amateur, and I don't want to. But there is more to it than mere subjectivity, one hopes. A movie critic is part mirror: a mirror that talks back to what it's reflecting, a mirror informed by all the images that have passed before it. Our readers and our editors may see us merely as consumer guides, but I still like to think that splitting the fine hairs of art takes us deeper into ourselves, can help us see the work—and by extension the world—with clearer eyes. Contrary to our enemies, critics (or at least the ones I care to read) are not frustrated artists picking apart art because we don't have the stuff to make it ourselves. We're more likely to be frustrated, wildly promiscuous lovers, in perpetual pursuit of the one we can lose our hearts to, one eye fixed on the object of our desire, panting to be seduced, the other coolly judging the quality and terms of the seduction.

Memorable reviews (I say this as a reader) are well-written reviews. I was infuriated by Pauline Kael's putdown of *Hiroshima, Mon Amour* when I read it as a fourteen-year-old, and I knew instantly she was someone whose views I was compelled to contend with. It's a review I've learned from, argued with and never forgotten. A memorable review opens doors in your head, pulls the rug of received opinion out from under your feet, supplies a context to bounce your own ideas off of. It helps, of course (I say this as a critic) to have a memorable movie (good or bad) to write about; something you can sink your teeth into. By the time you get to contemplating shopworn summer sequels (whose audience couldn't care less what any critic thinks), your muse may feel a little punch-drunk. Still, hopefully, there will always be something going on inside or behind the movie you are writing about that bears scrutiny and can charge your mental batteries. The last part of your question (politics vs. entertainment) can be answered only on a case-by-case basis. There shouldn't be one answer to that question. The best critical minds are supple enough to juggle all these balls in the air at the same time, responding freshly to the matter at hand; the doctrinaire critic refuses to take a movie on its own terms, holding all up to the same predetermined notion of what Good Art (or Good Politics) is supposed to be. Little of interest can come of this. 4

Lopsided. That's the relationship today, now more than ever. Hollywood has all the power, much as they flatter you by misquoting your reviews in ads. It seems every year the big wannabe blockbusters, with their $40-million marketing campaigns, become more and more critic-proof. It simply didn't matter what anybody had to 5 say about *Mission: Impossible 2.* Its success was eerily predetermined: Paramount succeeded in marketing a commodity the nation felt obliged to see, don't ask me why. The strange and scary thing was that the biggest hit of the summer was a movie nobody in the country was genuinely excited by: I've yet to encounter anyone who loved it. Say what you will about *The Phantom Menace* (I say it stinks) it at least evoked some honest enthusiasm. The critic's real power in Hollywood isn't about influencing grosses; it's about making reputations. As others have observed, it's really ego, not money, that runs the movie industry. One can never overestimate the easily bruised egos of filmmakers and studio executives, or how much they need us to feel good about themselves in the morning. There was nothing more revealing than the hissy fit James Cameron threw in the pages of *The Los Angeles Times* in retaliation for Ken Turan's attacks on *Titanic.* The entire world had fallen in love with his movie, he was drowning in money and Academy Awards, and the fact that Turan thought his movie was shit drove him mad: he literally called for the *Times* to serve up Turan's head on a platter. He wanted him fired.

Our relationship with foreign and independent films is another story. Lacking the millions for marketing, the smaller distributors need good reviews (and almost as important, good placement on page one of the Friday entertainment section) to sell their movies. A pan from *The New York Times* of a foreign art film can not only kill the movie in New York, it also may mean the movie never opens anywhere else in the country. (It took years for Leos Carax's *Les Amants de Pont Neuf* to even open in New York after Vincent Canby savaged it at its New York Film Festival premiere.) 6

In a newsweekly, the biggest obstacle is space. Is there a magazine outside of *The New Yorker* or *The Atlantic* that hasn't seen the pictures get larger, and the text smaller, in the past twenty years? There are wonderful movies I simply haven't been able to review because there was no room that week in the magazine. A last-minute breaking news story can rob your three columns in the back of the book. (It happened as I was writing this.) I was happy to get in a plug for Human Resources, but the review was literally two sentences long, accompanied by four stars: I had to be content to be a consumer guide, but I certainly wasn't being a critic. There are good journalistic reasons to choose to review the movies everyone will turn up to see, but was it more interesting to write a two-column review of *Gone in 60 Seconds* than it would have been to write about *Aimee and Jaguar,* a film that never quite made it into the magazine? Do I need to answer? 7

One of the great services that critics can provide is turning the audience on to the best, freshest, most exciting new work in movies. Journalism used to be about that. But there's been a profound shift in 8 the culture. Most editors today are more concerned with second guessing their readers: what's the hot movie going to be? The media wants to be on the side of the winners. Magazines and newspapers think exactly like the studio execs: what sells tickets sells magazines. In the process, journalism has increasingly abdicated its power to set the agenda, to serve as a guide, to highlight what it considers to be the most worthwhile in favor of pandering to what it guesses will be the most popular. God forbid someone accuse you of elitism! In coverage of the arts, the monotone rules: everyone is lusting after the same stories, the same movies, the same stars to profile. Critics are by nature hierarchical. We have an innate belief in esthetic priorities. And we are swimming against the tide. The harsh fact is, the culture doesn't have much use for real criticism these days. We're cheerleaders or spoilsports, but we don't really matter the way we once did. But as Gilda Radner used to say, "Never mind." Pissing and moaning aside, it's a great gig. Sillier still, I believe in it.

JAY CARR, *THE BOSTON GLOBE*[2]

I write film criticism because it is by now as natural as eating and drinking and talking with my friends. In fact, it began years ago in New York, when not going to a new film and not talking about it for hours with your friends was unthinkable. You never know whom you're going to reach. Nor would you want to. One of the fringe benefits of writing, especially now that the Internet has been added to the mix, is that you never know who's going to read what you write. I like to be surprised by this, no less than I like being surprised by a film. 9

Your questions, please forgive me, seem naive in a few respects. The relationship between critics and the film industry should always be mutually uneasy and best avoided, or minimized. Each is working a different side of the street. They're trying to sell their film. You're trying to evaluate it, or capture your response to it—phenomenological, political, sociological, wherever the ball lands. It's a mistake to go into a film with an agenda. Go in honestly, demandingly, with a sense of perspective and film history. Learn to ignore the hype and buzz. It only interferes with your job, which is to respond to a film. 10

Writing about films, especially for a daily newspaper, has never been an ideal situation, apart from the fact that you're paid to do it. Does my publication require delivery of my copy on a short deadline 11

---

[2]Jay Carr, after reviewing film, theater and music for *The Detroit News*, joined *The Boston Globe* in 1993. Each year, Carr writes more than 300 reviews, profiles, and essays for the Arts pages of *The Globe*. He also is film critic for New England Cable News.

after only one screening? All the time. I write more than 300 pieces a year. No point in whining about it. It just goes with the territory. You do the best you can. The stuff gets written, usually in the best way when you trust your perceptual and instinctual equipment and just let the film act on you. Once you do that, the review writes itself, taking its cue from the interaction between the film and your sensibility, wiring, intelligence, empathetic capacity, background, imagination, etc. Worst of all is to overlay the process with some agenda or filter. Just let it happen and you'd be surprised how often the review emerges from whatever subterranean level it takes shape at. All you have to do is stand back and let it come, shaping the language a little bit.

Serious critical voices are used to being marginalized. They should be. They should stand off to one side of the mainstream, or at least stay out of bed with industry people adept at turning them into marketing adjuncts. The best critics usually are not celebrities. You can only be co-opted by the film industry if you allow yourself to be. So don't allow it. Just stand your ground, call your own shots, don't let people shove you around. There's no crisis in film criticism that hasn't always been part of the landscape, apart, that is, from finding a place that will pay you a decent salary and then leave you alone to do your job. There are fewer living-wage jobs for critics than there are for actors. That's the crisis. In the end, the stuff is out there with your name on it, finding its proper level. You put yourself on the line and let your writing do the talking—and the audience selection—for you. 12

DAVID DENBY, *THE NEW YORKER*[3]

Let's distinguish between self-pity and regret. The first is ridiculous and unworthy—we're all lucky enough to make a living by doing what we love. Initially, no one wanted or needed us, and we imposed ourselves, often in the face of disdain or indifference. So we've fought to become whatever it is we've become, and at this point, our survival is itself some sort of achievement, since, again, no one but a few enlightened editors and a minority of fervent readers really wants a serious movie critic around at this point. So self-pity should be easily 13

[3]David Denby has been a film critic and staff writer for *The New Yorker* since 1998. In the past, he was film critic for *The Atlantic, The Boston Phoenix,* and *New York.* His 1996 book on the undergraduate curriculum debates, *Great Books,* has been translated into nine languages.

extinguished by defiance. But regret is another story. To say that we live in a second-rate film culture that diminishes us all may be true or false, but the statement is not in itself a sign of weakness—it's a reflection on history. Nostalgia may be a muted form of grief.

Of course there are always good things coming out; there are always interesting things to write about. But as a culture, it's a shadow of what it was. Anyone who can't see that, admit that, live with that, is afraid that simple candor will propel him right out of a job. Yes, it would be nice if it were 1968 again and Godard were still riding high in the saddle, or 1972, with Coppola, De Palma, Scorsese, et al., breaking through, a time when critics were avidly read, argued over, played off against one another, even turned into minor household icons, etc. But we're a long way from those eras, and nothing like them is likely to appear in the immediate future. As I write this, it is the second week of October 2000, more than nine months into the year, and what has been released in the American cinema this year that one can unequivocally call first-rate? (That's a rhetorical question that may not need answering.) Or even inventive, bold, exciting? Nineteen ninety-nine, it turns out, was an anomaly: Everyone in Hollywood was afraid of competing with *Phantom Menace,* and so a number of big stupid projects were cancelled or pulled back, and great things came out at the periphery of the studios, from the classics divisions or independents. In 2000, it's back to business as usual. I have no idea what the Internet and digital filmmaking will bring, but at the moment, despite all the ballyhoo about independent film and the democratization of production, producers are in control; no director, even if he or she has the talent, is likely to become an auteur in this system, and some of the best actors are fleeing to television. At the critical end, one result of the collapse has been the overpraise of mediocre movies—the feeble, repugnant *Chuck & Buck,* the soft and temporizing *Almost Famous.* These would not have been seen as good movies twenty-five years ago. 14

A severe downturn in quality hits an ambitious critic like an ax. He cannot fire up his work without being obsessed with his subject, yet in a bad period the movies do not always repay obsession. If he is very resourceful, and has the Devil's own wit, he can write his way out of trouble; or he can join the Righteous, disappearing into a film-festival and cultural-institute regimen of austere, or merely high-minded films, praising 'interesting' movies from Egypt—an arrogant form of denial. But if the dream of a great popular art form—the dream that animated Griffith, Chaplin, Keaton, Eisenstein, Gance, Renoir, Lubitsch, Ford, Welles, Truffaut, Kurosawa, Fellini, Scorsese—has died, then critics are dying too, for that dream also inspired Gilbert Seldes, James Agee, Robert Warshow, Andrew Sarris, and 15

Pauline Kael. Formerly, a critic who got angry was in a good state of health—he was honestly expressing the betrayal of his hopes when something better was possible. But if the possibility of art is evaporating, if the system has no use for it, doesn't want to produce it, and wouldn't know what to do with it if anyone did produce it, then what is the point of a critic's putting down bad movies week after week or day after day? In such a case, rage threatens to go stale and collapse into ill humor—the prig's offended nostrils at the cotton-candy media carnival. At the moment, the movies are hardly good enough in general for a critic to say with love and hope in his heart that they are bad in particular. But we do it, of course. We do it, because we have to. But we face a relentless tide.

Like it or not, we are enmeshed in marketing, which has become 16
not just a way of getting products to consumers but an ethos, a way of life, a law, a metaphysical imperative. To question its workings is to risk the charge of extreme naivete. Yet the terrible thing about marketing is that most of it is indiscriminate, without special feeling for the product or the audience. There is a loud, agitated, relentless, and wearying quality now to the cycle of movie publicity, release, and withdrawal, a powerful disgust built into the operation of the huge machine itself. Whirlwinds of promotion often lead to a sudden collapse—all to be repeated the following week with a new movie, the instant monumental dissolved and reborn, dissolved and reborn. Critics want to stop the world and get off, but they can't. The marketing cycle controls most of them-us—as well, The studios have either marginalized us as cranks or reduced us to semiirrelevance by surrounding us with hacks whom they create, nourish, and promote with junkets and blurbs. Most criticism has been pulled into the marketing system.

The situation may be particularly severe at daily newspapers. 17
Newspapers are in desperate competition with other media merely to survive, and editors and writers at some papers may come under tremendous pressure to stupefy their movie coverage. A talented critic who is instinctively honest can get trapped as completely as a mediocity. Editors, perhaps pressured by publishers (with marketing studies in hand), may ask critics to shorten and punch up their reviews, assign star or letter grades to the movies, omit qualifying paragraphs, lines of reasoning, evocation—everything that makes a review criticism and not thumbs-up-or-thumbs-down hackwork. The editor would be of much greater value to the critic and to the paper if he challenged him to become a provocative writer, thereby attracting new readers, but publishers may not see it that way, and all too often editors cut critics down to size any way they can. Frightened that readers will feel outclassed by a strongly worded opinion, they may tell the critic that he's

'lost touch' with the audience; or they may publish opinions by ordinary folk or students to reveal the voice of 'the people.' What they really want—what they think readers need—are not reviews at all but endless feature coverage of movies and interviews with stars, so they require the critics to do double duty and join publicity junkets in New York or Los Angeles. The meaningless stories and fake interviews on local TV channels proliferate like kudzu.

Gently, ever so gently, with cunning and diplomacy, critics have to remind editors, and through them, if possible, publishers, that movies, however threadbare at the moment, can still be a great art form; that critics play a small but necessary role in the art of movies; and that newspapers and magazines have a responsibility to the audience—to defend the best possibilities of movies—that the audience isn't necessarily aware of. If editors won't trust the tastes of their critics, they could at least trust their own tastes, rather than follow the chimera of 'what the public wants'—which is often just a meaningless rumble created by past hits, star power, and promotion. Critics handing out blurbs will stop playing the fool if only editors will ask them to stop. 18

It is a strange profession. The critic is a creature of the city, dipping in and out of shadows, seeking enchantment through long moods of sardonic disaffection. He is devoted by necessity to craft, not (usually) to philosophy, and to steady work and small victories, not to triumph. For him, there is no triumph; instead there is service, a calling—though certainly not a humble calling—and the exacting toil of precision, fairness, and wit. A critic who can't write has little value as a judge. 19

Drama critics, by tradition, affect the debonair; they are men and women of the city, too—boulevardiers. But movie critics slouch and vegetate, cultivating endless memory and odd loyalties. They also cultivate hope. Obsessed with a performing art, critics need to feel that something is breaking out, that something good is opening. They may be outsiders, but the surge of excitement surrounding a new movie sweetens their moods as much as it does that of people working in show business. And like players everywhere, they hope to get luck; they want to feel, exultantly, that they are riding the crest of a movement, or helping some new taste or sensibility make its way in the world, or perhaps marking the stages in a great director's or actress's career. In his own head (and even if the world will never agree), the critic likes to think he is playing some role in the way new movies are made and discussed. It's hard, at times, to think that now, but without thinking it, critics do not greet gently their moods at morning when they first sit down to write. 20

STUART KLAWANS, *THE NATION*[4]

Film critics sometimes speak of publications as 'vehicles' for reviews. We also call our employers a 'berth.' Apparently, we can't decide: Are we the merchant or the cargo ship, the dispatcher or the product? 21

This ambivalence is a defining mark of today's American film criticism: a showy, self-advertising form of writing, whose main business is to whistle up customers for a publication, and whose allure is borrowed, sometimes guiltily, from the supposed glamor of the subject matter. I know how quickly a name (however small) can be made in journalism, once you've taken a bit part in the movie business, since I spent my early years in obscurity as a book reviewer. Did my prose improve with the change from literature to film; did my ideas deepen? Unfortunately, no. The modest repute I suddenly enjoyed, along with invitations to parties and festivals, was owed to my objects of study. So much for critical distance. Though I may profess disdain for 'critics' who are mere puff-writers, I recognize that my publication and I both use the movies—just as the blurb-o-mats do—and are used in turn. 22

For me, this confusion in identity and mission has been a happy one, because my berth (or vehicle) is *The Nation*, a magazine that allows its writers complete freedom within strict limits. On the one hand, *The Nation* has a dauntingly impressive (though discontinuous) history of publishing film criticism, going back to Siegfried Kracauer, James Agee, Manny Farber, and Susan Sontag, a history that the magazine honors today by letting its contributors run loose. The editors may occasionally question my diction or syntax; but they never interfere in my choice of films to review (the selection is left entirely in my hands), they never challenge my judgments, and they never expect me to serve as a reliable consumer guide. As for politics, broadly construed: Should I venture an opinion that the editors and subscribers find reprehensible, the explicit policy is to let the effrontery stand. 23

On the other hand, I rarely venture such an opinion. I write for *The Nation* because no other publication will have me, but also because I am a typical *Nation* reader. We're not what you'd call movie brats. Though committed to an inclusionary politics and perennially hopeful of mass appeal, we are (relatively speaking) an old, pale, and academic crowd, who reveal our demographic skew through an elitist tone and 24

---

[4]*The Nation*'s film critic Stuart Klawans is a New York *Daily News* columnist and regular contributor to *The Village Voice*, NPR, WBAI, *Grand Street* and the *Times Literary Supplement*. Klawans's book *Film Follies* was nominated for a 1999 National Book Critics Circle Award for Criticism.

taste. When we enjoy a big, studio-made movie, we rush to congratulate ourselves on being in touch with the people. But, more often, we're proud to be out of touch, preferring the small, the independent, and the foreign to anything that carries the scent of money.

A lot of the pleasure I've taken in writing for *The Nation* has come from toying with these prejudices, which are of course my own. For example, I have avoided writing about John Sayles's well-meaning and honorable films, except for *Lone Star,* which was a big enough hit that I could afford to give it a drubbing. (When artistic angels are lifeless, there's good fun in being of the devil's party.) An example from the opposite end of my reviewing might be the lengthy, enthusiastic notice I gave to *Bill & Ted's Bogus Journey.* Not even a *Nation* reader could score points for liking that one. 25

Does this mean I'm practicing a form of self-mortification? God forbid. I'm merely suggesting that criticism is a continual questioning of one's situation in the world: a situation that's always being rediscovered through one's relationships to a single film, to a body of films, to an industry, to a publishing business, to one's readers, to oneself. Is the situation often intellectually dubious and morally compromised? That, too, is part of life. One's job is to keep the questions in play—and I'm fortunate to work for one of the few publications that encourage such writing. 26

That said, the logistics aren't great. Because *The Nation* cannot afford to put me on staff or provide medical insurance, I subsidize the habit of film criticism by maintaining a demanding full-time job. My employer, though patient, sometimes suffers from my inattention; and so does *The Nation,* since paid work interferes like hell with moviegoing. I struggle to keep up even a pretense of following the new releases, and I write my copy in the minutes snatched between distraction and exhaustion. Fortunately, my editors allow me to file at the last possible moment (ten days before the issue mails), so long as the word count hovers between 1400 and 1600. The editors also put up with my wholesale rewrites on galleys; but even so, the great majority of my pieces come straight off the top of my head. 27

Given these circumstances, I don't look to Farber, Kael, Bazin, Daney, or any of the fashionable critics as my model. I think instead of Vincent Canby, who wrote extraordinarily well, on short deadline, for year after year and never once felt impressed by himself. If you want to marvel at the insight he could bring to the most difficult pictures, look up his review of Aleksandr Sokurov's *Save and Protect.* But if you want to see what I value most in Canby's work, dig up the 200 words he wrote about a little picture titled *Love Your Mother:* a heartfelt, thoroughly amateurish movie produced in Chicago by some people who had hired an industrial filmmaker to direct their script. Most other critics would have crushed this movie and moved on. Canby, while 28 quietly letting his readers know that they would not want to watch this film, conveyed a sense that real human beings had poured themselves into *Love Your Mother* and that they deserved respect. I think his review, headline included, ran all of six column inches. It did as much as criticism could.

RICHARD SCHICKEL, *TIME*[5]

A definition: critics write for people who have seen or read or heard the object they are writing about; reviewers write for people who are perhaps thinking about—but probably won't—expose themselves to the movie or book or symphony in question. The contributors to this symposium are, most of the time, reviewers, not critics, so your title is misleading—and perhaps a little pretentious. 29

I, for example, may have written a little movie criticism over the past few decades, but for thirty-five years I've mostly plied the humbler craft of reviewing. Over that time, it has become something of a habit with me. It's not quite as mundane as brushing my teeth every day. It's more like my Tuesday tennis game—something I look forward to, engage in passionately for a finite amount of time, then pretty much forget until the next week. Another way of putting that is that you have to take the task seriously while you're doing it, but it's self-deluding—no, self-aggrandizing—to take it seriously after it's done. 30

Still, as jobs go, it's not a bad one. You get to shoot your mouth off without causing anyone any lasting harm—least of all yourself. Sometimes you even get to do a little minor good—bringing attention to a neglected film or advancing a worthwhile young career. I also value the work because it keeps me involved, week-in, week-out, in what passes for public life in our times. Without having to get out and see movies I would probably spend a lot more time in bed with the covers pulled over my head. Also I like seeing my name regularly in print in a major American magazine, a privilege not vouchsafed to many. Finally, movies, being the capacious medium they are, provide a nice variety of socio-political-esthetic topics to write about at least glancingly. 31

But that's about it. To make any larger claims for reviewing is to reveal yourself as a pompous ninny. This is a breed not entirely unknown in the trade, and it is one reason reviewing has always been a 32

[5]Richard Schickel is film critic for *Time* magazine and is the author of numerous books, including biographies of Marlon Brando, James Cagney, D. W. Griffith, Walt Disney, and Clint Eastwood. Two of his newest books, *Matinee Idylls* and *Intimate Strangers: The Culture of Celebrity*, have just appeared in paperback.

part-time job for me. It is an occupation that should not become an exclusive preoccupation.

To that end I have, from the beginning, spent more time writing books and writing, producing, and directing television documentaries than I have reviewing. Sometimes in these other jobs I make broader critical gestures than I do when I'm reviewing. I certainly think that making films for television has made me a better reviewer, more alert to the processes—and the often sly tricks—by which movies are put together. These other activities also serve a need I have to make things that are a little larger and more complicated to construct than a movie review, to express myself in ways that reviewing cannot fully accommodate. 33

Given my rather modest and solipsistic definition of the reviewer's job, the question of what makes a "critique" (a loathsomely pretentious word, by the way) "memorable" strikes me as moot. I can't think of a review I have ever read that I thought ought to outlive, in toto, the shelf-life of the publication in which it appeared. Some old reviews (Agee's, Otis Ferguson's, Manny Farber's) are helpful to the historian and sometimes these writers spin some very nice apercus. But when I go back to them I generally find myself arguing with them. 34

Politely, of course. Like me, these people were doing their jobs as best they could. That is to say, contingently, in a hurry. They undervalued films we now regard as masterpieces. And vice versa. They had no idea they were writing for the long run. Most of them, indeed, wanted to be doing something else—writing a novel, say, or painting a picture. They were not lifers. They thought there must be an existence beyond the jute mill. Which may, paradoxically, account for the wacky grace of the best prose. They often just grabbed a thought out of thin air and ran with it until the deadline or exhaustion stopped them. 35

I don't know that any of them particularly confronted the insoluble contradiction that lies at the center of movie reviewing. Which is that words are an awkward and frustrating tool with which to confront an essentially visual medium, a medium that usually creates its best effects through sub- and non-verbal means. All of us who review movies are trapped in narrative—the who, what, why, and whens of the plot—which is often silly and misleading, obliged for reasons of space (and literary logic) to skip the shot or the cut or the series of same where a movie's most profound, if flickering and accidental, logic lies. 36

Because of this, I am pretty much convinced that it is impossible to write sensible movie reviews—or for that matter art or music reviews—at a very high level. Logically, you would have to paint or compose a response to a painting or a symphony. Perhaps only literary criticism—words applied to words—is possible. 37

Doubtless, I'm exaggerating this argument for effect. But the thought is, I think, usefully instructive. At the least, it keeps one's own 38 self-regard decently within bounds. All I try to do when I'm reviewing is turn a nice phrase or two, make the pieces as pleasurable to read as I can and offer an honest first word—not a definitive last word—on whatever movie I'm talking about, something that perhaps helps set the terms of any argument that may develop over a given movie—which these days are not many or particularly illuminating.

Eventually, if you are a reviewer who appears regularly in a significant publication, you establish yourself not by isolated acts of brilliant writing or thinking, but by a sort of reliability. People get used to your voice, grow accustomed to your quirks and you become a source against which they measure their own taste: "If that guy likes it, I probably will, too." Or, conversely, "If he likes it, I know I'm going to hate it." 39

The best short definition of movies I ever heard was offered by Joseph Campbell, the scholar of myth, in a lecture he gave not long before he died: "The genial imaging of enormous ideas." I know, of course, that many great movies are short on "geniality." But even they offer the shimmer and sheen of their imaging, a quality that disarms and seduces us, makes us willing accomplices in their explorations of "enormous"—though often hard to define—"ideas." 40

I'm thinking now of pictures like *Bonnie and Clyde, Chinatown,* and *Fargo, Double Indemnity, Hail the Conquering Hero,* and *White Heat*—allusive, elusive movies that offer curiously subversive visions of American blandness and terror, permanently nourish our memories and entirely evade firm theoretical and ideological definition. It's the duty of the reviewer to be alert to these rarities, to single them out of the endless rush of film passing before him. That may not be a big deal. But it is not entirely an inconsequential one, either. 41

For a movie must either live up to its first notices or live them down as it seeks such place as it may have in history. If we are responsible reviewers we must strive not to make too many egregious errors as we confront the new releases. You're bound to make some, of course, but you don't want to be a laughing stock after you're gone; it will embarrass your children. 42

Beyond that, what? Well, I think it is important to make it difficult for distributors to pull quotes from your pieces to adorn their ads. Who wants to be an unpaid adjunct to their marketing departments? It is also important to be intellectually flexible. Any reviewer who insists on approaching all movies from a fixed ideological perspective—Marxist, structuralist, feminist, auteurist, what-have-you—is by my definition, totally—and joylessly—wet. And bound to miss the delightful point most of the time. 43

I think reviewing is an instinctive occupation. We respond to a movie viscerally: we like it, we don't like it. Then comes the hard part: 44

analyzing both the movie itself and our response to it. It makes it more interesting if that response is complicated by having seen lots of movies, by having a sense of the careers, the cultural exigencies, that has brought the anxious—not to say quaking—object to its moment of scrutiny. But the main thing is to stay in touch with your instincts. By them—largely—do we find out why a movie works or doesn't work, why it gives us pain or pleasure.

But movie reviewing, even of this modest sort, is in decline—perhaps even approaching that "crisis" the editors speak of in their invitation to contribute. In the Sixties and Seventies, when the literati—as usual well behind the cultural curve—discovered (or permitted themselves to admit) that movies were an 'art form,' more prestige attached to movie reviewing than it now enjoys. Movies, of course, were more stirring then. People were really trying to get a handle on the then-flourishing modern masters of the form—Bergman, Godard, Kurosawa, et al. Also the American movie was in an inspiringly unsettled state and was trying to expand and redefine its generic boundaries. The services of reviewers as mediators and explicators were more centrally interesting to readers then than they are now, when imported films struggle for attention and the American film has settled into largely vulgar display. 45

Other unpleasant circumstances have also arisen. I don't know if many reviewers have been, as *Cineaste*'s editors darkly suspect, "co-opted" by the industry, but television has created hundreds of 'critics,' most of whom are what the publicists scornfully call "quote whores"—people who will give you something to run in the ads even before they have written the rest of their imbecilic notices. It is also true that the new pattern of release—2,500 or so prints of a major film going out on the same Friday, a movie's commercial future foretold in that first weekend—diminishes the role of the reviewer, enhances the role of pure hype in drawing crowds. By the time the public gets around to reading the few serious reviewers who are left (who also may have less space than ever for their views), the die has been long since cast. We are, at that point, playing catch-up ball, at best. The studios, we might note, are aware of this and if, as I do, you write for an influential magazine they make it as difficult as possible for you to see the film in time to publish before that first weekend. I suspect our views are irrelevant to the success or failure of the movies on which they have gambled the most money, are therefore most nervous about, but those birds aren't taking any chances. 46

I don't know if this constitutes an authentic "crisis." But then, I'm not at all certain that movies—let alone movie reviewing—have much of a future. I suppose theatrical distribution of films—almost certainly in some digital format—will continue, if only because adolescents will al- 47 ways require a dating destination. But whether movies for this audience will require attentive reviewers I doubt. Whether movies in general will survive as a genuine art form—with products appealing to every element of a vast audience, some portion of which welcomed serious reviewing as a goad to their own thinking—is also dubious, I think.

The studios and distributors would, naturally, be glad to be rid of us—to turn movie journalism exclusively into a branch of celebrity journalism. And I think a lot of newspapers and magazines would be glad to be done with our gesturings (or are they merely posturings?) as well. It takes up valuable space and annoys some readers. Something punchy in the jejune dot-com manner—consumer guidance rendered in a superficially subjective, purely populist style—would do almost everyone just as well. 48

Will you miss us when we're gone, you rascals you? Maybe more than you know—the rattle of more or less informed, more or less cogently expressed opinion, appearing in generally accessible venues, has its mysterious, indefinable uses in societies that maintain the democratic pretense. It keeps people buzzing, hopping, stirred up in ways that an in-depth profile of Britney Spears never will. Maybe it's not much. But I'm bound to think, given the time I've devoted to this curious occupation—next to Andrew Sarris and John Simon I guess I'm the longest continuously serving reviewer around—that it is not nothing, either. 49

ARMOND WHITE, *NEW YORK PRESS*[6]

As hits go by—on a weekly basis, without sticking to the ribs or memory—film critics have become virtually useless. They no longer retain the culture, providing historical or esthetic contexts for new releases or, more importantly, for younger, uninformed audiences. To be a mainstream film critic with popular influence, one is required to cooperate with the industry's manipulation of ignorant, gullible viewers for whom every chase film, every film noir, every sex comedy, every blockbuster disaster flick is a 'new,' 'astonishing' experience (*Titanic, Armageddon, Gladiator*). As a result, 'hype' is now the definition of what 'criticism' means to most people. 50

Perfect example of the process behind that perversion can be seen in the different media response to Alan Rudolph's *Trixie* and Neil 51

[6]Armond White is a film critic for *New York Press.* Formerly the Arts Editor for *The City Sun,* he has written for numerous publications, including *The New York Times, Film Comment, Essence, Rolling Stone, Vibe* and *The Nation.* He is the author of *The Resistance: Ten Years of Pop Culture That Shook the World* and *Rebel for the Hell of It: The Art-Life of Tupac Shakur.* A member of The National Society of Film Critics, he was also Chairman of The New York Film Critics Circle in 1994.

LaBute's *Nurse Betty.* Most critics accepted the failed aims of the latter rather than trying to figure out the themes of the former. In plain terms, critics no longer attend to art. Instead of figuring out Rudolph's eccentric use of language as a key to how contemporary media-bred fantasies isolate us socially and politically, critics celebrated LaBute's castigation and sentimental condescension toward those who are unsophisticated media junkies. Conventional cynical pathology was preferred to politicized humanism; LaBute's crude mise-en-scene was praised while Rudolph's subtle visual elegance was ignored. Guile appreciated over sincerity.

There used to be two cinemas: commercial Hollywood which overwhelms us, and another competing cinema, the art cinema we had to purposely seek out. *Pulp Fiction* (1994) signified the merging of the two. Since that moment, the increased self-consciousness of American movies (which had been happening since Hollywood swallowed the French New Wave whole) has turned everyone—journalists, filmmakers, audiences—paradoxically skeptical of craft and style yet more than ever susceptible to formula and technique. Serious critical approaches such as Pauline Kael's and Andrew Sarris's became part of mainstream film lingo, yet their rigor has been diluted—thus Ebert and Siskel and the Internet kids promote a film culture of consumption rather than inquiry and sensitivity. 52

But all this is prelude to the abyss. 53

In the May 13–19, 1999, issue of *New Times Los Angeles,* a Help Wanted ad appeared that blew the profession into oblivion. 54

Its entirety: 55

> **Film Reviewer Wanted**
>
> Are you sick and tired of the movie reviews you read in the *L.A. Times* or even in these very pages? Are you annoyed by reviewers who believe that movies must aspire to high art to be valid, that the auteur theory still pertains? Are you more interested in *Go* and *Very Bad Things* than *Titanic* and *The Truman Show*?
>
> *New Times* is looking for a new voice to join our weekly mix of critics. If you think movies are the greatest form of pop culture we have, and if you can write with energy and wit, you are a candidate to become our newest film critic.
>
> Please send (no phone calls) cover letter, clips, and resume to *New Times Los Angeles*—FILM, Suzanne Mantell, Arts Editor. 1950 Sawtelle Blvd., Suite 200, Los Angeles, CA 90025.

It's difficult to know what Ms. Mantell wanted, given her inane requirements (anti-aspiration, pro-validation) and contradictory requests (the "greatest form of pop culture" yet antagonistic to "high 56 art"). But her ad's attitude, plainly, stinks. Like most people in the contemporary filmgoing audience, she's looking for someone to give her and her readers permission to go to the movies and not think. That ad doesn't seek a reviewer but a huckster in the guise of a critic—the latest evolution of that Sixties-Seventies movie love and pop savvy into idiocy. And the attitude is rampant. Once, criticism was a practice that denoted Agee-Kael-Sarris intellection and literacy, now it's all thumbs.

Foolishness (film savvy that anyone can claim) explains the confusion of that *New Times'* ad as it pits the flip cynicism of *Very Bad Things* against the flip cynicism of *The Truman Show;* as it imagines *Titanic*'s sentimentality was somehow less popular than the (now proven unpopular) humanist comedy in Doug Liman's *Go.* But these are not the major upsets in our cultural climate. What makes moviegoing uninspiring, repellant these days is the nonsense in pictures like *Leaving Las Vegas, The Sweet Hereafter, In the Company of Men, Affliction* or *Payback*—all critical hits that destroy one's artistic and social and humane hopes. Bad critics who praised those films then hold no responsibility for the bilge that follows have set a tone of gaseous criticism and dishonesty. 57

And there are practical difficulties to being a critic in this insane era—the treadmill effect of tending to the market's new fast turnover makes it almost impossible to cultivate an appreciation of film. Reviewers have altogether given up probing movies so that even a race-and-religion-based hit like *The Matrix* lingers vacantly—like a going-out-of-business sign—because critics can't see anything in it beyond visual noise; they've stopped thinking of movies as expressions of social fear or desire. They're content seeing movies as product—as in the delimited response to *The Phantom Menace.* 58

Sigourney Weaver's threat in *Alien*—"Blow it the fuck into outer space!"—is what most reviewers tried to do to George Lucas. Trashing *The Phantom Menace* became 'smart' critics' inglorious, pathetic way of salvaging integrity. But it was too late; the profession had already sunk under the weight of its own corrupt collusion. You know: going along with a manufactured zeitgeist, giving print space and air time to something that is, primarily, of commercial interest. 59

Taste (what's that?) wasn't offended by *The Phantom Menace.* In Y2K desperation, critics needed a way to convince themselves they have not been had. (So Jar Jar Binks became the new Milli Vannilli.) Breathlessly straining on the hype treadmill, there's no time to make cultural significance of most films. Critics are stuck following the industry's dictates rather than encouraging erudition, thought. This *Star Wars* mess is especially saddening, not because millionaire Lucas is stuck addressing a degraded pop audience when he really wants to do abstract meta-narratives, but because out of our entire critical 60 constabulary no one understood his frustration. Critics reacted like unenlightened children, complaining *Phantom Menace* isn't exactly like the Star Wars movies before it, that the thrill ride doesn't go fast enough.

These turnabout disses implied that previous coverage of *Star* 61
Wars was something else—news. But this is typically disingenuous. The release of a multimillion dollar Hollywood film is never news, yet collusive media workers continuously promote a brother industry and in that sense a review, negative or positive, is just more promotion. Criticism thus loses its significance; that's why it doesn't matter what critics say about *Phantom Menace* (it eventually grossed over $600 million); the profession has conspired in its own paralysis. Media exists only to sell product; that's what *New Times* knows.

In an imaginary world, far, far away, the amount of money spent 62
making and promoting a movie would not correlate to the media attention a film received; *Star Wars* would be treated as indifferently and inconspicuously as a film by Ira Sachs, a book by Richard Dyer, a CD by The Wedding Present. In other words, reviewers would operate on individual taste, not marketing. Maybe then a film could be appreciated on its own merits, and we could stop this heedless consumption frenzy.

It's hard to explain these things to generations born into hype, 63
who think it's a normal process and not a pernicious outgrowth of capitalist indoctrination. To be a mainstream journalist has come to mean one's complicity with this system rather than a detached view of it. Today's young moviegoers (courted by Hollywood and the media) don't realize that even in an artificial, commercial environment some things are, if not unnatural, then culturally untenable.

Pop permissiveness, the new form of anti-intellectuality, was 64
first apparent in the herd response to *Pulp Fiction*; and it has infected much neo-con critical writing as a rejection of liberal sanctimony. But it most nefariously expresses libertarian license given to the ever-mounting corporate domination and monopoly that melds filmmaking, journalism, and marketing. Hypercapitalism. Criticism's downfall proves our culture's submission to insensitivity, the media's abdication of intellectual life. Perhaps that's why *New Times* shamelessly advertised its complicity. Editors who control film journalism do so to promote the film industry.

A common question in this era—"Does it live up to the hype?"— 65
is not even a rational thought. A film ought to present itself—ideas, images, sensibility. Naive moviegoers thus reveal their inherent gullibility. You can't talk them against hype; because they believe the hype actually has something to do with the film that was made. Conformity has become the law of cinemaland; people would rather get tattooed

than admit that *Beloved* was the best film of the past year or that *The Phantom Menace* isn't that bad.

You may have noticed that in many newspapers, the label "reviewer" or "critic" has been struck from many bylines. Under hyper-capitalism criticizing a product simply isn't allowed. Forty-five years after James Agee's death the badge 'critic' has been retired. We have movie writers, staff writers—anything that won't be misconstrued "nay-sayer" or "thinker." No matter the new vistas digital-era film can create, this isn't a democracy that turns everyone into a critic, it's a bazaar. Though we all may have Internet access to mass audiences making moviegoers, more than ever, their own critical experts, the fact is, we are lost in space. 66

Examining the Text

1. Refer back to Mark Schaefermeyer's distinction between movie reviewers and film critics, then re-read paragraph 1 of this *Cineaste* essay. How do the editors of *Cineaste* handle this distinction? In what ways do the critics/reviewers in this piece grapple with this distinction? Do any of these critics/reviewers seem to fit clearly into one or the other category of film critic or movie reviewer? If so, how?

2. Why does Armond White of the *New York Press* feel that the ad he saw in *New Times Los Angeles* seeking a film reviewer "blew the profession into oblivion"? (59)

3. Look over the questions that *Cineaste* poses and discuss which questions the critics/reviewers seem to focus upon most. Discuss some notable similarities and differences between their responses to the more popular questions.

4. Discuss the critics'/reviewers' apparent relationship to the publications for which they write. To what extent do they feel their audience—and their editors' and publishers' perceptions about their audience—affects the ways they write about movies?

For Group Discussion

Imagine you are a group of movie reviewers for a popular newspaper, such as *USA Today*. Discuss how you might respond to some of the questions *Cineaste* posed to the reviewers here. How would your responses differ if you were a film critic writing for an academic—rather than popular—audience?

Writing Suggestion

Choose one of the film critics/reviewers featured in this article and read several examples of his work. Write a short paper discussing how the critic's views on particular movies seem to reflect their ideas on their role as critics. Are there ways in which their published movie reviews or critiques conflict with the ideas they espouse in this *Cineaste* article?

The Horror Movie

Why We Crave Horror Movies

Stephen King

A hotel with ghosts as its guests, a downtrodden teenager whose telekinetic powers wreak havoc at her prom, a giant dog from hell, a satanic antique store owner . . . all are products of the fertile (and some would say twisted) imagination of Stephen King, whose books are so widely read—and the movies made from them so popularly viewed—that his creations may well have become part of the American collective consciousness. In the following article, King takes a break from story-telling to reflect on the genre that has brought him worldwide recognition.

King begins by stating a bold and not entirely tongue-in-cheek premise: "I think that we are all mentally ill." Underneath a frequently thin veneer of civilization, he suggests, we all have fears, homicidal rages, and sexual desires"—baser urges which he calls "anticivilization emotions"—and the function of horror movies is to appeal to those dark elements within ourselves and therefore reduce their psychic energy. Thus purged of our negative impulses, we can go on to engage in positive feelings of love, friendship, loyalty and kindness. According to King, then, horror movies serve an important regulating function, defusing people's destructive urges and helping to maintain a society's psychic equilibrium.

***Before you read** this article, consider your own feelings about portrayals of the macabre, especially in films. If you enjoy horror movies, are you drawn to them for the reasons Stephen King suggests—that is, do you have deep-seated fears, angry urges, or inappropriate sexual drives that need defusing—or are there other factors involved which King has not considered? More to the point, how do you respond to King's basic premise: that everyone is in some sense mentally ill?*

I think that we're all mentally ill; those of us outside the asylums only hide it a little better—and maybe not all that much better, after all. We've all known people who talk to themselves, people who sometimes squinch their faces into horrible grimaces when they believe no one is watching, people who have some hysterical fear—of snakes, the dark, the tight place, the long drop . . . and, of course, 1 those final worms and grubs that are waiting so patiently underground.

When we pay our four or five bucks and seat ourselves at tenth-row center in a theater showing a horror movie, we are daring the nightmare. 2

Why? Some of the reasons are simple and obvious. To show that we can, that we are not afraid, that we can ride this roller coaster. Which is not to say that a really good horror movie may not surprise a scream out of us at some point, the way we may scream when the roller coaster twists through a complete 360 or plows through a lake at the bottom of the drop. And horror movies, like roller coasters, have always been the special province of the young; by the time one turns 40 or 50, one's appetite for double twists or 360-degree loops may be considerably depleted. 3

We also go to re-establish our feelings of essential normality; the horror movie is innately conservative, even reactionary. Freda Jackson as the horrible melting woman in *Die, Monster, Die!* confirms for us that no matter how far we may be removed from the beauty of a Robert Redford or a Diana Ross, we are still light-years from true ugliness. 4

And we go to have fun. 5

Ah, but this is where the ground starts to slope away, isn't it? Because this is a very peculiar sort of fun indeed. The fun comes from seeing others menaced—sometimes killed. One critic has suggested that if pro football has become the voyeur's version of combat, then the horror film has become the modern version of the public lynching. 6

It is true that the mythic, "fairytale" horror film intends to take away the shades of gray . . . It urges us to put away our more civilized and adult penchant for analysis and to become children again, seeing things in pure blacks and whites. It may be that horror movies provide psychic relief on this level because this invitation to lapse into simplicity, irrationality and even outright madness is extended so rarely. We are told we may allow our emotions a free rein . . . or no rein at all. 7

If we are all insane, then sanity becomes a matter of degree. If your insanity leads you to carve up women like Jack the Ripper or the Cleveland Torso Murderer, we clap you away in the funny farm (but neither of those two amateur-night surgeons was ever caught, heh-heh-heh); if, on the other hand your insanity leads you only to talk to yourself when you're under stress or to pick your nose on the morning bus, then you are left alone to go about your business . . . though it is doubtful that you will ever be invited to the best parties. 8

The potential lyncher is in almost all of us (excluding saints, past and present; but then, most saints have been crazy in their own ways), 9 and every now and then, he has to be let loose to scream and roll around in the grass. Our emotions and our fears form their own body, and we recognize that it demands its own exercise to maintain proper muscle tone. Certain of these emotional muscles are accepted—even exalted—in civilized society; they are, of course, the emotions that tend to maintain the status quo of civilization itself. Love, friendship, loyalty, kindness—these are all the emotions that we applaud, emotions that have been immortalized in the couplets of Hallmark cards and in the verses (I don't dare call it poetry) of Leonard Nimoy.

When we exhibit these emotions, society showers us with positive reinforcement; we learn this even before we get out of diapers. 10 When, as children, we hug our rotten little puke of a sister and give her a kiss, all the aunts and uncles smile and twit and cry, "Isn't he the sweetest little thing?" Such coveted treats as chocolate-covered graham crackers often follow. But if we deliberately slam the rotten little puke of a sister's fingers in the door, sanctions follow—angry remonstrance from parents, aunts and uncles; instead of a chocolate-covered graham cracker, a spanking.

But anticivilization emotions don't go away, and they demand periodic exercise. 11 We have such "sick" jokes as, "What's the difference between a truckload of bowling balls and a truckload of dead babies? (You can't unload a truckload of bowling balls with a pitchfork . . . a joke, by the way, that I heard originally from a ten-year-old.) Such a joke may surprise a laugh or a grin out of us even as we recoil, a possibility that confirms the thesis: If we share a brotherhood of man, then we also share an insanity of man. None of which is intended as a defense of either the sick joke or insanity but merely as an explanation of why the best horror films, like the best fairy tales, manage to be reactionary, anarchistic, and revolutionary all at the same time.

The mythic horror movie, like the sick joke, has a dirty job to do. 12 It deliberately appeals to all that is worst in us. It is morbidity unchained, our most base instincts let free, our nastiest fantasies realized . . . and it all happens, fittingly enough, in the dark. For those reasons, good liberals often shy away from horror films. For myself, I like to see the most aggressive of them—*Dawn of the Dead,* for instance—as lifting a trap door in the civilized forebrain and throwing a basket of raw meat to the hungry alligators swimming around in that subterranean river beneath.

Why bother? Because it keeps them from getting out, man. It 13 keeps them down there and me up here. It was Lennon and McCartney who said that all you need is love, and I would agree with that.

As long as you keep the gators fed. 14

Examining the Text

1. How seriously do you think King expects readers to take his opening statement? What evidence does he offer to support his assertion? Does disagreeing with him here mean that you must automatically reject the rest of his argument about the appeal of horror movies?

2. King states that the horror movie is "innately conservative, even reactionary" (paragraph 4). Is he using these terms politically or in another sense? In what ways can horror movies be seen as "reactionary, anarchistic, and revolutionary all at the same time" (11)?

3. King basically offers three reasons for the popularity of horror movies (3, 4, and 5–14); obviously the third is his main thesis. Summarize King's three reasons. Which do you find most persuasive, and why? Can you offer any other reasons?

4. King's tone throughout this essay is quite informal (it was originally published, by the way, in *Playboy* magazine). Find several examples that illustrate his informality and describe the overall effect.

For Group Discussion

For the sake of discussion, accept King's premise that we all have "anticivilization emotions" (11). List as a group some other things besides horror movies and "sick" jokes that we use to purge these emotions and "keep the gators fed." As a class, consider the extent to which these examples are products of contemporary society and what this suggests about how our psychic behaves differ from those of people who lived a century or more ago.

Writing Suggestion

Consider several of your favorite horror movies. In an essay analyze these in light of King's theories about the horror genre's appeal. Do your examples support or disprove King's point about the daredevil, normative, and psychological function of horror movies?

Monster Movies: A Sexual Theory

Walter Evans

In an essay earlier in this chapter, Mark Schaefermeyer breaks film criticism down into three categories: semiotic critics look for signs and relationships among images in films; contextual critics examine movies in a specific context, focusing, for example, on a director's style or on a movie as a representative of a particular genre; and structuralists look at films from the perspective of a certain theory or belief system, whether mythic, political, psychological, or historical. Walter Evans, the author of the following essay, belongs to the last of these camps. In "Monster Movies: A Sexual Theory," he relies on a psychological approach to human sexual development to explain why monster movies are especially appealing to adolescents. Compared with Stephen King's explanation, Evans's is both more limited and more detailed.

Evans's central thesis is that monster movies embody many of the powerful—and sometimes socially unacceptable—impulses that preoccupy teenagers as they begin to mature, to experience unprecedented physical changes, and to be pulled by unfamiliar drives and urges. "The key to monster movies and the adolescents which understandably dote upon them," says Evans, "is the theme of horrible and mysterious psychological and physical change; the most important of these is the monstrous transformation . . . directly associated with secondary sexual characteristics and with the onset of aggressive erotic behavior." Since most of those aggressive, animalistic impulses cannot be acted upon in "civilized" society, Evans believes that monster movies serve as an outlet through which teenagers can ritually act out those drives.

Evans relates each of the various aspects of the movie monster's aggressive behavior to a specific adolescent erotic impulse or physical change—the onset of menstruation, the impulse to masturbate, the drive to marry and to create life. He then examines two specific film "monsters," Frankenstein and Dracula, from this perspective. The former, he says, must "give up dangerous private experiments on the human body" and learn to "deal safely and normally with the 'secret of life,'" just as adolescents must move from secretive masturbatory practices to more socially acceptable forms of sexuality: marriage and child rearing. Similarly, Dracula is like an adolescent, thrust into "a world he does not understand, torturing him with desires he cannot satisfy or even admit."

***As you read** these interpretations, consider your own intellectual response to them: do you believe that Evans makes some valid points in using adolescent developmental psychology to explain the attraction of monster movies, or is he forcing his belief system on the genre?*

The key to monster movies and the adolescents which understandably dote upon them is the theme of horrible and mysterious psychological and physical change; the most important of these is the monstrous transformation which is directly associated with secondary sexual characteristics and with the onset of aggressive erotic behavior.[1] 1

[1]Though many critics focus on adult themes in monster movies, I believe that adolescents provide the bulk of the audience for such films, particularly the classic films shown on late night television all across America. Adolescents, of course, may be of any age.

The Wolfman, for example, sprouts a heavy coat of hair, can hardly be contained within his clothing, and when wholly a wolf is, of course, wholly naked. Comparatively innocent and asexual females become, after contact with a vampire (his kiss redly marked on their necks) or werewolf (as in *Cry of the Werewolf*), quite sexy, aggressive, seductive—literally female "Vamps" and "wolves."[2]

As adolescence is defined as "developing from childhood to maturity,"[3] so the transformation is cinematically, defined as movement from a state of innocence and purity associated with whiteness and clarity to darkness and obscurity associated with evil and threatening physical aggression. In the words of *The Wolf Man*'s gypsy: 2

> Even a man who is pure at heart
> And says his prayers by night
> May become a wolf when the wolfbane blooms
> And the moon is full and bright

The monsters are generally sympathetic, in large part because they themselves suffer the change as unwilling victims, all peace destroyed by the horrible physical and psychological alterations thrust upon them. Even Dracula, in a rare moment of self-revelation, is driven to comment: "To die, to be really dead. That must be glorious. . . . There are far worse things awaiting man, than death." Much suffering arises from the monster's overwhelming sense of alienation; totally an outcast, he painfully embodies the adolescent's nightmare of being hated and hunted by the society which he so desperately wishes to join. 3

Various aspects of the monster's attack are clearly sexual. The monster invariably prefers to attack individuals of the opposite sex, to 4

---

[2]The transformation is less obvious, and perhaps for this reason more powerful, in *King Kong* (1933). Kong himself is safe while hidden deep in the prehistoric depths of Skull Island, but an unappeasable sexual desire (made explicit in the cuts restored in the film's most recent release) turns him into an enemy of civilization until, trapped on the world's hugest phallic symbol, he is destroyed. The psychological transformation of Ann Darrow (Fay Wray) is much more subtle. While alone immediately after exchanging vows of love with a tough sailor she closes her eyes and, as in a dream vision, above her appears the hideously savage face of a black native who takes possession of her in preparation for the riotous wedding to the great hairy ape. Significantly, only when civilization destroys the fearful, grossly physical beast is she finally able to marry the newly tuxedoed sailor.

[3]*Webster's New World Dictionary of the American Language,* 2nd College Edition (Englewood Cliffs, N.J.: Prentice Hall, 1970). Interesting, in view of the fiery death of Frankenstein's monster and others, is one of the earlier meanings of the root word: "be kindled, burn."

attack them at night, and to attack them in their beds. The attack itself is specifically physical; Dracula, for instance, must be in immediate bodily contact with his victim to effect his perverted kiss; Frankenstein, the Wolfman, the Mummy, King Kong, have no weapons but their bodies. The aspect of the attack most disturbing to the monster, and perhaps most clearly sexual, is the choice of victim: "The werewolf instinctively seeks to kill the thing it loves best" (Dr. Yogami in *The Werewolf of London*). *Dracula*'s Mina Seward must attack her fiance, John. The Mummy must physically possess the body of the woman in whom his spiritual bride has been reincarnated. Even more disturbing are the random threats to children scattered throughout the formula, more disturbing largely because the attacks are so perversely sexual and addressed to beings themselves soon destined for adolescence.

The effects of the attack may be directly related to adolescent sex- 5
ual experimentation. The aggressor is riddled with shame, guilt, and anguish; the victim, once initiated, is generally transformed into another aggressor.[4] Regaining innocence before death seems, in the best films, almost as inconceivable as retrieving virginity.

Many formulaic elements of the monster movies have affinities 6
with two central features of adolescent sexuality, masturbation and menstruation. From time immemorial underground lore has asserted that masturbation leads to feeblemindedness or mental derangement; the monster's transformation is generally associated with madness; scientists are generally secretive recluses whose private experiments on the human body have driven them mad. Masturbation is also widely (and, of course, fallaciously) associated with "weakness of the spine," a fact which helps explain not only Fritz of *Frankenstein* but the army of feebleminded hunchbacks which pervades the formula. The Wolfman, and sometimes Dracula, are identifiable (as, according to underground lore, masturbating boys may be identified) by hairy palms.

Ernest Jones explains the vampire myth largely in terms of a 7
mysterious physical and psychological development which startles many adolescents, nocturnal emissions: "A nightly visit from a beautiful or frightful being, who first exhausts the sleeper with passionate embraces and then withdraws from him a vital fluid: all this can point only to a natural and common process, namely to nocturnal emissions accompanied with dreams of a more or less erotic nature. In the un-

[4]It is interesting, and perhaps significant that the taint of vampirism and lycanthropy have an aura of sin and shame not unlike that of VD. The good doctor who traces the taint, communicable only through direct physical contact, back to the original carrier is not unlike a physician fighting VD.

conscious mind blood is commonly an equivalent for semen...."[5] The vampire's bloodletting of women who suddenly enter full sexuality, the werewolf's bloody attacks—which occur regularly every month—are certainly related to the menstrual cycle which suddenly and mysteriously commands the body of every adolescent girl.

Monster movies characteristically involve another highly significant feature which may initially seem irrelevant to the theme of sexual change: the faintly philosophical struggle between reason and the darker emotional truths. Gypsies, superstitious peasants, and others associated with the imagination eternally triumph over smugly conventional rationalists who ignorantly deny the possible existence of walking mummies, stalking vampires, and bloodthirsty werewolves. The audience clearly sympathizes with those who realize the limits of reason, of convention, of security—for the adolescent's experiences with irrational desires, fears, urges which are incomprehensible yet clearly stronger than the barriers erected by reason or by society, are deeper and more painful than adults are likely to realize. Stubborn reason vainly struggles to deny the adolescent's most private experiences, mysterious and dynamic conflicts between normal and abnormal, good and evil, known and unknown. 8

Two of the most important features normally associated with monster movies are the closely related searches for the "secret of life" and "that which man was not meant to know." Monster movies unconsciously exploit the fact that most adolescents already know the "secret of life" which is, indeed, the "forbidden knowledge" of sex. The driving need to master the "forbidden knowledge" of "the secret of life," a need which seems to increase in importance as the wedding day approaches, is closely related to a major theme of monster movies: marriage. 9

For the adolescent audience the marriage which looms just beyond the last reel of the finer monster movies is much more than a mindless cliche wrap-up. As the monster's death necessarily precedes marriage and a happy ending, so the adolescent realizes that a kind of peace is to be obtained only with a second transformation. Only marriage can free Henry Frankenstein from his perverted compulsion for private experimentation on the human body; only marriage can save Mina Harker after her dalliance with the count. Only upon the death of adolescence, the mysterious madness which has possessed them, can they enter into a mature state where sexuality is tamed and sancti- 10

[5]See Ernest Jones, "On the Nightmare of Bloodsucking" in *Focus on the Horror Film,* 59.

fied by marriage.[6] The marriage theme, and the complex interrelationship of various other formulaic elements, may perhaps be best approached through a close analysis of two seminal classics, *Frankenstein* and *Dracula*.

11 Two events dominate the movie *Frankenstein* (1931), creation of the monster and celebration of the marriage of Henry Frankenstein and his fiancee Elizabeth. The fact that the first endangers the second provides for most of the conflict throughout the movie, conflict much richer and more powerful, perhaps even profound, when the key thematic relationship between the two is made clear: creation of life. As Frankenstein's perverse nightly experiments on the monstrous body hidden beneath the sheets are centered on the creation of life, so is the marriage, as the old Baron twice makes clear in a toast (once immediately after the monster struggles out of the old mill and begins wandering toward an incredible meeting with Henry's fiancee Elizabeth; again, after the monster is destroyed, in the last speech of the film): "Here's to a son to the House of Frankenstein!"[7]

12 Frankenstein's fatuous father, whose naive declarations are frequently frighteningly prescient (he predicts the dancing peasants will soon be fighting; on seeing a torch in the old mill he asks if Henry is trying to burn it down), declares, when hearing of the extent to which his son's experiments are taking precedence over his fiancee: "I understand perfectly well. Must be another woman. Pretty sort of experiments they must be." Later, after receiving the burgomaster's beaming report on the village's preparations for celebration of the marriage, he

---

[6]In "The Child and the Book," *Only Connect*, Sheila Egoff, ed., G. T. Stubbs, and L. F. Ashley (New York: Oxford UP, 1969) noted psychiatrist Anthony Storr has discussed a precursor of monster movies, fairy tales, in a similar context.

> Why is it that the stories which children enjoy are so often full of horror? We know that from the very beginning of life the child possesses an inner world of fantasy and the fantasies of the child mind are by no means the pretty stories with which the prolific Miss Blyton regales us. They are both richer and more primitive, and the driving forces behind them are those of sexuality and the aggressive urge to power: the forces which ultimately determine the emergence of the individual as a separate entity. For, in the long process of development, the child has two main tasks to perform if he is to reach maturity. He has to prove his strength, and he has to win a mate; and in order to do this he has to overcome the obstacles of his infantile dependency upon, and his infantile erotic attachment to, his parents.... The typical fairy story ends with the winning of the princess just as the typical Victorian novel ends with the marriage. It is only at this point that adult sexuality begins... It is not surprising that fairy stories should be both erotic and violent, or that they should appeal so powerfully to children. For the archetyal themes with which they deal mirror the contents of the childish psyche; and the same unconscious source gives origin to both the fairy tale and the fantasy life of the child." (93–4)

[7]The dialogue is followed by a close-up of a painfully embarrassed Henry Frankenstein.

again associates his son's experiments with forbidden sexuality: "There is another woman. And I'm going to find her."

There is, of course, no other woman. The movie's horror is fundamentally based on the fact that the monster's life has come without benefit of a mother's womb. At one point Frankenstein madly and pointedly gloats over his solitary, specifically manual, achievements: "the brain of a dead man, ready to live again in a body I made with my hands, my own hands!" 13

Significantly, a troubled search for the "secret of life" is what keeps Henry Frankenstein separated from his fiancee; it literally proves impossible for Henry to provide for "a son to the House of Frankenstein" before he has discovered the "secret of life." Having discovered the "secret of life," he ironically discovers that its embodiment is a frightening monster horrible enough to threaten "normal" relations between himself and Elizabeth. Henry's attempt to lock the monster deep in the mill's nether regions are finally thwarted, and, in a wholly irrational and dramatically inexplicable (yet psychologically apt and profound) scene, the monster—a grotesque embodiment of Frankenstein's newly discovered sexuality—begins to move threateningly toward the innocent bride who is bedecked in the purest of white, then quite as irrationally, it withdraws. On his return Henry promises his wildly distracted fiancee that there will be no wedding "while this horrible creation of mine is still alive." 14

The monster is, of course, finally, pitilessly, destroyed,[8] and Henry is only ready for marriage when his own body is horribly battered and weakened, when he is transformed from the vigorous, 15

---

[8]Significantly, the monster himself is pitifully sympathetic, suffering as adolescents believe only they can suffer, from unattractive physical appearance, bodies they don't understand, repulsed attempts at love, general misunderstanding. Though endowed by his single antagonistic parent with a "criminal brain," the monster is clearly guilty of little but ugliness and ignorance, and is by any terms less culpable than the normal human beings surrounding him. He does not so much murder Fritz as attempt to defend himself against completely unwarranted torchings and beatings; he kills Dr. Valdeman only after that worthy believes he has "painlessly destroyed" the monster (a euphemism for murder), and as the doctor is preparing to dissect him; the homicide which propels his destruction, the drowning of the little girl, is certainly the result of clumsiness and ignorance. She had taught him to sail flowers on the lake and, flowers failing, in a visual metaphor worthy of an Elizabethan courtier, the monster in his ignorant joy had certainly meant only for the girl, the only being who had ever shown him not only love, but even affection, to sail on the lake as had the flowers. His joyful lurch toward her after having sailed his flower is, beyond all doubt, the most pathetic and poignant lurch in the history of film.

courageous, inspired hero he represented early in the film to an enervated figure approaching the impotent fatuity of his father and grandfather (there is plenty of fine wine for the wedding feast, Frankenstein's grandmother would never allow grandfather to drink any), prepared to renounce abnormal life as potent as the monster in favor of creating a more normal "son to the House of Frankenstein."

The message is clear. In order to lead a normal, healthy life, Henry Frankenstein must—and can—give up dangerous private experiments on the human body in dark rooms hidden away from family and friends. He must learn to deal safely and normally with the "secret of life," however revolting, however evil, however it might seem to frighten and actually threaten pure, virgin womanhood; only then, in the enervated bosom of normality, is it possible to marry and to produce an acceptable "son to the House of Frankenstein." 16

Dracula's much more mature approach to womankind is clearly aimed at psyches which have overcome Henry Frankenstein's debilitating problem. *Dracula* (1931), obviously enough, is a seduction fantasy vitally concerned with the conditions and consequences of 17

Movie poster for the 1958 film, *The Blob*

premarital indulgence in forbidden physical relations with attractive members of the opposite sex.

Of all the movie monsters Dracula seems to be the most attractive to women, and his appeal is not difficult to understand, for he embodies the chief characteristics of the standard Gothic hero: tall, dark, handsome, titled, wealthy, cultured, attentive, mannered, with an air of command, an aura of sin and secret suffering; perhaps most important of all he is invariably impeccably dressed. With such a seductive and eligible male around it is certainly no wonder that somewhere in the translation from fiction to film Dr. Seward has become Mina's father and thus leaves Lucy, who also lost the two other suitors Bram Stoker allowed her, free to accept the Count's attentions. Certainly any woman can sympathize with Lucy's swift infatuation ("Laugh all you like, I think he's fascinating.") and Mina's easy acceptance of Dracula as her friend's suitor ("Countess, I'll leave you to your count, and your ruined abbey."). 18

Having left three wives behind in Transylvania, Dracula is obviously not one to be sated with his second English conquest (the first was an innocent flower girl, ravaged immediately before he meets Lucy and Mina), and he proceeds to seduce Mina, working a change in her which does not go unnoticed, or unappreciated, by her innocent fiance: "Mina, you're so—like a changed girl. So wonderful—." Mina agrees that indeed she is changed, and, on the romantic terrace, alone with her fiance beneath the moon and stars, begins, one is certain, the first physical aggression of their courtship. John is suitably impressed. "I'm so glad to see you like this!" Discovered and exposed by Professor Van Helsing, Mina can only admit that (having had relations with Dracula and thus become a Vamp) she has, indeed, suffered the proverbial fate worse than death, and shamefully alerts her innocent, naive fiance: "John, you must go away from me." 19

Only when John and his older, respected helpmate foil the horrible mock elopement—Dracula and Mina are rushing to the abbey preparing to "sleep," he even carries her limp body across the abbey's threshold—only when the castrating stake destroys the seducer and with him the maid's dishonor, is Mina free to return to the honest, innocent, suitor who will accept her past, marry her in the public light of day, and make an honest woman of her. 20

Lucy, who has no selfless suitor to forgive her, marry her, and make an honest woman of her, is much less successful. When last seen she has become a child molester, a woman of the night who exchanges chocolate for horrible initiations. 21

The thematic importance of such innocent victims turned monster as Lucy and Mina, Dr. Frankenstein's creation, King Kong, the Wolfman and others points directly to one of the most commonly ob- 22 served and perhaps least understood phenomena of monster movies, one which has been repeatedly noted in this paper. In those classics which are best loved and closest to true art the audience clearly identifies with the monster. Child, adult or adolescent, in disembodied sympathetic fascination, we all watch the first Karloff Frankenstein who stumbles with adolescent clumsiness, who suffers the savage misunderstanding and rejection of both society and the creator whose name he bears, and whose fumbling and innocent attempts at love with the little girl by the lakeside turn to terrible, bitter, and mysterious tragedy.

Clearly the monster offers the sexually confused adolescent a 23
sympathetic, and at best a tragic, imitation of his life by representing a mysterious and irreversible change which forever isolates him from what he identifies as normality, security, and goodness, a change thrusting him into a world he does not understand, torturing him with desires he cannot satisfy or even admit, a world in which dark psychological and strange physical changes seem to conspire with society to destroy him.

Examining the Text

1. In his first footnote, Evans states his belief that "adolescents provide the bulk of the audience" for monster movies. Do you think this is so? Why, according to Evans, are adolescents especially drawn to monster movies? In what ways do movie monsters reflect adolescent problems and concerns? Do you find Evans's evidence convincing?

2. Evans wrote this essay in 1975, drawing all his examples from classic monster movies of the 1930s and 1940s: the Wolfman, Frankenstein, Dracula, the Mummy, King Kong. What do these have in common, and what do they represent for Evans? Is his thesis generally supported by more contemporary movie monsters—Jason, Freddy Krueger, Chuckie, and others? Or might they suggest some evolution in adolescent sexuality since the 1930s and 1940s?

3. One of Evans's main points is that in classic monster movies, which, he says "are best loved and the closest to true art, the audience clearly identifies with the monster" (paragraph 22). Do you agree? Does this hold true for contemporary movie monsters? Why or why not?

For Group Discussion

Taking into account Stephen King's ideas about the appeal of horror movies as well as Evans's connection of monster movies to adolescent sexuality, broaden your scope to include both classic and contemporary examples and then, as a group, explain why adolescents seem to be particularly attracted to monster/horror movies. Bring your own knowledge of such movies and first-hand experience and observation of adolescent behavior into the discussion. As a class, see if you can agree on a ranking of your reasons.

Writing Suggestion

Apply a psychological critical model to another genre of film with which you are familiar, such as futuristic action pictures, *Airplane-* or *Naked Gun-*style satires, menaced-female thrillers, bratty kid comedies, *Rambo-*esque revenge stories, and so on. In an essay, account for the genre's popularity by discussing its specific appeals to an audience's basic emotional needs. Like Evans, you may want to focus on a specific audience with which your genre seems most popular.

The Blair Witch Project Project

J. P. Telotte

Web sites are now a common marketing tool for movies. At the end of trailers and TV ads announcing a new movie, we are now typically shown URLs named after the new movie—the studio's implicit invitation for us to click our way to the movie's site. Once there, the studios hope we'll become more excited about the movie, we'll tell our friends, and, of course, we'll be compelled to go and pay the ticket price at the local multiplex. As Telotte points out, the complexity and interactivity of these Web sites vary widely. Some function just like movie posters, simply offering information about a movie, whereas others feature contests, links, and downloads, making the movie's Web site itself an interesting experience, and more fully capitalizing on the Internet's capabilities. Still, Telotte concludes that all these Web sites preserve the "hierarchical entertainment value of the movie itself," as they all point to the movie as the site where the real fun will be had.

This discussion of movies and the Internet leads Telotte to his specific concern: the unique ways in which the studio marketing The Blair Witch Project *used the Internet in its highly successful advertising campaign. Such success has helped lead to more widespread use of Internet movie Web sites, but Telotte contends that such sites aren't able to duplicate* The Blair Witch Project*'s success because the unique features of this particular movie made its Web content extraordinarily effective in its promotion. Telotte argues that* The Blair Witch Project, *rather than preserving the hierarchy of film over Web sites and other cultural productions, blurs the distinctions between these productions, distinguishing both the film and the Web site from other horror films and other movie Web sites.*

Telotte uses these points about the movie's actual relationship to Internet technology—and the audience of The Blair Witch Project*'s actual rela-*

tion to technology—to segue to his main concern: The Blair Witch Project'*s narrative style and its thematic commentary on technology. In essence, he argues that both the film and the Web site use forms of electronic narrative to draw us into a "world that [. . .] is coextensive with our own" (15) in order to advance a theme in which our reliance on and comfort with technology—including film and the Internet—is questioned.*

As you read, *notice the ways in which Telotte relies upon theories of electronic narrative, the ideas of other film critics and movie reviewers, and his own close reading of the movie itself to support his points. How successful is he in building support for his complex ideas?*

In discussing the structure and workings of the New Hollywood, Janet Wesko cautions against attending too much to the sort of stories it is producing or the myths it so readily fosters about how those movies are being made. As she notes, "by accepting the myths or concentrating primarily on aesthetic aspects of film technology, corporate influences on film activities, as well as the actual power structure of the industry, can be obscured."[1] It is a caution that can serve us well when thinking about one of the most popular movie phenomena of recent times, *The Blair Witch Project.* A cheaply produced, independent horror film, done by a couple of film school graduates from the low-profile University of Central Florida, it grossed nearly $150 million in 1999, garnered favorable critical commentary, turned its female protagonist into an overnight star, and even earned both sequel and television deals for its co-writers/directors. And some measure of that public embrace of the film has to do with its apparently humble independent origins: its approximately $35,000 production cost, unsophisticated look, and unknown actors. It is, after all, manifestly unlike the high-budget Hollywood gloss with which we are so familiar and which has tended to dominate the recent box office. Yet, as the comment by Wasko might suggest, the story of *The Blair Witch Project* and its seemingly overnight success is far more complex, and that success a far larger lesson about what is happening in the American film industry, particularly in its marketing efforts, than would initially seem to be the case. 1

In an era that has become practically defined not only by the effects of "mass media" but by the interweaving of many media, by multimedia, films today seldom really stand alone. Each new release operates—if it is to be at all successful—within a complex web of information sites: radio spots, theatrical trailers, various sorts of television promotions, billboards, product tie-ins, and increasingly the Internet. Certainly, the latter of these is the newest marketing ploy, yet it is one that combines the lures of many more traditional advertising 2 techniques: the graphic pull of posters, the hyped language of the old-fashioned press release, interviews with stars via live-time chat rooms, publicity stills, sneak previews via downloadable video clips, offers of movie-related giveaways, and selections from film soundtracks. In fact, today almost no major film is released unaccompanied by its own carefully fashioned "official" Web site—one that can provide an extremely cost-efficient yet information-intensive medium for promoting the movie—and often by a variety of fan-created and fan-driven unofficial sites as well. The official Web site especially not only offers potential viewers the sort of information or lures that would, after the fashion of traditional film advertising, make them want to rush out and see the film. It can also effectively tell the "story" of the film, that is, as the film's makers and/or distributors see it and want it to be understood. For it can frame the film narrative within a context designed to condition our viewing or "reading" of it, even to determine the sort of pleasures we might derive from it. This establishing of context, this seemingly secondary "project," has been one readily acknowledged factor in the larger success of *The Blair Witch Project,* and one that merits further consideration for its comments on marketing in the contemporary film industry.

Before we examine this secondary project, however, we need to note other factors that came into play in the case of *Blair Witch.* When Artisan Entertainment picked up *The Blair Witch Project* for distribution after its screening at the Sundance Film Festival for approximately $1.1 million, it continued a pattern for that minor-major studio of cheaply acquiring projects with an easily identifiable audience and then extensively promoting them to achieve a predictable if modest profit, as we see in the case of such films as *Pi* and *The Limey,* the latter of which also benefited from an elaborate Web site. In the instance of *Blair Witch,* that promotional project relied heavily on an extensive elaboration of a Web site already developed by the film's producers—hardly an uncommon add-on to the publicity push by this time, but one that has been given most of the credit for this film's success. Yet most accounts of the film's promotion overlook the extent of its *conventional* marketing project, one which included television advertising, especially on MTV; a series of ads in major college newspapers, alternative weeklies, and magazines with a young readership like *Rolling Stone;* and widely distributed posters for the "missing" principals of the film. As Dwight Cairns, vice-president of Sony's new Internet Marketing Strategy Group, notes, "people tend to forget that the offline campaign . . . was so well integrated into what they did on the Web—the missing posters of the unknown cast, the TV spots perpetuating the myth that missing footage was found and they they should go to the site to see more. The Web was just another channel to deliver the 3 message."[2] Indeed, Amorette Jones, head of the Artisan marketing campaign for *The Blair Witch Project* and a veteran of marketing at such major studios as Universal, Columbia/Tri-Star, and MGM/UA, acknowledges a hardly modest $20 million marketing campaign for the film, one which included a series of ever-more-elaborate trailers, some of which were pointedly tied to playdates for *Star Wars: Episode One* in hopes of drawing in that same audience. As Jones admits, Artisan "did commercial things; we just did them in a non-commercial way."[3]

This admission of the extent of the film's conventional publicity campaign perhaps helps to explain why other films have had trouble emulating the success of *Blair Witch*. Creating a "fun" Web site to lure young viewers, after all, is a relatively inexpensive and easy path for advertising, one which even allows the studio to begin to gauge—through a "hit" counter—the extent of potential viewer interest. And given Artisan's success, it is little wonder that other studios would try to follow suit, although as yet without similarly spectacular results. Marc Graser and Dade Hayes offer a partial explanation, noting that "calmer heads are realizing that the 'Blair Witch' site was not an added-on marketing tool, but was designed as part of the film experience—one that tapped into fans of the horror genre."[4] I would go a bit further and suggest that the selling of *The Blair Witch Project* and the *telling* of that film, its narrative construction, were from the start a careful match or "project," one that better explains both the film's success and why that success was so quickly and easily laid at the door of the now almost equally famous Web site. 4

Before pursuing this other project, the match between the filmic narrative and its electronic marketing, we first need to consider how such Web sites typically work, and thus why this Web site in particular might have played such a significant role in the film's success, quickly inspiring other film companies to follow suit in an effort to reach a key audience demographic online. As I have already noted, almost every major release today is preceded by a site designed to build audience anticipation for the film and, even after it has been released, to support that interest by feeding viewers additional information (behind-the-scenes facts, technical data, playdates for various markets, even the opportunity to purchase film-related souvenirs), and later to open up yet another avenue for profits by marketing tape and DVD copies of the film. 5

A selection of Web sites for similarly-themed films released in the same general period shows several typical levels of presentation. Those for *The Haunting* and *Stigmata* (both 1999), like the majority of official Web pages, are largely advertisements with little animation, offering basic data about the story, opening dates, and advance ticket-ordering information. Replicating the films' key advertising graphics 6 against red or black backgrounds—colors obviously keyed to the films' horror genre—they seem like little more than electronic posters. The official *Urban Legend* (1998) and *Deep Blue Sea* (1999) sites provide a slightly higher level of information. The former, against a black and gold background, lists showtimes, offers credits and "behind the scenes" images, provides a library of contemporary urban legends, and invites visitors to participate in a sweepstakes contest. The latter, against a black and green background, offers images, text, and interviews with many of those involved in the production. Both are essentially press kits for the digital age, providing the sort of deep background typically found in their conventional counterparts. However, the Web sites for such films as *Lake Placid, House on Haunted Hill,* and *The Mummy* (all 1999) are far more complex affairs, not only providing the same sort of fundamental information—and measurably more—found in the previously noted sites, but also inviting a level of viewer interaction. These more elaborate sites all offer a story line, cast list, background on the filmmakers, clips from the films, various electronic giveaways (such as downloadable screensavers and electronic postcards), chat rooms, and games keyed to the films' plotlines, set against the generically-familiar black or dark red screens that immediately establish the horror film tone. Such sites invite their visitors to linger, to explore, and, often with a few simple mouse clicks, to call the sites—and thus the films—to the attention of friends; they try to be fun and encourage visitors to share the fun by viewing the sites and then, naturally, seeing the films.

Of course, such linkage is precisely the purpose. Thus, even as 7
sites like those for *Lake Placid, The House on Haunted Hill,* and *The Mummy* provide their own level of entertainment to visitors, they also ultimately point to the film experience and suggest that we see their narratives within a tradition of cinematic horror. *The House on Haunted Hill* Web page quickly announces that the film is "a spine-tingling remake of William Castle's 1958 classic horror tale"; *The Mummy*'s site describes it as "a full-scale re-imagining of Universal Pictures' seminal 1932 film"; and *Deep Blue Sea*'s producer, Akiva Goldsman; explains that the movie is a "classic old style horror film." While their games and on-line trailers afford net surfers a hint of the movies' atmosphere and some brief entertainment, these sites, in keeping with the long tradition of movie advertising, are basically "teasers," lures suggesting that the real thrills are to be found in the movies themselves—and in a *tradition* of similar movies. They *guide* our experience by situating their films in the context of the film industry and pointing to the entertainment power of the movies, particularly their special ability—one implicitly unmatched by the Internet—to transport us into another realm.

Artisan's own ambitious marketing campaign, and especially its Internet strategy, seems to have been designed to employ an element of this contextualizing, while also moving visitors in a direction different from the advertising sites just described. In fact, it seems to have been fashioned precisely to avoid the sort of situating at which these similar sites aim (including the hierarchical entertainment value of the movie itself that the established film industry would prefer to affirm), seeking instead to capitalize on the particular characteristics of this film. That campaign, which ended up as a television project as well, pitches the fictional movie as a documentary about three real student filmmakers who vanished while working on a documentary about a legendary witch near the town of Burkittsville, Maryland. The story unfolds through their own footage, accidentally discovered by student anthropologists a year after their disappearance and then pieced together by Artisan. The Web site that became the hub, although hardly the sole focus, of the campaign offered much additional material about the case of the missing filmmakers: information on the "Mythology" surrounding the Blair Witch legend, background on "The Filmmakers" who disappeared, a summary of "The Aftermath" of the disappearance, and a tour of "The Legacy" of these mysterious events, that is, of the various materials recovered in the search for the student filmmakers.[5] All of these elements, the film's *backstory,* if you will, elaborately propagate the notion of authenticity, attesting to the film as, quite literally, a "found-footage" type of documentary rather than a fictional work, and more particularly, as a different sort of attraction than the movies usually offer, a reality far stranger than that found in any "classic old-style horror film." Rather, they suggest we see the film *not as film,* but as one more artifact, along with the materials gathered together at the Web site, which we might view in order to better understand a kind of repressed or hidden reality. 8

Thus *The Blair Witch* site, in contrast to those noted above, points in various ways away from the film's privileged status as a product of the entertainment industry. Or more precisely, its "project" is to blur such common discrimination, to suggest, in effect, that this particular film is as much a part of everyday life as the Internet, that it extends the sort of unfettered knowledge access that the Internet seems to offer, and that its pleasures, in fact, closely resemble those of the electronic medium with which its core audience is so familiar. *Blair Witch* co-creator Eduardo Sanchez has hinted as much when discussing the importance of his film's Web site. He offers, "it gave us a lot of hype for a little movie," while he also points to the fact that the site was effective primarily because it was so very different from other publicity pages with which Web surfers were familiar. Rather than "just a behind the scenes thing with bios," he notes, they aimed to create "a 9 completely autonomous experience from the film. You don't have to see the film to actually have fun on the Web site, and investigate it and get creeped out. And that's kind of what you have to do" with such independent films.[6] While operating within what has quickly become an established, if still evolving electronic genre—that of the official film Web site—the *Blair Witch* page does rather more. It seems pointedly designed to suggest a level of difference from other sites, and to imply as well that the film, precisely insofar as it is *like* the Web site, *differs* from other films, even those within the horror genre.[7] While it does provide what might be thought of as a kind of gaming experience, it does so in a far more complicated way than other sites; moreover, its key emphasis is on the complicated and mysterious nature of a world that would inspire such an experience. Thus, the *Blair Witch* site offered to those who had not yet seen the film but who might have heard some of the hype, as well as those who had already seen it, a path of further investigation and a source of other, similarly creepy sensations—in effect, a *different context* for viewing the film.

10 And even as the site suggests that we see this film differently from other, more conventional works, it also points to the key terms of that difference, the central strategies shared by both Web site and film. To isolate these effects and better consider their implications for the film, I want to draw on Janet Murray's study of electronic narrative forms, wherein she describes how such texts, generally much more sophisticated than a typical advertising site, usually rely upon three "aesthetic principles" or characteristic "pleasures" for their lure—what she terms "immersion, agency, and transformation."[8] The term "immersion" refers to the "experience of being submerged" in the world of the text, and thus to a certain delight in "the movement out of our familiar world" and into another realm,[9] such as the complexly detailed medieval world of a game like *The Legend of Zelda.* By "agency" she means our ability to participate in the text, something we "do not usually expect to experience . . . within a narrative environment,"[10] but which is fundamental to the participatory investigation of a mysterious environment in a game like *Myst.* And "transformation" indicates the ability electronic texts give us to "switch positions,"[11] to change identities, role play, or become a shape-shifter—as freely happens in games like *Donkey Kong* and *Mortal Kombat*—within a world that is itself marked by a constant transformative potential. While not quite a game in the sense of those noted above, the *Blair Witch* site, largely because it does function as part of a larger narrative context, draws to varying degrees on each of these "pleasures" which, it forecasts to those who have grown up with the computer and the Internet, extend into the world of the film as well.

While employing the same sort of dark and suggestive color scheme as other sites, the *Blair Witch* page especially distinguishes itself by its power of immersion. Rather than pointing to the entertainment industry, it lures visitors into a world that is, on the surface, deceptively like our own, and even anchors us in that realm of normalcy with maps, police reports, found objects, and characters who evoke the film's target audience of teenagers or young adults (the missing student filmmakers and the University of Maryland anthropology class that, we learn, later discovered their film and various other artifacts). After establishing this real-world context and giving it authority, the site shifts from that anchorage into a completely "other" world, one of witchcraft, one connected to the repressed history of the mysteriously abandoned town of Blair, and one with a mythology all its own, attested to by a collection of woodcuts depicting witchcraft in the region and selections from the supposed book *The Blair Witch Cult,* which we are told is "on display at the Maryland Historical Society Museum." As site visitors move within that realm, they increasingly exercise an element of agency, exploring, like the missing filmmakers themselves, different dimensions of the mystery: gathering background on the region; pursuing the public debate about the missing students through interviews with Burkittsville locals, parents of the students, college professors of anthropology and folklore; reading pages of Heather's diary; looking over evidence accumulated by the local sheriff, the anthropology students, and the private investigator hired by Heather's mother. Through this agency effect, wherein we sort through a wealth of clues in any order we wish and try to put the pieces of a puzzle together, much in the fashion of *Myst,* we determine precisely how much we want to be "creeped out" by the materials made available to us. And in that "creeped out" effect, we glimpse both the site's limited version of "transformation," as well as its key difference from the film itself. 11

Despite the densely structured nature of this world and its invitation to navigate its cyberspace, the site never quite gives us a full range of that other "characteristic pleasure of digital environments," of transformation.[12] Here we cannot morph into another figure or become one of the three central characters; the best we can do is to become the anonymous surfer of cyberspace, or to settle into the role of an investigator and adopt that posture as a satisfactory shift out of the self. The various interviews offered here—with, for example, Bill Barnes, Executive Director of the Burkittsville Historical Society; Charles Moorehouse, a Professor of Folklore; or private investigator Buck Buchanon, among others—all place us in the typical position of the documentary audience, as recipients of the direct address of these 12 speakers. To do otherwise, to allow us, even as a kind of investigative experiment, to temporarily "become" one of the lost students, would, of course, rub against the very texture of the film toward which this site does ultimately and so successfully point. For making the experience immediate rather than mediated could reassert a kind of cinematic context, reminding us of the extent to which subject position is always constructed by point of view in film, and would thus show the film not as another artifact, co-terminous with the site, but as a kind of game played with—or on—us by the film industry. Simply put, it would work against the film's reality context. More to the point, the site mainly hints at the power of transformation because that closely allied "pleasure" is the payoff at the core of the film itself.

The Web site's ultimate aim, of course, is to encourage viewing 13
the film, to help build its audience, which it does so effectively not only by allowing us these electronic pleasures, but by suggesting we might also find them, and perhaps something *more,* a content for this creepy context, in the film itself.[13] Indeed, what *The Blair Witch Project* offers is some variation on the thrills of its Web site, along with a surprising level of transformation. In fact, after a number of studios tried to emulate the Internet-heavy approach of *The Blair Witch Project,* usually without reaping the same benefits, many in the industry recognized that its success derives from the way the Web site and film function together, *share* certain key attractions. As Marc Graser and Dade Hayes explain, an initial industry frenzy to mimic the *Blair Witch* Internet campaign has given way to a recognition "that the 'Blair Witch' site was not an added-on marketing tool but was designed as part of the film experience—one that tapped into fans of the horror genre" in a special way.[14]

In his review of *The Blair Witch Project,* Richard Corliss notes two 14
"rigorous rules" that, he believes, account for its effectiveness as a horror film: "It will show only what the team could plausibly have filmed, and it will not reveal any sources of outside terror—no monsters or maniacs."[15] That same sense of a restricted and thus logical agency and of a real rather than fantastic situation into which we can move are also crucial to the Web site. In effect, they point toward some of the ways in which those issues of immersion, agency, and transformation, all central to the context the Web site establishes, are key components of the film, contributing to its real-world context and conveying its specific pleasures.

The film offers us "no monsters or maniacs," no horror movie 15
fare of mad slashers, incarnate devils, or outsized monsters, because it is trying to immerse us in a world that, to all appearances, is coextensive with our own. In fact, the young filmmaker Heather worries specifically about making her film look too much like traditional hor-

ror movies. "I don't want to go too cheesy," she says, in a way that echoes the site's constant insistence on the real; "I want to present this in as straightforward a way as possible . . . the legend is unsettling enough." In keeping with this attitude, the film begins with domestic scenes: at Heather's house with Josh ("This is my home, which I am leaving the comforts of," she says as the film opens); at Mike's home as they pick him up and ask if they can meet his mother; at the grocery as they stock up on food for their excursion, the emphasis on buying marshmallows suggesting a typical boy (or girl) scout camping trip. It then carefully moves us into another realm with the "ceremonial first slate" of the movie, used to introduce Burkittsville (which is, as Heather intones, "much like a small quiet town anywhere"), with interviews of locals in the town, and with the scene in the motel room before the filmmakers head into the woods. This location is pointedly different—the cemetery against which Heather films her introductory remarks in 16mm black and white quickly establishes that—but it remains a fairly known, sufficiently commonplace world, one of shopkeepers, waitresses, local fishermen. But the narrative quickly shifts into a realm in which neither the students nor the viewers can ever quite get their bearings, as the filmmakers "start out off the map," repeatedly get lost, find they are going in circles, lose their map, and can make no sense out of their surroundings. And the shifting between black and white film and color video images only reinforces that disorientation. Finally, the climactic scene, in which Mike and Heather enter the ruined old house in the woods, recalls and mocks those initial domestic images of Heather's and Mike's homes with their implications of safety and security. We are simply left immersed in a world that has been completely transformed, one Josh had earlier, and quite accurately, summed up as "fucking crazy shit."

If the Web page is driven in large part by agency, the film links 16
that thrust precisely to the powers of transformation. As Murray reminds us, "the more realized the immersive environment, the more active we want to be within it."[16] Yet here, after a fashion long familiar from other horror films and their limited use of subjective camera, agency is evoked only to be frustrated, creating a sense of helplessness that is fertile psychic ground for horror. Although we find ourselves moving about in this world through our subjective incarnation as the filmmakers, we exercise no real control; as in so many slasher films, and as the *Scream* films repeatedly note and parody, we cannot stop these teenagers from running out into the dangerous dark where their fates are cinematically sealed. In its use of this effect the film recalls an earlier, landmark assay in this sort of cinematic narration, Robert Montgomery's subjective private-eye film *The Lady in the Lake* (1947). That film's experiment with agency, we might recall, fell flat with au-

diences, as one reviewer's frustrated feeling explains: "*You* do get into the story and see things pretty much the way its protagonist, Philip Marlowe, does, but *you* don't . . . get a chance to put your arms around Audrey Totter. . . . After all, the movie makers, for all their ingenuity, can go just so far."[17] Here, though, the "pleasure"—along with the frustration—of agency dissolves into transformation, as we do indeed "become," by turns, Josh, Heather, and Mike, sharing their points of view and often even exchanging identities and point of view within the same scene, as one character's vantage through the color video camera shifts to that of another, filming in 16mm black and white, almost as if we were "team-playing" a video game.

That instability allows us to shift and share sympathies, as when 17
Josh, filming Heather, upbraids her for getting them lost, while it also allows us another register of feeling when, from her subjective vantage, we see the familiar scenery that indicates they have gone in a circle, and the faces of Josh and Mike accusingly look to Heather. That same systemic instability allows as well for our acceptance of the shifty environment in which these events transpire, for our sense of a world that seems to operate from different principles and to speak in an indecipherable language of rock piles, stick figures, scrawled symbols, and strange voices. Transformation, especially via the extended subjective shot, then, becomes a key impulse that drives *The Blair Witch Project,* and a link as much to the realm of contemporary electronic narrative as to traditional horror films.

What may be just as significant as these simple alterations of ex- 18
tended subjective shot, though, is the film's self-consciousness, which constantly pulls us back from the typical film experience, as if it were trying to reach for a more realistic context, one beyond the camera and its limited field of vision, one perhaps more in keeping with the Internet and its seemingly transparent access to the world. For while the camera is a device that appears to let us capture the real, to chronicle it in "as straightforward a way as possible," it also constrains our experience by restricting what we can see, as is literally the case when Josh, Heather, and Mike run out into the night and we can see only as far as the limited light on their camera. Thus Josh tells Heather that he knows why she likes the video camera: "it's like a totally filtered reality."

In fact, the film ultimately challenges, even attacks our relation- 19
ship to the cinema, the technological in general, and their usual filtering effect. For its three filmmaker-protagonists eventually prove ill equipped for dealing with a natural and transformative world: their car can only take them so far; their map and compass prove unavailing; their cameras and sound equipment, designed to record the real, offer no insulation against a mysterious, perhaps even supernatural realm. And by funneling our relation to the natural world, even to one

another, through the technological, the narrative evokes our own sense of being lost in the mediated contemporary world. Attacked for her near attachment to the camera—an attachment that makes possible the film itself, we cannot forget—Heather is told to turn it off, put it down, help figure out their position and determine how to get out of it. Her reply, "No, I'm not turning the camera off. I want to mark this occasion," seems the response of someone who is already fully lost to and within the cinematic. From behind the camera, just as back in her home, she feels temporarily secure, pointed in a safe direction, able to document the "creeped out" experience of her companions while remaining immune from its menace. And yet she is in the midst of that experience herself and unable, or unwilling, to face her own contingent situation, to see herself as lost and endangered here. Consequently, the extreme close-up of her face—cold, shaking, nose running—at the film's climax, as she turns the camera on herself, works another and most effective "transformation" here. It shows her, and perhaps by extension us as well, as a frail contemporary human, immersed beyond all insulation by her technology, involved to such an extent that she can no longer find a safe distance, transformed from skeptical reporter to helpless victim of this quaint bit of local folklore.

20 In describing the success of *The Blair Witch Project,* Libby Gelman-Waxner has also linked the film's technological bent and its successful computer-based promotion. As she comments, its success must be "partially attributed to the heavy promotion of the movie on the Internet, and that makes sense: It's a movie for men and women . . . who prefer to see the world entirely through technology—it's nature downloaded."[18] That is, it seems to present us with a kind of raw human experience framed by technology, a technology that allows us a safe, almost aesthetic distance on events—much as we might find on the Internet. That distance, with its built-in controls and a carefully established context, does seem a key to the film, albeit one whose import she does not quite fully gauge. For while that sense of distance suggests the film's packaging for Internet consumption, it also opens onto the film's own critique of a mediated environment, particularly of the cinema, essential to its context of difference. Perhaps it goes without saying that today's moviegoers, situated within a pervasive multimedia environment, experience the cinematic text differently, even much more sceptically than other generations of moviegoers. Certainly, the success of the *Scream* films suggests as much. But the link I have explored here points not simply to the measurably different ways in which we are now viewing and decoding those texts, but also to how our viewing experience and capacity for such decoding depend on a whole different register of experience, how various voices assist in constructing our experience, even constructing our critique of that

experience. With *The Blair Witch Project*'s project, we can begin to gauge the dimensions of that construction, begin to make out what is so often obscured by mechanisms that are changing both the movies and our experience of them.

Paul Virilio has recently described the postmodern experience as like living in "the shadow of the Tower of Babel,"[19] not simply as a result of the many and different voices with which the multimedia environment bombards us but because of a certain dislocation that accompanies those various voices. For the electronic experience, he believes, with its tendency to bring together many and different places, to bind us within what he terms "glocalization,"[20] also leaves us without a real place—decentered and lost. *The Blair Witch Project,* along with its Internet shadow, seems to have effectively captured, and capitalized on, this sensibility. For it recalls the nature of the typical electronic document, the hypertext, which consists of a series of documents connected to one another by links; that is, it is a text of many fragments but no whole, no master text. And by virtue of its very lack of center, its absence of what Murray terms "the clear-cut trail,"[21] the hypertext invites us to find our own way, even to find some pleasure or profit in its very decenteredness. That absence of a center—or the lostness which the hypertext user shares in part with the three protagonists of *Blair Witch*—is simply part of the great capital of the Internet experience, something it typically barters with, plays upon by alternately denying and opening onto it. Here it is the stuff that can effectively "creep out" an audience. It is also something that the movie industry is quickly taking the measure of in its larger project of providing the postmodern audience with its peculiarly postmodern pleasures. 21

With this essay, more than simply describing the relationship between film and Web site, the product and its marketing, I hope to shed some light on the contemporary film industry. In today's wide-open media marketplace, the small, virtually unknown filmmaker often seems to function as successfully as the big studio in finding a venue for his or her work. Certainly, the proliferation of independent film festivals, the opening up of direct-to-video distribution possibilities, the appearance of media outlets like the Independent Film Channel on cable television, and even the industry-feared Internet distribution of digitized films all support this notion and, in truth, lend it some substance. The well-made, small-budget, independently produced, and star-less movie does have a chance to be seen, picked up by a national distributor or cable outlet, and then offered to a wide audience. Yet reaching that wide audience remains a troublesome project, one with which the power structure of the industry is 22 growing familiar, and for which it is constantly developing new strategies. These strategies then must take into account the changing nature of the entertainment form itself, particularly the increasingly substantial role of the computer and its offspring, the Internet—a medium that also threatens, much as television did, to supplant the film industry, in part by offering its own pleasures to a young audience that has grown up with electronic narratives. As Murray reminds us, "the computer is chameleonic. It can be seen as a theater, a town hall, an unraveling book, an animated wonderland, a sports arena, and even a potential life form. But it is first and foremost a representational medium, a means for modeling the world that added its own potent properties to the traditional media it has assimilated so quickly."[22] And, I would add, it is a medium that, through the Internet and much as film has traditionally done, has begun to assert its own model for the world. It powerfully affirms its own authority, its own truth, its own priority at affording access to the world.

NOTES

1. *Hollywood in the Information Age: Beyond the Silver Screen* (Austin: University of Texas Press, 1994), p. 19.
2. Quoted in Marc Graser and Dade Hayes' "No Scratch from 'Witch' Itch," *Variety*, Feb. 28, 2000, p. 1.
3. Quoted in Nicholas Maiese's "*Blair Witch* Casts Its Spell," *Advertising Age*, Mar. 20, 2000, S8. Much of the commentary here on the advertising campaign derives from this piece.
4. "No Scratch from 'Witch' Itch," p. 1.
5. The four categories of material cited here correspond to the names of the four links that the main Web page offers visitors. Each one opens onto an elaborate display of images, text, streaming video, and sound files that essentially extends the experience of the movie, or as I suggest here, even offers an alternate, if parallel experience to the film.
6. Prairie Miller, "*Blair Witch Project:* An Interview with Eduardo Sanchez," *http:allmovie.com/cq/x.dll?uid=12:53:34/pm&p=avg&sq/ =m1 vll/176036*
7. In this context, see Wasko's reminder about the influence of television and the cable industry on film aesthetics; as she notes, "the way a film is shot and edited definitely has been influenced by new distribution outlets such as video and cable." See *Hollywood in the Information Age*, p. 38.

8. *Hamlet on the Holodeck: The Future of Narrative in Cyberspace* (Cambridge: MIT Press, 1997), p. 181.
9. Ibid., pp. 98–99.
10. Ibid., p. 126.
11. Ibid., p. 180.
12. Ibid., p. 154.
13. As a measure of effectiveness, we might note the Nielsen ranking of the *Blair Witch* site. As reported in *Variety,* the Nielsen NetRating for the week ending August 1, 1999, ranked the site the 45th most popular on the Web and second among movie sites, trailing only that of *Star Wars: Episode One–The Phantom Menace.* The typical visitor in this period averaged more than 16 minutes at the site. See Richard Katz's " 'Blair' Fare a Big Hit on Web," *Variety,* Aug. 10, 1999, p. 13.
14. " 'Witch' Hunting: Studios Fail to Match 'Blair' Flair on 'Net,' " *Variety,* Mar. 2, 2000, p. 1.
15. "There's Something About Scary," *Time.* July 12, 1999, *www.time.com/time/magazine/articles/0,3266,27736,00.html*
16. *Hamlet on the Holodeck,* p. 126.
17. Anon., review of *The Lady in the Lake, New York Times,* 24 Jan. 1947, p. 18.
18. "'Witch' and Famous," *Premiere* 13.3 (1999), pp. 80–81.
19. *Open Sky,* trans. Julie Rose (New York: Semiotext(e), 1997), p. 145.
20. Ibid., p. 144.
21. *Hamlet on the Holodeck,* p. 91.
22. Ibid., p. 284.

Examining the Text

1. Describe your own experience with movie Web sites (including, if applicable, the Web site for *The Blair Witch Project*), and discuss how it fits in with the observations Telotte makes in the first part of his essay. In what ways do most of these sites function as glorified movie posters, and in what ways do they go beyond that static medium? Has a movie Web site ever persuaded you to see a movie you weren't all that interested in seeing before viewing the site? If so, how did it accomplish this? What made you go to the movie Web site in the first place? If you've never or rarely viewed any movie Web sites, discuss why they don't interest you.

2. Define Janet Murray's three "aesthetic principles" of electronic narrative forms. Discuss the ways in which Telotte applies these terms to *The Blair Witch Project*'s Web site and film.

3. Review the semiotic, structural, and contextual critical approaches as defined by Mark Schaefermeyer. In what ways does Telotte's approach to film criticism fit into any of these schools of thought? Is there a neat fit here or does Telotte's approach contain elements from some or all three critical theories? Give examples to support your conclusions.

For Group Discussion

Telotte's analysis leads to an interesting, somewhat paradoxical conclusion: while *The Blair Witch Project* is a film that is intimately connected to current technology, it ultimately puts forth a message that questions, even critiques, our reliance on such technology. Think about other examples of movies where computer technology figures prominently, such as *Minority Report, Swordfish, Antitrust,* and less recent examples such as *The Net,* and *Enemy of the State.* What kinds of attitudes do these movies adopt toward the technology with which they're concerned? Discuss themes, plots, and characterizations within these movies in order to arrive at some conclusions about the movies' attitudes towards technology. Do these movies display differing stances towards technology, or do you detect patterns overall? How do these movies' messages compare to *The Blair Witch Project*'s?

Writing Suggestion

The Blair Witch Project's Web site is still up and active, in part to help promote the movie's sequel, *Book of Shadows: Blair Witch 2.* Review the Web site (*www.blairwitch.com*) and write an essay analyzing how the current version of the site uses the electronic narrative forms of "immersion, agency, and transformation." You might push your examination further by comparing and contrasting your analysis of the current site with Telotte's analysis of the original site.

The "Witchcraft" of Media Manipulation: *Pamela* and *The Blair Witch Project*

Martin Harris

In 1740, the British writer Samuel Richardson caused quite a sensation when he published his novel Pamela: or, Virtue Rewarded, *which was written to make it appear that the title character was actually sharing her letters and diary entries. In these writings, Pamela Andrews, a maidservant for a wealthy family, describes the long assault on her virtue carried out by the master of the household, referred to only as Mr. B. Pamela consistently resists these advances, and her virtue ultimately converts Mr. B., who reforms and does the proper thing by marrying the lowly, but beautiful, Pamela—thus is her virtue ostensibly rewarded. The book aroused controversy on a number of levels, but confusion over the fictional status of Pamela is the issue most pertinent to Harris's comparison of* The Blair Witch Project *and* Pamela.

As Harris describes, while Pamela's writings were the invention of Richardson, the author sought to obscure this fact through a number of means—just as the creators and distributors of The Blair Witch Project *used the blurred lines between truth and fiction to promote interest in their film. Such confusion over the truth claims of works such as these help to explain their appeal, Harris argues.*

*As Harris examines the similarities in the promotion, production, and reception of the two works, he extends his points further. Finding "uncanny" similarities in the style of storytelling used in both works, Harris posits that such convergences indicate a shared project: both works attempt to engage a large audience, and both position themselves as correctives to the failings of the genre in which they fit—*Pamela *attempts to improve upon novels and romances of the eighteenth century, and* The Blair Witch Project *addresses what its creators see as failings in the late twentieth-century genre of horror films.*

***As you read,** notice the ways in which Harris uses the rhetorical techniques of comparison and contrast, with an emphasis on comparison—Harris calls his essay a "comparative analysis" (3). As he shifts between describing elements of* The Blair Witch Project *and* Pamela, *how persuasive do you find his accumulation of descriptive details? How does Harris deal with any contrasts that arise between the works?*

> *I have done nothing but read it to others, and hear others again read it, to me, ever since it came into my Hands; and I find I am likely to do nothing else, for I know not how long yet to come: because, if I lay the Book down, it comes after me. — When it has dwelt all Day long upon the Ear, It takes Possession, all Night, of the Fancy. — It has Witchcraft in every page of it: but it is the Witchcraft of Passion and Meaning.*
>
> —Aaron Hill, to the Editor of *Pamela*[1]

From the perspective of the American news media, the sudden, phenomenal commercial success of *The Blair Witch Project* (1999, dir. Daniel Myrick and Eduardo Sanchez) represented a story as absorbing and suggestive as the one told by the film itself. In its first weekend of wide release, the film (the directors' first, and the first from their company, Haxan Films) earned nearly $30 million, an amount which according to some estimates represented approximately one thousand times that spent to produce the film.[2] Per theater earnings for the 1 film's opening week were reportedly the highest ever enjoyed by a nationally-released film.[3] After only two months of theatrical release, *The Blair Witch Project* already had become the highest-grossing independent film ever.[4] Generally speaking, the media responds to the unexpected, "sleeper" success of films such as *The Blair Witch Project* with ruminations about best-selling formulas and the mysterious vagaries of popular taste.[5] Such discussions often yield one of two possible conclusions about the cultural product whose surprising success is being investigated: 1) that the product has managed to uncover a new strategy for creating a commercial success, in which case, identifiable aberrations in the product (e.g., of technique) will be instinctively interpreted as "innovative" and therefore crucial to the product's having procured a large audience; 2) that formulas for commercial success are either non-existent or if they do exist they are inaccessible, in which case the product's success will be described as incomprehensible, the result of cultural forces too complex to grasp.

Initial reaction to *The Blair Witch Project*'s success largely followed these two patterns of response, with reviewers and commentators either attributing its popularity to one or more "unique" elements of its production and/or marketing strategy,[6] or regarding the entire question of its success as simply unanswerable.[7] However, it is possible to analyze both *The Blair Witch Project* and its sudden, unprecedented popularity without reducing its achievement to its stylistic or marketing "innovations." Nor should the film's popularity be understood as proof that forces influencing public taste are best regarded in the same way the filmmakers seem to have regarded the Blair Witch herself, that is, as a mystery whose meaning is utterly unavailable to us.[8] Rather, the film's critical and commercial successes can both be explained by analyzing its creators' masterful exploitation of an archetypal paradigm for creating a mass media entertainment, a paradigm exemplified most readily by Samuel Richardson's 1740 "sleeper" hit, *Pamela, or Virtue Rewarded.*[9] As occurred with Richardson's novel, the creators of *The Blair Witch Project* manipulated the various media through which its narrative was presented in a manner that encouraged initial audiences to experience its fictional story as if it were nonfictional. In both cases, such "truth" claims abetted the works' commercial success while also enabling their creators to interrogate contemporary debates about a specific kind of cultural production (i.e., the novel and the horror film). 2

What follows is a comparative analysis of the "media events" of *Pamela* and *The Blair Witch Project* which highlights similarities between the works and the circumstances surrounding the publication of each.[10] The analysis is divided into three sections, each of which considers one phase of the media event. The first section documents simi- 3 larities between pre-publication strategies for advertising both *Pamela* and *The Blair Witch Project* and how these strategies helped foster speculation about the "truth" of their fictional stories. The second section addresses the works themselves, concentrating primarily upon how both *Pamela* and *The Blair Witch Project* manipulate audience identification in ways that can be interpreted as morally appealing and therefore, I argue, commercially advantageous. The final section compares the reception of each work and offers explanation and analysis of the extreme positive and negative responses both works tended initially to elicit. Such a comparison will allow an initial avenue of inquiry into the *Blair Witch* film, its marketing, and its unprecedented commercial success that resists characterizing the entire event as either the result of technical and/or promotional sleight-of-hand or as simply impenetrable to analysis. That is to say, much as Aaron Hill does with regard to *Pamela,* I would qualify *The Blair Witch Project*'s "Witchcraft" or "spell" over its initial audience as one that in fact possesses actual, understandable "Meaning."

PROMOTION

When *The Blair Witch Project* was screened at the 1999 Cannes film festival, one aspect of the film's promotion caused a minor controversy amongst the assembled press corps. Following a procedure initially established at the film's premiere at the Sundance Film Festival five months earlier, fliers advertising the film were posted around Cannes which drew upon what Amir Maim, co-president of Artisan Entertainment (the film's distributor), called "the great conceit of Blair Witch," namely, that it is "a real documentary" (Ascher-Walsh 36). Across the top of the flier read a headline, "MISSING," under which were placed photos of the film's three principal stars (Heather Donahue, Joshua Leonard, and Michael Williams). Information beneath the photographs enigmatically reported the trio's disappearance, with the film's title in small capitals being positioned along the bottom edge of the advertisement.[11] The fliers therefore described *The Blair Witch Project*'s premise—that the film is composed of footage shot by three amateur filmmakers who "were never heard from again"—as if it were not a premise at all, but rather genuine historical fact. The morning after the fliers were posted in Cannes, however, they had mysteriously vanished. As Gregg Hale, one of the film's producers, would later learn, a television industry executive had in fact been kidnapped weeks earlier at a local convention: the handbills had been removed out of respect for this highly-publicized case involving an actual missing person. (The executive was subsequently rescued.) Hale responded to the inci- 4 dent by attempting to clarify the intentions behind the film's promotion: "We've never intended this as a hoax," he said, though went on to add an important qualification: "We allow people the illusion it's all real."[12]

Such had been the strategy at Sundance, where *The Blair Witch* 5
Project's entry marked the first time a horror film had ever been accepted to participate in the influential festival. After Artisan bought distribution rights for the film (within hours of its Sundance premiere,[13] "Malin convinced the filmmakers to move the film's opening credits to the end, adding to Blair's home-video-like realism" (Ascher-Walsh 36.)[14] Soon after buying the rights to distribute the film, Artisan also took over from the directors the management of the film's Web site (*www.blairwitch.com*), originally launched by the directors in June 1998. Artisan had followed a similar pattern the previous year following its purchase at Sundance of distribution rights to π [Pi] (1998, dir. Darren Aronofsky), also a low-budgeted, independent film which became a moderate commercial success in the summer of 1998.[15] Since the early 1990s, the creation of "official" Web sites for feature films has become a fixture of promotional campaigns, and Artisan's elaborate site for π [Pi] was widely considered as central to creating successful publicity for the film. However, Artisan's handling of the *The Blair Witch Project* Web site was decidedly different than it had been with the site they had created for π [Pi]—indeed, possibly unlike that of any other film previously promoted on the Internet. As the proliferation of computer virus hoaxes, celebrity death rumors, and investment scams have repeatedly shown, the Internet has proven a highly susceptible vehicle for rapid, widespread dissemination of fraudulent information. Unlike other media, the Internet allows for anonymous broadcast with no editorial policy governing its truth content, a fact which allowed Artisan to exploit the film's "great conceit" without having to worry about their message being taken down as happened in the streets of Cannes. In an on-line journal, Dan Myrick describes the directors' collaboration with Artisan to alter the original Web site. According to Myrick, Artisan added material primarily designed to "compliment [sic] the film and reinforce the backstory of the Blair folklore" (2 March 1999). This material included fictional items such as police reports, interviews with the "missing" filmmakers' parents, a time line extending back to the eighteenth century, and other data bearing some relation to the story told by the film though not depicted onscreen. Speaking of the Web site around the time of *The Blair Witch Project*'s nationwide premiere, Myrick noted "It's all fiction . . . but people are getting confused. We kind of count on that" (Ascher-Walsh 36).

Anecdotes about audiences "getting confused" about *The Blair* 6
Witch Project's fictional status began to circulate even before the film

was completed. Upon receiving a demo tape called "The Blair Witch Project" from Myrick in the summer of 1997, John Pierson, host of the cable television show Split Screen, which airs on Bravo and the Independent Film Channel, reportedly "both loved it and was spooked by it—initially believing it really was an 'unsolved mystery.'"[16] Pierson later would qualify the description of his initial response: "The eerie and compelling quality of the original sample made me suspend my disbelief" (para. 1). On 15 August 1997, Split Screen aired the entire eight-minute demo, along with commentary afterward from Myrick, Sanchez, and Hale, who spoke of the found footage and "what they hoped (or feared) they'd find on the film and tapes" (Grainy Pictures, para. 5). Grainy Pictures, producers of Split Screen, supplied Haxan $10,000 to film the alluded-to footage, which was completed in October 1997. A second eight-minute edited excerpt of the "found" footage was then aired on Split Screen on 6 April 1998, after which Pierson equivocally expressed skepticism about the footage's validity and invited viewers to visit Grainy Pictures's Web site and post their views on the matter. Hundreds did, including some who expressed concern over the ethical ambiguity of Split Screen's having presented fiction as fact. In May 1998, the producers were reportedly contacted by an Albany private investigator who had spent weeks looking for the "missing" filmmakers.[17] Later, at the film's premiere at Sundance in January 1999, came further reports of audience confusion over the story's truth, despite the festival catalogue's description of the film as an "edited compendium of the purported filmmaker's findings" that "[b]rilliantly blur[red] the lines between fact and fiction" (Yeldham, para. 2, 3).[18] On 11 July 1999, days before the film's initial, limited release, a special produced by Haxan, "Curse of the Blair Witch," was aired on another cable network, the Sci-Fi Channel. Following the format of other sensationalist documentary programming such as the television show *In Search Of* (1976–82) and the film *Legend of Boggy Creek* (1972, dir. Charles B. Pierce), both of which were routinely cited by the directors as being among their direct influences, the special further perpetuated the conceit by presenting interviews with law enforcement officials, inhabitants of Burkittsville (an actual town in Maryland which provides the film's setting), and "newsreel" footage of a character alluded to in the film, a child-murderer named Rustin Parr.[19] According to "Curse of the Blair Witch," the fact of the filmmakers' disappearance is understood; rather, it is the truth of the "legend" of the Blair Witch that the special seeks to interrogate, much as *Legend of Boggy Creek* presents itself as an investigation into the existence of a Sasquatch-type monster. Meanwhile, Artisan's revised Web site reinforcing the film's non-fictional "back story" had not only become the most-accessed film Web site of the year, but according to Nielsen NetRatings was among the top fifty most used sites on the entire Internet during the week preceding the film's national release, all of which helped fuel still further chatroom and listserve discussions about the film's fictional status (e.g., "Re: the answer to if *The Blair Witch Project* is true!!!").[20]

As *The Blair Witch Project* successfully utilized print advertising, cable television, and the Internet to suggest to audiences the "truth" of its narrative, so, too, was the publication of Richardson's novel accompanied by a similar exploitation of media technology designed to impress upon readers the veracity of Pamela's letters. The story of how a fifty-year-old London printer interrupted the composition of a conduct book to write what would become one of the eighteenth century's most influential prose fictional works has been rehearsed often.[21] It is significant, of course, that when writing *Pamela: or, Virtue Rewarded* (first published 6 November 1740), Richardson conceived of the project as being not unlike what he had been pursuing in *Letters Written To and For Particular Friends, On the Most Important Occasions* (often referred to as *Familiar Letters*). The idea for the letter-writing guide originally had been suggested to Richardson by a pair of booksellers, who requested the author create "a little volume of Letters, in a common style, on such subjects as might be of use to those country readers, who were unable to indite for themselves."[22] In his reply to the booksellers, Richardson suggested that such a book might also be fashioned so as to "instruct them [his readers] how they should think and act in common cases, as well as indite" (Barbauld lii). It was while brainstorming such "common cases" that Richardson is said to have recalled an actual incident involving the attempted seduction of a waiting maid by her master. Such a case would indeed have been "common" if not for its outcome, namely, the master himself being "subdued" by the maid's "noble resistance, watchfulness, and excellent qualities" into marrying her.[23] Attracted to this unusual instance of "virtue rewarded," Richardson retold the story as a true account, presenting the maid's letters as if he had merely edited them. As he would do with *Familiar Letters,* Richardson withheld his name from the title page of *Pamela.* In both cases, Richardson's intent was to suggest to readers that the letters were reproductions, not inventions, and thereby reinforce each work's potential status as especially exemplary because factual. 7

As would be the case with *The Blair Witch Project,* speculation about the "true" identity of Pamela Andrews predated the novel's initial appearance. In the 11 October 1740 issue of the *Weekly Miscellany* there appeared an anonymous letter, likely composed by Rev. William 8

Webster, a friend of Richardson's. In the letter, the writer conveys having "sympathiz'd with the pretty Heroine" in a manner which implies his impression that the story was factual:

> It is an astonishing Matter, and well worth our most serious Consideration, that a young beautiful Girl, in the low Scene of Life and Circumstance in which Fortune placed her . . . could after having a Taste of Ease and Plenty . . . resolve to return to her primitive Poverty, rather than give up her Innocence.[24]

For this reader, that the case being related is not "common" 9
makes Pamela Andrews's story noteworthy, though by no means causes him to suspect that his friend the printer had himself composed the letters. In fact, the letter writer is so convinced of Pamela's existence he suggests to the "Editor"[25] that he put to rest all urges to edit the letters any further: "No; let us have Pamela as Pamela wrote it; in her own Words, without Amputation, or Addition" (7). When *Pamela* did appear on 6 November, this letter was prefixed to it, along with another letter "To the Editor of the Piece intitled, Pamela" by "J.B.D.F." (Jean Baptiste de Freval) in which the letter writer insists that "the Hints you have given me, should also be prefatorily be given to the Publick," namely, those regarding the letters' veracity. Like the footage which makes up *The Blair Witch Project, Pamela* also is presented as consisting of actual, "found" writings, altered only to the extent that the "editor" was, as J.B.D.F. explains, "obliged to vary some of the Names of Persons, Places, &c. and to disguise a few of the Circumstances, in order to avoid giving Offence to some Persons" (5). Finally, Richardson himself added a most effective, if infamous, endorsement of the letters' legitimacy in the form of a "Preface by the Editor." After a lengthy list of reasons for having published the letters, the Preface concludes with a heartfelt recommendation of their merit, with Richardson disingenously explaining his qualification to offer such praise "because an Editor may reasonably be supposed to judge with an Impartiality which is rarely to be met with in an Author towards his own Works" (3).[26]

It is clear that despite the ridicule which it would later bring him 10
(e.g., Shamela's "The Editor to Himself"), the "Preface by the Editor" was central to Richardson's strategy for advancing *Pamela*'s didactic purpose. In the 13 December 1740 issue of the *Weekly Miscellany,* alongside another commendatory letter from Rev. Webster, Richardson reprinted the "Preface" as a means to advertise the work, confident in the assumption that Pamela Andrews's story would more effectively "cultivate the Principles of Virtue and Religion in the Minds of the Youth of Both Sexes" if the letters were thought genuine.[27]

As was the case at initial screenings of *The Blair Witch Project,* people were "getting confused" about whether or not the story was a fiction. Like Rev. Webster, Richardson's friend Aaron Hill originally thought Pamela to be an actual person, only to be later disabused of the notion by Richardson.[28] Even after Richardson's authorship had become widely-known, the author continued to receive letters asking whether the story was indeed factual. A letter written by "six ladies in Reading" to Richardson following the publication of his sequel to *Pamela* in December 1741 shows readers still puzzling over the fictional status of his invented characters: "You seem to speak at the beginning of your First and Third Volumes, as if ye Story was Fact . . . [however,] we can't think that People of the Distinction that Mr. and Mrs. B. seem to be of, wou'd care to be pointed at as they must be, by people . . . conversant in the Polite world, notwithstanding your altering some of the Incidents, Names, and Places."[29] The much-repeated story of country villagers having rung church bells to celebrate Pamela's wedding seems also to indicate the ambiguous status of Richardson's fictional creation. The anecdote recalls other stories of audiences responding to fictional cultural productions in ways that would appear more appropriately reserved for real events. Examples include the construction of a grave in the Trinity Churchyard in New York for the title character of Susanna Rowson's highly-popular *Charlotte Temple,* subtitled *A Tale of Truth;* a similar display of public grief in response to the publication of chapters 71 and 72 of Charles Dickens's *The Old Curiosity Shop* in which the death of Little Nell is described; and reports of listeners' having taken flight upon listening to Orson Welles's 1939 radio broadcast of *The War of the Worlds.* To such a list one might add stories concerning *The Blair Witch Project,* for example, the Frederick County sheriff's office having received "30 to 40 calls a day about the film" during the height of its popularity. "Many still think it's a true story," said one Frederick County official. "When you tell them the truth, they think there's a conspiracy and a cover-up."[30]

Richardson would eventually express tentative misgivings over 11
the confusion wrought by his "bold stroke . . . [of] having the umbrage of the editor's character to screen myself behind"; however, as Richardson wrote to Aaron Hill, it was also the case that he thought the story, if written in an easy and natural manner, suitably to the simplicity of it, might possibly introduce a new species of writing, that might possibly turn young people into a course of reading different from the pomp and parade of romance-writing, and dismissing the improbable and marvellous, with which novels generally abound, might tend to promote the cause of religion and virtue.[31]

Richardson believed the decision to present his story as "A Narra- 12
tive which has its Foundation in Truth and Nature" (as the title page

announces) was integral to his attempt to reform the flights of fictional fancy then associated with "romance-writing." While both Richardson and the creators of *The Blair Witch Project* were successful in their respective efforts to promote and present their cultural objects as containing some element of truth, it is tempting initially to interpret the filmmakers' aims as having been much narrower (i.e., strictly commercial) than were Richardson's. Such seems to be the implication of sentiments like those expressed by Sanchez regarding the illusion of *The Blair Witch Project*'s factuality: "It seems real, it looks real, it feels real. We're not saying it's the truth, and we're not saying it's not. We were smart enough, as we were making the film, to realize we have something different here" (Elias). However, motivations for Richardson and the creators of *The Blair Witch Project* to perpetuate their respective works' "great conceit" are in fact more similar than they are different, insofar as in both cases the suggestion of truth proved crucial to their creators' commercial aspirations as well as to their reformative projects.

To suggest that Richardson did not betray professional interests 13
in the promotion of his first novel is to ignore the author's own statements about the literary marketplace. To Hill, a poet whose publications repeatedly proved less than popular, Richardson tried to assuage his friend by describing his poetry as too intellectually challenging for the average reader: "Your writings require thought to read, and to take in their whole force; and the world has no thought to bestow. Simplicity is all their cry. . . . I am of opinion that it is necessary for a genius to accommodate itself to the mode and taste of the world it is cast into, since works published in this age must take root in it, to flourish in the next."[32] Richardson's distinction, one often evoked by cultural theorists when delineating mass and elite culture, well indicates the professional printer's acquaintance with how the marketplace's general preference for "Simplicity" might be exploited not just for commercial purposes (the work "must take root") but for more far-reaching aims (to allow the work "to flourish in the next"). In other words, for Richardson, didactic and commercial interests need not be viewed as incommensurable. With *Pamela,* Richardson explicitly hoped to reform the novel, creating a "new species of writing" whose trajectory was morally instructive; yet he also recognized that in order for his message to reach his intended audience ("the Youth of Both Sexes"), it was vital that he "accommodate" the telling of Pamela's story "to the mode and taste of the world it is cast into." Later, Richardson would directly address the necessity to convey one's instructive message in an accessible form:

> I am endeavouring to write a Story, which shall catch young and airy Minds, and when Passions run high in them, to shew how they may be

> directed to laudable Meanings and Purposes, in order to decry such Novels and Romances, as have a Tendency to inflame and corrupt: And if I were to be too spiritual, I doubt I should catch none but Grandmothers, for the Granddaughters would put my Girl indeed in better Company, such as that of the graver Writers, and there they would leave her.[33]

Thus did Richardson connect the dissemination of his moral message to practical, commercial purposes, with the "bold stroke" of presenting his fictional story as true proving crucial to the attempt to "catch" as many young readers as he possibly could.

By the same token, it would be unfair to the creators of *The Blair Witch Project* to interpret their precociousness about the film's truth content as having been entirely financially-motivated. Like Richardson's novel, *The Blair Witch Project* consciously targeted a youth market, and it can be argued that the film's creators likewise considered the film's truth conceit a ready way "to catch young and airy minds."[34] However, Sanchez's description of the directors' revelation "we have something different here" also indicates the creators' desire to interrogate genre conventions and, as the Sundance film catalogue description of the film indicates, produce a work that "redefines the horror genre" (Yeldham, para. 3). In interviews the directors consciously positioned their film in opposition to current examples of cinematic horror. When describing their aims with *The Blair Witch Project,* the film's directors made it a custom to state their grievance that "too many recent horror films have used satire and humor to re-invigorate a genre that had become predictable and repetitive" (Elias). The film's creators thereby articulated their "project" as an attempt to deliver an alternative entertainment, with the film's realism "conceit" being central to the desire to produce a cultural product which would be perceived as neither predictable nor repetitive. Thus did Artisan fashion a promotional campaign designed to intensify and not lessen viewers impression of a film that stylistically "seems real," "looks real," and "feels real." Like Richardson, what the filmmakers "were going after was identifiability," as Myrick noted to an interviewer (Beale), deliberately avoiding stylistic cliches (gory special effects, *Psycho*-styled music, "tinglers") which according to *The Blair Witch Project*'s creators have the function of distancing audiences from identifying or empathizing with the characters' plight. To paraphrase Richardson, *The Blair Witch Project* "dismiss[es] the improbable and marvelous, with which [horror films] generally abound" in order to realize a specific, aesthetic purpose, namely, to evoke a correspondingly more "real" response from audiences. 14

By presenting and promoting their works as factually-based, then, both Richardson and *The Blair Witch Project*'s creators invested 15 their cultural products with a characteristic much valued by their respective cultures, namely, a respect for the worlds in which their audiences lived and breathed. In both instances was this recognition of the importance of the "real" or the "true" motivated both by commercial interests and what can be described as aesthetic objectives. Richardson recognized that "romance-writing," though popular, could never capture genuine mainstream success because of its fundamental resistance to realism. Similarly did the makers of *The Blair Witch Project* view contemporary horror film's stylized disconnection with actual human experience as having evolved into a commercial liability. Since realism often will increase the likelihood of "identifiability," cultural products exhibiting a realistic style will often carry greater cultural capital by increasing the potential demographic of its audience. Richardson instructs Hill that if a writer's story is perceived of as being true, that writer has a greater opportunity to attract the attentions of more than just "Grandmothers." Similarly did *The Blair Witch Project*'s commitment to a "realistic" style better its chances to "become the Elvis, the E.T., the Pet Rock of 1999," as a *Time* cover story about the film suggested (59).[35] However, in neither case did the decision to present "A Narrative which has its Foundation in Truth" ensure mainstream appeal. As I argue below, while the petition to realism certainly helped rapidly attract large audiences to both works, more central to both *Pamela* and *The Blair Witch Project*'s widespread commercial successes was the fundamentally conservative moral stance informing each work's attempt to reform its respective genre of popular entertainment. In other words, both works can be said to exemplify how audiences respond most positively to those cultural productions whose aesthetic can be readily (though not exclusively) interpreted as indicating a conservative or "moral" interpretation of the cultural role of popular entertainments.

PRODUCTION

If the methods by which *Pamela* and *The Blair Witch Project* were promoted can be said to have borne similarities, parallels between the two works' plots, styles, and scenarios might be considered downright uncanny. Each work features a narrative whose rhythm is essentially episodic, with the telling of each story being marked by numerous gaps and pauses. In each case, such gaps are generally explained within the narrative itself: Pamela often concludes letters and journal entries with accounts of the external constraints under which she had composed them;[36] similarly has the student filmmakers' "footage" been edited together in a way that visually "explains" its chronology, 16 with many of the edits exemplifying continuity editing or match on action.[37] Relatedly, both plots are especially forward-looking, with the ominous "end" always looming over the presently-narrated moment. Much as the announcement of the student filmmakers' disappearance which opens *The Blair Witch Project* concentrates the audience's attention throughout the film upon the story's conclusion, so too does Pamela punctuate her narrative with many premature "ends" in which she describes herself as signing off her journal for what may be the last time.[38] Both works also feature a deliberately "natural" or amateurish style, what Richardson calls "an easy and natural manner" especially suitable to his protagonistnarrator. Such a similarity is directly consequent to both works' having positioned the tellers of their stories within the stories themselves.

Unlike narrators who retrospectively narrate their tales, neither Pamela nor the student filmmakers have access to how their stories will end, and in both cases such narrative uncertainty is further thematized by the narratives' style. The much-noted "shaky camera" style of *The Blair Witch Project* connotes both the student filmmakers' uncertainty about the use of their equipment as well as uncertainty about what exactly they are filming or their own personal safety. Pamela likewise finds herself unsure about what she is writing, and often self-reflexively comments upon her own narrative skills: "I can hardly write," she complains, "yet as I can do nothing else, I know not how to forbear!—Yet I cannot hold my Pen!—How crooked and trembling the Lines!" (159–60). Like the student filmmakers', Pamela's uncertainty reveals itself both structurally and stylistically as a series of fits and starts, and in both works the intended, cumulative effect of such narrative self-doubt is to heighten audience identification with their respective protagonists' predicaments. Both works also feature similar scenarios in which young, vulnerable, and impetuous protagonists find themselves besieged by villains whose characterization is deliberately lesser developed than their own. Much as the true identity of *The Blair Witch Project*'s "villain" is never revealed, so too is Mr. B most often interpreted as more of a stock figure than a fully-developed character, and in both cases does the mysterious quality of the protagonists' tormentors embellish their (and the empathizing audience's) fears.[39] Finally, both narratives additionally position their protagonists as addressing their narratives to their parents, significantly impacting the "intimate" or personal quality of their stories.[40] 17

Yet rather than make the dubious argument that all of these parallels indicate evidence of a specific "formula" for creating commercially successful cultural products, it is more fruitful to consider how these narrative similarities in fact emerged from similar theories regarding the "Meanings and Purposes" of commercial storytelling. 18

Both *Pamela* and *The Blair Witch Project* can be interpreted as exemplifying their tellers' notions of how best to "catch" the widest possible audience while at the same time "decry[ing]" the respective genre of popular entertainment to which each presents itself as belonging. Regarding the latter purpose, the promotion and publication of both works aimed to provide a conservative corrective to the genre of popular entertainment which might be described as forming a significant part of the "the world it [each work] is cast into" (for Richardson, "Novels and Romances"; for *The Blair Witch Project*'s creators, "recent horror films"). To this end, it is important to recognize that while each work's plot, style, and scenario are calculated to encourage audience identification, in both cases is such identification primarily associated with the "victims" narrating the respective stories.

Similarities of narrative technique between *Pamela* and *The Blair Witch Project* are therefore direct exponents of their creators' corresponding attitudes toward what they considered morally-questionable qualities associated with their respective genres. Both works deliberately attempt to avoid a glorification of vice by attempting to withhold from their audiences the perspective of the "villain," and instead choose a narrative course which delivers their audiences exclusive and sustained acquaintance with the emotional, mental, and even physical devastation potentially wrought by villainous behavior.[41] That is to say, it is not each work's technical "innovation" or even the sensation-causing confusion over the works' "truth" that can be said entirely to explain their immediate, unprecedented commercial successes; rather it is the essentially conservative approach both works took toward the task of "reforming" a particular genre of popular entertainment that directly encouraged the kind of word-of-mouth publicity generally required for the "sleeper" to succeed. 19

By encouraging audience identification with Pamela Andrews, Richardson explicitly attempts to counter the voyeuristic qualities of the romance or "amatory fiction,"[42] such as had been written by popular authors like Mary de la Riviere Manley and Eliza Haywood, which had proven so captivating to younger readers. In a new introduction to his study of "Popular Fiction Before Richardson," John J. Richetti considers how such commercially-successful "formula fiction . . . must have been in some way a challenge to an increasingly restricted and measured actuality" Richardson pursued in *Pamela,* a novel which demonstrates "a refusal of that easy plenitude and bounding eroticism for the constraints of realism" (xxviii). It is important to recognize that Richardson was not interested in promoting realism as such, but rather a particular mode of realistic narrative "restricted" or "measured" by a moral vision. Like Richardson, writers of romance also sometimes tried to capture the attentions of youthful readers by cast- 20 ing their narratives as recognizable, "realistic" representations of the world in which they lived; however, Richardson objected to what he felt was often the result of such representations, namely, a too vivid depiction of the seducer's morally-degraded perspective upon such intrigues. Later, Samuel Johnson would take up a similar argument in his famous Rambler essay No. 4 (31 March 1750) and describe how the technique of realism should be selectively applied. According to Johnson, fiction writers should try to avoid depicting vice in ways that might encourage "the temptation to practise it"(13). In *Pamela,* Richardson's technique quite purposefully excludes all perspectives but that of his heroine: even when Mr. B., her seducer, speaks, it is Pamela who reports his words. In this way does Richardson attempt to control the depiction of Mr. B.'s licentiousness in the first half of the book by showing all of Mr. B.'s behaviors as they are interpreted through the virtuous lens of Pamela Andrews, whose descriptions of his behavior are appropriately disapproving. Richardson thereby enacts Johnson's subsequent petition to fiction writers "to distinguish those parts of nature, which are most proper for imitation," and exert "greater care . . . in representing life, which is so often discoloured by passion, or deformed by weakness"(12).

Similarly does *The Blair Witch Project* insist that its audience iden- 21
tify with its "victims" in order to counter what its creators viewed to be a prevailing and unsatisfactory trend in contemporary horror films, namely, the encouragement of audiences to identify with villainous characters, usually murderers, and by implication sanction violent behavior rather than be forced to explore its "real" consequences. In interviews and press releases, *The Blair Witch Project*'s creators most often pointed to American horror films from the 1970s and '80s, specifically the "slasher" variety of killer-perspective horror film most famously exemplified by *Halloween* (1978, dir. John Carpenter) and *Friday the 13th* (1980, dir. Sean S. Cunningham), as the specific type of horror film they wished most readily to position *The Blair Witch Project* against. In the Sundance catalogue description, this contrast is deliberately evoked when *The Blair Witch Project*'s "pure, unadulterated, primordial horror" is clarified with the statement: " '*Friday the 13th,*' eat your heart out" (Yeldham, para. 1). Much as Richardson's choice to target "romance-writing" or "amatory fiction" distinguished for himself a clearly-defined position regarding the genre of popular entertainment whose audience he wished to capture with *Pamela,* so too did the evocation of a film like *Friday the 13th* as an antithetical example allow *The Blair Witch Project*'s creators to forge for themselves a specific position regarding the contemporary horror film.[43] Additionally, by citing examples of late '70s/early '80s mainstream, stylized "slasher" films as the variety of cinematic horror *The Blair Witch Project*

sets itself out to improve upon, its creators also positioned their film against a couple of other more recent trends in popular culture in ways that afforded such pronouncements a certain moral valence perhaps only partially intended by the *The Blair Witch Project*'s creators.

First, such a position directly opposed the implied stance represented by more recent, mainstream successes such as *Scream* (1996, dir. Wes Craven) and its imitators. Unlike *The Blair Witch Project,* films like *Scream* articulate—sometimes literally in their dialogue—a nostalgically-tinged appreciation of films such as *Friday the 13th* via self-reflexive reference and stylistic imitation. (Such were the films obviously targeted by Myrick's complaint about "recent horror films" employing satire as a means to revive the horror genre.) A second trend countered by *The Blair Witch Project*'s deliberate adoption of the victim's point of view is represented by the recent, significant rise in popularity of so-called "first-person shooter" computer games such as *Doom* or *Quake.* Following a spate of school shootings, including the April 1999 tragedy at Littleton High School in Colorado, President Clinton delivered a speech on 1 June 1999, echoing many sentiments which had already been widely-circulated by the American news media regarding the film and computer game industries. Citing "somewhere over 300 studies" showing "a link between sustained exposure . . . to violent entertainment and violent behavior" in children, as well as numerous poor-taste advertisements for first-person shooter games (e.g., "Kill your friends guilt-free"), Clinton urged "members of the entertainment industry . . . [to] do their part" by eliminating what he described as the "violent appeal" contained in their cultural productions. 22

Six weeks after Clinton's speech, *The Blair Witch Project* arrived. Myrick and Sanchez often described their primary goal with the film as being an aesthetic one: "[W]e decided that there hadn't really been [a horror film] that scared us, really scared us, since we were kids," said Myrick (Elias), implying that *The Blair Witch Project* and its promotion were constructed with the intention of "really" scaring audiences who came to see it. This aesthetic purpose was dually served both by the film's "realism" conceit and by the encouragement of audience identification with the film's victims. Yet the means by which *The Blair Witch Project* achieved this purpose could also be perceived as a response to an overwhelming "call" to the entertainment industry to temper its depictions of violence and to discourage identification with fictional characters who commit violent acts. Otherwise casual criticisms such as Myrick's complaint that "All the recent horror films have been sex-ridden and cool to watch. We didn't want that" (Weinraub) functioned to further an impression already available to viewers via the film itself that *The Blair Witch Project,* by encouraging an extreme identification with those characters being victimized by (and not 23 perpetrating) its horror, marked a morally-favorable, "pure" and "unadulterated" alternative to those popular entertainments which the American news media and government officials had so conspicuously condemned in the weeks leading up to the film's premiere. By its contact with such powerful moral touchstones (e.g., no encouragement to identify with violent characters, no explicit gore, no sex), *The Blair Witch Project* could therefore be readily interpreted as a message from its creators deliberate in its intention "to decry such [entertainments] as have a Tendency to inflame and corrupt."

RECEPTION

The Blair Witch Project's initial reviewers concentrated their attentions 24
upon the filmmakers' seemingly serendipitous discovery of an aesthetic that matched the financial limitations under which they were forced to operate.[44] As far as concerns the technical presentation of *The Blair Witch Project*'s narrative, there was much to distinguish the film from other contemporary films receiving national release. For one, *The Blair Witch Project* was exclusively shot using 16mm black-and-white film and High-8 color video, neither of which produce the preferred resolution of industry-standard 35mm. Secondly, all of the footage was filmed using hand-held cameras, a fact emphasized by the aforementioned not-so-steady handling of the cameras. Also, the film's soundtrack entirely shuns the use of non-diegetic sound, perhaps the most-sustained example of such a technique in a nationally-released film since Alfred Hitchcock's *Rear Window*.[45] Positive reviews of the film invariably fore-grounded these technical limitations, largely agreeing with Malin that they helped to further the "realism" conceit to great effect. Often these reviews described the experience of watching the film in physiological terms.[46] Such reception echoed the spirit of Aaron Hill's response to reading *Pamela*, which he likens to being subjected to a "Possession." Said one reviewer, "There's no denying the terror in '*The Blair Witch Project*.' It's fierce, it's palpable and it gets deep under the skin in a way few movies do" (Guthmann).

Equally captivating to the film's initial reviewers was the un- 25
usual "theory" which its creators had said informed its production. As was explained in numerous pre and post-release interviews, as well as in press kits distributed to members of the press in advance of their screening of the film, The Blair Witch Project was created using a process the Haxan filmmakers dubbed "Method Filmmaking," whereby the actors were given cameras and were instructed to film each other responding to situations devised by the directors.[47] As Myrick, Sanchez, the principal actors, and the film's publicists

explained, the camping trip portrayed onscreen and comprising the majority of the film's narrative was edited from an actual eight-day excursion in which the actors moved from site to site through Maryland's Seneca Creek State Park. Rather than have the actors follow a completed script, the directors instead offered them information on a "need to know" basis.[48] Aided by Global Positioning System technology, a computerized navigational system which allowed the actors to move from location to location in the state park without direct contact with the directors, the actors were individually supplied notes on character, vague references about what to expect from their colleagues, and information describing how to get to the next location. As Joshua Leonard (one of the actors) explained, the result was "like one of those 'Choose Your Own Adventure' books" whereby the actors themselves were allowed to make decisions affecting their characters' development (Mannes, para. 11). The result was to establish genuine uncertainty about the "reality" of some of the exchanges portrayed onscreen, as well as confusion regarding the difference between the characters' relationships and that of the actors.[49]

When assessing reviewers' response to *The Blair Witch Project,* it 26
is tempting to extend the creators' "Method" to Artisan's ingenious prerelease marketing of the film and compare the instructions supplied to the actors to the press kits supplied to its reviewers.[50] Both sets of "guidelines" performed a similar function, helping to shape their recipients' experiences in ways preferred by the filmmakers, if not entirely controlled by them. To this strategy one might compare Richardson's decision to reprint Aaron Hill's letter (along with other, similar plaudits) before the second duodecimo edition of his *Pamela* (published 14 February 1741), as well as Richardson's own "Preface by the Editor," items which William Warner has characterized as collectively constituting a "reader's guide" to the novel (203). Much as advance publicity for *The Blair Witch Project* concentrated attentions upon the material circumstances of the film's production, so too did the prefatory items placed before *Pamela*'s first letter cause Richardson's readers to focus first upon the book's method, and then upon its content. Indeed, immediate response to *Pamela* primarily revolved around the narrative technique which Richardson would later describe as "writing to the moment," thereby creating a hugely divisive reaction to the book. Since method was fore-grounded, readers had first to decide whether or not they accepted Richardson's "new species of writing," with one's choice upon technique generally deciding one's evaluation of the book's content. Those who accepted Richardson's technique (such as did Hill) accepted in turn its moral message. Those who questioned Richardson's technique (such as did the author of *An Apology*

for the Life of Mrs. Shamela Andrews) were less likely to embrace *Pamela*'s lesson of "virtue rewarded."

Similarly does recognizing the overt attention afforded to the material circumstances of *The Blair Witch Project*'s production encouraged by its publicists help to explain the extremely divided response the film evoked from its initial audiences. Even when acclaimed as "a rough masterpiece of suggestion," such praises were consistently accompanied by a careful rehearsal of the film's use of "commonplace materials" (sticks, rocks, KY jelly, primitive film equipment, amateur actors, amateur camera operators), items which some reviewers insisted were somehow more intrinsically "suggestive" than other, less familiar materials.[51] In this manner were the filmmakers' aesthetic decisions routinely subordinated to reiterations of the limited technical means available to them, with respondents finding the film "a very clever solution to the problem of how to make a movie on next to no money" (Taylor, para. 2). Even the choice of genre could be made to appear the consequence of material restraints: "The horror genre is ideal for the bare-bones (pardon the expression) nature of this undertaking," noted one reviewer, since "It enabled the filmmakers to turn a near-total absence of resources into a creative advantage." Both dramatically and materially was the film championed as "a nifty example of how to make something out of nothing" (Maslin, "Blair Witch"). This mode of response offered little in the way of analysis, either of the film or of its phenomenal commercial success, though it might be noted that reviews written to accompany film premieres often do bear a closer affinity to advertising than to analysis. Instead, rehearsals of the film's technical and methodological novelties had the function of reducing the work to a "gimmick" status, indicating to audiences the need to prepare themselves to experience the film much as they might prepare themselves to witness a magician perform a trick: Those who can resist the temptation to try and "figure it out" will find the experience most rewarding, while those who cannot overcome such temptation will find themselves incapable of satisfying the creators' intentions, which in the case *The Blair Witch Project* was "really" to scare the audience by encouraging intense identification with its protagonist-narrators. 27

Thus were evaluations of the film often couched inside of theoretical statements of purpose regarding the use of film entertainments, generally speaking. The film's admirers spoke of its "touch[ing] on something serious—filmmaking as passion" (Denby 87), and having bought the premise and suspended disbelief, they unequivocally appreciated the fictional world created by the filmmakers as if it were not fictional at all. Such evaluations are qualitatively similar to Aaron 28

Hill's response to reading *Pamela,* an experience which Hill also found absorbing yet meaningful. It is important to note that after having described the experience of having his fancy possessed by *Pamela,* Hill then proceeds to query Richardson who might be "the wonderful AUTHOR of *Pamela*" (10), demonstrating how an awareness of the fiction need not necessarily disturb one's experience of the story's "truth . . . [52] On the other hand, those who disliked *The Blair Witch Project* generally tended to doubt its "cinematic" qualities altogether, with such conclusions generally serving to explain their having "failed" to connect, sympathize, or identify with the story or its characters. One such reviewer wondered aloud about the film's success, surmising that one needed to be suitably "entranced" to enjoy it, and that "the movie seems to cast a spell on some viewers, eager to make it a cult object."[53] Such responses recall Oscar Wilde's belated evaluation of *The Old Curiosity Shop* that it would require a heart of stone to read of Little Nell's death without laughing. Wilde's implication that those who cried in the streets at the news of Nell's passing were the victims of a momentary, culturally-induced hysteria or "spell" is not unlike the position of *The Blair Witch Project*'s initial reviewers who found it difficult to articulate their dissatisfaction with the film in terms understandable to those whose opinions they opposed.

Because both *Pamela* and *The Blair Witch Project* foregrounded un- 29
usual narrative techniques in order both to increase their potential audiences and to advance "projects" to reform their respective genres, both works managed to evoke highly-divisive responses which in turn served further to promote their commercial successes, thereby elevating both *Pamela* and *The Blair Witch Project* to the status of "media events." In the context of discussing *Pamela* and eighteenth-century literary entertainments, William Warner defines a media event as containing three necessary elements: 1) a media production (e.g., publication of a book, public screening of a motion picture); 2) interest in the production which "feeds upon itself," making the media production into "an ambient, pervasive phenomenon"; and 3) further interest in the production evidenced by its having "trigger[ed] repetitions and simulations" and its "becom[ing] the focus of critical commentary and interpretation" (178). Both *Pamela* and *The Blair Witch Project* certainly satisfy all three of Warner's criteria. Both were media productions that generated a culturally-inclusive brand of curiosity such as is alluded to by Aaron Hill ("I have done nothing but read it to others, and hear others again read it"). Additionally, both instantly inspired imitations, often of a critical nature. The remarkable propagation of "Pamelas" and "Anti-Pamelas" following the publication of Richardson's novel has been well-documented.[54] Print technology fos-

tered rapid appropriation of the "Pamela" name, with many who did so drawing upon the medium's capacity to convey the impression of truth as a means to validate their own publications.[55] Indeed, over a dozen parodies, burlesques, criticisms, and spurious sequels to Richardson's novel appeared before the author himself could weigh in a year later with his own sequel, *Pamela . . . in Her Exalted Condition.*[56]

Similarly, the same technologies which were used so success- 30
fully to promote *The Blair Witch Project* also allowed for the swift proliferation of parodies. Within a month of its release, spoofs had already begun to appear on American television, with several networks (ABC, NBC, CBS, Fox, and ESPN) airing promotions mimicking *The Blair Witch Project*'s technique and premise. In advertisements for its September 1999 Video Music Awards show, MTV parodied the parodies, showing the program's hosts going into a wooded area to film a satirical promotion only to discover other networks' crews already there doing the same.[57] Within two months of the film's release, it was reported that "a cauldron of wannabe filmmakers have whipped up short satires to impress producers or studio execs" with titles such as *The Blair Princess Project, The Blair Hype Project, The Watts Bitch Project,* and *The Blair Witch Ripoff* (Landau). Indeed, in the tradition of novels such as *Anti-Pamela: Or Feign'd Innocence Detected* (likely by Eliza Haywood), soon after the film's debut there appeared The Anti-Blair Witch Project (Wood), a Web site dedicated to providing a facetious list of "scary moments" from the film (e.g., "Heather screaming," "Faint, inaudible noises at night," "Looking up Heather's nose").

Much as the "Anti-Pamelist" productions did little to dissuade 31
readers from seeking out Richardson's novel (five editions would be exhausted within a year of its debut), negative evaluations of *The Blair Witch Project* concentrating on the film's unusual narrative technique not only failed to diminish interest, but more likely encouraged those who had not seen the film to see it for themselves. Criticism of Pamela Andrews's "virtue" often took issue with the way Pamela told her own story, which for some readers had the effect of making the heroine's self-proclaimed "artlessness" seem anything but. *An Apology for the Life of Mrs. Shamela Andrews* (probably by Henry Fielding) exemplifies this mode of response. In *Shamela,* questions about the heroine's morality are routinely couched inside mocking illustrations of Richardson's "writing to the moment," indicating the technique's utter ineffectiveness with *Shamela*'s author:

> "Odsbobs!" exclaims Shamela, "I hear him just coming in at the Door. You see I write in the present Tense, as Parson Williams says. Well, he

> [Mr. B, here rechristened "Mr. Booby"] is in Bed between us, we both shamming a Sleep, he steals a Hand into my Bosom." (15)

Such farce clearly communicates the author's dissatisfaction with 32
Pamela as an emblem of "virtue." Yet by concentrating its energies upon the novelty of the character's "writ[ing] in the present tense," Shamela's criticism possessed the additional function of advertising the novel to those curious about what the experience of reading such a book must be like. In a similar fashion does The Anti-Blair Witch Project's humorously dispassionate cataloguing of the film's "scary moments" tend to pinpoint the film's technique as a main obstacle to identification with its protagonists, thereby inviting others to consider for themselves how they might respond to "Faint, inaudible noises at night." By concentrating their criticisms upon the works' technical and promotional strategies to encourage audience identification, neither criticism functioned to dissuade those unacquainted with the works from testing their own responses.

It is a characteristic of both *Pamela* and *The Blair Witch Project* that 32
their narrators stubbornly insist upon recording their stories regardless of how desperate their situations become. Indeed, in both works, the protagonists draw the audience's attention to the persistence with which they pursue their documentary activities. Especially during the period of her "imprisonment," Pamela repeatedly remarks how "my Pen and Ink (in my now doubly secur'd Closet) is all that I have" (150); likewise do the student filmmakers query each other regarding the need to continue filming (e.g., to Josh's incredulous complaint to Mike that "She's still making movies here man!" Heather replies "It's all I fucking have left!").[58] Whether or not they identified with the protagonist-narrators of *Pamela* and *The Blair Witch Project,* both works' initial audiences discovered it difficult to resist the temptation, advanced via promotional campaigns and self-consciously within the works themselves, to scrutinize the means by which their narratives were created. That audiences came away from both *Pamela* and *The Blair Witch Project* with a great deal to say about their narrative techniques seems initially to explain how, in both cases, word-of-mouth publicity increased sales regardless of its evaluative content. Especially low exit poll ratings following the first week of *The Blair Witch Project*'s release seem to support the argument that because audiences' attentions were focused upon narrative technique and questions of the film's status as a fiction, both positive and negative responses communicated information about the film which in either case had the function of attracting still more viewers.[59] In addition, the implication that the film was, despite its creators' intentions, not "really" scary might also be said to have encouraged non-horror fans to see the film. Indeed, some review-

ers noted how the film tended not to shock the viewer, but instead "deliver[ed] rich, pleasurable doses of fear" (Denby 87). It appears that the film's self-conscious exclusion of the villain's perspective made it difficult for even its strongest detractors to employ convincing, "moral" arguments to dissuade others from seeing it.

As Warner implies, there comes a point in the development of any highly-successful "media event" when the media production appears to become divorced from its creators' control, after which time the work will be described as having taken on a "life" of its own. Comments such as Sanchez's that "we didn't know what we had until we started showing it to audiences and hearing their reactions" often function to encourage such a perception and further advance the position that commercial success is indeed the result of "Witchcraft."[60] A significant portion of *Pamela*'s critical legacy reflects an opinion, delivered in numerous critical contexts, that Richardson did not know what he was doing when writing his first novel—that "*Pamela* itself was something of an accident" (Watt 55). Indeed, the entire "rise of the novel" discourse which posits *Pamela* as the "first" example of novelistic writing includes an assumption of a certain degree of authorial ignorance about the work as a prerequisite to the discussion. Just as *Pamela* eventually had "Meanings and Purposes" subsequently assigned to it which were not envisioned by its creator, so too has *The Blair Witch Project* already been assigned significances perhaps unimagined by its creators, a process which will undoubtedly continue to occur. This circumstance does not, however, preclude the possibility of analysis; in other words, I disagree with John Pierson, the host of Split Screen, who responded to *The Blair Witch Project*'s unprecedented commercial success by pronouncing that "There is no good lesson to learn here."[61] Much as Richardson successfully intervened into discussions about the dangers of novel reading with *Pamela,* the creators of *The Blair Witch Project,* unwittingly or otherwise, tapped into public fears about the effects of exposure to violent entertainments. Both works consequently functioned to provide morally "safe," alternative entertainments which expressly encouraged identification with victims and not villains. As did Richardson's *Pamela, The Blair Witch Project* "media event" (i.e., the promotion, production, and reception of the film) exemplified a successful manipulation of media to produce a stylistically "real" narrative that could be interpreted as directly addressing contemporary concerns about popular entertainments. That both works could be understood as delivering conservative or "moral" messages about the uses and purposes of popular entertainment appears the most ready explanation for their both having achieved immediate and widespread commercial success. 33

NOTES

1. Richardson, *Pamela,* 9–10. The second edition of *Pamela* reprints Hill's letter. Eaves and Kimpel's *Pamela* (1971), based on the first edition, also includes the second edition's prefatory matter.
2. Haxan Films was founded by fellow University of Central Florida film students Myrick, Sanchez, Gregg Hale, and Robin Cowie (the film's producers), and Michael Monello (co-producer). *The Blair Witch Project* earned $29.2 million (domestic) during its first weekend ("Variety Box Office," 9–15 August). In pre-release interviews, Myrick and Sanchez were humorously evasive about the film's budget. Said Myrick at the film's Cannes premiere, "I've seen people here wearing more than the movie cost" (Maslin, "Fascinating"). Meanwhile, a publicist informed David Denby the film was made "for less than your mortgage" (86). $35,000 is the most-often quoted estimate of the actual production costs for *The Blair Witch Project,* though Artisan's heavy promotion campaign has driven the overall costs for the film much higher, possibly in excess of $15 million (Weinraub).
3. Mathews. The film earned an average of $44,295 from each of the 1,101 theaters in which it was shown 30 July–5 August 1999 ("Variety Box Office," 9–15 August).
4. By 30 September 1999, *The Blair Witch Project* had earned in excess of $140 million worldwide, surpassing the previous high for an independent film, Miramax's *Good Will Hunting* ($138 million) ("Variety Box Office," 4–10 October 1999). The designation of a film as "independent" generally indicates its having been financed and developed outside the Hollywood studio system, although recent co-production deals between independents and majors (e.g., Miramax and MGM) have caused the distinction to become less rigid.
5. Malcolm Gladwell's recent *New Yorker* piece, "The Science of the Sleeper," describes how a new marketing tool called "collaborative filtering" may increase the number of "sleeper" hits in both fiction and film. Though Gladwell does not mention *The Blair Witch Project* in his essay, he betrays the film's influence when he lists the "obscure Belgian comedy" *C'est Arrive Pres de Chez Vous* as a film recommended to him by a collaborative filtering computer program designed to suggest titles to moviegoers based on films they have seen (55). See below, note 57.
6. Responding to *The Blair Witch Project*'s phenomenal opening weekend, Charles Lyons concluded in article for *Variety* that "The pic's success is due to risk-taking: by the filmmakers for

their stylistic choices, their creative uses of the Internet, their marketing instincts; by Artisan for trusting the filmmakers while developing its own full-fledged, tailored marketing campaign" ("Spooked" 7). Reviewers of the film tended to agree with Lyons; for examples, see Denby, Ebert, Elliott, Guthmann, Maslin ("Blair Witch"), and Mary Williams.

7. In his *Time* cover story, "Blair Witch Craft," Richard Corliss readily represents the position which regards popular culture trends as utterly mystifying, interpreting the film's success as an example of "true Witch Craft" possessing "no profound meaning for the future of film" (64).
8. "Who is the killer in the end? The witch, or an imposter?" an online chat participant asks the film's co-director Eduardo Sanchez; he replies, "Something possesses them [the victims]—whether it's the witch's spirit or Rustin Parr's—who knows?" ("Blair Witch: Behind the Scenes," para. 25).
9. References to *The Blair Witch Project*'s "creators" refer both to Myrick and Sanchez and to others responsible for the film and its marketing, including representatives from the film's distributing company, Artisan Entertainment, who played a significant role in helping fashion the Blair Witch "event." References to the "student filmmakers" refer to the film's principal characters.
10. As I discuss below, I am using the term "media event" as William Warner defines it in his discussion of Richardson's novel and the "Pamela media event." See 176–230, especially 178–80.
11. Fliers posted in Park City at the Sundance Film Festival included additional information about the film's Web site, under the heading "EVIDENCE EXISTS. . . ."
12. "Witch Publicity Thwarted" (para. 5). Jay Boyar also reports on the Cannes incident, adding an anecdote from "a press conference at Cannes, [where] a journalist who felt she had been tricked took them [Myrick and Sanchez] publicly to task" (para. 49).
13. Lyons, "Every 'Witch' Way." Artisan reportedly paid $1.1 million for distribution rights (Ressner).
14. In lieu of an opening credit sequence, *The Blair Witch Project* opens with a brief disclaimer: "In October of 1994, three student filmmakers disappeared in the woods near Burkittsville, Maryland, while shooting a documentary called 'The Blair Witch Project.' A year later their footage was found." One presumes the film that follows to be comprised entirely of that footage. End credits do not describe the film as fictional, though they do identify its having been "Written, Directed and Edited by Daniel Myrick & Eduardo Sanchez."

15. Such terms are relative to the present context: Despite a production budget of $60,000, π [Pi]'s domestic gross exceeded $3 million during the period of its theatrical release.
16. Mark Williams, para. 8. Grainy Pictures, which produces Split Screen, reports on its Web site how "Pierson, a Maryland native who should have known better, fell for it hook, line, and sinker" (para. 4).
17. Grainy Pictures, para. 9. The Internet Movie Database entry for *The Blair Witch Project* had originally listed its three principal actors as deceased, a designation which has since been corrected (Mannes, para. 3).
18. Another unique element to *The Blair Witch Project*'s promotion was the decision of Kevin J. Foxe, the film's executive producer, not to pre-screen the film to potential distributors prior to its showing at Sundance at midnight the night of 24 January 1999: "In other words . . . [Foxe] was going to make them [representatives of Fine Line, Miramax, Artisan, and other distributors] come to the midnight screenings at Park City, driven by what he calls a 'must have, can't have' feel around the picture" (Mark Williams, para. 24). A similar release strategy was employed for the film's national release: "Instead of opening the film in New York and L.A. and then expanding it across the country, Artisan determined that the best way to build buzz was to release the film in 24 markets on 27 screens. 'We wanted to make it a hard ticket,' says Main [of Artisan Entertainment]. 'We wanted people to go to the theaters and have it be sold out. In this summer's cluster of movies, we want to make our picture an event'" (Ascher-Walsh 36). In both cases, this "must have, can't have" strategy not only successfully increased the commercial worth of the film, but also helped fuel confusion about the film's "documentary" status.
19. Like the theatrical film, the special also has its own "official" Web site (*http://www.scifi.com/blairwitch/*), which similarly minimizes reference to the works' "creators."
20. "According to Nielsen NetRatings for the week ending Aug. 1 [1999]. . . . Blairwitch.com was the 45th most used site on the Web. The site's unique audience hit 647,997. with 10.4 million page views and an average time of each person visiting of 16 minutes and 8 seconds" (Katz and Ault, para. 2). Grainy Pictures hosts a sample of on-line debate over *The Blair Witch Project*'s truth content on its Web site.
21. For an overview, see chapter V of Eaves and Kimpel's biography of Richardson ("The Composition and Publication of *Pamela* and the *Familiar Letters*," 87–99).

22. Reported by Barbauld in a biographical introduction to her edition of Richardson's letters (lii). Richardson describes the booksellers' request to Aaron Hill in his letter of 15 January 1740 (Selected Letters 39–42).
23. Richardson to Hill, 15 January 1741 (Selected Letters 40).
24. The *Weekly Miscellany* letter is reprinted in *Pamela,* ed. Eaves and Kimpel (6–8).
25. When published in the *Weekly Miscellany,* the letter originally had been addressed "To my worthy friend, the Author of *Pamela*"; however, when later reprinted as part of the prefatory material before the first edition of the book, its addressee was altered from "Author" to "Editor," a subtle yet significant change not unlike the one proposed by Artisan for the creators of *The Blair Witch Project* to move the film's credits to its conclusion. In both cases, the "conceit" of truth had been comprehensively established by the time the work was debuted to the public, thereby charging such last-minute revisions with special significance.
26. When Richardson's friend the Reverend Benjamin Slocock famously recommended *Pamela* from the pulpit of St. Saviour's in Southwark (likely sometime during December 1740), Richardson was brought under further suspicion of having unethically manipulated the promotion of his novel (see Sabor). The creators of *The Blair Witch Project* have similarly been accused of manipulating Internet "buzz" about the film (see Dilucchio).
27. Richardson, *Pamela* (title page), 1. A third letter from Webster appeared in the 28 February 1741 issue of the *Weekly Miscellany* (Eaves and Kimpel, 124). According to Eaves and Kimpel, Richardson "adequately" advertised *Pamela*—primarily posting announcements in the *Daily Gazetter* whenever a new edition was being published—though did not publicize his book as widely as he had works he had printed for others. As Eaves and Kimpel describe it, word-of-mouth publicity caught on quickly; thus, as far as print advertisement was concerned, "the book did not need it" (124).
28. In a letter (dated 22 December 1740) responding to Hill's praise-filled request to learn the true source of the story, Richardson modestly responded "how can I comply with your Commands, and name the Writer?" (qtd. by Eaves and Kimpel in their edition of *Pamela,* 11n).
29. Qtd. in Koretsky 37.
30. August. Frederick County is where Burkittsville, Maryland, is located, and where *The Blair Witch Project* suggests the student filmmakers disappeared.
31. Richardson to Hill, 15 January 1741 (Selected Letters 41).

32. Richardson to Hill, 27 October 1741 (Selected Letters 98).
33. Richardson to George Cheyne, 31 August 1741 (Selected Letters 46–47).
34. At the Cannes festival, the film was awarded the Prix de la Jeunesse, a special prize decided upon by a panel of European judges aged 18 to 25. "It means a lot to us," said Myrick of the award. "I mean, that's our target audience" (Boyar, pan. 11).
35. Of course, appearing on the cover of *Time* magazine in and of itself would appear to confirm the film's "mainstream" appeal, as *Time*'s editors immodestly recognize when they include amongst a time line of important events contributing to the *The Blair Witch Project* phenomenon "the film's directors appear on the cover of *Time*" (61). One might also point to the fact that *The Blair Witch Project* marked the first time a horror film had ever been accepted to play at the Sundance Film Festival as further evidence of its status as a "mainstream" cultural product.
36. Eg., "I am forc'd to break off, hastily" (36); "John is come back, and I'll soon send you some of what I have written.—I find he is going early in the Morning; and so I'll close here" (59).
37. Such match on action edits between the two cameras used by the student filmmakers also readily establish a "continuity" of cinematic space, a technique which (unlike montage editing) generally adumbrates a "realistic" visual narrative.
38. "God bless you both! and send us a happy Meeting; if not here, in his heavenly Kingdom. Amen" (180).
39. While Pamela's frequent expostulations ("Save then, my Innocence, good God. . . . [M]y presaging Mind bodes horrid Mischiefs!—Everything looks dark around me" [141]) receive a somewhat different emphasis in *The Blair Witch Project* (such as when a noise in the dark causes Josh to wonder aloud: "Jesus Christ! What the fuck is that?! FUCK!"), both serve a decidedly similar function to heighten audience anxiety about the protagonists' situations. Interestingly, both works received specific criticism regarding the necessity of such effusive outbursts. Richardson received an anonymous letter, reprinted in the second edition of *Pamela,* which criticized Pamela's overuse of the word "God": "if the sacred Name were seldomer repeated, it would be better" (12). "For the second edition Richardson considerably abridged *Pamela*'s piety—eighty-five mentions of God are either cut or altered by changing to word 'God' to 'Heaven'" (Eaves and Kimpel, 12n). In a review of *The Blair Witch Project,* Janet Maslin similarly lamented one "byproduct" of the filmmakers' realistic method: "the gratingly limited vocabulary, full of

virtually nonstop bleepables, which makes the film somewhat hard on the ears" ("Blair Witch").

40. Of course, in terms of implied audience, the narrative trajectories of *Pamela* and *The Blair Witch Project* move in opposite directions. While *Pamela*'s narrative begins as a private correspondence between herself and her parents, only to become a relatively more "public" account read by other characters in the story, the student filmmakers in *The Blair Witch Project* set out to make a commercial documentary about the Blair witch, only to find themselves readjusting the "story" they are filming toward a more private audience. Thanks to the film's promotional campaign, the moment Heather (the documentary's "director") signals this change of address—in a monologue often described as her "confessional" ("I just want to apologize to Mike's mom and Josh's mom and my mom and I'm sorry to everyone. I was very naive")—has been elevated to nearly iconic status.
41. The fact that not all readers of *Pamela* or viewers of *The Blair Witch Project* were suitably persuaded to identify with the stories' protagonist-narrators is discussed below (see section III).
42. A term introduced by Rosalind Ballaster to distinguish the more eroticized variety of popular fiction from female "pious" fiction (eg., sentimental tales ending in marriage).
43. Besides appealing to opponents of *Friday the 13th* and similar fare, such an advertisement can have the effect of intriguing those who are fans of this variety of horror film as well, thereby excluding no potential audience in its promotion of the film.
44. Guthmann's review is emblematic: After briefly describing the film's premise, the reviewer prematurely concludes his or her analysis of the film in order to question why the film is so affecting. In this case, Guthmann asks how first-time actors managed to be so effective: "Is it just brilliantly good acting—the kind that John Cassavetes drew from his actors—or did Myrick and Sanchez scare the living hell out of them?" The question is then answered with a discussion of "Method Filmmaking" (see below).
45. A term used in film criticism and theory, "diegesis" refers to the physical world experienced by the characters in a film. Diegesis is not limited to sound (e.g., a film's credits can be referred to as "non-diegetic" since they exceed the characters' experience).
46. One article about *The Blair Witch Project* (McManaman) even provides advice from a otolaryngologist for how to stave off motion sickness when watching the film. (Take a "vestibular depressant" before viewing, says the doctor.)

47. "Much of the credit for the revolutionary technique that the team calls 'method filmmaking' must go to producer Hale, who drew upon his military experience" (Boyar, para. 32).
48. Pincus, para. 15. For further information regarding the details of "Method Filmmaking," see the transcript of the ABC on-line chat with Sanchez, or reviews by Beale, Lim, Mannes, and Pincus.
49. That the conditions for the camping trip were reportedly less than ideal, with the actors being supplied only a limited (though not dangerously so) cache of provisions, added to audience confusion about the degree to which the discomfort of the actors was distinct from that being expressed by the characters. ("Your safety is our concern. Your comfort is not," the directors reportedly told their cast.) For interviews with the *The Blair Witch Project*'s cast, see Lim, Mannes. For an interesting, disapproving look at the ethics of "Method Filmmaking," see Taylor.
50. Reporting on how the producers initially shopped *The Blair Witch Project* to potential investors in a manner that "didn't actually tell the potential investors that the footage was genuine, [though] some of them might reasonably have drawn that conclusion," Boyer suggests, "Perhaps we should call [this] . . . technique 'method salesmanship'" (para. 40). It should be noted that the eventual promotion and marketing of the film appears to have been a highly-collaborative effort, engineered in the main by Artisan (who, for example, prepared and distributed the press kits).
51. Denby 86, 87. See also Ebert.
52. Hill here provides a perfect model for Richardson's own theory of fiction-reading, exhibiting "that kind of Historical Faith which Fiction itself is generally read with, tho' we know it to be a Fiction" (Richardson to William Warbuton, 19 April 1748, Selected Letters, 85).
53. Elliott. Interestingly, as did many who reviewed the film negatively, Elliott cannot resist asking questions about its premise ("Why are the flashlights so minuscule? How come nobody can ignite a fire? Why are the men such doofy whiners?") which seem better applied to a genuine documentary than to a fictional story.
54. See McKillop (42–106), Sale (111–35), Eaves and Kimpel (119–53), Kreissman, Turner, and Gooding.
55. For instance, spurious sequels such as the two-volumed *Pamela's Conduct in High Life* (likely by John Kelly) or the anonymous *Pamela in High Life: Or, Virtue Rewarded* exploited Richardson's own realism conceit (which had been greatly facilitated by his own access to print technology) when their title pages an-

nounced their works as having reproducing *Pamela*'s "original" letters or manuscripts. For a comprehensive chronology of the "Pamela Vogue" in England, see Eaves and Kimpel's introduction to *Pamela,* xvii–xxii.

56. A second film, titled *Book of Shadows: Blair Witch 2,* premiered in October 2000. Haxan and Artisan had in fact announced plans for a second Blair film (a sequel or a prequel) even before the first film had premiered, a decision which Sanchez initially responded to with resigned acceptance: "I've got a feeling . . . that we're going to be dealing with Blair Witch, in one way or another, for the rest of our lives" (Boyar, para. 64). See also "Blair Witch: Behind the Scenes," Lyons ("Spooked"), Pincus, and Wolk.
57. Landau. The MTV spot has its own antecedent in the Belgian film *C'est Arrive Pres de Chez Vous* (1992, dir. Remy Belvaux, Andre Bonzel, and Benoit Poelvoorde), also known as *Man Bites Dog,* with which *The Blair Witch Project* shares several affinities. Also a low-budget, "unedited" faux-documentary featuring characters who share their actors names filming each other, *Man Bites Dog* portrays in a darkly-humorous fashion the actions of a serial killer (Poelvoorde). Late in the film, the filmmakers discover their documentary being interrupted by the intrusion of another trio of filmmakers making another documentary about another serial killer.
58. See *Pamela* 60, 76, 85, 95, 105, 134. Josh's complaint to Heather follows an especially self-reflexive moment during which his character has apparently just described the actors' "real" situation: "We walked for 15 hours today, we ended up in the same place! There's no one here to help you! That's your motivation!"
59. Cinemascore, Inc., a company that distributes exit-poll information to the media and film industry, polled theatergoers in three cities during the first week of *The Blair Witch Project*'s national release, finding "that while 60% of the 600 respondents said they 'couldn't wait' to see the movie, they only gave it a grade of C. People who came along with them gave it an F" (Mathews).
60. "Blair Witch: Behind the Scenes," para. 31.
61. Qtd. in Corliss, 63.

WORKS CITED

Ascher-Walsh, Rebecca. "Rhymes with Rich." *Entertainment Weekly* 30 July 1999: 34–36.

August, Melissa. "Welcome to Burkittsville." *Time* 16 Aug. 1999: 62.

Ballaster, Rosalind. *Seductive Forms: Women's Amatory Fiction from 1684–1740.* Oxford: Clarendon, 1992.

Barbauld, Anna Loetitia. "Life of Samuel Richardson." *The Correspondence of Samuel Richardson.* 6 vols. Ed. Barbauld. London, 1804. 1: vii–ccxil.

Beale, Lewis. "Frightful Fellows." *New York Daily News* 11 July 1999, Showtime: 5.

"Blair Witch: Behind the Scenes: A Chat with the Film's Co-Director, Ed Sanchez." ABCNEWS.com. 19 Aug. 1999. <*http://more.abcnews.go.com/sections/us/DailyNews/chat_blairwitch.html*>. 7 Oct. 1999.

The Blair Witch Project. Dir. Dan Myrick and Eduardo Sanchez. Perf. Heather Donahue, Michael C. Williams, Joshua Leonard. Artisan Entertainment. 1999.

The Blair Witch Project. Posted June 1998. <*http:11www.blairwitch.com/*>. 2 Oct. 1999.

Boyar, Jay. "Bewitching Cinema." *The Orlando Sentinel.* Posted 4 June 1999. <*http://www.orlandosentinel.com/calendar/060699_boyar06 . . . 51.htm*>. 2 Oct. 1999.

Clinton, Bill, and Hillary Clinton. "Remarks by the President and Mrs. Clinton on Children, Violence and Marketing." *The Rose Garden.* 1 June 1999.

Corliss, Richard. "Blair Witch Craft." *Time* 16 Aug. 1999: 59–64.

Curse of the Blair Witch. Perf. Heather Donahue, Michael C. Williams, Joshua Leonard. Sci-Fi Channel. 11 July 1999.

Curse of the Blair Witch. Posted July 1999. <*http://www.scifi.com/blairwitch/*>. 1 Oct. 1999.

Denby, David. "Last Waltz." Rev. of *The Blair Witch Project. The New Yorker* 26 July 1999: 84–87.

Dilucchio, Patrizia. "Did 'The Blair Witch Project' fake its online fan base?" *Salon.* Posted 16 July 1999. <*http://www.salon.com/tech/feature/1999/07/16/blair_marketing/index2.html*>. 29 Sept. 1999.

Eaves, T. C. Duncan, and Ben D. Kimpel. *Samuel Richardson: A Biography.* Oxford: Clarendon, 1971.

Ebert, Roger. "Oh, the Horror of 'Blair Witch.' " Rev. of *The Blair Witch project. Chicago Sun-Times* 16 July 1999, late ed.: 30.

Elias, Justine. "Making Horror Horrible Again: Into a Forest Full of Witchery." *The New York Times* 11 July 1999, sect. 2:13.

Elliott, David. "Heavy-handed Horror Dogs Blair from Takeoff." Rev. of *The Blair Witch Project. San Diego Union-Tribune* 15 July 1999: 24.

[Fielding, Henry.] *An Apology for the Life of Mrs. Shamela Andrews.* 1741. New York: Garland, 1974.

Gladwell, Malcolm. "The Science of the Sleeper." *The New Yorker* 4 Oct. 1999: 48–55.

Gooding, Richard. "Pamela, Shamela, and the Politics of the Pamela Vogue." *Eighteenth-Century Fiction* 7.2 (Jan. 1995): 109–30.

Grainy Pictures, Inc. "The Blair Witch Connection." *<http://www.grainypictures.com/blairwitch/index.html>*. 13 Oct. 1999.

Guthmann, Edward. "Primal Fear Runs Amok In 'Witch." ' Rev. of *The Blair Witch Project. San Francisco Chronicle* 16 July 1999: C1.

Johnson, Samuel. *Essays from the Rambler, Adventurer, and Idler.* Ed. W. J. Bate. New Haven: Yale UP, 1968.

Katz, Richard, and Susanne Adult. " 'Blair' Fare a Big Hit on Web." Posted 10 Aug. 1999. *<http://www.dbmedia.org/finalcut/newswire/august99/blair/>*. 29 Sept. 1999.

[Kelly, John.] *Pamela's Conduct in High Life.* 2 vols. 1741. New York: Garland, 1975.

Koretsky, Allen C. "Poverty, Wealth, and Virtue: Richardson's Social Outlook in *Pamela.*" *English Studies in Canada* 9.1 (Mar. 1983): 36–56.

Kreissman, Bernard. *Pamela-Shamela: A Study of the Criticisms, Burlesques, Parodies, and Adaptations of Richardson's "Pamela."* Lincoln: U of Nebraska P, 1960.

Landau, Peter. "Schtick Figure." *Entertainment Weekly* 10 Sept. 1999: 22.

Lim, Dennis. "Heather Donahue Casts a Spell." *Village Voice* 20 July 1999: 50+.

Lyons, Charles. "Every 'Witch' Way to the Top." *Variety* 9–15 Aug. 1999:8.

———. "Spooked by 'Witch." ' *Variety* 9–15 Aug. 1999: 7–8.

Mannes, Brett. "Something Wicked." Salon. Posted 13 July 1999. *<http://www.salon.com/ent/movies/int/1999/07/13/witch_actor/index.htm l>*. 29 Sept. 1999.

Maslin, Janet. " 'The Blair Witch Project': Where Panic Meets Imagination." Rev. of The Blair Witch Project. *New York Times* 14 July 1999: El.

———. "Fascinating Features on Sidelines Outsparkle Main Event at Cannes." *New York Times* 21 May 1999: E1.

Mathews, Jack. " 'Witch's' Brew Hard for Many to Swallow." *New York* Now 5 Aug. 1999: 46.

McKillop, Adam Dugald. *Samuel Richardson: Printer and Novelist.* Chapel Hill: U of North Carolina P, 1936.

McManaman, Angela. "For Some Film Viewers, Fright of 'Blair Witch' Is an Upset Stomach." *Milwaukee Journal Sentinel* 14 Aug. 1999, final ed.: 1.

Myrick, Dan. Home page. "Online Journal." *<http://www.danmyrick.com>*. 4 Oct. 1999.

Pamela in High Life. 1741. New York: Garland, 1975.

Pierson, John. "John Responds (Blair Witch and Haxan Films)." Posted 7 May 1998. *<http://www.grainypictures.com/answers/may7.html>*. 13 Oct. 1999.

Pincus, Adam. "Off the Beaten Track: The Blair Witch Project." *Independent Video and Film.* Posted July 1999. *<http://www.aivf.org/the_independent/9907/july99_blairwitch.html>*. 19 Aug. 1999.

Ressner, Jeffrey. "They Believed in Magic." *Time* 16 Aug. 1999: 63.

Richardson, Samuel. *The Correspondence of Samuel Richardson.* Ed. Letitia Barbauld. 6 vols. London: R. Phillips, 1804.

———. *Familiar Letters on Important Occasions.* 1741. Rpt., with introduction by Brian W. Downs. New York: Dodd, Mead, and Co., 1928.

———. *Pamela.* 1740. Ed. T. C. Duncan Eaves and Ben D. Kimpel. Boston: Houghton Mifflin, 1971.

———. *Selected Letters of Samuel Richardson.* Ed. John Carroll. Oxford: Clarendon, 1964.

Richetti, John J. *Popular Fiction before Richardson. Narrative Patterns:* 1700–739. Oxford: Oxford UP, 1992.

Sabor, Peter. "Did Richardson Bribe Dr. Slocock?" *Notes & Queries* 26 (1979):29–31.

Sale, William Merritt, Jr. *Samuel Richardson: A Bibliographical Record of His Literary Career with Historical Notes.* New Haven: Yale UP, 1936.

Taylor, Charles. "Method Madness." *Salon.* Posted 14 July 1999. *<http://www.salon.com/ent/movies/feature/1999/07/14/blair_essay/index.html>*. 29 Sept. 1999.

Turner, James. "Novel Panic: Picture and Performance in the Reception of Pamela." *Representations 48* (Fall 1994): 70–96.

"Variety Box Office." *Variety* 9–15 Aug. 1999: 9.

"Variety Box Office." *Variety* 4–10 Oct. 1999: 13.

Warner, William. *Licensing Entertainment: The Elevation of Novel Reading in Britain, 1684–1750.* Berkeley: U of California P, 1998.

Watt, Ian. *The Rise of the Novel: Studies in Defoe, Richardson, and Fielding.* Berkeley: U of California P, 1957.

Weinraub, Bernard. "A Witch's Cauldron of Success Boils Over." *New York Times:* E1+.

Williams, Mark London. "Out of the Trees into Sundance: The Blair Witch Project." *Rough Cut.* Posted 17 Feb. 1999. *<http://www.roughcut.com/features/stories/blair_witch_project.html>*. 13 Oct. 1999.

Williams, Mary Elizabeth. " 'The Blair Witch Project.' " Rev. of The Blair Witch Project. *Salon.* Posted 13 July 1999. *<http://www.salon.com/ent/movies/review/1999/07/13/blair/index.html>*. 9 Oct. 1999.

"Witch Publicity Thwarted; Spike on Sam." *Mr. Showbiz.* Posted 20 May 1999. *<http://mrshowbix.go.com/news/Todays_Stories/990520/cannes052099.html>*. 9 Oct. 1999.

Wolk, Josh. " 'Blair' Warning." *Entertainment Weekly Online.* 4 Aug. 1999. *<http://www.pathfinder.com/ew/daily/0,2514,1801,sequelplansalawsuit.html>*. 9 Oct. 1999.

Wood, Jan, and Pete Wood. The Anti-Blair Witch Project. *<http://creativehomeliving.com/blair/antiblair.htm>*. 6 Oct. 1999.

Yeldham, Rebecca. "The Blair Witch Project." Sundance Film Festival 1999 Film Guide. *<http://www.sundancechannel.com/festival99/>*. Jan. 1999.

Examining the Text

1. Sum up and compare the major points in the production and promotion of *Pamela* and *The Blair Witch Project.*

2. Harris argues that the creators of *The Blair Witch Project* use realism as an attempt to "re-invigorate" the horror film genre, to rescue the horror film from repetition and predictability. Discuss the ways in which he says the movie achieves this; in other words, how is *The Blair Witch Project* different from other horror films? In what ways is it similar?

3. Explain what Harris means when he states that both works took an "essentially conservative approach" toward the task of "reforming" their respective genres of popular entertainment (19). How, according to Harris, does this approach lead to commercial success?

For Group Discussion

As Harris points out, *The Blair Witch Project*—like all horror movies—aimed to capture the "youth market." Discuss elements of the movie that are most likely to appeal to this audience. Use terms from Evans essay if you like, as well as your own ideas about what appeals to a young audience.

Writing Suggestion

Based on your reading of Stephen King and Walter Evans in the two previous articles, and your own viewing experiences, develop a "treatment" for the first in a series of successful new horror/monster movies. Define the prime audience for the movie; devise one or more monsters or villains and describe him/her/it/them in detail; create a cast of non-monster characters; decide on a setting; and roughly outline a plot. End your "treatment" with a section justifying your choices by discussing the assumptions you made about your movie's audience.

ADDITIONAL SUGGESTIONS FOR WRITING ABOUT MOVIES

1. In an interpretative essay, compare and contrast several movies dealing with similar themes or issues. For instance, you might compare several films about the Vietnam War, or about the lives of the current generation of "Twentysomethings," or about inner-city gangs, or about parent-child relationships. Choose movies that interest you and, ideally, that you can see again. You might want to structure your essay as an argument aimed at convincing your readers that one movie is in some way "better" than the others. Or you might use your comparison of the movies to draw some larger point about popular culture and the images it presents to us.

2. In a research or "I-search" essay, consider the complex relationship between film and social morality. Do you agree with *The Blair Witch Project* creators (as cited by Harris, paragraph 21) that "slasher" movies (such as the *Halloween* and *Friday the 13th*) tend to encourage audience identification with the villain and help "sanction violent behavior"? Harris suggests that violent "first-person shooter" video games are also part of a trend in media against which *The Blair Witch Project* is working (22). Explore what other experts say about the relationship between real and fictional violence. Can you find specific current events that support your arguments?

3. Based on your reading of the essays by Mark J. Schaefermeyer, Walter Evans, J. P. Telotte, and Martin Harris, evaluate this kind of intellectual criticism.

4. Just as Stephen King looks at "Why We Crave Horror Movies," in an essay of your own, explore why we crave another popular genre of movies: futuristic techno-thrillers, movies based on television sitcoms and cartoons, chase movies, menaced-female dramas, psychotic-killer stories, romantic comedies, supernatural comedies, and so forth. Choose a type of movie familiar to you so that you can offer as many specific examples as possible. In approaching this assignment, try to answer some of the same questions King does: What is the "fun" of seeing this type of movie? What sort of "psychic relief" does it deliver? Are there specific types of people who are likely to enjoy the genre more than others? Does the genre serve any function for society? In what ways do movies in this genre affect us, changing our thoughts or feelings after we've seen them?

5. Compare and contrast several movie reviews of *The Blair Witch Project* with either J. P. Telotte or Martin Harris's piece of film criticism. Consider the similarities and differences between the reviews and the criticism in terms of form as well as content. In other words, compare and contrast not only their points about the films, but also the ways in which they make and support their points.

Internet Activities

1. These days, anyone with a Web site has the power to post a movie review. Choose several online reviews—written by both professional movie critics and "regular" moviegoers such as yourself—for a movie you've seen (some options are available on the *Common Culture* Web site). Write an essay in which you note the primary differences between the reviews done by professionals and those done by the regular fan(s). What aspects of the film do the professionals focus on? Are they the same as those of the regular fan or do they vary? Does one group emphasize certain elements, such as the emotions encouraged by the film, the acting, or the cinematography? Which of the reviews most closely reflects your opinion of the movie? Why do you think these reviews are the ones with which you best identify?

2. Vist a Web site for a new film you're interested in seeing and write a review of the site (some options are available on the *Common Culture* Web site). What is offered on the Web site that a potential audience wouldn't get from any other form of media? What do you like best about the Web site? What would you change? Describe the advantages of having a Web site for a new film. Are there any disadvantages? How do you feel movie Web sites will influence which movies we want to watch?

Reading Images

Write an essay in which you "read" the poster for the 1931 movie version of *Dracula* (p. CI-8). The assignment for this essay: make specific connections between the Peter Cushing/Christopher Lee poster and Walter Evans's article, "Monster Movies: A Sexual Theory" in this chapter.

In interpreting this poster's messages, you will want to undertake many, if not all, of the activities suggested in the "Reading Images" section in Chapter 1. However, before launching into that analytic process, your first task in writing this essay will be to identify within the Evans essay a specific thematic thread that you can then relate to the image. What are Evans's main points about sexuality as revealed through horror movies in general, and the Dracula movies in particular? Study the poster carefully for several minutes, letting its overall impressions wash over you, and then re-read the Evans essay, noting any themes that seem especially pertinent to this poster.

Once you have identified one or several relevant points in the Evans essay, look again the movie poster, this time noting specific items: first its overall colors and dimensions and then specific physical objects, especially the central characters. While the sexuality implicit in the central image is obvious, take care to note subtleties here: what is implied by the skin tones of the two central figures, by the direction in which Dracula is looking, by the placement of clothing, by facial expressions, hair arrangements, and so forth? Finally, read the actual text in the poster, to discover ways in which it helps to put forth the implied sexual message(s).

For Further Reading: A Common Culture Bibliography

CHAPTER 2: ADVERTISING

Barthel, Diane. *Putting on Appearances: Gender and Advertising*. Philadelphia, PA: Temple University Press, 1988.

Berger, Arthur Asa. *Ads, Fads, and Consumer Culture: Advertising's Impact on American Character and Society*. Lanham, MD: Rowman & Littlefield, 2000.

Cortese, Anthony Joseph Paul. *Provocateur: Images of Women and Minorities in Advertising*. Lanham, MD: Rowman & Littlefield Publishers, 1999.

Cook, Guy. *The Discourse of Advertising*. London: Routledge, 2001.

Ewen, Stuart and Elizabeth Ewen. *Channels of Desire: Mass Images and the Shaping of American Consciousness*. 2nd edition. Minneapolis, MN: University of Minnesota Press, 1992.

Fowles, Jib. *Advertising and Popular Culture*. Thousand Oaks, CA: Sage, 1996.

Fox, Roy. *Mediaspeak: Three American Voices*. Westport, CT: Praeger, 2001.

Kilbourne, Jean, director. *Still Killing Us Softly*. Cambridge, MA: Cambridge Documentary Films, 1992 Videocassette.

—. *Deadly Persuasion: Why Women and Girls Must Fight the Addictive Power of Advertising*. New York: Free Press, 1999.

Lasn, Kalle. *Culture Jam: The Uncooling of America*. New York: Eagle Brook, 1999.

Mitchell, Arthur. *The Nine American Lifestyles: Who We Are and Where We're Going*. New York: Warner Books, 1983.

Myers, Greg. *Words in Ads*. New York: Routledge, 1994.

O'Shaughnessy, John. *The Marketing Power of Emotion*. Oxford: Oxford University Press, 2003.

Rampton, Sheldon and John Stauber. *Trust Us, We're Experts!: How Industry Manipulates Science and Gambles with Your Future*. New York: Jeremy P. Tarcher/Putnam, 2001.

Sivulka, Juliann. *Soap, Sex, and Cigarettes: A Cultural History of American Advertising*. Belmont, CA: Wadsworth, 1998.

Turow, Joseph. *Breaking up America:Advertisers and the New Media World*. Chicago, IL: University of Chicago Press, 1997.

CHAPTER 3: TELEVISION

Abt, Vicki and Leonard Mustazza. *Coming after Oprah: Cultural Fallout in the Age of the TV Talk Show*. Bowling Green, OH: Bowling Green State University Popular Press, 1997.

Batten, Frank with Jeffrey L. Cruikshank. *The Weather Channel: The Improbably Rise of a Media Phenomenon*. Boston, MA: Harvard Business School Press, 2002.

Cantor, Paul A. *Gilligan Unbound: Pop Culture in the Age of Globalization*. Lanham, MD: Rowman & Littlefield, 2001.

Edgerton, Gary R. and Peter C. Rollins (Eds.). *Television Histories: Shaping Collective Memory in the Media Age*. Lexington, KY: University of Kentucky Press, 2001.

Gamson, Joshua. *Freaks Talk Back: Tabloid Talk Shows and Sexual Nonconformity*. Chicago, IL: University of Chicago Press, 1998.

Gitlin, Todd. *Inside Prime Time*. 2nd edition. New York: Pantheon, 1994.

Hartley, John. *Uses of Television*. London: Routledge, 1999.

Mander, Jerry. *Four Arguments for the Elimination of Television*. New York: Morrow, 1978.

Miller, Mark Crispin. *Boxed In: The Culture of TV*. Evanston, IL: Northwestern University Press, 1988.

Monaco, Paul. *Understanding Society, Culture, and Television*. Westport, CT: Praeger, 1998.

Morreale, Joanne (Ed.). *Critiquing the Sitcom: A Reader*. Syracuse, NY: Syracuse University Press, 2003.

Morse, Margaret. *Virtualities: Television, Media Art, and Cyberculture*. Bloomington, IN: Indiana University Press, 1998.

O'Neill, John. *Plato's Cave: Television and Its Discontents*. Cresskill, NJ: Hampton Press, 2002.

Oppenheimer, Jerry. *Seinfeld: The Making of an American Idol*. New York: HarperCollins, 2002.

Parks, Lisa and Shanti Kumar. *Planet TV: A Global Television Reader*. New York: New York University Press, 2003.

Postman, Neil. *Amusing Ourselves to Death*. New York: Penguin Books, 1985.

Williams, Raymond. *Television: Technology and Cultural Form*. New York: Schocken Books, 1975.

CHAPTER 4: POPULAR MUSIC

Baker, Houston A., Jr. *Black Studies, Rap, and the Academy*. Chicago: University of Chicago Press, 1993.

Brightman, Carol. *Sweet Chaos: The Grateful Dead's American Adventure*. New York: Random House/Clarkson Potter, 1998.

Chang, Kevin and Wayne Chen. *Reggae Routes: The Story of Jamaican Music*. Philadelphia: Temple University Press, 1998.

Chuck D. and Yusaf Jah. *Fight the Power: Rap, Race, and Reality*. New York: Delacorte Press, 1997.

Cloonan, Martin and Reebee Garofalo. *Policing Pop*. Philadelphia: Temple University Press, 2003.

Colegrave, Stephen and Chris Sullivan. *Punk: The Definitive Record of a Revolution*. Boston: Thunder's Mouth Press, 2001.

Costello, Mark and David Foster Wallace. *Signifying Rappers: Rap and Race in the Urban Present*. New York: Ecco Press, 1997.

Dickerson, James. *Women On Top: The Quiet Revolution That's Rocking the American Music Industry*. New York: Billboard Books, 1999.

Fernando, S. H. Jr. *The New Beats: Exploring the Music, Culture, and Attitudes of Hip-Hop*. New York: Anchor, 1994.

Forman, Murray. *The 'Hood Comes First: Race, Space, and Place in Rap and Hip-Hop.* Middletown: Wesleyan University Press, 2002.
George, Nelson. *Hip Hop America.* New York: Viking Press, 1998.
Goodman, Fred. "La explosion pop Latino." *Rolling Stone,* n812 (May 13, 1999): 21.
Heylin, Clinton. *From the Velvets to the Voidoids: A Pre-Punk History for a Post-Punk World.* New York: Penguin, 1993.
Jones, Quincey and the Editors of *Vibe* Magazine. *Tupac Amaru Shakur 1971–1996.* Pittsburgh: Three Rivers Press, 1998.
Krims, Adam. *Rap Music and the Poetics of Identity.* Cambridge University Press, 2003.
Loza, Steven. *Barrio Rhythm: Mexican American Music in Los Angeles.* Urbana-Champaign: University of Illinois Press, 1993.
Marcus, Greil. *Mystery Train: Images of America in Rock 'N' Roll Music.* New York: Plume, 1997.
Marcus, Greil. *In the Fascist Bathroom: Punk in Pop Music, 1977–1992.* Cambridge, Massachusetts: Harvard University Press, 1999.
McNeil, Legs and Gillian McCain. *Please Kill Me: The Uncensored Oral History of Punk.* New York: Penguin, 1997.
Moore, Allan F. *Analyzing Popular Music.* Boston: Cambridge University Press, 2003.
Neal, Mark Anthony. *Soul Babies: Black Popular Culture and the Post-Soul Aesthetic.* New York: Routledge, 2002.
Perkins, William Eric. *Droppin' Science: Critical Essays on Rap Music and Hip Hop Culture.* Philadelphia: Temple Univ Press, 1996.
Posner, Gerald L. *Motown: Money, Power, Sex, and Music.* New York: Random House, 2002.
Potter, Russell A. *Spectacular Vernaculars: Hip-Hop and the Politics of Postmodernism.* New York: State Univ of New York Press, 1995.
Queen Latifah. *Ladies First: Revelations from a Strong Woman.* New York: William Morrow & Company, 1999.
Reynolds, Simon. *Generation Ecstasy: Into the World of Techno and Rave Culture.* New York: Little Brown & Company, 1998.
Rose, Tricia. *Black Noise: Rap Music and Black Culture in Contemporary America.* Middletown, Connecticut: Wesleyan University Press, 1994.
Savage, Jon. *England's Dreaming: Anarchy, Sex Pistols, Punk Rock, and Beyond.* New York: St. Martin's Press, 2002.
Sicko, Dan. *Techno Rebels: The Renegades of Electronic Funk.* New York: Billboard Books, 1999.
Ward, Brian. *Just My Soul Responding: Rhythm and Blues, Black Consciousness, and Race Relations.* Berkeley: University of California Press, 1998.

CHAPTER 5: CYBERCULTURE

Armstrong, Sara (Ed.). *Edutopia: Success Stories for Learning in the Digital Age.* San Francisco, CA: Jossey-Bass, 2002.
Barrett, Neil. *Digital Crime: Policing the Cybernation.* London: Kogan Page, 1997.
Cherny, Lynn and Elizabeth Reba Weise, eds. *Wired_Women: Gender and New Realities in Cyberspace.* Seattle, WA; Seal Press, 1996.
Chayko, Mary. *Connecting: How We Form Social Bonds and Communities in the Internet Age.* Albany, NY: State University of New York Press, 2002.
Coupland, Douglas. *Microserfs.* New York: HarperCollins, 1995.

Dery, Mark. *Escape Velocity: Cyberculture at the End of the Century*. New York: Grove Press, 1996.

Dutton, William H. and Brian D. Loader. *Digital Academe: The New Media and Institutions of Higher Education and Learning*. London: Routledge, 2002.

Fornas, Johan (Ed.) *Digital Borderlands: Cultural Studies of Identity and Interactivity on the Internet*. New York: Peter Lang, 2002.

Holloway, Sarah L. and Gill Valentine. *Cyberkids: Children in the Information Age*. London: Routledge, 2003.

Jordan, Tim. *Cyberpower: The Culture and Politics of Cyberspace and the Internet*. London New York: Routledge, 1999.

Moore, Dinty W. *The Emperor's Virtual Clothes: The Naked Truth about Internet Culture.* Chapel Hill, NC: Algonquin Books, 1995.

Rheingold, Howard. *The Virtual Community: Homesteading on the Electronic Frontier.* Reading, MA: Addison-Wesley, 1993.

Smolan, Rick and Jennifer Erwitt (Eds.). *24 Hours in Cyberspace: Photographed on One Day by 150 of the World's Leading Photojournalists.* QUE Macmillan: Against All Odds Productions, 1996.

Zucker, Andrew and Robert Kozma with Louise Yarnall. *The Virtual High School: Teaching Generation V*. New York: Teachers College Press, 2003.

CHAPTER 6: SPORTS

Baker, Aaron and Todd Boyd. *Out of Bounds: Sports, Media, and the Politics of Identity*. Bloomington: Indiana University Press, 1997.

Bolin, Anne and Jane Granskog. *Athletic Intruders: Ethnographic Research on Women, Culture, and Exercise.* New York: State University of New York Press, 2003.

Bloom, John and Michael Nevin Willard. *Sports Matters: Race, Recreation, and Culture.* New York: NYU Press, 2002.

Cahn, Susan K. *Coming on Strong: Gender and Sexuality in Twentieth-Century American Sports*. New York: Macmillan, 1994.

Coakley, Jay J. *Sport in Society: Issues and Controversies*. Boston: Irwin/McGraw-Hill, 1998.

Gerdy, John R. *Sports: The All-American Addiction.* Mississippi: University Press of Mississippi, 2002.

Leifer, Eric Matheson. *Making the Majors: The Transformation of Team Sports in America*. Cambridge: Harvard University Press, 1995.

Lupica, Mike. *Mad as Hell: How Sports Got Away From the Fans—and How We Get it Back.* New York: Putnam, 1996.

Miller, Toby. *Sportsex*. Philadelphia: Temple University Press, 2002.

Nelson, Mariah Burton. *The Stronger Women Get, the More Men Love Football: Sexism and the American Culture of Sports.* New York: Harcourt Brace, 1994.

Platt, Larry. *New Jack Jocks: Rebels, Race, and the American Athlete.* Philadelphia: Temple University Press, 2002.

Oleksak, Michael M and Mary Adams Oleksak. *Beisbol: Latin Americans and the Grand Old Game*. Grand Rapids: Masters Press, 1991.

Quirk, James P. and Rodney Fort. *Hard Ball: The Abuse of Power in Pro Team Sports.* Princeton: Princeton University Press, 1999.

Rinehart, Robert E. and Synthia Sydnor. *To the Extreme: Alternative Sports, Inside and Out.* New York: State University of New York Press, 2003.

Smith, Lissa. *Nike is a Goddess: The History of Women in Sports*. New York: Atlantic Monthly Press, 1998.

Sugden, John and Alan Tomlinson. *A Critical Sociology of Sport.* New York: Routledge, 2002.
Weyland, Jocko. *The Answer Is Never: A Skateboarder's History of the World.* New York: Grove Press, 2002.
Wilcox, Ralph C. et al. *Sporting Dystopias: The Making and Meaning of Urban Sport Cultures.* New York: State University of New York Press, 2003.

CHAPTER 7: MOVIES

Denzin, Norman K. *Images of Postmodern Society: Social Theory and Contemporary Cinema.* New York: Sage Publications, 2001.
Dixon, Wheeler Winston. *Straight: Constructions of Heterosexuality in the Cinema.* New York: State University of New York Press, 2003.
Dunne, John Gregory. *Monster: Living Off the Big Screen.* New York: Random House, 1997.
Dunne, Michael. *Intertextual Encounters in American Fiction, Film, and Popular Culture.* Bowling Green: Popular Press, 2001.
Gabler, Neal. *Life, the Movie: How Entertainment Conquered Reality.* New York: Knopf, 1998.
Grundmann, Roy. *Andy Warhol's Blow Job: Culture and the Moving Image.* Philadelphia: Temple University Press, 2003.
Lopate, Phillip. *Totally, Tenderly, Tragically: Essays and Criticism from a Lifelong Love Affair with the Movies.* New York: Anchor Books, 1998.
Martinez, Gerald. *What It Is . . . What It Was! The Black Film Explosion of the '70s in Words and Pictures.* New York: Hyperion, 1998.
May, Larry. *Screening Out the Past: The Birth of Mass Culture and the Motion Picture Industry.* Chicago: University of Chicago Press, 1983.
Muller, Eddie. *Dark City: The Lost World of Film Noir.* St. Martin's Press, 1998.
Naremore, James. *More Than Night: Film Noir in Its Contexts.* Berkeley: University of California Press, 1998.
Natoli, Joseph P. *Memory's Orbit: Film and Culture, 1999–2000.* New York: State University of New York Press, 2003.
Rueschmann, Eva. *Moving Pictures, Migrating Identities.* Mississippi: University Press of Mississippi, 2003.
Scorsese, Martin. *A Personal Journey with Martin Scorsese through American Movies.* New York: Hyperion, 1997.
Skal, David. *The Monster Show: A Cultural History of Horror.* Boston: Faber & Faber, 2001.
Skal, David J. *Screams of Reason: Mad Science in Modern Culture.* New York: W.W. Norton & Company, 1998.
Slotkin, Richard. *Gunfighter Nation: The Myth of the Frontier in Twentieth-Century America.* Norman: University of Oklahoma Press, 1998.
Tarkovsky, Andrey. *Sculpting in Time: Reflections on the Cinema.* Austin: University of Texas Press, 1989.
Trice, Ashton D. and Samuel A. Holland. *Heroes, Antiheroes and Dolts: Portrayals of Masculinity in American Popular Films 1921–1999.* New York: McFarland & Company, 2001.

Acknowledgments

TEXT CREDITS

p. 10 Tham, Hilary, "Barbie's Shoes," from MEN AND OTHER STRANGE MYTHS. Copyright © 1994 by Hilary Tham Goldberg. Reprinted by permission of Lynne Rienner Publishers, Inc.

p. 13 Leo, John. "The Indignation of Barbie," by John Leo from U.S. NEWS AND WORLD REPORT. Copyright © October 12, 1992 U.S. NEWS & WORLD REPORT. Reprinted by permission.

p. 16 Motz, Marilyn Ferris. "Seen Through Rose-Colored Glasses: The Barbie Doll in American Society," Marilyn Ferris Motz which appeared in POPULAR CULTURE: AN INTRODUCTORY TEXT by Jack Bachbar and Kevin Lause. Copyright © 1992 by Bowling Green State University Press Popular Press. Reprinted by permission.

p. 44 Carolyn Muhlstein, "Role-Model Barbie: Now and Forever?" Reprinted with the permission of the author.

p. 51 Kalle Lasn, "The Cult You're In" from CULTURE JAM: The Uncooling of America, New York: Eagle Brook Press, 1999, pp. 51–57.

p. 56 Roy Fox, "Salespeak" from MEDIASPEAK. Westport, CT: Praeger, 2001, pp. 87–116, as edited (pp. 105–108 omitted)

p. 78 Fowles, Jib. "Advertising's Fifteen Basic Appeals," by Jib Fowles, from ETC: A REVIEW OF GENERAL SEMANTICS, 39, no. 3. Reprinted by permission of the International Society for General Semantics, Concord, California.

p. 97 John E. Calfee, "How Advertising Informs to our Benefit," CONSUMERS' RESEARCH MAGAZINE, April 1998, v. 81, n. 4.

p. 110 Damian Ward Hey, "Virtual Product Placement," TELEVISION QUARTERLY, Winter 2002, v. 32, i.4.

p. 119 Jennifer L. Pozner, You're Soaking In It" from SALON.com, January 30, 2001.

p. 129 Miller, Mark Crispen, "Getting Dirty," from BOXED IN: THE CULTURE OF TV, by Mark Crispen Miller, pp. 43–50. Copyright © 1989 by Mark Crispen Miller. Reprinted by permission of Northwestern University Press.

p. 137 Gloria Steinem, "Sex, Lies, and Advertising," by Gloria Steinem, from MS. MAGAZINE 1, No. 1 (1990). Copyright © 1990 by Gloria Steinem. Reprinted by permission of the author and Ms. Magazine.

p. 160 Barbara Ehrenreich. "Spudding Out" from THE WORST YEARS OF OUR LIVES by Barbara Ehrenreich. Copyright © 1990 by Barbara Ehrenreich. Reprinted by permission of International Creative Management, Inc.

p. 163 Robert Kubey & Mihaly Csikszentmihalyi, "Television Addiction is No Mere Metaphor" from SCIENTIFIC AMERICAN, Feb. 2002, v. 286 i2.

p. 172 Waters, Harry. "Life According to TV" by Harry Waters from NEWSWEEK, Dec. 6, 1982. Copyright © 1982 by Newsweek, Inc. All rights reserved. Reprinted by permission.

p. 182 John Kelly, "Interactive Television: Is it Coming or Not?" from TELEVISION QUARTERLY, Winter 2002, v 32 i4.

p. 189 Rebecca Gardyn, "The Tribe Has Spoken," AMERICAN DEMOGRAPHICS, September 1, 2001, pp. 34–40, including five tables with data contained in article.

p. 200 Robert Samuels, "Keeping it Real"

p. 208 Paul A. Cantor, "The Simpsons: Atomistic Politics and the Nuclear Family," POLITICAL THEORY, December 1999, v27, n6: 734

p. 226 Lisa Frank," The Evolution of the Seven Deadly Sins: From God to the Simpsons," JOURNAL OF POPULAR CULTURE, Summer 2001, v35 il.

p. 244 Gavin James Campbell, "I'm Just a Louisiana Girl: the Southern World of Britney Spears," SOUTHERN CULTURE, Winter 2001, v7, i4: 81

p. 258 Michael Slinger and Amy Hillman, "Napster: Catalyst for a New Industry or Just Another Dot-com" from IVEY BUSINESS JOURNAL v66, n3 (Jan–Feb, 2002): 45

p. 278 Gary Burns, "Marilyn Manson and the Apt Pupils of Littleton," POPULAR MUSIC AND SOCIETY, Fall 1999, v23, n3:3. Reprinted by permission of Taylor & Francis, Ltd., <*www.tandf.co.uk/journals*>.

p. 285 Melissa McCray Pattacini, "Deadheads Yesterday and Today: An Audience Study," POPULAR MUSIC AND SOCIETY, Spring 2000, v. 241, n1. Reprinted by permission of Taylor & Francis Ltd., <*http://www.tandf.co.uk/journals*>.

p. 300 August, Melissa, Leslie Everton Brice, Laird Harrison, Todd Murphy, and David E. Thigpen, "Hip-Hop Nation: There's More to Rap than Just Rythms and Rhymes," TIME 153, No.5 (February 8, 1999). Copyright © 1999 Time, Inc. Reprinted by permission.

p. 313 Evelyn Jamilah, "The Miseducation of Hip-Hop," BLACK ISSUES IN HIGHER EDUCATION, Dec. 7, 2000, v17 121:24.

p. 322 Polly E. McLean, "Age Ain't Nothing But a Number," POPULAR MUSIC AND SOCIETY, Summer 1997, v21, n2: 1. Reprinted by permission of Taylor & Francis Ltd., <*http://wwwtandf.co.uk/journals*>.

p. 345 Kenneth Gergen, "The Self in the Age of Information," THE WASHINGTON QUARTERLY, 2000, v23: 201–214.

p. 361 Barlow, John Perry, "Cyberhood vs. Neighborhood," from UTNE READER No. 58 (March-April 1995). Reprinted by permission of the author.

p. 369 "Virtuality and Its Discontents," by Sherry Turkle, from THE AMERICAN PROSPECT. Reprinted by permission of THE AMERICAN PROSPECT 24 (Winter, 1996) and the author. Copyright © 1996 The American Prospect, PO Box 772, Boston, MA 02102-0772. All rights reserved.

p. 381 "Black Studies in Cyberspace: Cyber-Segregation and Cyber-Nazis," by Colin Beckles, WESTERN JOURNAL OF BLACK STUDIES v21, n1 (Spring, 1997): 12. Reprinted by permission.

p. 397 Claudia Wallis, "The Learning Revolution," from "Welcome to Cyberspace," TIME MAGAZINE, Spring 1995 special issue.

p. 403 Neil Postman, "Virtual Students: Digital Classroom," THE NATION, 1995, v261: 377.

p. 413 Richard A. Lanham, "Undergraduate Teaching in the Electronic Age." Source: *http://www.cni.org/docs/tsh/Lanham.html*

p. 425 John D. Solomon, "The Sports Market is Looking Soggy," from NEW YORK TIMES, April 21, 2002.

p. 432 Choonghoon Lim and Douglas Michele Turco, "The Next Generation in Sport: Y," CYBERJOURNAL OF SPORTS MARKETING, *www.cjsm.com/vol3/lim34.htm*

p. 443 Kate Rounds, "Why Men Fear Women's Teams," MS. MAGAZINE, Jan/Feb. 1991, p. 43. Copyright © 1991 by Ms. Magazine. Reprinted by permission of Ms. Magazine.

p. 450 T.R. Young, "The Sociology of Sport," SOCIOLOGICAL PERSPECTIVES, 1986, v1: 3

p. 470 Robert M. Fernquist, "Geographical Relocation, Suicide, and Homicide." Source: *http://physed.otago.ac.nz/sosol/v4i2/v4i2Fernquist.htm*

p. 486 Maya Angelou, "Champion of the World," from I KNOW WHY THE CAGED BIRD SINGS. Copyright © 1969 by Maya Angelou. Reprinted with permission of Random House, Inc.

p. 490 Jay Nordlinger, "Tiger Time: The Wonder of an American Hero," NATIONAL REVIEW, April 30, 2001, v53 n8.

p. 497 William Dowell et al, "Life on the Edge," TIME, September 6, 1999, v154 i10: 28.

p. 506 Paul Roberts, "Risk," from PSYCHOLOGY TODAY 27, No. 6 (November-December 1994). Reprinted with permission from PSYCHOLOGY TODAY MAGAZINE. Copyright © 1994 Sussex Publishers, Inc.

p. 520 Sydney Pollack, "The Way We Are," by Sydney Pollack, from THE AMERICAN ENTERPRISE, vol. 3, #3 May-June 1992. Copyright 1992 The American Enterprise. Distributed and reprinted by permission of the New York Times Special Features/Syndication Sales.

p. 530 Schaefermeyer, Mark J., "Film Criticism," by Mark J. Schaefermeyer, from Alan Wells, ed., MASS MEDIA AND SOCIETY (Boston: Lexington Books, 1987). Reprinted by permission.

p. 542 David Ansen et al, "Film Criticism in America Today: A Critical Symposium," CINEASTE, Winter 2000, v26 nl: 27, as edited.

p. 563 Stephen King, "Why We Crave Horror Movies," from PLAYBOY (1982). Copyright © 1982 Stephen King. All Rights Reserved.

p. 566 Walter Evans, "Monster Movies: A Sexual Theory," from JOURNAL OF POPULAR FILM AND TELEVISION 2, No. 4 (Fall 1973). Copyright © 1973. Reprinted by permission.

p. 576 J.P. Telotte, "The Blair Witch Project Project" from FILM QUARTERLY, Spring 2001, v54 i3: 32.

p. 591 Martin Harris, "The 'Witchcraft' of Media Manipulation: Pamela and the Blair Witch Project," JOURNAL OF POPULAR CULTURE, Spring 2001, v34 i4: 33.

PHOTOGRAPH AND ILLUSTRATION CREDITS

Chapter 1: p. 1 Nicole Miller/Globe Photos, Inc. 1994

Chapter 2: p. 47 Timex Corporation; p. 56 Adbusters, Inc. p. 128 The Mary Boone Gallery, New York

Chapter 3: p. 158 The New Yorker Magazine, Inc./The Cartoon Bank; p. 225 Twentieth Century Fox/Neal Peters Collection

Chapter 4: p. 242 The Lord Group; p. 246 AP/Wide World Photos; p. 281 AP/Wide World Photos

Chapter 5: p. 342 Randy Glasbergen; p. 354 Machine Talker, Inc.; p. 409 Roger Ressmeyer/CORBIS; p. 416 James Capparell

Chapter 6: p. 423 Mark J. Terrill/AP/Wide World Photos; p. 488 AP/Wide World Photos; p. 499 AP/Wide World Photos; p. 501 John Storey/TimePix

Chapter 7: p. 518 Universal City Studios, Inc./Photofest; p. 526 Getty Images, Inc./Hutton Archive Photos; p. 573 Picture Desk, Inc./Kobal Collection

Color insert: p. CI-1 (top) Mattel, Inc.; (bottom) Kimmy McCann; p. CI-2 (top) Adbusters, Inc.; (bottom) Tom Allison and Chris Gomien/Carl Solway Gallery; p. CI-3 Jeff Christensen/Reuters/TimePix; p. CI-4 DMI/TimePix; p. CI-5 Picture Desk, Inc./Kobal Collection; p. CI-6 Picture Desk, Inc./Kobal Collection; p. CI-7 Jim Bourg/Reuters/TimePix; p. CI-8 Picture Desk, Inc./Kobal Collection

Index by Author and Title

Index by Academic Discipline

Political Science

Pop Cultural Criticism

Psychology

Semiotic Analysis/Cultural Studies

Sociology/Communications

Gender Studies

Index by Rhetorical Mode